SECOND EDITION

Assessing and Screening Preschoolers

Psychological and Educational Dimensions

Edited by

Ena Vazquez Nuttall
Northeastern University

Ivonne Romero
Interamerican University of Puerto Rico

Joanne Kalesnik
Department of Defense Educational Activity
Seoul, South Korea

Allyn and Bacon

Boston ▪ London ▪ Toronto ▪ Sydney ▪ Tokyo ▪ Singapore

Series Editorial Assistant: Susan Hutchinson
Manufacturing Buyer: Suzanne Lareau
Editorial-Production Service: Omegatype Typography, Inc.

Copyright © 1999, 1992 by Allyn & Bacon
A Viacom Company
160 Gould Street
Needham Heights, MA 02494

Internet: www.abacon.com

Library of Congress Cataloging-in-Publication Data

Assessing and screening preschoolers : psychological and educational
    dimensions / edited by Ena Vazquez Nuttall, Ivonne Romero, Joanne
    Kalesnik. – 2nd ed.
      p.   cm.
    Includes bibliographical references and index.
    ISBN 0-205-26676-2
    1. Psychological tests for children.   2. Preschool children—
Psychological testing.   I. Nuttall, Ena Vazquez,   II. Romero,
Ivonne.   III.   Kalesnik, Joanne.
    BF722.A85 1999
    155.42'3'0287–DC21   98-25701
                                                          CIP

Printed in the United States of America
10   9   8   7   6   5   4   3   2   03   02   01   00   99

CONTENTS

P R E F A C E

The last 35 years have witnessed an upsurge in the development of tests for preschool children. The expansion of services for children with developmental disabilities, the creation of the Headstart Program and the passing of federal legislation Public Law (P.L.) 94-142 and P.L. 99-457 and the reauthorizations P.L. 101-476 and recently P.L. 105-17, have contributed and will continue to contribute to interest in the area of preschool assessment. Because of the provisions of these pieces of legislation, the realms of infant, preschool, and family assessment are flourishing.

These changes demand that professionals serving preschool children with disabilities hone their assessment skills and intervention practices in order to serve this population. This revision of this book intends to help professionals become more competent in assessing preschoolers ages 3 to 5 who have special needs. The book emphasizes the ecological model and incorporates multicultural issues in many of its chapters. This revision includes new chapters on family-focused assessment and transdisciplinary play-based assessment. All chapters have been updated and many have been completely rewritten.

The book is organized into six sections, containing 22 chapters. It is intended primarily for graduate students and professionals who already have taken an introductory course in psychological or educational assessment that covered the basic psychometric concepts of validity, reliability, and standardization. The *Introduction* section defines the process of assessment, reviews the history of preschool evaluation and the current status of preschool measures, and presents an ecological model that can be used to guide the assessment process.

Part II, *Normal, Delayed, and Different Development of Preschoolers*, starts with Chapter 2, which describes the stages of normal development in five major realms: physical and motor, cognitive, language, social and moral knowledge, and emotional development. Chapter 3, on abnormal development, covers the most important categories described in federal laws P.L. 94-142 and 99-457, in reauthorizations P.L. 101-476 and 105-17, and in the *Diagnostic and Statistical Manual of Mental Disorders,* Fourth Edition (DSM-IV), which are pertinent to children aged 0 to 5. There is some unavoidable overlap between this chapter and those presented in Section V, *Evaluating Special Populations.* The intent of Section II, which focuses on human development, is to provide readers with a good foundation so that they can competently determine when development is proceeding well and when it is not.

The third part, *Ethical and Technical Issues in Preschool Assessment,* covers ethical issues involved in preschool assessment, procedures to follow when evaluating young children, and general issues in screening. The section starts with Chapter 4, on the ethical and legal issues that pertain to conducting assessments at the preschool level. The authors focus on the ethical principles of the American Psychological Association, the National Association of School Psychologists, and pertinent national legislation in order to inform readers about how to conduct their work according to the highest professional and legal standards.

Chapter 5 presents an overview of the testing procedures involved in the individual assessment of preschoolers aged 3 to 5. This chapter presents a step-by-step progression of the testing process and gives some practical suggestions on administration.

Screening is the major topic of Chapter 6. It contains a review of the area including a rationale for preschool screening, a typical preschool screening program, "people" issues in screening, procedural issues, screening outcomes, and the future of screening.

The focus of Part IV, *Assessment of Major Areas of Functioning,* is the comprehensive assessment of the major behavior realms, including developmental history, family issues, social and emotional factors, cognitive skills, speech and language, and visual and fine motor skills. Other areas also covered in this section are academic readiness, neuropsychological assessment, and a new chapter on play assessment.

Chapter 7 focuses on obtaining a developmental history. Developmental and medical interview techniques are discussed. Chapter 8 presents the important area of family assessment and views it from a systemic perspective. Chapter 8 discusses all the important factors to consider when conducting family assessments, including culture, family composition, socio-economic status (SES), area of residence, roles and responsibilities, stressors, and sources of support. In addition, topics such as how to assess family strengths and weaknesses, as well as the most popular formal assessment procedures, are presented.

Social and emotional functioning and adaptive behavior are the topics covered in Chapter 9. From an ecological and behavioral perspective, the author discusses direct observation, clinical interviews, behavior rating scales, behavioral observation approaches, projective techniques, and adaptive behavior scales. Chapter 10 is a new chapter that focuses on the use of transdisciplinary play-based assessment with preschool children.

Chapter 11 discusses the principal cognitive tests administered to preschool children. It is the longest and one of the most important chapters of the book. It reviews the Wechsler Preschool and Primary Scale of Intelligence—Revised, the Woodcock-Johnson Psychoeducational Battery—Revised, the Stanford-Binet Intelligence Scale (Fourth Edition), the Differential Ability Scales, and the Bayley Scales of Infant Development (Second Edition). The impact of socio-cultural variables on intelligence measures is seriously considered.

Speech and language skills are covered in Chapter 12. The major language measures used at this developmental level are reviewed, and issues of assessing speech and language are discussed.

Visual, fine, and gross motor development are the foci of Chapter 13, which includes an extensive discussion of normal and abnormal development in these areas and a review of the major assessment tools in these three realms. Chapter 14 reviews academic and readiness measures appropriate for preschoolers.

The neuropsychological assessment of preschool children is the theme of Chapter 15. This chapter presents a unique approach to the clinical assessment of the preschool child with suspected or identified developmental deficits. Methods and procedures for integrating and interpreting assessment data are provided. An illustrative case report is included.

Part V concentrates on *Evaluating Special Populations.* The special populations covered include the culturally different, those with developmental disabilities and at-risk conditions, those with hearing and vision impairments, and those who have been sexually or physically abused.

Chapter 16 focuses on the culturally different. It includes a definition of the level of multicultural competence that is needed for working with culturally and linguistically different students, a decision-making tree for conducting these types of assessments, and a review of available measures, which—although limited in many ways—can be used with minority children with disabilities.

Chapter 17 concentrates on the assessment of preschoolers with developmental disabilities and at-risk conditions, focusing on children with autism, orthopedic impediments, traumatic brain injury, HIV, prematurity, parental alcohol and drug exposure, and lead poisoning. A multidimensional and multilevel approach to assessment is advocated.

Chapter 18 centers on the evaluation of preschool children with hearing losses. It discusses general issues in the assessment of these children and reviews the most frequently used measures. A counterpart to this chapter is Chapter 19, which focuses on the assessment of preschool children with visual impairments. This chapter continues the same format, discussing the definition of visual impairment, developmental issues, and major measures used in assessment.

The assessment of maltreatment and neglect in the preschool population is the major focus of Chapter 20. This chapter defines sexual and physical abuse in legal terms, discusses the reporting law, the impact of abuse, and assessment procedures.

Part VI, *Writing and Implementing Assessment Results,* addresses writing individual assessment reports and implementing evaluation findings. In Chapter 21, the different parts of a typical assessment report are described; an integrated case report with multiple measures is presented and discussed. Chapter 22 focuses on the implementation of screening and assessment results and covers the development of IEPs, team meetings, and consultation practices.

For the reader's convenience, tables describing tests in specific realms have been included. A table describing screening measures appears in the Appendix.

Professors wishing to use this book as a textbook for a one-semester course are advised to use Parts I through IV, skip V, and continue to VI. For year-long courses, we recommend the whole book, with supplementary materials from other texts covering specific measures or techniques for testing, legislation, and other areas of choice. We strongly recommend that instructors use a series of videotapes entitled *Young and Special,* distributed by the American Guidance Service, to supplement the course. These videotapes present typical and atypical development as well as assessment and remediation in the major areas covered in Part IV.

Our hope is that users who are newcomers to the field will learn how to competently assess and screen preschool children after reading this book.

As a final note, we would like to thank the testing companies that provided us with information and granted us permission to use their materials in our book. The expert reviews of our manuscript by Lisa G. Bischoff of Indiana State University and by Stephen B. Olsen of the Alexander Center for Child Development and Behavior of Bloomington, Minnesota, are greatly appreciated. The editorial and clerical assistance of Anat Hampel, Kim Nuttall-Vazquez, Sandra Pierce-Jordan, David Shriberg, and Arminda Gomes also helped in making this book possible. Last but not least, the support and encouragement received from our respective nuclear and extended families were critical to the initiation and completion of this manuscript. Any deficiencies found are strictly our own responsibility or that of the collaborating authors.

E.V.N., I.R., & J.K.

CONTRIBUTORS

Vincent C. Alfonso, Ph.D., is assistant professor of school psychology at Fordham University where he coordinates the masters degree program in preschool psychology. In addition, he is executive director of the Rosa A. Haggin School Consultation Center and the Early Childhood Center at Fordham. Dr. Alfonso received his Ph.D. in the combined clinical and school psychology program at Hofstra University in 1990. Most recently he was appointed associate editor of *The School Psychologist,* Division 16's newsletter. He has held several positions in various psychology organizations including the New York State Psychological Association, the New York Association of School Psychologists, and the School Psychology Educators Council of New York State. Dr. Alfonso's research interests include preschool psychology, psychological and educational assessment, and subjective well being.

Jayne E. Bucy, Ph.D., is an assistant professor of psychology at Illinois State University in Normal, Illinois. She is a graduate of the University of North Carolina at Chapel Hill, earning her Ph.D. in School Psychology with a specialization in early intervention. As a school psychologist, she has worked with infants, toddlers, preschoolers, and their families since 1984. Her research interests include rituals in families with young children, and Asperger's Disease.

Michelle Cardona, M.S., is a bilingual school psychology M.S./C.A.G.S. graduate of Northeastern University. She has a B.A. in psychology from Sacred Heart University in San Juan, Puerto Rico. In the past two years she has completed two internships, an early intervention practicum and certificate, and a school psychology practicum in the Brookline public schools. She currently works as a Latino child coordinator for the Children's Home and Community Intensive Family Support Service program that serves the Department of Mental Retardation in Region VI—Merimack Valley in Haverhill, Massachusetts.

Tiffany Chenneville, M.A., has a Masters degree in clinical psychology from the University of Hartford and a Masters degree in school psychology from the University of South Florida. Her primary areas of interest include pediatric HIV/AIDS and legal and ethical issues in psychology.

Stephen T. DeMers, Ed.D., is a professor and director of the school psychology program at the University of Kentucky. He teaches courses in legal and ethical issues in psychology and has authored or co-authored numerous articles and book chapters on legal and ethical aspects of professional practice in psychology.

Jennifer L. Devaney, M.S., received her Master of Science and CAGS in school psychology from Northeastern University in 1994. Currently, she works as a school psychologist with preschool and elementary school children in a suburb of Boston.

Winnie Dunn, Ph.D., OTR, FAOTA, is a professor and the chairperson of the Occupational Therapy Education department for the University of Kansas Medical Center in Kansas City, Kansas. Dr. Dunn specializes in pediatric occupational therapy and is the author of the *Sensory Profile.*

Carolyn Pope Edwards, Ed.D., is a professor of psychology and family and consumer sciences at the University of Nebraska, Lincoln. She has also taught at the University of

Massachusetts, Amherst, and the University of Kentucky, and has held research appointments at the University of Nairobi, the National Research Council (Rome), and the Centre for Advanced Study (Oslo). Her fields of study are early childhood education and child development.

Catherine Fiorello, Ph.D., received her doctoral degree from the University of Kentucky in December, 1992. She has completed clinical post-doctoral studies in ADHD, worked in private practice, and taught part-time at the University of Kentucky. In the fall of 1996, she began an appointment as an assistant professor at Temple University, teaching and supervising interns in the school psychology program, including the early childhood specialization.

Dawn P. Flanagan, Ph.D., is an associate professor of school psychology at St. John's University in New York. Dr. Flanagan conducts research on the structure of intelligence, psychoeducational and preschool assessment, and professional issues in school psychology. Her articles and chapters on these topics appear in school and clinical psychology journals and books. She is senior editor of *Contemporary Intellectual Assessment: Theories, Test, & Issues,* co-author (with Kevin McGrew) of the forthcoming book, *The Intelligence Test Desk Reference (ITDR): Gf-Gc Cross-Battery Assessment,* and co-guest editor (with Judy Genshaft) of the 1997 School Psychology Review mini-series, *Issues in the Use and Interpretation of Intelligence Testing in the Schools.* Dr. Flanagan received the Lightner Witmer Award from the American Psychological Association at the 1997 annual meeting for her early achievements and outstanding scholarly contributions to the field.

Cheri Gilman, Ph.D., is an assistant professor in child and family studies at St. Cloud State University, where she teaches undergraduate and graduate courses in assessment and early childhood special education. Her research interests include linking assessment to intervention, and early childhood outcomes for all children including those with disabilities.

Vickie Gregory, Ph.D., J.D., obtained her Master of Science and doctoral degrees in psychology from Iowa State University. She obtained her Juris Doctor degree from the University of Utah. Dr. Gregory is presently in private practice in Salt Lake City, Utah, where she specializes in forensic neuropsychology and consultation.

Anat Hampel, M.S., received her B.A. in psychology and completed the education and women's studies programs at Brandeis University in 1994. She received her M.S. in school psychology at Northeastern University in 1996. She is currently completing a Ph.D. at Northeastern University in school and counseling psychology. Her research interests are in the field of neuropsychology. She is currently conducting research on the neuropsychological deficits resulting from chronic asthma and hypoxia.

Ceri B. Holm, Ed.S., earned a degree in school psychology from the University of Northern Colorado. She is a doctoral candidate at the University of Denver. Ms. Holm was a school psychologist in Colorado and an intervention specialist for National Civilian Community Corps, an Americorps Program. Currently, Ms. Holm is the assistant director of special education in Bryn Athyn, Pennsylvania.

Jennifer J. Johnson, M.A., is presently a psychologist doctoral intern working with the Kyrene school district in Tempe, Arizona. She received her Masters degree from the University of South Florida's school psychology program. She has published articles in *Women's Health: Research on Gender, Behavior, and Policy.*

Joanne Kalesnik, Ph.D., is a licensed psychologist who earned her masters and doctoral degrees in school psychology at the University of Massachusetts, Amherst. She worked as a school psychologist for the Amherst public schools and in private practice in Texas. She has been a part-time instructor for the University of Texas in Denton. Her work for the Easter Seal Society in Texas focused mostly on preschool children with disabilities. In this role she conducted hundreds of assessments of preschool children and their diverse families and helped determine appropriate placements and interventions. During the last two years, Dr. Kalesnik has been practicing school psychology in Seoul, Korea, by serving the children of United States military personnel. She travels throughout South Korea consulting with parents and teachers as well as assessing and treating preschoolers.

Howard M. Knoff, Ph.D., is director of the school psychology program at the University of South Florida, professor of school psychology, and a past president of the National Association of School Psychologists. He specializes in organizational consultation and school reform processes, personality assessment with children and adolescents, and behavior management and classroom discipline interventions, and has published extensively in these areas.

Louis J. Kruger, Psy.D., is an associate professor at Northeastern University, where he is a faculty member in both the specialist and doctoral programs in school psychology. His areas of interest are teamwork, computer-mediated collaboration, and organizational change. He is the founder of the first global computer network for school psychologists.

Marianne LaRoche, Ed.D., received her doctorate in school psychology from the University of Massachusetts, Amherst, in 1989. She is currently a practicing school psychologist and consultant. Dr. LaRoche resides in Northhampton, Massachusetts, with her two children, Aaron and Maggie.

Steven Landau, Ph.D., is a professor of psychology at Illinois State University. His current research focuses on the psychological sequelæ of children with attention-deficit/ hyperactivity disorder (ADHD) and school-based issues surrounding pediatric HIV. He formerly served as associate editor of the *School Psychology Review.*

Chieh Li, Ed.D., is an assistant professor in the school psychology program at Northeastern University. She has experience and expertise in psychological assessment, counseling, and consultation with culturally diverse children and parents, especially with Asian children and families. She publishes in both English and Chinese.

Karen Lifter, Ph.D., is an associate professor in the counseling psychology, rehabilitation, and special education program at Northeastern University. She received her B.A. in biology from Temple University and her Ph.D. in developmental psychology from Columbia University, and completed a post-doctoral specialization in developmental disabilities at the University of Massachusetts, Amherst. At Northeastern, she is principal investigator and director of the federally funded, interdisciplinary preparation program entitled "PROJECT TEAM: Teams Preparing Teams of Personnel to Serve Infants and Toddlers with Disabilities, and Their Families, from Linguistically and Culturally Diverse Backgrounds." She also directs the doctoral program in school and counseling psychology and the Masters' level teacher preparation program in special needs. Her research program centers on descriptive studies of children's play, language, and social development, and on intervention studies in which play activities are taught to young children with disabilities to facilitate their developments in cognition, language, and social competence. She developed the Developmental Play Assessment (DPA) tool as a result of her research program.

Toni Linder, Ed.D., is the chairperson of the child and family studies program and the graduate coordinator in the College of Education at the University of Denver. She is the author of *Early Childhood Special Education: Program Development and Administration* (1983), *Transdisciplinary Play-Based Assessment* (1990, 1993), and *Transdisciplinary Play-Based Intervention* (1993). Dr. Linder consults nationally on issues related to assessment and intervention and has worked with children with disabilities, high risk infants, and children exposed prenatally to drugs. She serves on several state advisory groups and is actively involved in many interagency efforts. Dr. Linder has also directed a school for children with disabilities and an inner-city Denver project for high risk infants. She has directed personnel preparation training grants for over 15 years.

Nancy Malatesta, CAGS, is a practicing elementary school psychologist in a western suburb of Boston, Massachusetts. She is also a licensed certified social worker and national board certified counselor. She provides psychological assessments for preschoolers and school-aged children, individual and group counseling and consultation. Childhood learning disabilities and social skills deficits are her professional areas of interest.

Glenn A. Masse, M.A., has a Master's degree in clinical psychology from the University of Massachusetts, Dartmouth, with an emphasis in Applied Behavioral Analysis. He is currently a doctoral candidate at Northeastern University in the combined school and counseling psychology program while working part-time as a behavioral consultant and service coordinator at an early intervention program in southeastern Massachusetts. This work primarily consists of consulting with parents, teachers, and therapists from other disciplines regarding family-system and child development issues. Previous work experience includes several positions providing psychological services for developmentally delayed children and their families.

Marcia Collins Moore, Ph.D., is a licensed psychologist in private practice in Oklahoma City, Oklahoma. Her experience involving children with visual impairments includes psychological and educational evaluation and program planning; individual, group, and family therapy; low-vision evaluation and treatment; parent workshops and retreats; consultation and in-service training with physicians and educators; and participation in local and national advocacy groups.

Yvonne Mullen, Ed.D., is the director of the psychology division at the Clarke School for the Deaf in Northampton, Massachusetts. She is a lecturer in the graduate teacher education program at Smith College and supervises school psychology interns from local graduate training programs as well as Gallaudet University. Dr. Mullen is a graduate of the University of Massachusetts, Amherst, earning a doctorate in school psychology with a focus on the successful mainstreaming of students with hearing impairments. A practicing school psychologist since 1972, she has worked with children, families, and educators in both public and specialized school settings. Her research interests include assessment, deafness, and ADHD.

Ena Vazquez Nuttall, Ed.D., obtained her doctoral degree in school psychology and counseling from Boston University. She is currently associate dean and director of the graduate school at the Bouvé College of Pharmacy and Health Sciences at Northeastern University. She is treasurer of Division 16 (School Psychology) of the American Psychological Association and has worked on several APA Committees, including chairing the Education and

Training Group of the Commission on Ethnic Minority Recruitment, Retention and Training. She was also a member of the Children, Youth, and Families committee. She has published widely and serves on the editorial board of *School Psychology Review* and *School Psychology Quarterly*. She is a member of the accreditation committee of the American Psychological Association. Involvement in the National Association of School Psychologists has included acting as delegate from Massachusetts and as a charter member of the National School Psychology Certification Board.

Kim Nuttall-Vazquez, M.S., received her Master's degree in counseling psychology in June, 1998, from Northeastern University. She received her Bachelor's degree in English literature from Boston College in 1991 and has several years of business experience. Currently she is completing an internship at the Simmons College Counseling Center.

Celiane Rey-Casserly, Ph.D., is director of postdoctoral training in neuropsychology at Children's Hospital, Boston and an instructor in psychiatry at Harvard Medical School. She has a diploma in clinical neuropsychology from the American Board of Professional Psychology. She serves on the American Psychological Association Task Force on Test User Qualifications.

Ivonne Romero, Ed.D., is the director of the Interamerican Psychology Clinic, a university-affiliated internship site at the Interamerican University of Puerto Rico, Metropolitan Campus. She has a doctorate in school psychology from the University of Massachusetts, Amherst, and a post-doctorate in child clinical neuropsychology from Harvard Medical School and Boston Children's Hospital. She has worked as a school psychologist at several school systems in Massachusetts and as a child clinical neuropsychologist at Boston Children's Hospital. She has been involved in research and publications centered on preschool assessment and on the neuropsychological sequelæ of childhood disorders such as leukemia.

Harry N. Seymour, Ph.D., is chairman of the department of communication disorders at the University of Massachusetts, Amherst, and a well-known researcher and author in the areas of child language development, disorders, and dialects. He is a Fellow of the American Speech-Language-Hearing Association.

Patricia Silver, Ed.D., is a professor in the School of Education at the University of Massachusetts and the director of Learning Disabilities Support Services. She has published on language and reading learning disabilities and assessment, and has conducted research in accommodating students with disabilities in higher education.

Tina Smith, Ph.D., is an assistant professor of school psychology in the College of Education at the University of Florida. She received her doctorate in school psychology with an emphasis on early childhood from the University of North Carolina.

Stephanie A. Stollar, Ph.D., is an educational consultant with the Southwest Ohio Special Education Regional Resource Center in Cincinnati, Ohio. Her current work involves providing technical assistance to school personnel who are using collaborative problem solving to support individual learners and systems-level change efforts.

Martha Thurlow, Ph.D., is an associate research fellow in educational psychology at the University of Minnesota. She has conducted research for over 25 years in a variety of areas, including assessment and decision making and learning disabilities in general education settings. She currently is editor of *Exceptional Children,* the research journal of the Council for Exceptional Children.

Ann H. Tyler, Ph.D., is affiliated with the Neuropsychiatric Institute of the University of Utah in Salt Lake City. She works extensively in the areas of violence and child maltreatment. A diplomate of the American Board of Psychological Specialties, Dr. Tyler's expertise is often utilized in forensic settings.

Kelly Walsh, M.S., is completing her doctorate in child and family studies at the University of Denver. She is currently living in New Mexico performing developmental assessments and follow-up for children in the Los Pasos Program, which provides medical, developmental, and social support to the families of children who have been exposed to drugs and alcohol.

Joan Riley Walton, Ed.D., has been practicing multicultural, bilingual psychology in the schools for over 20 years. She taught preschool assessment to school psychology students at Northeastern University and now teaches a practicum seminar. She lived in El Salvador, where she founded and consulted with eight preschool classes. Dr. Walton now works with the Taunton public schools and also has a bilingual counseling practice in the same town.

Toya A. Wyatt, Ph.D., is an associate professor in the communicative disorders program at California State University, Fullerton. Her primary areas of teaching and research include child language development, disorders, and assessment, with a special emphasis on the language development and assessment of African-American and bilingual children. Dr. Wyatt has presented numerous workshops and conference papers and has a number of publications dealing with these issues.

CHAPTER

1 Introduction

ENA VAZQUEZ NUTTALL

KIM NUTTALL-VAZQUEZ

ANAT HAMPEL

All children will be ready to learn.
—U.S. Congress, *Goals 2000: Educate America Act,* 1994

Why focus attention on young children? Why write a book on preschool assessment? The answer is, *one has to.* The Zeitgeist has converged to make this an ideal time to focus on identifying and helping children early in their lives (Peterson, 1987) so they will enter school ready to learn. Many factors have contributed to this favorable climate toward preschool and early childhood assessment and education services.

Among them is the concern for the quality of education of *all* children in the United States. North American children are not achieving educationally as well as those from other countries (IEA Third International Mathematics and Science Study, TIMSS, 1998). In the TIMSS study, involving 45 countries and more than a million students, American seventh and eighth graders scored 24th and 28th, respectively, in math achievement and 13th and 17th, respectively, in science. These low achievement levels prompted government officials and educational experts to develop national goals which include:

1. All children will be ready to learn.
3. Students in grades 4, 8, and 12 will have demonstrated competency over challenging subject matter including English, mathematics, science, foreign language, civics and government, economics, arts, history, and geography.
8. Every school will promote a partnership that will increase parents' involvement and participation.

The negative political and economic repercussions of this low academic achievement cannot be overstated. Starting to educate children early, especially poor children, is seen as the best way of ameliorating this serious situation.

1

A second factor to consider is the increasing number of children living in poverty. The Census Bureau has estimated that there were 14.6 million children in the United States (12.9% of the population) living in poverty during 1992 (Children's Defense Fund [CDF], 1994). However, when these figures are partitioned by age and race, black children younger than eighteen had a poverty rate of 39.8%, Hispanic children 32.2%, and white children 12.5% (CDF, 1994). Because of the strong link between poverty, disabling conditions, and learning problems, these high figures are cause for worry. According to a study published by the U.S. Department of Education, "Family income is a far more powerful correlate of a child's IQ at age five than maternal education, ethnicity, and growing up in a single parent family home" (CDF, 1994, p. 3).

A third factor is the increasing failure of schools to educate minority children properly. Statistics reveal that among major urban school systems, dropout rates range from one-third to two-fifths of the student population (Bowen in *Time,* February 1988). Since out of school usually means out of work, this high drop-out rate constitutes a serious national problem ("Here They Come", 1986). Helping children early is beginning to be seen as one of the few solutions to this problem. Studies have also shown that early educational intervention can significantly reduce later juvenile crime rates. These findings continue to support the assertion that early childhood services are rewarding in the social and financial arenas.

Regardless of financial condition, children with special needs and delays in cognition, perceptual-motor, language, social-emotional and other areas need early intervention programs. If the needs of these children are left unaddressed, the original disabilities will become more severe and secondary handicaps will appear. Their parents need to develop constructive child rearing practices early (Peterson, 1987).

On the positive side, there is a growing sense of confidence in the educational and financial effectiveness of early intervention services. The work of the Perry Preschool Project (Berrueta-Clement, Schweinhart, Barnett, Epstein, & Weikart, 1984) has shown that children who participated needed less costly special education services later, had higher projected lifetime earnings, and their parents had a greater amount of release time.

The passing of P.L. 94-142, the Education of the Handicapped Law, its amendments P.L. 99-457, and its re-authorizations P.L. 101-476 and recently P.L. 105-17, which mandate early intervention and preschool programs for children 0 to 5, reflect the continuing and increasing commitment to children with special needs by the federal government in the last 25 years.

All of these factors attest to the importance of concentrating attention on the education and services offered to preschoolers. Part of this effort involves providing excellence in training to personnel who work with preschool aged children. Among the activities which are important to serve these children and their families are early screening and assessment of their strengths and disabilities. This book aims at preparing professionals to provide competent and thorough assessments.

Definitions of Assessment

Early psychological scholars used the term "psychological testing" to refer to what is now known as psychological assessment. In 1982, Anastasi stated that "the function of psychological tests has been to measure differences between individuals or between the reactions of the same individual on different occasions" (p. 3). Palmer (1970) defined psychological assessment as "the use of scientific knowledge and methods in order to study the behavior problems of an individual child" (p. 3). Both authors view assessment as the search for differences and deficits, in contrast to the present perspective which is to identify problems in children and families and use this information to create interventions to solve them.

Many scholars have attempted to define the term *assessment* (Anastasi, 1988; Maloney & Ward, 1976; McReynolds, 1968; Salvia & Ysseldyke, 1995; Sattler, 1992), emphasizing different aspects of the process in their definitions. For example, Maloney and Ward (1976) define assessment as:

> psychological assessment is a process of solving problems (answering questions) in which psychological tests are often used as one of the methods of collecting relevant data. (p. 5)

One of the most important aspects of this definition is its emphasis on assessment as a way of finding solutions to problems. Assessments should be conducted with a specific purpose in mind; they should not be unplanned safaris or boring rituals. Another important distinction they make is that persons conducting assessments should include more than psychological tests in their approach. Assessment should not be synonymous with the administration of formal tests.

Another perspective is provided by McReynolds (1968) who defines psychological assessment as:

> the systematic use of a variety of special techniques in order to better understand a given individual, group, or psychological ecology. (p. 2)

McReynolds's (1968) definition is useful because it emphasizes that testing is a systematic activity which is planned and organized in advance. Consistent with Maloney and Ward (1976), McReynolds highlights the use of a variety of assessment techniques in the process of evaluation, in contrast to the sole use of formal tests. In addition, he underscores that assessment does not have to focus on the individual, it can include units of different sizes, such as a child, a family, a classroom, or a whole social system.

Salvia and Ysseldyke (1995) are more specific in their definition:

> Assessment is the process of collecting data for the purpose of making decisions about students. (p. 5)

They emphasize the function of assessment as a decision making tool in educational and psychological intervention. The decisions made with assessment data commonly include: pre-referral, classroom decisions, entitlement decisions, post-entitlement classroom decisions, and accountability decisions. Problem areas assessed typically include academic problems, behavior problems, and physical problems.

Knoff (in this volume) emphasizes that assessment should be multi-method, multi-source, and multi-setting. This implies that different methods should be used when obtaining data, including interviews, observations, examination of records, and informal and formal testing. Different sources should also be involved, including the child, family, teachers, therapists, and other pertinent personnel. Multi-setting means that the child should be observed and tested in different settings, including the home, school, playground, hospital, and elsewhere. Knoff emphasizes that the new mission of assessment is to solve problems and design interventions.

Meisels and Provence (1989), experts in young children at risk and with disabilities, affirm the change in function of the assessment process by stating:

> Screening and assessment should be viewed as services—as part of the intervention—and not only as means of identification and measurement.... Assessment, in particular, should be approached as an ongoing, dynamic process with multiple components, including case management, family support, transitional programs, and the development of the IFSP/IEP. (p. 23)

This author defines preschool assessment as the process of obtaining information from different levels, through different means, and in different contexts, to identify the problems experienced by children who are at risk or with disabilities and by their families, and to design solutions to solve those problems.

In this section, we have reviewed the definitions of assessment, starting with a narrow conceptualization of the process as solely to identify and measure individual differences, to the current ecologically based definitions that emphasize different contexts and levels and the active implementation of assessment findings. In the next section, we will review the history of assessment instruments and the issues of validity and reliability within these instruments.

History and Current Status of Preschool Assessment

The history of preschool assessment is not long. Kelley and Surbeck (1991), in an extensive review of this history, identify two periods of high productivity in a field that has been dominated by the assessment of school age children. The first period of high development includes the contribution of Arnold Gessell (1925), who at the Yale Clinic for Child Development created a "developmental schedule" that contained approximately 150 items in four areas: motor development, language development, adaptive behavior, and personal-social behavior. His work, which spanned a period of about 40 years, influenced and is still influencing the construction of tests for preschool children.

Kelley and Surbeck (1991) point out other assessment instruments for infants and preschoolers developed during this period: the Merrill-Palmer Scale of Mental Tests (Stutsman, 1931), the Minnesota Preschool Scale (Goodenough, Maurer, & Van Wagemen, 1940), the Goodenough-Draw-a-Man Test (Goodenough, 1926), the California First Year Mental Scale (Bayley, 1933), and the Iowa Tests for Young Children (Fillmore, 1936). The central concern of the field at that time was the reliability, predictive validity, and stability of the tests.

The 1960s was a golden age for preschool assessment (Anastasi, 1988). The funding of the 1964 Child Health and Mental Retardation Act and of the Head Start and Follow Through Programs created great need for preschool tests for diagnosis, monitoring, and program evaluation. Tests were designed to measure the taxonomy of goals included in Head Start instruction: the affective, intellectual, psychomotor, and subject achievement domains (Hoepfner, Stern, & Nummedal, 1971).

The Center for the Study of Evaluation at the University of California in Los Angeles reviewed over 120 preschool and kindergarten tests (Hoepfner et al., 1971). Of these 120 tests (comprised of 630 subtests), only 7 subtests were rated as providing good validity. Most tests were rated poor or fair for normed technical excellence. The old problems of inadequate validity and standardization procedures had not been solved (Kelley & Surbeck, 1991).

The present status of preschool assessment instruments still leaves much to be desired (Bracken, 1987; Lehr, Ysseldyke, & Thurlow, 1986; Thurlow & Ysseldyke, 1979). In 1979, Thurlow and Ysseldyke evaluated the validity, reliability, and norms of the most frequently used tests in federally funded Child Service Demonstration Centers (CSDC) and found that only 7 of the 28 tests reviewed were technically adequate in all psychometric properties. A similar analysis by Lehr, Ysseldyke, and Thurlow in 1986 using Handicapped Children's Early Education Program demonstration projects across the United States revealed that among the 19 most commonly used devices, only 3 (Vineland, McCarthy, and K-ABC) were technically adequate.

In a similar study, Bracken (1987) analyzed the 10 most commonly used preschool instruments, focusing on total test and subtest internal consistency, test-retest reliability, floor adequacy, the steepness of subtest item gradients, and the presence of validity information. He concluded that many of the tests designed for preschool use are severely limited in floor, item gradient, and reliability, especially at the lower age levels. Preschool assessment below the age of 4 presents the greatest psychometric problems.

Concern over the problem of psychometric and practical appropriateness of norm-referenced tests has intensified, due to a study conducted by Bagnato and Neisworth (1994) on the treatment invalidity of intelligence testing for early intervention. On a national consumer study of preschool psychologists (n = 185), they found that early intelligence tests failed to be workable or acceptable tools 43% of the time and failed to document the eligibility for early intervention of over 3,000 young children. Although this study focused only on the validity of the intelligence tests and did not also address this question for all the other possible measures, the findings underscore the need to use other types of measures. Assessment personnel working with preschool children should be mindful of the poor psychometric status and the treatment invalidity of early preschool assessment norm-referenced measures. Care should be taken to select the best normed, criterion-referenced and judgment-based instruments available and to supplement them with observations, interviews, play assessments, examination of records, and informal measures.

Introducing the Ecological Model

Many assessment scholars are advocating the use of an ecological model to guide the assessment of children and adolescents (e.g., Knoff, this volume; Paget & Nagle, 1986). Vazquez-Nuttall and Nuttall propose an ecologically based assessment approach which has been greatly influenced by the work of Bronfenbrenner (1977, 1979), Brim (1975), and Barker and associates (1978).

Bronfenbrenner (1977) has noted the nested arrangement of structures that constitute an ecological system. He states that the smallest element (in this context) is the *microsystem,* which "is the complex of relations between the developing person and environment in an immediate setting containing that person (e.g., home, school, work place, etc.)" A *setting* is defined as "a place with particular physical features in which participants engage in particular roles (e.g., daughter, parent, teacher, employee, etc.) for particular periods of time. The factors of place, time, physical features, activity, participant, and role constitute the elements of setting" (p. 514).

Above the microsystem level are *mesosystems,* which are the interrelations among the major settings containing a person at any given point in time. The next level up are the *exosystems,* which include the formal and informal specific social structures that impinge on the target person.

Also included in the Bronfenbrenner model are the concepts of *macrosystems,* which he defines as the overarching institutional patterns of the culture or subculture that generally carry information and endow meaning and motivation to institutions and activities.

Figure 1.1 presents the Vazquez-Nuttall version of the Bronfenbrenner model adapted to the preschool child and his or her family. This model borrows from earlier work (Vazquez-Nuttall & Nuttall, 1979) conducted with Italian and Hispanic handicapped children and their families. The innermost circle of the model addresses the individual child and the realms of behavior that are important to include in assessment and that, if found to be deficient, will be

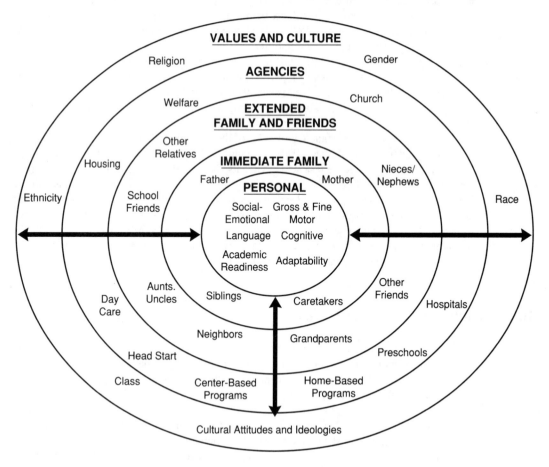

FIGURE 1.1 The Ecomap of Child and Family Functioning

Adapted from Knopf, H., *The Assessment of Child and Adolescent Personality,* 1986, p. 16

addressed in the interventions. These realms are cognitive, social-emotional, language, gross and fine motor skills, academic readiness, and adaptability. Most of the assessment done at this level focuses on the child. The child may be tested directly with formal and informal tests, or be observed in the home, classroom, hospital and/or playground. The family or child caretakers are usually asked to report on the present and past performance of the child in these areas. P.L. 99-457, the Education of the Handicapped Act Amendments (ERIC, 1988), and its reauthorizations (P.L. 101-476 and P.L. 105-17) stipulate that for children 0 to 3, a statement of the child's present level of development must be obtained for inclusion in the Individual Family Service Plan (IFSP).

The second circle of the model, the immediate family, focuses on those people who are in direct charge of the child, including parents, step-parents, foster parents, relatives or other primary caretakers. The legislation is very specific as to the information to be obtained at this level for children 0 to 3: a statement of the family strengths and needs relating to enhancing the child's development, and of the major outcomes expected to be achieved by the child and family. For older preschoolers, information to be obtained at this level usually includes developmental history and the structure and dynamics of the family. This information is usually obtained through formal and informal interviews and family observations.

The extended family and friends of both parents are included within the third circle. The literature on family support systems (Vazquez-Nuttall & Nuttall, 1979; Lynch & Hanson, 1992) underscores the importance of relatives, especially in families of culturally and linguistically different backgrounds, in helping deal with the stresses and demands of caring for a child with special needs. Availability, type, and quality of support, or the absence of such, is important information to be obtained during the family interview. Inquiries should also be made about friends, neighbors, and work mates since they often can play significant roles in helping parents cope with a child with disabilities.

Agencies, the next focus, are extremely important because parents of preschool handicapped children especially need the services of child-care agencies and schools. Availability of public education is mandated by federal legislation (P.L. 101-476 (IDEA) and P.L. 105-17) which requires all states to ensure a free and appropriate education for all children with handicaps aged 3 to 5. The assessment process should include information about the location of the family and the presence and nature of preschool services available in the city or town where the child lives.

The outermost circle of the model is concerned with values and culture. Infants and preschool children are more purely products of their particular culture than children who have been socialized for several years into American culture by the schools. Evaluators assessing multicultural preschoolers need to be careful in their assessments, since most developmental norms have been obtained on mainstream children only (Westby, 1986). It is important to understand the family structure and dynamics of different ethnic groups (McGoldrick, Pearce, & Giordano, 1996; Lynch & Hanson, 1992), as well as their child rearing patterns. It is also important to be cognizant of the differences in patterns of development of children from different cultures (Field, Sostek, Vietze, & Leiderman, 1981). For instance, studies have shown that black infants are generally more motorically advanced in comparison to other ethnic or cultural groups (Brazelton, Koslowski, & Tronick, 1976).

It is crucial for persons conducting assessments to obtain information about the racial and ethnic background of the child and to take this data into consideration when administering and interpreting assessment results. This information is also extremely important when a person is designing service delivery plans.

In summary, the ecological model presented here offers a comprehensive guide to the assessment and intervention of preschool children with special needs. It includes the different settings, factors, agencies, and people which need to be considered when designing a reliable, valid, and useful evaluation and service plan.

Summary

This introductory chapter defined assessment as a process directed at solving problems using multiple sources and measures while taking into account the child and family and the context in which they function. A review of the short history of preschool assessment concluded that the state of the art of the field is in great need of improvement and assessment personnel need to use multiple measures to increase the validity and accuracy of evaluations. Sole reliance on intelligence tests should be abandoned.

Assessment is an activity that demands much knowledge—of normal and abnormal development, ethical and legal issues, cultural and social aspects of behavior, psychometric concepts, and many different kinds of measures and techniques—as well as many skills involving the ability to analyze and interpret all information and to write and present it in terms of action plans. This book supplies the foundation for meeting these demands.

2 Development in the Preschool Years

The Typical Path

CAROLYN POPE EDWARDS

The preschool years are a time of far-reaching and dramatic changes in thought and behavior. Physically, the child develops from a round-bellied toddler with wide stance and swaying walk, into a school-age child of slimmer and more mature proportions, able to run and leap, hop, twirl, and skip. Under family guidance, the child takes those first steps toward self-reliance—whether in eating, dressing, hygiene, toileting, sleeping alone, or helping around the house—that are defined as "must do's" by the culture. The beginning communicator limited to one- or two-word phrases is transformed into one capable of complex sentences embodying knowledge of rules and relationships. Less obvious, but equally important, the child's sense of self is born, including commitment to standards of right and wrong; empathy for the feelings and desires of others; and awareness of basic social categories such as age, sex, and race. Underlying all these changes are measurable changes in brain size and structure changes that make possible successive waves of reorganization in cognitive capacity and in emotionality and emotion regulation.

Although various domains of development—physical, motor, cognitive, linguistic, social, moral, and emotional—are thus distinguished for the purposes of study and discussion, they are actually inseparable. Each aspect of development influences and is influenced by the others. It is difficult to argue that one area of development is "more basic" or more important to the practitioner who works with children.

This chapter, however, will begin with a sketch of the physical and motor changes, because they have been the longest studied. Following is a discussion of cognitive change, because it is the author's view that the three basic cognitive reorganizations of the preschool years provide insight into the other areas of development. This framework may help professionals to remember, recognize, and support desirable growth in many facets of thought and action during the preschool years, across all the areas of development, including linguistic, social, moral, and emotional. A holistic visual panorama of child development—with many scenarios drawn from cultures around the world—can be found in the video series, *Childhood* (Public Broadcasting System, 1991), accompanied by the text (Konner, 1991).

Physical and Motor Development

Height and Weight

In the first two years of life, babies quadruple their weight and increase their height by two-thirds. During the next 4 years, growth still takes place rapidly (but at a continually slower and slower rate). The average 2-year-old child in North America weighs 27 pounds and is 34 inches tall. By age 6, this child has typically gained 20 pounds and grown 12 inches (Hamill, Drizd, Johnson, Reed, Roche, & Moore, 1979). Sex differences are slight, although boys on average are a bit taller, heavier, and more muscular.

Physical growth normally takes place rather smoothly and gradually. One normal irregularity is that children grow almost three times faster in the spring than in the fall! This has something to do with the way seasonal changes in sunlight are experienced, because the springtime growth spurt is not seen in blind children or in children who live near the equator. Stress and emotional neglect can affect growth in a negative way. When high familial stress blocks the parent–child relationship, the young child may become weak and apathetic and may fail to "thrive" and grow. This condition, reversible if not too prolonged and severe, is labeled Reactive Attachment Disorder of Infancy and Early Childhood in the *Diagnostic and Statistical Manual of Mental Disorders,* fourth edition (DSM-IV; American Psychiatric Association, 1994). Of course, population trends in physical growth are affected primarily by heredity: On average, children of African descent are tallest, those of Asian descent shortest, and those of European and North American descent fall in between. Children are affected secondarily by their environment, as major differences in health care and nutrition create variations in physical growth.

Brain Growth

The brain grows especially rapidly during the early years. By age 2, the brain is already about 75% of its adult size, and by age 6 about 90% (Tanner, 1978). Brain growth is not steady but occurs in distinct waves. There seems to be one spurt at about 2 years and a large one between 3 and 5 years of age (Fischer & Lazerson, 1984). As we shall see, these spurts are associated with periods of major cognitive development.

Much of the brain increase results from *myelinization,* the growth of insulating covers around nerve fibers to allow them to conduct impulses more efficiently. The nerve fibers that connect the higher and lower cortex are not completely myelinated until age 4 or later; these are the fibers that assist the fine motor skills of drawing and writing necessary for school. In addition to myelinization, changes take place in the organization and size of nerve cells. They extend their interconnections and acquire more nutrition-bearing capillaries nearby. Under the microscope, the brain looks increasingly dense and complex.

Another major structural change in the brain is the beginning of *hemispheric lateralization,* the tendency for the two halves of the brain to perform different functions. The left side comes to deal increasingly with information in a sequential or linear way. The right side identifies patterns or relationships holistically.

Lateral preferences (behaviors best performed with one side of the body) also emerge during the preschool years. Most people are neither totally right- nor totally left-handed. A right-handed person may be left-eared (in listening to the telephone) or left-eyed (in peering through a telescope). Only rarely, however, do people show a lack of lateral preference, for example, in being able to write equally well with both hands.

Motor Development

As the brain matures, it allows for better control and coordination of movement with sensory information. The welcome result for the child are major strides in large and fine motor skills. These improvements take place gradually, however, because they also require learning and opportunities for practice or training.

Following are some sample large muscle activities the average North American child demonstrates: At age 2, jump 12 inches, throw ball overhand; at age 3, balance on one foot for one second, walk on tiptoe, and hop on both feet three times; at age 4, descend stairs with alternating feet, and hop on one foot up to six times; at age 5, skip smoothly, balance on one foot for several seconds, hop on one foot many times, and start, stop, and turn effectively in games. Here are some examples of fine motor skills: At age 2, scribble spontaneously, hold a glass with one hand, and construct a tower of 6 to 8 blocks; at age 3, copy a circle, eat with a spoon, and smear and daub paint; at age 4, draw shapes and simple figures, cut on a line with scissors, and use blocks to make buildings; at age 5, copy squares, letters and numbers, string beads, and use utensils and tools correctly. Although exceptional skill in motor tasks does not indicate superior intelligence, practitioners should watch for motor skill development because severe delays may indicate a need for medical and/or educational intervention. For more in-depth information on gross and fine motor development, read Chapter 13.

Skeletal Age and Maturity

Throughout childhood, physical size correlates strongly with age, but it is not the most accurate indicator of the child's physical maturity. The most accurate indicator is skeletal age, estimated by the percentage of cartilage replaced by bone. In most children, chronological age, skeletal age, and size correlate well, but for children whose growth is abnormal, knowing their skeletal age may be useful. For example, it can indicate whether a very short boy (from an adequate environment) is simply a slow and late maturer, or whether he suffers from an inadequate amount of growth hormones.

An interesting fact about skeletal age is that it confirms that girls are maturationally ahead of boys throughout childhood (Fischer & Lazerson, 1984). At birth, girls are already four weeks ahead of boys in skeletal age, and at age 13 they are almost two years ahead. This developmental difference is not just confined to bones. Girls' teeth erupt earlier. Baby girls achieve half their adult height at about 1.9 years, versus 2.5 years for baby boys. Girls perform almost all motor skills earlier than boys, on average: creeping, sitting, walking, talking, toileting, dressing, writing. Boys have the advantage only in large muscle activities (running, throwing, climbing) because of their slightly greater strength and better large muscle coordination.

Given these facts, it should not be surprising to find out that in cultural communities around the world—rural and urban, Western and non-Western—mothers generally expect daughters to show more mature and responsible social behavior than sons of the same age (Whiting & Edwards, 1988). Observations of mother–child behavior indicate that the most universal sex difference lies in young girls receiving earlier and more serious training to participate in subsistence and household work of all kinds (except care of large animals), and to take social responsibility that requires self-control and accommodation to the needs of others (e.g., care of infant and toddler siblings). Girls are also seen to be more cooperative with maternal requests for socially mature behavior. We mention the sex difference in developmental rate not to exaggerate it or give it undue significance, but to remind the reader of the interconnectedness of development.

Cognitive Development

During the years the child is shooting physically out of toddlerhood, he or she is also taking another kind of giant step mentally. Intellectual processes change profoundly during the years between 2 and 6. Two processes basic to learning, *memory* and *attention,* show greatly improved power. The preschooler can remember more things than before. For instance, in one of the most common tests of "memory span," the subject must repeat a list of numbers or words immediately after hearing it. This task is part of many IQ tests. At age 3 children typically have a span of about 3 items, at age 4 about 4 items, at age 6 about 5 items, and at age 8 about 6 items. Furthermore, the preschooler can do more complex remembering than the infant (e.g., recalling action sequences instead of single acts) and begins to have conscious strategies for remembering (e.g., saying something over and over to him- or herself, or drawing a picture).

The improved power of attention with age is something especially noticeable to adults. *Attention span* for a focused task increases from about a quarter-hour at age 3 up to an hour by age 6, while at the same time *selective attention* also increases, involving increased ability to focus attention on critical information and ignore irrelevant information (Sigelman & Shaffer, 1994). From age 4 onwards, furthermore, *systematic attention* increases, involving increased ability to plan and carry out systematic perceptual searches. By the end of the preschool years, children become much easier to teach, to interview, and to test because they can follow adult directions and/or sustain a group task longer, with less distractibility, and with more self-control.

But the intellectual changes most fascinating to teachers and parents involve not those quiet, quantitative improvements in memory and attention, but the dramatic, qualitative changes in how children think about and understand their world. There, the key breakthrough of early childhood is *symbolization,* the use of images, words, or mental actions to represent events or experiences. Children begin to break out of the strait-jacket of here-and-now, sensorimotor intelligence at around 18 months or 2 years of age. Their new potential is seen when they begin to pretend in play, imitate actions they observed earlier, search with determination for missing objects, and put words together to talk about the world. Yet the ways in which they form and connect their thoughts still show many limitations that can make their statements humorous or incomprehensible to adults.

The cognitive theorist who surely has most advanced our understanding of the special qualities of preschool thinking is Jean Piaget (1896–1980). Piaget (1983) argued that the development of intelligence involves qualitative changes in the way that people think, not merely quantitative changes in how much they know. He characterized the preschool child in terms of his second stage, "preoperational intelligence," meaning the child does not yet command the logical operations of thought that underlie reasoning and the concepts of time, space, causality, and number.

In a helpful metaphor, Piaget compared the child's thinking to a slow-motion movie projector, with its series of static images going by in succession. During the sensorimotor stage, the infant can only process (that is, look at) one image at a time. When the infant moves on to the next image, he forgets the first one. During the preoperational stage, the preschool mind becomes able to move along with the succession of images and remember their order. But the child still does not grasp what transformations take place between the beginning and end of the film. During the concrete operational stage, the mind of the schoolchild takes control of the projector. Now the child can run the film forward and backward at will and can recognize the connections sequences. The child can remember individual frames as well as what part each plays in the film as a whole. Finally (to add to Piaget's metaphor) we can say that during the formal operational state, the adolescent becomes the film director, able not only to understand the one concrete film, but also to make an abstract map of other hypothetical plots, staging plans, and characterizations.

Piaget's theory has aroused controversy and dispute. Yet many have found the hypotheses of the active, constructive mind, qualitative change, and equilibration processes to be compelling, along with much of the specific description of each age period. It is noteworthy, for example, that virtually all of the current texts in child development devote the bulk of their discussions of preschool mental development to Piagetian theory.

Building on Piaget's theory, many cognitive theorists have attempted to create revisions that respond to the major criticisms, account for new research findings, and integrate the strong points of alternative theories and perspectives on cognitive development. Well-known examples include Jerome Bruner, Jerome Kagan, and Howard Gardner.

One neo-Piagetian theorist currently active is Robbie Case, whose account retains the Piagetian notion of *central conceptual structures* (defined as semantic nodes and relations that represent core knowledge in a domain and that can be applied to all cognitive tasks in that domain). Major transformations of core structures are hypothesized to take place as children enter each new stage of development (Case & Okamoto, 1996). Once formed, new structures influence all subsequent knowledge acquisition via dynamic processes in which general and specific insights are reciprocally coupled, each enhancing the other. Thus, cognitive development involves both stage-like changes and continuous skill acquisitions—each exerting a "bootstrapping effect" on the other side.

Another influential neo-Piagetian is Kurt Fischer, whose system is useful because it presents the most detailed explanations of the changes that take place within the early childhood years. Fischer (1980) and Fischer, Hand, Watson, Van Parys, and Tucker (1984) present 10 hierarchical cognitive "skill" levels, organized into three tiers. A *skill* is an organized ability, under voluntary control, tied to a context. The *sensorimotor* tier (typical of infancy, and corresponding to Piaget's sensorimotor stage) consists of skills composed of sensory perceptions and motoric actions on objects, events, or people in the real world. The *representational* tier (typical of early and middle childhood, and corresponding to Piaget's preoperational and concrete operational stages) consists of skills composed of symbolic concepts with concrete referents by which children can think of things independently of looking at or acting on them. The *abstract* tier (typical of adolescence and adulthood, and corresponding to Piaget's formal operational stage) consists of skills composed of concepts that apply to broad categories of objects, events, or people, such as *cruelty* and *symmetry*. Abstract concepts can be manipulated, analyzed, and compared independent of the particular concrete instances to which they apply.

These ten skill levels underlie all thinking. Fischer argues, however, that the concept of "level" is preferable to "stage" because the latter implies that children will tend to use one level of thinking across all subject areas. In fact, development is usually uneven: Children are never at the same skill level for all subject areas. But individual children do have one highest or optimal level of which they are capable at a given time; and as their brains mature and their powers of memory increase, their optimal level increases. An important hypothesis is that during periods of rapid change, such as the early childhood years, children's optimal level in spontaneous play closely matches their optimal level as assessed by formal tests. Young children use play as a context for pushing their intelligence forward; thus, their play can be a good indicator of their optimal level.

Language Development

Language is the main way that human beings around the world communicate and demonstrate their preeminent representational competence. Already by the end of the first year of life, babies may know and use many single words—*dog, no, out, up*. They typically use their single words in a simple presymbolic way (saying "*Up!*" to be lifted), comparable to their use of action routines like pointing to the door to go out, or reaching up to be held (Fischer & Lazerson, 1984). But language really takes off at around 18 months or 2 years, when children simultaneously begin to show symbolic capacities in play and such social behaviors as imitation and pretending.

A true explosion is evident in the young child's growth of vocabulary. At 18 months, the child's vocabulary is usually more than 3 words but less than 50. Average spoken vocabulary then increases rapidly, from about 200 to 300 words at age 2, to about 1,600 words at age 4, to over 2,500 words at age 6 (Moskowitz, 1978). Carey (1977) estimated that her sample of 6-year-olds had a comprehension vocabulary of between 8,000 and 14,000 words. Preschool children are very sensitive to new words and will begin to use them before they fully understand their meaning. This is one of the reasons that young children can learn a second language so easily.

In order to convey their ideas, children must now begin to put their words together into phrases and sentences, resulting in their showing steadily increasing mean length of utterance (MLU). Speaking in sentences requires them to learn their language's grammar. Children everywhere learn grammar, without being explicitly taught, through a combination of listening, imitation, inference, and trial and error. This process of gradually mastering grammatical rules has been the focus of much study, fortunately not limited to English-speaking children but rather extended to 40 different languages, possessing vastly different grammatical structures.

After the single-word stage, children move on to 2- or 3-word phrases that leave out "little words" (articles, conjunctions) to express the essentials of meaning. This *telegraphic speech* tends to express a limited range of kinds of ideas no matter what language the child is learning, suggesting that these basic meanings reflect the 2-year-old's view of what is important. Here are the most frequent types, with examples (deVilliers & deVilliers, 1979, p. 47).

action-agent "me fall"	*recurrence* "more milk"
action-object "bump table"	*labeling* "this truck"
possession "my teddy"	*nonexistence* "no more soup"
location "cup in box"	

Telegraphic speech also reflects the young child's first response to the grammar challenge. In English, where word order is such an important way of conveying correct meaning, young children demonstrate the *subject-action-object* order as their first strong rule, before they use grammatical inflections. In Russian, where word endings are more important than word order, young children use endings correctly in their telegraphic speech but their word orders are more variable (Slobin, 1982). Most of the early language milestones are culturally universal; all babies coo, babble, understand before speaking, speak their first word at about 12 months, go through the one-word phase beginning about 18 months before joining words, and pay more attention to the ends of words than the beginnings, so that they learn suffixes before they learn prefixes. But cultural variations become evident with respect to syntactical learning and in children's early attempts to construct sentences in the language they are hearing.

Furthermore, cultural diversity is seen in the manner in which children interact with others to learn language (Owens, 1992). For example, not all cultures within the United States place the same emphasis on verbal communication. Among some Latinos and Native Americans, silence is associated with self-restraint, and children are encouraged to be silent and thoughtful, to listen, and to pause before speaking. Mothers' roles in language teaching vary also; in some groups of African American and inner-city Puerto Rican background, the mother does not view herself as the main communication partner for toddlers; rather, this role should be taken by peers and siblings. Social class differences are prominent, too; middle class children come to schools prepared to tell topic-oriented, sequentially organized narratives, but children from lower or working class backgrounds may have less skill in organizing their material logically, though they show competence in selecting vivid examples and using humor or other dramatic modes to embellish their stories. Children from Hispanic and some Native American cultures may be more visually than verbally oriented when they start school.

Regardless of cultural or socioeconomic background and verbal style, however, children's speech develops in predictable ways as they grow older. Their speech becomes less telegraphic and they add more elements to their speech, such as pronouns, prepositions, articles, auxiliary verbs, and the grammatical morphemes (prefixes or suffixes) called *inflections*. They elaborate the basic structure of the sentence to reflect more complex relational knowledge.

One especially significant way that children express this knowledge is by use of "relational words" (deVilliers & deVilliers, 1979). They gradually come to use words like *big/little, short/tall, young/old, hot/cold,* whose correct application depends on what is being described; for example, a small truck is actually bigger than a large apple. Most of the development of use of these opposite concepts takes place after age 3. Other relational words, like *this/that* and *here/there,* shift their reference according to the speaker's (not the listener's) location. Young children first use these words correctly to describe locations relative to themselves as speakers, before they correctly interpret them with reference to other speakers. A third class of words that shift their reference according to context is pronouns. Normal children have little difficulty in correctly using *I/you* and *mine/your* by age 2 or 3. Autistic children, in contrast, may grow up reversing *I* and *you,* or saying *he* or *she* when *you* is the appropriate pronoun, suggesting a fundamental difficulty in conceptualizing relational knowledge about the social situation (deVilliers & deVilliers, 1979).

Children's speech also comes to embody ever more complex grammatical rules. Children learn simpler rules first, where the grammatical simplicity as well as the simplicity of the underlying meaning is the issue. Because the complexity of a grammatical rule depends on what language is being spoken, the age at which children typically master a rule depends partly on their language.

After word order, English-speaking children customarily begin to add inflections to their words to express grammatical information. The plural *-s* and progressive *-ing* almost always appear first, followed by the prepositions *in* and *on,* the articles *a* and *the,* and then the verb markers such as the past regular *-ed* and the third person singular *s.* At the same time, they gradually expand the length of their sentences. They construct simple noun phrases to substitute for single nouns, first at the end of sentences (*"I saw that brown dog"*), later at the beginning (*"That brown dog is mine."*) After adding verb inflections, they go on to add the verb auxiliaries *can, do, will, may,* and later the more difficult ones such as *would, should, have, has, had.* They express negation in progressively more complex ways: first by saying *no* or *not;* later by using auxiliaries such as *won't, can't, don't;* and much later by using the negative with indefinites such as *some, none, any.* They ask questions: first by means of simple rising voice inflection (*"I have some?"*), later by using the *wh* words (*where, what, whose, who, why, how, when*). The first four of these are simpler for children to use because they are answered by specifying a place, object, action, or person. The latter three are more complex because they require a reason, manner in which, or time. Children also master techniques for joining thoughts together in sentence clauses, conjunctions of two sentences, connectives, and pronominalizations. As the preschool period ends, they typically begin to express reversible passives (*"The boy was chased by the bear"*) and indirect object–direct object constructions (*"The man showed his son the book"*).

In acquiring all of these rules, children seem to act on a basic operating principle: "Avoid exceptions!" They exhibit the well-known behavior of overregularization, the over-application of a rule even where it does not correctly apply. Overregularization actually indicates that a child knows a rule. Before a child knows it, he may use correctly a few words that are "exceptions" to a rule but were learned by rote. For example, the 3-year-old may say, correctly, "two *feet*" or "I *broke* it." Later, when he begins to apply the rules for pluralization and past tense, he will overregularize and say "two *feets*" and "I *breaked* it." By the time the child reaches school age, he usually has the correct noun plurals and past tenses again, but other errors will persist into later years. For example, he may still say, "I would have *broke* it" or "She shouldn't have *came.*"

Social and Moral Knowledge

Self-Awareness

The preschool period dawns, in a social sense, with the child's revolutionary discovery that he or she is a separate being from other people, a "self." No doubt, even infants associate the feelings of their body with the sight of their limbs and their own sounds, but this body consciousness does not mean they differentiate themselves from others.

A sense of self is not acquired all at once. The concept of self, as it develops, comes to be multifaceted and to involve feelings as much as thoughts. *Self-recognition* is an essential first step. At about 18 months or 2 years, children begin to use the mirror as if they know it reflects their own image (Lewis & Brooks, 1974). The great apes are the only other animals with this capacity.

Psychological self-awareness is more difficult to see from the outside. Do toddlers have a concept of an inner self that thinks and feels in privacy from others? Psychoanalytically oriented observers claim that 2-year-olds undergo a crisis of self-confidence when they realize that they are not omnipotent and that their parents operate under separate control (Mahler, Pine, & Bergman, 1975). By age 3, children appear to have a rudimentary concept of a private, thinking self (Maccoby, 1980), but not until well into the school years do they describe themselves in terms of stable personality traits. When younger children are asked to describe themselves, they list facts about their bodies, what they can do, their possessions, their likes and dislikes, and other concrete characteristics. This fits with Piaget's claim that concrete operations are needed to conserve psychological dispositions such as "kindness" and intelligence.

As the self-concept develops during the preschool years, its component dimensions emerge and begin to be important. Disturbances in any of them can lead to the development of an emotionally or behaviorally troubled child. Yet preschool children are particularly resilient and are good subjects for treatment because their self-concept is still fluid and changeable.

Self-esteem—one's feelings of self-approval—is the evaluative dimension. The preschooler does not yet have the cognitive capacity for a stable understanding of how she is (the "real self"), or stable notions of what she wants to be (the "ideal self") (Perry & Bussey, 1984). So although she is sensitive to the kind of acceptance, approval, and respect she receives from beloved adults and can easily be made to feel good or bad, proud or ashamed, about what she has done, it is not until the school years that she can construct evaluations of self-worth that are conscious, based on society's standards, and resistant to change (Coopersmith, 1967).

Locus of control is a dimension of belief about whether one "internally" controls one's behavior and its outcomes, or whether one is "externally" controlled by fate, luck, or other circumstances. This dimension correlates strongly with school success, and its foundations may be laid down as early as infancy (Perry & Bussey, 1984). Infants and toddlers whose mothers respond quickly to their calls become more secure in their belief that their mother is controllable, and are more cooperative with adult requests. Infants who discover they can direct the action of toys and mobiles show more motivation to master new and challenging learning situations than infants who have the experience of helplessness.

Social comparison is the process of comparing self and others. Children begin to engage in social comparison at about age 4. Comparisons concerning the concrete, overt, and physical (e.g., "I'm bigger than you," "My picture is better," "You have a dog but I don't") comprise the interest and focus of preschool children.

Social and Moral Concepts

Social development involves a spiraling increase of knowledge of both self and others. Throughout life, new knowledge about the self transforms and illuminates one's understanding of others, and vice versa. This is the dialectic of personal growth.

How do young children make sense of the immense flux that goes into creating what adults call the social world? Preschool children are able to focus on only the most concrete and immediate cues when assessing self and others, analyzing social interaction, and understanding moral terms, relationships, and rules. Adults can categorize the social world by classifying people in terms of occupational group, ethnicity, social class, religion, and other abstract categories. Adults understand connections between people in terms of institutions of government, the legal system, the economy, and they understand moral dilemmas in terms of basic issues such as justice and virtue, convention and law, role and reciprocal obligation. Yet all of these concepts are much too abstract and general for young children (Edwards, 1986). Instead, *familiarity, age, gender,* and *race* may be the first categories children employ.

Family and *friendship* are the first social connections they understand. *Authority* and *fairness* may be central to children's notions of right and wrong in our society (Damon, 1977, 1988).

All of the basic social and moral categories and concepts witness major transformations during the preschool years. The changes are summarized in Table 2.1. The concepts are important because they are so close to the child and to the heart of the child's working model of the world. Perhaps professionals who work with children could better help them if they understood more clearly the special nature of young children's social and moral knowledge (Edwards, 1986).

The Early Preschool Period.   At age 2 or 3, the child's social and moral concepts are typically at Fischer's (1980) level of "single representations" (skill level 4). Children study the overt and visible differences between people; they want to discover how to identify self and others in terms of the labeling words that people around them emphasize. Age terms (*baby/child/grownup*) seem most salient and interesting to young children, along with gender categories (*man/woman/boy/girl*). For some children, racially-related skin or appearance differences (connected to categories of *African/Asian/European American*) or language (e.g., *Spanish-/English-speaking*) may also be salient, especially as children become more capable of social comparison, at age 4 or 5.

TABLE 2.1   Summary of Developmental Changes in Social Knowledge During the Early Childhood Years

	Early Preschool Level[1] 2–3 Years Old	Later Preschool Level[1] 4–5 Years Old	Early School Level[1] 6–8 Years Old
Cognitive Skill Level	Fisher's Level 4. The child cognitively focuses on and controls one symbolic representation at a time.	Fisher's Level 5. The child cognitively controls, compares, or coordinates two symbolic representations at a time.	Fisher's Level 6. The child controls and coordinates three or more representations at a time, and constructs systems of representations about social categories.
Social and Moral Concerns			
1. Gaining Age, Gender, and Racial Awareness	What am I? What are you? What do different categories of people do? (Behavioral roles)	What will I (and you) become? What am I not? What do different categories of people want or like to do?	What defines one's identity? What changes, what stays the same? What should different categories of people do (as role members)?
2. Understanding Family Ties	What are you called? (mother/father/brother/sister/etc.)	Are you my relative? (Mother/father/brother/sister/etc.)	What defines why we are relatives; what is the connection?
3. Understanding Friendship Bonds	Whom can I call 'friend'?	Are you my friend right now?	What should friends do for each other?
4. Making Decisions about Obedience to Authority	What do the adults I care about say to do?	What do I want to do? What do adults want me to do?	What should I do in order to be good & earn praise from people I respect and admire?
5. Making Decisions about Justice	Is it my turn? How much is my portion?	Whose turn is it? How much is everyone's portion?	Has everyone had equal turns? Does everyone have equal portions?

[1]These ages are not exact and would not be expected to be the same for all children. Children vary in the rate at which they develop. Moreover, children are typically not even in their development; they progress more rapidly in some content areas than in others.

The young child associates stereotyped aspects of behavior and role with each category to construct a first, shared model of the social world. But the child still thinks about each concept in isolation, not of the relation between categories. For instance, she does not know that age is really about years of life (not "bigness") and involves a continuous, slow transformation. She does not know that race and gender are permanent features of identity, and may think that dark skin can be lightened by washing or dyeing or that a girl can grow up to be a daddy.

In terms of family and kinship concepts, the child uses the most familiar terms (*mother/sister/grandmother,* etc.) as simple labels for age and sex groups. He defines a father as a "man" without realizing that, to *be* a father, a man must *have* a child. The child thinks of a family as a clump of people: father, mother, sister, brother. He applies the word *friend* to any special person who has been so labeled for him. He tends not to talk about friendship much, although he may have favorite peers and strong attachments.

Moral concepts are very simple at this level. Yet 2- to 3-year-olds are strongly motivated to learn the standards that adults emphasize with them. They regard adults with genuine awe and believe that the essence of being "good" is following adult wishes and commands (Piaget, 1948; Kohlberg, 1981, 1984). Because they cannot keep two people's perspectives in mind at once, however, they tend to forget about the adult's commands when he or she is out of sight, and so they are not very trustworthy or obedient. In their relations with peers, they are aware that parents, teachers, and friends are most concerned about "sharing" and "taking turns," but they tend to use these terms in an egocentric way: "*You* share with me and give me that tricycle." They define fairness as what the self wants right now.

The Later Preschool Period.   By age 4 or 5, the child often displays thinking at Fischer's (1980) level of "simple relations of representations" (skill level 5) with regard to specific social and moral concepts. The challenge now felt by the child is how to coordinate two categories. She will understand that *boy* and *girl* are exclusive categories (a child must be one or the other). She also understands that a *boy* grows up to be a *man.* She attaches strong preferences to some sex-typed behaviors selected by herself ("I hate video games and girls don't play with them." "Girls love red dresses; I do.") The child also becomes interested in racial and ethnic categories, and understands that if she is called *black* or *African American,* that means she is not *white,* and that she will be a *black* person like her parents when she grows up. But the child cannot coordinate three or more roles simultaneously. So, when thinking about the male-female distinction, for instance, he cannot also keep track of the young-old dimension. He may plan to marry his mother when he grows up; he forgets that she will be growing into a grandmother during this time. The child is thus cognitively predisposed for the Oedipal conflict (Fischer & Lazerson, 1984).

In terms of family concepts, the child now realizes that kinship terms involve a relationship of some kind, but because her thinking is still so concrete, she tends to define the relationship in terms of "closeness." People are relatives because they "live in the same house," "love each other so much," or "want to be." They can become nonrelatives just as easily through becoming unclose in some way. If the parents separate and one moves out, the child may have difficulty grasping how her father is related to her mother and even how that parent remains related to her.

A "friend" is defined as someone liked right now or someone with whom one is playing. When the child gets angry, she may say, "You're not my friend!" but she does not intend anything about her future feelings. Friendships are easily and quickly repaired in the preschool years.

During this period, children's moral concepts become slightly more elaborated. Because they can now compare two people's perspectives, these children realize that sometimes what they want opposes what authorities want. They may consciously regard their parents and teachers as obstacles to the self's rightful desires, and so as "unfair." In relations with peers, they still define fairness as what the self wants, but they struggle to attach a reason to justify their choice, something beyond, "I should get it because I want it."

The Early School Years. When children enter Fischer's (1980) level of "systems of representations" (skill level 6, equivalent to Piaget's concrete operations) with regard to specific social concepts, their thinking takes a quantum leap forward. They disentangle age and physical size and begin to construct a quantitative linear scale based on years of life. They achieve gender and racial constancy when they comprehend the necessary permanence of these categories and their basis in invariant bodily differences. They realize, for example, that their racial or ethnic category (e.g., African American, Hispanic) is permanent and will remain the same despite superficial transformations (e.g., getting a sun tan, learning another language). Children may or may not hold rigid stereotypes or negative attitudes about the categories, depending on the emotional commitment they are taught to hold for them, but many will move on to less primitive and stereotyped preferences (e.g., on doll preference tasks that ask, "Which doll is like you? Which doll do you like best?") as a result of their increasing cognitive maturity and flexibility (Aboud, 1988).

Children move away from "closeness" definitions of family ties toward kinship definitions, and understand that each person has a place in the kinship system of his or her family, with multiple connections. They define friendship in terms of reciprocity: friends are people who are kind or helpful to each other. Whereas at first the focus in friendship is on the exchange of concrete goods and services, gradually over the years the focus shifts toward more intangible kinds of exchange (good feelings, secrets, promises) and the long-term nature of commitment.

During the school years, children usually move toward more mature authority concepts, where they see moral standards as external and binding on both adults and children (Kohlberg, 1981, 1984). They consider authorities as having the right to be obeyed because of their superior knowledge and age as well as their power. They begin to apply notions of reciprocity to authority and to believe that children "owe" parents obedience in return for the concrete help, care, and good things bestowed. They also construct concepts of justice based on equality and reciprocity. Because they can simultaneously see more than one perspective, they painfully experience conflicts about what is fair. They rigidly insist on "tit for tat" and, when dividing resources, demand strictly equal shares, no matter what. Gradually in later years they will move toward more complex ideas of fairness as "equity," balancing strict equality with considerations of mercy, merit, and need.

Emotional Development

The Psychosocial Stages

Recent years have seen a resurgence of interest in the topic of emotional development. Among the major developmental theories, psychoanalytic theory most emphasizes emotion and motivation, explaining why this perspective has always remained important to practitioners in schools and clinics. For example Erik Erikson's (1963) theory of psychosocial development, based on Freud's psychosexual stages, is still considered useful to those who work with young children.

In Erikson's account, two of life's major developmental crises take place during the preschool years. The crisis of *autonomy versus shame and doubt* takes place during the toddler period and centers on the child's first attempts at self-control; the issue is whether these attempts result in his being made to feel competent and worthy or incompetent and ashamed. In some cultures, toilet training can be the central battleground; in others, the focus is elsewhere. The crisis of *initiative versus guilt* takes place during the later preschool years and centers on the child's use of her boundless new energy and initiative in exploring a wider world. The issue is whether this leads to her feeling strong and proud, or guilty over aggression and other "bad" deeds or thoughts. The crisis of *industry versus inferiority* begins as the child emerges into middle childhood and desires to win approval in new, adult-like skills and responsibilities defined by her culture as important—for example, caring for the baby skillfully or learning to read and write well enough to avoid feelings of failure.

Developmental Sequence of the Emergence of Basic Emotions

Although recent years have seen a surge of research on emotion, there is still no agreement on the best way to define and measure it. One leading theorist, Carol Izard (1978), defines emotion as an inborn type of complex, unlearned, motivating response. Universal primary emotions emerge in infancy as they become adaptive in the life of the infant and the infant's interaction with caregivers and the environment. Each primary emotion consists of specific facial expressions, neurophysiological changes, and inner states: interest, joy, surprise, distress, anger, disgust, contempt, fear, shame (shyness), and guilt.

Jerome Kagan (1984), a prominent cognitive theorist, has criticized this position because it omits emotions that other cultural groups regard as equally fundamental (Kitayama & Marcus, 1994). For example, modern Japanese regard the emotion of *amae* (the feeling of mutual interdependence with another) as primary. Ifalukians of Micronesia stress *ngach* (a feeling aroused by being alone, overworked, ill, hot, or bored; see Lutz, 1982).

Kagan (1984) would define emotions in ways that specify the eliciting context, the "incentive." This leads to an outline of emotional growth in which new emotions emerge as the child's capacities for memory and comparison improve. Kagan's list resembles Izard's (1978). The fundamental emotions are considered to serve adaptive and survival functions and to be culturally universal, but we need not accept these assumptions to find the scheme useful for understanding development in American society. Kagan emphasizes the unity of emotional, cognitive, and social development, and his scheme matches aspects of Erikson's stages.

During the first 3 or 4 months of life, several coherent reaction profiles emerge: *distress* to physical privation, *relaxation* to gratification, *surprise* to the unexpected, *joy* of understanding, and *excitement* to assimilation of the unexpected. At 4 to 10 months, two important new reactions come in: *fear* (or *wariness)* to the unfamiliar; and *anger* (*rage*) to frustration or disappointment. During the second year, the most important new emotion is *depression* (to the loss of a familiar person). As the child approaches 2, we see *shame* (when reprimanded), *defiance* (or *testing,* of adult authority), *anxiety* when rules are broken or property destroyed, and *pride* when the child succeeds. After age 4, a still more advanced response to violation appears: *guilt* at the recognition that one has voluntarily deviated from a standard. It requires one to recognize that he or she could have behaved differently from the course chosen.

The next group of reaction sets emerges at age 5, 6, or later. These reactions, aroused when the child compares the self to others, are *insecurity, inferiority, humility, pride, confidence, jealousy,* and *envy.*

Emotion Regulation

Besides studying the growth of the separate emotions and their importance for mature development, researchers have discovered that the early childhood years are a key time for developing capacities to *control* and *regulate* emotions. Not only are particular emotions (such as empathy, pride, and guilt) necessary for emotional maturity, but the expression of all the emotions must become increasingly mature—more flexible (not stereotyped and fixed), responsive to situations (not rigid), and appropriately modulated (not over- or under-arousing) (Thompson, 1994). This involves children gaining increasing capacity to monitor and evaluate themselves, and then modulate and manage such attributes as the quality, intensity, timing, and recovery of their emotions in ways considered appropriate by their family and cultural community, in order to function adaptively in their world. Emotion regulation is not a single, unified skill, but rather a broad set of loosely related skills and processes that slowly and gradually emerge over the course of childhood. These skills have, at their core, neurophysiological processes that have evolved to regulate physiological arousal.

While there is no definitive account of the processes nor timetable for their achievement, the following is a list of some of the most important changes seen during the preschool years, with examples (taken from Thompson, 1994):

1. *Managing the intake of emotionally arousing information,* by redirecting attention in arousing situations (covering eyes or ears; removing distressing stimuli; withdrawing from situation).
2. *Altering the interpretation of an emotionally arousing situation,* by changing one's goals (e.g., deciding one would rather play by oneself than with a too-busy parent).
3. *Accessing coping resources when in an emotionally arousing situation,* by seeking attachment figures when distressed, using the body to self-comfort (rocking, thumb-sucking), or using transitional objects (blankets, stuffed animals).
4. *Regulating the emotional demands of the situation* by seeking out settings and contexts that are optimally arousing (e.g., avoiding the playroom at daycare where the too-rough children play, or seeking to go outside when bored).
5. *Selecting adaptive and appropriate responses* by trying to use and follow cultural-display rules (e.g., trying to control crying and tantruming, to control expressions of anger, to use words instead of screaming or hitting, and not to laugh at the wrong times).

Summary

The preschool years witness enormous changes across all aspects of development. Children's bodies and brains grow rapidly (if at a slower rate than during infancy), with only slight sex differences seen in overall height and weight but with definite sex differences (favoring girls) in general physical and social maturity. Powers of short- and long-term memory increase, not only in terms of the number of items that can be remembered, but also in how children can use their memories; this sets the stage for the "cognitive revolution" that occurs around 18 months of age in children's capacities to symbolize or to use representation as a tool for learning and thinking. This is clearly a key part of language development, for, after months of slowly building up a small, idiosyncratic vocabulary during the one-word stage, the older toddler's language suddenly begins to explode in terms of rapidly expanding vocabulary and increasing mastery of syntactic rules, until by age 6 most children know thousands of words and have a near-adult command of grammar. The cognitive reorganizations of the preschool years also make possible the following profound changes in children:

> their understanding of social and moral categories, relations, and rules
>
> their capacity for complex emotions involving comparison of the self to other people and also of the self's actions against internalized norms and ideals
>
> their capacity for emotion regulation, which allows them to function effectively in their social world.

Although these domains of development have been distinguished for the purposes of description, nevertheless they must be understood as inseparable. Although the field of child development still lacks an integrated theory and language for describing all that is known about childhood, nevertheless at last it seems to be moving toward a more balanced perspective and recognition of the need for a new synthesis of knowledge. The opposing theoretical schools are becoming more integrated. At last one can hope that a scientific understanding of the whole child will soon be within reach.

3 Descriptions of Preschool Children with Disabilities or At-Risk for Developmental Delay

How Should a Child Be Called?

KARIN LIFTER

Preschool children come in a variety of shapes and sizes, and are equally varied in their physical, cognitive, communication, social, emotional, and adaptive developments, despite a fairly narrow age range. Some preschoolers, however, do not clearly fit within the range encompassed by what are considered standard developmental patterns. Instead, they develop more slowly than or differently from their peers in obvious or subtle ways. For some children, the variation observed is great enough to warrant the designation of disability, either at birth or by the time of the preschool period. For other children, the differences observed may not be considered significant, but certain conditions render the child "at risk" for later difficulties.

This chapter describes preschool children who are developing more slowly than or differently from their peers. Its purpose is to provide descriptions that aid clinicians and educators in (1) the identification of preschoolers with disabilities or at-risk for developmental delay, and (2) the development of service plans for these children. The factors that influence the need for, and the nature of, the various descriptions in current use will be reviewed first. Then follows a listing of the categories of disability that are used to describe preschool children with special needs, organized according to those categories specified by the legislative mandates (P.L. 105-17, the 1997 amendments to IDEA) and those categories specified by the *Diagnostic and Statistical Manual for Mental Disorders* (DSM-IV, American Psychiatric Association [APA], 1994). Finally, the relevance of different descriptors to the nature of services that are developed for these children will be considered.

The author is especially grateful to the children, families, teachers, and staff of the May Center for Early Childhood Education, Arlington, Massachusetts, and the May Institute, South Harwich, Massachusetts, for their enthusiasm and support for the study of the play, language and social development in preschoolers who are developing more slowly than or differently from their peers.

The Need for and Nature of Descriptions

Several factors influence the need for, and the nature of, the descriptions that are used for children with disabilities or at-risk for developmental delay. The *need* for descriptions is derived from legislative mandates, in particular, but also from the more global commitments of educators and clinicians to help children who are developing with difficulty, and from the concerns of researchers that center on (1) examining the etiology, characteristics, and sequelae of various disabilities that affect young children, and (2) evaluating the quality and success of intervention efforts. The *nature* of descriptions usually emphasize either a differentiation of children into various categories of disability or a grouping of children according to risk factors and delays in developmental domains. Descriptions that emphasize the distinguishing features of the different categories of disabilities (e.g., mental retardation, autism) are regarded as categorical descriptions. In contrast, those descriptions that group children according to parameters that can be applied to children regardless of their particular category of disability (e.g., progress in language, quality of play activities) are called noncategorical or cross-categorical descriptions. Each of the foregoing factors will be described in turn.

Descriptions Resulting from Legislative Mandates

The legislative mandates regarding disabilities provide the societal framework for description and, as a result, make explicit *who* must be served. The federal laws, most notably P.L. 94-142, P.L. 99-457, P.L. 101-476, P.L. 102-119, and P.L. 105-17 (the 1997 amendments to The Individuals with Disabilities Education Act: IDEA), affirmed this nation's commitment to the intrinsic worth of each individual, and particularly to children and youth with, or at risk for, disabilities. These laws set the guidelines for those children and youth entitled to special services. P.L. 94-142, the Education of All Handicapped Children Act of 1975 (the 1975 amendments to the Education of the Handicapped Act [EHA]), guaranteed a "free appropriate education" to all children and youth with disabilities who require it. P.L. 99-457, the 1986 amendments to the EHA, extended the right of a free appropriate education to preschool children with disabilities, and established the Handicapped Infants and Toddlers Program (Part H). Fundamental to the law was that the educational, psychological, and social problems many children face in school can be identified and remediated at an earlier point in time. P.L. 101-476 (IDEA) changed the name of the laws to emphasize person-first language, and expanded the rights under law to include children with autism and children with traumatic brain injury more fully as children to be served. P.L. 102-119, the 1992 amendments to IDEA, primarily addressed the Part H program, and renamed it the Early Intervention Program for Infants and Toddlers with Disabilities. P.L. 105-17, the 1997 amendments to IDEA, changed the description of who should be served from "children with disabilities" to "child with a disability," allowed states and local school districts "to utilize 'developmental delay' eligibility criteria as an alternative to specific disability through age 9," and emphasized the importance of a child's involvement and progress in the general curriculum (Federal Register, October 22, 1997).

The current legal descriptions of *who* must be served were detailed in the 1997 amendments to IDEA, enacted into P.L. 105-17 on June 4, 1997. The term "child with disability," given appropriate evaluations, is a child:

having mental retardation, a hearing impairment including deafness, a speech or language impairment, a visual impairment including blindness, serious emotional disturbance (hereafter referred to as emotional disturbance), an orthopedic impairment, autism, traumatic brain injury, an other health impairment, a specific learning disability, deaf-blindness, or a multiple disability, and who because of that impairment needs special education and related services. (Federal Register, October 22, 1997, p. 55069)

Each of these categories of disability is defined in the regulations, and these more detailed descriptions are presented later in this chapter. These descriptions were derived originally in relation to school-age children (P.L. 94-142, 1975). Indeed, the specific descriptions of each category include phrases regarding the impact of the disability to the effect that it "adversely affects a child's educational performance."

With the passage of P.L. 99-457 in 1986, the categorical descriptors for school-age children were extended to preschool children. Educators and clinicians raised concerns regarding the appropriateness of these descriptors for the preschool age group (Snyder, Bailey, & Auer, 1994). In addition, because each categorical description included the phrase "adversely affects a child's educational performance," the lack of specificity for what "educational performance" and an "adverse affect" constituted on educational performance at the preschool level became a problem.

However, the regulations did provide the term "developmental delay" as an alternative description to categorical descriptions identified above, "as part of a unified approach [which would] allow the special education and related services to be directly related to the child's needs and prevent locking the child into an eligibility category which may be inappropriate or incorrect, and could actually reduce later referrals of children with disabilities to special education" (Federal Register, October 22, 1997, p. 55070). The term "developmental delay," now extended to include children from age 3 to age 9 for "a child with a disability," may include a child:

> who is experiencing developmental delays, as defined by the State and as measured by appropriate diagnostic instruments and procedures, in one or more of the following areas: physical development, cognitive development, communication development, social or emotional development, or adaptive development; and who, for that reason, needs special education and related services; and, if the State adopts the terms for children of this age range (or a subset of that range) and the LEA (Lead Education Agency) chooses to use the term. (Federal Register, October 22, 1997, p. 55069)

As a result, preschoolers with disabilities may be described according to progress in developmental domains instead of in terms of educational performance relative to school-age children. (Note: A state may not require an LEA to use the term "developmental delay." On the other hand, if a state does not adopt the term, the LEAs cannot use it).

Thus, the legislative mandates allow for both categorical and noncategorical descriptions to describe preschoolers with disabilities or at-risk for developmental delay: descriptions that differentiate children from one another according to categories of disability, and descriptions that group children according to progress in one or another developmental domain. Despite this option, most states continue to use categorical descriptions for preschool-age children (Snyder et al., 1994). However, the use of noncategorical descriptions may facilitate the child's involvement and progress in the general curriculum, a specification included in the 1997 amendments to IDEA.

Descriptions Resulting from Diagnostic and Educational Needs

A second need for describing preschoolers with disabilities arises from the concerns of clinicians and educators. Prior to, and concomitant with, the federal legislation that specified who should be served, clinicians and educators had been serving children who were developing with difficulties. Their tasks were usually two-fold: (1) identifying those children in need of services, which usually requires a diagnostic description or a description of eligibility; and (2) developing plans of intervention to help these children, which usually requires a more functional or curriculum-based description (McLean, 1996; Bucy, Smith, & Landau, this volume).

Diagnostic Descriptions Needed for Identification.   The identification of children in need of services usually requires the determination of a "category" of disability, whether it is a specific category of disability (e.g., mental retardation) or a more global category of need (i.e., "developmental delay"). The categorical systems available for purposes of identification include those provided in the legislative mandates, described earlier, and those provided by particular diagnostic systems. Three diagnostic systems in common use are the DSM-IV (American Psychiatric Association [APA], 1994), the ICD-10 (World Health Organization [WHO], 1994), and the Diagnostic Classification of Mental Health and Developmental Disorders of Infancy and Early Childhood (Zero to Three, 1994).

The DSM-IV (APA, 1994) is a classification system for disorders of childhood, adolescence, and adulthood, and it is used predominantly in clinical as opposed to educational settings. This system is significant for several reasons: it has been widely used by school and clinical personnel since 1952; it represents a common language among professionals; the descriptions have been employed in many research studies that have documented the developmental sequelae of children with specific disabilities; and the categories overlap with the categories presented in the legislative mandates. Of particular relevance for the purposes of this chapter are those disorders that manifest before or during the preschool period. They are grouped in DSM-IV as "Disorders Usually First Diagnosed in Infancy, Childhood, or Adolescence" (APA, 1994, p. 37), and will be described later. The ICD-10 (WHO, 1994) categorical system has not been used with preschoolers to the same extent as the DSM classification systems and will not be described here. The Diagnostic Classification of Mental Health and Developmental Disorders of Infancy and Early Childhood (Zero to Three, 1994) is designed for infants and toddlers and focuses on concerns centered on developmental issues, and complements both DSM-IV and ICD-10. It is most concerned with "dynamic processes, such as relationship and developmentally based conceptualizations of adaptive patterns (i.e., functional emotional development level) (which) are therefore of central importance" (p. 14–15).

Educational Descriptions Needed for Intervention.   Once a child has been diagnosed with a particular disability, or the child has been determined to be eligible for special education services, different kinds of descriptions are needed to address the developmental and/or educational needs of the child. Intervention plans generally require descriptions according to some functional skills (e.g., Bailey & Wolery, 1992), according to a child's progress in an appropriate "curriculum" (e.g., Neisworth & Bagnato, 1988), or according to a child's progress in developmental sequences, such as language (Bloom & Lahey, 1978; Lahey, 1988) and play (Fewell & Kaminski, 1988; Lifter, 1996; Linder, 1993b). Skills are often grouped into the broad developmental domain areas described for "children with disabilities": physical development, cognitive development, communication development, social or emotional development, or adaptive development. Thus, in contrast to categorical descriptors that tend to be used for identification, descriptors that address the developmental and/or educational needs of children with disabilities tend to consider children independently of a particular category of disability.

Descriptions Resulting from Research Needs

The concerns of researchers centered on (1) describing children's development, (2) specifying the etiology, characteristics, and sequelae of various disabilities that affect young children, and/or (3) evaluating the quality and success of various intervention methods. The use of categorical or noncategorical descriptions were influenced by the different research emphases.

Developmental Psychology.   Many descriptive studies of children's development have come from developmental psychology, as is apparent in Chapter 2. The utility of such studies centers on the detailed descriptions provided of children's development in the various domains. Domains that have been described include language behaviors (Bloom, 1973; Bloom & Lahey, 1978; Brown, 1973), play behaviors (Fein & Apfel, 1979; Lifter & Bloom, 1989; Nicolich, 1977), relationships between play and language (McCune, 1995; Lifter & Bloom, 1989), displays of affect (e.g., Piaget & Inhelder, 1969), emotional behaviors (Haviland, 1976), social behaviors (e.g., Howes & Matheson, 1992; Lorimier, Doyle, & Tessier, 1995), motor skills (Case-Smith, 1994), and the integration among developmental domains (Bloom, 1993). The resulting developmental sequences have served as important resources for clinicians and educators who use developmental sequences for evaluating a child's progress and setting intervention goals (e.g., Bloom & Lahey, 1978; Dyer, Santarcangelo, & Luce, 1987; Lifter, Sulzer-Azaroff, Anderson, & Cowdery, 1993). They also lend themselves to curriculum-based evaluation inasmuch as developmental sequences *are* the curricula of the preschool period.

Descriptive Studies of Children Developing with Disabilities or Risks.   Much descriptive research on the etiology, characteristics, and sequelae of the various disability conditions that affect young children have provided researchers and practitioners with an extensive knowledge base of the manifestations of delays and differences in development, and the relationships of these delays and differences to various risk conditions and events. These studies have made use of descriptors according to the timing of the insult, the probability of risk, or the particular clinical category in identifying different groups of children for study.

Many events that occur in a child's life can render the child at risk for delays and differences in various developmental domains (Shonkoff & Marshall, 1990). These events can be described according to the timing of the insult; they can occur prenatally (before birth), perinatally (defined as the period from birth through the first month of life), or postnatally (beginning at 28 days of life) (Kopp, 1983; Werner, 1986). Prenatal events include (1) genetic factors ("chromosomal disorders, inborn errors of metabolism, [and] neural tube defects") and (2) environmental factors ("harmful drugs, maternal infections, metabolic disorders, nutritional deprivation, radiation, [and] toxic chemicals"). Perinatal events include "asphyxia, cardiopulmonary problems, congenital malformations, disorders of labor and delivery, low birth weight, pre-term birth, infections, metabolic disorders, neonatal intracranial hemorrhage, [and] neonatal medications." Postnatal events include (1) biological factors ("accidents, chronic disease, failure to thrive, infections, protein-energy malnutrition, [and] toxic substances") and (2) psychosocial factors ("family dysfunctions, illiteracy, parental psychopathology, [and] poverty") (Werner, 1986, p. 3).

The events described above can be reorganized according to probability factors where certain risks carry high probabilities for subsequent delays, such as trisomy 21 (Down syndrome), or variable probabilities for subsequent delays as seen in prematurity. Tjossem (1976) offered the terms "established risk," "biological risk," and "environmental risk" to characterize children with various risk factors, and these terms are used widely to describe infants and children who are eligible for intervention services. Children with "established risk" are "those with diagnosed medical disorders (usually of known etiology) for which expectancies for physical and developmental insults are known," such as is the case for Down syndrome. Children with "biological risk" are "those with prenatal, perinatal, or postnatal histories signaling potential biological insults or underlying problems, for example the occurrence of rubella prenatally, low birth weight or prematurity perinatally, or the ingestion of toxic substances (e.g., lead) postnatally." Children at "environmental risk" are "those who are biologically and genetically normal and intact at birth but whose early life experiences and environmental surroundings impose a threat to their physical and developmental well-being," for example, children who are neglected physically and/or psychologically (Peterson, 1987, p. 139). Factors such as malnutrition, lead poisoning, maternal depression, and family violence "occur more commonly among children living in poverty and often lead to developmental delay, behavioral disturbance, and subsequent school failure" (Kaplan-Sanoff & Nigro, 1988, p. 2).

A wealth of descriptive studies have provided detailed accounts of the sequelae of children diagnosed with particular disabilities or clinical syndromes. Children with Down syndrome have been studied extensively (e.g., Cicchetti & Beeghly, 1990). There are also studies of children with autism or Asperger's syndrome (e.g., Dawson, 1989; Restall & Magill-Evans, 1993; Szatmari, Archer, Fisman, Streiner, & Wilson, 1995; Ungerer & Sigman, 1981), children with ADHD (e.g., Stein, Szumowski, Blondis, & Roizen, 1995), children with visual impairments (Crocker & Orr, 1996), and children with communication disorders (Guralnick, Connor, Hammond, Gottman, & Kinnish, 1996) as well as studies and reviews of children categorized into more global categories of disability or risk, such as children born prematurely (Kopp, 1983), children with developmental disabilities (Johnson, Lubetsky, & Sacco, 1995), children with developmental language disorders (Rapin, 1996), children with mild delays (e.g., Guralnick & Groom, 1987), and children with developmental delays (Kopp, Baker, & Brown, 1992). In addition, various developmental domains have been described for children with different categories of disability, such as for adaptive skills (Vig & Jedrysek, 1995).

In the bulk of these descriptive studies, the same descriptors that are used to describe the development of children without disabilities are not only used to describe the development of children diagnosed with disabilities, but they are also used to describe the development of children with distinctly different disability conditions. As a result, such descriptions provide an important source of information for delays and differences within the developmental domains that can be evaluated across categories of disability.

Studies of Intervention. Researchers and practitioners have long been concerned with the quality and success of intervention efforts. Like the descriptive studies, descriptions of children according to categories of disabilities has been applied differentially. Some studies have examined intervention methods as they apply to children with autism (Lifter et al., 1993; Odom, McConnell, & McEvoy, 1992), while other studies have evaluated interventions for children with disabilities more generally (Warren, Yoder, Gazdag, Kim, & Jones, 1993). The relevance of categorical descriptions to intervention efforts is debatable (Snyder et al., 1994). If children are considered as children first, then intervention efforts planned and evaluated according to progress in developmental domains (e.g., developmental sequences) should be applicable to all children.

Summary of Descriptors

The foregoing overview of the need for, and the nature of, descriptions of preschoolers with disabilities or at-risk for developmental delay has resulted in basically two kinds of descriptors: categorical descriptors that differentiate children from one another, and noncategorical descriptors that group children according to risk factors and delays in developmental domains. Questions regarding the usefulness of categorical descriptions may include whether the impact of a particular disability has a unique impact on a developmental domain distinct from other disability conditions. If so, the characteristics of the particular disability category remain critical for developing an intervention plan. If not, the developmental domain as a descriptor may be regarded as a more important descriptor because of the direct links to an intervention plan that may be established.

Although the usefulness of categorical descriptions continues to be debated, they have served both clinical and research purposes in providing a common language and specific descriptors for serving and studying the developmental course of children with various syndromes (Bernheimer & Keogh, 1986). Because categories of disabilities continue to be applied to preschoolers, those categories detailed in the legislative mandates, and their correspondences to the categories described in the DSM-IV, are presented next.

Categories of Disability

The categories used to describe preschool children with disabilities are presented here and in Table 3.1 according to the terms used in the legislative mandates (P.L. 105-17), complemented with the diagnostic classification system of the DSM-IV (APA, 1994). The order of presentation begins with the categories of disability that can be grouped under a diagnosed physical condition, followed by those categories of disability that can be grouped according to a diagnosed mental condition. This division is not used in the federal mandates, where 13 categories are presented in alphabetical order, but is imposed here for the purpose of examining correspondences between the two categorical systems. The DSM-IV is focused on categories of disability that are regarded as mental conditions, and the section of the DSM-IV

TABLE 3.1   Categories of Disability

1997 Amendments to IDEA (P.L. 105-17)	DSM-IV (1994)

Physical Conditions
  Deafness
  Hearing Impairment
  Visual Impairment Including Blindness
  Deaf-Blindness
  Orthopedic Impairment
    Cerebral Palsy; Spinal Cord Damage
  Other Health Impairment
    Chronic/Acute Health Problems
      Epilepsy/Lead Poisoning
      Cystic Fibrosis/AIDS
      FAS/Cocaine Exposure/some ADD,
      ADHD
    Traumatic Brain Injury
    Multiple Disability	

Mental Conditions
  Mental Retardation
    Down Syndrome
    Fragile X Syndrome/Other Syndromes
	Mental Retardation
	  (Mild, Moderate, Severe, Profound)

Autism	Pervasive Developmental Disorders
	  Autistic Disorder
	  Rett's Disorder
	  Childhood Disintegrative Disorder
	  Asperger's Disorder
	  Pervasive Developmental Disorder Not Otherwise Specified

Speech or Language Impairment	Communication Disorders
	  Expressive Language Disorder
	  Mixed Receptive-Expressive Language Disorder
	  Phonological Disorder
	  Stuttering
	  Communication Disorder Not Otherwise Specified

Specific Learning Disability
  (Some ADHD/ADD)
	Learning Disorders
	  Reading Disorder
	  Mathematics Disorder
	  Disorder of Written Expression
	  Learning Disorder Not Otherwise Specified
	Motor Skills Disorder
	  Developmental Coordination Disorder

Emotional Disturbance[1]
  (Some ADHD/ADD)
	Attention Deficit and Disruptive Behavior Disorders
	  Attention-Deficit Hyperactivity Disorder
	    Predominantly Inattentive Type
	    Predominantly Hyperactive-Impulsive Type
	    Combined Type

Conduct Disorder
  Oppositional Defiant Disorder
  Attention-Deficit Hyperactivity Disorder Not Otherwise
    Specified
  Disruptive Behavior Disorder Not Otherwise Specified

Feeding and Eating Disorders of Infancy and Early Childhood
  Pica
  Rumination Disorder
  Feeding Disorder of Infancy or Early Childhood

Tic Disorders
  Tourette's Disorder
  Chronic Motor or Vocal Tic Disorder
  Transient Tic Disorder
  Tic Disorder Not Otherwise Specified

Elimination Disorders
  Encopresis
  Enuresis

Other Disorders of Infancy, Childhood, or Adolescence
  Separation Anxiety Disorder
  Selective Mutism
  Reactive Attachment Disorder of Infancy or Early Childhood
  Stereotypic Movement Disorder
  Disorders of Infancy, Childhood or Adolescence
    Not Otherwise Specified

Note: The distinction of physical versus mental conditions does not appear in the 1997 amendments to IDEA, but it is used in this chapter for comparison with DSM-IV, which concerns mental conditions only.
[1]The category "Emotional disturbance" does not correspond to a particular disorder listed in DSM-IV, but overlaps with many of these disorders.

entitled "Disorders Usually First Diagnosed in Infancy, Childhood, or Adolescence" is included here. The legislative mandates include a wider range of categories to include those that are imposed by particular physical conditions. The categories will be presented according to their defining characteristics and according to their impact on the developmental tasks of the preschool period. Much of the information on etiology and prevalence of the various disorders to be presented here has been taken from the Batshaw (1997a) volume on children with disabilities.

Physical Conditions

The categories of disabilities included here are those impairments which have a physical basis and that can be diagnosed medically.

Deafness and Hearing Impairment.   Hearing disabilities include two categories: deafness and hearing impairment. "'Deafness' means a hearing impairment so severe that the child is impaired in processing linguistic information through hearing, with or without amplification, that adversely affects educational performance." "'Hearing impairment' means an impairment in hearing, whether permanent or fluctuating, that adversely affects a child's educational performance but that is not included under the definition of deafness in this section" (Federal Register, Oct. 22, 1997, p. 55069).

Hearing loss may be congenital, acquired, or due to unknown causes. Congenital causes include cleft palate and Down syndrome, noise pollution, and infections (Steinberg & Knightly, 1997). Most of acquired hearing loss is a result of middle ear infections, with the remainder due to prematurity, anoxia, some antibiotics, and trauma. Causes are unknown for approximately half the children with this disorder. Obviously, hearing loss in its more severe form (i.e., deafness) is easier to identify than an impairment in hearing. Substantial hearing loss can usually be identified by the time the child is two and one half years old. Approximately 1.8% of children (those younger than 18), have some sort of hearing impairment.

The sensory impairment of deafness, especially in its severe forms, has major impacts on language and social development. A child with a hearing impairment will not have the full benefit, if at all, of hearing the words and sentences that describe the ongoing events with people and objects in the environment with whom the child actively engages. This sound-meaning mapping of hearing words that express ongoing events represents a critical relationship in understanding language and using language, and is especially important in infancy and early childhood (Bloom, 1974; Stark, 1979). Children with hearing impairments are delayed in the onset and rate of development at which they learn auditory-vocal language (Lahey, 1988). However, children with hearing impairments "...raised in an environment where sign language is their native language would not, necessarily, demonstrate a language disorder; they may have no difference at all learning their native language, which is not dependent on the auditory modality" (Lahey, 1988, p. 60).

The quality of the social relationships and the nature of the educational placement that children with hearing impairments and deafness have, will be influenced by the child's and the interactant's facility with the communication system used (i.e., vocal versus gestural). Total communication systems—a combination of vocal and gestural systems—are being used increasingly, which allow for a greater range of participants in the child's social world along with a greater range of educational placement options.

Difficulties in academic subjects—especially reading, which is language-based— have been observed for children with hearing impairments (e.g., Furth, 1971). For-in depth information on the assessment of hearing impaired children see the chapter in this text by Mullen.

Visual Impairment Including Blindness.   "'Visual impairment including blindness' means an impairment in vision that, even with correction, adversely affects a child's educational performance. The term includes both partial sight and blindness" (Federal Register, Oct. 22, 1997, p. 55070). Of those children who are blind, approximately half are born blind, and the other half lose their sight before their first birthdays. The most common congenital causes of blindness are due to infections and eye malformations. Other causes are due to retinopathy of prematurity (damage from oxygen that was used to treat respiratory distress syndrome), trauma, tumors, and nutritional disorders. The overall incidence of blindness in children is one in 3,000. Approximately half the children who have a visual impairment also have a developmental disability (Menacker & Batshaw, 1997).

Impairments in vision manifest themselves in development very differently from impairments in hearing. A primary impact of a visual impairment is on the rate and extent of cognitive development. Sighted infants use their hands to reach out to objects and people in their environments as they act on and learn about their worlds. Children who are blind are much slower to reach out and to explore. The reason they are slower is that they require more advanced conceptual development to reach out, and this conceptual development includes knowing about the existence and permanence of people and objects (Fraiberg, 1977). Children who are blind are accordingly delayed in the development of language, such as in vocabulary, syntax, and the use of words to communicate wants and needs (Lahey, 1988). Fortunately, there is considerable "catch up" of these children by the time of the preschool period (Landau & Gleitman, 1985).

The sensory impairment of blindness also influences social development, in that the infant or child who is blind is limited in the behavioral displays the child can provide for caregivers to respond to, and is limited in responses the child can provide to caregivers' gestural displays. For more information on the preschool child with visual impairments, see Chapter 19.

Deaf-Blindness. " 'Deaf-blindness' means concomitant hearing and visual impairments, the combination of which causes such severe communication and other developmental and educational problems that [the child] cannot be accommodated in special education programs solely for children with deafness or children with blindness" (Federal Register, Oct. 22, 1997, p. 55069).

Children who are deaf and blind are enormously disadvantaged in their abilities to engage with their caregivers and to act on the objects and events in their worlds. Such impairments will have profound effects on all aspects of development. Children who are deaf and blind will also have difficulties in acquiring word meanings and in using language to comment on ongoing events and to make their needs known.

Orthopedic Impairment. " 'Orthopedic impairment' means a severe orthopedic impairment that adversely affects a child's educational performance. The term includes impairments caused by congenital anomaly (e.g., clubfoot, absence of some member, etc.), impairments caused by disease (e.g., poliomyelitis, bone tuberculosis, etc.), and impairments from other causes (e.g., cerebral palsy, amputations, and fractures or burns that cause contractures" (Federal Register, Oct. 22, 1997, p. 55069). There are several disorders that would be considered under orthopedic impairment.

Cerebral Palsy. This is a non-progressive disorder of varying etiology resulting in "paralysis, weakness, or incoordination of the motor system as a result of intracranial lesions" manifesting primarily in impairments in fine and gross motor coordination (Peterson, 1987, p. 207). Damage to the brain may occur prenatally, perinatally, or postnatally, but does occur before the child's brain has fully matured. Most causes are accounted for by prematurity due to problems during intrauterine development, at approximately 26 to 32 weeks gestation, when the areas of the brain that are important for motor control are in critical stages of development. Between 1.4 to 2.4 children per 1,000 have cerebral palsy, but an increasing percentage of these children are represented by children who were born prematurely (Pellegrino, 1997).

Cerebral palsy is commonly further described according to the area of the brain that is damaged, "pyramidal" (having to do with spasticity and the initiation of movement), "extrapyramidal" (having to do with regulating movement and maintaining posture), and "mixed-type" involving both brain areas, and the resulting quality of the motor impairment and limbs involved (Batshaw & Perret, 1992). It is often associated with mental retardation. Approximately 60% of children with cerebral palsy have mental retardation of varying degrees. There is also a high incidence of hearing, speech, language, visual, feeding, growth, behavioral, and emotional problems associated with cerebral palsy (Pellegrino, 1997).

Neural Tube Defects.   Orthopedic impairments may also result from neural tube defects (NTDs). NTDs result if the neural tube does not close completely, which should occur by 26 days after fertilization. The three major forms of NTD are spina bifida, encephalocele, and anencephaly. Spina bifida is the most common and is the result of a separation of a section of the vertebral arches. It may be associated with myelomeningocele, which is a fluid-filled sac protruding from the spine. Encephalocele consists of a malformation in the skull which allows a portion of the brain to protrude, and it is associated with mental retardation, hydrocephalus, spastic diplegia, and seizures. Anencephaly consists of an even greater malformation of the skull and brain, which results in spontaneous abortion or rare survival beyond infancy (Liptak, 1997).

Other Orthopedic Impairments.   Still other orthopedic impairments may be caused by infections (e.g., polio) and by diseases that affect movement (e.g., muscular dystrophy). Muscular dystrophy, which involves a progressive degeneration of the voluntary muscles, is the best known of the muscle diseases; its most common form is Duchenne muscular dystrophy. Muscular dystrophy is a sex-linked disorder and occurs in one in 3,000 male children. It is associated with learning disabilities and cognitive impairments (Dormans & Batshaw, 1997). Early symptoms, which include awkward, clumsy walking and running, and walking on tiptoe, may appear in children as young as three years of age. Most children are in wheelchairs by age 10, due to muscle weakness (Peterson, 1987). Included also in childhood muscle diseases are congenital myopathies, which are characterized by decreased muscle tone and strength (Dormans & Batshaw, 1997).

The conditions of cerebral palsy and other orthopedic impairments have major impacts on development. Infants and children learn by doing. A child who has difficulty with or is prevented from moving about is severely restricted in acting on the world. The extent of motor impairment, learning problems, and mental retardation influences the extent of delays and differences in all other aspects of development, including adaptive development.

Other Health Impairment.   " 'Other health impairment' means having limited strength, vitality, or alertness, due to chronic or acute health problems such as a heart condition, tuberculosis, rheumatic fever, nephritis, asthma, sickle cell anemia, hemophilia, epilepsy, lead poisoning, leukemia, or diabetes that adversely affects a child's educational performance" (Federal Register, Oct. 22, 1997, pp. 55069–70). The conditions cystic fibrosis and AIDS (Acquired Immune Deficiency Syndrome) would also be included under 'Other health impairment.' It is noted in P.L. 105-17 that children with ADD or ADHD may be classified as eligible for services within this category if their problems in educational performance are due to excessive fatigue (e.g., from drug therapy). Many factors that have been identified as causes of health impairments (e.g., lead, alcohol) are thought to predispose a child to ADHD (Blum & Mercugliano, 1997).

Diseases and conditions classified as "Other health impaired" have obvious implications on a child's vitality for development and learning. As is the case for all physical conditions, problems of social and emotional adjustment frequently occur, which may, in turn, influence a child's learning potential. Six conditions in this category—epilepsy, lead poisoning, cystic fibrosis, AIDS, Fetal Alcohol Syndrome, and cocaine exposure—are described next.

Epilepsy.   Epilepsy is defined as repeated unprovoked seizures, rendering it a seizure disorder in contrast to the isolated seizures that result from high fevers (Brown, 1997). A seizure consists of an "excessive and periodic (electrical) discharge...from the neurons in the cortex of the brain." Seizures "may lead to loss of consciousness, behavior changes, involuntary movements, altered muscle tone, or abnormal sensory phenomena," and are categorized according to how much of the cortex (all or part) is affected. Seizures are caused by "developmental brain abnormalities, anoxia, hypoglycemia, inborn errors of metabolism, trauma, and infections" (Batshaw & Perret, 1992, pp. 490–491). Seizures are categorized as either generalized or partial. Generalized seizures involve the entire cortex from the outset, and account for approximately 40% of epilepsy. Partial seizures begin in a single location and are more common. Seizure disorders may start in infancy or in later childhood, and are controlled, by and large, with anti-epileptic medication. Approximately 50% of individuals with a seizure disorder are within the standard range of intelligence. Also associated with seizure disorders is mental retardation, and a higher incidence of learning, behavior, and psychological problems (Brown, 1997). The impacts of epilepsy on learning and development center on reduced time available for learning and a variety of side effects, such as fatigue and reduced attention, resulting from anti-epileptic medications.

Lead Poisoning.   Lead poisoning may manifest in lethargy, clumsiness, anemia, seizures, language delays, and other developmental disabilities. It is caused by the ingestion of lead (i.e., toddlers eating old paint chips, containing lead, from peeling walls) which can cause damage to the brain, resulting in seizures and coma at high levels, to fatigue, irritability and weight loss, among other things at more moderate levels (Farber, Yanni, & Batshaw, 1997). Lead poisoning also results in "deficits in psychometric intelligence scores, speech and language processing, attention and classroom performance" (Needleman, Schell, Bellinger, Levinton, & Allred, 1990, p. 83). Manifestations of lead poisoning are difficult to identify and often coexist with other risk factors, such as poverty (Kaplan-Sanoff & Nigro, 1988). Infants and children with eating disorders (i.e., "Pica," described later) are particularly susceptible to lead poisoning when living in older homes with peeling lead paint.

Cystic Fibrosis.   This is a "recessive heredity disorder...characterized by abnormal mucus secretion by all secreting glands except those that secrete into the bloodstream." Major problems include "a dry nonproductive cough; susceptibility to acute infection; and bronchial obstruction" which are controlled by medical treatment, diet, and exercise (Best, Bigge, & Sirvis, 1990, p. 295). The sequelae of this disorder are in social and emotional adjustment to the disease rather than in learning potential specifically.

AIDS (Acquired Immune Deficiency Syndrome).   AIDS represents a serious threat to increasing numbers of children, especially those born to parents who are carriers of HIV (Human Immune deficiency Virus), which attacks the immune system. There is no known cure for it. Approximately 7,000 infants are born each year at risk for the development of HIV infection, and 1,000 new cases of AIDS are identified in children younger than 13 years of age. Children with AIDS usually suffer from progressive motor, communicative, and cognitive impairments (Rutstein, Conlon, & Batshaw, 1997). Although children with AIDS are highly susceptible to a variety of infections, they should be encouraged to participate in school during periods of good health (Best, Bigge, & Sirvis, 1990).

AIDS and HIV infection also impose serious threats to psychosocial development. The families of persons with AIDS or HIV infection are often isolated socially and the children are often shunned in school, despite the fact that the risk of transmission is negligible. The parents face guilt about their own behaviors, grief about their children's chronic illness and likely death, and fear about their own likely deaths. The affected children may also exhibit emotional problems.

Fetal Alcohol Syndrome (FAS).   FAS is a leading cause of developmental disabilities. In addition to mental retardation, children with FAS are characterized by physical abnormalities (especially in facial features), stereotypic behaviors, and behavior problems. The term Fetal Alcohol Effects (FAE) is used to describe children with milder cognitive impairments that are associated with learning and behavior problems, but who do not have the particular physical characteristics associated with FAS (Batshaw & Conlon, 1997).

Cocaine Exposure.   This is a new problem compared to FAS. Children exposed to cocaine prenatally are at risk for "abruption, prematurity, LBW (low birth weight), and decreased head size," and may be at increased risk for "subsequent impairments in language and motor skills, attention span, organizational strategies, and interpersonal relationships" (Batshaw & Conlon, 1997, p. 153). However, studies also suggest that most of the children exposed prenatally to cocaine will have average cognitive functioning and no significant physical problems at school entry (Batshaw & Conlon, 1997).

Traumatic Brain Injury.   "'Traumatic brain injury' means an acquired injury to the brain caused by an external physical force, resulting in total or partial functional disability or psychosocial impairment, or both, that adversely affects a child's educational performance. The term applies to open or closed head injuries resulting in impairments in one or more areas, such as cognition; language; memory; attention; reasoning; abstract thinking; judgment; problem-solving; sensory, perceptual and motor abilities; psychosocial behavior; physical functions; information processing; and speech. The term does not apply to brain injuries that are congenital or degenerative, or brain injuries induced by birth trauma" (Federal Register, Oct. 22, 1997, p. 55070).

Traumatic brain injury currently constitutes the most common acquired disability in childhood, with approximately one in 25 children receiving medical attention because of a head injury (Michaud, Duhaime, & Lazar, 1997). For preschoolers, the most common cause of head injury is falls from heights, but other causes include physical abuse and neglect. Risks to young children increase as a result of impulsive behavior. Causes attributable to sports and motor accidents increase with increasing age. The trauma is severe enough to cause a change in consciousness (coma) or cause an anatomical change in the brain. It is imperative that a child be treated promptly after the injury to reduce the possibility of resulting physical and cognitive impairments. Physical impairments include motor deficits, feeding disorders, and problems with vision and/or hearing. Cognitive impairments include problems with attention, memory, problem solving, and judgement. A severe head injury should be suspected if the child is "lethargic, confused or irritable; has a severe headache; demonstrates acute impairments in speech, vision, or movements of the arms or legs; has significant bleeding from the wound; or vomits repeatedly" (Michaud, Duhaime, & Lazar, 1997, p. 600). Outcomes of a severe head injury range from complete recovery to a variety of functional disabilities including "motor, communication, cognitive, behavior, and sensory impairments" (ibid., p. 613).

Multiple Disability.   "'Multiple disability' means concomitant impairments (such as mental retardation-blindness, mental retardation-orthopedic impairment, etc.), the combination of which causes such severe educational problems that the problems cannot be accommodated in special education programs solely for one of the impairments. The term does not include deaf-blindness." (Federal Register, Oct. 22, 1997, p. 55069). More information on multiple disabilities and other health impairments appears in Chapter 17. This category overlaps with both physical and mental conditions.

Mental Conditions

The categories included under mental conditions are those presented in P.L. 105-17, IDEA amendments (1997), and that overlap with those presented in DSM-IV (APA, 1994).

Mental Retardation.   "'Mental retardation' means significantly subaverage general intellectual functioning existing concurrently with deficits in adaptive behavior and manifested during the developmental period that adversely affects a child's educational performance" (Federal Register, Oct. 22, 1997, p. 55069).

The category "Mental retardation" appears in both IDEA and DSM-IV, and involves general delays. Its essential features in DSM-IV are: "A. Significantly subaverage general intellectual functioning: an IQ of approximately 70 or below on an individually administered IQ test (for infants, a clinical judgment of significantly subaverage intellectual functioning). B. Concurrent deficits or impairments in present adaptive functioning (i.e., the person's effectiveness in meeting the standards expected for his or her age by his or her cultural group) in at least two of the following areas: communication, self-care, home living, social/interpersonal skills, use of community resources, self-direction, functional academic skills, work, leisure, health and safety. C. The onset is before 18 years." (APA, 1994, p. 46). Mental retardation is coded in DSM-IV according to "degree of severity reflecting level of intellectual impairment" and includes the following cattegories: Mild Mental Retardation (IQ 50–55 to 70); Moderate Mental Retardation (IQ 35–40 to 50–55); Severe Mental Retardation (IQ 20–25 to 35–40); Profound Mental Retardation (IQ below 20 or 25); and Mental Retardation, Severity Unspecified (presumption of mental retardation but the person's intelligence is regarded as untestable) (APA, 1994).

Mental retardation has been distinguished as either organically based (for example, due to birth injuries, inborn errors of metabolism, and infections) caused by chromosomal abnormalities as in Down syndrome and fragile X syndrome (Batshaw & Perrett, 1992), or "cultural-familial," in which there is no organic or genetic basis; 75% of children with mental retardation are in this last category (Zigler & Balla, 1982). Mental retardation is associated with many other impairments that "include cerebral palsy, visual impairments, seizure disorders, communication impairments, feeding difficulties, psychiatric disorders and attention-deficit/hyperactivity disorder (ADHD)," (Batshaw & Shapiro, 1997, p. 349).

Most individuals with mental retardation fit the classification of "mild." Regarding language development, preschool children with mild retardation achieve developmental milestones but somewhat later than their peers. Children with moderate retardation have difficulty with aspects of communication identified in the preschool period (e.g., narratives). Children with severe and profound retardation, however, demonstrate motor delays that influence speech development, develop language late (i.e., school age), and are rarely competent at conversation (Lahey, 1988). Similarly with play activities, delays will occur, but to varying extents, depending on the degree of retardation. The assessment of children with mental retardation is treated more thoroughly in Chapter 17.

The most common presentation of mental retardation in the preschool period is in terms of developmental delays in the developmental tasks of the preschool period. Early identification is important. Children with mental retardation are characterized by delays in essentially all areas of development, but the nature and course of development is essentially the same. For example, children with Down syndrome have been noted to "undergo developmental patterns and sequences that are highly similar to those of normal children" (Beeghly, Weiss-Perry, & Cicchetti, 1990, p. 333). The extent of delay, however, will be influenced by the extent of retardation.

Down Syndrome.   This is a particular genetic abnormality, also known as trisomy 21, that usually results in mental retardation, although of varying degrees of severity. The prevalence is approximately 0.92 per 1,000, having decreased from 1.33 per 1,000 since the early 1970s (Roizen, 1997). Research has demonstrated that the malformations on the X-chromosome are "a consequence of incomplete embryogenesis rather than deviant development," and, given an examination of brain tissue, a relative "immaturity of neurons and their synaptic connections" (Batshaw & Perret, 1992, p. 273). There are physical characteristics associated with Down syndrome, and they include relatively small heads; small ears, mouth, hands and feet; and epicanthal folds at the inner corners of the eyes. Down syndrome is also associated with increased risk of medical problems that include congenital heart problems, sensory impairments, endocrine abnormalities, orthopedic problems, and gastrointestinal malformations (Roizen, 1997).

A considerable amount of research has been dedicated to describing development in children with Down syndrome to elucidate delays and differences, in general (Cicchetti & Beeghly, 1990), and symbolic development, in particular (Beeghly & Cicchetti, 1981). The social-interactive abilities of children with Down syndrome are usually higher than would be expected. Because much is known about the development of children with Down syndrome and the condition can be identified prenatally (by chromosomal abnormalities) or at birth (by the physical characteristics), Down syndrome is characterized as an "established risk." As a result, intervention services for children with Down syndrome are customarily begun early.

Other chromosomal abnormalities associated with mental retardation are fragile X syndrome, cri-du-chat (cat's cry) syndrome (resulting in a retardation in growth), Klinefelter syndrome (resulting in a thin appearance and underdeveloped sex organs) (Patton, Beirne-Smith, & Payne, 1990), Rett Syndrome (characterized by stereotypical hand wringing and hand flapping), Prader-Willi Syndrome (characterized by marked obesity and excessive demand for food), and Lesch-Nyan Syndrome (characterized by compulsive biting of lips and fingers) (Batshaw & Perrett, 1992). Attention to *fragile X syndrome* has increased in recent years. It is the second most identifiable cause of mental retardation (following Down syndrome), and is inherited as a sex-linked disorder. Like Down syndrome, fragile X syndrome is also associated with physical characteristics (elongated face, long ears, and prominent jaws). It represents one third of all X-linked causes of mental retardation. Children with fragile X syndrome generally have mental retardation at the severe level. Communication delays are common (as a result of cognitive and motor delays), difficulties with attention and problem solving are usual, and the children lack social skills (Batshaw, 1997b).

Autism.   "'Autism' means a developmental disability significantly affecting verbal and nonverbal communication and social interaction, generally evident before age 3, that adversely affects a child's educational performance. Other characteristics often associated with autism are engagement in repetitive activities and stereotyped movements, resistance to environmental change or change in daily routines, and unusual responses to sensory experiences. The term does not apply if a child's educational performance is adversely affected primarily because the child has an emotional disturbance, as defined...(by that category)" (Federal Register, Oct. 22, 1997, p. 55069). P.L. 105-17 notes that the category may still apply for identification after the age of 3, given that the foregoing criteria still apply. The condition "autism" was removed from the category "Seriously emotionally disturbed" and moved to the category "Other health impaired" in 1987 (U.S. Department of Education, 1987). This change was based, in part, "in research reflecting a biochemical etiology" (Best, Bigge, & Sirvis, 1990, p. 297), and on behaviors supporting a biological explanation (Peterson, 1987). "Autism" was listed as a category in its own right in P.L. 101-476 (1991).

Autism corresponds to "Autistic Disorder" in DSM-IV, and is included as one of the Pervasive Developmental Disorders (APA, 1994). The Pervasive Developmental Disorders "are characterized by severe deficits and pervasive impairment in multiple areas of development. These include impairment in reciprocal social interaction, impairment in communication, and the presence of stereotyped behavior, interests, and activities. The specific disorders included in this section are Autistic Disorder, Rett's Disorder, Childhood Disintegrative Disorder, Asperger's Disorder, and Pervasive Developmental Disorder Not Otherwise Specified" (APA, 1994, p. 38).

The DSM-IV criteria for *Autistic Disorder* include

A. ...qualitative impairment in social interaction,...qualitative impairments in communication,...(and) restricted repetitive and stereotyped patterns of behavior, interests, and activities...

B. Delays or abnormal functioning in at least one of the following areas, with onset prior to age 3 years: (1) social interaction, (2) language as used in social communication, or (3) symbolic or imaginative play; and C. The disturbance is not better accounted for by Rett's Disorder or Childhood Disintegrative Disorder. (APA, 1994, pp. 70–71)

The prevalence of autism is determined to be one in 1,000 live births. The biological basis of autism is attributed to a combination of genetic and developmental factors. Certain complications during fetal development such as exposure to thalidomide and various infections are associated with Pervasive Developmental Disorder (Mauk, Reber, & Batshaw, 1997).

Autism is distinguished from the other developmental disabilities by characteristic social and behavioral problems, and by impairments in the pragmatics of language. Preschool children with autism have been characterized as having "core deficits" in social cognition, that is "deficits in social understanding and symbolic representation of other individuals" (Sigman & Mundy, 1987, p. 44). Such deficits will manifest themselves in language (Tager-Flusberg, 1989), play activities (Ungerer & Sigman, 1991), and social interaction (Strain, 1985). The language development of children with autism has been described by Lahey (1988) as involving "more than late onset" and as differing in "form, content, and use and in the interactions among these components" (p. 77). Often language is used "out of context," in that a child will produce a well-formed sentence that has no meaning in relation to ongoing linguistic and non-linguistic events. This kind of language may be described as "delayed echolalia" where the child repeats someone else's utterance, verbatim, but separated in time from the original event. It should be noted, however, that there is considerable variation among the language development of children with autism, and there is no one syndrome of language behaviors to describe the language of these children (Lahey, 1988).

The play activities of children with autism has been characterized as predominating in manipulative play, and as limited in the frequency and variety of symbolic play activities (Ungerer & Sigman, 1981). Research has also indicated deficits in joint attention, between child and caregiver, in play activities (Sigman & Mundy, 1987).

Deficits in social attachment comprise a major feature in identifying children with autism, manifesting in depressed levels of attachment to caregivers and in interactions with other children. Affective behavior has been described as flattened, inappropriate, or excessive and labile (Schreibman, Koegel, & Koegel, 1989). (See Dawson, 1989, and Schreibman et al., 1989, for comprehensive reviews of autism).

Rett's Disorder. Rett's Disorder is characterized as "the development of multiple specific deficits following a period of normal functioning after birth; there is a loss of previously acquired purposeful hand skills between ages 5 and 30 months, with the subsequent development of characteristic stereotyped hand movements resembling hand-wringing or hand washing" (APA, 1994, p. 71). Interest in the social environment usually diminishes after the onset of the disorder but may reappear later. There is also impairment in expressive and receptive language development, problems with gait and trunk movements, and psychomotor retardation (APA, 1994).

Childhood Disintegrative Disorder. This is "marked by regression in multiple areas of functioning following a period of at least 2 years of apparently normal development. Apparently normal development is reflected in age-appropriate verbal and nonverbal communication, social relationships, play, and adaptive behavior. After the first two years of life (but before age 10 years), the child has a clinically significant loss of previously acquired skills" in two or more areas (APA, 1994, p. 73). Children with this disorder manifest social, communicative, and behavioral deficits associated with Autistic Disorder.

Asperger's Disorder. This is distinguished by "severe and sustained impairment in social interaction and the development of restricted, repetitive patterns of behavior, interests, and activities," and affects social, occupational, and other areas of important functioning (APA, 1994, p. 75). It is differentiated from Autistic Disorder because there are not clinically significant delays in language, cognitive development, self-help skills, adaptive behavior, and curiosity about the environment.

Speech or Language Impairment. "'Speech or language impairment' means a communication disorder such as stuttering, impaired articulation, a language impairment, or a voice impairment that adversely affects a child's educational performance" (Federal Register, Oct. 22, 1997, p. 55070).

The *Communication Disorders* (APA, 1994) correspond directly to "speech or language impairment," because they are characterized simply "by difficulties in speech or language (p. 38). As in the "learning disorders," the emphasis is on a discrepancy between performance, measured using a standardized assessment, and what would be expected, also measured using standardized assessments. The communication disorders include the following: Expressive Language Disorder, Mixed Receptive-Expressive Language Disorder, Phonological Disorder, Stuttering, and Communication Disorder Not Otherwise Specified.

A related description is "Specific-language-impaired" (SLI), which is a diagnostic category used by speech pathologists to characterize children "who appear to develop normally in all respects except language" (Lahey, 1988, p. 49).

Expressive Language Disorder. Of the Communication Disorders, Expressive Language Disorder is characterized by "an impairment in expressive language development," and may manifest in "a markedly limited vocabulary, making errors in tense, or having difficulty recalling words or producing sentences with developmentally appropriate length or complexity" (APA, 1994, p. 58). The child with Expressive Language Disorder is assumed to have normal comprehension abilities and to be cognitively intact. What is apparent is a discrepancy between what the child knows and the expression of that knowledge using language. Mixed Receptive-Expressive Language Disorder includes the symptoms for Expressive Language Disorder "as well as difficulty understanding words, sentences, or specific types of words, such as spatial terms" (p. 60). The impairment is specific to language in that the child's cognitive development is assessed as normal. The identified discrepancy is between relatively low performance in language comprehension, given what one would expect based on a nonverbal assessment of the child's intelligence.

Phonological Disorder. Phonological Disorder is characterized by "a failure to use developmentally expected speech sounds that are appropriate for the individual's age and dialect" (APA, 1994, p. 61). This disorder is a speech disorder, in contrast to the language disorders described previously. Stuttering is defined as "a disturbance in the normal fluency and time patterning of speech that is inappropriate for the individual's age" (p. 63), and is characterized by frequent occurrences of sound and syllable repetitions, sound prolongations, interjections, broken words, audible or silent blocking (i.e., "filled or unfilled pauses in speech"), circumlocutions (i.e., word substitutions), "words produced with an excess of physical tension," and "monosyllabic whole-word repetitions" (p. 65).

Specific Learning Disability.

(i) General. The term means a disorder in one or more of the basic psychological processes involved in understanding or in using language, spoken or written, that may manifest itself in an imperfect ability to listen, think, speak, read, write, spell, or do mathematical calculations, including such conditions as perceptual disabilities, brain injury, minimal brain dysfunction, dyslexia, and developmental aphasia. (ii) Disorders not included. The term does not include learning problems that are primarily the result of visual, hearing, or motor disabilities, of mental retardation, of emotional disturbance, or of environmental, cultural, or economic disadvantage (Federal Register, Oct. 22, 1997, p. 55070).

The term "perceptual disabilities" appears in this definition: these are noted as problems in auditory and visual-spatial perception, to be distinguished from impairments in hearing or vision. "Specific learning disability" is defined mostly in terms of what it is not, rather than what it is, and the definition does not address the etiology of the disorder (Church, Lewis, & Batshaw, 1997).

It was noted in P.L. 105-17 that children with ADD or ADHD may be designated as a child with a disability if they meet the criteria, specified above, for specific learning disability. P.L. 105-17 does not recognize ADHD/ADD as a specific category of disability.

Specific learning disability is defined customarily in terms of a discrepancy between ability and achievement. Achievement relates to achievement in school subjects, as in literacy and numeric skills. Achievement during the preschool period can be defined in terms of pre-academic skills or in terms of the developmental tasks of the period. States differ on whether this category is recognized and used for eligibility purposes at the preschool level, rendering the term controversial at the preschool level (Snyder et al., 1994). The term "learning disabled" is sometimes applied to the syndrome of "specific language impairment" (Lahey, 1988).

Learning Disorders encompasses several disorders in the DSM-IV categorization system that overlap with "specific learning disability." "These disorders are characterized by academic functioning that is substantially below that expected given the person's chronological age, measured intelligence, and age-appropriate education" (APA, 1994, p. 38). These disorders all have to do with achievement, measured by a standardized test, as substantially below what would be expected, and they include the following: Reading Disorder, Mathematics Disorder, Disorder of Written Expression, and Learning Disorder Not Otherwise Specified.

"Specific learning disability" and the "learning disorders" apply more to school-age children than to preschool-age children. It is thought that approximately 4 to 5% of the school-age population has learning disabilities. Each of these disorders significantly interferes with academic achievement or the activities of daily living that require reading skills, mathematical ability, or the composition of written texts. Specific reading disability is the most common of the learning disabilities. However, during the preschool period, the core symptoms of learning disabilities are manifest in delays in language, attention, behavior, social interaction, motor skills, and impulse control (Church, Lewis, & Batshaw, 1997). In fact, there is a growing body of research linking delays and differences in language during the preschool period to later problems in school (e.g., Scarborough, 1990; Vellutino, 1987). Problems in learning language have been distinguished as problems in learning, which often result in problems in learning school subjects (Bloom, 1980).

Motor Skills Disorder.   "Motor Skills Disorder" (APA, 1994) does not appear as a separate category in the categories of disability delineated in P.L. 105-17. Motor Skills Disorder "includes 'Developmental Coordination Disorder,' which is characterized by motor coordination that is substantially below that expected given the person's chronological age and measured intelligence" (APA, 1994, p. 38). It is similar to the "learning disorders" described above in its emphasis on performance as below expectation. The essential feature "...is a marked impairment in the development of motor coordination...[that]...significantly interferes with academic achievement or activities of daily living" (APA, 1994, p. 53). Motor Skills Disorder is considered separately from any association with a medical condition (e.g., cerebral palsy), and the diagnosis is not made if the criteria for Pervasive Developmental Disorder has been made. The disorder is manifest in problems in fine and gross motor activities that are not characterized by the clumsiness due to distractibility and impulsiveness.

Emotional Disturbance.

'Emotional disturbance'...means a condition exhibiting one or more of the following characteristics over a long period of time and to a marked degree that adversely affects a child's educational performance: (A) An inability to learn that cannot be explained by intellectual, sensory, or health factors; (B) An inability to build or maintain satisfactory interpersonal relationships with peers and teachers; (C) Inappropriate types of behavior or feelings under normal circumstances; (D) A general pervasive mood of unhappiness or depression; (E) A tendency to develop physical symptoms or fears associated with personal or school problems. The term includes schizophrenia. The term does not apply to children who are socially maladjusted, unless it is determined that they have an emotional disturbance (Federal Register, Oct. 22, 1997, p. 55069).

"Emotional disturbance" is the last of the 13 categories presented in P.L. 105-17. The change from "Serious emotional disturbance" to "emotional disturbance" was noted in P.L. 105-17 as "intended strictly to eliminate the pejorative connotation of the term 'serious'" (Federal Register, Oct. 22, 1997, p. 55070). It was also noted that children with ADD or ADHD may be designated as a child with a disability if they meet the criteria, specified above, for emotional disturbance.

Identification of preschoolers with emotional disturbance is extremely difficult, due to several factors: there is a tremendous range of "normal" behavior; children's behaviors are influenced by parental expectations and cultural values; children's behaviors are highly individualistic unless contextual constraints (e.g., day care) require conformity; social-emotional and personality characteristics are continuing to evolve in the preschool period; many behavior problems may be transient in the period; and manifestations of various impairments cut across different disorders (Peterson, 1987). Common developmental behavior problems include eating problems, fears, temper tantrums and aggressive behavior, withdrawal and isolation, problems with elimination (enuresis and encopresis), and hyperactivity. However, "in severely disturbed children the same behaviors are manifest in greater numbers and in more exaggerated, severe, and perseverative forms" (p. 234).

There are several categories that remain under the heading "Disorders Usually First Diagnosed in Infancy, Childhood, or Adolescence" in the DSM-IV classification system. These disorders do not correspond to, but overlap with the category "Emotional Disturbance."

Attention-Deficit and Disruptive Behavior Disorders. The Attention-Deficit Disorders include Attention-Deficit Hyperactivity Disorder and Attention-Deficit Hyperactivity Disorder Not Otherwise Specified. The Disruptive Behavior Disorders are focused on the identification of behaviors that are socially disruptive, and generally pertain to school-age children and youth. Two subcategories—Conduct Disorder ("characterized by a pattern of behavior that violates the basic rights of others or major age-appropriate societal norms or rules") and Oppositional Defiant Disorder ("characterized by a pattern of negativistic, hostile, and defiant behavior") (APA, 1994, p. 38)—pertain to school-age children and youth, and are not discussed here.

Attention-Deficit/Hyperactivity Disorder is "characterized by prominent symptoms of inattention and/or hyperactivity-impulsivity." Symptoms of inattention must persist for a period of 6 months or more "to a degree that is maladaptive and inconsistent with developmental level" (p. 83). These symptoms include difficulties with the following activities: paying close enough attention to details, sustaining attention in tasks or play activities, listening, following through on instructions, organizing tasks and activities, participating in activities that require sustained mental effort, remembering things needed for a task, not being distracted by extraneous stimuli, and remembering the components of daily activities.

Symptoms of hyperactivity/impulsivity must also persist for a period of "at least 6 months to a degree that is maladaptive and inconsistent with developmental level" (APA,

1994, p. 84). Symptoms of hyperactivity include the following behaviors: fidgeting with hands or feet or squirming in seat, leaving one's seat when remaining in one's seat is expected, running about or climbing excessively, difficulty in playing or engaging in leisure activities quietly, often "on the go," and often talking excessively. Symptoms of impulsivity include the following behaviors: blurting out answers before question has been completed, difficulty with waiting for one's turn, and interrupting or intruding on others. Subtypes are provided for specifying the predominant symptom presentation: Predominantly Inattentive Type, Predominantly Hyperactive-Impulsive Type, and Combined Type (APA, 1994, p. 38).

ADHD is the most common disorder of childhood, and coexists with other learning, emotion, and behavior problems. It is estimated that 3 to 5 % of school-age children have ADHD. It was originally thought to be caused by a brain injury, but it is now regarded as having a genetic basis. However, certain factors that influence brain development (e.g., lead, alcohol, cocaine, low birth weight, prematurity) are associated with ADHD (Blum & Mercugliano, 1997).

A child with ADHD experiences extreme difficulty sitting quietly and sustaining attention to a task, and frequently shifts from one activity to another. Behaviors are often impulsive, such as grabbing toys from other children; taking turns or waiting become very difficult tasks. Because of impulsivity and difficulties sustaining attention, children with Attention-Deficit Hyperactivity Disorder experience difficulty in learning across the board, which is a significant factor distinguishing it from learning disabilities. However, approximately 25% of children with ADHD have learning disabilities, while another 25% have other academic problems. Its presence will influence the course of development in all aspects of cognition, language, social, motor, and self-help skills.

Feeding and Eating Disorders of Infancy or Early Childhood.   The Feeding and Eating Disorders of Infancy or Childhood are characterized by persistent disturbances in feeding and eating (APA, 1994, p. 38). The specific disorders include Pica, Rumination Disorder, and Feeding Disorder of Infancy or Early Childhood.

Pica is characterized by the "persistent eating of non-nutritive substances for a period of at least 1 month" (APA, 1994, p. 95), such as dust, string, and cloth; in addition, the eating of non-nutritive substances is inappropriate for the age level and is not part of a culturally sanctioned practice. Predisposing factors include neglect and mental retardation. Although most infants and toddlers will mouth many objects in their explorations, the distinguishing feature in Pica is the persistence and frequency with which non-food objects are ingested.

Rumination Disorder is defined as "repeated regurgitation and rechewing of food that develops in an infant or child after a period of normal functioning and lasts for at least 1 month" (APA, 1994, p. 96). This disorder is most commonly seen in infants. The infant behaves as if he or she gains satisfaction from the sucking movements made with the tongue which causes the regurgitation. Aside from weight loss, complications also include alienation of caregivers from the infant due to difficulty in feeding and the noxious odor of regurgitated food.

Feeding Disorder of Infancy or Early Childhood is characterized by "the persistent failure to eat adequately, as reflected in significant failure to gain weight or significant weight loss over at least 1 month" (APA, 1994, p. 98). It is important to distinguish that this disturbance is not associated with a gastrointestinal or other general medical condition.

Tic Disorders. Tic Disorders "are characterized by vocal and/or motor tics...(and include)...Tourette's Disorder, Chronic Motor or Vocal Tic Disorder, Transient Tic Disorder, and Tic Disorder Not Otherwise Specified." Common to all Tic disorders is a "sudden, rapid, recurrent, nonrhythmic, stereotyped motor movement or vocalization. It is experienced as irresistible but can be suppressed for varying lengths of time. All forms of tic may be exacerbated by stress and attenuated during absorbing activities" (APA, 1994, p. 100).

In *Tourette's Disorder* the tics are a combination of motor movements (e.g., eye-blinking) and vocalizations (e.g., clicks, grunts, yelps). The occurrence of the tics ranges from several times a day to intermittent occurrence through a year. *Chronic Motor or Vocal Tic Disorder* is characterized by either motor or vocal tics but not both as in Tourette's Disorder, and is usually of a less severe type. In *Transient Tic Disorder,* "single or multiple motor and/or vocal tics... occur many times a day, nearly every day for at least 4 weeks, but for no longer than 12 consecutive months" (APA, 1994, p. 104), unlike Tourette's Disorder and Chronic Motor or Vocal Tic Disorder which require a duration of greater than one year.

Elimination Disorders. The Elimination Disorders include Encopresis and Enuresis. Encopresis is characterized by the "repeated passage of feces into inappropriate places ...the event must occur once a month for at least 3 months" (APA, 1994, p. 106). Additional requirements for the diagnosis include a chronological and mental age of at least four years of age and the absence of physical problems that could cause incontinence. This pattern may develop because of anxiety about defecating or it may reflect a pattern of oppositional behavior. Deliberate incontinence is often associated with antisocial behavior.

Enuresis is "repeated voiding of urine during the day or at night into bed or clothes" (APA, 1994, p. 108). The frequency of episodes required for this diagnosis is twice per week for at least 3 months. Continence is generally expected by age five for preschool children.

Others Disorders of Infancy, Childhood, or Adolescence. These disorders include Separation Anxiety Disorder, Selective Mutism, Reactive Attachment Disorder of Infancy or Early Childhood, Stereotypic Movement Disorder, and Disorder of Infancy, Childhood, or Adolescence Not Otherwise Specified.

Separation Anxiety Disorder can be identified in the preschool period, and is characterized by "developmentally inappropriate and excessive anxiety concerning separation from home or from those to whom the child is attached" (APA, 1994, p. 39). The "disturbance must last for a period of at least four weeks... and cause significant distress or impairment in social, academic (occupational), or other important areas of functioning" (p. 110). The child has unrealistic or persistent worries that he or she will be separated from major attachment figures or that serious harm will befall these figures. The occurrence of the disorder is often preceded by some form of life stress (e.g., death of a family member, a move to another city). Such stressors of infancy and childhood (i.e., separation) are the focus of considerable contemporary research (Garmezy, 1988; Kagan, 1988). There are important cultural variations "in the degree to which it is considered desirable to tolerate separation" (p. 111).

Selective Mutism is defined as "consistent failure to speak in specific social situations (in which there is an expectation for speaking, e.g., at school) despite speaking in other situations" (APA, 1994, p. 115). This disorder is rare and is usually not identified until the child is required to be in contexts outside of the home (e.g., school). Occasionally children with this disorder have language or speech disorders, but usually develop language normally.

Failure to communicate in school obviously influences the child's development in many areas, particularly social skills.

Reactive Attachment Disorder of Infancy or Early Childhood is characterized by "markedly disturbed and developmentally inappropriate social relatedness in most contexts, beginning before age 5 years" (APA, 1994, p. 118). There is persistent failure to initiate or respond in social interactions. Children with this disorder can be recognized by the depressed occurrence or absence of the social interactive behaviors typically established in infancy and early childhood (e.g., visual tracking, response to caregiver's voice, attention, interest, and reciprocal gaze). This disorder is presumed to be related to grossly pathogenic care which interferes with the emotional development of the child in relation to the primary caregiver. The conditions of Mental Retardation and Pervasive Developmental Disorder must be ruled out for the diagnosis to be made.

Stereotypic Movement Disorder is defined by "repetitive, seemingly driven, and nonfunctional motor behavior (e.g., hand shaking or waving, body rocking, head banging, mouthing of objects, self-biting, picking at skin or bodily orifices, hitting own body)" (APA, 1994, p. 121). Some of these behaviors, however, may be observed in infants and children who are developing without disabilities (e.g., rocking before sleep, teeth grinding as new teeth are coming in). The occurrence of the disorder is often associated with mental retardation, interferes with the development of social and self-help skills, and may result in injury to the child.

Relevance of Descriptors to the Nature of Services Developed

The final section of this chapter concerns the relevance of various descriptors to the nature of services that are provided for preschoolers with disabilities or at-risk for developmental delay. Services for these children center on the selection of goals and the implementation of these goals. The importance of the early involvement of the children's families in all aspects of this process cannot be overstated.

Relevance of Descriptors to the Selection of Goals

The selection of goals for preschoolers is related to how a preschooler with disabilities is described. If preschoolers are described as school-age children, the categorical descriptions presented in P.L. 105-17 apply. For each of these categorical descriptions, the phrase that the disability "adversely affects educational performance" was included. Consequently, if preschoolers are to be described as school-age children, and if goals for them are to be written in terms of a remediation of the impact of the disability on educational performance, then these goals will be focused more likely on pre-academic skills, such as pre-literacy and pre-numeric skills.

In contrast, preschoolers with disabilities may be described as "children who are experiencing developmental delays" in one or more of the developmental domains, following the alternative, noncategorical description offered in P.L. 105-17. If preschoolers are described in terms of delays and differences in developmental domains, then goals will likely focus on what is needed to facilitate progress in these domains. Practitioners may also write goals in terms of classroom behaviors appropriate for the preschool age group, such as mastery activities and goals of social interaction (Bronson, Hauser-Cram, & Warfield, 1995).

Relevance of Descriptors to the Implementation of Goals

The implementation of goals for preschoolers with disabilities is also related to how they are described. Implementation of goals includes whether the goals are embedded into everyday contexts of the classroom, and whether the goals allow for children to be included fully in the classroom activities.

The context of service delivery for preschoolers with disabilities generally is either in an integrated setting or a separate setting. Integrated settings tend to emphasize the children as children first, and as children with disabilities second. As a result, descriptions in terms of progress in development domains are highlighted because they can be applied to all the children. In contrast, segregated settings may place greater attention on the particular disability of the participating children, thereby emphasizing a categorical focus.

How goals are implemented includes whether goals are embedded into the context of everyday activities for implementation. Embedding individualized goals into preschool activities (i.e., play activities; social/communicative activities; self-help activities), provides a venue for addressing learning goals while supporting the children's inclusion in the activities of their peers (Lifter et al., 1997).

Finally, goals need to be designed so that they allow children with disabilities to be full participants in classroom activities. Full participation means the children understand what they are doing and can be actively engaged in ongoing events; goals are written not simply in terms of what children need to learn but also in terms of what children are ready to learn from a developmental point of view. Such an approach is advocated by Lifter and Bloom (1998) for identifying play and language objectives for intervention. Describing preschoolers with disabilities in terms of progress in areas of developmental functioning represents a way in which one truly can use the descriptions of children developing "more slowly than" or "differently from" their peers; children with and without disabilities are described along the same continuum. Researchers and practitioners are in a strategic position to develop and to expand intervention programs for children with various delays and differences that regard them as children first. How these children are described will influence how they are served.

Summary

This chapter began with a summary of the legislative mandates pertaining to children with disabilities as they provide a framework for describing preschoolers developing with difficulty. Factors that influence the need for, and the nature of, descriptions were reviewed. The categories of disabilities, set forth in P.L. 105-17 and DSM-IV (APA, 1994), were presented, and included descriptions of the developmental sequelae of children with these disabilities. The relevance of categorical and noncategorical descriptors to the nature of services developed was discussed.

4 Legal and Ethical Issues in Preschool Assessment and Screening

STEPHEN T. DEMERS

CATHERINE FIORELLO

The assessment of preschool children presents some special legal and ethical consider-ations for the practitioner who provides such services. Such assessments involve working with children who are suspected of being developmentally delayed, and who often come from racial or ethnic minority populations. The fact that the individuals being assessed are legal minors, possibly disabled and often racial/ethnic minorities results in the imposition of extraordinary legal and ethical safeguards and protections. Consequently, psychologists and other diagnostic specialists need to be familiar with the special legal and ethical man-dates affecting assessment services with young children.

While assessment personnel perform these assessments in order to benefit children and their families as well as the schools and agencies that serve them, such services carry the potential for harm if not provided with competence and concern for the welfare of oth-ers. Also, the lay person is often unable to evaluate the appropriateness of the assessment services they receive because of the technical nature of many testing practices. Therefore, professionals, like psychologists, have developed a code of ethics and standards of practice through professional associations (like the American Psychological Association and the National Association of School Psychologists) to guide practitioners and protect the pub-lic. In addition, certain legal statutes, both federal and state, have set limits on how profes-sionals may practice.

This chapter introduces the reader to the major legal and ethical issues to be consid-ered when conducting preschool assessments and screening. The section on legal mandates includes a brief discussion of relevant federal legislation, including the Individuals with Disabilities Education Act (IDEA), and the Family Educational Rights and Privacy Act (or FERPA). The section on ethical principles focuses on several problematic areas like use of appropriately normed and validated procedures, obtaining informed consent, confidential-ity and privacy issues, and so on, and discusses these in light of the ethical standards pro-mulgated by relevant professional associations.

Federal Legislation Affecting Preschool Assessment and Screening

Legal intervention in the work of public institutions like the schools (as well as that of expert professionals such as psychologists) has a relatively short history (Bersoff & Hofer, 1990; DeMers & Bersoff, 1985). The courts have typically intervened in public school operations only when an issue of constitutional protection has been raised. Psychologists and other diagnostic specialists who work in the schools are often involved in situations where such constitutional issues may arise. Assessment for special education placement, disciplinary hearings, and the confidential aspects of assessment and counseling services all raise potential claims of equal protection or due process violations. Much of the legislation affecting psychological and educational assessment of children in schools has resulted from legal challenges raised at the state and local level through litigation by parents on behalf of their disabled children. (See Bersoff & Hofer, 1990; DeMers & Bersoff, 1985; and Jacob-Timm & Hartshorne, 1994 for a detailed discussion of these cases.)

Two major pieces of federal legislation have the most impact on the assessment and screening of preschool children, namely, The Individuals with Disabilities Education Act (IDEA) and the Family Educational Rights and Privacy Act (FERPA).

Individuals with Disabilities Education Act (IDEA)

The Individuals with Disabilities Education Act, or IDEA, replaced the original federal special education legislation known as P.L. 94-142 which passed in 1974 and dramatically affected the way all school personnel provide special education services (Jacob-Timm & Hartshorne, 1994). P.L. 94-142 has been amended several times since 1974, including one major revision in 1986 known as P.L. 99-457 which extended special education services to those from birth to age 21. IDEA was passed in 1990 and has recently been amended (i.e., Individuals with Disabilities Education Act Amendments of 1997). IDEA incorporates all the prior amendments of P.L. 94-142 including those mandating special education services to preschool children. IDEA as originally passed in 1990 included other modifications of P.L. 94-142 such as replacing the term *handicapped* with *disabled* and adding several new categories of disability (i.e., autism and traumatic brain injury). The 1997 amendments to IDEA add an emphasis on demonstrating effectiveness of educational programming in meeting the needs of disabled students. For the first time, both state and local education plans for serving disabled students under IDEA must indicate methods for accountability in assessing progress towards meeting goals set for students in their individual education plans. Other aspects of the amendments to IDEA may have an impact on preschool assessment and screening, such as provisions for use of paraprofessionals in the delivery of services to disabled students and an expanded notion of related services. However, the regulations designed to implement the statutory changes made in IDEA in 1997 have not been finalized.

IDEA maintains the protections originally offered to children and parents under P.L. 94-142 that related to nondiscriminatory assessment, qualified assessment procedures and personnel, and informed consent for services. With regard to nondiscriminatory assessment, IDEA still requires that tests be administered in the child's native language and by trained personnel in accordance with procedures described by the test publisher. Tests also must be validated for the specific purpose for which they are used and the assessment must be comprehensive, multifactored, and conducted by a multidisciplinary team. Because of this federal law, school systems across the country began using multidisciplinary teams and comprehensive assessment batteries to evaluate students for special education. Bersoff and Hofer (1990) noted that the majority of court cases related to assessment are concerned with the issues of nondiscriminatory assessment, and using qualified examiners and appropriately validated tests. Another major feature of IDEA is the expansion of parental rights in the decision making related to special education placement. The law requires that parents be notified in writing and in the language typically used in the home whenever the schools seek to initiate, change, or deny a parent's request for the evaluation or placement of a child.

Given our focus on preschool assessment and services, the sections of IDEA dealing with services to preschool children and their families are of central importance. IDEA Part B extends the right to a free and appropriate education to all children aged 3 years and above. Under Part B of IDEA, children aged 3 to 5 years must be afforded the same opportunities for identification and intervention as those provided to children 5 to 21 years of age. School districts are obligated through their state-approved plan to make reasonable efforts to identify preschool children who may be experiencing developmental delays. In addition, children aged 3 to 5 years may be classified as "children with disabilities," a more generic classification than the specific disability classifications of mental retardation or learning disability, for example, that are required of children 5 years and above.

Under Part B, an Individual Education Plan (IEP) is required for each child (aged 3 to 5 years) served, although the multidisciplinary team may include a family needs component in the IEP for this age group. A variety of service providers may be employed in the IEP for this population, with much flexibility given to determining the kind of program that may best meet the child's needs at a given level of development. Allen and Hudd (1987) recommend that parent involvement be individualized, with training and support available to those parents who want to participate, and professionals available to replace parents who cannot or will not participate.

The Early Intervention Program for Infants and Toddlers under Part C (formerly Part H) of IDEA incorporates the provisions of P.L. 99-457 which afforded services to infants and toddlers. Part C of IDEA provides funds for states to develop early intervention services for all infants and toddlers up to 2 years of age who are developmentally delayed, have physical conditions that typically result in delay, or are at risk for substantial developmental delay. The primary components of Part C of IDEA include:

1. A state determined definition of developmental delay
2. A multidisciplinary assessment
3. Development of an Individualized Family Service Plan
4. Appointment of a case manager
5. Establishment of a state interagency coordinating council to facilitate interagency management of services
6. Development of a comprehensive, statewide child find system to guarantee identification of all eligible children

Each family served under Part C of IDEA must have an Individualized Family Service Plan (IFSP) based on assessment of the needs and resources of the family. Support services available to the children are varied, with members of an interagency multidisciplinary team determining the type and extent of services needed. Monies are available for parent training to assist parents in developing additional skills as well as becoming knowledgeable and effective advocates for their disabled child. Families can decline permission for some services under the IFSP without jeopardizing access to other services. Funds are also available under IDEA for the development, adaptation, and implementation of assessment materials and instruments for determining the needs of individual children and the strengths and weaknesses of families served under an Individualized Family Service Plan.

Due process procedures in Part C differ from Part B in several important ways. The procedural safeguards regarding informed consent and prior notice remain essentially unchanged; however, the law specifically provides for situations where the parents are unknown or unavailable and provides for continuation of some services during disputes. Part C protects the rights of a child whose parents are unknown or unavailable by assigning a surrogate to act in the place of a parent or guardian. The law also states that infants and toddlers obviously needing services will not experience a delay in services while the required assessment is being completed. Finally, the law guarantees that, in disputed cases, the child shall continue to receive all early intervention services unrelated to the dispute.

Family Educational Rights and Privacy Act

The Family Educational Rights and Privacy Act (FERPA, 1974) is especially relevant to the innovative preschool services authorized under IDEA. FERPA was designed to regulate treatment of educational records by all public educational institutions. Specifically, it allows parents of minor students access to their child's official school records, provides parents the opportunity to challenge inaccurate or misleading information, and requires written parental consent before records are released to a third party. Given the emphasis in IDEA upon family involvement and assessment for preschool children, as well as interagency cooperation, the issue of confidentiality and access to records becomes paramount.

IDEA encourages states to use existing agencies for serving disabled preschool children, but does this mean such agencies are now considered "public educational institutions" under the mandates of FERPA? What records shall be developed and maintained regarding the assessment of family strengths and weaknesses and who shall have access to such records? Whose needs will be of primary importance, the family's right to privacy or the child's need for intervention if parents do not allow access to information deemed pertinent by the assessment team? Who determines what is an "educational record" versus other kinds of records (e.g., medical, social, etc.)? All of these questions remain essentially unanswered and indicate the need for Congress or the U.S. Department of Education to address specifically the relationship between FERPA and IDEA. Meanwhile, school districts, agencies, and individual professionals must use their best judgment in handling these controversial issues—risking possible litigation from parents who feel wronged. Perhaps such service providers should establish policies prior to any dispute to show that the actions taken were carefully considered in light of the conflicting legal mandates.

A second major aspect of FERPA is the provision for parents to amend educational records (Jacob-Timm & Hartshorne, 1994). At a hearing to amend the information they consider inaccurate, misleading, or an undue invasion of privacy, parents are entitled to legal representation at their own expense. If consensus is not reached, then parents have a right to add a comment to existing information and this comment must be included when the child's file is released to anyone.

The "disclosure of information" section of FERPA is particularly relevant to the assessment of preschoolers and their families under IDEA. FERPA allows disclosure of a student's record without parental permission to a school official with a legitimate educational interest (Jacob-Timm & Hartshorne, 1994; Overcast, Sales, & Sacken 1990). Such disclosure is intended to allow discussion and consultation among interested professionals who share responsibility for meeting the child's educational needs, without mandating specific parental consent in each instance. Given the variety of service agencies that may be involved with the preschool child and family, plus the different and possibly conflicting policies each agency has related to release of information, the extension of FERPA disclosure provisions to agencies participating under IDEA services to preschool children may need further definition. Questions to be addressed include: Are all community agency personnel involved in preschool assessments now considered "school officials" and able to review records without parental permission? Are agency records now "educational records"? How can a parent's right to privacy be adequately protected in a program providing for diverse, loosely coordinated interagency services? Again, schools and agencies are advised to consider the letter and spirit of FERPA and establish policies governing the sharing, disclosure, and amendment of records generated by the new preschool services.

Ethical Issues in Preschool Assessment and Screening

Ethical codes are established by professional groups to guide the practice of their members. Because professional work is often technical in nature, the public depends on professional associations or regulatory boards to decide when professionals have acted inappropriately. Because a variety of professionals may be involved in preschool services, it is impossible to address all the potentially relevant ethical codes. We have chosen to examine the ethical considerations of preschool assessment and screening from the perspective of professional psychology because of the prominent role psychologists, especially school psychologists, play in special education assessment in most states. In addition, both the American Psychological Association (APA) and the National Association of School Psychologists (NASP) have ethical codes that address issues relevant to preschool assessment, and have established procedures and mechanisms for enforcing their ethical codes.

Interestingly, ethical principles typically complement legal mandates, although sometimes glaring exceptions occur—such as conflicts between a client's right to confidentiality and legal requirements to report child abuse or potentially violent clients to proper officials (DeMers, 1986). With regard to preschool assessment, many of the legal requirements outlined above also constitute ethical obligations on the part of psychologists. For example, psychologists are ethically bound to use appropriately normed and validated tests, to inform clients adequately of the potential benefits and risks of specific diagnostic and treatment procedures, and to maintain—within legal limits—the confidentiality of information gained about clients and their families. Thus, the legal requirements for test validation, informed consent, and proper protection and disclosure of sensitive information are mirrored in the ethical requirements discussed in the sections below.

Test Validation

Psychologists have an ethical obligation to use tests appropriately in assessing and screening preschool children. APA's Ethical Principles of Psychologists and Code of Conduct (1992) state in Standard 2.04 that

> Psychologists who…use assessment techniques are familiar with the reliability, validation,…and proper use of the techniques they use.

Similarly, the NASP Principles for Professional Ethics (1997) state that,

> School psychologists are knowledgeable about the validity and reliability of their instruments and techniques choosing those that have up-to-date standardization data and are applicable and appropriate for the benefit of the student/client. (IV.B.2.)

The issue of using appropriately normed and validated tests is particularly relevant to preschool assessment because of the lack of appropriate, technically adequate instruments designed for use with this age group (Bracken, 1988; Thurman & Widerstrom, 1985). As Prasse (1983) points out, most assessment information and expertise relative to the psychological and educational evaluation of preschool children has been extrapolated from well-established procedures used with school-aged children. Furthermore, Dunst and Trivette (1985) acknowledge that instruments designed to assess families and home environments as required by the preschool legislation are in short supply.

In addition, the changeable and inconsistent nature of many developmental and behavioral characteristics of preschool children make reliable assessment inherently more difficult than assessing school-aged children. Paget and Nagle (1986) suggest that assessment strategies with preschool children should focus on situational differences in order to develop and prioritize interventions, rather than assuming that unreliability is something to be minimized or eliminated. Bagnato, Neisworth, and Munson (1989) suggest that curriculum-based assessment may be more relevant than the use of norm referenced standardized tests in developing appropriate interventions for young children.

Assessment instruments must be developed and normed on appropriate minority and disability populations in order to be useful. Children from different racial, ethnic, or cultural groups must be assessed by persons knowledgeable about that population and using instruments validated on those groups (Jacob-Timm & Hartshorne, 1994). Referral to another professional who is familiar with this subgroup may be necessary in order to meet this ethical obligation. In addition, comprehensive assessments are necessary to ensure that standardized tests are not identifying cultural differences as deficits (Thurman & Widerstrom, 1985). Physical handicaps such as sensory impairments must also be considered as a test validation issue. Reynolds and Clark (1983) note that few preschool assessment instruments are normed and validated on children with sensory impairments, nor are many psychologists adequately trained to work with such children.

Finally, psychologists are ethically required to remain familiar with current literature regarding assessment instruments and techniques. Current assessment practices with the preschool population are rapidly changing, with new instruments and validity studies appearing frequently (see Bagnato, Neisworth, & Munson, 1989; Dunst, McWilliam, & Holbert, 1986; and Dunst & Trivette, 1985). Especially for psychologists who conduct few preschool assessments, remaining current will be a difficult task, perhaps necessitating referral to or consultation with colleagues more familiar with the preschool literature.

Informed Consent

Informed consent refers to the legal requirement to obtain permission to perform some action (such as assessing a preschool child) only after fully explaining what is to be done, the purpose for the action, and the potential risks. It is the psychologist's ethical responsibility to ensure that the explanation has been understood and that consent has been freely given. Although not legally required, the child's consent should be sought where possible. NASP's ethical code states explicitly that "... school psychologists understand their obligation to respect the rights of a student or client to initiate, participate in, or discontinue services voluntarily" (III.B.3).

According to the procedural safeguards contained in IDEA, notice must be given to the parents in their native language and in nontechnical terms before any assessments are done or placements are initiated or modified. Psychologists have a similar ethical responsibility as described in APA's ethical code as follows:

> psychologists ensure that an explanation of results is provided in language that is reasonably understandable to the person assessed or to another legally authorized person on behalf of the client. (Standard 2.09)

Given the lack of many adequately normed and validated preschool and family assessment techniques and the sensitive nature of some of the family dynamics of interest to the assessment team, gaining the informed consent of parents for comprehensive preschool assessments could prove to be difficult.

Confidentiality

Psychologists have a clear ethical responsibility to maintain the confidentiality of information obtained about their clients. However, in the case of minor children, information about the child cannot legally be denied to parents except in certain specified cases such as suspected child abuse. Thus, while psychologists may feel an ethical obligation to keep confidential from parents the information shared between the psychologist and their client who is a minor, they may have little legal basis for doing so. Such a legal/ethical conflict is a good example of the differences between a psychologist's ethical obligation to maintain confidentiality and their legal right to claim privileged communication (DeMers, 1986; DeMers & Bersoff, 1985).

Both APA and NASP codes of ethics describe the obligation to maintain confidentiality of clients within the limits allowed by law. APA's code states that psychologists reveal confidential information without the consent of the person only as mandated by law (Standard 5.05). NASP's ethical code requires that the "school psychologists inform their clients of the limits of confidentiality" (III.A.11). Fortunately for those interested in preschool assessment, conflicts between children and their parents over confidential information shared with the psychologist are more typical of older children, particularly adolescents. A more likely ethical/legal conflict may arise in situations where a family assessment under the preschool legislation has revealed information about the family that falls under one of the mandatory reporting statutes such as duty to warn of potential harm to self or others and child abuse laws (DeMers, 1986). Obviously, the ethical codes acknowledge the precedence of legal requirements over ethical obligations. But this precedence in itself creates an ethical obligation for the psychologist to discuss the limits of confidentiality with all clients prior to obtaining the confidential information.

The prevalence of divorce, shared custody, and blended/step families also complicates the psychologist's responsibility to maintain confidentiality. Since Part C of IDEA places such a heavy emphasis on family assessment and intervention, it becomes necessary to define "family" in light of the current nontraditional custodial arrangements. Knapp and VandeCreek (1987) discuss many aspects of privileged communication, confidentiality, and minor children, noting that the courts are not currently clear about rights to privacy in cases of parental dispute and shared custody.

The interdisciplinary and interagency aspects of the preschool services under IDEA present some peculiar ethical concerns. Drew and Turnbull (1987) discuss some of the ethical complications that may arise in an interdisciplinary setting. For example, in situations where several different professions are represented on the multidisciplinary team, how are ethical dilemmas to be resolved when each professional subscribes to a separate ethical code or perhaps has no specific ethical code accepted by that profession? Drew and Turnbull (1987) suggest it is not at all clear in such situations what behavior is appropriate nor which professional is responsible. Different policies and procedures across separate social service agencies about access to records and release of client information present similar concerns.

Obviously, many other ethical principles can also apply to preschool assessment and screening—such as appropriate advertising and claims for services offered, appropriate relationships with other professionals, responsible and fair financial arrangements where services are not free, and so on. All professionals who offer preschool assessment services should take time to review their ethical code and reflect on the ethical implications of their conduct during such assessments.

Summary

We have presented a number of legal and ethical mandates and expectations that must be considered when conducting preschool assessments. However, as we have seen, the law and the ethical codes do not address all the important issues, and several unanswered questions remain. The following scenarios illustrate some possible problematic situations one might actually encounter in practice.

1. The diagnostic or assessment team is legally bound to provide a comprehensive, multifactored assessment, but no valid or appropriate tests are available.
2. The assessment team member is requested to evaluate a preschooler from an ethnic minority group (or with a sensory impairment) with which he or she is unfamiliar and no competent professional is available for referral.
3. A preschooler's parents are separated and only one parent will give consent for the evaluation.
4. A psychologist extends confidentiality to a client and discovers sensitive information relevant to the case, but is uncertain whether the information should be shared with the team.
5. A "family needs" assessment of a custodial parent is made and the noncustodial parent sues for custody using information obtained at the team meeting from the family assessment.
6. A multidisciplinary team member behaves in a way that another team member feels is unethical, but the team members belong to different professional groups where the behavior in question is only clearly inappropriate for the complaining professional.

Each of these situations highlights the complicated legal and ethical considerations that could arise while conducting some preschool assessments. Unfortunately, there are no easy answers on how to resolve such dilemmas. Individual practitioners as well as school districts and agencies are encouraged to investigate the relevant state and federal legal mandates as well as the ethical codes that various team members will follow. Then, considering the possible legal and ethical dilemmas that may arise, policies and procedures should be developed and formally adopted so as to prevent obvious abuses and to deal with the questionable situations when they arise. Finally, over time, more definitive regulatory language as well as legal decisions resulting from possible litigation will help to clarify what constitutes appropriate professional behavior in the conduct of child and family assessments under the current initiatives to provide comprehensive services to preschool children.

5 Individual Assessment Procedures with Preschool Children

IVONNE ROMERO

This chapter presents an overview of the testing procedures involved in the individual assessment of 3- to 5-year-old children. It begins with a discussion of the behavioral characteristics that make preschoolers a unique population, and the impact of those characteristics in the individual testing session. The rest of the chapter presents a step-by-step progression of the testing process and gives some practical suggestions on how to go about it.

Characteristics of Preschool Children

Although individual preschool children vary considerably, they share some characteristics and common responses that have an impact on the individual testing situation. Some of those shared behavioral patterns that make this population unique will be discussed in this section.

Wide Variability in Performance

A common characteristic of young children is the wide range of individual differences they possess—in other words, their distinctiveness. Preschoolers come to the testing situation with diverse rates of maturation, different experiential and cultural backgrounds, and varied levels of exposure to environments outside the home. Some have attended or are attending preschool programs, or have had many outside contacts with adults, whereas for others the testing session is their first introduction to strange adults and settings. They lack the comparable and somewhat homogenizing experiences that school-aged children have developed through their years in school. Therefore, preschoolers' behavior and ultimately their performance during the testing situation (levels of fatigue, ease in separating from caretaker, verbal facility) will be quite diverse.

Reactions to the Demands of the Testing Situation

Several investigators have described preschoolers as having limitations in their understanding of "assessment cues," given that the demands of the testing situation are new to

59

them (Martin, 1986). Because they lack experience with a "structured question–answer task–reward testing format" (Rogers, 1982), they tend not to seek feedback from the examiner to determine if the answer was understood and are not too concerned about providing a "correct" answer (Ulrey & Schnell, 1982).

To assume that a preschooler will correctly answer questions and perform, just because that is the expected test-taking behavior, is a serious mistake for the preschool examiner. As Ulrey and Schnell (1982) point out, examiners must be flexible and creative in order to elicit cooperation and to determine accurately what the young child really knows. The focus must move away from mechanically noting right and wrong answers, to determining why the child failed a task and how the task was understood by him or her.

Motivation

Unlike the case of the school-aged child, the preschool child's motivation and interest in the testing procedures is less contingent on a desire for mastery of the task than on the intrinsic appeal of the task itself. Although some preschoolers have learned to be "reinforced" by pleasing an adult who has won their trust and regard, the examiner cannot always count on that factor. This can be due to variations in the young child's previous experiences or can occur because the child might not associate the examiner's responses of pleasure or displeasure (smiles, nods of approval) with performance (Ulrey, 1982). As Ulrey points out, at times "the involvement with a task at a level he or she can understand may be more reinforcing than a general social reinforcer" (p. 26). Some practical suggestions on how to enhance preschoolers' motivation and interest in the tasks involved in the testing procedures will be presented later in this chapter.

Can't versus Won't

The process of distinguishing the young child's inability from his or her refusal to cooperate is a hard one, particularly for inexperienced examiners. It is certainly challenging to determine when responses like "I don't know" or "I can't" really do mean that, and when they mean "I don't want to" or "I won't." In the same fashion, nonverbal behaviors such as a shrug of the shoulders or a silent nonresponse might have varied meanings, ranging from the resistance of an uncooperative child to the painful self-acknowledgment of a bright child that he or she does not really know the answer.

Although there is no unequivocal way of knowing whether a child is not cooperating, is too frightened to respond, or is sincerely trying but still failing, examiners who have experience with preschoolers and thorough knowledge of the testing instruments being administered will be able to discern more clearly the child's intent and motives.

Assessment Procedures: Preparing for Testing

The production of useful assessment data depends to a large extent on the amount of information one has gathered prior to the individual testing session. This section outlines a series of steps, modified from Vazquez Nuttall (1997), that should be followed in preparation for the actual testing. Following these pretesting activities will ensure assessors a final product that will be relevant to the referral sources and helpful to the child.

Obtain a clear and specific referral question. Most requests for assessments do not contain sufficient information to enable the examiner to do an informed evaluation. Many times, because of lack of familiarity with the assessment process, the referring person provides a very brief and vague description of the type of information he or she wants to obtain—for example, "I would like to find out why this child is not doing well in preschool."

It is imperative that when examiners encounter this type of referral, they interview the referral source, preferably in person. It is important to find out what the person wants and what problem is being addressed. In the example presented—"I would like to find out why this child is not doing well in preschool"—it is important to know several things. What specific behaviors are of concern? What are the circumstances under which they occur? What factors are prompting this person to make a referral? Why does he or she want an assessment now? What kinds of decisions will be made on the basis of this assessment?

This first interview, in addition to providing an opportunity to clarify the nature of the referral, gives the examiner a chance to begin to establish a relationship with the referral source. This initial contact is of utmost importance in linking assessment to intervention. It will enable the examiner to obtain more complete information, which can be transformed into a program for the child and practical help for his or her parents and teachers. Furthermore, a successful initial contact will lead to a greater likelihood that the assessment findings will be accepted and the program recommendations followed. For an in-depth review regarding principles and techniques of interviewing, refer to Sattler (1998).

Study already available data. In preparation for conducting an assessment, it is extremely important that the examiner read all the data available on the preschooler. With a clear referral question in mind, examination of previous records helps the professional determine an appropriate testing strategy. For instance, if the child has any diagnosed condition, such as cerebral palsy, the assessor may need to adapt the testing procedures and/or use specialized tests to assess this child adequately. Furthermore, the examiner may discover that obtaining certain information from other professionals is crucial for the case before selecting assessment techniques. For example, when a review of records suggests possible vision problems, a referral for an ophthalmological examination prior to psychological assessment would be appropriate. In many instances, careful scrutiny of the available data will suggest hypotheses to guide the testing process.

Identify all the relevant people to be included in the assessment. Who should be involved in the assessment process? Everyone who seems to be needed in order to obtain a clear idea of the problem. Preschool assessment referrals necessitate obtaining information from more than just the child. For instance, young children who are referred to determine the status of their cognitive, educational, and psychosocial development will not be able by themselves to provide answers to all these questions. Likely persons to be called upon to help unravel this puzzle are the parents, past and present day care or preschool teachers, pediatricians, and other pertinent professionals.

It is extremely important that these people, particularly the parents, be interviewed to obtain a developmental history of the child. Because of its importance, the process of gathering a developmental and medical history of the child is described in detail in Chapter 7 by Kalesnik.

Identify all areas that need to be emphasized. Although assessment information should be obtained in each of several areas or domains (cognitive, social-emotional, motor, adaptive, language) and in different environments, one or several of those areas may need to be emphasized in order to gain diagnostic knowledge about the problem and to plan adequate interventions.

As part of the process of clarifying the referral question, the assessor should obtain a clear idea of all the areas that need to be covered in the assessment. Should the testing mainly emphasize the social-emotional domain? Should a neuropsychological workup be included? Is a more in-depth evaluation of family dynamics necessary to help understand the problem? Only after interviewing the referral source, examining the child's records and developmental history, and obtaining a clear idea of uses of the testing will the examiner be able to determine all areas that may need additional thorough assessment.

Determine an overall testing strategy.   As a result of performing the previous activities outlined in this section, the examiner will be able to develop a clear assessment strategy. At this stage, decisions need to be made regarding which methods of assessment will be useful in obtaining different types of information. How many people will be interviewed? What specific tests should be used and in what order should they be administered? Will physical adaptations or specialized tests be needed? Once areas, techniques, and persons are determined, the examiner is ready to make an appointment with the child to begin the individual assessment sessions.

The Testing Session

After a successful gathering of pretesting information, the actual examining session is ready to commence. By now the examiner has a clear testing strategy in mind and knows which instruments will be used. He or she must have excellent knowledge of standardized testing procedures and of the rules for testing administration and scoring. Furthermore, the multiple aspects of test administration—arranging materials, performing demonstrations, applying discontinuing and scoring rules, knowing when to probe—must become "second nature to the examiner" (Lichtenstein & Ireton, 1984, p. 75). This will enable the examiner to proceed smoothly and quickly through the tests, paying closer attention to the child than to the test manual.

Apart from making sure that standardized testing procedures are known "by heart," the examiner must carefully prepare the testing materials and setting before bringing the child into the room. These environmental considerations will be discussed in the following section.

Preparing the Test Setting and Materials

Ideal Room.   The testing room should be attractive but free of too many distractions, such as background noise and excessive numbers of pictures or toys. The room should be brightly lit and have a temperature comfortable for the child. Paget (1991) recommends that the room temperature be set "a few degrees lower than what might normally be comfortable for an adult," due to young children's warmer body temperatures (p. 35). Tables and chairs should be of appropriate size for preschool children, so that their feet touch the floor (Preator & McAllister, 1995).

Materials.   Apart from the standard testing materials, which should be kept at hand but out of the child's sight and reach, it is useful to have additional toys or interesting materials like picture books and large crayons. Goodenough (1949, p. 299) suggests that additional toys and materials not only are good for establishing rapport prior to beginning testing, but also can be used during breaks or as a reward for task completion.

Beginning the testing session.   Excellent preschool assessment guidelines have been provided by Bagnato and Neisworth (1991), Bracken (1991), Goodenough (1949), Lichtenstein and Ireton (1984), McCarthy (1972), Paget (1991), and Sattler (1992). They are summarized here in the form of practical suggestions.

Approach the preschool child with confidence.   It is useful to approach young children confidently, assuming that they will enjoy the games and activities that comprise the testing session. Preschoolers tend to be very perceptive about signs of apprehension or tension from the examiner, which are likely to result in resistance or negativism on their part.

Begin testing when the child is ready.   Trying too hard or too soon to get the child's cooperation, before he or she is ready to begin, makes for a bad start. With some preschoolers, those with whom rapport is easily established, test administration can begin fairly quickly after an introduction period. That introduction can consist of telling the child about the puzzles, blocks, and other games they will be playing with and how some questions will be asked. In many instances, however, a warm-up period is needed before the introduction and subsequent testing can occur. In that case the child must be given ample opportunity to

© National Association of School Psychologists. Reprinted by permission of the publisher.

examine the room. When he or she appears to be at ease, the examiner could call the child's attention to a couple of toys placed on the table. Some verbal interaction may be elicited through the child's involvement with the toy. The examiner can then ask the child questions about the toy but should not insist that the child respond. When spontaneous verbalizations and responses start occurring, giving the examiner an indication that the child is at ease responding, then testing can safely begin.

Carefully observe and record the child's behavior.   Direct observation of the preschooler's behavior can provide examiners with invaluable information that cannot be obtained through standardized tests. A behavioral observation checklist is included in the appendix at the end of this chapter to aid examiners with their in-session observations. Following the checklist there is a list of questions to help the examiner use this instrument. During the testing session, the examiner should be noting the child's ability to separate from the caretaker and to shift from one task to another, as well as the child's attentiveness, motivation, interest, activity level, task approach, responsiveness, and other idiosyncratic behaviors. However, it must be understood that in-session observations, though important, represent only a limited sample of the preschooler's behavior. Because of the unfamiliar and somewhat contrived nature of the examining session, these observations may represent atypical behaviors that are not easily generalizable to other situations. This underscores the need to also observe the child in non-test situations, preferably natural settings such as the daycare or preschool playground, the classroom, or the home.

Be sensitive to the child's needs.   With young children, the examiner should be watching for early signs of fatigue, boredom, distress, or physical discomfort. Introducing breaks into the testing session, such as a trip to the bathroom or water fountain, might prevent those conditions.

Provide adequate praise and reinforcement.   For praise to be effective it must be genuine, varied, and well timed, and must fit naturally into the conversational flow. It should never be expressed in a mechanical or monotonous tone, or through stereotyped phrases that will soon lose any reinforcing value. Most important, praise should be contingent not on success but on effort. With some children, praise and examiner approval are not enough to maintain their interest, particularly on tasks that have little intrinsic appeal. In those cases the use of other reinforcers like gestures such as handclapping, hand-shakes, "high fives" and "thumbs up" may work well. Another useful strategy is to establish a reward system, in which the child is allowed to play with preferred toys or to obtain a tangible reinforcer, such as attractive stickers, after completing the tasks at hand.

Slow down or speed up the pace accordingly.   The pace of administration must be adapted to the child's needs and style. Timid or shy children tend to respond more readily and may be less confused if the examiner slows down the tempo. Active children may need a quicker administration and presentation of materials to hold their attention and interest.

Establish structure and limits while remaining friendly.   Young children are often distractible and seek to test the limits of a novel situation. Thus, the examiner has to provide them with clear, positive directions and enough structure to help them complete tasks successfully.

Determine the length of the testing session.   Factors like fatigue, short attention span, and active participation exhibited by the child will greatly determine the length of the session.

Some young children cannot be tested for more than 20 minutes at once, while others can tolerate a longer session. Since obtaining an optimal performance from the preschooler is of crucial importance, often testing sessions may need to be scheduled with great flexibility. Short periods over several days may need to be allowed. However, this might be easier if testing is done in the child's preschool rather than in a hospital or clinic setting. It is recommended that any subsequent sessions be scheduled as soon as possible, and no more than one week apart.

Summary

This chapter has presented general testing guidelines, useful in the individual assessment of preschool-aged children. They are by no means an exhaustive list of what to do in every single instance during the assessment situation. The examiner, as an expert in early childhood development and assessment procedures, must use his or her expertise, sensitivity, and creativity to deal with the special challenges posed by the examination of young children.

For specific suggestions on assessment procedures with special preschool children (for example, those who are culturally different or those who have multiple handicaps, visual, hearing, or neurological disabilities), see part V of this book.

APPENDIX 5A

Behavioral Observation Checklist for Different Domains:
Language, Motor, Task Approach, Social/Emotional, General*

Name _____ DOB _____ Age _____ Gender _____

Primary Language _____ Ethnicity _____ Hand preference _____

Examiner _____ Date(s) of Evaluation _____

Referral Reason _____

Place an X under the appropriate number for each behavior. Omit items for behaviors not observed or not applicable.

Descriptions of Child's Test Behavior

Test Behavior	Adequate (Not Problematic) 1	2	Occasionally Problematic 3	4	Problematic 5
Language: Expressive					
Syntax	_____	_____	_____	_____	_____
Grammar	_____	_____	_____	_____	_____
Voice quality (volume, pitch)	_____	_____	_____	_____	_____

(continued)

*Designed by Ivonne Romero. May be reproduced without permission.

APPENDIX 5A   Continued

	Adequate (Not Problematic)		*Occasionally Problematic*		*Problematic*
Test Behavior	*1*	*2*	*3*	*4*	*5*

Descriptions of Child's Test Behavior

Language: Expressive

Speech intelligibility

Articulation

Vocabulary
(extent, word choice)

Spontaneous communication
(vs. limited answering)

Ability to express ideas
(fluency)

Latency of response

Elaboration of response

Use of unusual language
(echolalia, bizarre, ritualistic, obscene)

Language: Receptive

Understanding of
spoken information

Need for modified language
(repetitions, clarifications)

Motor: Fine Motor

Fluidity of movement
(fumbling, tremor)

Bilateral hand coordination
(dexterity and speed)

Hand grasp

Motor: Gross Control

Gait

Posture

Movement in space
(precise vs. knocks
objects, awkward)

Motor: Graphomotor

Pencil grip
(tripod vs. fisted, pencil
held loosely or too tight)

Handwriting/drawing
    (fluid vs. labored)   _____ _____ _____ _____ _____

Line quality
    (trembly, over-shoots)   _____ _____ _____ _____ _____

Task Approach

Initiation (deliberate
    vs. impulsive)   _____ _____ _____ _____ _____

Style (organized
    vs. disorganized)   _____ _____ _____ _____ _____

Problem solving
    (efficient vs. inefficient)   _____ _____ _____ _____ _____

Ability to benefit
    from feedback   _____ _____ _____ _____ _____

Attention   _____ _____ _____ _____ _____

Persistence   _____ _____ _____ _____ _____

Flexibility   _____ _____ _____ _____ _____

Ability to shift   _____ _____ _____ _____ _____

Interest   _____ _____ _____ _____ _____

Effort   _____ _____ _____ _____ _____

Social-Emotional

Affect   _____ _____ _____ _____ _____

Mood   _____ _____ _____ _____ _____

Ability to separate
    from parents   _____ _____ _____ _____ _____

Relationship with parents
    (warm vs. detached)   _____ _____ _____ _____ _____

Expression of feelings   _____ _____ _____ _____ _____

Sociability
    (confident vs. insecure)   _____ _____ _____ _____ _____

Ability to regulate and
    modulate behaviors   _____ _____ _____ _____ _____

Bizarre or unusual behaviors   _____ _____ _____ _____ _____

General

Appearance: _____ _____ _____ _____ _____

    Grooming   _____ _____ _____ _____ _____

    Height   _____ _____ _____ _____ _____

    Weight   _____ _____ _____ _____ _____

    Facies   _____ _____ _____ _____ _____

Visual acuity   _____ _____ _____ _____ _____

Hearing acuity   _____ _____ _____ _____ _____

(continued)

APPENDIX 5A   Continued

Descriptions of Child's Test Behavior

Test Behavior	Adequate (Not Problematic) 1	2	Occasionally Problematic 3	4	Problematic 5
General					
Eye contact					
Activity level					
Compliance					
Need for limit setting					
Need for reassurance					
Need for structure					
Response to praise					
Reaction to examiner					
Reaction to test materials					
Approach to a new situation (relaxed vs. tense)					
Curiosity					
Degree of cooperation					

Other observed test behaviors not mentioned above (please describe):

_____

_____

_____

_____

APPENDIX 5B

Questions to Supplement Behavioral Observation Checklist

In completing the *Behavioral Observation Checklist,* the rater is required to make three judgments; is the child's behavior more or less *Adequate (not problematic), Occasionally Problematic* or *Problematic?* In order to make that determination it is helpful to ask the questions in this appendix as each item is completed. In addition, the rater should use his or her own words as applicable in describing the quality of the child's behavior. Those qualitative observations could be noted on the margins or below each description of test behavior on the checklist.

Language: Expressive

1. *Syntax:* How was the child's ability to manipulate syntactical structures? How were the words in the child's phrases or sentences organized?

2. *Grammar:* How was the child's ability to manipulate grammatical structures? (For example, were the verb and noun coordinated?)
3. *Voice quality:* What was the child's voice like? Was the volume unusually loud, or soft? Was the pitch unusually high or low?
4. *Speech:* How intelligible (understandable) was the child's speech?
5. *Articulation:* Did the child have any speech impediments? Were the words articulated clearly? Were there any sound substitutions?
6. *Vocabulary:* What was the extent of the child's vocabulary and use of words; limited for age, or advanced?
7. *Spontaneous communication:* Did the child communicate freely or did the child prefer to answer direct questions rather than volunteering information?
8. *Ability to express ideas:* Could the child express ideas with fluency?
9. *Latency of response:* How quickly did the child answer the questions posed?
10. *Elaboration of response:* Could the child elaborate or add to a response given to a question posed? Was the child's answer brief and with very little elaboration? When asked to elaborate further, was the child able to do it?
11. *Use of unusual language:* How was the general tone and content of the child's language? (Observe for echolalia, obscene or ritualistic language, bizarre use of words, neologisms, loose associations, clang associations, rambling, tangentiality, vagueness, perseveration, irrelevance, incoherence, circumstantiality.)

Language: Receptive

12. *Understanding of spoken information:* Could the child understand and fully grasp the information being presented orally?
13. *Need for modified language:* Did the child need frequent repetitions and clarifications?

Motor: Fine Motor

14. *Fluidity of movement:* How were the child's fine motor (finger, hand and arm) movements? Were they fluid and graceful or awkward and clumsy?
15. *Bilateral hand coordination:* What were the child's dexterity and speed in the use of both the dominant and non-dominant hand? (Note for signs of tremor, particularly in the manipulation of small objects)
16. *Hand grasp:* What was the child's ability to grasp objects (pencil, blocks, etc.)? (For example, observe the type of grasp, pincer vs. fisted, etc.). For a review of grasping patterns please refer to Chapter 13 in this book.

Motor: Gross Control

17. *Gait:* How adequate was the child's ability to walk?
18. *Posture:* What was the child's posture?
19. *Movement in space:* How did the child move and ambulate? Were his or her movements precise or awkward? Did he or she ambulate gracefully, without knocking objects? (Also observe for exaggerated or repetitive movements [tics, twitches, tremors].)

Motor: Graphomotor

20. *Pencil grip:* How did the child hold a pencil when writing or drawing? (Observe for tripod, fisted, or pincer grasp and for pressure. Note if pencil was held loosely or too tight.)

21. *Handwriting/drawing:* How would you characterize the child's use of writing utensils? How much control did the child exhibit over the writing utensil? Was the handwriting or drawing easy to produce (fluid) or hard (labored)?

22. *Line quality:* How do the writing or drawing strokes look? Do the traces look trembly? Are there many overshoots?

Task Approach

23. *Initiation:* How did the child begin a task? Was the child's initial approach to tasks deliberate or impulsive ?

24. *Style:* What style did the child exhibit in approaching tasks throughout the testing session? Was the child's style organized or disorganized?

25. *Problem solving:* How were the child's problem-solving abilities? Was the child efficient or inefficient? What problem-solving strategy did the child use? (For example, trial-and-error.)

26. *Ability to benefit from feedback:* Did the child benefit from corrective feedback from the examiner? Was a change in problem solving strategy observed after feedback was provided?

27. *Attention:* How was the child's attention throughout the testing session? Was the child able to focus appropriately? Was the child able to sustain his or her attention?

28. *Persistence:* How was the child's persistence? Was the child persistent or did he or she give up easily? Was the child able to give up when everything else failed?

29. *Flexibility:* Was the child flexible in approaching tasks? Did the child try different alternative solutions?

30. *Ability to shift:* Did the child shift set (problem-solving strategies, for example) when task parameters changed?

31. *Interest:* What was the child's level of interest in the tasks presented?

32. *Effort:* What was the child's level of effort? Did the child have to mobilize much effort or none in order to complete the task at hand?

Social-Emotional

33. *Affect:* What was the general affect of the child? (For example, was it flat, blunted, broad, expansive). Was the child's affect consistent with his or her speech and content of communications?

34. *Mood:* What was the general mood of the child? (For example, was the child sad, cheerful, indifferent, angry, tense, distressed, irritable, energetic?)

35. *Ability to separate from caretaker:* Was the child able to separate from parents or caretakers during the evaluation session?

36. *Relationship with parents:* What was the child's relationship with parents? (For example, was it warm, detached, hostile, insecure?)

37. *Expression of feelings:* How was the child able to express his feelings? What did the child express about his or her mood and feelings?

38. *Sociability:* How sociable was the child with the examiner? Did the child present himself or herself as confident, insecure, shy, reticent, friendly?

39. *Ability to modulate and regulate behaviors:* What was the child's ability to modulate and regulate his or her behaviors in the context of the testing demands?

40. *Bizarre or unusual behaviors:* Were there any bizarre or unusual behaviors observed during the evaluation? (Note, for example, bizarre gestures or actions, repetitive

movements [motor or verbal tics], disruptive behavior, tantrums, inappropriate laughter, abnormally slow movements or extremely excited behavior.)

General

41. *Appearance:* How did the child present himself or herself? How did the child look generally? (Note, for example, the child's grooming, height, weight, facial appearance [facies], physical handicaps.)
42. *Visual acuity:* How intact is the child's sight?
43. *Hearing acuity:* How intact is the child's hearing?
44. *Eye contact:* Did the child establish eye contact with the examiner?
45. *Activity level:* What was the child's level of activity?
46. *Compliance:* Was the child able to comply with the testing demands? Was the child able to comply with the behavioral limits established?
47. *Need for limit setting:* Did the child require much or little limit setting?
48. *Need for reassurance:* Did the child require much or little reassurance?
49. *Response to praise:* What was the child's response to praise? (For example, did the child feel uncomfortable or elated when praised?) Was praise reinforcing to this child?
50. *Reaction to examiner:* How did the child relate to the examiner? (For example, was the child cooperative, friendly, resistant, wary, attentive, fearful, suspicious, warm, indifferent, manipulative, hostile?)
51. *Reaction to test materials:* How did the child relate to test materials? (For example, was the child interested, enthused, challenged, indifferent, habituated easily, needed to change materials often to sustain interest and effort?)
52. *Approach to a new situation:* How did the child approach the testing situation? (For example, was the child relaxed, tense, trusting, guarded, submissive, cautious, fearful.)
53. *Curiosity:* Was the child curious about the testing situation and procedures?
54. *Degree of cooperation:* What was the degree of cooperation elicited?

6 Issues and Practices in the Screening of Preschool Children

MARTHA L. THURLOW

CHERI J. GILMAN

Preschool screening is now an accepted part of a child's journey toward adulthood. Since the mid 1970s, when the need for screening became apparent, the number of preschool screening programs and the services available to the public have increased dramatically. The recognition of the importance of identifying young children who might otherwise enter school without the benefit of needed early interventions, in part, led to Goal 1 of the eight national education goals (first identified by President Bush and the nation's governors in 1989, and later reaffirmed by President Clinton with the enactment of Public Law 103-227, *Goals 2000: Educate America Act*): By the year 2000, all children in America will start school ready to learn. The concern about readiness for school focuses on more than just cognitive development—it includes the physical, social, and emotional well being of children before they enter school (e.g., National Center for Education Statistics, 1993; Office of Research, 1993; Zero to Three, 1992).

One of the reasons for emphasizing preschool screening is the belief that it is a successful way to identify children with disabilities and children at risk for developing disabilities. Since fiscal year 1992, states must make available a free and appropriate public education (FAPE) for 3- to 5-year-old children with disabilities. Most states actually began serving these children long before 1992 (U.S. Department of Education, 1995). In 1993–94, when approximately 5.4 million children and youth received special education and related services overall (the most recent year for which data are available), about 9.2% (493,425) of these children were in the age range from 3 to 5 years. This represents an 8.3% increase from 1992–93.

The changing characteristics of young children heighten the importance of preschool screening. Increasing numbers of new births are of Hispanic/Chicano, African American, and other cultural backgrounds (Hodgkinson, 1992; Hodgkinson & Outtz, 1992). Children are over-represented among the poor (Hodgkinson & Outtz, 1992), and poverty is the major predictor of who will be at risk of school and health failure (Children's Defense Fund, 1994). The trends for major indicators of risk, such as births to unmarried teens and low birth-weight babies, also are increasing (Annie E. Casey Foundation, 1995).

Despite our acceptance of preschool screening, there continue to be many issues surrounding these programs, and much variability in practice. The purpose of this chapter is to explore these issues, and to examine current practices in preschool screening programs, all with an eye toward developing recommendations for model practices. Toward this end, we first look at preschool screening as one piece of a puzzle, that being the "assessment to intervention to outcomes" linkage. In addition, we provide a quick overview of current screening programs and the research knowledge base about these programs. This information serves as a backdrop for looking at key issues and practices related to the people, procedures, and outcomes involved in the screening of preschool children, and in turn, toward proposing recommendations for model practices.

Screening as One Piece of a Puzzle

The Puzzle: Assessment to Intervention

Preschool screening is but one part of a larger process designed to provide special services to those young children who need them and only to those who need them. Generally, screening is viewed as a relatively brief and inexpensive assessment of large numbers of children in terms of their vision, hearing, physical health, and development in speech and language, motor skills, social and emotional growth, and cognitive skills. Although terminology difficulties have been a major stumbling block to clear communication about programs for preschool children with disabilities (Peterson, 1987), most uses of the term *preschool screening* are fairly consistent. "The goal of early childhood screening is to identify normal aspects of a child's health and development while sorting out potential problems that need further evaluation" (Luehr & Hoxie, 1995, p. 1).

The defining characteristics of "screening" in comparison to "diagnostic assessment" are specified in a guide to developmental screening published by the National Association for the Education of Young Children. In that report, Meisels (1985) defined early childhood developmental screening as a "brief assessment procedure designed to identify children who, because of the risk of a possible learning problem or handicapping condition, should proceed to a more intensive level of diagnostic assessment" (p. 1). Most definitions of screening are in agreement that it is a relatively limited procedure designed to reduce the number of children who are given full comprehensive assessments.

In recent years, early childhood screening has evolved into a process that, in addition to screening for health and developmental concerns, includes a review of risk factors (e.g., access to health care, family resources and needs, child care and early education experiences) that might affect the child's learning and development (Luehr & Hoxie, 1995). The addition of a family assessment was initially viewed as a great challenge for schools, and seen as intrusive by some parents. In light of those obstacles, family components in assessments are more likely to be considered optional. There have also been changes in how health screening information is obtained. While sensory screening and developmental screening generally have not changed, concerns about increasing costs in many places have resulted in replacing actual physical assessments with health histories.

Figure 6.1 is a depiction of the decision-making process, from assessment to intervention with key decision points noted. When confusion has arisen about the scope of screening activities or their place within the larger puzzle, the confusion usually has been in distinguishing screening from the preceding step (case finding) or the step that follows it (diagnosis). These distinctions are important, for they help feed into several critical issues related to the screening of preschool children, Also, there is evidence that the distinctions often

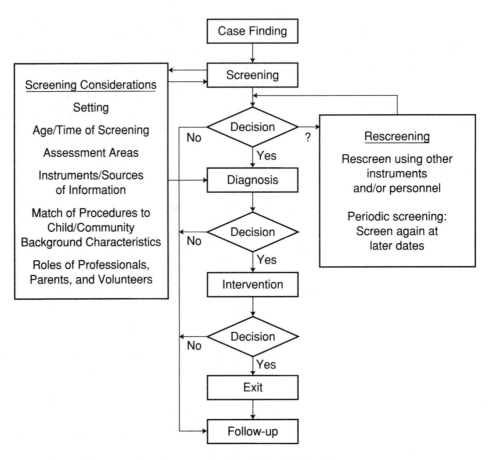

FIGURE 6.1   **"Assessment to Intervention" Decision-Making Process**

become blurred or ignored in practice (Keogh & Daley, 1983). Case finding (also called *outreach*) is the step in which children who are eligible for screening are identified. Outreach is an intensive effort to notify all parents of the requirement for screening, of their options for services, and to encourage participation at designated ages. It is in relation to those children who literally must be found that many of the "people issues" in preschool screening arise. Diagnosis is the step in which those children who need more intensive evaluations are assessed. It is in relation to these children that "outcome" issues in preschool screening arise. This chapter does not focus on either case finding or diagnosis, but they are mentioned in relation to the key issues and practices that they bring into the process of preschool screening.

P.L. 94-142 provided impetus to states to find ways to identify and serve children with disabilities. P.L. 99-457 expanded the focus on preschool children. Since these federal laws did not specify how to screen, procedures vary widely across states, and screening and diagnosis are often inappropriately combined into one process, causing ambiguity and confusion (Wortham, 1990).

Rationale for Preschool Screening

Before 1975, when services for children with disabilities down to age 3 first were included in P.L. 94-142, many children were entering school with problems that directly affected their capacity to learn, and many others were already in school with problems that could have been remediated at an earlier age (see Thurlow, 1992). With the assumption that it is not possible to give extensive diagnostic assessments to all children to determine who needs early childhood special education services, the major argument for preschool screening was that it was a cost-efficient process for identifying children in need of more intensive evaluations. The belief in the need for this screening was further supported by demonstrations of the effectiveness of early childhood programs for children in general (Campbell & Ramey, 1993; Schweinhart & Weikart, 1998; Weiss, 1981) and for children with disabilities in particular (e.g., Casto & Mastropieri, 1986; White & Greenspan, 1986).

Most screening programs today seem to have adopted the model that they must identify those youngsters who, if they do not receive special services, are at risk for school failure. Thus, screening programs have assumed the burden not just of identifying for further assessment those who probably have a disability, but also of predicting which children already have a problem that will continue as the child matures, and those who might have a particular combination of characteristics that likely will result in problems in the future. This tendency is suggested by the finding that children served in many early childhood special education programs are youngsters with mild language, cognitive, and developmental delays (see Ysseldyke, Thurlow, Weiss, Lehr, & Bursaw, 1985).

Recently, a broader purpose has been attributed to preschool screening programs—that of assisting parents and communities in improving the educational readiness and health of young children through early detection of factors that may interfere with a child's learning and development. By detecting potential problems early, school and community personnel can assist in linking children and families to appropriate education and health programs and enable parents to be aware of the connections between health, development and learning.

Despite these refinements in focus of preschool screening programs, we have virtually no information on the effects of preschool screening. In one of the few studies conducted (Kochanek & Hennen, 1998), preschool screening data obtained in the spring prior to kindergarten entrance predicted special education need two years later. Whether the same outcome would be realized if the screening had been conducted earlier (thus allowing time for service provision) is unknown. It is clear that much less attention has been paid to the efficacy of preschool screening than to the efficacy of early intervention (see Lichtenstein & Ireton, 1984). While some argue that it would be just as effective to provide early childhood services only to those children in certain risk categories (e.g., low SES, children in single-parent families, etc.), thereby saving the costs of screening all children, others argue that without a screening process, many problems will go undetected because these problems are not limited to specific targeted populations (Suzukamo, 1996).

A Typical Preschool Screening Program

Even though some preschool screening programs have been in place since the late 1970s, it is difficult to describe a typical preschool screening program. Most states mandate preschool screening, but not all have explicit guidelines for the programs. The research that we have on these programs is limited, most of it being conducted in the early to mid 1980s. The findings that were obtained then, for the most part, remain true today. Actual practices and procedures are not specified by law. It is not surprising, then, that preschool screening practices vary widely from state to state. Even within a single state, screening practices vary considerably.

One portrait of preschool screening was painted by a set of studies conducted in the mid 1980s (see Thurlow, O'Sullivan, & Ysseldyke, 1986). The studies focused on one state, Minnesota, which has a long history (since 1977) in required public preschool screening programs. Yet, Thurlow, Ysseldyke, and O'Sullivan (1985) found that large variability existed among the more than 400 districts in the rates of problem identification (0% to 100%, with an average of 31.2%) and referral (0% to 85.7%, with an average of 24.3%). Factors derived from various social, economic, and educational characteristics of school districts in which the preschool programs studied by Thurlow et al. (1985) were located did not predict referral rates, or even which preschool programs had the highest and the lowest referral rates (Ysseldyke & O'Sullivan, 1987). Furthermore, referral rates across time (3 years) showed large differences in some districts, but not always in the same direction (i.e., some districts showed increases in referral rates from one year to 3 years later, while other districts showed decreases).

Ecological case studies involving observations, interviews, file searches, and parent surveys provided a picture of the entire decision-making sequence in four Minnesota school districts—from initial outreach case finding efforts to programming and transition into elementary schools (Ysseldyke, Thurlow, Lehr, et al., 1986). The preschool screening programs in these districts (Ysseldyke, Thurlow, & O'Sullivan, 1987) all were part of the state-administered program, which provided partial reimbursement for screening costs. The state program required that districts offer health and developmental screening to all children at least once before kindergarten entry, with six required screening components—vision, hearing, growth (height, weight), health history, and developmental screening (speech/language, cognitive, gross and fine motor, social-emotional development). Optional components could be added, such as dental inspection, nutritional screening, and laboratory tests (urine, blood). Three of the four case study programs added one or more of these optional components.

There was great variability among the four case study programs. Of particular note are variations in the numbers of dates that screening was conducted (5 to 160 days), participation rates (54% to 88%), average screening times (30 minutes to 120 minutes), screening personnel (from 2 nurses to 6 multidisciplinary professionals to 15 volunteers), and referral rates (2% to 11%). Other sources of variability involve such factors as whether the screening process included all children or a limited set of children (e.g., one district did not screen anyone who had been in a program for children with severe developmental disabilities), whether the process incorporated an automatic rescreening check (one district rescreened only for hearing problems, another for both hearing and vision, another for any developmental failure in five areas), and who made the final referral decision (special education coordinator, nurse, multidisciplinary team). These kinds of variability point toward some of the issues related to the screening of preschool children. They are also supported on a larger scale from the results of a survey of 398 school districts in Minnesota (Ysseldyke, Thurlow, O'Sullivan, & Bursaw, 1986), and from surveys of assessment practices in model early childhood special education programs across the nation (Lehr, Ysseldyke, & Thurlow, 1986).

The research that has been conducted on preschool screening has indicated that screening programs differ significantly in their purposes, their attitudes about special education services for young children, and their relationships with other service providers. One screening program may strive to provide early childhood special education services as soon as possible to all children with potential disabilities. Another may operate with the belief that screening should pick up only those children with significant developmental delays. Administrators of screening programs also hold differing beliefs about the proportions of children who need further assessment, perhaps leading to more lenient referral criteria in some years and to more restrictive criteria in other years.

Moving Toward a New Look at Preschool Screening

As our nation has moved toward a set of common goals, such as readiness for school (Goal 1), it also is moving toward a more concise view of what constitutes a model preschool program. In conceptualizing the model preschool screening program, it is important to understand the issues and the practices in three broad areas: the procedures of screening, the people of screening, and the outcomes of screening.

Procedural Issues and Practices in the Screening of Preschool Children

Issues related to the procedures used in the screening of preschool children usually are the first ones to be raised. The primary concern is with the instruments used for screening, particularly in terms of validity, reliability, and representativeness of the standardization population. These issues are not addressed here, other than in a tangential manner; they are presented in Appendix A. The focus of this section is on issues and practices related to (1) where and when screening occurs, (2) what areas are screened and how administration procedures are organized, (3) commonly used instruments and other sources of information for screening, and (4) communicating results.

Where and When Screening Occurs

Characteristics of the ideal assessment environment have been described many times. Meisels (1985) speaks directly of the screening environment when he suggests that the environment must be high in respect and professional competence and low in anxiety and confusion. In reality, the extent to which these descriptors can be used for any given screening program is influenced by a number of factors.

Where Screening Occurs

The "where" of testing becomes important in this regard. Conducting the child's entire screening at one time and at one site permits the integration of screening results to obtain a total picture of the child's health and developmental status (Luehr & Hoxie, 1995).

Screening programs sometimes occupy several rooms, and the child is moved from one room to the next for each component of the screening process. Sometimes these rooms are in a regular school building; sometimes they are in a local church. Sometimes there are not separate rooms, but one room in which the child moves around from station to station. Sometimes space issues result in screening being conducted in hallways or other makeshift spaces.

© National Association of School Psychologists.
Reprinted by permission of the publisher.

Two general approaches have been used to organize the preschool screening setting. One is a station approach in which the child moves from one station to the next with a different assessor and a different focus (e.g., fine motor skills) at each station. An alternative to the station approach is to have the child interact with only one assessor who administers all parts of the screening in one or several areas of the room.

Screening settings can also be characterized on a continuum of informal to formal. In planning for screening, consideration needs to be given to conducting screening in settings that are familiar and comfortable for children and families More informal settings might involve screening young children in homes or in their nursery school or daycare groups by their teachers rather than in public facilities unfamiliar to the child and family (Meisels & Provence, 1989). Clearly, the range of settings is immense. Might one not expect that differences in the setting of screening would be related in some way to the results of the screening process?

When Screening Occurs

The "when" of screening refers here not to the age of the child, but, rather, to the time that assessment is conducted. Keogh (1977) noted that performance on screening tests is related to the time of year that testing is conducted. Lichtenstein and Ireton (1984) argue that screening should occur as close in time as possible to follow-up assessment and services; thus spring screening is not recommended if services are not available until fall. The Arizona Department of Education (1992) recommends that screening be scheduled at the time of year when attendance would be best. In Minnesota, many districts add late spring, summer, and early fall screening clinics in order to screen children who had been missed earlier or who had recently moved into the district (Luehr & Hoxie, 1995). The time of year also is influenced by administrative considerations about mass screening versus spread-out screening; the latter is recommended when the numbers to be screened are relatively large. Mass screenings may not support the goal of screening each child at an optimal age in order to provide the benefits of any needed intervention a full year before school entry. Lichtenstein and Ireton recommend that the timing of screening always be coordinated with both the follow-up assessment and intervention program schedules, with the guiding principle being to minimize the interval between screening and intervention.

Addressing the "when" as if it were a discrete event also raises issues about the inappropriateness of viewing screening as a process young children experience only once during their early years. The follow-up component is critical for those children about whom issues emerge. Developmental screening should more appropriately be viewed as a recurrent or periodic process (Meisels & Provence, 1989).

But there are other "time" issues to address. For example, is it better to screen young children in the morning or the afternoon? Or is it better to adjust the time of screening to each child's individual schedule? There is much folklore, and even the beginnings of some data, on the effect of time of day on the performance of elementary-age children (Davis, 1987). Certainly, it is also possible that similar effects influence outcomes of screening for preschool children.

Areas Assessed and Administration Procedures

Comprehensive screening ensures that all aspects of a child's development are assessed, albeit briefly. On the other hand, it is argued that screening should cover only those areas for which services are available. The issue of which areas to assess is still an important one. If no services are available, should assessment be conducted? Similarly, if a technically adequate instrument does not exist for a particular area, should assessment occur in that area? These are questions that screening programs must address.

Several areas have been proposed as important outcomes for young children. Taking these models one step further leads to the identification of possible areas of focus for preschool screening programs. For example, Kagan, Moore, and Bredekamp (1995) proposed five dimensions of early learning:

1. Physical well-being and motor development
2. Social and emotional development
3. Approaches toward learning
4. Language usage
5. Cognitive and general knowledge

The National Center on Educational Outcomes (NCEO) also identified developmental outcomes in broad domains, including some with child-oriented and some with more family and community-oriented indicators of success:

- Presence and participation
- Family involvement/accommodations and adaptations
- Physical health
- Responsibility and independence
- Contribution and citizenship

- Academic and functional literacy
- Personal and social development
- Presence and participation (Ysseldyke, Thurlow, & Gilman, 1993a, 1993b)

Among the reasons for taking a comprehensive approach to looking at outcomes are that it is less likely to produce a narrowing of the curriculum for programs that serve children identified through preschool screening, and a comprehensive approach better reflects the "complex interconnectedness of early development and learning" (Kagan et al., 1995). These approaches reflect the recent trend toward including information on family factors and on family and community-oriented outcomes. Family factors include information on: child care and early childhood education; health care coverage, access and utilization; family strengths and resources including literacy, economic base, living arrangements (Luehr & Hoxie, 1995). Family and community-oriented outcomes involve: access to resources; family involvement and support for the child's needs; and family, provider and community satisfaction with early educational services (Ysseldyke, Thurlow, & Gilman, 1993a, 1993b).

With regard to administration procedures, Peterson (1987) argued that a series of short testing sessions is more realistic for young children because of their reactivity to new and unfamiliar situations. She also noted that young children are not usually responsive to strangers, and thus will require more time for extended rapport building. Rosenkoetter and Wanska (1992) highlight these and other characteristics of young children (e.g., their lack of opportunity and experience in testing situations, hour-by-hour variability in performance, lack of motivation to please examiner) that influence screening outcomes. If these considerations are applied to screening, they support using one screener rather than a station approach with many screeners, and/or breaking up the screening into separate identifiable sections. Regardless of layout, or number of screeners, it is still critical that the entire screening time period is relatively short.

Screening Instruments and Other Sources of Information

In other sections of this book there are summaries of specific tests and other procedures available for screening or for comprehensive assessments. The purpose of this section is to look at the adequacy of instruments and procedures currently being used for screening. Are they technically adequate? Should screening programs develop their own screening instruments?

In a survey of assessment practices in 54 model early childhood special education programs (Lehr et al., 1986), it was found that "other" procedures (e.g., record reviews, observations, parent involvement) were used about as often as specific tests for screening. Most of the commercial instruments used for screening did not have the level of reliability (.80) needed, or appropriate standardization populations. These kinds of difficulties with commercially developed instruments no doubt led many screening programs to develop their own instruments. But the same standards for technical adequacy apply to self-developed tests.

The use of alternative procedures has been promoted for assessment of young children. The extent to which these really are appropriate for screening similarly must be addressed, as well as the issue of how one can even judge the technical adequacy of these alternative assessment approaches. Other kinds of requirements that instruments might meet, such as "community fit" (Pennsylvania Department of Education, 1992), have been identified by some states.

Peterson (1987) indicated that screening procedures and instruments should be selected in relationship to four factors: (1) age range of the population screened, (2) dispersion of that population in the geographic area to be served, (3) means available for gaining access to the population, and (4) predicted prevalence of conditions for which screening is to be done. It is also noted, at least in a cursory fashion, that screening instruments must be appropriate to the child's cultural and language background. If all of the criteria are applied, it is unlikely that one will be left with any satisfactory instruments or procedures to use for screening.

Appropriate practices in using multiple sources of information in the decision-making process shift the focus from consideration of only child-focused norm-referenced developmental assessments. Screening typically includes child-focused developmental screening but also includes various formal and informal sources such as observation, interview, developmental history, checklists, and family-focused screening and reports (Pennsylvania Department of Education, 1992). For children from culturally diverse populations, these other screening processes may yield more accurate information than any of the available norm-referenced tests that are not appropriately normed for particular cultural groups (Anderson & Goldberg, 1991).

Meisels (1984) has suggested adjusting norms to meet the needs of an area. This is part of what he refers to as a transactional approach to screening. Developers of screening instruments who provide norms for different subgroups reflect this approach (Lichtenstein & Ireton, 1984; Mardell-Czudnowski & Goldenberg, 1990).

Communicating Results

Screening professionals should be keenly aware that interactions with parents during screening, including the sharing of results at the conclusion, set the tone for future interactions between school and health professionals and parents. Parent-professional partnerships are recognized as critical components in facilitating child success and learning progress. Immediate feedback on the screening decision is considered appropriate practice for preschool screening programs (Pennsylvania Department of Education, 1992).

Parents who have received feedback can leave the screening site with information on areas of possible concern, and what the necessary follow-up steps are, including when, where, and possible costs. Clarification of what screening is and is not is critical at this point. While screening professionals generally are aware that the screening process will identify some children as needing further evaluation when there is no problem, few parents are aware of this. It is important for professionals to convey to parents that a screening decision that uses terms such as "potential problem" or "suspect" does not imply there is a confirmed problem or diagnosis. It cannot be assumed that parents will interpret the screening in the same manner as the professionals. Therefore, communications must be explicit.

For those parents whose screening decision is a "no follow-up" or similar indication that the child is "okay," it is equally important to encourage parents to continue to monitor and attend to their child's development and health. Professionals know that screening does not identify all problems, and that parents must continue to attend to their child's health and development. These parents too should leave the screening site with information on referral sources and available community programs so that they will know where to go if they become concerned about their child's development or health.

Important Considerations for Appropriate Practice

Many issues and practices have been identified in this section on procedures in the screening process. Among them, there are several considerations for appropriate practice:

- The purpose of the preschool screening program must be clearly defined, and all procedures kept consistent with the defined purpose.
- The setting for screening should be the one that is least distracting and most comfortable for the child and parents. Often, this will mean the screening will be in a community setting other than a school.
- When feasible, screening should be conducted at the time that is best for individual children rather than for the convenience of the program. This is easier to do in larger screening programs.
- The time period should be minimized between screening and further evaluation or intervention, and enough time should be left for sufficient early childhood intervention to occur.
- Ideally, developmental screening is a periodic process, implying that preschool screening should occur several times during the preschool years.
- The time of day when screening is conducted should be taken into consideration when interpreting results.
- Consensus among stakeholders should be reached regarding the areas that a preschool program will assess, based on community needs and family factors.
- Screening time should be designed to be brief, but allow for the child's adjustment to the situation and for building rapport with screening personnel.
- Screening instruments should be selected carefully, taking into consideration the targeted age and technical characteristics of the instrument.
- Multiple sources of information should be used to make screening decisions.
- Information on the results of screening should be immediately shared with parents.

People Issues and Practices in the Screening of Preschool Children

People issues and practices in screening preschool children obviously revolve around the individuals who are screened and those who do the screening. A key aspect necessarily involves the match and/or the nature of the interactions between the two. In this section, a brief overview is provided of the most salient of the issues and practices related to people involved in preschool screening: "Who is screened?" and "Who does the screening?"

Who Is Screened?

An array of characteristics that might be used to describe individual children could be addressed in this section. Rather than attempt to produce what would probably be an unending list, two primary factors will be discussed—the age of the child being screened, and the background of the child being screened. Those young children who end up going through the screening process almost always are a subset of the population of children who could be screened. Thus, it is important also to address the issue of participation rates in screening programs, and to note the characteristics of nonparticipants in the screening process.

Age. Age is an obvious child characteristic that influences screening results. Most obvious is the fact that the preschool age means that assessors are working with youngsters who, simply because of their age, are apt to be more influenced by distractibility, inattention, lack of motivation, unwillingness to work with strangers, and fatigue (Lidz, 1983). However, age also constitutes an issue in a more specific sense, in that screening programs make decisions about what ages to include in screening and those decisions have significant implications for screening procedures.

The challenges to assessing young children described earlier, together with the effort to screen children and provide any needed intervention a full year before school entry, often have resulted in targeting a very specific age for screening (e.g., 3 years 10 months). For children who are missed at the target age or age range, some states have instituted mandatory screening that extends the screening process into the first 30 days after kindergarten entry (Luehr & Hoxie, 1995). The age range covered by screening tools of choice also affects the target screening age, with appropriate practice dictating that children should not be at the extremes of the screening ranges covered by the assessment tool.

The specific implications of directing screening efforts toward different age groups have not been addressed. Some measurement experts have noted that for children younger than 3 years of age without obvious disabilities, there are few good predictor instruments (see Goodman & Cameron, 1978; Kochanek, Kobacoff, & Lipsitt, 1990; Stixrud, 1982). With the push toward services for children younger than 3 years of age, this issue becomes even more relevant. The increased emphasis on Child Find efforts to identify and intervene with children from birth to age 3 as a result of federal legislation P.L. 99-457 and its amendments have created a periodic screening and referral system for children who have some risk characteristics. Children who are part of an early tracking system are referred for multidisciplinary evaluation at anytime between the ages of birth and age 5, as it becomes necessary (Pennsylvania Department of Education, 1992).

Background. The background knowledge and experiences with which the young child approaches the screening situation also have a definite impact on screening outcomes. These factors can also be the source of unintended bias when screening is conducted and when decisions are made (Pianta & Reeve, 1993). Two of the more obvious background characteristics that may influence screening outcomes are the language and cultural backgrounds of the children being screened, particularly when these are different from those of the screeners. Although federal and state laws require that assessment be nondiscriminatory, unintended biases may occur when background differences exist, particularly for children with limited English proficiency and with significant cultural differences (see Anderson & Goldberg, 1991; Meisels & Provence, 1989).

It is a generally accepted guideline that children be screened in their native language (see Fallen & Umansky, 1985), yet there are few screening programs with this capability, and few with any kind of coordination between preschool screening programs and programs for linguistic minority groups (see Nuttall, Landurand, & Goldman, 1984). Assessment of the young culturally different child is discussed in much greater detail in Chapter 16.

There are other background characteristics that may influence preschool screening. For example, there is considerable variability in young children's familiarity with expectations similar to those that arise in a testing situation (Shepard, 1994). Dreisbach and Keogh (1982) conducted a study in which one group of kindergarten children whose families were from Mexican American backgrounds was trained in test-taking skills and another group was not. All children then were tested in Spanish and English on a standardized readiness test, with order effects controlled. On both the Spanish and the English administrations, the children who had received training on test-taking skills performed significantly better than the untrained children. Further, those children who were tested first on the Spanish version did better on the English version than did those who were tested first on the English version. It is unclear whether similar results would be obtained with bilingual preschoolers. However, the point made by Dreisbach and Keogh is that both opportunity and experience, not just ability, affect screening outcomes.

An even more prevalent background characteristic that sorts young children today is experience with early childhood education programs. According to national studies (Hofferth, West, Henke, & Kaufman, 1994; West, Wright, & Hausken, 1995), children's participation in center-based programs increases with household income and mother's education.

Characteristics of Nonparticipants

If families with certain characteristics tend not to participate in preschool screening, then the outcomes of screening efforts will be biased. For example, if residents with limited English proficiency are unable to read brochures or letters about preschool screening in their school district, it is unlikely that they will participate in screening. If screening is held only during certain hours of the day, single-parent families or families in which both parents work may not be able to bring their child in during scheduled screening times. Unplanned nonparticipation means that some subset of the population will not be targeted for further assessment efforts.

In general, good data do not exist on screening program participation rates. For most screening programs, the identification of who should be notified about and participate in preschool screening involves the use of census information on who lives in the district and the ages of children in various residences. When mobility rates are high, as they usually are in inner city and urban areas (Kerbow, 1996), there is difficulty in knowing what the target population looks like and who should be in it. In one study, the 61% rate of participation in a preschool screening program was attributed to a variety of factors, including the high mobility rates of Native American families who move to and from reservations, some first-time mothers, some children in private day care homes, and some "needy/high-risk" families (Ysseldyke, Thurlow, Lehr, et al., 1986). Yet, in another preschool screening program with a similar rate of participation, the reasons for nonparticipation could be attributed to lack of interest, children already screened through other avenues (e.g., family doctors), and working parents. Comparable participation rates do not necessarily mean that the characteristics of the nonparticipants are the same.

In one of the few recent studies of screening program participation (Wilder Foundation, 1996), it was found that one in three young children did not participate in preschool screening in time to benefit from possible learning readiness opportunities. Ten percent of the 16,185 children screened in the three counties surrounding the eastern Minneapolis-St. Paul metropolitan area were not screened until they entered kindergarten. These 1600+ children are those who could be Considered "non-participants" or those who are "missed." The Wilder Foundation obtained these statistics through the early childhood screening reports submitted to the state department of education by local districts. Districts estimate that about 5% of children are screened through other sources, such as health care providers, and that the number may increase as links are made with other community service providers for comparable screening (Luehr & Hoxie, 1995).

In a follow-up to the Wilder study (Suzukamo, 1996), it was reported that white children were more likely to be screened in time than were children of color. The difference in participation in screening programs is even more dramatic in urban areas. For example, in St. Paul, where considerable effort is expended to make preschool screening accessible (e.g., holding night screenings, using translators for Hmong, Spanish, and Vietnamese, and visiting homes to encourage parents to bring in their children), it was found that nearly 25% of kindergartners had to be screened after they entered school (Suzukamo, 1996).

The better informed a preschool screening program is of its success in reaching all possible participants (case finding), and the more it knows about those who "choose" not to participate, the more likely it is to be able to address the issues that arise from not reaching certain segments of the population, and to devise ways to reach these groups and promote participation.

Who Does the Screening?

Typically, when "Who does the screening?" is asked, the focus is on the individual characteristics and qualities desired in the examiner. At the point of conducting an in-depth comprehensive evaluation of a child, it is crucial to pay attention to desired examiner qualities. Particular attention must be given to such issues as the examiner's familiarity with the child (see Fuchs, Featherstone, Garwick, & Fuchs, 1984; Fuchs & Fuchs, 1986; Fuchs, Fuchs, Dailey, & Power, 1985; Fuchs, Fuchs, Garwick, & Featherstone, 1983; Fuchs, Zern, & Fuchs, 1983), the assessor's language and style in relationship to the child's ethnic background (see Nuttall et al., 1984; Roth, McCaul, & Barnes, 1993), and the assessor's knowledge and background in the area of child development (see Fallen & Umansky, 1985; Meisels, 1985). Some have argued that the same kinds of characteristics are desired in those involved in preschool screening (Meisels, 1985). The possibility of requiring such characteristics from those who conduct preschool screening is an issue. The question of who screens is addressed by focusing in this section on three factors: (1) parental roles in the screening process, (2) the use of volunteers versus paid professionals, and (3) professional background of the screening administrator and/or decision maker(s).

Parental Role in Screening. Meisels (1985) and others have argued that the important screening role for parents or caregivers occurs during the questionnaire and feedback stages of the screening process. Parents have information about the child that should be considered during screening (e.g., Diamond, 1993; Glascoe, MacLean, & Stone, 1991). However, it is also the case that parents or other caregivers can provide information about the child's environment that should be considered during screening, such as the availability to the child of broader support networks (Kochanek, 1992).

Some might argue that parents have a legitimate role to play during the actual assessments that take place during screening, in order to alleviate fear of strangers and to provide a validity check on information collected. Even when parents are at the screening program site, parental involvement may vary considerably, from completing a parent information questionnaire, to observing from a distance to clarify and interpret behaviors, to remaining with the child throughout the screening process (e.g., Frankenburg et al., 1992; Mardell-Czudnowski & Goldenberg, 1990). It has been found that children performed significantly better when their mothers were involved in the actual data collection (as examiners) than when a professional examiner conducted all assessment without a parent present (Stoneman

& Gibson, 1978). Others, however, have found that the presence of parents tends to inhibit the child's spontaneity (Paget, 1983). The reality is that all mothers and/or fathers are not available to participate in screening (as was evidenced by the need for the large, case-study school district to go to day cares to pick up children for screening). Results from screenings in which some parents participate and others do not may reflect another form of bias in screening. The question of whether to involve parents in any or all aspects of preschool screening is a real issue that must be addressed by preschool screening programs.

It is important to recognize, and to convey to parents as well, that even when screening is required for entrance into public school (as in Minnesota, for example), the requirement can be met without participating in the preschool screening program. Alternative approaches include having the child screened by a regular health care provider or by documenting for the school that the child has not been screened because of "conscientiously held beliefs" (e.g., Luehr & Hoxie, 1995).

Volunteers versus Paid Professionals.   Screening, by definition, is supposed to be a relatively brief, cost-efficient set of assessment procedures designed to identify those children in need of further assessment. A viable alternative to staffing a preschool screening program with professionals is to use volunteers to assist in the assessment procedures. The extent to which this can be implemented depends, in part, on the procedures used for screening and the clear definition of roles for volunteers. Few would question the need to pay careful attention to the appropriateness of the assessment instruments used during screening. Fallen and Umansky (1985) imply in their discussion of assessment techniques that screening personnel who administer assessment instruments must be trained, and that guidelines set forth in most assessment device manuals must be followed in regard to the qualifications required to use the device.

Lichtenstein and Ireton (1984) see a role for nonprofessionals in certain activities that require interpersonal skills but not technical skills, such as scheduling, assisting parents with questionnaires, and escorting children between screening stations. They also acknowledge, however, that given certain screening procedures (those less difficult to master), careful selection, and sufficient training, nonprofessionals might be used as screening examiners. Still, they note, it is not necessarily more cost effective to use volunteers. With volunteers, the costs include recruitment, training and supervision, and rescreening of the child by a professional whenever the volunteer notes a problem (Luehr & Hoxie, 1995).

Coordinators of preschool screening programs tend to believe that the use of volunteers influences the frequency of problem identification, and ultimately, referral rates (Ysseldyke et al., 1985), even though research indicates that there is no obvious relationship between the use of volunteers and the referral rate for developmental problems (Ysseldyke et al., 1986). The potential influence of the "front-line personnel" is not yet known because the data needed to know exactly the nature of that influence are not currently available. The relationship, in fact, may vary with the specific individuals involved or with other contextual factors. This seems to be an unknown that could become known if programs collected their own data.

Professional Background of Administrator.   Another important issue related to "Who screens?" involves the person who is the coordinator of the screening program, as well as the key decision maker(s) in the determination of whether to submit a referral. The decision maker(s), and the professional background of the decision maker(s), is a factor that has been implicated as being related both to the extent to which problems are identified and to the

Important Considerations for Appropriate Practice

Many issues and practices have been identified in this section on people in the screening process. Among them, there are several considerations for appropriate practice:

- The ideal age for preschool screening is between 3 and 5 years of age. [This assumes that an adequate infant screening program is in place, and that preschool screening is a one-time event for a child.]
- Earlier screening should be made available for children whose parents are concerned about the child's development.
- Preschool screening should be sensitive to the child's first language, and conducted by individuals familiar with and adaptable to the family's cultural background.
- Children should be provided sufficient opportunity to become familiar with preschool screening personnel before being asked to participate in the screening process,
- Continued special efforts (e.g., moving screening to familiar community sites) must be made to encourage timely participation of those most likely to be missed.
- The role of parents during assessments of the child must be defined. Given the conflicting recommendations in the literature, this might be a topic for discussion by a focus group involving school personnel, parents, and other community members.
- Parents, and sometimes other family members, should be requested to provide information about the child as part of the screening process.
- The use of paid professionals should be balanced with the use of volunteers to meet the personnel needs of preschool screening.

rate of referrals for further evaluation (see Ysseldyke et al., 1985). In general, districts with higher referral rates vested more decision-making power in the hands of teachers and speech clinicians. Those districts referring a lower percentage of children relied more heavily on the judgment of the school nurse or the consensus of a team of professionals.

Outcome Issues in Screening of Preschool Children

The outcome of preschool screening typically is viewed as the decision about whether a youngster should receive additional assessment procedures (usually referred to as in-depth diagnostic or comprehensive assessment). Today, however, with the emphasis on National Education Goal 1 (starting school ready to learn), we are more often viewing preschool screening as the test of whether a child will be ready for school when he or she enters kindergarten. There are fears expressed about the inappropriate results of taking this perspective, including keeping children out of school beyond school entrance age, developing pre-kindergarten programs, and other approaches that suggest it is the child's responsibility to be ready for school rather than the responsibility of schools to be ready to work with all young children (see Shepard, 1994). Parental perspectives regarding developmental screening often reflect the belief that such tests are indicators of readiness for school (Suzukamo, 1996).

When viewing the major outcome of preschool screening as the determination of whether a child needs a more in-depth assessment, we talk about the *hit rate* (where hit rate refers to making the correct decision) (see Figure 6.2). Correct decisions regarding referral

FIGURE 6.2   Possible Outcomes of Screening

| | *Screening Outcome* | |
Actual Status of Child	Refer (+)	Do Not Refer (−)
Needs Further Assessment	True Positive **Correct Decision**	False Negative (Under-referral)
Does Not Need Further Assessment	False Positive (Over-referral)	True Negative **Correct Decision**

Hit Rate = Number in "Correct Decision" Cells/Number in All Cells
Sensitivity = Number in "True Positive" Cell/Number Not Needing Further Assessment
Specificity = Number in "True Negative" Cell/Number Not Needing Further Assessment

for assessment is one way to look at hit rate; but, the ultimate correct decision with respect to hit rate is a follow-up of all children to determine that those needing services actually receive them (i.e., to make sure children are not falling through the cracks during the screening process). When looking at outcomes, we traditionally also look at the rates of false positives and false negatives. A *false positive* refers to the case in which a child who does not really need special services is referred as a result of preschool screening procedures. A *false negative* refers to the case of a child who really needs special services but is not referred as a result of preschool screening procedures. Screening programs that have many false positives are *over-referring*. Those that have many false negatives are *under-referring*. These types of outcomes are to be avoided.

The desirable outcomes of preschool screening reflect *sensitivity* (referring children who do need special services) and *specificity* (not referring children who do not need special services) (see Lichtenstein & Ireton, 1984, for a fuller discussion of these issues). Sensitivity is a major concern in screening because it reflects the extent to which further assessment will be given to those needing it. Because of this, it is not enough to calculate only a hit rate. Knowing how many children fit into each of the two "Correct Decision" cells has implications for the screening program. If the rate of correct nonreferrals (true negatives) is high, an overall hit rate can mask a low rate of correct referrals (true positives) (Stone, Gridley, & Treloar, 1992).

The basic notions of false positives and false negatives indeed are important because they relate to other possible outcomes of screening preschool children. In this section, five major topics will be addressed: (1) accuracy and predictive value, (2) labeling, (3) referral rates, (4) cost effectiveness, and (5) evaluation.

Accuracy and Predictive Value

On one hand, we know that intellectual and performance tests have limited predictive ability for young children (Goodman & Cameron, 1978; Peterson, 1987; Stixrud, 1982). On the other hand, we have persuasive documentation of the benefits derived from early intervention programs for young children (see Barnett, 1995; Casto & Mastropieri, 1986; Schweinhart &

Weikert, 1981; Weiss, 1981). At issue is where to draw the line between guessing that a child might have or develop a disability, and providing services for that child. Screening affords the opportunity to make the guessing process a little less expensive than it would be if a complete diagnostic assessment were conducted on every preschool child. All of this relates to the predictive value of preschool screening. As Meisels (1985) notes, however, the needs for screening measures to be brief, efficient, low cost, developmental, and to have objective scoring, may make the goal of long-term predictive accuracy unattainable. Despite this, most states now are collecting data not only on the numbers of children screened, and the hit rate, but also on the effectiveness of screening in the identification of potential problems, referrals, and results for children and families.

Labeling

The positive and negative effects associated with labeling children as having disabilities, and, even more specifically, as having a disability with an identified label (e.g., learning disability, mental retardation, emotional disturbance) has received considerable attention in the special education literature (see Ysseldyke, 1987; Ysseldyke & Algozzine, 1982, 1990; Ysseldyke, Algozzine, & Thurlow, 1992). Labeling issues become even more critical for young children, who have much more time for the effects of labeling to multiply over years.

Current opinion is that labeling is inappropriate for preschool children. Meisels (1985) notes the limited implications that can be drawn from screening results and also points to the labeling issue when he states: "Screening should not be used to label children, place them in particular programs, or develop specific intervention procedures" (p. 5).

These concerns have been voiced by numerous others, often with special reference to very young children (Stixrud, 1982). In fact, probably as a result of many of these concerns, in 1990 the Individuals with Disabilities Education Act was amended to allow for the use of the more general category "developmental delay" for preschool-age children. And, in 1996, Congress was considering two new amendments related to the labeling of children. One proposal which was approved was to allow states to use the label "developmental delay" for children up to eight years of age; another proposal was to eliminate the use of labels in child counts totally, and instead to provide funds based on a percentage of the total population of children.

These opinions and proposals for changes in law certainly reflect the concern about people's tendency to categorize and explain events through labeling. Professionals must be sensitive to possible parent perceptions that a screening decision indicating a potential problem implies a label or diagnosis. Continued attention to labeling issues may be needed (including special training) to remove the tendency to label children, particularly those who are young.

Referral Rates

Referral rates from preschool screening programs have been found to vary tremendously, even within the same state and even within the same geographical area (see Thurlow et al., 1985). It has been noted that children from families of low socioeconomic status (SES) tend to be referred more often than are children from high-SES families (Lichtenstein & Ireton, 1984). Few relationships between referral rates and broader social, economic, political, or educational factors have been identified (Ysseldyke & O'Sullivan, 1987). High referral rates suggest over-referral, and low referral rates suggest under-referral. But whether one of these is the case is not easy to determine because there are no standards that tell us what an appropriate referral rate is, and because the appropriate referral rate probably would vary from one place to the next anyway.

Once a referral rate is determined, steps can be taken to change the rate. If the number indicates that the referral rate is too low, criteria for identification of a problem can be relaxed, or additional screening procedures can be implemented to identify additional problem areas (see Lichtenstein & Ireton, 1984). If the number indicates that the referral rate is too high, criteria can be made more stringent, or fewer areas might be checked. Whether these approaches are considered ethical is another matter.

Rescreening is one of the more popular ways to adjust for overreferrals. Rescreening refers to the use of a second-level assessment prior to referring a child for a more in-depth diagnostic assessment. The second-level screening uses assessment procedures that may be slightly more time consuming than those used in the original screening, and may use personnel who are more highly trained (at least compared to nonprofessional screeners, if those are the personnel used in the original screening). Research (Teska & Stonebruner, 1980; Ysseldyke, Thurlow, & O'Sullivan, 1987) has suggested that rescreening practices reduce referral rates.

Cost-Effectiveness of Preschool Screening

Are current screening efforts meeting the criterion of low cost? State reimbursements for screening typically do not cover the entire cost per child. In a 1986 study (Ysseldyke, Thurlow, Lehr, et al.), the state provided reimbursement for screening at the rate of about $15 per child screened, but that rate of reimbursement was expected to decline. However, during 1994–95, the same state was reimbursing at the rate of $25 per child screened; still, the estimated cost of just the screening was about $38 per child (Suzukamo, 1996). Thus, preschool screening is a cost to each district, above the amount that the state reimburses.

Another way to look at the costs of screening is to look at what happens when over-referral or under-referral occurs. Teska and Stonebruner (1980) estimated that each over-referral from screening costs an estimated $100 to $200 per child. This figure probably is much higher today. These costs are associated with the costs of conducting the more in-depth diagnostic assessments that follow from many referrals. On the opposite side of the coin, under-referrals can result in even more significant financial consequences. If early intervention occurs and is successful in eliminating the need for further special education services in school (see Peterson, 1987, who cites Antley & DuBose, 1981; Weber, Foster, & Weikart, 1978; Wood, 1981), the savings per child would range from about $15,000 to nearly $30,000 per child. These cost studies have focused on those children who receive services. Cost-effectiveness and benefit-cost studies apparently have not been conducted for preschool screening programs.

Evaluation of Screening Programs

It is very surprising that there has been so little evaluation of preschool screening, particularly since it now has a relatively long history. Evaluation of preschool programs is not the same as evaluation of preschool screening programs. The need for evaluation of screening becomes more important as other methods (such as identifying those children living in poverty) are proposed to identify children in need of intervention, or even those in need of further assessment.

Important Considerations for Achieving Appropriate Outcomes

Many issues and practices have been identified in this section on outcomes related to preschool screening. Among them, there are several considerations for achieving appropriate outcomes:

- Screening programs should be designed to maximize the hit rate (accurate referrals and non-referrals).
- Screening programs should collect and report data on referral rates.
- Screening programs should not label children.
- Every program should keep track of costs, periodically bring together focus groups to discuss benefits in relation to costs.
- Screening programs should develop evaluation plans that they adhere to, with a focus on percent of target population screened, referral rates, costs, and hit rates.
- Collection and use of information other than child-focused data, such as the satisfaction of constituencies (e.g., parents, service providers) with the results of preschool screening, should be a critical component of an evaluation plan.

What is needed in a good evaluation of a preschool screening program? Calculation of hit rates is just one of many pieces that should be considered in a good evaluation (see Lichtenstein & Ireton, 1984). It is equally important to evaluate the percentage of the target population that is actually screened, and the number of over- and under-referrals. Additional information on those not screened is important, and can help to inform a program about changes that may be needed to more successfully reach a broader part of the target population. Information on whether and when follow-up to a screening decision occurs (either rescreening or diagnostic assessment), is also an important piece of the evaluation process.

Information of the costs of screening programs is important. At some point, programs need to seriously judge the cost-benefit of simply pulling a portion of the target population, based on characteristics that do not need to be measured (e.g., income level, number of parents in the home, etc.), versus the cost-benefit of carefully screening each child on an individual basis on a set of characteristics that need to be measured (e.g., visual acuity, language development, etc.). Serious cost-benefit analyses, however, require assigning value to some effects that cannot easily be assigned monetary values (e.g., parent satisfaction).

Obviously, satisfaction is another important variable that needs to be included in any evaluation of preschool screening programs (Lichtenstein & Ireton, 1984; Ysseldyke, Thurlow, & Gilman, 1993a, b). Parent satisfaction, school district satisfaction, and even child satisfaction are all legitimate goals of a preschool screening program, and therefore should be evaluated.

As resources become more scarce, the need for evaluation information will increase. Preschool screening programs would be wise to develop evaluation plans now, and to slowly ease the necessary data collection for evaluation into their everyday procedures.

A New Look at Preschool Screening

Preschool screening today is much more accepted and expected than it was just 10 years ago. While there are still many issues that surround preschool programs and what is best practice, there are many existing practices to examine and to use as a basis for making recommendations about what needs to be considered when implementing programs. In this chapter, we identified issues and practices within the broad areas of people, procedures, and outcomes. And, preschool screening was placed within the larger context of assessment in general.

Where is the field now, compared to where it was ten years ago? There are several answers to this question. First, preschool screening, now more than before, is focused on identifying "at risk" children, rather than children with obvious disabilities. Second, the focus of preschool screening is broader than just the child, expanding to include family factors and supports. Third, preschool screening programs, in general, remain without answers to some relatively simple questions. And, finally, preschool screening programs have made little progress in justifying themselves.

Special education services are now available to young children beginning at birth. This should mean that there is increased attention to evidence of more obvious disabilities. By the time children get to preschool age, obvious disabilities should have been recognized, more indepth assessments should have already occurred, and services should have been and should continue to be provided to these children. Therefore, the focus of preschool screening is more likely to be on identifying children at risk of developing disabilities as they progress toward and into school. This, of course, is conjecture. We have no data to verify that this is the case. However, one might expect, in general, that this would be a characteristic of preschool screening today.

As preschool screening has built up a history, it has become increasingly obvious that parents and family support are important aspects of a child's life and adjustment. Attempting to screen and assess a child in isolation from family factors is like getting only part of the picture. While most screening programs view family factors as optional, information on family resources, strengths, economic status, education, and literacy are significant contextual factors that help to interpret the child's status. Even for children who do not qualify for further assessment/intervention as a result of the screening process, screening itself can be a form of intervention if it affirms or supports the parents' view of their child's abilities and needs.

Despite added years of experience, preschool screening programs still do not have "answers" to some relatively simple questions. An underlying issue for screening continues to be how to merge the need for quick, inexpensive procedures with what one knows works best for assessing young children. This means that there is a need for answers to questions such as, "Can a program use volunteers rather than professionals and still get comparable results?" "Which instruments are quick yet valid and reliable?" "What is the best way to encourage participation in screening of those most likely to need preschool services?" These are questions that can be answered through research. Yet, we see virtually no research on preschool screening within the past 6 to 8 years. Research and evaluation must assume greater roles in preschool screening.

The need for research and evaluation flows directly into the fourth descriptor of where preschool screening programs are today: They have made little progress in justifying themselves. Without sound evaluation data, or at least research to support existing practices, preschool screening programs are relying on the documented benefits of early childhood intervention programs. Policymakers may begin to question whether it is cheaper and just as effective to target children for early intervention programs in ways other than through individualized screening procedures that require personnel, facilities, and many other resources. The need for thoughtful evaluation plans and the collection of data is now more urgent than ever before. Within the current context of changing demographics, the identification of children at birth and shortly after, and the press toward school readiness as part of Goal 1, the role and purpose of preschool screening may be redefined in the future. The added benefit of having data is that the data can help formulate improved procedures and decision making, not just better justification for program existence.

Summary

In this chapter we identified issues and described practices in the screening of preschool children. Preschool screening is one piece of a larger puzzle of assessment to intervention, with screening as a quick, inexpensive assessment of large numbers of children to determine who needs further in-depth diagnostic evaluation. Despite a strong rationale for preschool screening and its acceptance today, it is difficult to find a "typical" preschool screening program because there is so much variability in practice. This variability is what leads to many of the issues identified in this chapter. The limited research that exists provides the basis for some considerations about appropriate preschool screening practice in each issue area.

Three areas of issues were presented: procedural, people, and outcomes. The key procedural issues addressed were where and when screening occurs, areas assessed and administration procedures, screening instruments and other sources of information, and communicating results. The key issues discussed within the area of "people" were who is screened (age, background, characteristics of nonparticipants), and who does the screening (parental role, volunteers versus paid professionals, professional background of administrator). Outcome issues include accuracy and predictive value, labeling, referral rates, cost effectiveness, and evaluation. Consideration of these issues in light of current practice brings us to a new look at preschool screening within the broader context of national education reform goals, such as all children starting school ready to learn.

7 Developmental History

JOANNE KALESNIK

The behavior and functioning of preschool-aged children is complex. Good preschool assessments explore this complexity by simultaneously evaluating multiple domains of development such as cognitive, speech, language, adaptive behavior, motor skills, and social-emotional. When pieced together, information obtained from this type of multi-perspective assessment yields a total picture of the child and thus, a greater understanding of why he or she is presently functioning and behaving in manners that are causing concern. For example, a child may be referred for preschool assessment based on the concern that he appears socially immature compared to other children his age and shows little interest in readiness activities such as coloring, pretend play, and looking at picture books. Once the child is evaluated, test results might indicate the presence of significant language delays, visual-perceptual difficulties, and below-age-level cognitive skills.

Yet, what about information related to the child's past functioning and development, prior to the time he or she is referred for preschool assessment? The cornerstone of a thorough evaluation is a complete case history (Nuttall & Ivey, 1986), however this is often the shortest section of assessment reports. Even when report writers include detailed background information, they often fall short in linking it to current test results or the recommendations they make. This chapter presents a component of the data collection process referred to as "Developmental History." In written reports, this section should precede the reporting of tests administered and results obtained. Its purpose is to present information related to the child's history of development beginning from conception, through the pregnancy and birth, the newborn period, and up until the time the child is referred for preschool assessment.

Typically included under Developmental History are the following age-related subcomponents: prenatal development, which pertains to all aspects of conception and pregnancy; perinatal development, which focuses on the actual birth and delivery; postnatal development, which has to do with the newborn's first weeks of life; and infancy through early childhood development, which pertains to everything from the first months of life through the child's present age, including his or her attainment of key developmental milestones. Information related to each of these subcomponents can provide background clues that help to explain the child's present behaviors and shed some light on current levels of developmental functioning.

Background information is typically elicited by reviewing the child's past records, interviewing parents and caretakers, and having them complete child history forms. The practice of involving parents and caretakers in an interview process serves an important twofold purpose. First, it allows for initial rapport building and lays the foundation for a working partnership early in the overall assessment. It connects parents to the evaluation that is underway and enables them to contribute and become active participants in helping their child. From the outset, parents and caretakers thus become important members of the multidisciplinary team.

Secondly, detailed background information allows for current test results, once obtained, to be framed within a larger, more meaningful and historical context. It expands what is known about the child's current behaviors and functioning and provides all members of the preschool team with direction for the evaluations they will be conducting. More importantly, detailed background information shifts attention away from the current testing data so that the child is viewed as having been connected to past experiences and, in some cases, to systems (hospitals, programs, centers) other than the preschool program currently evaluating the child.

Gathering Information for a Developmental History

There are several ways to go about obtaining relevant background information in order to construct a case history of the child. A practical starting point is to review the child's existing records. These would include, for example, medical and hospital records and those from any previous assessments and interventions done by private therapists or public programs such as Early Childhood Intervention (birth to 3) centers. In cases of adoption or foster care placement, a thorough review of past records and agency files is especially important because biological parents and family-of-origin members may not be available to interview. When information obtained from a review of records is cited within the developmental history section of written reports, it should be preceded by a phrase indicating the source, such as "According to pediatrician records...." If the child has formally undergone an assessment similar to the one being conducted, both the instruments used and results obtained should be reported. Such information will help to guide preschool evaluators in their choice of instruments and serve as baseline data for the current assessment.

Often, it is necessary to ask parents if past records or files are available on the child and, if so, how they might be accessed. Some parents may not realize the relevance and importance of past information to the preschool assessment currently underway. Parental consent and permission must always be obtained for the release and review of any record pertaining to the child. Chapter 4 of this text addresses legal and ethical issues associated with obtaining parental consent, confidentiality, and the release or records between agencies and professionals serving the child.

In addition to reviewing past records, parents should serve as another good source of background information through interviewing and, if they can read and write, completing child history forms. Parents, however, may not always be (or have been) the primary caregivers and thus, may not be the sole sources of information. In some families, grandparents, aunts, cousins, or older siblings serve as caretakers and, for this reason, should play an active role in providing background information. This may be particularly relevant in the case of children from culturally or racially diverse backgrounds or more nontraditional family compositions such as teenage parenting, adoptive and foster parenting, same sex parenting or single-parenting. Other situations that might require special consideration in identifying who can or should be interviewed to obtain relevant background information on the child are those involving divorce, shared custody, blended stepfamilies, and parental disputes between the custodial and noncustodial parent(s).

When past records related to the child are available for review, inconsistencies or contradictions between them and what parents or caretakers report during the interview process should be noted and made clear. The amount of background information parents are able to report and can remember about their child may be important in understanding their level of involvement and interest in the child's development. It may also reflect the degree to which the parent is capable of understanding issues related to child development, such as the attainment of key developmental milestones, or the impact which pre-, peri-, and postnatal conditions can have on later developmental status. Whether parents and caretakers agree upon and report the same information is equally important, as this provides insight into their perceptions and areas of greatest concern regarding the child. For example, a father may focus primarily on the child's lack of motor coordination and poor motor planning skills, whereas the mother is most concerned about the child's delayed speech and language abilities.

Types of Background Information

When past records, including previous evaluation or treatment reports, are reviewed and parents have been interviewed and asked to complete child history forms, the background information elicited typically falls under two broad categories, *medical history* and *developmental milestones*. Information related to the child's medical background and his or her attainment of earlier developmental milestones should be reported for each of the four developmental periods, as applicable: prenatal, perinatal, postnatal, and infancy through early childhood.

Medical history would include, for example, information from records and the parent interview pertaining to any type of complication or special circumstance related to the child's conception, the mother's pregnancy, the delivery and birthing procedures, and the newborn's need for placement in a neonatal intensive care unit (NICU) or special care nursery immediately after birth. Also included within the category of medical history might be reported events such as hospital stays, surgeries, special tests performed (for example, in genetics or neurology), visits to specialists such as ophthalmologists, audiologists, endocrinologists, and cardiologists, previous interventions provided by allied health professionals such as physical therapists and occupational therapists, special equipment which the child required or currently uses (such as feeding tubes, orthotics, hearing aids, and catheters), current medications and treatments, or any type of serious injury or illness occurring since the time of birth up until the child's present age.

Appendix 7B of this chapter presents a simple structure, "Intake Form for a Medical History," which can be followed when parents are interviewed for this type of information. If parents can read and write, they can also be asked to complete the form themselves, separate from the interview process. As can be seen, the "Intake Form for a Medical History" is divided into the four general developmental periods: Prenatal; Perinatal; Postnatal; and Infancy and Early Childhood. It covers many specific medical areas and conditions, yet can be modified from its existing format to suit particular settings and purposes for preschool assessment.

The second category of background information, *developmental milestones,* includes information pertaining to the age at which the child is reported to have accomplished certain degrees of functioning in the main developmental areas of feeding/eating, sleeping, dressing, toileting, gross and fine motor skills, speech, language usage, play, and social interaction. Other areas commonly noted under developmental milestones include the child's early temperament, style of expressing emotion, and activity level. Appendix 7A of this chapter presents a sample structure, "Checklist for the Accomplishment of Early Developmental Milestones," which can be used as a guideline while interviewing parents for this type of information. Parents can also be asked to complete the form themselves, separate from the interview process. As can be seen, the checklist is fairly comprehensive and specific, yet can certainly be modified from its existing format for use in particular preschool settings. In the sections that follow, the categories of medical history and developmental milestones as they pertain to constructing the child's developmental history will be discussed further.

Medical History

Some children referred for preschool assessment will arrive with well-documented medical histories because they have an already diagnosed condition such as spina bifida, cerebral palsy, Down syndrome, visual or hearing impairment, metabolic disorder, or a specific chromosomal abnormality. Often, under the guidelines of Special Education, these children are classified as Other Health Impairment (OHI). In the case of a child with an already identified medical condition, it is important to gather specific information related to the level of severity, such as mild, moderate, or severe; current functional impairments and their implications; prognosis; current medications and equipment needs; and what impact medical personnel see the condition as having on the child's rate of growth in each area of development which the preschool assessment team will be evaluating. Additionally, some children within this group will carry multiple diagnoses, such as visually and hearing impaired or cerebral palsy and seizure disorder, which should be noted and thoroughly described.

   Apart from reviewing existing medical records on children referred for preschool assessment who already have a diagnosed condition(s), additional records likely exist from previous treatment centers such as Early Childhood Intervention (birth to 3) programs, hospital-based programs such as gait training or speech therapy, and private therapists who have worked, or are continuing to work, with the child in the areas of physical therapy, occupational therapy, or speech-language therapy. Thus, these records should also be obtained and reviewed along with input provided by parents and caretakers during the interview process.

   A second group of children referred for preschool assessment will arrive with no particular condition such as cerebral palsy or Down syndrome, but will nonetheless have significant medical histories stemming from the prenatal, perinatal, postnatal, or infancy and early childhood periods. Examples include children whose mothers ingested alcohol and drugs while pregnant and children born prematurely, weighing less than four pounds at birth, due to a condition in the mother such as placenta previa. Also included within this group might be children with long histories of reoccurring inner ear infections (otitis media) which have been resolved through antibiotic therapy or ear tubes, but which negatively impact the child's speech and language development. Other children may have been born full-term and in a healthy and stable state, yet later suffered a serious injury or illness which interrupted normal developmental progression during the time of occurrence or caused permanent developmental damage. This would include, for example, children who have experienced a near drowning, head trauma, high fevers, meningitis, or lead poisoning.

   A third group of children referred for preschool assessment will arrive with no documented medical diagnosis and no significant medical history stemming from earlier developmental periods. They will, in fact, simply be "developmentally delayed" in the absence of any known biological condition or medical cause. Children within this group are certainly cause for concern, and even more so if the child's developmental delays are discrepant to a significant degree from the personal norms of the family's cultural expectations. In cases where the developmental delay has no known etiology, the preschool assessment team might make a recommendation for testing by a specialist—for example pediatric neurology—if the child's parents indicate that no previous testing of this type has been done. Although in many cases the actual cause of the developmental delays will remain unknown, it is nonetheless helpful to rule out underlying medical conditions by subjecting the child to the appropriate medical tests.

Detailed information related to a child's medical history is extremely important to the preschool assessment being conducted. However, this type of information comprises only one part of the child's full developmental history. Other factors related to his or her accomplishment of past developmental milestones must also be identified and discussed.

Developmental Milestones

Background history related to developmental milestones provides a broader picture of past experiences that the preschool child brings to the current assessment. By indicating how and when the child accomplished earlier developmental milestones, a historical account of rate of development can be constructed. Typically, information related to history of developmental milestones focuses on the period of infancy and early childhood; that is, from the time the child is born up until his or her present age. When it is determined that a child has been late in reaching certain developmental milestones, such judgment is usually based on what age-related graphs and charts portray as normal developmental progression. Charts of this type which outline stages of normal development are commonly seen hanging on the walls of pediatrician's offices, in the waiting rooms of public health centers, and appear in almost every book written for parents about child development. (For information related to normal development, see Chapter 2 of this text.)

However, determination of developmental delay should not only be based on what graphs and charts portray as normal progression, but should also take into account the values and expectations of the child's culture and ethnicity, when applicable. Some children may reach developmental milestones in a manner which provides for optimal adjustment and success in their home culture, which may not always be the majority culture. Thus, when working with children of diverse cultural and ethnic backgrounds, it becomes necessary to view their history of development within the context of innate abilities as well as environmental and situational factors. If preschool evaluators have little knowledge about the expectations and values of a child's specific culture or ethnicity, family members should be asked, "Did this child learn to walk or talk as your other children did, or did she or he learn more slowly or in some different way? Are you and other family members concerned about your child's development and, if so, why? What specifically concerns you?" Open-ended questions of this type will hopefully elicit information from parents and caregivers as to whether they feel the child has been progressing in a normal manner and why.

Background information related to a child's attainment of earlier developmental milestones can be recorded on informal or formal instruments. Informal instruments, such as the checklist appearing in Appendix 7A of this chapter, have not been standardized or normed on sample populations and thus have no documented validity or reliability data. Informal instruments simply indicate *when* a child successfully accomplished *which* specific milestones. Informal instruments do not tell how the child's development compares to that of other children.

It is a relatively common practice among preschools and early childhood education centers to use informal instruments for obtaining relevant background information. That is, they design their own developmental checklists to suit the needs to their particular setting and the children they serve. An example of a center-developed informal instrument is the *Parent Inventory of Child Development in Nonschool Environments* (Vincent, Davis, Brown, Broome, Funkhouser, Miller, & Gruenewald, 1988) developed for use by the Madison (Wisconsin) Public Schools and the Department of Rehabilitation Psychology and Special Education at the University of Wisconsin in Madison. Figure 7.1 is a sample page from the self-help area of the third section, "Age of Beginning Independence—37 to 48 Months."

Apart from informal checklists, preschool programs and early childhood centers also use formal instruments to gather and record relevant background information related to developmental milestones. With formal instruments, the developmental accomplishments of a referred child can be compared to those of a sample population. Formal instruments are commercially marketed, come with manuals and recording forms, and provide standardized norms. In most cases, computer scoring packages are available for these instruments which convert raw data (parent responses) into scaled scores, percentile ranks, and plotted profiles indicating whether the child's development in a particular area is advanced, within normal limits, or delayed.

An example of one such instrument is the *Child Development Inventory* (CDI) (Ireton & Thwing, 1992), a 300-item questionnaire which parents complete about their child's development in eight different areas: social, self-help, gross motor, fine motor, expressive language, language comprehension, letters, and numbers. The CDI also yields a general development index so that, globally, the child's developmental status can be compared to same-aged peers. A briefer parent questionnaire available from the same company that markets the CDI is the *Preschool Development Inventory* (PDI) (Ireton, 1988). The PDI contains a 60-item general development scale and a 24-item symptom and behavior problems list. The PDI is designed to allow for parent input related to additional concerns they have about their child which were not covered by items in the questionnaire.

Another standardized instrument, the *Developmental Observation Checklist System* (DOCS) (Hresko, Miguel, Sherbenou, & Burton, 1994), is a questionnaire completed by parents based on their observations of the child's functioning in the areas of language, motor, social, and cognitive development. The DOCS also contains scales related to the child's adjustment behaviors and levels of family stress and support. The *AAMR Adaptive Behavior Scales-School: Second Edition* (ABS-S:2) (Lambert, Nihira, & Leland, 1993) is another standardized instrument in which parents check items pertaining to developmental milestones their preschool child has accomplished in areas such as independent functioning, sensory and motor abilities, language, socialization, self-direction, and responsibility. The ABS-S:2 is divided into two parts: Part One focuses on personal independence and coping skills considered important for daily living; and Part Two focuses on content related to level of social adaptation. A special feature of the ABS-S:2 is that its manual provides detailed information about how score results can be used in instructional planning and IEP development.

The *Developmental Profile II* (DP-II) (Alpern, Boll, & Shearer, 1986) is yet another formal instrument which can be used to compare a child's development to that of other children who are the same age. The DP-II consists of 186 items which describe specific skills in five key areas: muscle and motor abilities, self-help, social, cognitive/intellectual,

FIGURE 7.1   Sample from the Parent Inventory of Child Development in Nonschool Environments

Age of Beginning Independence — Self Help — My Child:	Does this consistently.	Does this sometimes.	Is starting to do this.	Does not do this.	I would like this to be a goal for my child	I'm not sure why this is important for my child to do.
1. Drinks from all drinking utensils independently.						
2. Eats most kinds of food.						
3. Will feed him/herself independently with fork and spoon.						
4. Will pour him/herself a glass of juice or milk but needs help in getting the juice or milk container from the refrigerator.						
5. Needs some assistance when dressing—shoes/socks, determining front/back, button/zipping/snaps/belts.						
6. Will undress independently.						
7. When requested, will wipe nose and cover mouth when he/she has a cold.						
8. Will independently wash and dry face and hands.						
9. Will bathe and dry him/herself with frequent assistance.						
10. Will comb and brush hair with frequent assistance.						
11. Will hold toothbrush and brush teeth with adult assistance.						
12. Independently takes care of all bathroom needs.						
13. Goes to bed easily (might awaken in the middle of the night either with a bad dream or to go to the bathroom).						
14. Has a consistent bedroom—e.g., puts toys away, reads a story, kisses goodnight.						
15. Gets ready for bed with little help—e.g., undresses and gets pajamas on.						

Source: L. Vincent, J. Davis, P. Brown, K. Broome, K. Funkhouser, J. Miller, and L. Gruenewald, *Parent Inventory of Child Development in Nonschool Environments* (Madison, WI: Madison Metropolitan School District Early Childhood Program and the Department of Rehabilitation Psychology and Special Education, University of Wisconsin, 1988.)

and expressive and receptive communication. When completing the DP-II, parents indicate whether or not their child has mastered the skill in question. As is the case with standardized instruments, parent responses are then converted to scaled scores which are plotted onto a profile indicating whether the child's development in any of the five key areas is normal or delayed.

Another instrument, the *Battelle Developmental Inventory* (BDI) (Newborg, Stock, Wnek, Guidubaldi, & Svinicki, 1984) is a nationally standardized developmental battery with scales in five domains: personal-social, adaptive, motor, communication, and cognitive. Each of these domains is further divided into specific skill components. Although items on the BDI are typically administered directly to the child by a preschool evaluator, in many instances parents must be interviewed to provide additional information about skills not displayed by the child during the evaluation session. The *Scales of Independent Behavior* (SIB) (Bruininks, Woodcock, Weatherman, & Hill, 1984) comprise another nationally standardized developmental battery in which parent input is necessary. The SIB contains fourteen subscales in the broad areas of motor skills, language, social interaction, personal self-care, self-help, and orientation to home/community.

In summary, a good developmental history presents information related to milestones the child has already mastered and at what ages. Information of this kind can be recorded on informal (non-standardized) instruments (see Appendix 7A) or formal (standardized) instruments in which parents serve as the primary respondents. Apart from providing information related to their child's past developmental accomplishments, parents can also be interviewed and, if they can read and write, asked to complete forms about their child's medical history, beginning at the time of conception, through the pregnancy and birth, and into the infancy and early childhood periods (see Appendix 7B). The following case study illustrates how the developmental history section would appear and be woven into the overall preschool assessment report.

Case Study

Reason for Referral

At the recommendation of her pediatrician, Peggy was referred for preschool assessment at the age of 3 years, 4 months due to delayed language development, articulation (speech) difficulties, and motor coordination concerns such as difficulty balancing, climbing stairs upright, and using hand and finger skills for feeding herself and grasping objects such as utensils, large crayons, small toys, and pullstrings. Peggy just recently became fully toilet trained for bladder and bowel.

Developmental History

In gathering information related to Peggy's developmental history, her parents were interviewed and, as they could read and write, also completed an "Intake Form for a Medical History" (see Appendix 7B) in their primary language, English. They also signed consent forms so that Peggy's medical records could be obtained from the hospital where she was born and from the pediatrician who referred her for preschool assessment. Additionally, Peggy's parents completed a "Checklist for the Accomplishment of Early Developmental

Milestones" (see Appendix 7A). During the interview, Peggy's parents reported that no previous developmental assessments have been done and that Peggy has received no past developmental therapies. There is no reported history of her participation in an Early Childhood Intervention (birth to 3) center or any type of preschool program.

From input provided during the interview with Peggy's parents and based on information they shared on the medical history forms they were asked to complete, it appears that the pregnancy of Peggy was planned and she was conceived naturally. Peggy was the mother's fifth pregnancy and is the third of three children. Two miscarriages occurred prior to the birth of the family's oldest child, for unknown reason. The mother states that she did not use nicotine, alcohol, or any other drug while pregnant. Reportedly, the pregnancy with Peggy was normal and uncomplicated until the seventh month when amniotic fluid began leaking and her mother was ordered on total bed rest. After approximately three weeks of bed rest, Peggy's mother began having contractions and was hospitalized. Hospital monitors indicated fetal distress so labor was allowed. Vaginal delivery became complicated, fetal distress increased, and it was determined that the umbilical cord had become wrapped around Peggy's neck. Therefore, Peggy was immediately delivered via an emergency C-section.

Once she was born, Peggy's parents report that she experienced breathing problems, irregular heart rate, and had swallowed some of the amniotic fluid. They recall that Peggy's APGAR's were 5/7 and her birthweight was 5 pounds, 0 ounces. According to hospital records, Peggy was placed in the neonatal intensive care unit (NICU) for a period of six days following her delivery. During her stay in the NICU, records indicate that Peggy was placed on a respirator and maintained a fever for approximately three days, for which she received antibiotic therapy. By the fourth day, records indicate that the fever resolved and her breathing improved. Peggy was thus downgraded from the respirator to an oxygen halo. After six days, Peggy was discharged and went home with her mother who had remained in the hospital to recover from her C-section delivery.

According to pediatrician records and information provided by Peggy's parents during the interview, once home from the hospital Peggy experienced colic and fussiness during her newborn and early infancy period. She reportedly had difficulty establishing a sleep and feeding schedule. Several formulas had to be tried due to reflux and what her parents describe as "allergic reactions" to feedings including rashes, gas, and constipation. By the time Peggy was 8 months old, these difficulties reportedly resolved. However, her parents stated that she continues to be a "picky eater" and a "light sleeper."

Pediatrician records indicate that Peggy began experiencing chronic and reoccurring ear infections (otitis media) at 10 months of age. Such infections were initially treated with antibiotic therapies until PE tubes were placed, bilaterally, when she was 22 months old. After approximately 6 months, the ear tubes fell out, so another surgery was required to place a second set. Since that time, Peggy reportedly has experienced "only a handful" of ear infections. When Peggy was 25 months old, pediatrician records indicate that she was hospitalized for a period of three days due to unexplained high fever and subsequent dehydration. Reportedly, meningitis was first suspected as a cause, but later ruled out.

There is no reported history of other significant illnesses, surgeries, or hospitalizations. However, Peggy's parents point out that she has "always been clumsy" and thus, has experienced a series of falls and tumbles resulting in minor cuts, bruises, and abrasions. Vision and hearing tests conducted at her pediatrician's office last month were each within normal limits.

In regard to Peggy's accomplishment of early developmental milestones, the checklist completed by her parents (see Appendix 7A) indicates delays or complication in all areas of development since infancy: feeding and eating, sleeping, gross and fine motor skills, toileting, speech, language, dressing, and social interaction and communication. For example, Peggy is 3 years, 4 months old and according to her parents, is still not fully using her fingers or utensils to feed herself. She has not yet mastered drinking from an open cup and thus prefers a bottle or sipper-cup. Reportedly, Peggy does not consistently sleep through the night and "every little noise will wake her up."

In regard to motor skill development, Peggy did not begin walking until 15 months of age and still experiences difficulty with motor movement, balance, and coordination. Toilet training did not begin until Peggy was 2½ years old and was just recently fully accomplished. Peggy's parents also report that she was a late talker and, since the beginning, her speech has been difficult to understand due to articulation error. Because Peggy reportedly has difficulty with hand and finger skills, she cannot yet dress herself using buttons, zippers, ties, or socks.

In regard to social interaction, Peggy's parents note that other children and adults find her speech difficult to understand; when playing with children her same age, Peggy appears "more immature" and "not up to their level." Finally, Peggy's parents report that due to some of her earlier health concerns (colic, feeding problems, ear infections), they may have overprotected her and "treated her more like a baby" than they should have. They now wonder if not requiring more of Peggy could have caused some of her current difficulties and the delayed onset of past development milestones such as walking and talking.

At the close of the interview, Peggy's parents were thanked for their thorough input and for completing the forms related to her developmental and medical history. It was explained to them that the next step in the process would be for Peggy to undergo a comprehensive evaluation by the preschool assessment team in order to further investigate the nature and extent of her developmental delays. Each member of the preschool assessment team will be able to review the information contained in Peggy's developmental history to assist them in selecting appropriate evaluation measures. As test results become available, the developmental history section of the written report will provide a meaningful and historical context in which to frame them.

Summary

This chapter assumed an ecological perspective to child assessment, one that recognizes an entire range of factors that can influence and affect developmental status and functioning. In regard to conducting preschool assessments, it presented a component of the data collection process referred to as "Background Information." When included in written reports, this information source focuses on factors related to the child's prenatal period (conception and pregnancy), perinatal period (actual delivery and birth), postnatal period (the newborn's first weeks of life), and infancy through early childhood, including the attainment of key development milestones. The importance of obtaining information of this kind is summarized as follows:

- It necessitates contact with the child's parents and primary caretakers early in the assessment process, thereby actively involving them in helping their child and establishing their role as important members of the multidisciplinary team.
- It presents a developmental and medical history of the child which may provide background clues and shed light on current functioning and developmental status.
- It guides preschool evaluators in selecting appropriate test instruments and measures for the current assessment.

- It provides a broader and more meaningful context in which to interpret the results obtained from testing.
- It guides the formulation of recommendations and action plans for the child later in the assessment process.

APPENDIX 7A

Checklist for the Accomplishment of Early Developmental Milestones*

Child _____ DOB _____ Age _____ Sex _____

Primary Language _____ Other Language(s) _____ Ethnicity/Race _____

Any existing condition or disability _____

Interviewer _____ Date and Place of Interview _____

Respondent(s) _____ Relationship to Child _____

Directions: Check only those skills child has mastered and the age at which he or she did so.

		0–3 mo.	4–6 mo.	7–12 mo.	13–18 mo.	19–24 mo.	2–3 yr.	3–4 yr.	4–5 yr.	Cannot say
I.	***Feeding and Eating***									
1.	Weaning: Breast									
	Bottle									
2.	Eating solid foods									
3.	Using fingers to feed self									
4.	Using a spoon; fork									
5.	Drinking from a cup									
6.	Getting food for self (helpings, snacks)									

Any early problems related to feeding and eating, appetite, or certain foods?

II.	***Sleeping***									
7.	Sleeping all night									
8.	Sleeping in a bed (not a crib)									
9.	Predictable length of sleep									

Any early problems related to sleeping?

_____ Nightmares   _____ Restlessness   _____ Rocking

_____ Sleepwalking   _____ Heavy sleep   _____ Others

*Designed by Joanne Kalesnik. May be reproduced without permission.

	0–3 mo.	4–6 mo.	7–12 mo.	13–18 mo.	19–24 mo.	2–3 yr.	3–4 yr.	4–5 yr.	Cannot say

III. *Gross and Fine Motor*

	0–3 mo.	4–6 mo.	7–12 mo.	13–18 mo.	19–24 mo.	2–3 yr.	3–4 yr.	4–5 yr.	Cannot say
10. Rolling over by self									
11. Sitting up without help									
12. Crawling									
13. Walking without help									
14. Walking up stairs by self									
15. Riding a tricycle (three-wheeler)									
16. Catching a big ball (e.g., beach ball)									
17. Throwing a big ball									
18. Cutting with knife (e.g., food, play-dough)									
19. Running									
20. Balancing (e.g., walking a curbing)									
21. Gripping a crayon or pencil to draw									

Any early problems related to the motor areas?

_____ Frequent falling _____ Lack of balance

_____ Weak grip _____ Hand tremors _____ Others

IV. *Toileting*

22. Fully bladder trained									
23. Fully bowel trained									

Any early problems related to toileting?

V. *Speech and Language*

24. Babbling at people or to noises									
25. Speaking first words (e.g., Mama; Dada; wawa)									
26. Putting words together (e.g., me cookie; me go)									
27. Speaking two- or three-word sentences									
28. Speaking clearly so strangers understand									
29. Finding the right words for things									

Any early problems related to speech and language?

(continued)

APPENDIX 7A   Continued

	0–3 mo.	4–6 mo.	7–12 mo.	13–18 mo.	19–24 mo.	2–3 yr.	3–4 yr.	4–5 yr.	Cannot say
VI. *Dressing*									
30. Putting on pants									
31. Putting on shirt									
32. Putting on socks; shoes									
33. Knowing left from right									
34. Doing snaps									
35. Buttoning									
36. Zippering									
37. Tying shoelaces									
38. Picking out own clothes									

Any early problems related to dressing?

VII.   *Social Interaction and Communication*

39. Showing an interest in others									
40. Playing with other children									
41. Playing with adults and older people									
42. Sharing									
43. Getting points of view across									
44. Following the rules of a game									
45. Letting others know about wants and needs									

Any early problems related to social interaction and communication?

Additional Information:

A.   *Child's early temperament or disposition:*

_____ Calm, quiet, reserved   _____ Overactive, "antsy"   _____ Irritable, colicky

_____ Moody   _____ Happy, carefree   _____ Nervous, anxious

Was anyone concerned about child's early temperament or disposition? If so, why?

B.   *Child's early style of expressing feelings:*

_____ Held them inside   _____ Cried a lot   _____ Acted them out

_____ Talked about them   _____ Had temper tantrums

Was anyone concerned about child's early style of expressing feelings? If so, why?

C. *Child's early contacts outside the home:*

—In the neighborhood (with playmates, babysitters, etc.)

—Within the extended family (e.g., with aunts, uncles, cousins, grandparents)

—Day care or nursery school

—Supervised and structured playgroups

—Early intervention programs

—Medical treatment centers or programs

Ask Respondent(s):

"Do you feel [this child] learned all of these skills we've been talking about in a normal or typical manner?" If not, "Why? What was different about the way he/she learned them?"

"Have you been concerned about [this child's] development?" If yes, "Why and in what ways?"

APPENDIX 7 B

Intake Form for a Medical History*

Child _____ DOB _____ Age _____ Sex _____

Primary Language _____ Other Language(s) _____ Ethnicity/Race _____

Any Existing Condition or Disability _____

Interviewer _____ Date and Place of Interview _____

Respondent(s) _____ Relationship to Child _____

Are any medical records available on this child that would be helpful to the current assessment?

I. *Prenatal Period (Pregnancy)*	Yes	No	Cannot Say	Comments
1. Mother had a viral infection (specify)				
2. Mother had an illness (specify)				
3. Mother had toxemia				
4. Mother had bleeding (specify degree and frequency)				
5. Mother smoked (specify how much)				
6. Mother drank alcoholic beverages				
7. Mother took some kind of drug or medication (specify)				
8. Mother's nutritional state was generally good				
9. Mother was under a lot of physical stress				
10. Mother was under a lot of emotional stress				

(continued)

*Designed by Joanne Kalesnik. May be reproduced without permission.

APPENDIX 7B   Continued

	Yes	No	Cannot Say	Comments
I. *Prenatal Period (Pregnancy)*				
11. The pregnancy was planned				
12. The pregnancy lasted 9 months (if not, then specify)				
13. The pregnancy was a hard one				
14. The pregnancy was mother's first (if not, specify others)				
15. The pregnancy was preceded by a miscarriage(s)				
16. There is a disease which runs in the family (specify)				
17. There is some condition which runs in the family (specify)				
II. *Perinatal Period (Delivery and Birth)*				
18. The labor and delivery were hard				
19. The labor lasted how long (specify)				
20. Labor was induced				
21. Mother was given medication for the delivery				
22. Mother was given anesthesia for the delivery				
23. Forceps were used				
24. Baby was breach				
25. A Caesarean section (C-section) was done				
26. Family were present during the labor and delivery				
27. How did family participate if present?				
28. Baby was premature (specify by how much)				
29. Baby weighed less than 5 pounds at birth (specify birth weight)				
30. Baby had breathing problems				
31. Baby had hypoxia (oxygen deprivation)				
32. Baby had asphyxia (unconsciousness due to lack of oxygen)				
33. Baby was jaundiced (yellow)				
34. Baby had cyanosis (was blue)				
35. Baby had a seizure				
36. Baby vomited right after being born				
37. Baby had diarrhea right after being born				
38. Baby was injured during the delivery (specify)				
39. Baby was born with an infection				
40. Baby was born with an illness				
41. Baby was born with a drug addiction				
42. Medications had to be given to baby just after birth				

III. *Postnatal Period (Following the Birth)*	Yes	No	Cannot Say	Comments
43. Baby needed an incubator (specify for how long)				
44. Baby was put on a respirator or ventilator				
45. Baby had a seizure(s)				
46. Baby vomited several times				
47. Baby often had diarrhea				
48. Medications had to be given to baby (specify)				
49. Baby had anemia (red blood cell deficiency)				
50. Baby had Rh incompatibility				
51. Baby needed blood transfusions				
52. Baby had surgery or special procedure performed (specify)				
53. A heart defect was found				
54. A heart murmur was detected				
55. Baby had an allergy (specify)				
56. Baby was addicted to a drug				
57. Baby developed a viral infection				
58. Baby developed a bacterial infection				
59. Baby developed a fungal infection				
60. Baby was diagnosed with a disease (specify)				
61. Baby was diagnosed with a condition (specify)				
62. Baby was fed intravenously				
63. Baby was nursed by mother or fed mother's milk				
64. Baby was nursed by a bottle with formula				
65. Mother was healthy following the delivery				
66. Mother developed complications following the delivery				
67. Baby received Apgar screening (specify scores)				
68. Baby received BNBAS screening (specify scores)				
69. Baby was separated from mother because of adoption				
70. Baby was transported to another hospital after being born				

IV. *Infancy and Early Childhood*				
71. Child has been weaned (specify when)				
72. Child had colic as an infant				
73. Child had and/or now has a good appetite				
74. Child's weight gains have been in the normal range				

(continued)

APPENDIX 7B   Continued

IV. *Infancy and Early Childhood*

	Yes	No	Cannot Say	Comments
75. Child's height gains have been in the normal range				
76. Child has had a lot of ear infections (otitis media)				
77. Child has had tubes put in his/her ears because of fluid				
78. Child had high fever(s) as an infant				
79. Child has had pneumonia (specify when and how many times)				
80. Child has had seizures, fits, or spells (clarify)				
81. Child has had a concussion				
82. Child has had some other type of head injury (specify)				
83. Child once took a blow to the head but later seemed O.K.				
84. Child once fainted momentarily after a head injury				
85. Child is prone to getting headaches				
87. Child tends to be moody, have mood swings				
88. Child is overly sensitive, cries easily, gets upset easily				
89. Child had or does have problems seeing				
90. Child has had an eye infection like pink-eye				
91. Vision problems run in the family				
92. Child had or does have problems hearing				
93. Hearing problems run in the family				
94. Child has asthma				
95. Child has an allergy (specify)				
96. Child used to, or still does, get rashes easily				
97. Child had or has kidney problems				
98. Child had or has heart problems				
99. Child has a low energy level, is lethargic				
100. Child has a high energy level, is overactive				
101. Child has been poisoned before (clarify)				
102. Child has had an overdose of some substance (specify)				
103. Child has been treated for dehydration in the past				
104. Child has been treated for malnourishment in the past				
105. Child has had a serious illness (e.g., meningitis)				
106. Child has had a serious injury (specify)				

IV. *Infancy and Early Childhood*	Yes	No	Cannot Say	Comments
107. Child has been hospitalized since infancy (specify)				
108. Child has had surgery since infancy (specify)				
109. Child has taken a medication over a long period of time (specify)				
110. Child has had a broken bone (specify)				

Ask Respondent(s):

"Whom might we contact for further medical information related to [this child]?"

"Will you sign a release (or consent form) which would permit us to contact this person/agency?"

"May we have access to the child's medical records which you mentioned earlier?"

"Is there anything that wasn't covered in this interview that you would like to add?"

8 Family Assessment

JOANNE KALESNIK

The focus of this chapter is the family system in which the child is embedded. Family systems typically consist of parents and siblings, but can also include other primary caretakers such as relatives, nannies, foster parents, neighbors, and government agencies such as Child Welfare. In keeping with an ecological model in which the family provides a context for human development (Bronfenbrenner, 1986; see Chapter 1 of this text), it is important to consider how the child who is referred for assessment both influences and is influenced by the family system in which he or she resides, and how family systems operate in relation to the child's development and functioning.

When children are referred for preschool assessment, they differ significantly not only in regard to their developmental histories, but also in relation to the uniqueness of their family systems. Families vary considerably across different structural dimensions. For example, level of parent education, parent age, gay and lesbian or heterosexual parents, family size, socioeconomic status (SES), area of residence (rural versus urban), family composition, marital and sibling subsystem functioning, family stressors, sources of both internal and outside support, style of responding to stress, and areas of strength as well as need.

In this chapter, each of these family dimensions will be addressed regarding its relevance to the individual child. It is important not to clinically analyze families in order to identify their levels of dysfunction and shortcomings. Rather, the goal in conducting a "Family Assessment" related to preschool children is to determine what the strengths and needs of the family are in order to recognize how they impact the child and which type of recommendations can be made to impact them in positive and helpful manners.

Rationale for Family Assessment

Educational institutions have long recognized the importance of the family as a primary learning environment and socializing agent for young children. The impact of a caregiving environment on child outcome along dimensions such as physical growth, health, cognitive development, and social-emotional functioning has been well researched in the past century (e.g., Bowlby, 1951; Chapin, 1915; Hunt, 1961; Sameroff, 1986; Spitz, 1946; Zeanah, 1993). A Committee Report (U.S. House of Representatives, 1986) pertaining to the development of Public Law 99-457 cited the family as the primary learning environment for infants and young children. It stated that a critical need existed for parents and professionals to function in a collaborative fashion. An intent to actively involve parents and families in childhood intervention programs and provide them with information and support led to the inclusion of Section 677, Part H, under Title I of the law. These provisions are now included in Part C of P.L. 105-17 (1997) and require that an Individualized Family Service Plan (IFSP) be developed for the families of all children with handicaps or at-risk conditions, from birth to age 3.

Although the IFSP requirement does not exist under Part B for the 3- to 5-year-old populations, it is the spirit of the law to foster a family focus in all preschool intervention efforts and programs. This position of fostering a family focus with 3- to 5-year-olds was further emphasized in Public Law 102-119, the amendments to Public Law 94-142 (IDEA) which were passed by Congress in 1991 and re-authorized as P.L. 105-17 in 1997. The family focus requirement formalizes, makes more systematic, and provides structure to a process that typically already occurs between most families and the early intervention programs which serve their children. It calls for "a statement of the family's strengths and needs relating to enhancing the development of the family's handicapped infant or toddler" (P.L. 105-17, Part C). Information pertaining to the identified strengths and needs is later used to specify family goals and services. Whereas this chapter concerns itself primarily with conducting a family assessment, the actual development of family service plans is addressed in Chapter 22.

Although preschool programs are not bound by law to formulate IFSPs, many follow the basic premise and ideology which the IFSP represents. That is, to foster a family focus when working with the individual child. Families with a child with special needs who are seeking services must continually expose themselves to the scrutiny of professionals. Thus, professionals should be sensitive about preserving the family's privacy to the greatest degree possible.

While gathering information related to the child's family system, issues might be disclosed or discovered which indicate that the family is experiencing significant difficulties of adjustment or stress that warrant professional help because they extend beyond the boundary of the parent–professional partnership or the level of training held by the preschool staff. In these instances, a referral could be made for assessment by a marriage and family therapist, clinical psychologist, child psychiatrist, or appropriate outside agency. Preschool programs should structure interagency partnerships that connect children and families with a full range of comprehensive services (Melaville & Blank, 1991). Parent or family counseling services provided through outside sources can certainly be recommended and also written directly into the family's service plan, when appropriate.

Gathering Family Assessment Information

The process by which family assessment information is obtained is critical. It is through this process of interaction that the relationship between the entire family system and the system providing services to the child begins to take form and be established. The more smoothly this process goes, the greater the depth of meaningful information that can be shared by both parties, not only during this first stage of interaction, but in all future interactions and service delivery. Further, such a process shifts the focus away from the individual child and places it on the broader context of a multitude of family variables which impact the child in a reciprocal fashion. General guidelines for gathering family assessment information are as follows:

- Set an appointment time that is convenient for the family and allows as many family members to be present as possible. Decide if the meeting will take place within the family's home setting or within the preschool assessment center. Be aware that family members may behave differently depending on the setting in which the session takes place.
- If necessary, arrange for an interpreter who speaks the family's primary language and specific dialect.
- Work on establishing rapport with families through small-talk and introductions. Some families may require more of this than others, for example, depending on their particular interaction style when familiarizing themselves with an outsider. Some families prefer physical contact such as a handshake or light touch, whereas others view lack of contact as a sign of respect. The same can be true of eye contact. Be sensitive to these issues as rapport is being established and follow the family's lead in terms of defining a comfort zone. Always allow time to place the family at ease.
- Have a conversation with the family rather than an interview. Allow the family to do most of the talking. Ask open-ended questions and encourage the expression of different viewpoints, when appropriate.
- If this is the family's first contact with the system that will be providing services to their child, avoid using professional jargon and terms that might be intimidating because they do not understand them. If terms are used, such as "IEP," explain fully and clearly to families what they mean.

© *National Association of School Psychologists.*
Reprinted by permission of the publisher.

- Be sensitive to parent level of education and language proficiency and adjust your approach accordingly—for example, how questions are phrased, the use of concrete and simple examples to illustrate concepts, and the pace at which questions are asked as the session proceeds.
- Clarify your role to the family and explain the rationale for gathering information related to their family system. Convey the notion that you are working to form a partnership with them so that, together, ideas can be generated that will help them to help their child.
- Maintain cross-cultural sensitivity and awareness. If you have limited information or experience with the family's culture and language, explain this to them and ask for their help in increasing your knowledge and understanding.
- Begin to build trust. For example, a family who has experienced prior involvement with Child Protective Services may be reluctant to share information or may fear that the information they do share could result in their child being removed from their home. Another family might be hesitant to open up if they feel that the professional is in charge or is in a one-up and expert position, thus making them feel somewhat inferior and intimidated by the process. Gay and lesbian parents will want to know how you respect parents of their sexual orientation.
- Respect the family's right to privacy and discuss with them issues related to confidentiality. Be sensitive about later placing delicate information into written reports which the family wishes to remain private and off-the-record. If the session is being videotaped, be sure that parents have signed the appropriate permission forms and have been informed about how the videotape will later be used, who will have access to viewing it, and how it will be stored or destroyed.
- Maintain healthy boundaries on interaction during the information gathering process. For example, do not be overly intrusive in reaction to a family who is distancing or is hesitant about sharing. Conversely, assure that the family does not become overly involved in the process, thereby turning it into a therapy session and sharing more information than is actually necessary or appropriate.
- Determine the family's perception of the identified child from their own perspective. For example, their beliefs about the child's handicapping condition and its source; their level of acceptance or denial about what is going on.
- Familiarize yourself with all aspects of the family structure including family composition, socioeconomic status, area of residence, family roles and responsibilities, stressors, and support systems. These are described later in this chapter.
- Observe family interaction patterns and style of relating while the session is being conducted and in specific relation to different topics of conversation. For example, does anxiety level or distractibility appear to increase when issues related to the child's handicapping condition are discussed? Do the children begin to exhibit behavior problems when the parents talk of their marital discord? Does one family member seem to be in charge of disseminating information and controlling the conversation?
- Conduct a survey of family strengths and needs using informal methods such as a self-designed questionnaire and/or formal instruments such as the "Family Needs Survey" or the "Family Resource Scale" which are described later in this chapter. Listen carefully in order to more accurately identify what the family is saying it needs.
- Observe needs which the family has, but did not identify for themselves when surveyed. For example, during the interview process, were parents able to place limits on the children's behavior and discipline them in an appropriate manner? Did a family

member break down and weep or describe chronic feelings of depression and despair? Did the adults have realistic expectations and basic knowledge related to child development issues? Were any issues related to attachment and bonding observed (such as lack of attachment or over-attachment)?

■ Place closure on the information gathering process by reviewing with the family the information obtained, the rationale for obtaining it, and how it will be used to formulate recommendations and design child interventions and family service plans.

Working with Nontraditional, Ethnic, and Culturally Diverse Families

There is a significant need for preschool interventionists to further develop their skills in working with nontraditional, ethnic, and culturally diverse families. The process of gathering family assessment information necessitates entry into a family's sphere and manner of functioning, which may not always be consistent with that of the practitioner. For example, family behaviors which are culture-specific could be wrongly interpreted as being atypical by the practitioner who lacks awareness of this kind. The potential for cultural, ethnic, gender, sexual orientation, and social class bias may increase when families and the professionals who serve them vary across these dimensions. The following demographics and family characteristics have been on the rise throughout the 1990s and are predicted to continue growing into the twenty-first century:

■ By the year 2000, it is estimated that almost 40% of the U.S. population under the age of eighteen will be non-Anglo whites and nonwhites (Research and Policy Committee, Committee for Economic Development, 1987).

■ The percentage of traditional nuclear families in the United States is decreasing while the percentage of nontraditional families, including single parents, step-parents, adoptive parents, grandparents, foster parents, and same-sex parents is increasing (Copeland & White, 1991; Flannagan & Miranda, 1994).

■ The average number of births per woman in the United States is decreasing among whites while increasing among other ethnic groups (Hanson & Lynch, 1992).

■ The rate of births to African American females under the age of 15 has been steadily increasing since 1983, and over 40% of African American females under the age of 19 become pregnant at least once (Osofsky, Hann, & Peebles, 1993).

■ Each year, the number of young children residing in households with incomes below the poverty line increases; almost two-thirds of these poor children live in mother-only families, while over two-thirds live in families supported by welfare (Halpern, 1993).

■ There has been a trend of increased immigration of non-Europeans to the United States in recent years (Huang & Gibbs, 1992).

As non-white, nontraditional, non-European immigrant, same-sex, and poor families have continued to increase and expand within the U.S. population, training programs in early childhood intervention which include students and parents of differing cultural, sexual orientation, ethnic, lower socioeconomic, and diverse language backgrounds have not (Hanson, 1992). By the year 2000, professionals providing services to these children and their families are predicted to be predominantly white, English-speaking Anglos (Flannagan & Miranda, 1994; Hanson, 1992). Developing cross-cultural competence does not happen overnight and practitioners cannot expect to know everything there is to know about every culture, ethnicity, and race (Flannagan & Miranda, 1994). When forming working partnerships with culturally diverse families, the key is to remain sensitive, aware, and responsive. General issues that should be taken under consideration include cultural characteristics, cultural patterns, languages, values, beliefs, attitudes, behaviors, and, in cases of immigrant families, level of acculturation. For example, when a family immigrates to the United States, it is not uncommon for the children to learn their new language and social roles more quickly than the parents and grandparents. This difference in rate of adjustment can create a certain degree of tension within the family, disrupting its traditional structure and hierarchy (Huang & Gibbs, 1992; Lynch & Hanson, 1992). Thus, sensitivity and awareness must be given to how all family members are reacting and adjusting to the new dominant culture and what level of acculturation each has achieved (Nuttall, DeLeon, & Valle, 1990).

In regard to cultural patterns, when meeting with an entire family to gather essential family information, it would not be uncommon in the case of an Asian American family for the father to present as the main speaker and conveyer of information even though, privately, the mother may actually be the key decision maker (Huang & Gibbs, 1992: Tseng & Hsu, 1991). In working with African American (Allen & Boykin, 1992; Frisby, 1992) and Latino (Garcia-Preto, 1982; Nuttall et al., 1990) families, it would not be uncommon to see a network of kinship links operating in relation to the child. That is, strong ties existing with extended family members such as grandparents, aunts, and uncles, all of whom may be actively involved in the family's matters and in caring for the child. Thus, maintaining an ethnic- and culture-oriented perspective of family systems is important to the information gathering process.

Types of Family Assessment Information

Preschool interventionists gather family assessment information to acquaint themselves with the child's family system so that, later, meaningful recommendations can be made and service plans written. The type of information that should be obtained for this purpose falls under the broad category of family structure. In regard to family structure, two levels can be conceptualized as existing. The first, family dynamics, is related to issues internal to the family—the emotional and psychological factors and primary relationships which circulate among, and impact the development and behaviors of each family member within the closed "nest" of the system. The second level is related to influences which are external to the family: economic, political, legal, educational, and sociocultural factors that bear down upon and exert their impact onto the family system. Each level of family structure—the internal and the external—is important to consider because of the significant role it plays in delineating a family's identity and thus, that of the child.

In regard to family structure, there are six basic elements to consider: family composition, socioeconomic status (SES), area of residence, family roles and responsibilities, stressors, and sources of support.

Family Composition

One element of family structure is who the members are, whether they are blood-relations or not, and what characteristics define them. Information related to family composition also identifies and then fully describes the specific caregivers forming the immediate reality in which the child exists. With increasing numbers of children coming from homes of divorced parents, some of whom then re-marry to create blended family situations, the task of describing "family members" may at times become complex. Typically, family composition includes a description of the parent(s) and sibling(s) who are blood relatives and/or with whom the child either resides or has visitation or frequent contact. In some cases, family composition might require multiple listings or dual home settings, and may include non-blood relations. Often included in this description are birth parents, adoptive or foster parents, step-parents, half- and step-brothers and sisters, and others who are living in the home such as boyfriends/girlfriends of the parent(s), extended family members such as grandparents or other relatives, and other adults who are in the role of primary caretaker of the child, such as a live-in nanny.

After a listing of this type is made, the characteristics of each of these persons is then further described, including their age, level of education, occupation, employment status, and other information that might be pertinent. For example, a parent or other family member who has a chronic illness, an impairment of some type (visual, hearing, physical), a level of mental retardation, drug, alcohol, or sexual addiction, mental illness, incarceration, or other special circumstance, such as a genetic or inherited disorder, which merits mentioning because of its special relevance to the child who is undergoing assessment. Components of family composition also include the child's birth order, family size (family-of-origin as well as secondary blended families), a delineation of the marital and sibling subsystems, languages spoken in the home (and by whom), and the child's cultural and ethnic identification.

Socioeconomic Status (SES)

Another element of a family's structure is its socioeconomic status (SES), which tends to correlate with variables such as parent age, parent level of education, family size, and area of residence (Case Foundation, 1992). As social class varies, so does the range of opportunities, the kind of choices, and the degree of challenges which are presented to children and their families (Bronfrenbrenner, 1991). Information pertaining to SES should be included in the description of a family for a variety of reasons. First, membership in a particular social class can have a profound impact on every variable that influences an individual's developmental accomplishments and well being (Johnson, Sum, & Weill, 1992). The literature is replete with research showing the devastating effects that poverty can have on families and children across several dimensions of functioning: social, emotional, behavioral, cognitive, educational, and physical (Klerman, 1991; National Center for Children in Poverty, 1990).

Second, information related to SES provides an indication of the resources, financial and otherwise, available to the family, the degree and manner in which they are utilizing them, and, in some cases, their eligibility to receive additional government support or assistance. Third, research on prenatal risk factors has shown that socioeconomic factors can be more important in predicting child outcome than early birth complications. For example, infants with problems at birth who show learning deficits in later years are more likely to be low-SES children whose life difficulties and home environments exacerbate their constitutional delays (Halpern, 1993). In middle-class samples, such continuity in problems from birth to the preschool age is seen to a lesser degree, most likely because the opportunities and richness of the home environment help to override the earlier problems (Hamburg, 1992; Schakel, 1986).

Because SES is often linked to level of parent education, higher-income parents can not only afford to provide more for their children, but also tend to have greater knowledge related to the availability and importance of early childhood services and how to access them compared to lower-SES, less educated parents (Mercer, 1990; Musick, 1993). Further, more educated, older, and higher-income parents tend to demonstrate a greater understanding of issues related to child development compared to parents with limited education and those who are younger or in the lower socioeconomic strata (Loan, 1992; McDonough, 1993; Provence & Naylor, 1983).

Area of Residence

Where a family lives is yet another element of its structure. Area of residence refers not only to type of dwelling or lack thereof (e.g., homelessness) in urban versus rural locations, but also to geographical locations within a country. The importance of being sensitive about this type of information is primarily related to two issues. First, where children live can play a role in the amount, type, and quality of early intervention services they receive, their parents' ability to access services, and the center's ability to access the family.

Children live within the context of their families and families exist within the context of the outer world (Winnicott, 1987). Thus, a second issue related to area of residence involves neighborhood and community variables such as the presence or nonpresence of crime, violence, gangs, drugs, overcrowding, incidence of teenage pregnancy, school dropout rates, employment opportunities, cost of living, and concentration of ethnic and minority groups, including race relations (e.g., see Jencks & Peterson, 1991). These sociocultural variables can exist as sources of stress outside of a family or be embedded within both its internal and external structures.

Family Roles and Responsibilities

Another element of family structure is related to the type of roles family members assume or are assigned pertaining to responsibilities and decision making. Information of this kind is relevant to understanding how the family functions in different situations. For example, who assumes the role of primary caretaker; who makes, and has made, critical decisions related to the child's development and needs; who decided to bring the child in for assessment and what was the level of agreement or support for such action; what are the expectations for child behavior; who is in charge of discipline; who handles the finances and is the breadwinner; and so on.

Families having a child with a handicapping condition are more vulnerable to experiencing role confusion and a disruption in roles than are families having no handicapped members (Brown, Goodman, & Kupper, 1993; Waterman, 1976). The roles that siblings assume in relation to the child with the handicap are equal in importance to parent roles, as siblings influence and shape behavior through interaction, modeling, and teaching. Processes of influence operate in a reciprocal fashion, in that the child with the handicap also shapes the behavior of his or her siblings and parents. Because the adaptation of siblings of children with handicapping conditions may not always be smooth or favorable, it is important to examine siblings' roles in order to promote their functioning as family members (Bailey & Simeonsson, 1988; Klein & Schleifer, 1993; NICHCY, 1991; Powell & Gallagher, 1993).

One technique for accessing information related to family roles is to ask members for a term or phrase that describes themselves within the family. In the case of infants and very young children, older family members can provide the response. Such a process provides an indication of the roles family members perceive themselves to be playing, how satisfied they feel, and whether they experience the role positively or negatively. It provides a sense of how responsibilities are divided among family members and who participates in decision making. It also allows for the observation of reactions to determine whether a unified impression or consensus exists among family members.

Stressors

Stressors are another element of family structure. Stressors are usually linked to events, such as the birth of a child with a handicapping condition, or to circumstances, such as living in poverty or isolated locations. There can be single stressors, or multiple stressors occurring simultaneously. Stressors can exist within the family, outside of it, be short-term in duration, or be chronic. Other elements of family structure already discussed in this chapter can exist as "stressors" in and of themselves. For example, characteristics of the family composition might include single mothers, same-sex parents, absent fathers, teenage parents (Werner & Smith, 1992); situations of divorce (Wallerstein, 1991) or custody battles (Hart, 1991); as well as voluntary abandonment of children (e.g., to the grandparents), legalized adoptions, or state findings of parental unfitness stemming from child abuse and neglect (Horner & Guyer, 1993). Families with a child who has special needs tend to have higher incidence of marital separation and divorce, stressors which can increase levels of tension and emotional distress for all members (Gallagher, 1990).

Existing within the family composition might be substance abuse, alcoholism, mental illness, or low level of parental education (Barnard, Morisset, & Spieker, 1993). The child with handicaps who is referred for preschool assessment may represent yet another stressor within the family system, particularly on an emotional level (Brown, Goodman, & Kupper, 1993; McAnaney, 1992; Smith, 1993). Depletion of financial resources, financial instability, homophobia and racism, lower socioeconomic status, and living on welfare can all be stressful situations for families (Simpson, 1990; Zill, Moore, Smith, Stief, & Coiro, 1991), as can factors related to a family's area of residence, including isolation in rural locales, high crime rates, homelessness, inadequate shelter, and overcrowding.

Dissatisfaction with family roles can create stress both within and among family members. Additional stressors may come from families being overburdened with responsibilities related to their child with a handicapping condition. In the face of single or multiple stressors, a final source of additional stress might derive from a lack of adequate support systems or the family's inability to effectively utilize sources of support which are available to them (Turnbull & Turnbull, 1991).

When gathering family assessment information pertaining to the type and degree of stressors a family is experiencing, preschool practitioners do not have to transform into the role of marriage and family therapist, clinical psychologist, or specialist in mental health interventions. However, preschool practitioners should remain sensitive to these kinds of issues and establish partnerships with outside agencies and community resources so that, when necessary, families who are overwhelmed by significant psychological stressors can be referred for the additional services they might need.

Sources of Support

The amount and type of support systems available to a family comprise a final element of its structure. Sources of support can exist both within (intrafamilial) and outside of the family (extrafamilial) and play a key role in how stressors are responded to and managed. Intrafamililal sources of support include the family's inner strengths, coping mechanisms, level of emotional cohesiveness, religious beliefs, spirituality, and ability to manage stress. In this category can also be included available financial resources, level of education, and other assets which the family can internally draw upon to function. Extrafamilial sources of support are external to the family and include relatives, kinship links, a social network of friends and neighbors, employers, church affiliations, charitable organizations, systems existing within the community such as schools, hospitals, or counseling centers, and public assistance programs such as welfare and Medicaid. When a child is referred for preschool assessment, the system providing the service becomes an external source of support and resources for the family.

Research has consistently shown that factors that influence a family's adjustment to having a child with a handicapping condition include not only the severity of the child's handicap, but also the support systems active within the family and those existing external to it (Dunst, Trivette, & Thompson, 1991; Schell, 1981; Turnbull, Patterson, Behr, Murphy, Marquis, & Blue-Banning, 1993). Understanding the support structures which a family utilizes is important to understanding how they cope and adjust in relation to their child's special needs and the associated stressors (Dunst & Trivette, 1990). When family assessment information is obtained, it is also relevant to note whether the family is drawing primarily upon its intrafamilial or extrafamilial resources. For example, some families rely heavily upon their own internal support structures, whereas others tip the scale in the opposite direction. When the balance of resources is weighted too heavily in one direction, recommendations can be made which help the family to achieve greater balance.

Conducting a Survey of Family Strengths and Needs

Once information related to the six different elements of family structure has been gathered, a survey of family strengths and needs can be conducted as it relates to enhancing the development of the referred child. Although the process of gathering information related to the element of family structure has been presented separately from this section pertaining to conducting a survey of family strengths and needs, the two typically occur simultaneously when a family intake session is conducted. The more experienced a preschool practitioner becomes with gathering family assessment information, the easier it becomes to weave together structure and survey information while the session is proceeding.

The ultimate goal of conducting a survey is to determine what the family needs in relation to their referred child. This stems from what they state their needs to be, as well as from the practitioner's professional insights about needs which the family has, but may be unaware of or fail to identify for themselves. For example, a teenage, single mother may identify a primary need for "respite care," that is, time away from her child. However, a skilled practitioner may identify that she also needs more information related to child development and appropriate discipline techniques. Another family may qualify for government benefits under a special program, yet be unaware that such financial resources even exist. Research has shown (e.g., Achenbach, Howell, Quay, & Conners, 1991) that parental perception of child behaviors and family circumstances may not always be consistent with what is actually going on. Thus, the preschool interventionist should strive to carefully blend what the family states its needs to be, with other needs it might have so that, together, a unified whole is created reflecting "total identified needs."

All families have strengths and resources. A second goal of conducting a survey is to explore and elicit strengths within families, even when stressful circumstances prevail. A family's internal strengths and coping strategies are affected by their external supports and resources and the degree to which they are utilizing them effectively.

Informal Methods

When conducting a survey of family strengths and needs, informal approaches such as family interviews and locally developed, self-designed questionnaires are commonly used, particularly because of the low availability of formal instruments that have been designed especially for the preschool population. Informal approaches can prove helpful in working with nontraditional, ethnic, and culturally diverse families for a couple of reasons. First, the majority of formal instruments which are available have been developed in relation to predominantly mainstream populations. Therefore, they tend to reflect somewhat narrow views with respect to differing value and belief structures. Second, if minority groups are under-represented in the standardization samples, the content of formal instruments may not be appropriate for identifying family strengths and needs within cultural and ethnic contexts. With formal instruments, there may not be enough compatibility between the design of the instrument and the family's belief system and goals for their child (Westby, 1986).

If the method chosen is an informal one, such as interviewing parents and other family members, the data collection process should have structure and focus to insure that all relevant information is collected, the major topics are touched upon, the interview proceeds with clear direction, and is conducted in a timely manner.

Formal Instruments

Preschool programs might choose formal instruments to conduct a survey of parent and family needs if a structured format is preferred or required. Table 8.1 presents instruments that are commercially available.

Summary

This chapter presented one component of the preschool evaluation process, that of gathering family assessment information. This information source focuses not just on the single child, but on the family system in which the child is embedded. The rationale for obtaining information related to a child's family is two-fold. First, it helps to frame the child in a broader sphere and more meaningful context of primary relationships and reciprocal forces of influence. Second, it allows for the identification of the family's strengths and needs so that appropriate recommendations can be made and intervention plans formulated. Obtaining family assessment information necessitates contact with the child's caregivers, thereby involving them, empowering them, and enabling them to contribute and become active participants in helping their child.

TABLE 8.1 **Instruments for Conducting a Survey of Parent and Family Needs**

Family Resource Scale (Dunst & Leet, 1987)	A 30-item scale designed to identify a family's needs for social support and resources. Subscales included Food and Shelter, Financial Resources, Time for Family, Child Care, Extrafamilial Support, Special Child Resources, and Luxuries. Ratings are made on a scale from "not at all adequate" to "almost always adequate." Overall reliability of the scale has been found to be .92; split-half reliability .95; and test–retest .52. Relationship of the scale to other measures have been found to be moderate (.57 with a measure of personal and well-being; .63 with a measure of commitment to intervention).
Family Support Scale (Dunst, Jenkins, & Trivette, 1984)	An 18-item rating scale designed to identify parents' perceptions of how help-ful various supports are in raising young children. Ratings are made on a scale from "not at all helpful" to "extremely helpful." Two indices of support are obtained from responses: how many sources of support parents feel they have; and a "helpfulness" index, which indicates how helpful they feel such sup-ports are to them. Subcategories of available sources of support include: for-mal and informal kinship; social organizations; the family; and professional services, either specialized or generic. Overall reliability of the scale has been found to be .85 for total scores; .75 split-half reliability; and .91 test–retest for total scores. The authors report significant correlations between this scale and subscales of personal and familial well-being from the Questionnaire on Resources and Stress (QRS; Holroyd, 1974).
Family Needs Survey (Bailey & Simeonsson, 1988)	A 35-item self-report measure designed to identify parents' needs in six dif-ferent areas: information; support from family, friends, other parents, or a minister; explaining about their child to others; community services; finan-cial; and family functioning. Responses are made on a scale from "definitely do not need help with this" to "definitely need help with this." Authors recom-mend that mothers and fathers complete the survey separately. (Reliability and validity data are not available.)
Family Information Preference Inventory (Turnbull & Turnbull, 1986)	A 37-item self-report measure in which parents rate the extent to which they need or want information related to five different areas: teaching the child at home, advocacy and working with professionals, planning for the future, help-ing the family relax and enjoy life to a greater degree, and finding and using more support. Space is provided for parents to describe any additional needs they may have that are not listed in the instrument. Ratings are made on a scale from "no interest in this information" to "this information is of high pri-ority." Parents also indicate how they would prefer to have their need for information met by meeting with other parents, in an individual meeting, or through written materials. This inventory is designed for parents with children through the high school age, so some items will not be applicable and should be eliminated before it is given to parents. (Reliability and validity data are not available.)

(continued)

TABLE 8.1 Continued

Inventory of Parents' Experiences (Kirkham, Schilling, Norelius, & Schinke, 1986)	A 54-item questionnaire designed to identify the social supports available to a parent from professionals, the neighborhood and community, friends, and the personal/marital relationship. The parent indicates the number of contacts with individuals in each area and the degree of satisfaction with each area of support. This inventory is a modified version of the 45-item measure developed by Crnic and others (Crnic, Ragozin, Greenberg, & Robinson, 1981). (Reliability and validity data are not available.)
Parent Needs Inventory—Revised (Robinson & Derosa, 1980)	This instrument consists of three sets of 25 statements related to three different areas: the grief process, knowledge of child development, and knowledge of local resources. Parents complete the inventory individually by sorting the sets of statements according to what their present situation is and what their ideal situation would be for each area. The inventory is designed to be administered to parents by a professional. Fewel (1981) has modified it into a self-rating scale, which parents complete at their convenience. Reliability of items in relation to the entire inventory has been found to be .64 for grief, .83 for child development, and .87 for local resources. Test–retest reliability has been found to be moderate to poor: .64 for grief, .33 for child development, and .47 for local resources. Information pertaining to the validity of items is not available.

A P P E N D I X 8 A

Family Assessment Resources

Videotapes

Family Focused Interview, developed by the Frank Porter Graham Child Development Center as a training tape for professionals.

Finding the Balance and Listen With Respect, a set of tapes which comes with a training manual, "Culturally Responsive Services for Children and Families."

On This Journey Together, a series of parent support tapes for parents and the professionals working with them.

Parent/Professional Partnerships, instructional tape for both parents and professionals with suggestions on how to work together collaboratively.

Resources for Families, provides concrete suggestions to parents about the process of seeking resources.

Videotapes available from:

Child Health and Development Educational
   Media (CHADEM)
5632 Van Nuys Blvd., Suite 286
Van Nuys, CA 91401
Telephone: (818) 994-0933

Building a Family Partnership From Listening to Families, and *Exploring Family Strengths From Listening to Families.* Both tapes demonstrate how professionals can develop a collaborative partnership with families

of young children with special needs. Highlighted in the tapes are families from African American, Hispanic/Latina, and European-American backgrounds from all income levels.

Videotapes available from:

Listening to Families Project
AAMFT Foundation, Suite 901
1100 17th Street, NW
Washington, DC 20036
Telephone: (202) 467-5127

Resources for Parents and Families

Dickman, I. (1993). *One miracle at a time: Getting help for a child with a disability* (rev. ed.). New York: Simon & Schuster. Available from Simon & Schuster, 200 Old Tappan Road, Old Tappan, NJ 07675. Telephone: 1-800-223-2336.

Lawrence, K., Johnson, G., & Stepanek, J. (Eds.) (1994). *Parent resource directory* (5th ed.). Bethesda, MD: Association for the Care of Children's Health. Available from Association for the Care of Children's Health, 7910 Woodmont Avenue, Suite 300, Bethesda, MD 20814. Telephone: (301) 654-6549.

Miller, N. B. (1994). *Nobody's perfect: Living and growing with children who have special needs.* Baltimore, MD: Paul H. Brookes. Available from Paul H. Brookes, P.O. Box 10624, Baltimore, MD 21285-0624. Telephone: 1-800-638-3775.

National Information Center for Children and Youth with Disabilities (published yearly). *A parent's guide: Accessing Programs for infants, toddlers, and preschoolers with disabilities.* Available from The National Information Center for Children and Youth with Disabilities, P.O. Box 1492, Washington, DC 20013-1492. Telephone: 1-800-695-0285.

National Parent Network on Disabilities. National organization which provides services and information about disability issues to families. Contact National Parent Network on Disabilities, 1600 Prince Street, Suite 115, Alexandria, VA 22314. Telephone: (703) 684-6763.

NICHCY News Digest. A collection of articles written for parents and families by professionals and published three times a year. Available from The National Information Center for Children and Youth with Disabilities, P.O. Box 1492, Washington, DC 20013-1492. Telephone: 1-800-999-5599.

The Exceptional Parent. A magazine published monthly for parents and families with children with handicaps. Available from The Exceptional Parent, P.O. Box 3000, Denville, NJ 07834. Telephone: 1-800-562-1973.

Turnbull, A. P., Patterson, J. M., Behr, S. K., Murphy, D. L., Marquis, J. G., & Blue-Banning, M. J. (Eds.) (1993). *Cognitive coping, families, and disability.* Baltimore, MD: Paul H. Brookes. Available from Paul H. Brookes, P.O. Box 10624, Baltimore, MD 21285-0624. Telephone: 1-800-638-3775.

Turnbull, A. P., & Turnbull III, H. R. (1990). *Families, professionals, and exceptionality: A special partnership* (2nd ed.). Columbus, OH: Merrill Publishing.

9 Assessment of Social-Emotional Functioning and Adaptive Behavior

HOWARD M. KNOFF

STEPHANIE A. STOLLAR

JENNIFER J. JOHNSON

TIFFANY A. CHENNEVILLE

The assessment of social-emotional and adaptive behavior functioning is critical during the preschool years because many of these affective and skill-related areas form a foundation that guides and influences children's later functioning in home, school, and community domains. More specifically, ongoing assessment in these areas is able to identify children's age-appropriate development or their atypical development in one or a number of areas. From a social-emotional perspective, atypical development may involve anxiety disorders, attachment disorders, pervasive developmental disorders (see DSM-IV; American Psychiatric Association, 1994). From a behavioral or functional perspective, atypical development may involve skill deficits, performance deficits, or deficits of self-control or self-management (Elliott, Racine, & Bruce, 1995). In total, the assessment process attempts to integrate all of these perspectives while evaluating the child in an objective and ecological context. This context will be discussed briefly first because of its importance to accurate, effective assessment. Then, this chapter will move on to more specific information on direct observation, clinical interviews, behavior rating scales, behavioral observation approaches, projective techniques, and adaptive behavior scales.

Assumptions, Purposes, and Approaches of Social-Emotional Assessment with Preschool Children

Social-emotional assessment with preschool children is guided by five primary assumptions and four major purposes. The assumptions are critical both to the conceptualization and operationalization of the assessment process, and they are discussed in various forms throughout this book. Briefly, these assumptions reflect the need for (1) *ecological/ environmental assessment* such that children are assessed within the contexts of the family, school, and community systems where they have grown up and now live; (2) *multimethod, multisource, multisetting assessment* to increase reliability and validity of the evaluation process; (3) *a developmental context to assessment* such that all evaluations are completed in the context of typical and atypical child development; (4) *a problem-solving and hypothesis testing approach to assessment* such that interventions are linked to assessments and are conducted only after the reasons why a referred problem is occurring has been empirically validated; and (5) *objective and observable assessment strategies.*

The four purposes of assessment (Mash & Terdal, 1988) are: (1) diagnosis, (2) prognosis, (3) treatment/intervention design, and (4) the evaluation of treatment/intervention effectiveness. While diagnosis may be important (e.g., under the Individuals with Disabilities Act—IDEA; Public Laws 94-142, 99-457, and 105-17) in order that preschool students receive services, diagnosis in the context of social-emotional assessment most often results only in a label. Indeed, given (1) that diagnostic labels are a conglomerate of possible behaviors and conditions, (2) that "normal" behavior is more broadly defined during the preschool years than at any other time, and (3) that labels do not directly result in *specific* interventions or treatment decisions, assessment for the purposes of diagnosis and prognosis should be de-emphasized in favor of assessment for treatment/intervention design and evaluation (Knoff, 1995). In fact, according to P.L. 105-17, chidren's social-emotional behavior needs to be *functionally assessed* such that all evaluations are directly linked to the treatments and interventions devised. In doing this, the importance of identifying replacement behaviors and of maintaining a preventive perspective is paramount (Batsche & Knoff, 1995).

Replacement behaviors are the desired, expected, necessary, and/or most adaptive behaviors for a specific social or interactive situation. As such, replacement behaviors are typically the *real* goal or focus of assessment as linked to intervention. From a behavioral perspective, if a preschooler is demonstrating a great deal of social withdrawal or isolated play, the evaluation should focus on a functional and ecological assessment of these behaviors, a determination of "why" these behaviors are occurring, and an analysis of the pervasiveness (across time, settings, individuals, expectations, etc.) of these behaviors. Relative to intervention, however, the focus will likely *not* be on decreasing or eliminating the withdrawal or isolated play behavior, but on increasing the *replacement* behavior—that is, the teaching and/or reinforcement of social initiation and cooperative play behavior. Critically, while social withdrawal or isolated play is a characteristic in a number of diagnostic entities, the ultimate intervention focuses not on the diagnosis, but on the behavior that the child needs to exhibit in order to continue to socially or behaviorally progress.

Similarly, linking assessment, intervention, and a preventive perspective is critical because early and successful preschool intervention is one of the best deterrents to later, more serious clinical problems. In order to develop and implement these interventions, assessment needs to be more focused on intervention than diagnosis. Indeed, very few clinical problems use the preschool years as the critical period (or "age of onset") when a diagnosis can be made. Thus, the importance of assessment for the purpose of developing interventions again is emphasized.

Relative to functional assessment, Cone (1978) created a comprehensive, three-dimensional model called the Behavioral Assessment Grid (BAG) that separates behavioral assessment into (1) behavioral contents, (2) behavioral methods, and (3) universes of generalization. Within this model, behavioral contents consist of children's cognitive, physiological, and motoric behavior. While it is clear that preschoolers have internal or private thoughts, beliefs, attitudes, expectations, images, and feelings, the reliable assessment of these cognitions is difficult due to young children's inability to accurately recognize, understand, and express them. Preschoolers' physiological and motor behaviors, meanwhile, are more easily observed and assessed. The behavioral methods noted in the model are separated into indirect and direct methods, respectively. The indirect methods include interview, self-report, and behavior rating scale approaches, while the direct methods include self-observation, analog role play and free play approaches, and naturalistic role play. Finally, the universes of generalization include generalization of scorer, item, time, setting, method, and dimension. All of these directly relate to the multimethod, multisource, multisetting assessment approach mentioned earlier.

Critically, the second dimension of the BAG, methods of assessment, conceptually interacts with the other two dimensions such that a child's cognitive, physiological, and motoric behavior can be assessed by multiple methods and sources, and in multiple settings. In this way, preschoolers' social-emotional (and adaptive behavior) status can be assessed reliably while maintaining a sensitivity to situation- and setting-specific behavior. Below, the assessment methods in the BAG are discussed as they relate to the effective and accurate assessment of preschoolers' social-emotional and adaptive behavior.

Clinical and Diagnostic Interview Methods

In a general sense, there are three types of interviews—unstructured, semistructured, and structured—which can occur across the assessment process, from the initial problem identification interview to the post-assessment, and from the pre-intervention interview to the post-intervention evaluation or termination interview (Sattler, 1990–1992). All of these interviews can focus on any number of social-emotional or adaptive behavior areas, and each one could involve the preschooler him or herself, a parent, or another individual critical to the referral or assessment process. Significantly, most social-emotional or adaptive behavior interviews are semistructured. That is, they have clearly defined assessment areas and numerous scripted questions, but they also allow the interviewer to pursue specific answers to scripted questions and to follow a logical line of questioning that maximizes the flow and direction of the interviewee's responses and style. Thus, the semistructured interview has an assessment agenda that must be completed but allows some flexibility for doing so in the most comfortable, facilitative way possible.

Diagnostic Interview Components, Goals, and Conceptualizations. Assuming that a preschooler has been referred for a social-emotional or adaptive behavior problem, in the initial problem identification and problem analysis interviews with a parent it is important for the interviewer to (1) develop rapport, (2) provide an overview of the goals and organization of the interviews themselves, (3) work toward identifying the concerns that prompted the referral, (4) move toward specifying hypotheses that might explain the concerns and ways that these hypotheses might be tested, and (5) complete the assessments that will test these hypotheses (Knoff, 1995; Knoff & Batsche, 1991). Early on in the interview process, numerous developmental and medical/health questions should be asked, for example, about the mother's pregnancy with the referred child; the birth process and post-natal course; the child's early feeding and sleeping patterns; the toilet training process; speech, motor, cognitive, and temperament development; the child's interpersonal and play behavior and skill;

and other health issues. Later on, the questioning process should become far more focused, working to define the specific concerns that motivated the referral and to understand these concerns, functionally and behaviorally. Ultimately, all of the interview questions should provide both a global understanding of the referred child's developmental history, and a specific understanding that can be integrated into a behavioral analysis that evaluates the child's development of behavioral skills and maintenance of specific behavioral patterns.

Within this behavioral context, a number of diagnostic interview goals are evident. During the problem identification and problem analysis stages, operational definitions of the referred concerns and explanatory hypotheses are necessary. While these concerns and hypotheses will be altered as appropriate during the entire assessment process, these definitions should be as specific as possible so that anyone could observe the referred child and reliably recognize the identified behaviors in question. As the analysis proceeds, these definitions should include descriptions of the frequency, duration, intensity, and setting specificity (as appropriate) of the behavior, and these characteristics should be developmentally and normatively compared to the child development research and the child's *in situ* peer group, respectively. Finally, a behavioral analysis of possible antecedent and consequent events that are child-specific, setting-specific, and system-specific must be accomplished such that it is possible to identify the contingencies directly or indirectly causing, supporting, or maintaining the concerns in question.

To guide the diagnostic interview process and to facilitate a functional analysis of referred and actual concerns, Kanfer and Saslow (1969) suggested an approach that incorporates dimensions relevant to referred children's current behavioral situations and their past developmental history. Among the interview and assessment dimensions outlined are: (1) an analysis of the referred problem concerns, including an assessment of the referred child's behavioral assets, excesses, and deficits; (2) clarification of the behavioral ecology that is maintaining the problem behaviors and situation; (3) a motivational analysis of the referred child and those who might be involved in any intervention programs; (4) a developmental analysis of the child including biological, sociological, and behavioral facets; (5) a self-control analysis of the child; (6) an analysis of the social relationships between and around the child and significant others; and (7) an analysis of the interrelationships of the social, cultural, and physical environment involving and around the child.

Two other paradigms commonly used to guide the interview process have been developed by Goldfried (1977) and Lazarus (1981). Goldfried uses a SORC paradigm that involves the assessment of Situational variables, Organismic (i.e., psychological and physiological) variables, Response or observable behaviors or variables, and Consequence variables. Lazarus suggests organizing the interview using components summarized by the acronym BASIC ID: Behavior, Affect, Sensation, Image, Cognition, Interpersonal Relationships, and Drugs/Biological Functioning.

Structured and Semi-Structured Ecobehavioral Interviews with Parents and Significant Others.

As noted previously, most diagnostic interviews are semistructured. However, depending on format and semantics, some "interviews" can be considered structured. Semistructured ecobehavioral interviews can provide a detailed description of behaviors across settings, they can clarify the concerns of caregivers, and they can encourage the participation of caregivers in the development of interventions. These interviews also help to sample numerous possible problem behaviors and circumstances, to analyze problem situations in depth, and to develop an overall picture of a child's and family's place in the community. Two ecobehavioral interviews, the *Waking Day Interview* and the *Problem*

Solving Interview are useful for the identification and analysis of ecobehavioral factors impacting social and adaptive behavior referrals.

In the Waking Day Interview (Barnett & Carey, 1992; Wahler & Cormier, 1970), the caregiver is asked to describe a typical day with the referred child, focusing on events, routines, and behaviors from waking to bedtime. The caregiver is asked to provide information about the home (and other) settings and the child's behavior during daily events such as entering daycare or school, class activities, transitions, lunch, and other activities. The events included in the interview (see Table 9.1) are generic but flexible, and they are adapted to reflect each referred child's personal schedule. The Waking Day Interview is useful for identifying behaviors that are of greatest concern to caregivers, selecting target behaviors, determining conditions needed to establish baseline information, and revealing environments that can support interventions (Barnett & Carey, 1992).

Ecobehavioral "Problem Solving" interviews, based on the work of Alessi and Kaye (1983) and Kanfer and Grimm (1977), are used to help further clarify and analyze the concerns of caregivers. As a follow-up to the Waking Day Interview, problem solving interviews allow further analysis of the problem situations identified by caregivers. Semistructured problem solving interviews assist with a functional analysis of the behavioral concerns identified by caregivers and others, and they can be modified for use in home or school settings. Critically, the importance of obtaining information from both family members and teachers or other caregivers is emphasized. Indeed, the sometimes conflicting information provided by different caregivers may provide insight into contextual factors that are maintaining or limiting a preschoolers' behavior, in addition to effec-

TABLE 9.1   Events and Information Included in the Waking Day Interview

Directions: Describe your child's behaviors in the following settings or situations:

Home Setting

Sleep patterns	In the car
Waking up time	During play
Breakfast	With siblings
Dressing	With peers
Transport to school	Alone
After school	Discipline techniques and when disciplined
Dinnertime	Chores
After dinner	When shopping
Bath time	In other community settings
Bedtime	With visitors/guests

School or Daycare Setting

On the bus	Large group activities
When entering the classroom	Small group activities
During organizational activities	Free-play activities
At transition times	During individual activities
Lunchroom	Out-of-classroom activities (e.g., gym, field trips)
Bathroom	When interacting with parents/adults

Source: From D. Barnett. (in press). *Early Intervention: A Practitioner's Guide.* Used by permission of Guilford Press.

tive caregiver strategies and interactions, and other unique aspects that inform both the assessment and a potential intervention. A twelve-part format for the problem solving interview is presented in Table 9.2.

Beyond the Waking Day Interview, the Problem Solving Interview, and other semi-structured interviews that exist within multidimension developmental scales (e.g., the Denver Developmental Screening Test—Revised, the Early Learning Accomplishment Profile), no known structured, diagnostic interviews have been standardized for use with preschoolers. Thus, it appears that preschool social-emotional assessment interviews depend primarily on semistructured formats. From a functional assessment perspective, this actually is preferred as these formats facilitate the process of understanding the unique ecology and situation of each child referred.

Relative to adaptive behavior, there are a number of structured interview measures available which can be used for preschool children. Among the most popular are the AAMD Adaptive Behavior Scales (Lambert, Windmiller, Tharinger, & Cole, 1981) and the Scales of Independent Behavior (Bruininks, Woodcock, Weatherman, & Hill, 1984), which can be completed by either a parent or a teacher. The Vineland Adaptive Behavior Scale (Sparrow, Balla, & Cicchetti, 1984) also can be considered a structured interview; however, its administration directions suggest that the Scale's questions be answered within the flow of the natural discussion, rather than in a rigid, sequential question-by-question style. All three of these measures have been standardized for the preschool ages and beyond, and each one has its own operationalization and focus on specific components of adaptive behavior. These three scales will be discussed further below. For the present, however, they do exemplify indirect methods of adaptive behavior assessment, an important component of the Behavioral Assessment Grid.

Diagnostic Interviewing with the Preschooler. Because preschoolers have difficulty verbalizing their thoughts and feelings, the "traditional" diagnostic interview with its focus on discussion and self-reflection is not recommended. Indeed, preschoolers are too concrete, egocentric, "black and white," and impressionable to provide valid and reliable interview information. Yet, alternative "interview" formats with the preschooler *can* provide useful information, usually in the form of hypotheses that need later validation or data that reinforce other information gathered during a multimethod, multisource, multisetting assessment process. Among the most-used alternative interview formats are those involving play—from symbolic play therapy to behavioral free-play interactions.

While play therapy typically emphasizes the symbolic content of a child's play and involves interpretations that often are indirect and presumptive (Axline, 1947; Moore, 1983), free-play interactions allow a number of social-emotional and adaptive behavior dimensions to be assessed in a more direct, less inferential manner. Significantly, during a free-play interview, the practitioner can develop rapport and discuss pertinent issues while playing with the child. Garbarino and Stott (1989) suggest that practitioners, when interviewing children, should use language and terms that are cognitively and socio-culturally appropriate, that they conduct the interview in a setting familiar and comfortable to the child, and that they refrain from asking the child, "Do you understand?" when needed and instead ask the child to repeat what was previously said. Communication skills, attitudes toward adults, emotional reactions to play situations, and cognitive problem-solving also can be evaluated by observing child–clinician interactions empirically and objectively. In fact, free-play interactions provide a necessary medium through which children can comfortably share their thoughts, feelings, and beliefs.

TABLE 9.2   A Format for the Problem Solving Interview

Step 1: Explain the interview and its purpose.

Example The purpose of this interview will be to talk about problems related to parenting (or teaching) so we can develop goals to make parenting easier or more enjoyable. In order to accomplish this, we need to discuss the areas of difficulty which bother you most, when they occur, how often they occur, and what you think might influence these behaviors.

Step 2: Define problem behavior.

Examples Please describe your greatest areas of difficulty related to your role as a parent. What exactly does your child do when he or she is acting this way?

Step 3: Prioritize multiple problems.

Examples Which bothers you the most? Which of these concerns are most pressing to you? Tell me which of these problems you think you could learn to manage most easily or successfully?

Step 4: Define severity of the problem.

Examples How often do you, or does your child. . . ? About how many times a day, week, etc., does this problem occur? Would you say this problem is starting to happen more often, less often, or is it staying about the same?

Step 5: Define generality of the problem.

Examples How long has this been going on? Where does the problem behavior usually come up? Do you observe the behavior at home? How about when visiting friends or family, or shopping?

Step 6: Explore determinants of the problem behavior.

Examples I want you to think about the times when the problem is worst. What sort of things are going on then? What about the times when the problem gets better? What kinds of things are happening then? What do you think is causing the problem? Think back to the last time the problem occurred. What was going on at the time? Where were you? Were there any other people around? Who? What were they doing? What were you thinking about at the time? How did you feel? What usually happens after the problem occurs? Does this happen consistently?

Step 7: Determine modification attempts.

Examples What things have you tried to stop this problem behavior? How long have you tried that? How well did it work? Have you tried anything else?

Step 8: Identify expectancies for improved behavior.

Examples In this kind of situation, what would you like [your child, yourself, spouse] to do instead of the problem behavior? If [child] were to improve, what would you notice first? What is the desired behavior you would like to see [your child, yourself] accomplish?

Step 9: Summarize caregiver's concerns.

Step 10: Explore the caregiver's commitment and motivation to work on the problem.

Examples How would solving this problem make your day easier? Were this problem to go away, how would this change your day? If this problem were to get worse, how would this affect your parenting/teaching? What do you think the chances are of resolving this problem?

Step 11: Have caregiver summarize problems, treatment goals, and plans.

Example In order to make sure I understand your concerns and goals, I would like you to summarize them for me. Please describe your impression or understanding of how the intervention will work.

Step 12: Discuss and mutually arrive at plans for the next steps.

Source: Reprinted with permission of the author and publisher from "Behavioral Observation for the School Psychologist: Responsive-Discrepancy Model" by Alessi, G. J., 1980, *School Psychology Review*, Vol. 9, pp. 31–45.

The information obtained when interviewing preschoolers is influenced by the purpose and context of the interview, the communication and interactive skills of the child, and the personal and professional skills of the clinician (Garbarino & Stott, 1989). While these interactions also allow the direct behavioral observation of other child-oriented dimensions (see the discussion that follows), they should not be underestimated in their ability to access significant social-emotional and adaptive behavior information. Critically, this information reflects some of the preschooler's unique perceptions of his or her world—perceptions that are important in any comprehensive assessment of a referred child's problems.

Behavior Rating Scale Methods

Behavior rating scales typically contain a number of specific behaviors or correlates of behavior organized into empirically-derived factors or scales which provide information about a child across numerous social-emotional or adaptive behavior dimensions. Most often, these scales have been developed from a review of the literature in the behavioral area of interest, and by accessing behavioral or clinical descriptors of children who are representative of the target population of the rating scale. These descriptors are then factor-analyzed and the resulting scales are evaluated for their psychometric soundness, especially their construct, content, concurrent, and discriminant validities. More pragmatically, respondents, usually parents or teachers, rate these behavioral descriptors as to what degree they are present (e.g., does your child hit other children very often, somewhat often, never?) and their answers are summed across the behavioral factors and then compared to some standardization sample or reference group. A behavioral profile results that can be compared and contrasted with other data collected within the BAG (Cone, 1978) taxonomy so that an accurate picture of the preschooler's behavior and affect results.

Before describing specific behavior rating scales for use with preschoolers, it is important to emphasize that most of these scales have very specific assessment goals and orientations, and that they differ along a number of critical characteristics. For example, Edelbrock (1983) noted that behavior rating scales should be analyzed a priori across the following dimensions:

1. What the behavior rating scale purports to measure and how it accomplishes this goal. Behavior rating scales may focus on clinical, home, and/or school concerns; they may be descriptive, prescriptive, or diagnostic; they may rate a child's behaviors or simply indicate that they exist; finally, they may be unidimensional in scope or multidimensional.
2. The technical adequacy of the behavior rating scale, including its development, construction, standardization, and norming.
3. The level or specificity of behavioral analysis reflected in the items of the behavior rating scale, along with the time frames used to assess target children (e.g., one month, six months, one year), and the respondents (e.g., mother, father, teacher) for which the scale is normed.
4. Whether the behavior rating scale makes provisions to control the different levels of response bias (e.g., halo effects, leniency or severity effects, and central tendency or range restriction effects), especially when multiple respondents are used.

Thus, behavior rating scales should be chosen so that they can answer case-specific referral questions and can address needed assessment dimensions. In all, there are an enormous number of behavior rating scales available for preschool populations, including some that evaluate very specific referral problems such as hyperactivity, autism, or self-concept. Unfortunately, many of these scales have questionable psychometric qualities, are not nationally standardized, and have not been constructed to encourage multimethod, multisource, multisetting analyses which lead to clear and effective intervention approaches. Below, four different behavior rating scales for the preschool ages are reviewed briefly (see Table 9.3 for each scale's standardization and psychometric background information). One scale is part of a multisetting, multisource, and multirespondent system (the Child Behavior Checklist; Achenbach, 1991; Achenbach & Edelbrock, 1981); one can be used in classroom settings (the Burks' Behavior Rating Scales, Preschool and Kindergarten Edition; Burks, 1977); one focuses specifically on assessing hyperactive and related behavior (The Conners' Rating Scales; Conners, 1990); and one evaluates social skills as a cluster of many specific, yet interrelated, behaviors (the Social Skills Rating System; Gresham & Elliott, 1990).

Child Behavior Checklist.   There are, in fact, five different behavior rating scales developed over the past decade by Achenbach and Edelbrock: the Child Behavior Checklist (ages 2 to 3), the Child Behavior Checklist (ages 4 to 18), the Teacher's Report Form (ages 5 to 18), the Youth Self-Report (ages 11 to 18), and the Direct Observation Form (ages 5 to 14). Of these, the first two can be used with preschool-aged children.

The Child Behavior Checklist for ages 2 to 3 (CBCL/2–3) consists of 99 items and one open-ended item describing various behaviors, emotional problems, or reactions to specific situations. It is completed by a child's parents. These 99 items are rated along a 3-point scale where the behavior is considered to be: 2–Very true or often true; 1–Somewhat true or sometimes true; or 0–Not true at the present time or over the last two months. The CBCL/2–3 has three global scales (Total Problems, Internalizing, and Externalizing) and six narrow-band scales (Social Withdrawal, Depressed, Sleep Problems, Somatic Problems, Aggressive, and Destructive), with the latter scales identified through a factor analysis of parents' ratings for 398 nonreferred, clinically-referred, and at-risk children. The CBCL/2-3 is scored similarly for both genders because no differences were found during the norming process.

The Child Behavior Checklist for ages 4 to 18 (CBCL/4–18) is actually somewhat different than the CBCL/2–3, as the two scales share only 59 items. The CBCL/4–18 has 118 problem statements and two open-ended items which are evaluated by parents along the same 3-point scale as the CBCL/2–3. The CBCL/4–18 also has a social competence section which evaluates children's play and home activities, social interactions, school and academic status, and total social competence. Using the 118 problem statements, the CBCL/4–18 was re-normed in 1991 on over 2,300 children from across the United States who had not received mental health or special remedial school classes within the preceding 12 months (Achenbach, 1991). Narrow- and broad-band clinical syndrome scales then were derived using a clinical sample of over 2,100 additional children and youth, matched to the normative sample, drawn from psychological clinics, mental health centers, and private and agency practices across the country. Many of the CBCLs in the clinical sample were used to determine the CBCL's clinical syndrome scales in 1983. Their CBCL profiles were reanalyzed in 1991, using two sets of principal components analyses, so that problem items, internalizing and externalizing groupings, and core clinical syndromes could be identified across the CBCL, the Youth Self-Report, and the Teacher's Report Form.

TABLE 9.3 Summary of the Standardization and Psychometric Properties of Select Preschool Behavior Rating Scale Assessment Instruments

The Child Behavior Checklist (CBCL; ages 2 to 3)

Standardization: Normed on 273 randomly selected nonreferred children.

Reliability data: Test-retest reliabilities for a one-week period with a nonreferred sample ranged from .79 (Destructive scale) to .92 (Sleep Problems scale) for the clinical scales, with correlations averaging .88 for the Internalizing and Externalizing scales, a .91 correlation for the Total Problems scale, and a mean correlation of .87 across the entire rating scale. Test-retest reliabilities for a 4- to 6-week period of time with a different, nonreferred sample were slightly lower, yet comparable (Crawford & Lee, 1991). One-year test-retest correlations (Achenbach, Edelbrock, & Howell, 1987) were lower, as expected, yet quite acceptable ranging from .56 (Depression scale) to .72 (Destructive scale) for the clinical scales, with a .76 for the Internalizing scale, a .70 for the Externalizing scale, a .76 for the Total Problems scale, and a mean correlation of .69 across the entire rating scale. Interparent correlations, meanwhile, averaged .47 at age 2 and .57 at age 3.

Validity data: Concurrent validity was assessed by comparing the CBCL/2–3 to the Minnesota Child Development Inventory, the Bayley Scales of Infant Development, and the McCarthy Scales of Children's Abilities. No significant areas of overlap, as expected, were found as the CBCL/2–3 was intended to measure social-emotional and behavioral problems and not the developmental/intellectual skills of the other three scales. Discriminant validity was assessed by comparing CBCL/2–3 scores of 96 normal and 96 clinically-referred children matched on age, sex, SES, and race. Regression analyses here were very positive indicating that up to 32% of the variance was accounted for by a child's referral status. Thus, the CBCL/2–3 significantly discriminated between the two samples, a major test of its validity and clinical utility (Achenbach, Edelbrock, & Howell, 1987).

The Child Behavior Checklist (CBCL; ages 4 to 18)

Standardization: Re-normed in 1991 on over 2,300 children from across the United States who had not received mental health or special remedial school classes within the preceding 12 months (Achenbach, 1991). Narrow- and broad-band clinical syndrome scales were derived using a clinical sample of over 2,100 additional children and youth, matched to the normative sample, drawn from psychological clinics, mental health centers, and private and agency practices across the country.

Reliability data: Test–retest reliabilities with a non-referred sample for a one-week period was .89 for the total problems, internalizing, and externalizing scales, and the eight core clinical syndromes; and .87 for all of the social competence scales. Using CBCLs completed by parents from both clinically-referred and general population samples, interparent agreement correlations averaged .87 for the social competence items and .65 for the problem behavior items, exceeding the mean correlations found in prior meta-analyses.

Validity data: The CBCL/4–18 was compared with the Conners Parent Questionnaire and the Quay-Peterson Revised Behavior Problem Checklist for a sample of clinically-referred 6- to 11-year-old children (Achenbach, 1991). The results revealed correlations ranging from .59 (CBCL Attention Problems scale with the Conners Impulsive-Hyperactive scale) to .86 (CBCL Aggressive scale with the Conners Conduct Problem scale), and from .59 (CBCL Delinquent Behavior

(continued)

TABLE 9.3   Continued

---

scale and the Quay-Peterson Socialized Aggression scale) to .88 (CBCL Aggressive Behavior scale with the Quay-Peterson Conduct Disorder scale) for the clinical syndromes across the two respective scale comparisons. The total problem scales for the CBCL and the Conners, meanwhile, correlated .82, while the total problem scales for the CBCL and the Quay-Peterson comparison correlated .81. Similar results were found (Costenbader & Keller, 1990) when the CBCL was correlated with the Conners for a different sample of 6- to 11-year-old children who were either non-referred or labeled emotionally handicapped or learning disabled.

Relative to discriminant validity, the CBCL/4–18 also demonstrates the ability to discriminate between clinical and non-clinical samples on all Social Competence and Behavior Problem scales (Achenbach, 1991). These results, once again, were supported by Costenbader and Keller's (1990) study relative to their non-referred versus special education samples.

The Burks' Behavior Rating Scale (BBRS)—Preschool and Kindergarten Edition

Standardization: The BBRS was standardized with 127 preschool children (70 boys and 57 girls) from San Bernardino County, California and with 337 kindergarten children (184 boys and 153 girls) from four school districts in Los Angeles and Orange Counties also in California.

Reliability data: The BBRS manual reports 10-day test–retest reliabilities ranging from .74 to .96 for 84 kindergarten children. In addition, previous research with the elementary school BBRS is described where another 10-day test–retest reliability study with 95 disturbed first- through sixth-graders resulted in an average correlation of .71.

Validity data: The manual cites research suggesting that the BBRS has both criterion-related and content validity. However, the data on its construct validity are more complete and suggestive of a sound factorial structure. Overall, the Preschool and Kindergarten Edition of the BBRS depends a great deal on the psychometric studies of its Elementary Edition.

Conners' Behavior Rating Scales: The Conners' Parent Rating Scales (CPRS) and the Conners' Teacher Rating Scales (CTRS)

Standardization: The CPRS was standardized on 578 children between the ages of 3 and 17 and the CTRS was standardized on 383 children between the ages of 3 and 17.

Reliability data: One year test–retest reliability coefficients, reported in the manual for the original form of the CPRS, ranged from .40 to .70. One month test–retest reliability coefficients, using the original form of the CTRS, ranged from .72 to .91 with significantly lower coefficients reported for the one year test–retest data (Conners, 1990). Beyond the manual, Brandon, Kehle, Jenson, and Clark (1990) reported acceptable test–retest reliability with a sample of 60 children twice-rated one week apart. They also found no evidence to support the presence of practice effects, statistical regression, warm-up impact, or teachers' expectations on repeated Conners' ratings.

Validity data: Acceptable concurrent validity was established between the Conners and the Achenbach scales by Costenbader and Keller (1990) for both the teacher and parent forms of each scale, respectively. In addition, predictive validity, discriminant validity, and construct validity all

(continued)

TABLE 9.3 Continued

are discussed in the Conners manual. These results, however, involved the original versions of the Conners' Rating Scales.

Social Skills Rating System: The Social Skills Rating System-Teacher (SSRS-T) and the Social Skills Rating System-Parent (SSRS-P)

Standardization: Norms for the SSRS were developed for both girls and boys using parents and teachers who rated 200 children from a national tryout sample (Gresham & Elliott, 1990).

Reliability data: The internal consistency of the scale was determined by using the normative sample and data described above. Overall, a relatively high degree of scale homogeneity was found based on coefficient alphas ranging from .83 to .94 for the Social Skills scale and .73 to .88 for the Problem Behaviors scale across all forms and levels. Predictably, the coefficients for the separate subscales were lower, with median correlations ranging from .78 to .84 for Cooperation, Assertion, Self-Control, and Externalizing Problems. On the SSRS-P at the preschool level, ratings on the Internalizing items differed according to gender, and alpha coefficients of .67 were found for girls and .48 for boys.

Relative to test–retest reliability, both the SSRS-T and the SSRS-P appear to have good to excellent stability. For example, reliability coefficients of .85 for the Social Skills scale and .84 for Problem Behaviors scale were reported for the SSRS-T with a sample tested and then retested after four weeks. The test-retest coefficients for the SSRS-P were .87 for the Social Skills scale and .65 for the Problem Behaviors scale. Significantly, however, these results were computed using the elementary level of the standardization sample and not the preschool level sample.

Validity data: Gresham and Elliott (1990) extensively documented the content, social, criterion-related, and construct validity of the SSRS in the manual. Content and social validity, for example, was demonstrated through teachers' and parents' ratings of the importance of the SSRS items relative to their inclusion in the scale. Criterion-related validity was documented by comparing the SSRS in various studies to the Social Behavior Assessment, the Harter Teacher Rating Scale, the Piers-Harris Children's Self-Concept Scale, and various forms of the Child Behavior Checklist. Finally, the evidence supporting the system's construct validity included factor analyses, convergent and discriminant correlation analyses, and comparisons of contrasted groups, along with the consistency of these analyses across the demographic characteristics (e.g., race, gender) of those children evaluated by the SSRS.

Relative to preschoolers, the content validity of the SSRS was documented by Elliott, Barnard, and Gresham (1989) who analyzed SSRS-T and SSRS-P ratings of a diverse sample of 212 preschool children. Results indicated that nearly all of the behavior items included on the SSRS-T and SSRS-P were rated as either "Critical" or "Important" by the respondents. Relative to concurrent validity, the same study compared the SSRS-T and SSRS-P to Burks' Behavior Ratings Scale responses. Significant positive correlations were found between the Interfering Behaviors factor (one of the pre-publication factors of the SSRS) on both the SSRS-T and SSRS-P and the three problem areas (Aggression, Inhibition, and Inattention) of the Burks. In addition, negative correlations were found between the prosocial factors on the SSRS-T and SSRS-P and the problem behaviors on the Burks. These findings provide support the concurrent validity of both forms of the SSRS at the preschool level.

In the end, the revised CBCL/4–18 has seven global scales: the Activities, Social, and School scales which then are summarized in the Total Competence scale; and the Internalizing and Externalizing scales which then are summarized in the Total Problems scale. Significantly, all 4 and 5 year olds *were omitted* from the competence scale norms because no significant differences were found between referred and non-referred children at these ages. Relative to the CBCL's clinical syndromes at the 4- to 5-year-old level, eight scales were identified by the factor analyses. These were labeled: Withdrawn, Somatic Complaints, Anxious/Depressed, Social Problems, Thought Problems, Attention Problems, Delinquent Behavior, and Aggressive Behavior. The first three of these syndromes correlated with the Internalizing scale, while the latter two correlated with the Externalizing scale. Critically, separate norms were developed for boys and girls aged 4 to 11 and 12 to 18, respectively.

In summary, the CBCL/2-3 and CBCL/4-18 behavior rating scales appear to be psychometrically strong and able to provide clinically useful information to a multimethod, multisource, multisetting assessment. Written at a fifth-grade reading level, either of the scales can be completed in approximately 20 minutes. Interpretively, the scales use the 98th percentile cutoff (70T) to determine clinical significance for the Clinical Syndrome scales, although a borderline range exists beginning at 67T. While interpretation of the broad- and narrow-band syndromes can facilitate an understanding of the referred child, it still is important to analyze individual item responses and, especially, responses in the "Other Problems" list which identifies significant problems which did not load on the core syndrome factor analysis. This focus on individual items is important, given that some scales need only two or three 2-point responses to be clinically significant for an entire syndrome. The Child Behavior Checklist is an important behavior rating scale in the preschool assessment battery. It evaluates children's assets and their problem behaviors, and its items generally can be easily validated in either home or school settings.

Burks' Behavior Rating Scales.   The Preschool and Kindergarten Edition of the Burks' Behavior Rating Scales (BBRS; Burks, 1977) consists of 105 items which describe various childhood behaviors and behavioral reactions. These items can be rated by both parents and teachers along a 5-point scale from "1–You have not noticed this behavior at all" to "5–You have noticed this behavior to a very large degree." Factor-analyzed into three broad-band factors (Aggressive-Disinhibited, Anxious-Immature, and Impulsive for preschool students; Aggressive-Disinhibited, Anxious-Inhibited-Immature, Inattentive for kindergarten students), the BBRS, nonetheless, is most often interpreted using its 18 factor analytically-derived narrow-band scales: Excessive Self-Blame, Excessive Anxiety, Excessive Withdrawal, Excessive Dependency, Poor Ego Strength, Poor Physical Strength, Poor Coordination, Poor Intellectuality, Poor Attention, Poor Impulse Control, Poor Reality Contact, Poor Sense of Identity, Excessive Suffering, Poor Anger Control, Excessive Sense of Persecution, Excessive Aggressiveness, Excessive Resistance, and Poor Social Conformity. These factors are listed on a profile sheet that plots each scale's total raw score across a "not significant" to "significant" to "very significant" spectrum, based on the instrument's norms. Separate profile sheets are not used for preschool versus kindergarten students nor for male versus female students. In fact, the BBRS manual attempts to explain the use of one profile sheet by comparing the distribution of each scale's scores by age and gender, deeming all differences as non-significant. Unfortunately, however, the manual does not provide the raw score means and standard deviations for the various scales across these variables so that this decision can be independently validated.

Psychometrically, the Preschool and Kindergarten Edition of the BBRS depends a great deal on relevant studies of its Elementary Edition. As all 18 scales from the Preschool/Kindergarten Edition appear on the Elementary Edition, this may seem logical. Nonetheless, future research with the Preschool and Kindergarten Edition must provide the necessary empirical support that will allow this instrument to stand alone psychometrically and clinically.

Interpretively, some caution must be used in analyzing data from the BBRS. At a specific item level, however, the test is very useful. The individual items are well written, the rating scale clearly identifies behaviors that are of concern or present to a large or very large degree, and all items can be followed up easily during an interview with either a parent or teacher. At a narrow-band scale level, however, the individual items that push a scale into the "significant" or "very significant" level must still be identified and analyzed. Given the absence of factor-analytic data and the use of the California samples for standardization, only tentative use of the 18 scales is suggested. However, with multimethod, multisource, multisetting confirmation, more confidence in BBRS conclusions is possible.

Overall, the BBRS has some important limitations that need to be addressed by additional research. This scale, however, does have the potential to be very useful in a multimethod, multisource, multisetting assessment, especially given its potential use across both sources and settings. In fact, as part of a functional assessment, the individual items on the BBRS provide a good, comprehensive screening of a preschooler's interactions with others across a wide range of behaviors. Thus, even if the 18 scales were ignored, the individual items of the BBRS help to assess important concerns that can be cross-validated through other assessments and observations from home and school environments. For the present, the BBRS is a scale of possibilities. Significantly, it provides an interesting example of both good and bad behavior rating scale characteristics (see Edelbrock, 1983 and the preceding section). For the future, the scale has a good functional foundation that additional research can build into a more psychometrically secure tool.

Conners' Behavior Rating Scales.   The Conners' Rating Scales consist of the Conners' Parent Rating Scales (CPRS) and the Conners' Teacher Rating Scales (CTRS). Although originally developed to help identify hyperactive children, the Conners' Rating Scales are useful in characterizing and evaluating other, related problem behaviors. There are two versions of each scale, a long form and a short form. The short forms will be discussed here because they have normative data available at the preschool level. The CPRS consists of 48 items rated along a 0 to 3 scale (0 = Not at All; 1 = Just a Little, 2 = Pretty Much, or 3 = Very Much) by a child's parent. Factor analyses have sorted the CPRS's items into five scales: Conduct Problem, Learning Problem, Psychosomatic, Impulsive-Hyperactive, and Anxiety. The CTRS consists of 28 items rated along the same 0 to 3 scale by a child's teacher. Factor analyses have sorted the CTRS's items into three scales: Conduct Problem, Hyperactivity, and Inattentive-Passive.

The CPRS was standardized on 578 children between the ages of 3 and 17 and the CTRS was standardized on 383 children between the ages of 3 and 17. Relative to reliability, one year test-retest reliability coefficients, reported in the manual for the original form of the CPRS, ranged from .40 to .70. One month test-retest reliability coefficients, using the original form of the CTRS, ranged from .72 to .91 with significantly lower coefficients reported for the one year test-retest data (Conners, 1990). Beyond the manual, Brandon, Kehle, Jenson, and Clark (1990) reported acceptable test-retest reliability with a sample of

60 children twice-rated one week apart. They also found no evidence to support the presence of practice effects, statistical regression, warm-up impact, or teachers' expectations on repeated Conners' ratings.

As discussed earlier, acceptable concurrent validity was established between the Conners and the Achenbach scales by Costenbader and Keller (1990) for both the teacher and parent forms of each scale, respectively. In addition, predictive validity, discriminant validity, and construct validity all are discussed in the Conners manual. These results, however, involved the original versions of the Conners' Rating Scales. Thus, additional research is needed to document the reliability and validity of the short forms of the Conners beyond the available normative data on preschool children.

Social Skills Rating System.   The Social Skills Rating System is a multi-rater inventory designed to screen and evaluate children's social skills in different settings and to assist in the development of interventions when social skills deficits are identified (Gresham & Elliott, 1990). Organized across three age levels (the Preschool, Elementary, and Secondary levels), the Social Skills Rating System is comprised of two behavior rating scale forms that are used at the preschool level: the Social Skills Rating System-Teacher (SSRS-T) and the Social Skills Rating System-Parent (SSRS-P). At this preschool level, the SSRS-T consists of 40 items made up of 30 prosocial behavior items (e.g., makes friends easily, receives criticism well, controls temper in conflict situations) and 10 problem behavior items (e.g., has temper tantrums, appears lonely, disturbs ongoing activities). The prosocial behavior items are rated according to their frequency (2 = Very Often, 1 = Sometimes, and 0 = Never) and their importance to success in the classroom (2 = Critical, 1 = Important, and 0 = Not important), while the problem behavior items are rated according to their frequency only. The SSRS-T has been factor-analyzed into the following scales: Cooperation, Assertion, and Self-Control for the Social Skills section, and Internalizing and Externalizing for the Problem Behaviors section.

Also at the preschool level, the SSRS-P consists of 49 items made up of 39 prosocial behavior items and 10 problem behavior items. Critically, 22 of the 39 prosocial behavior items on the SSRS-P have comparable items on the SSRS-T, and all 10 of the problem behavior items exactly duplicate those on the SSRS-T. The SSRS-P uses the same response formats for the prosocial and problem behavior items, respectively. Finally, the SSRS-P has been factor-analyzed into the Cooperation, Assertion, Responsibility, and Self-Control scales for the Social Skills section, and the Internalizing and Externalizing scales for the Problem Behaviors section.

While additional research is needed for the SSRS, it does demonstrate the potential to accurately assess the prosocial and problem behavior of preschoolers, across home and school environments and ratings, and to track these children's progress in these skills over time. The SSRS also may provide an important link between assessment and intervention, a critical need in preschool social-emotional and adaptive behavior assessment.

Behavioral Observation

Behavioral Observation Recording Methods.   While an extensive discussion is impossible for this chapter, there are six or more different methods of recording behavioral observations (Keller, 1986; Sattler, 1990). *Narrative recordings* are also referred to as anecdotal records. Here, observers descriptively write down anything that seems critical to a comprehensive understanding of a child or target behavior. Narrative recordings are typically running records of everything that is observed during a particular time. While they are infrequently quantified, they most often set the stage for a more molecular analysis of a particular target behavior during a later observation period.

Interval recording is used when an observer divides a predetermined observation period into equal time units. Specific target behaviors then are observed and recorded whenever they occur within each time unit such that a percentage of occurrence over the entire observation period can be calculated. Interval recording can be contrasted with *time-sampling recording* which also uses predetermined time units, but requires observers to record a target behavior's presence only when it occurs at a specific time during a time unit (e.g., only at the end of the time unit). Interval recording is used primarily for behaviors that occur with moderate frequency and which do not have clear beginning and end points. Time-sampling recording is used similarly, but allows for briefer observation times and the potential for more observation periods across a particular day. Sattler (1990) calls time-sampling recording *point-time interval sampling,* and considers it one of a number of interval recording methods (including partial-interval time sampling, whole-interval time sampling, momentary time interval sampling, and variable interoccasion interval time sampling).

Event recording involves an actual frequency count of the number of times a specific target behavior occurs across an observation period. This recording method is best used to observe discrete behaviors which occur in moderate frequencies. At some points, event recording may expand to include *duration and latency recordings,* thereby analyzing how long a target behavior lasts during an observation unit or how long it takes from an antecedent behavior, for example, to a desired target behavior, respectively. Event recording can track a specific target behavior over time, from assessment to intervention to generalization. It also can assess the rate and intensity of some behaviors such that a comprehensive behavioral analysis is possible.

Finally, *ratings recording* involves a predetermined observation period and the completion of a formal behavior rating scale or checklist based exclusively on the observations and behavior noted. The Child Behavior Checklist—Direct Observation Form (Achenbach, 1991) exemplifies this recording approach as a referred child is observed over a 10-minute period and then 96 specific problem items are rated on a 0-1-2-3 scale. While this tool has been standardized for ages 5 through 14, it does demonstrate that a ratings recording approach is feasible for younger ages and that a preschool-aged version can be developed for empirical and objective use.

Behavioral Observation Approaches.   Returning to the BAG (Cone, 1978), four approaches to behavioral observation are noted: naturalistic free behavior, naturalistic role play, analog free behavior, and analog role play. While behavioral observation may appear to be the easiest and most objective of all our assessment approaches, it is actually one of the most complex. Behavioral observation must assess the behavioral ecology of a specific situation—its antecedent conditions, environmental structures and interactions, overt and covert contingencies, planned and unplanned consequent conditions, cultural context, and its unintended effects. Further, it must objectively choose and analyze target behaviors that are both significantly responsible for the problems or concerns referred and able to be effectively assessed through an observation approach. Finally, behavioral observation must be sensitive to both the developmental and normative aspects of preschool behavior. That is, target behaviors and observation objectives must be consistent with the chronological or developmental age expectations of the child being observed (otherwise, they may be abnormally high or low and expected to be so), and they must allow comparisons to others in the peer group or behavioral setting (in order to control for idiosyncrasies within the behavioral ecology and to establish a sense of "local norms").

Naturalistic Observation.   *Naturalistic observation* involves observing preschoolers' behavior in the actual settings where they live, grow, and learn. Done effectively, such observation should utilize trained observers who collect data unobtrusively using recording strategies and protocols that require minimal inference for analysis (Keller, 1986). Naturalistic observations have the advantage of occurring in the child's natural environment where it is assumed that the behaviors sampled are most representative of the child's actual behaviors. They are, however, not always time- or cost-efficient because a target behavior might not always present itself "at the right time." Nonetheless, naturalistic observations are the most ecologically sound, and they offer a great deal to the social-emotional and/or adaptive behavior assessment process.

Barnett and Carey (1992) recommend a two-step sequence for naturalistic observation. In Step 1, preliminary observations are conducted to determine important behaviors and events using real-time recordings. In this context, real-time recording provides a running account of behavior as it occurs in a child's natural environment; it involves behavioral observations of the target child, the peer group, and the teacher; and it determines which aspects of behavior and the environment are important to record. On the recording protocol, each line contains one molar (meaningful and complete) unit of behavior, and each activity is recorded in a mutually exclusive (one event is recorded) and exhaustive (all the time is accounted for by recorded behaviors) fashion. Time notations are made in the left margin at pre-specified (e.g., one- or 2-minute) intervals, or at the beginning and end of a specific target behavior. In the end, real-time observations yield frequency counts, rates of occurrence, intervals of duration, prevalence rates, and inter-response times. This information helps to define target behaviors, to select structured observation approaches for subsequent observations, to conduct antecedent–behavior–consequence analyses, and to monitor later intervention effectiveness (Barnett & Carey, 1992; Suen & Ary, 1989).

In Step 2, data collected from the preliminary observations are integrated with ecobehavioral interview data resulting in the selection of the best format for a second, more structured observation. This second observation typically focuses more on specific target behaviors and might center on (a) environments; (b) play activities; (c) peer relationships; (d) relationships with adults; (e) responses to learning tasks, demands, and rules; (f) antecedent and consequent events for specific behaviors or functional analyses; and/or (g) pragmatic language use. A wide range of specific methods can be used for this second observation depending on the target behaviors, the ecological circumstances, and potential or needed intervention directions (Wolery, 1989). For example, the Preschool Observation Code (POC; Bramlett & Barnett, 1993) uses a standardized coding format that allows practitioners to observe and analyze frequently referred problems. The POC includes a momentary time sampling system for state behaviors, and frequency counts for event behaviors. State behaviors are coded at one pre-determined time during each observation interval, and the frequency of events is recorded within each of these intervals. Overall, the POC has acceptable technical adequacy and is useful for research and behavioral observations in the field.

Given the wide range of typical behavior during the preschool years and the impact of teacher and setting variables, it often is useful to compare the behavior of a referred child to a non-referred child. This can be done using momentary time sampling or interval sampling approaches, and the degree to which a referred child differs from other children can facilitate decisions regarding assessment questions, referrals, or potential interventions

(Walker & Hops, 1976). PLA-CHECK (Planned Activity Check) is a method for observing the social behavior of children in groups. At the end of a specified interval, a group of children is observed and the number of children engaged in a target behavior is counted. This number then is divided by the total number of children in the group to determine the percent of children engaged in the target behavior. Scan checking (Alessi, 1988; Alessi & Kaye, 1983) is an adaptation of the PLA-CHECK procedure in which a classroom is momentarily scanned every 2 minutes or so during an observation, and the number of children who are, for example, on-task is recorded as a percentage.

The functional assessment of preschoolers' social-emotional or adaptive behavior frequently involves analyzing their play development (see Table 9.4 for some possible focuses of observation). This may occur, for example, during a free play session at a water or sand table where an observer would attend to a referred child's play interactions with his peers, particularly his frequency and duration of unoccupied, solitary, onlooker, parallel, associative, and cooperative play (Yussen & Santrock, 1982). The observation also could assess specific antecedent and consequent conditions (e.g., peer invitation or positive teacher attention, respectively) that may encourage a particular level of play, and evaluate predetermined social skills behaviors that facilitated the play process. The observation data then could be compared (1) with developmental expectations, by looking at the literature that evaluates preschoolers' chronological age and play behavior across the six play categories (Yussen & Santrock, 1982); and/or (2) with normative expectations, by observing typical peers' play within the same class and with the same activities.

Analog Observation.   *Analog observation* occurs within the context of a controlled situation that is planned and executed in order to simulate a particular environment or behavioral/ecological condition. This analog situation attempts to elicit specific, referred behaviors for a detailed and comprehensive functional analysis, while working to minimize extraneous variables that interfere with this analysis. Naturally, the situation's ability to facilitate a child's typical behavior and behavioral reactions will go a long way in decreasing the amount of inference necessary during the data interpretation process. To this end, older children often are told to approach the analog situation by role playing or acting as if they were in their natural environment. For preschoolers, this may not be necessary as they may not discriminate between natural and analog situations and environments.

Analog observations are very time-efficient in that they are structured to increase the likelihood that a target behavior will be observed. In addition, they can be used to evaluate possible intervention strategies, thereby maximizing the assessment to intervention link. Analog observations, however, can be time-inefficient if a substantial amount of time is necessary to create the analog situation, if the situation does not appropriately simulate reality, and/or if too much interpretive inference is necessary such that conclusions are unreliable or invalid. These disadvantages can be overcome with sound problem identification and analysis procedures and with detailed planning that considers the preschooler's entire behavioral ecology and possible reactions.

An example of an analog observation might involve analyzing a preschooler's aggressive, altruistic, and other emotional reaction to a specially created incident arranged to induce conflict, distress, frustration, or enjoyment. Zahn-Waxler, McKnew, Cummings, Davenport, and Radke-Yarrow (1984) designed such a situation involving a referred child and his mother, a same-age peer and his mother, and selected staff interacting across nine sequenced interactive conditions: a novel environment; an affection and sharing environment; a neutral context; a hostile, angry, and rejecting climate; a second neutral context; a reconciliation

TABLE 9.4   Possible Observation Areas to Assess Children's Play

Entrance into the Play Room

- Does the child go into the playroom easily?
- Does the child ask to hold the mother's or interviewer's hand on the way?
- Does the child approach the toys, or does he or she cling to the mother?

Initiation of Play Activities

- Is the child a quick or slow starter?
- Does the child require help in getting started?
- Does the child need encouragement and approval?
- Is the child able to direct his or her own play?
- Does the child require active and steady guidance?
- Does the child show initiative, resourcefulness, or curiosity?
- Is the child impulsive?
- Does the child initiate many activities but seldom complete them, or does he or she maintain interest in a single activity?

Energy Expended in Play

- Does the child work at a fairly even pace, or does he or she use much energy in manipulating the play materials, making body movements, and making verbalizations?
- Does the child seem to pursue an activity to the point of tiring himself or herself?
- Does the child start to work slowly and then gain momentum until the actions are energetic, or does he or she gradually lose momentum?
- Does the child seem listless, lethargic, lacking in vitality?

Manipulative Actions in Play

- Is the child free or tense in handling the play materials?
- Are movements large and sweeping or small and precise?
- Are movements smooth?
- Are play materials used in conventional or unconventional ways?

Tempo of Play

- Does the child play rapidly or with deliberation?
- Is the pace of play hurried or leisurely?
- Does the pace of play vary with different activities or is it always about the same?

Body Movements in Play

- Does the child's body seem tense or relaxed?
- Are the child's movements constricted or free?
- Are the child's movements uncertain, jerky, or poorly coordinated?
- Are movements of hands and arms free, incorporating the whole body rhythmically, or are movements rigid, with only parts of the body being used?
- Does the child use the right hand, the left hand, or both hands?

Verbalizations

- Does the child sing, hum, use nonsense phrases, or use adult phrases as he or she plays?
- Does the child giggle appropriately?

- What is the general tone of the child's voice tones (for example, loud, shrill, excitable, soft, aggressive, tense, enthusiastic, more matter-of-fact)?
- What does the child say?
- What is the purpose of the child's verbalizations, judging from the intonation?

Tone of Play

- What is the general tone of the child's play (for example, angry, satisfied, hostile, impatient)?
- Does the child throw, tear, or destroy play materials?
- Is the child protective of play materials?
- If aggression is present, does it have a goal or is it random?
- Does aggression increase, causing the play to get out of hand and posing a threat of damage to the playroom or interviewer?

Integration of Play

- Is the play goal-directed or fragmentary?
- Does the play become more integrated over time?
- Does the play have form, or is it haphazard?
- Is the child's attention sustained or fleeting?
- Is the child easily distracted?
- Are there any peculiar elements to the play?

Creativity of Play

- Is the play imaginative or stereotyped?
- Does the child use simple objects for play, or are special toys needed?
- Does the play show elements of improvisation or constriction?

Products of Play

- What play materials are preferred?
- What objects are constructed or designs completed during play?
- Do the products have a recognizable form?
- How does the child achieve form?
- Does the child show interest in the product?
- Does the child tell a story about the product?
- Does the child show the interviewer and/or parent the product?
- Does the child want to save the product?
- Does the child want to give the product to someone?
- Does the child use the product for protective or aggressive purposes?
- Is the child overly concerned with nearness, alignment, or balance of the play materials?

Age Appropriateness of Play

- Is the play age-appropriate?
- Are there changes in the quality of the play?

Attitude Toward Adults Reflected in Play

- Does the child comply with adult request or do what he or she thinks adults expect of him or her?

(continued)

TABLE 9.4   Continued

■ Does the child imitate adult manners accurately
■ Does the child protect himself or herself from adults?
■ Does the child attempt to obtain tender responses from adults?
■ Does the child follow his or her own ideas independently of adults?

Source: Reprinted by permission of the publisher and author from *Assessment of Children,* 3rd edition—Revised, by J. M. Sattler, pp. 418–419. Copyright © 1992 by Jerome M. Sattler, Publisher.

interaction; a friend's separation experience; a mother separation experience, and a reunion with mother. Throughout these nine conditions, the referred child's behavioral reactions were specifically noted. These analog-free behavior observations then were compared with other, more naturalistic behavioral observations of the child such that a reliable and valid assessment was obtained. This approach provides another potential component to a comprehensive social-emotional and behavioral analysis of a referred preschool child.

Free Behavior versus Role Play Observations.   Quite simply, free behavior observations occur as the preschooler is allowed to freely react and interact within a chosen environment. That is, no artificial rules or constraints are placed on the child; he or she responds to situations in a way that we would expect is typical for that child. Naturalistic free behavior observations occur, for example, when preschoolers are observed in their unaltered, normal environments (e.g., at home, school, or on the playground). Analog-free behavior is observed, for example, when a structured or contrived situation (such as a game or an activity—the dress-up corner) is introduced to elicit a specific behavior or reaction, but the child is allowed to respond freely and without additional constraints.

Role play observations involve more inference than free behavior observations. Role plays are somewhat more structured and scripted, yet these characteristics may have less impact on preschoolers given their tendency toward fantasy, play, and make-believe. Naturalistic role play observations occur when individuals within a target child's environment are "scripted" to interact or respond in a specific, strategic way to a situation or activity that routinely occurs in the target child's life. Here, the target child is allowed to freely respond to the situation as he or she typically would. In an analog role play, scripted individuals would interact with a target child in a structured or contrived situation for the purposes of eliciting a specific behavior or reaction and to allow the target child's specific responses to be observed.

All four types of behavioral observations can potentially elicit important data for the social-emotional and/or adaptive behavior assessment. Clearly, in the context of the BAG (Cone, 1978), any behavioral observation approach will collect "more direct" data than any of the indirect approaches (i.e., interview, self-report, or behavior rating scale). This is assuming, however, that the observation has been done as effectively and objectively as possible. To do this, some attention must be spent on the observation method and protocol used in this process and on sources of observation error (see below).

Comprehensive Behavioral Observation Analyses.   Relative to a comprehensive analysis of behavior, there are numerous coding systems and protocols available for behavioral observation (e.g., Alessi, 1980; Keller, 1986). Most of these systems code (1) for children's behavior relative to themselves, their peers, adults, and home or school equipment and material; (2) for adults' (parent or teacher) behaviors and reactions to the referred child and others; and (3) for other peers' (or siblings') behaviors for comparison purposes. Figure 9.1 provides an example of one type of comprehensive behavioral observation protocol (Alessi, 1980). Note that this protocol allows for analyses (1) of multiple target behaviors; (2) of interactions between referred children, their teachers, and their peer group; (3) of various observation recording methods; and (4) of interobserver agreement and reliability.

Observing Classroom Environments. Because preschoolers' social-emotional and adaptive behavior skills are impacted, often interdependently, by their interactions within classroom environments, analyses of the classroom environment itself should be considered during any observation. To this end, the classroom environment can be divided into physical and social components. The physical component involves the fixed or programmatic aspects of the classroom. Observational targets here might include (1) the arrangement and accessibility of classroom space, (2) patterns of supervision, and (3) the availability of classroom materials (Moore, 1987). The social component involves the interactive characteristics of the classroom, including teacher and peer behavior. Observational targets here might include (1) the number and characteristics of available peers; (2) the responsiveness of the environment; and (3) the planning, scheduling, and classroom management techniques of the teacher (Olds, 1987).

Several coding systems have been developed to facilitate the observation and analysis of classroom environments. One ecobehavioral preschool code is the Ecobehavioral System for Complex Assessment of Preschool Environments (ESCAPE; Carta, Greenwood, & Atwater, 1992), developed to assess the interaction of children's behavior and environmental variables within the preschool classroom. Using momentary time sampling with 15-second time intervals to code specifically defined events, the ESCAPE provides both molar and molecular analyses of classroom environments. Significantly, Carta et al. (1992) suggest that the ESCAPE be used across an entire school day. While the ESCAPE results in a nonjudgmental picture of what is taking place in the classroom, it is a highly complex system and this may discourage some from using it. At the very least, this reinforces the importance of training and practice prior to the use of any behavioral observation system. Once again, while behavioral observation is the least inferential and most objective method of social-emotional assessment, a high degree of expertise is needed to use it clinically and effectively.

The Preschool Assessment of the Classroom Environment (PACE; McWilliam & Dunst, 1985) was designed to assess environments that serve children, from birth to age 6, with identified disabilities. The instrument consists of 70 items organized into 4 categories: (1) program organization (including program management, integration, and parent involvement); (2) environmental organization (including the physical environment, staffing patterns, scheduling, and transitions); (3) instruction (including growth and development, curriculum, plans for intervention, methods of instruction, and behavior management); and (4) program outcomes (including child engagement and program evaluation). Each item is scored on a 5-point rating scale, and all ratings are completed after observing the classroom environment, interviewing staff, and reviewing written materials.

The Early Childhood Environment Rating Scale (ECERS; Harms & Clifford, 1980) provides an analysis of the surroundings for children and adults in preschool settings. The ECERS examines the use of space, materials, and activities to enhance children's development, the effectiveness of the daily schedule, and supervision. Based on a review of the literature and input from caregivers, supervisors, and seven early childhood experts, the ECERS

FIGURE 9.1 **Example of a Comprehensive Behavior Observation Protocol**

Western Michigan University School Psychology Program
CLASSROOM OBSERVATION RECORD PROTOCOL

Pupil _____Mary_____   Comparison: _____C.J._____   Observer: _School Psychologist (L.C.)_

Age:_____6–10_____   Age: _____6–7_____   Reliability: _____Social Worker_____

Grade: _____2nd_____   Class Size:_____26_____

School: _____Westwood_____   Class Type: _____Regular ed._____

Teacher: _____Mrs. Kaput_____   Time Stop: _____10:23_____

Date: _____16/10/78_____   Time Start: _____

                                                                          Total Time: _____:10_____

Reason for observation (What questions do we want to answer?):

To confirm reported discrepancy between Mary's behavior and that of her classroom peers.

Classroom Activity and explicit rules in effect at time of observation:

Activity: Math. — See notes below for details. Rules: 1. Follow teacher's directions.
2. Work quietly. 3. Complete work.

Description of Observation Techniques: (interval or time sample and length)

30-minute interval for Mary and comparison. 2-minute time sample for class scan check.

Behavior Codes:	Grouping Codes:	Teacher Reaction Codes:
T = On Task	L = large group	AA = attention to all
V = Verbal Off task	S = small group	A+ = positive attention to pupil
M = Motor Off task	O = one-to-one	A- = negative attention to pupil
P = Passive Off task	I = independent act.	Ao = no attention to pupil
__ = _____	F = free-time	An = neutral attention to pupil
__ = _____	__ = _____	__ = _____

	Time	Pupil	Com-parison	Class Scan Check	Anecdotal notes on behavior	Grouping	Teacher Reaction
1.	10:13	P	T		_Ma not responding to teacher_	L	An
2.		M	T		_Standing up—other sitting_	L	Ao
3.	10:14	M	T		_Te leads ma back to desk_	L	An
4.		M	T	80%	_Standing up_	L	Ao
5.	10:15	P	T		_Sitting staring at others_	L	Ao
6.		T	N		_Looking at teacher_	S	Ao
7.	10:16	T	N	76%	_Sitting quietly and listening_	S	Ao
8.		T	T		_Working at desk_	S	Ao
9.	10:17	P	T		_Looking out window_	L	Ao
10.		T	T	83%	_Copying math problems_	L	Ao

FIGURE 9.1 Continued

	Time	Pupil	Com-parison	Class Scan Check	Anecdotal notes on behavior	Grouping	Teacher Reaction
11.	10:18	P	T		Staring at board	L	Ao
12.		M	T		On floor getting pencil	L	Ao
13.	10:19	M	T	80%	On floor getting pencil	L	Ao
14.		M	N		On floor poking other	L	Ao
15.	10:20	P	T		In seat staring	L	Ao
16.		P	T	88%	In seat staring	L	Ao
17.	10:21	T	T		Writing math	S	An
18.		T	T		Writing math	S	Ao
19.	10:22	M	T	80%	Walking in class	S	Ao
20.		T	T		Writing math	S	Ao
Summary:		35% (7/20)	85% (17/20)	81%		L = 13; S= 7	Ao =17; An = 3
Reliability =		83%					

Western Michigan University School Psychology Program
CLASSROOM OBSERVATION RECORD PROTOCOL

Observer: _____ *School Psychologist (K.A.)* _____   Date: _____ *28/10/78* _____
                                                                                  day   month   year
Reliability Observer: _____ *paraprofessional* _____

Teacher: _____ *Mrs. Graves* _____

School: _____ *Pine Elementary* _____   Time Stop: _____ *11:16* _____

Subject area: _____ *reading—seatwork* _____   Time Start: _____ *11:09* _____

Referred pupil (R): _ *Chelsea* _ Age: _ *8-6* _   Total time: _____ *:7* _____

Comparison pupil (C): _____ — _____ Age: _ *8-5* _

Class size: _____ *31* _____ Class Type: _ *regular* _   Observation recording method:
                                                                                  (circle one)

Grouping situation: Teacher Reaction Codes: (a) Interval: size _ *30″* _
(circle one)   (b) time sample: size _____
                           AA = attention to all   (c) event count _____
L = large group   A+ = positive attention to pupil **(d) duration for "out of seat"
S = small group   A- = negative attention to pupil   (e) latency
O = one-to-one   Ao = no attention to pupil
(I) = independent act.   An = neutral attention to pupil
F = free-time   __ = _____
__ = _____   __ = _____

Explicit classroom rules in effect during observation: _ *1. work quietly*   *2. sit at desks* _
        3. raise hand for help

(continued)

FIGURE 9.1   Continued

Teacher would like to see: less of _____ ; _____ ; more of _____ ; none; strengths;

Behaviors	Tot.		1	2	3	4	5	6	7	8	9	10	11	12	13	14	15
1. Verbal	8	R	X	O	O	X	X	O	O	X	X	O	O	X	X	O	X
Off Task	2	C	O	X	O	O	X	O	O	O	O	O	O	O	O	O	O
		T	Ao	Ao		Ao	An			Ao	Ao			Ao	An		Ao
2. Master	4	R	X	O	X	O	O	O	O	O	O	X	X	O	O	O	O
Off Task	1	C	O	O	O	O	O	O	O	O	O	O	O	O	X	O	O
		T	Ao		Ao							Ao	An	Ao			
3. Passive	1	R	O	O	O	O	O	X	O	O	O	O	O	O	O	O	O
Off Task	1	C	O	O	O	O	O	O	X	O	O	O	O	O	O	O	O
		T						Ao	An								
4. On Task	3	R	O	X	O	O	O	O	X	O	O	O	O	O	O	X	O
	11	C	X	O	X	X	O	X	O	X	X	X	X	O	X	X	X
		T	Ao	An	An	An		Ao		Ao	Ao	An	Ao		Ao	An	Ao
5. Ask questions	1	R	O	O	O	O	O	O	O	O	O	X	O	O	O	O	O
	3	C	O	O	O	X	O	O	O	O	O	O	X	O	O	X	O
		T				An						An	An			An	
6.		R															
		C															
		T															
7. Out-of-seat	53"	R	14"	8"	22"	9"											
(duration)	6"	C	6"														
		T	A-	A-	An	A-											
8. Raising hand	1	R	O	O	O	O	O	O	O	O	O	O	X	O	O	O	O
for help	2	C	O	O	O	X	O	O	O	O	O	O	O	O	O	X	O
		T				An							An			An	
9.		R															
		C															
		T															

Were reliability data collected? (Yes) No   If yes, interobserver % agreement = 83%.

**Specific behavior definitions included on back, as well as comments (strengths, contextual observations, etc.).

Source: Reprinted with permission of the author and publisher from "Behavioral Observation for the School Psychologist: Responsive-Discrepancy Model" by Alessi, G. J., 1980, *School Psychology Review,* Vol. 9, pp. 31–45.

has 37 items arranged into 7 subscales: (1) personal care routines, (2) furnishings and display, (3) language-reasoning experiences, (4) fine and gross motor activities, (5) creative activities, (6) social development, and (7) adult needs. Each item is scored on a scale from 1 (inadequate) to 7 (excellent), and the authors recommend that classroom observations and staff interviews be completed before rating the items. The inter-rater reliability of the ECERS was found to be .88 and the test–retest reliability was .96 (Harms & Clifford, 1980).

Several studies have investigated the ECERS's ability to evaluate dimensions of environmental quality. In a study of 166 preschool children in nine daycare centers, McCartney (1984) found a moderate relationship ($r = .70$, $p < .10$) between overall ratings of day care environment, as measured by the ECERS, and the interactive speech between caregivers and children, as measured by the Preschool Language Assessment Instrument. However, low correlations were reported between the ECERS and the Peabody Picture Vocabulary Test ($r = .23$, $p < .05$), the overall score on the Preschool Language Assessment Instrument ($r = .23$, $p < .01$), and caregiver ratings of language development on the Adaptive Language Inventory ($r = .35$, $p < .001$). According to the authors, additional research is needed to determine the efficacy of the ECERS for evaluating preschool environments and the relationship between the environment and developmental outcomes for children.

The ECERS also was used to compare the classroom environments for typically-developing preschoolers and those for children with disabilities. Bailey, Clifford, and Harms (1982) reported that the overall environmental ratings for 56 classrooms of typical children were significantly higher than of 25 classrooms for children with disabilities. While the authors suggested that the preschool environments appeared less normalized than those for the typical children, item comparisons between the two types of programs revealed significant differences on only 12 of 37 ECERS items. In the end, the authors suggested that the ECERS may not be entirely appropriate for rating the environments of handicapped children. Nonetheless, the results of this study should be considered exploratory; future research is clearly indicated.

Sources of Observation Error.   As with behavior rating scales, there are numerous sources of error that can totally undermine the reliability and validity of a behavioral observation. For example, behavioral observations are as susceptible to halo effects, leniency or severity effects, and central tendency or range restriction effects as behavior rating scales. In addition, the following sources of error must be defended against when completing behavioral observations: observer drift, omissions, coding errors, expectations, and reactivity; protocol complexity, irrelevance, and invalidity; and parent, teacher, referred child, or peer group reactivity (Sattler, 1992). The latter error source is particularly important. Many times, referred children and others manifest atypical behavior due to the fact that they are being observed. This is a critical phenomenon for any age group, but especially for preschoolers. Preschoolers are particularly interested in new and interesting adults. All behavioral observations must be organized so that a representative sample of typical behavior is manifested and assessed. This involves desensitizing children to new adults, to the observation, and to following directions when a new adult is present in the environment. With planning and attention to the various sources of error above, appropriate and significant data can be obtained through behavioral observations.

To summarize this section, behavioral observation is the most direct way to evaluate a preschooler's social-emotional and adaptive behavior. Not without its potential liabilities, behavioral observation also requires the least amount of inference relative to interpretation and analysis. Every preschool referral should have a behavioral observation as part of the comprehensive analysis process. Then, combined with other assessment methods from the BAG (Cone, 1978), an objective and meaningful assessment can be completed, leading to direct and logical linkages with the interventions to follow.

Empirical/Behavioral Methods

Returning to the indirect assessment methods of the BAG, it is extremely important to recognize the availability of objective or empirically-derived behavior assessment methods. As noted above, these tools are typically developed by subjecting a large pool of social-emotional and adaptive behavior characteristics and descriptors to factor analysis in order to identify clusters of related behaviors at specific ages and for specific individuals. In the section below, two objective assessment tools are reviewed: one, the Personality Inventory for Children that was empirically derived, and the other, the Temperament Assessment Battery for Children that was theoretically derived.

The Personality Inventory for Children.   One of the better known and researched clinical assessment tools available at the preschool level, the Personality Inventory for Children (PIC; Wirt, Lachar, Klinedinst, & Seat, 1984) is an objective, multidimensional measure of behavior, affect, ability, and family functioning. The PIC consists of 600 true/false items which typically are answered by a referred child's mother. Organized such that increasing parts of its 20 scales (four factor scales, four validity and screening scales, and 12 clinical scales) can be scored with 131, 280, or 420 items, respectively, the PIC has been normed separately for males and females from the ages of 3 to 5, and 6 through 16.

Based on its most current norms, the PIC consists of the following scales:

1. *Factor Scales*: Undisciplined/Poor Self-Control, Social Incompetence, Internalization/Somatic Symptoms, and Cognitive Development
2. *Validity and Screening Scales*: Lie, Frequency, Defensiveness, and Adjustment
3. *Clinical Scales*: Achievement, Intellectual Screening, Development, Somatic Concerns, Depression, Family Relations, Delinquency, Withdrawal, Anxiety, Psychosis, Hyperactivity, and Social Skills

This allows the PIC to provide diagnostic information on a preschool child from an individual item, a clinical scale, a scale cluster (e.g., the "cognitive triad" consisting of the Achievement, Intellectual Screening, and Development scales), and a factor-level perspective. In addition, because the PIC's scales were independently developed and validated, they can be analyzed and interpreted individually, without the need to consider inter-scale correlations or effects.

Overall, the PIC contributes important and clinically useful information to a social-emotional and/or adaptive behavior assessment. As an empirically based scale, the PIC has good psychometric properties (see Table 9.5), and its validity scales can detect a respondent (i.e., a parent) who is either exaggerating or defensive. As an objective scale, the PIC can be used to confirm hypotheses that have been generated through less reliable means. Finally, as a behavior rating scale of sorts, the PIC is a low inference tool; it can validate the presence of specific referral problems or concerns, and its factor structure can assess the more global aspects of personality assessment.

The Temperament Assessment Battery for Children.   The Temperament Assessment Battery for Children (TABC; Martin, 1988) was designed to parallel Thomas and Chess' (1977) model of temperament that relates the behavioral and emotional reactivity of infants and children to interactions with individuals (usually adults) and/or environmental

TABLE 9.5   Summary of the Standardization and Psychometric Properties of Select Empirical Preschool Assessment Instruments

The Personality Inventory for Children (PIC; ages 3 to 16)

Standardization: The PIC has been normed separately for males and females from the ages of 3 to 5, and 6 through 16. At the 3- to 5-year-old preschool level, the PIC was normed in 1979 based on a sample of 102 boys and 90 girls. The upper extension of the PIC was normed on an extremely large sample of 2,390 children from the greater Minneapolis area (81.5% from the Minneapolis Public Schools and the majority of the rest from a local medical center), with approximately 100 boys and 100 girls at each of 11 age levels between the ages of 5½ and 16½ years.

Reliability data: Most of the published studies have investigated PIC protocols at the 6- to 16-year-old level. Summarizing across three studies cited in the PIC manual, test-retest reliabilities ranged from .46 (Defensiveness) to .94, with a mean reliability coefficient of .86, for a psychiatric, outpatient sample (N = 34); from .50 (Defensiveness) to .89, with a mean of .71, for a sample of normal children (N = 46); and from .68 (Somatic Concerns) to .97, with a mean of .89, for a different sample of normal children. Across these studies, the length of time between two testings ranged from an average of 15 days to 51 days.

One internal consistency study, based on a heterogeneous clinic sample (N = 1,226), reported correlations ranging from .57 (Intellectual Screening) to .86, with a mean alpha of .74. Finally, a number of studies evaluating mother versus father interrater reliabilities reported correlations ranging from .34 (Frequency) to .68, with a mean of .57 for a sample of normal children (N = 146); ranging from .21 (Defensiveness) to .79, with a mean of .64, for a clinical sample (N = 84); and averaging .66 for the 13 clinical scales for a sample of children seen for a psychiatric evaluation (N = 360).

Validity data: The PIC manual documents a vast array of studies, most specific to its separate scales and related to their construction, and most addressing concurrent, convergent, or discriminant validity. The four final broad-band factors were generated through a factor analysis of data from a sample of 1,226 children evaluated at the Lafayette Clinic (MI), and generally, they overlap significantly with those factors typically reported by other objective, empirically-based personality assessment tools. Overall, the PIC has an excellent foundation of documented validity across its scales.

The Temperament Assessment Battery for Children (TABC; ages 3 to 7)

Standardization: While no national norms have been developed, the manual (Martin, 1988) reports data from several studies that involve (1) the Parent Form (1,381 male and female children from the Northeastern, Southeastern, and Rocky Mountain regions of the country); (2) the Teacher Form (577 male and female children from the Southeastern and Rocky Mountain regions); and (3) the Clinician Form (153 male and female children from the Southeastern region of the country).

Reliability data: The internal consistency of the TABC was estimated using coefficient alphas that ranged from .54 to .87, with alphas for the Teacher Form being somewhat higher on average than those for the Parent and Clinician Forms.

(continued)

TABLE 9.5   Continued

The stability of the Teacher Form was documented by 6 month test–retest reliability coefficients ranging from .69 to .87; one year test–retest reliability coefficients for the Parent Form ranged from .43 to .70 for mothers and .37 to .62 for fathers (test–retest reliability coefficients for the Clinician Form were not reported).

Finally, inter-rater reliability coefficients, as expected, were low (median mother–father correlations of .43, median parent–teacher correlations of .35, median teacher correlations of .79, and median same–parent correlations of .58 after one to two years) due to variability in the scale's items, children's behavior across settings, and differences in rater perceptions and experience with a child.

Validity data: The TABC manual provides examples of concurrent validity (e.g., with the Quay-Peterson Behavior Problem Checklist and the Bristol Social Adjustment Scale), and the relationship of the scale to observed behavior, teacher attitudes, assessments of psychopathology, and student achievement. More critically, while intra-test correlations between the different TABC scales were evident, results from confirmatory factor analyses reported in the manual did not support the factor structure of the scale.

circumstances. Critically, Thomas and Chess found that, when they longitudinally evaluated a group of children during their first years of life, seven of their nine temperament dimensions significantly predicted which children, at age five, were identified with symptoms of emotional or behavioral problems. The TABC can be used with children between the ages of 3 and 7 and is comprised of three forms: the Parent Form, the Teacher Form, and the Clinician Form. The Parent and Teacher forms each consist of 48 items which describe the frequency of children's behavior at home and in school, respectively, along a 7-point scale (Hardly Ever, Infrequently, Once in a While, Sometimes, Often, Very Often, or Almost Always). The same 7-point scale is included on the Clinician Form, which is essentially a questionnaire completed by psychologists or other mental health practitioners who have observed the child's behavior during a performance activity (e.g., a psychoeducational evaluation or in a classroom or play environment).

The TABC is organized into six scales (Activity, Adaptability, Approach/Withdrawal, Emotional Intensity, Distractibility or Ease-of-Management Through Distraction, and Persistence) that reflect six of nine Thomas and Chess temperament dimensions. Because the TABC has no national norms, depending instead on regional studies involving samples that were small and lacked representativeness (see Table 9.5), the author (Martin, 1988) noted that the results cannot be generalized to the preschool population at large. Thus, at best, the TABC can be used as a screening device that provides some functional, multisetting and multisource perspectives on the behavioral reactivity of a preschool child.

While temperament is an important construct in child development that does relate to children's behavior and interpersonal styles, the current standardization and psychometric properties of the TABC argue for the conservative use of this scale. Indeed, any data, results, or conclusions drawn from the TABC need to be cross-validated and confirmed through other assessments and observations that establish a consistent pattern of behavior or social-emotional interactions. Over time, it is hoped that an improved TABC or a new scale assessing children's temperament will be developed to provide functional and diagnostic information in this important area.

Summary and a Brief Note about Projective Tests

Clearly, the focus of this discussion has been on a behavioral perspective of preschool social-emotional assessment. And, given the primary assumptions discussed above, this is where the assessment process should be focused. Direct, one-on-one, verbal assessment with preschoolers is difficult, at best, due to their relative inexperience, their inability to comprehend the complexities of their social-emotional status both individually and in the context of peer and family interactions, and their limited communication and language skills. Thus, behavioral assessment, as operationalized by the Behavior Assessment Grid and completed within a multimethod, multisource, multisetting framework, offers the most reliable and valid approach to accurate and appropriate problem identification and analysis.

A behavioral approach to social-emotional and adaptive behavior assessment with preschoolers suggests a very limited role for projective assessment. Projective tests are best used to identify hypotheses about children's cognitions regarding their past, present, and future; their home, school, and "other" settings; their family, peers, and significant others; and about themselves—their internalizing and externalizing behavior, affect, or interactions (Knoff, 1986, 1990). These cognitions primarily involve their attitudes, beliefs, expectations, attributions, and memories, and these hypotheses must be validated by other more objective and empirically based assessments. Projective tests also are dependent on (1) children's understanding of somewhat vague or ambiguous test directions and expectations; (2) test stimuli that may be so novel that they elicit contaminated response sets; and (3) verbal or drawing responses. This latter area is especially important given preschoolers' developmental maturation in language and drawing (visual-motor skill). For example, how does one know if a projective drawing is "significant" because of the child's visual-motor skill, some social-emotional determinant, or some combination of the two? There is no reliable way to determine this in most cases; the integrity of the assessment process would suggest that the practitioner never be faced with this dilemma. Finally and in general, projective tests (1) lack appropriate standardizations, norms, and psychometric properties; (2) need substantial practitioner inference and subjective interpretation; and again (3) generate hypotheses, not conclusions, for the comprehensive assessment process.

Although projective assessment can be useful with children of elementary school ages and adolescents, they are not recommended at the preschool level. Direct and indirect behavior assessment, as summarized and operationalized in the BAG (Cone, 1978) is the most effective, accurate, and defensible assessment approaches for referred preschoolers. Such tests have relatively low inference levels, can be replicated and objectively evaluated, can directly assess behaviors and affects of concern, and provide a direct linkage between assessment and intervention in the vast majority of cases.

Assessing Adaptive Behavior

Adaptive behavior involves children's ability to function independently to a developmentally appropriate degree, to effectively meet the social and natural demands of the environments wherein they interact, and to adjust and function within the cultural constraints of society (AAMR, 1992; Sattler, 1990). Adaptive behavior is primarily assessed through adaptive behavior scales that integrate diagnostic interview, behavior checklist, behavior rating scale, and direct observation approaches. At the preschool level, the most used and best adaptive behavior scales are standardized, normed, and psychometrically tested. They may use both parents and teachers as informants, and they may be interested exclusively in adaptive behavior or may be part of a comprehensive tool measuring multifaceted domains. Although the discussion in this section will focus on a number of standardized scales that exclusively measure adaptive behavior, a few notable others will be briefly reviewed.

The Revised BRIGANCE® Diagnostic Inventory of Early Development (Brigance, 1991) is a developmental scale that assesses psychomotor, self-help, speech and language, general knowledge and comprehension, social and emotional development, and readiness and early academic skills for children from birth to age 6. Constructed by drawing from and integrating over 50 other developmental scales, the BRIGANCE® is primarily a criterion-referenced list of skills that are developmentally organized to facilitate a maturational comparison between the Inventory and an evaluated child. The self-help area of the BRIGANCE® evaluates feeding and eating skills, dressing and undressing skills, fastening and unfastening skills, toileting and bathing and grooming skills, household and classroom chore skills, and safety skills. The social and emotional development area evaluates general social and emotional development, play skills and behaviors, and work-related skills and behaviors. An evaluation using the BRIGANCE® typically results in (1) a global developmental placement of the child in the self-help and social-emotional areas, respectively; (2) a specific profile of the self-help and social-emotional skills and behaviors that the child knows or can demonstrate; (3) task analyses of the sequence of skills that are prerequisite or needed by children to attain certain developmental levels; and (4) appropriate intervention directions to teach or encourage those prerequisite or needed skills.

Two examples of more comprehensive tests with adaptive behavior components are the Denver Developmental Screening Test—Revised (Frankenburg, Dodds, Fandal, Kazuk, & Cohrs, 1975) and the Battelle Developmental Inventory (Newborg, Stock, Wnek, Guidubaldi, & Svinicki, 1984). The former test can be used with children from birth to age 6, and its personal-social domain (23 items) evaluates the child's ability to socialize with others, to play appropriately, and to perform self-care tasks. The latter scale can be used with children from birth to age 8, and it has two domains of interest: the Personal-Social domain (85 items) and the Adaptive domain (59 items). The Personal-Social domain evaluates children's skills in adult interaction, expression of feelings and affect, self-concept, peer interaction, coping, and social roles. The Adaptive domain evaluates skills in attention, eating, dressing, personal responsibility, and toileting. The Denver Developmental Screening Test—Revised depends heavily on parent report and very little is known about its psychometric properties. The Battelle Developmental Inventory was normed using 1981 census data and appears to be standardized adequately. Good test–retest reliability, content validity, and concurrent validity are reported in its manual. More construct validation and general research support appears to be in order for this test at this time.

AAMD Adaptive Behavior Scale

The AAMD Adaptive Behavior Scale (ABS; Nihira, Foster, Shellhaas, & Leland, 1974) can be used to assess individuals with mental retardation, emotional disturbance, and developmental disabilities from 3 to 69 years old. Organized in two parts, the ABS can be completed in approximately 30 minutes in a behavior rating scale or interview format, and it can be given to more than one individual for a multisetting, multisource assessment. The ABS was standardized on approximately 4,000 mentally retarded individuals from 68 facilities across the country. Although its inter-rater reliability is acceptable ($r = .86$ for Part I and $r = .57$ for Part II), as is its discriminant validity (Sattler, 1990), its construct validity appears questionable and its overall psychometric properties need further investigation. From a criterion-based perspective, however, the ABS provides a wealth of information. Because many of the assessed skills are hierarchically and developmentally arranged, the ABS is able to identify what skills a child has mastered, for example, in dressing and undressing, and what skills are emerging and need further instruction or maturation.

As noted above, the ABS is divided into two parts. Part I assesses independent functioning (eating, toilet use, cleanliness, appearance, care of clothing, dressing and undressing, travel, and general independent functioning), physical development (sensory and motor development), economic activity (money handling, budgeting, and shopping skills), language development (expression, comprehension, and social language skills), number and time knowledge and skill, domestic activity (cleaning, kitchen and other domestic duties), vocational activity, self-direction (initiative, perseverance, and use of leisure time), responsibility, and socialization. Part II assesses 14 domains related to personality and behavior disorders: violent and destructive behavior, antisocial behavior, rebellious behavior, untrustworthy behavior, withdrawal, stereotyped behavior and odd mannerisms, inappropriate interpersonal manners, unacceptable vocal habits, unacceptable or eccentric habits, self-abusive behavior, hyperactive tendencies, sexually aberrant behavior, psychological disturbances, and use of medications. In general, Part I is more useful than Part II. It has a satisfactory floor and ceiling for preschool populations and it provides skill hierarchies that are descriptively helpful and useful for further task analysis and intervention. Part II is now somewhat dated. It does not analyze the severity of the maladaptive behaviors identified, it does not sample enough of the various areas to be reliable or definitive, and its norms are skewed given the mentally retarded sample with which the test was standardized.

Overall, the ABS has some important strengths and weaknesses. At the present time, it is probably best used as a criterion-referenced tool. From a norm-referenced perspective, its norms are now dated and were derived from a limited population; its psychometric soundness is questionable at best. In order to return to maximal utility, the ABS clearly needs to be updated and re-researched.

AAMD Adaptive Behavior Scale—School Edition

The AAMD Adaptive Behavior Scale—School Edition (ABS-SE; Lambert, Windmiller, Tharinger, & Cole, 1981) can be used to assess children and adolescents from 3 years 3 months to 17 years and 2 months old. Normed on 6,500 children attending regular, Educable Mentally Retarded (EMR), and Trainable Mentally Retarded (TMR) classes primarily in California and Florida, the ABS-SE evaluates the same domains as the ABS (see preceding section) except for the deletions of the Domestic Activity domain in Part I and the Self-Abusive Behavior and Sexually Aberrant Behavior domains in Part II. The ABS-SE has separate norm tables for regular, EMR, and TMR students, except that there are no EMR norms for the ages 3 through 6 because no children in that age range were assigned to the programs used in the standardization process. Beyond the separate scaled scores provided for each of the 21 adaptive behavior domains, ABS-SE data can be further evaluated using five empirically-derived factors: Personal Self-Sufficiency, Community Self-Sufficiency, Personal–Social Responsibility, Social Adjustment, and Personal Adjustment. Finally, a comparison score is available, reflecting a child's general level of adaptive behavior as compared to children of similar age and made up of the Community Self-Sufficiency, Personal Self-Sufficiency, and Personal–Social Responsibility factors. The Comparison Score discriminates among regular, EMR, and TMR students; for preschoolers, it can predict a child's comparability to regular versus TMR populations.

Relative to the preschool ages (3 to 5), the ABS-SE was standardized on 429 regular education students and 91 TMR students from California and Florida. Factor score reliabilities ranged from .59 (Personal Adjustment at age 4) to .95 (Social Adjustment for age 5) for regular students, and from .54 (Personal Adjustment at ages 4 and 5) to .91 (Social Adjustment at age 4) for TMR students. Across the entire scale, median reliabilities were .81 for Personal Self-Sufficiency, .89 for Community Self-Sufficiency, .88 for Personal-Social Responsibility, .94 for Social Adjustment, and .65 for Personal Adjustment. No reliability coefficients were reported in the manual for the 21 individual domain scores or for the comparison score, nor were any test–retest scores reported. In the validity area, most of the reported studies preceded the 1981 revision of the ABS-SE. One study suggested that IQ was most related to the Language Development (.39), Self-Direction and Socialization (.38), and Economic Activity (.36) domains for children aged 3 to 6; but overall, there was a very weak relationship between IQ and the ABS-SE's various domains. No studies' discriminant validity data were provided for the preschool ages, and no appropriate concurrent validity studies were reported.

Overall, the ABS-SE has some significant psychometric problems. It should not be used for making diagnostic decisions, and it cannot be used for EMR preschool assessment or comparison. The ABS-SE, however, can be used more descriptively to identify referred students' specific adaptive behavior strengths and weaknesses. In this way, the ABS-SE will be used correctly, until some of its current weaknesses are corrected.

Vineland Adaptive Behavior Scales

The Vineland Adaptive Behavior Scales (VABS; Sparrow, Balla, & Cicchetti, 1984) come in three versions (the Survey Form, Expanded Form, and Classroom Edition) that can be used to assess the ability of handicapped and nonhandicapped children to perform the daily activities required for personal and social sufficiency from the ages of birth through 19. All three VABS versions measure adaptive behavior using four specific domains, Communication, Daily Living Skills, Socialization, and Motor Skills (this latter scale for children from birth through age 6), which then are summed to create an Adaptive Behavior Composite. In addition, the Survey and Expanded Forms of the VABS have an optional Maladaptive Behavior domain. The Survey Form (comprising 297 items and taking up to one hour to administer) and the Expanded Form (280 items beyond the Survey Form's 297 items, taking up to 90 minutes to administer) are both completed as a semistructured interview with a parent or significant caregiver. The Classroom Edition (244 items taking about 20 minutes to complete) is completed as a questionnaire by a teacher and can be used for children 3 to 13 years of age.

The Survey and Expanded Forms of the VABS were standardized on 3,000 individuals who were stratified by sex, race or ethnic group, community size, region of the country, and parents' level of education to match the 1980 U.S. Census. The Classroom Edition was standardized on 3,000 students with the same stratification characteristics. Unfortunately, this stratification process resulted in some inequities as students from the South, Hispanic students, rural students, and students from lower socioeconomic status homes were all underrepresented. Descriptively, each of the four primary VABS domains contain specific subdomains. The Communication Domain is divided into receptive, expressive, and written subdomains; the Daily Living Skills domain is divided into personal, domestic, and community subdomains; the Socialization domain is divided into interpersonal relationships, play and leisure time, and coping skills subdomains; and the Motor Skills domain is divided into gross and fine motor subdomains.

Psychometrically, the median split-half reliabilities of the VABS ranged from .83 to .90 (median Adaptive Behavior Composite: .94) and .91 to .95 (median Adaptive Behavior Composite: .97) for the Survey and Expanded Forms, respectively. For the Classroom Edition, the median split-half reliabilities ranged from .80 to .95 with an Adaptive Behavior Composite coefficient of .98. Test–retest reliabilities for the Survey Form, with 2- to 4-week retest intervals, were in the .80s and .90s, whereas inter-rater reliabilities for the Survey and Expanded Forms ranged from .62 to .75. Relative to validity, both construct and concurrent validities are reported. Specific to the latter, the VABS was correlated with the original VABS, the AAMD Adaptive Behavior Scale, the K-ABC, the WISC-R, and the PPVT-R. All of the correlations were moderate and positive. It appears that the VABS and the AAMD ABS are assessing different aspects of adaptive behavior. The moderate correlations with the intelligence and achievement measures are anticipated given the different constructs that are measured by each type of scale.

Overall, the VABS is a well-developed scale that needs additional psychometric research before it can be used diagnostically. The Vineland Interview Edition and the Vineland Classroom Edition yielded relatively low correlations ranging from –.05 to .54. This indicates that a multisource, multisetting evaluation using these two Vineland editions will be difficult as they may not compare very well. For preschoolers, some of the domains may have inadequate floors. For example, the written subdomain of the Communication domain begins with the child's ability to recite the letters of the alphabet and identify all printed letters of the alphabet—both upper and lowercase. This clearly presents both psychometric and diagnostic problems with preschoolers. The VABS, however, will provide important information in many other domains. And with separate norms for mentally retarded, emotionally disturbed, and physically handicapped children and adults, much of its potential has yet to be tapped.

Scales of Independent Behavior—Revised

The Scales of Independent Behavior—Revised (SIB; Bruininks, Woodcock, Weatherman, & Hill, 1984) uses parents or teachers to assess the independent functioning of individuals, from infancy to late adulthood, in home, social, and community settings. The full form of the SIB contains four adaptive behavior clusters with 14 subscales (Motor Skills: gross and fine motor; Social Interaction and Communication Skills: social interaction, language comprehension and expression; Personal Living Skills: eating, toileting, dressing, personal self-care, and domestic skills; and Community Living Skills: time and punctuality, money and value, work skills, home/community orientation) and three problem behavior clusters with eight subscales (Internalized Maladaptive Behavior: hurtful to self, unusual or repetitive habits, withdrawal or inattentive behavior; Asocial Maladaptive Behavior: socially offensive behavior and uncooperative behavior; and Externalized Maladaptive Behavior: hurtful to others, destructive to property, and disruptive behavior). A Broad Independence cluster score is generated from the adaptive behavior areas, while a Maladaptive Index is generated from the problem behavior areas. Overall, the full SIB takes about one hour to complete.

In addition to the full SIB, there is also a 40-item Short Form which can be completed for individuals at any developmental level. There is also an Early Developmental scale of adaptive behavior which was developed to assess children aged 2½ or younger or individuals who are developmentally functioning at the 2½ year old level or below.

Psychometrically, the split-half reliabilities for the four adaptive behavior clusters and the full-scale scores are adequate (ranging from .85 to .97), but the same reliabilities for individual subscales are much lower. Test–retest reliabilities over 4 weeks for a sample of typical elementary school children ranged from .96 to .98, and inter-rater reliabilities were quite good—in the .90s. Relative to validity, the SIB appears to have good construct validity, and its concurrent validity was demonstrated with comparisons to the Adaptive Behavior Scale—School Edition and the Quay-Peterson Revised Behavior Problem Checklist.

Overall, the SIB should be useful in assessing preschoolers' adaptive and problem behaviors. Additional research is definitely needed for this population especially, however, and its utility within a multimethod, multisource, multisetting assessment remains to be seen.

Summary

Social-emotional and adaptive behavior assessment with preschoolers challenges every practitioner's knowledge, skill, confidence, and objectivity. It must be done with a working knowledge of the assessment tools and approaches existing in the field, and their respective psychometric and clinical utility and effectiveness. These assessments also require a working knowledge of child and abnormal development, an ecological/systems perspective, and expertise in successfully consulting with and involving parents and child care workers. Across the age span, preschoolers have the widest range of "typical" behavior. We must be careful to look at preschoolers' social-emotional and adaptive behavior within their developmental and ecological contexts. An educational or psychological label often means relatively little to preschool services. Accurate and effective programs for needy preschoolers mean far more. These programs are based on sound problem solving—an approach that systematically identifies and analyzes the actual behaviors of concern, and that systematically develops interventions that are directly linked to those analyses.

10 Transdisciplinary Play-Based Assessment

TONI W. LINDER

CERI B. HOLM

KELLY A. WALSH

Infants and preschoolers are unique. Their attention span, motivation, interests, locus of control, and attachment and affiliation with their parents all differ from the school-aged child. Early childhood professionals need a method or assessment that responds to the distinctive developmental demands of young children. The following chapter will examine the concept of play-based assessment in relation to other forms of assessment, discuss various models of play-based assessment, and delineate the components and processes of one specific model: the Transdisciplinary Play-based Assessment (Linder, 1993a).

Role of Play

An increasing number of states have begun to identify and serve infants, toddlers, and preschoolers with disabilities, and, in some cases, those young children who are at-risk for developmental delay. In response to this increase in early childhood services and identification, professionals are finding that the "traditional" tests do not always give valid, reliable, or even appropriate information (Linder, 1993a, 1994). Procedures involving play observation are being used more frequently, as the child, the parents, and the evaluation team find the process and results less stressful, more comprehensive, and more reflective of the child's actual skills and behaviors (Myers, McBride, & Peterson, 1996).

What is play and why is it important to assessment? Pugmire-Stoy (1992) defined play as "the eager engagement in pleasurable physical or mental effort to obtain emotional satisfaction" (p. 4). Other researchers have described typical characteristics of play, such as: (a) valued by the players, (b) a pleasurable activity, (c) spontaneous and voluntary, d) requiring active engagement (Bronfenbrenner, 1979; Trawick-Smith, 1994), e) intrinsically motivating (Smith, 1977), and f) involving an object or activity. (Wolery & Bailey, 1989)

Many theorists and researchers have investigated play and its importance in child development. Froebel (1887), was the first to develop the theory that children learn through play (as cited in Tizard, 1977). Both Froebel (1887) and Vygotsky (1967) regarded play as the highest level of child development. Play has also been considered the best avenue of learning (Trawick-Smith, 1994) and as a precursor to most productive work (Sylva, 1977). The benefits of play include increases in cognitive, language, and social development; problem solving; creativity; healthy personality formation; reading (Trawick-Smith, 1994); perspective taking; attention span; cooperation; empathy; impulse control; and emotional adjustment (Smilansky, 1990).

Almost 20 years ago, Kalverboer (1977) explained that play is a potentially rich source of information regarding a child's developmental level, capacity to organize behavior within diverse environments, and emotional world and state. Additionally, he stated that play is important for normal development to occur and that the lack of progressively complex play behaviors may indicate cognitive, social, physical, or emotional difficulties. More recently, Hutinger (1994) stated that play activities are a positive means of providing domain-integrated services and, therefore, play "should become the hallmark of early intervention activities" (p. 90). Play can provide an important link between assessment of a child's developmental abilities and the most appropriate means of intervention.

The Role of Play in Assessment

Philosophically, play is the medium that allows movement from a naturalistic assessment of young children to a naturalistic intervention. According to Kalverboer (1977, p. 100), play has been neglected in the past as a tool of assessment and topic of study due to the following reasoning:

1. The individual who selects his own activities does not fit easily into a discipline governed by a rather simple stimulus-response pattern.
2. The organization of play behavior is very complex, and is unsuited to an 'abstracting' psychology which attempts to describe behavior patterns in terms of elementary functions such as perception, attention, memory, and so on.
3. Play behavior is difficult to define and changes dramatically during ontogeny. The behavior patterns involved vary in duration and external orientation and cannot be easily standardized and quantified, as required by reductionist psychology.

Play is currently gaining acceptance for use in assessments and program interventions (Hutinger, 1994; Linder, 1993b). The observation of play is useful for understanding the needs and abilities of all children, especially those with special needs. Children with special needs are often considered untestable by common standards of assessment. Conversely, play-based assessments can offer a great deal of useful information regarding abilities and challenges for all children (Kalverboer, 1977).

Traditional Assessment vs. Play-Based Assessment

Proponents of traditional assessment have noted several advantages of the typical assessment processes. Johnson and LaMontagne (1994) describe some of the traditional test benefits as including: (a) easy to administer, (b) provides concrete definition of strengths and needs, and (c) offers some measure of objectivity and rigor.

Despite the positive attributes of traditional testing, such assessment instruments have been commonly criticized. Linder (1994) described several of the reasons why traditional testing may not always be appropriate, including that tests (a) may penalize children with special needs, (b) may be used inappropriately with children with disabilities, (c) fail to view the child in a holistic manner, (d) lack a relationship between results and intervention, (e) often omit functional assessments, (f) have poor predictive validity, (g) have inappropriate structure and content, (h) use formal procedures, (i) lack process information, (j) are deficient of personality and social information, and finally, (k) require significant cost and time.

The Need for Alternative Approaches

The above limitations denote a need for a wider variety of valid measures to gain a broader range of information regarding young children. Play-based assessments and other alternative assessment methods are considered necessary to minimize many of the disadvantages of traditional assessment (Hutinger, 1994). Some of the alternative assessment techniques include (a) observation in natural environments; (b) arena assessment; (c) observational instruments which consider child-parent interactions, child-peer interactions, and isolated play; (d) parent interviews and rating scales; and (e) videotaped sessions of a child's performance compared over time (Hutinger, 1994).

Many early childhood specialists appear to be moving away from the exclusive use of standardized or criterion referenced tests and relying more on a combination of traditional techniques with experiential, observational approaches. A survey of school psychologists found that play-based assessment was one of the most frequently cited alternative options (44% of the time) used in conjunction with, or instead of, standardized measures in the assessment of infants and preschool children (Bagnato & Neisworth, 1994). In general, the field of early childhood assessment is giving more credence to qualitative procedures, and current legislation is emphasizing the need to develop alternative procedures for ongoing and naturalistic assessment (Hutinger, 1994).

Play and Children with Disabilities

Play for children is developmental, natural, functional, and universally common. A move toward a holistic model for assessment of young children should include observation of a child's play. The observation of play is particularly important for children with disabilities, as research has demonstrated key differences in the actual play of children with disabilities when compared to their non-disabled peers.

Lerner, Mardell-Czudnowski, and Goldenberg (1987) describe several functions of play for children with disabilities which include (a) facilitating growth of desirable behaviors in motor, language, cognitive, and social skills; (b) reinforcing instructional activities; (c) inhibiting socially inappropriate behaviors; and (d) providing pleasure or joy. Although all children utilize these functions within their play, children with various types of disabilities display some differences in content and structure of their play. A brief summary of the research on play and children with disabilities will highlight these differences.

Children with Developmental Disabilities

Although children with developmental delays appear to progress through the same stages of development as children who do not have developmental delays (Sigman & Ungerer, 1984), several differences in their play have been noted. For example, Li (1981) found that the play of children with mental retardation was characterized by a restricted repertoire of play skills, reduced language during play, less sophisticated representational play, and a limited selection of play materials. Differences in attention span also affect the play of children with developmental delays (Krakow & Kopp, 1983). The play of children with severe and profound delays may include stereotyped behaviors (Thompson & Berkson, 1985).

Children with Physical Disabilities

The play of children with physical disabilities is often restricted by their ability to move or to maintain their position. The inability to move may affect a child's ability to look at, track, grasp, release, or explore an object. Physical disabilities may also impact social interactions due to an inability to physically follow peers as they move around in the play environment. Furthermore, a child with a physical disability may not even be able to follow a peer visually, due to poor positioning (Linder, 1994).

Play of Children with Visual Impairments

Because children with visual impairments may not be aware of objects or persons near them, they have no incentive to reach out for or move to get interesting objects (Campos, Svejda, Campos, & Bertenthal, 1982). Children with visual impairments often do not let go of toys because it is difficult to find them again. Additionally, they often reveal different ways of exploring objects such as holding them close to their body, biting or licking objects, or rubbing the objects against their face or eyes (Newson & Head, 1979). Because blindness or a severe visual impairment results in an inability to observe others in play, such children may exhibit fewer play exchanges and, therefore, increased solitary play (Fewell & Kaminski, 1988).

Play of Children with Language Delays or Hearing Impairments

A study by Kennedy, Sheridan, Radlinski, and Beeghly (1991) showed a relationship between the complexity of children's play schemes and the length of their verbal utterances. They found that children who combined schemes in play also tended to produce multiword utterances. At the same time, children who produced single schemes in their play, tended to also produce single-word utterances. Lovell, Hoyle, and Siddall (1968) found that those children with language delays tend to engage in less symbolic play and more solitary play when compared to their peers. They also tend to make fewer social contacts, and to have less organized play than their same-aged peers who do not have language delays (Lovell et al., 1968; Williams, 1980).

Play of Children with Attention Deficit Hyperactivity Disorder (ADHD)

Decreased attention has been associated with developmental delays in both the cognitive and social levels of play in children with ADHD (Allesandri, 1992). Allesandri further found that the cognitive play of children with ADHD tends to be less symbolic in form, and to involve primarily functional or sensorimotor activities such as repetitive muscle movements with or without objects. Children with ADHD also tended to engage in less group and parallel play, and to engage in fewer peer conversations than children without ADHD.

Play of Children with Autism

Children with autism may also show differences in their play abilities. Many autistic children exhibit behaviors that may inhibit meaningful play activities and social contacts (Weiner, Ottinger, & Tilton, 1969). Such behaviors may include rocking movements, head banging or shaking, finger flicking, hand flapping, and the flicking or spinning of objects close to their face (Newson & Head, 1979). Furthermore, children with autism may exhibit low frequencies of verbal play behavior and variable nonverbal play behaviors (Coe, Matson, Craigie, & Gossen, 1991). Children with autism also tend to demonstrate specific sensorimotor deficits in imitations skills, especially those requiring symbolic substitution of objects (Sigman & Ungerer, 1984). Additionally, they may reveal fewer play sequences, less diverse play schemes, less time in advanced play skills, and less symbolic play related to dolls or people (Sigman & Ungerer, 1984).

The above characteristics of the play of children with disabilities is interesting not only from a descriptive standpoint, but also because these characteristics have implications for what professionals need to address in assessment and intervention. If the play aspects that differentiate these children from their typical peers can be identified in the assessment, professionals are more likely to target these play processes in the interventions and, thereby, increase the qualitative aspects of the child's play skills, sequences, and means of interacting.

Parameters of Play-Based Assessment

Choosing an assessment measure is often dictated by the child's age, nature of referral, purpose of testing, and program philosophy (Hutinger, 1994). Several characteristics help to differentiate assessment methods. Assessments may vary in purpose; content; degree of structure; role of the professionals, the child, and the parents in the assessment process; method by which a total evaluation of the child is obtained; and the location where the assessment is conducted. In other words, the what, who, how, where, and why of the assessment are key elements that need to be addressed when selecting or designing an assessment process. Each of these elements will be examined in order to clarify the differences inherent in play-based assessments.

What?

Play-based assessments vary from traditional assessments, in that specific items are not presented. The child is observed doing whatever the child typically does in the environment. In some play-based assessments, specific toy sets are presented according to developmental expectations (Fewell, 1984). In other play-based assessments, the play facilitator may present certain toys, materials, or situations relevant for a child's developmental level, but the content is prescribed by the interests of the child and the child's background and experiences (Linder, 1993a). A play-based arena assessment requires much planning and forethought. If a play-based assessment is conducted to determine initial eligibility, a standardized assessment instrument may be part of the assessment. Play-based assessments typically incorporate information gained from observing the child interacting with his or her parent(s), the assessment team, and possibly a peer or sibling(s).

After the assessment is complete, all team members meet and share information gained during the process related to the child's strengths and needs (McGonigel, Woodruff, & Roszmann-Millican, 1994). Giving immediate feedback to the families is considered an important aspect of best practices (Turnbull, 1991). The written report is the final step in the evaluation process and involves all members providing information and one or more team members integrating it into a report (McGonigel, Woodruff, & Roszmann-Millican, 1994).

Who?

Play-based assessments are most often conducted in an arena fashion in which the child, family, and all team members are together in one room. Team members may include an early childhood specialist, speech/language therapist, occupational therapist, psychologist, and parents. The team members work together as they observe and record the child's behavior rather than working individually with the child and family (Johnson, 1994). Many behavioral and developmental perspectives are incorporated and integrated when all members observe the child's behaviors, skills, and interactions (McLean & McCormick, 1993). The traditional clinical format has individual disciplines conducting assessments within their own area of expertise and then combining information and sharing information with parents after the completion of the assessment process. The shift toward a more integrated view of a child and the need for more meaningful parent involvement has necessitated a change in the ways teams function.

The family is considered to play a key role in the play-based assessment process. The family-centered approach (Turnbull, 1991) views families as team members that are invited to participate in the assessment process to the extent they feel comfortable. If parents choose to participate, the play interaction with their child provides unique information and a more natural environment for the child. Linder (1993a) involves parents in the play-based assessment as an observer, an informer, a facilitator, and an interpreter. A sibling may also take on the role of play facilitator (Hutinger, 1994). Caregiver-completed developmental questionnaires are often used to supplement the play-based assessment (Squires, Nickel, & Bricker, 1990).

Preparing families to participate in a play-based assessment is essential to a smooth assessment. Checklists have been developed for professionals to use when introducing families to various arena assessments (Garland, McGonigel, Frank, & Buck, 1989; Kjerland & Kovack, 1987). Before a Transdisciplinary Play-Based Assessment is conducted, families are asked about the best time of day for the assessment, the child's favorite toys and snacks, the activities the child enjoys, and how the family would like to interact with the child during the assessment (Linder, 1993a).

The roles that each team member (including the parents) plays varies in the different types of assessments. The roles and interactions also depend somewhat on where and how the assessment is conducted. Team members share an equal sense of participation and responsibility for the preparation and outcome of the assessment (McGonigel, Woodruff, & Roszmann-Millican, 1994). The trend toward increased family involvement and team interaction has resulted in a modification of typical assessment models.

Transdisciplinary Team Model.   Play-based assessments can be conducted by individuals or teams. When teams are used however, the transdisciplinary approach to observation, discussion, and planning makes the most sense. A transdisciplinary play-based assessment is a holistic, integrated approach which leads directly into functional, developmental, ecological, and transdisciplinary intervention.

There are two fundamental beliefs of the transdisciplinary model of service delivery. The first belief is that children's development is interactive and integrated among domains and, therefore, assessment is completed in a holistic fashion. The second cornerstone is that children are to be viewed within the context of family (McGonigel, Woodruff, & Roszmann-Millican, 1994) and, therefore, the family's concerns, priorities, and involvement are central to the transdisciplinary process (Bruder & Bologna, 1993). The family-centered approach and focus on cross-disciplinary work is consistent with Part H of IDEA and its reauthorization, P.L. 105-17, and with best practices in early childhood assessment (Bruder & Bologna, 1993; Linder, 1990; McGonigel, Kaufmann, & Johnson, 1991). Therefore, the transdisciplinary method may be the most appropriate model in relation to what is envisioned by Part C (formerly H) for early intervention (Garland et al., 1989; Woodruff, Hunson, McGonigel, & Sterzin, 1990).

In order for the transdisciplinary team model to be successful, team members, according to Benner (1992), must reach agreements in the following five areas: (a) acceptance of differences in skills, (b) acceptance of differences in approach, (c) willingness not to try to know everything, (d) an ability to call on others for assistance and ongoing knowledge, and (e) the creation of nonthreatening opportunities for discussion of these areas. Team consensus for all assessments, program planning, implementation, and evaluations is another driving force of the team (Garland et al., 1989). When consensus is not possible, best practices in family-centered early intervention would indicate that the family's preference should be followed (Kramer, McGonigel, & Kaufmann, 1991).

All team members participate in the assessment and design the intervention plan, but the plan is frequently carried out or coordinated by one designated primary service provider (any appropriate team member) and the family (McGonigel, Woodruff, & Roszmann-Millican, 1994). Therefore, having a primary service provider with knowledge and understanding of all the domain areas and intervention strategies is crucial to the successful implementation of the team plan. The primary service provider does not try to replace the other specialists, but rather attempts to continually pool information and skills between specialists to better develop and implement a service plan. And, if direct "hands-on" interventions are needed, then the actual professional from the discipline of need will provide those services (McGonigel, Woodruff, & Roszmann-Millican, 1994).

To become a successful transdisciplinary team requires continual attention to team building to diminish professional turf issues (Johnson, 1994). Therefore, there must be a commitment from the administrative staff to grant the necessary time, training, and support for team development (McGonigel, Woodruff, & Roszmann-Millican, 1994). The six transdisciplinary team development components include: role extension, role enrichment, role expansion, role exchange, role release, and role support (Linder, 1993a; McGonigel, Woodruff, & Roszmann-Millican, 1994).

Clearly, one of the major drawbacks of the transdisciplinary process is the necessary time commitment it takes to form a successful team (Benner, 1992). But as individuals add to their own repertoire of expertise by incorporating information and skills offered by other team members, (McGonigel, Woodruff, & Roszmann-Millican, 1994) they tend to advocate the benefits of the transdisciplinary model. Additionally, the transdisciplinary model significantly reduces the communication problems of the multidisciplinary and interdisciplinary approaches due to its focus on moving beyond disciplinary boundaries (Orelove & Sobsey, 1991).

How?

Formal–Informal Play.   Play-based assessments may be conducted on a continuum from formal to informal. In a formal play assessment the child may be presented with a series of play objects and directed by the assessor to "feed the baby," or play with the materials in a specific way, making the procedures standardized. In contrast, more informal play assessments involve the assessor in a facilitative role in which they often observe, imitate, suggest, model, or comment on the child's play. The less formal assessments often include the use of information from intermediate sources, such as caregiver interviews and questionnaires about the child's play and interactions. Such indirect information can provide necessary insights into the child's behavior in settings that are unavailable for direct observation by the examiner (Benner, 1992).

Structured Elicitation and Free-Play.   Along the same lines as the formal to informal dimensions, play models function within a range from structured elicitation to free play. Through elicited play models, the evaluator attempts to elicit an optimal level of performance by modeling or verbally describing a certain activity to the child. According to Bond, Creasey, and Abrams (1990) the advantages of elicited play include:

- A decreased likelihood that differences observed in play are a result of the environment.
- Encouragement of more sophisticated play from children who don't have access to stimulating objects or persons.
- The examiner may make inferences about motivational level.
- The assessor can compare the differences between the highest level of play obtained during free play versus elicited play.

Specific assessment tools using elicited play techniques were reviewed by Bond et al. (1990) and include: Belsky, Garduque, and Hrncir (1984) Executive Capacity Play; Yarrow, McQuiston, MacTurk, McCarthy, Klien, and Vietze (1983) Mastery Motivation Task; Watson and Fischer (1980) Elicitation Procedure (see Table 10.1).

In free-play models children are observed as they play at home, school, or child care, with their own toys. Children are generally unaware that they are being watched, and the evaluator does not interact directly with the child (Bond et al., 1990). The free play method has several advantages:

- The evaluator can observe how the child functions in their everyday life.
- The assessment can be completed at any time or place with few resources other than the observer.
- The assessment can provide information across settings and, therefore, can determine variations within a child across various environmental contexts.

In an example of this model, Bond, Kelly, Teti, and Gibbs (1983), found that observations of infants playing with their own toys were a significantly better predictor of the

TABLE 10.1   Play-Based Assessments Instruments

Assessment Instrument/Resource	Description
Ainsworth, M. D. S., Blehar, M. C., Waters, E., & Wall, S. (1978). *Patterns of attachments: A psychological study of the stranger situation.* Hillsdale, NJ: Lawrence Erlbaum Associates.	Examines patterns of attachment between children (birth to 1-year-old) and their primary caregiver. Eight episodes of observation which includes separation and reunion between caregiver and child.
Atlas, J. A. (1990). Play in assessment and intervention in childhood psychoses. *Child Psychiatry and Human Development,* 21(2), 119–133.	Children interact with a specified set of 10 toys. Play is then rated as not symbolic play, stereotyped play, or pretend play.
Belsky, J., Garduque, L., & Hrncir, E. (1984). Assessing performance, competence, and executive capacity in infant play: Relations to home environment and security of attachment. *Developmental Psychology, 20,* 406–417.	10-minute observation of free play followed by a competence examination where the examiner attempts to engage the child in more sophisticated play.
Belsky, J., & Most, R. K. (1981). From exploration to play: A cross-sectional study of infant free play behavior. *Developmental Psychology, 17*(5), 630–639.	A 12-step sequence of developmental exploration and play that begins with infant explorations and concludes with pretend substitutions. A set of toys is specified.
Bricker, D. (Ed.) (1993). *Assessment, Evaluation, and Programming System (AEPS): Measurement for Birth to Three Years.* Baltimore: Paul H. Brookes.	A 3-point scale rating various objectives from six developmental domains.
Bromwich, R. M., Fust, S., Khokha, E., & Walden, M. H. (1981). *Play Assessment Checklist for Infants.* Unpublished document. Northridge, CA: California State University.	An observation instrument to be used in free-play situations. A checklist is used in conjunction with a specified toy set.
Dixon, W. E., & Shore, C. (1990). Measuring symbolic play style in infancy: A methodological approach. *The Journal of Genetic Psychology, 152*(2), 191–205.	Provides three scenarios (breakfast, bath, and bed) under three conditions (spontaneous, modeled, and modeled with inappropriate object). Evaluates child's competence in symbolic play.
Fewell, R., & Rich, J. S. (1987). Play assessment as a procedure for examining cognitive, communication, and social skills in multi-handicapped children. *Journal of Psychoeducational Assessment, 5,* 107–118.	45 developmentally sequenced items. The child is observed playing with toys under spontaneous and elicited conditions.
Fewell, R. (1986). *Play Assessment Scale (5th revision).* Unpublished manuscript, University of Washington, Seattle.	Children interact with specified toy sets. The scale looks at sequences of play behaviors and produces a play age.
Flannery, K. A., & Watson, M. W. (1992). Are individual differences in fantasy play related to peer acceptance level? *Journal of Genetic Psychology, 54*(3), 407–416.	Codes child's free-play behaviors for frequency of fantasy play and non-fantasy play, and for the unreality level and unfamiliar level of the fantasy play.

(continued)

TABLE 10.1   Continued

Assessment Instrument/Resource	Description
Gowan, J. W., & Schoen, D. (1984). *Levels of Child Object Play.* Unpublished coding scheme manuscript. Chapel Hill, NC: Carolina Institute for Research on Early Education of the Handicapped, Frank Porter Graham Child Development Center.	Observational study of play using content, signifiers, and modes of representational analysis. The child is evaluated in an unstructured free-play situation.
Kearsley, R. B. (1984). *The systematic observation of children's play.* Unpublished scoring manual. (Available from author, Child Health Services, Manchester, NH.)	Standardized procedure of introducing the child to six sets of prearranged toys. Mother and child are observed for 10-minutes for four categories of play: stereotypical, relational, functional, and functional/symbolic.
Largo, R. H., & Howard, J. A. (1979). Developmental progression in play behavior of children between nine and thirty months. *Developmental Medicine and Child Neurology, 21,* 299–310.	Using a specified toy set, the tool accesses play behavior in the categories of exploratory functional, spatial, and nonspecific play behavior.
Lifter, K., Sulzer-Azaroff, B., Cowdery, G., Avery, D., & Anderson, S. R. (1994). The Developmental Play Assessment (DPA) Instrument (2nd Rev.). Unpublished manuscript, Northeastern University, Boston, MA.	Progress through a sequence of 14 play categories determined from a quantitative analysis of a 30-minute sample of unstructured play activities. Useful for identifying goals for interventions in play.
Lowe, M., & Costello, A. J. (1976). The *Symbolic Play Test.* Windsor, England: NFR-Nelson Publishing Co.	An evaluation of children's spontaneous, non-verbal play activities with four specified sets of miniature objects.
Lunzer, E. A. (1958). A scale of the organization of behavior for use in the study of play. *Educational Review, 11,* 205–217.	An abstract instrument that provides a 9-point developmental scale of the complexity play. of play emphasizing adaptiveness and the use/integration of materials.
Mayes, S. D. (1991). Play assessment of preschool hyperactivity. In C. E. Schaefer, K. P. Gitlin, & A. Sandgrund (Eds.). *Play Diagnosis Assessment.* 249–281. New York: Wiley.	A small area is arranged with 7 manipulative toys. While the child is exploring the toys, the child's behavior is being coded by the examiner for level of activity.
McCune-Nicolich, L.(1983). *A Manual for Analyzing Free Play.* New Brunswick, NJ: Department of Educational Psychology, Rutgers University.	An organized format for analyzing children's symbolic play according to Piagetian stages. A specified toy set is used.
Morgan, G. A., Harmon, R. J., & Bennett, C. A. (1976). A system for coding and scoring infants' spontaneous play with objects. JSAS *Catalog of Selected Documents in Psychology, 6,* 105 (Ms. No. 1355).	A free-play assessment for 8 to 24-month-olds. 40-minute observation of free play with standardized set of toys to distinguish between exploratory and cognitively mature play.

Morgan, G. A., Harmon, R. J., & Maslin, C. A. (1987, July). *Measuring mastery motivation in infants and young children.* Paper presented at the International Society of Behavioral Development, Tokyo.

Parent rating scales of the child's general persistence, mastery pleasure, independent mastery, and competence during play.

Mulhern, R. K., Fairclough, D. L., Friedman, A. G., & Leigh, L. D. P. (1990). Play performance scale as an index of quality of life of children with cancer. *Psychological Assessment, 2*(2), 149–155.

Parent rating scale of the child's sensorimotor cognitive/imaginative, affective, and social aspects of child's play behavior.

Parten, M. B. (1932). Social participation among pre-school children. *Journal of Abnormal and Social Psychology. 27,* 243–269.

Six different levels of play including unoccupied, solitary, onlooker, parallel, associative, and cooperative. Play is described in relation to how the child interacts with peers.

Rogers, S. J. (1984). *Play Observation Scale.* Denver: University of Colorado Health Sciences Center.

Assesses sensorimotor and symbolic stages of play and includes a set of items on social/communicative behavior.

Rubenstein, J., & Howes, C. (1976). The effects of peers on toddler interactions with mothers and toys. *Child Development, 47,* 597–605.

Play is coded on a 5-point scale: oral contact, passive tactile contact, active manipulation, exploiting unique properties of an object, and creative or imaginative play. Compares solitary free-play with play with peer or mother.

Rubin, K. H. (1989). *Play Observation Scale.* Ontario, Canada: University of Waterloo.

Assesses play and non-play categories in an unstructured environment.

Ruff, H. A., & Lawson, K. R. (1990). The development of sustained, focused, attention during free play in young children. *Developmental Psychology, 26,* 85–93.

Involves recording the amount of time the infant plays with and deliberately manipulates three to four objects.

Seagoe, M. (1970). An instrument for the analysis of children's play as an index of degree of socialization. *Journal of School Psychology, 8*(2), 129–144.

Five-question interview about play choices. Responses are coded for the child and who the child is playing with for each response.

Waston, M. W., & Fischer, K. W. (1977). A developmental sequence of agent use in late infancy. *Child Development, 48,* 828–836.

Four phased play procedure: familiarization, modeling, free-play, and requested-imitation. Coded by four types of agents: self, passive other, passive substitute, and active agent. Designed to capture Piaget's decentration notion.

Westby, C. E. (1980). Symbolic Play Checklist: Assessment of cognitive and language abilities through play. *Language, Speech, and Hearing Services in the Schools, 11,* 154–168.

Integrates language, cognitive, and social aspects of play in a 10-step hierarchy. Includes 9- to 60-month-olds.

Yarrow, L. J., McQuiston, S., MacTurk, R. H., McCarthy, M., Klein, R. P., & Vietze, P. M. (1983). Assessment of mastery motivation during the first year of life: Contemporaneous and cross-aged relationships. *Developmental Psychology, 19,* 159–171.

A number of tasks are modeled, one at a time. The child is then presented with the objects and observed in undisturbed, free-play. Behaviors coded included: nontask, visual attention, task-directed, and success or solution of task/problem.

Bayley MDI than when they were playing with the standardized set of toys. Bond et al. (1990) listed specific tools using free-play techniques which included: Rubenstein and Howes Procedure (1976); Kearsley Procedure (1984); Belsky and Most Free-Play Procedure (1981); Morgan, Harmon, and Bennett Procedure (1976); Lowe and Costello Symbolic Play Test (1976); and McCune-Nicolich Procedure (1983) (see Table 10.1).

The assessment process for a given child may include a variety of formal, informal, structured, and unstructured assessments. Furthermore, the total assessment process may include the administration of a standardized, norm-referenced test; systematic observations of the child in naturalistic settings and test situations; structured interviews; and environmental and interactional assessments.

Where?

The environment in which the child is assessed can have an impact on the results of the test (Linder, 1990; 1993a). Most traditional tests are conducted in a non-stimulating environment, so as not to distract the child from the test items being presented. For some children, this environment is anxiety-provoking and, thus may lead to a less than maximum performance. This clinical assessment may allow for a more standardized assessment, but the stress caused by the novel experience and lack of parental proximity may produce inaccurate results. Parents are frequently discouraged from directly participating in the standardized approach other than completing developmental histories and behavioral checklists.

A play-based assessment is a naturalistic assessment which refers to the observation of young children in their natural environments such as within the home, day care, school, and community. Such an assessment may better determine a child's actual functioning level due to familiarity of the environment and objects within the setting and, therefore, enhance their comfort level and an anxiety-reduced performance. The parents are encouraged to be involved with their child, for at least a portion of the assessment.

Why?

Play-based assessment is usually used as a component of an evaluation for identification, placement, program planning, and program evaluation. In addition, play-based assessment can provide useful information related to family strengths and needs, environmental issues, the child's learning style, and the child's mastery motivation. Developmental guidelines and age tables can provide a reference for identifying developmental delays. Observations of the child's learning style can inform placement decisions. Furthermore, information about demonstrated skills and mastery motivation offer direction for intervention planning. Inclusion of the parents in the process can also help establish family strengths and needs. Play-based assessment can be used in conjunction with other approaches to ensure a more holistic view of the child and, therefore, more valid results. In some cases, when the child is unable to perform in a more structured test situation, the play-based assessment and parent input may provide the majority of information about the child.

An arena assessment is not always the best assessment procedure for all children. Some children are simply too shy, sensitive, or distractible to allow for a successful and useful arena assessment. Furthermore, some families may be too uncomfortable in the presence of many professionals and choose not to participate. Therefore, the transdisciplinary team needs to be sensitive to the exceptions of the transdisciplinary model's typical assessment approach (McGonigel, Woodruff, & Roszmann-Millican, 1994). An alternative to having all the team members present at the assessment would be to videotape the play assessment with a few team members in the room, and have the other team members view the tape at another time.

Overview of One Play-Based Model: Transdisciplinary Play-Based Assessment

Parts B and C of IDEA and its reauthorization, P.L. 105-17, mandates that basic content areas be covered in the IEP or IFSP including:

1. A statement of the child's present cognitive, speech-language, psychosocial, motor, and adaptive (self-help) skills.
2. A statement of the family's resources, priorities, and concerns related to enhancing the child's development.
3. A statement of objectives to be achieved for the child and family, and the criteria, procedures, and timeliness for evaluating growth.
4. The particular interventions necessary to meet the needs of the child and family, including the what, when, and how of the services.
5. A statement of the natural environments where the early intervention services will be provided.
6. The anticipated dates of initiation and duration of services.
7. The designation of the service coordinator.
8. A statement of the transition procedures from the infant intervention program into the next placement.

Transdisciplinary Play-Based Assessment (TPBA) (Linder, 1990, 1993a) addresses all of these mandates, in a manner that is family-friendly and team-oriented.

Transdisciplinary Play-Based Assessment is one form of play-based assessment which draws on previous work by Ainsworth, Blehar, Waters, and Wall (1978), Belsky and Most (1981), Calhoun and Newson (1984), Fewell (1984), McCune-Nicolich (1980), Nicolich (1977), Parten (1932), Rogers (1986), and Westby (1980). Although TPBA differs from these works in the total number and range of domains observed, the philosophical base remains the same. The TPBA model was chosen as the most advantageous model of play-assessment because it minimizes many of the problems associated with traditional individualized assessment.

Transdisciplinary Play-Based Assessment is a natural and functional assessment process designed for children between the ages of one month and 6 years old. During the play-based assessment, the team (including the parents) examines the child's development across cognitive, social-emotional, language and communication, and sensorimotor domains as the child interacts with a play facilitator, a care giver, and a peer or group of peers. The TPBA process allows the child to lead the play, while the facilitator keeps the child interested and motivated by joining in the play. The facilitator alternates between observing free play and attempting to elicit the child's highest levels of performance.

Advantages of Transdisciplinary Play-Based Assessment

The advantages of TPBA are many. Linder (1993a) notes ten advantages:

1. *Natural environment.* TPBA is conducted in a natural environment that is familiar to the child, and where the child feels comfortable. Such environments may include day care centers, infant programs, preschools, the family's home, or any other setting containing materials that are familiar and/or appealing to the child. This type of environment is conducive to eliciting the child's highest skill level.

2. *Ease of rapport.* The TPBA process provides a greater likelihood of establishing rapport between the examiner and the child. Although examiners in both traditional assessment and TPBA may be unfamiliar to the child, TPBA allows the child to interact with only one facilitator (examiner), rather than a variety of different professionals. TPBA also allows the child to lead the activities and to be in the directive role, rather than having the examiner lead all activities. Through the process of TPBA, the facilitator imitates, models, suggests, and only rarely requests.

3. *Flexible approach.* Unlike standardized tests that require the examiner to follow a prescribed set of tasks in a specific manner, TPBA allows different sets of materials, varying conditions, variations in language, and alteration of sequence and content depending upon the child. It can, therefore, be adapted to the needs of diverse children and different disabling conditions.

4. *Holistic approach.* Under the TPBA model, all team members observe the same behaviors at the same time. With traditional assessment, each team member evaluates separate aspects of the child at different times, which can result in a fragmented and sometimes contradictory view of the child's abilities and disabilities. The TPBA, however, allows the team of professionals and parents to view the child at the same time, and then discuss how the strengths and concerns observed may be interrelated. Having the same frame of reference, therefore, gives everyone the same foundation, and improves team communication.

5. *Parental involvement.* TPBA actively involves the parents in the assessment process. Parents can both observe and participate in all aspects of the TPBA process, depending on their comfort level. This can benefit both the child and the parents in that it allows the child to visually or verbally "check in" with the parent when the child needs to, while the parents get an opportunity to observe the TPBA process and contribute their personal insights regarding their child. In addition, the parents play with their child, which allows the team to observe any differences in the child when interacting with a familiar adult. The parents discuss what is being seen with a parent facilitator and have an opportunity to obtain insights and share information about their child. Parents can also validate whether what is being seen is typical behavior on the part of the child. In a recent study, parents gave higher ratings to transdisciplinary play-based assessment over traditional assessment, particularly in relation to a feeling of comfort in seeking information from team members and in feeling that important goals were identified from the assessment (Myers, McBride, & Peterson, 1996).

6. *Process information.* Along with providing information concerning the child's cognitive, social-emotional, communication and language, and sensorimotor development, the guidelines for TPBA observation also addresses how the child processes information. Such "process" information might include the child's learning style, temperament

characteristics, mastery motivation, and interaction patterns. TPBA also looks at qualitative information, such as the underlying cognitive, social, and physical processes, or developmental components related to the development of skills in each area.

7. *All children are testable.* TPBA proceeds from whatever the child is capable of doing within the play setting. Regardless of the child's level of development or range of disabilities, the facilitator experiments with a variety of toys and equipment to ascertain what the child can do under different circumstances, with different materials and with different interaction patterns.

8. *Link between assessment and intervention.* The results of TPBA are useful in planning interventions. As noted above, many traditional forms of assessment often do not result in useful recommendations for intervention. TPBA, however, provides a strong base for a functional, play-based intervention approach. The information obtained from a TPBA is functional, process-based, skill-oriented, and relates to both the classroom and home.

9. *Transdisciplinary team model.* TPBA utilizes a transdisciplinary team model in which professionals from different disciplines support each other in assessing and designing interventions for the child in a holistic approach. Such a team approach considers a child in an integrated fashion, as it does not divide and separate the interdependent domains of assessment. Therefore the TPBA results are holistic, and provide for functional intervention recommendations.

10. *Focus on child's strengths and readiness areas.* The results of a TPBA are not worded in terms of the child's deficits and, therefore, the child is not talked about in negative terms. Although developmental age ranges are provided and can be used when needed, the most important information about the child is shared in terms of "Strengths" (current functioning), and "What I'm Ready For" (current needs).

Limitations of Transdisciplinary Play-Based Assessment

Depending on the needs of the child, TPBA can function as either a partial or a total evaluation. Some states require standardized testing that provides psychometric data comparing the child to other children of the same age and may require a specific "cut-off" in order to document or confirm a delay or disability. Other states have more flexible guidelines and may even identify "at-risk" children (those who are biologically or environmentally "at-risk" for developing a delay). Where state guidelines mandate standardized testing, the TPBA can still be a part of the total evaluation by providing information on underlying processes and functional use of skills, by involving parents in the assessment and planning process, and providing the forum for transdisciplinary collaboration.

If TPBA is the primary means of assessment, additional testing still may provide information not derived from the play session. For example, the range of receptive language skills, as well as specific sensory integration issues, may not be fully tapped through a TPBA. Also, physical and occupational therapists may like to spend additional time with a child who has motor problems to get a better "feel" for the child's muscle tone, range of motion, and so on. TPBA provides much valuable information, but the process is not always sufficient unto itself. TPBA is designed so that the team, materials, and format can be modified to fit diverse state requirements, variable staffing patterns, and the individual needs of children and families.

Validity and Reliability

The TPBA model utilizes observation guidelines, age tables, and professional judgment to determine the child's strengths and needs. In several studies, the validity and reliability of the TPBA process has been examined. Examining content validity, Friedli (1994) and (Linder, Green, & Friedli, 1996) found that the TPBA guidelines were supported by early childhood professionals most likely to use the process, such as psychologists, educators, speech-language therapists, and motor specialists. These experts rated the developmental domains and subcategories for relevance, clarity, and comprehensiveness on a scale from one to 7. All of the subcategories were judged favorably (higher than 4), with most ratings between 6 and 7.

The concurrent validity of TPBA was measured by comparing the outcomes of play-based assessment to traditional standardized and norm-referenced tests for children with and without disabilities. Friedli (1994) found that the TPBA was as accurate as standardized measures for determining whether a child was eligible for services. In fact, in her study, the TPBA was actually more accurate in identifying one child with social-emotional concerns.

Reliability of the TPBA process across time and raters has also been studied (Friedli, 1994; Linder, Green, & Friedli, 1996). TPBA was well supported in both test–retest and inter-rater conditions. The results indicate that TPBA can be used to assess the underlying developmental competencies of young children, despite the differences in their play performance and specific setting during the assessments.

The inter-rater reliability of TPBA was also examined using videotapes of TPBA sessions, with independent raters assessing each child. It was revealed that the reliability for the language, motor, and combined domains met the strictest criteria for tests used to make eligibility decisions. Of special interest was the finding that professionals across disciplines, given specific guidelines for observation, were as accurate in rating young children's developmental competence in diverse domains as were the specific domain experts.

A study by Myers, McBride, and Peterson (1996) also provides support for the social validity, or validation by "consumers," of transdisciplinary play-based assessment. Their study revealed that parents and staff rated the transdisciplinary play-based assessment higher than standardized testing on 13 of 17 items addressed in a questionnaire about the process and results. The functional utility of assessment reports also was rated higher, particularly for ease of obtaining an overview of the child's abilities, ease of determining which developmental areas were of concern, the number of developmental areas discussed in the report, the report being written in jargon-free language, the integration of discipline-specific information, and the objectives being clearly based on the child's strengths and weaknesses. In addition, greater agreement was found between parents and professionals on individual profile items, along with greater congruence in judgment-based ratings between team members. The validity and reliability data discussed previously provides support for the use of Transdisciplinary Play-Based Assessment as part of the assessment of young children.

Components of Transdisciplinary
Play-Based Assessment

Preparation for the Play Session

A pre-assessment planning session is important to the success of a play-based assessment. A planning meeting before the play session allows the team to discuss the activities and materials to be included in the play assessment, the information gained from parents about behaviors or learning style, the structure of the session, and the assignment of roles to team members. Through the use of a parent-completed developmental inventory assessing the child's abilities at home, the team can determine an approximation of the child's developmental level and the parent's primary concerns and goals for the child. This information helps the team to plan the structure and setting of the session, to select appropriate materials, and to provide a basis for discussions with the parents during and after the play session. The team also uses this time to identify the facilitators, the video camera operator, and any other resource team roles desired. This pre-assessment planning meeting, therefore, allows the team to coordinate the efforts of the team members in order to maximize their observations during the play session.

The Team

The Transdisciplinary Play-Based Assessment model usually utilizes the family and one professional to interact with the child. Through a reduction of multiple child-professional interactions, the TPBA assessment is often less disruptive to the child. In fact, many believe that not having to continually adjust to strangers may enhance the performance of the child (Linder, 1990; McGonigel, Woodruff, & Roszmann-Millican, 1994).

An advantage of TPBA is that it adapts to the composition of any team. Team composition begins with the parent(s), and should include other necessary professionals, such as a speech-language pathologist, occupational or physical therapist, and a teacher and/or psychologist. Other team members may also include a social worker, nurse, vision therapist, etc. Depending on the number of team members available, a variety of roles are assumed, including the play facilitator, the parent facilitator, observing team members, and the video camera operator. Each of the team members works together in a transdisciplinary manner.

Parents.   As stated previously, the parents are involved in TPBA process as both information providers, assessment participants, and intervention designers. Parents are given the opportunity to choose their level of participation and, therefore, may be involved in several diverse ways including the following: (a) participating with the child throughout the assessment if the age or behavior of the child necessitates the parents staying with the child, (b) seated to the side within the playroom, or (c) watching from behind a one-way mirror with participation in the play session when called for. Although parent participation is not required, it is preferred. This allows team members to observe parent-child interaction, as well as the child's "check in" behavior with the parent. The parents also participate by observing and discussing the play session, and comparing the child's current behaviors and activities in the play session to their child's behaviors typically seen in the home environment.

At some point during the session, parents will also be asked to leave the room for a few minutes. The team can then observe the child's reaction to separation and reunion with the parent. The parent may also be asked to teach the child a task or do a more structured activity with their child during the TPBA. The child's response to the parent's increased structure is observed, and then compared to interactions with the facilitator and peer.

Parent Facilitator.   The parent facilitator contacts the family prior to the evaluation to gain information regarding toy preferences and the best time for the evaluation, and discusses the TPBA process. On the day of the assessment, the parent facilitator greets the family and shows them and the child to the playroom where the rest of the team waits for them. The parent facilitator reminds the family what will happen in the play session, obtains additional information about the child while they are observing, and involves the parents in the actual assessment when the parents are ready to become more actively involved in the play session. Throughout the session, the parent facilitator explains the TPBA process, clarifies information received, answers any parent questions, and investigates whether the behaviors observed are typical of the child.

Play Facilitator.   The play facilitator, on the other hand, works directly with the child by imitating the child's responses, modeling new behaviors, or, in some cases, eliciting a new skill. The play facilitator is chosen on the basis of who has the most enticing manner with children, who represents the discipline most closely related to the child's reason for referral, who is the most familiar to the child, or for other pertinent reasons. Other team members can enter the process, if necessary or the child chooses, but this is minimized whenever possible in order to reduce the number of unfamiliar adults involved with the child. With only one facilitator involved, it is more likely that the child will exhibit higher levels of performance. The other team members can then cue the play facilitator to elicit behaviors from the child which will provide specific information needed.

The play facilitator is sensitive to the child, following his or her lead whenever possible. In this way, it may be possible to elicit a sample of behavior that is spontaneous, functional, and interactive. Following the child's lead also allows the facilitator to establish rapport more easily and encourages the child to demonstrate his or her higher-level skills. The use of directives are minimized, and are used only when the play facilitator feels that the child will respond well. The play facilitator helps to structure the environment by encouraging play, providing props, commenting on the child's actions, and elaborating or extending the child's play. Typically the play facilitator will observe what the child does spontaneously in each of the play areas, before modeling or suggesting alternative actions.

The play facilitator also acts as the moderator of the different phases of the assessment process including (a) unstructured facilitation, (b) structured facilitation, (c) child–child interaction, (d) parent–child interaction, (e) motor play, and (f) snack. With prompting from team members, the facilitator decides when enough information has been obtained from specific toys or activities, and when it is appropriate to move to new toys and materials or onto another phase of the assessment. Feedback from the other team members regarding what information they still need also helps the moderating process.

Observing Team Members.   Although all team members observe the child's behavior, those who are not directly interacting with the child or parents are responsible for documenting behavioral observations. They act as consultants to the play facilitator, cueing him or her to do specific activities if additional information is desired. Worksheets are provided for each developmental area which help team members to document specific aspects of the child's performance. Team members are primarily responsible for observing "their" area of expertise, but all members observe all developmental areas and contribute to the transdisciplinary discussion after the play session.

Video Camera Operator.   Linder (1993a) recommends that all TPBA sessions be video taped. This allows team members to review sections as needed, allows the tapes to be available for parent discussion, and provides an on-going record of the child's progress. In addition, many parents request copies of these tapes for their home use. Furthermore, play sessions held in small play rooms or in families' homes may not be large enough to accommodate an entire team and family. The video can be used in these situations to allow fewer people to be in attendance and yet still allow those not present to observe the TPBA session on tape.

The video camera operator, usually a member of the team, should be familiar with the basics of operating the camera. The team member should also have a good understanding of what is being sought from various activities. For example, fine motor activities may require a close-up of the hands, or the physical therapist may want to see the child's full profile. By discussing missing elements after each evaluation, all team members will become more skilled in this process.

The Facility

TPBA is best suited for a large, well-equiped playroom, but can also be conducted in the child's home or any other room that can be set up with portable materials. The space should be large enough to arrange the materials in a way that encourages the child to choose from several distinct activity areas. Such areas might include a house area, a block area with trucks and buildings, an art area, a sand and/or water table area, a work table area with puzzles and manipulatives, and a gross motor area. The room should be adaptable, so that areas can be covered or partitioned off, or in some way covered for children who are easily overstimulated.

When conducting a play assessment in the home, the team can bring materials with them, but should also use the furniture and space available in the home. Home observations allow parents to see how the high chair, coffee table, couch, etc. can be used to promote motor, cognitive, language, and social activities.

The Materials

The room(s) in which a TPBA is conducted should contain a variety of interesting and colorful toys and equipment including, but not be limited to representational toys, construction toys, sensory toys and materials, manipulatives, and gross motor equipment. The room is most often broken up into different areas, each of which contains certain types of toys. Parents may also bring some of the child's favorite toys from home.

Representational Area.   This area, usually a "house" area, may include a table and chairs, sink, stove, refrigerator, doll bed, tools, and other toys that encourage the re-creation of activities that are familiar to the child. Adult and child clothing may also help to encourage dramatic play. Miniature houses, garages, and farm sets also promote dramatic play as they require the child to direct dolls through actions with objects. Other settings or action figures with which the child is familiar may encourage the use of spontaneous behaviors that are already part of the child's repertoire. New and/or unusual role plays and objects may also be introduced in order to encourage the use of problem-solving behaviors.

Construction Area.   Sometimes referred to as the block area, this area contains construction toys of various types including blocks (of different shapes, sizes, and weights), paper, paste, beads, and string. It allows the team to observe the child's ability to combine objects, to construct a representation of something else, and to problem-solve spatial relations. The availability of a variety of options enables the facilitator to experiment and change materials to determine which materials best enhance the child's expression of developmental skills.

Sensory Toys and Materials. The sensory toys and materials may be broken up into a few different locations which may include a painting, sand/water table, a swing, rocking boat, and a music area. These activities provide different tactile, visual, auditory, vestibular, proprioceptive, and olfactory input to the child. These materials are important as they allow the team to look at the child's interests and motivations with regard to sensory input, and also provide important information for program planning for home and school.

Manipulatives Area. Providing manipulatives of various types enables the team to look at fine motor skills, problem solving, and visual-motor abilities. Puzzles and peg boards are traditional manipulatives, but cause-and-effect toys that allow the child to cause something to happen are typically more motivating. Toys with switches, handles, levers, knobs, and parts that require twisting, turning, pushing, poking, and pulling are often quite useful in determining a child's strengths and needs.

Gross Motor Area. Gross motor equipment is needed to enable the team to look at how the child moves his or her body, understands the position of his or her body in space, and plans movements through challenging activities. Gross motor activities enable the team to look at muscle tone, strength, endurance, flexibility, transitioning from one position to another, and the child's ability to perform age-appropriate motor skills.

In the home environment, the team may augment the materials available in the home with toys brought in for specific purposes. As previously noted, the furniture in the house can provide opportunities to observe the child's movements from one place to another such as climbing, crawling under, on top of, and around. The toys and objects found in the home can be used to represent the above-mentioned areas as well. Pots, pans, and spoons can be used for making noise, putting things in, on, and hiding things. Cardboard toilet paper tubes can be combined and made into towers, chutes, or a telescope. By using the materials available in the home, the team is also modeling how these everyday objects can be used in educational ways.

The TPBA Play Session Process

A TPBA session typically lasts approximately one hour. The structure of the play session should be flexible to adapt to the needs of the child. The session usually encompasses the following: (a) unstructured play with the facilitator, (b) structured play with the facilitator, (c) parent–child interaction, (d) separation from the parent, (e) play with a peer, (f) motor activities, and (g) snack. With infants, children who have difficulty separating from parents, parents who have difficulty separating from their child, and children with more severe disabilities, the play begins with the parent as a triadic play partner. With children who feel comfortable playing with the facilitator from the beginning, the parents can move to the side to sit with the parent facilitator. For some children, beginning with motor activities may be advisable with others, it may be best to wait until the end of the assessment to engage in motor activities. The important key to remember is to respond to the needs of the child and family, so the session is as comfortable as possible.

　　It is advisable to consider two other points before the parents bring the child into the session. Motor therapists typically like to look at the posture and alignment of the body without the child's clothes on. For infants and toddlers, undressing the child down to diapers during the session is not problematic. For preschool children, however, the team may want to recommend that the child wear a bathing suit under his or her clothes, so that at the water table or some other appropriate time, the child can remove the outer garments without concern. Another recommendation is to have the parents bring a snack for the child and the utensils the child typically uses for eating. This avoids the problem of children being allergic to snacks provided by the team, and allows the team to see what the child eats and drinks using utensils with which the child is familiar.

Unstructured Facilitation

During the first phase of the play session, and with each transition to a new activity, the facilitator allows the child to take the lead in play. The facilitator follows and/or imitates the child's behavior or vocalizations, engages in conversation, and interacts with the toys in parallel, associative, or cooperative play, depending upon the child's developmental level. The facilitator uses this time to try to build rapport, as well as to try to gently "bump up" the child's level of play through modeling a slightly higher level of skill. During unstructured facilitation, the child is free to move from area to area at will. The observers note which behaviors and skills the child spontaneously initiates and which behaviors he or she performs in imitation.

Structured Facilitation

Structured facilitation is needed to make sure the child interacts with a full range of materials in a variety of activities. Here, the facilitator is more directive as he or she attempts to engage the child in cognitive, social emotional, and language activities that were not observed during unstructured play. Structured facilitation is incorporated after spontaneous play in each area, and may also be used when enough information has been gained from a particular activity, or when the child is beginning to perseverate. The facilitator may then select alternative tasks and motivate the child to engage in this new activity. Typical activities that the child may not have selected spontaneously may include spatial tasks such as puzzles or drawings, cause-and-effect tasks involving understanding how things work, higher-level problem-solving skills, and pre-academic and other developmentally appropriate skills.

Child–Child Interaction

At some point in the session, when the child is engaged in social activity such as role play, another peer is introduced into the play. Research has demonstrated that a child who is familiar, of the same sex as the target child, and at a slightly higher developmental level, is the best choice for a role model type of a peer. In some cases, however, it may not be possible to find a child who fits all of the aforementioned criteria and, therefore, a peer who fits most of the criteria is brought in. Observation of peer interaction allows the team to observe the child's play interactions, social patterns, and any unique cognitive, speech/language, and motor behaviors when compared to parent–child and facilitator–child interaction.

　　If no spontaneous interaction takes place between the two children, the facilitator can take a more active role in the process by attempting to initiate and reinforce interaction. The introduction of toys that encourage interaction such as balls, cars, phones, and so on, often help to promote interaction. Guidelines are also provided for observation of the child in a group such as a preschool or day care center, should that be needed.

Parent–Child Interaction

Children may also exhibit different levels of skill when interacting with a parent or guardian than when they are interacting with other children or the facilitator. Some shy children, for example, may engage in higher levels of play when interacting with a parent than when interacting with the facilitator. Other children, who tend to be oppositional with familiar adults, may reveal higher levels of cooperation and, therefore, engage in more difficult tasks with someone with whom they are less familiar, such as the play facilitator. At some point in the session the caregiver is invited to join in play with their child. This parent–child play usually occurs when the parents indicate that the child is playing with something they typically play with at home. If both parents are present, they may each choose to play at a different time and in unique ways.

The parent(s) should be involved in the child's play only if they feel comfortable doing so. When the parent facilitator explains that the team frequently sees more language and higher level play behaviors when the child is playing with the parents, most parents will understand the importance of their involvement. During this phase, the parent is also asked to engage with the child in a more structured activity that is slightly challenging to the child. Teaching strategies, parent and child responsiveness, and parent–child interaction patterns are also observed at this time. Observation of the child's response to the more structured tasks with the parent may provide helpful guidance when planning interventions.

A third aspect of the parent–child interaction component is observing the child's reaction to the parents' departure. This should never occur at the beginning of the session, and should only occur when the parents feel the child is comfortable with the facilitator. If the parent reports difficulty with separation, this aspect is saved until the end or is omitted altogether in order to avoid inaccurate results due to the child's distress. When the parents feel that they can leave for a few minutes, they tell the child that they are leaving to do something and will be back in a few minutes. The team observes the child's reaction to the departure and subsequent return of the parents. The child's and parents' reactions to this separation may also provide insight into emotional support needs for the child and family.

Motor Play

During the motor play phase, both unstructured and structured motor play is observed. In unstructured activities, the play facilitator follows, encourages, and, when necessary, initiates various types of play with the child. After several minutes of unstructured motor play, the facilitator may introduce motor activities that have not yet been observed, or that the child has avoided. If the motor therapist is not the play facilitator, he or she may also choose to participate during this phase in order to better observe the child's muscle tone, equilibrium, etc. The introduction of new team members should be done only at the initiation of the child, in triadic interaction with the familiar facilitator, or at the end of the session, so as not to increase the child's anxiety about interacting with a new person. Some children, however, adapt easily to the introduction of new people at any time in the session. Team members, therefore, need to use discretion in deciding when additional people can interact with the child.

Snack

The final phase of the play assessment allows the team to observe the child eating a snack. Having a snack at the end of the TPBA helps to provide closure to the play session. The snack can also be incorporated at an earlier time in the session, such as during house play. It is sometimes difficult to get the child to stop playing without a good reason such as food! During snack time, the child may again be joined by the peer who was previously played with and/or the family members. This allows for additional observations of social interactions, self-help skills, adaptive behavior, and oral motor skills.

Recording the Observations

During each of the phases discussed above, professional team members record the child's skills and behaviors. TPBA observation guidelines assist team members to organize their observations across all domains of cognitive, social-emotional, communication and language, and sensorimotor development. TPBA worksheets coincide with each set of observation guidelines, and assist the team to focus on *how* the child performs a skill or engages in a type of behavior. The worksheets may also be used after the session when watching the video tape. For instance, the play facilitator is not able to take notes while playing with the child, and, therefore, may need an opportunity to watch and reflect on the play session.

Summary forms for each domain are also available. The summary forms allow the team members to describe the child's strengths, rate the child's abilities with regard to developmental level, provide a justification for the rating (or identify areas that are in need of further evaluation), and note what the child is ready for next. It is recommended that the summary sheets be completed immediately after the play session while observations are still recent in memory. The summary sheets provide a direct link between the assessment and intervention planning. Furthermore, the summary sheets can be used in future IFSP or IEP meetings with parents. After the assessment is completed and the summary sheets are filled out, the information is integrated and discussed with the family. The video tape of the TPBA can be used to point out specific developmental issues, effective interaction patterns, and intervention approaches. Finally, a formal report is written, providing both a quantitative and qualitative description of the child's abilities, concerns or areas of readiness, instructional targets, learning style, environmental demands, and recommendations. A case report is included here to illustrate the TPBA process.

Case Study

Kassandra M. is a 4 year-8-month-old child with a rare condition called cardio-facio-cutaneous syndrome. She has numerous allergies, skin problems, heart, kidney, and gastric disorders. As a result of these and other issues, Kassandra is a tiny girl, weighing only 23 pounds. Kassandra lives in a small apartment with her father, mother, and brother. She has been in an early intervention program since infancy and is currently beginning to use some words and has moved out of her wheel chair to work on beginning walking skills.

Kassandra participated in a transdisciplinary play-based assessment with a team consisting of her teacher, speech therapist, occupational therapist, and one of the authors. A nurse was also involved in her evaluation.

Kassandra was able to walk with assistance as she moved from activity to activity. She preferred to scoot backward while sitting by pushing with her arms and legs or to scoot forward, pushing with her right hand and bearing more weight on her right hip. When her movement was observed, increased tone in her shoulders could be seen to pull them forward and up, restricting the range of movement of her arms. Throughout the observation her extremities and trunk, however, revealed low tone, which affected her movement. She stands with a wide base of support, with feet turned out and weight on the inside borders of her feet. As a result of the effort required to move, Kassandra prefers to sit and play with small objects. This isolated play keeps her from socially interacting with her peers.

Both fine motor and cognitive skills were observed in her play with toys and her attempts at using signs. She was observed to reach for, grasp, and connect tubes in Marble Works, and used a pincer grasp, (with pads of her index finger and thumb together) to pick up and insert marbles into the tube. Kassandra was able to combine objects such as shapes in a shape box (her mother reports she can do all fourteen shapes in her shape ball at home) and put pieces in a simple separate-piece puzzle. She was observed to give a doll a bottle, to put a hat on her head, to turn pages of a book, and to point to pictures in a book with her index finger. Her thought sequences were limited to performing two related actions before she repeated the same actions or moved to another activity.

Kassandra's play interactions primarily relied on the adult facilitator to prompt her to interact with the materials. She was very social and interactive with the adults in the room, smiling, imitating their actions and seeking to continue the play by vocalizing and verbalizing sounds and single-word utterances. She appeared to maintain interactions with adults by using the words from her repertoire, particularly names ("Katie," and "Mommy"). In her classroom, it is reported that she plays alone unless her peers approach her and entice her to play. Pragmatically, Kassandra used her words to greet ("hi"), to request objects ("baw" for ball) or actions (signed "more" to continue a song), to comment ("ma knee" for my knee) and to protest (vocalizing and turning away). With a peer Kassandra was less vocal and interactive, but did respond to requests and encouragement from her friends.

From the play-based assessment, numerous recommendations were made to increase Kassandra's skills and the quality of her movement, communication, and play. Suggestions were turned into activities that would increase Kassandra's motivation to stand unsupported and to increase balance and tone in her trunk. In addition, the team offered ideas for activities that would increase hand strength and require the use of both hands together. They also recommended toys (such as cause-and-effect toys) requiring more than one or two steps to operate. Language was encouraged through turn-taking interactions with peers and imitation of familiar words and signs. It was also suggested that Kassandra be taught phases such as "What's that?" to encourage her to request vocabulary such as labels for objects, and "Let's play" to enable her to engage peers in play.

From this case study, one can see that a functional assessment can lead to functional recommendations that can be implemented in a variety of settings.

*For a copy of the tape of Kassandra's TPBA and full report, call Paul H. Brookes (800) 638-3775.

Implications

The discussion and suggestions within this chapter are not without implications. The evolution described is not universal, as other factors within the service delivery system may not be consistent with a play-based assessment model. Although it is not the intent of this chapter to delve into these issues, they deserve mention.

- The use of team-based arena models of assessment require the system, which is in many instances set up for individual assessments, to restructure so that teams have time to meet together.
- The philosophy of child-centered play-based approaches to assessment needs to be integrated into pre-service and inservice models of training.
- The importance of qualitative as well as quantitative data needs to be acknowledged by states, local school districts, and direct service providers.
- The involvement of parents before, during, and after an assessment requires training of staff in how to more effectively and sensitively incorporate families into the assessment process. In addition, the structure and time for assessments may need to be adjusted.

All of the above issues are important if play-based assessments are to become a standard, accepted approach to intervention. Professionals, therefore, need to address these realities of implementation along with the corresponding philosophical priorities.

Summary

Over the past twenty years, as professionals have begun to assess and serve infants, toddlers, and preschoolers who are at-risk for or have disabilities, we have begun to understand that the methods and instruments used to identify school-aged children with special needs are inadequate for younger children. An evolution of philosophy, process, and procedures has occurred which has involved a shift in the content or the type of data and information we gather about children; and a change in the context of assessment; a modification of the way we assess children; and a change in the role of the child, the family, and professionals during and after the assessment process. Ultimately, as a result of this evolution, this has changed the way we provide services to children and families. In this chapter, we have tried to illustrate some of the reasons for this evolution and the growing importance of play both in assessment and intervention with children and families. Although many different play instruments exist, the Transdisciplinary Play-Based Assessment model was highlighted, as TPBA is a comprehensive process that not only helps to assess where the child is currently functioning, but also provides a basis to determine eligibility for services, describe child and family needs, document changes over time, and develop intervention plans.

The use of play-based assessments as a part of a comprehensive evaluation of young children is a growing trend. This trend is supported on theoretical, philosophical, and research grounds on the basis that play-based approaches are developmentally responsive, family and child friendly, provide relevant information about the child, and provide a means for fusion of assessment and intervention processes.

CHAPTER

11 Assessment of Cognitive Functioning in Preschoolers

VINCENT C. ALFONSO

DAWN P. FLANAGAN

The purpose of this chapter is to provide readers with a quantitative and qualitative description and critical evaluation of intelligence tests that are used to assess the cognitive functioning of preschool children (e.g., aged 2-6 [2 years 6 months] to 5-6). It is important to evaluate

BUFORD'S FAMILY HONORS HIS LAST REQUEST THAT HE BE LAID OUT THE WAY MOST OF HIS FRIENDS WOULD REMEMBER HIM

© National Association of School Psycologists.
Reprinted by permission of the publisher.

the psychometric properties of our instruments because most states (n = 31) identify pre-schoolers who need special education services through the use of quantitative criteria (e.g., two standard deviations below the mean on a standardized norm-referenced test) (Danaher, 1995). Because decisions regarding program eligibility are made using norm-referenced tests of cognitive ability, it is important that these tests be psychometrically sound. The *quantitative* characteristics (i.e., psychometric properties) of intelligence tests reviewed here include stan-dardization, norm table age divisions, reliability, subtest, scale, and total test floors, item gra-dients, and validity. These characteristics are important to evaluate at all ages for which an instrument is designed. However, quantitative characteristics are *especially* important to examine when intelligence tests are used to assess the cognitive functioning of *preschoolers* for the following reasons: (1) young children's abilities change rapidly and instruments have to be sensitive to these subtle changes; (2) many traditional instruments represent downward extensions of subtests that were designed for older children and, therefore, were not designed with the preschool child in mind; and (3) traditional intelligence tests have been criticized extensively for use with young children due to poor psychometric properties.

For example, test floors (i.e., subtest, scale, total test) and item gradients, two impor-tant quantitative characteristics of instruments used for assessing preschoolers (Bracken, 1987), continue to be rated the weakest by independent reviewers (Flanagan & Alfonso, 1995). Adequate test floors are critical to any cognitive test because they allow examiners to distinguish among children at different levels of cognitive functioning (e.g., average, low average, borderline, mentally retarded). When test floors are inadequate, children may obtain standard scores that overestimate ability because the instrument does not contain a sufficient number of easy items to detect differences across ability levels. This is especially true when examiners are attempting to estimate the cognitive functioning of individuals with various degrees of mental retardation (i.e., mild, moderate, severe). In addition, tests with inadequate floors usually provide more information regarding what a child cannot do rather than what a child can do. Relatedly, a subtest's item gradients reflect its ability to detect fine gradations in cognitive performance within and across ability levels. Specifically, an item gradient refers to the amount of change in a child's standard score that is associated with a one unit change in his/her raw score. When a child's raw score increases by one point and the corresponding standard score increase is small, subtle differences in a child's ability can be observed. There-fore, knowledge of a test's item gradient *violations* provides crucial information regarding the *insensitivity* of the instrument to detect small differences in performance. An item gradi-ent violation occurs when standard scores increase more than one-third standard deviation for every one point increase in raw scores (Bracken, 1987). Tests with item gradient viola-tions that occur close to the mean are more problematic than those that occur 2 to 3 standard deviations below the mean, because they do not detect fine gradations in ability within the average and low average ranges of functioning—let alone the borderline and mental retarda-tion ranges (Flanagan & Alfonso, 1995).

With regard to the validity of intelligence tests, we first report whether each instrument has evidence of content, criterion-related, and construct validity. Next, we provide an evalua-tive judgment of a test's validity based on the presence or absence of these types of validity evidence, as well as our own evaluation of the available data provided in the test manuals and extant literature. In general, the criteria that exist for specifying the conditions under which an instrument is determined to be valid are arbitrary and often confusing (see Flanagan & Alfonso, 1995). Therefore, it is difficult to set an acceptable validity criterion (Bracken, 1987). Thus, our criteria for evaluating a test's validity as well as our overall judgments of the quality of validity evidence across tests may not be corroborated by other researchers and practitioners. Notwithstanding, it is important to keep in mind that validity is a process, and evidence of a test's validity accumulates gradually (Anastasi, 1988). As such, the present evaluation of the validity of intelligence tests reflects only the validity evidence that is available currently and will likely change as validity studies mount.

In addition to quantitative characteristics, it is necessary to review the *qualitative* characteristics of intelligence tests for preschoolers. Because many intelligence tests are used to assess the cognitive functioning of individuals across a large age range, many preschool scales represent downward extensions of scales designed for older individuals rather than separately designed scales for very young children. Therefore, a critical review of their qualitative characteristics, such as whether or not they contain varied and manipulative materials for young children, seems warranted (Bracken & Walker, 1997; Harrison, Flanagan, & Genshaft, 1997). The qualitative characteristics of intelligence tests reviewed here are organized according to two broad areas, namely, "Test Construction and Format" and "Administration." Examples of Test Construction and Format characteristics are the attractiveness of test materials and the inclusion of an appropriate nonverbal scale. Examples of Administration characteristics include opportunities for teaching the tasks tested, and receptive and expressive language requirements.

One of the most important qualitative characteristics of intelligence tests is the level of complexity of subtest directions. For example, children may not earn credit for particular items or sets of items because they did not *understand* the test directions rather than because they have less than average ability in the domain being assessed (Flanagan, Alfonso, Kaminer, & Rader, 1995). Thus, the validity of test results may be questionable for a child who does not understand one or more basic concepts contained in the directions of a subtest(s) (see Flanagan et al., 1995 and Bracken, 1986 for a discussion).

Finally, because the cultural composition of the preschool population that receives special education services is diverse and will continue to diversify (Children's Defense Fund, 1989), intelligence tests should be evaluated vis a vis their applicability for use with multicultural populations. Therefore, in an attempt to aid practitioners in selecting the most appropriate tests for evaluating culturally diverse populations, the subtests and composites of intelligence tests were classified here according to the extent to which exposure to mainstream North American society influences test performance. For example, an individual's performance on subtests that assess receptive and expressive language skills or general fund of information is highly influenced by exposure to North American culture, whereas an individual's performance on subtests that assess novel problem solving ability is less influenced by exposure to North American culture (Hessler, 1993; Horn, 1991).

The major intelligence tests reviewed here are: (1) Stanford-Binet Intelligence Scale: Fourth Edition (SB:IV; Thorndike, Hagen, & Sattler, 1986); (2) Wechsler Preschool and Primary Scale of Intelligence—Revised (WPPSI-R; Wechsler, 1989); (3) Woodcock-Johnson Psycho-Educational Battery—Revised: Tests of Cognitive Ability (WJ-R COG; Woodcock & Johnson, 1989); (4) Differential Ability Scales (DAS; Elliott, 1990a); and (5) Bayley Scales of Infant Development—Second Edition (BSID-II; Bayley, 1993).

Quantitative Characteristics of Intelligence Tests for Preschoolers

The following sources were used to make evaluative judgments about the quantitative characteristics of the previously mentioned intelligence tests: (a) *Standards for Educational and*

Psychological Testing (American Educational Research Association, American Psychological Association, and National Council on Measurement in Education [AERA, APA, & NCME], 1985); (b) *A Consumer's Guide to Tests in Print* (Hammill, Brown, & Bryant, 1992); (c) Bracken's (1987), Bracken and Walker's (1997), and Flanagan and Alfonso's (1995) critical reviews of the technical characteristics of intelligence tests for preschoolers; and (d) the authors' review of the most recent literature pertaining to the assessment of cognitive functioning of young children.

Based on these sources, a set of criteria was compiled and used to evaluate the technical adequacy of intelligence tests for preschoolers. Table 11.1 contains a list of the quantitative characteristics reviewed, the criteria that were used to evaluate each characteristic, and the evaluative classification assigned to each criterion. A discussion of how the criteria presented in Table 11.1 were developed, as well as how the evaluative judgments were determined for each quantitative characteristic, are beyond the scope of this chapter. Therefore, the reader is directed to primary sources such as Bracken (1987), Bracken and Walker (1997), and Flanagan and Alfonso (1995) for a complete discussion of these issues.

Qualitative Characteristics of Intelligence Tests for Preschoolers

The qualitative characteristics of intelligence tests for preschoolers have received less attention in the intelligence test and preschool assessment literature. To date, we have found only one comprehensive *summary* of qualitative characteristics of intelligence tests that includes corresponding suggestions for making evaluative judgments (i.e., Bracken & Walker, 1997). Most investigators have focused on only *one or two* qualitative characteristics that are relevant to the use of intelligence tests with preschoolers (e.g., Bracken, 1986; Kaufman, 1990).

Based on a review of the available literature in this area, we have compiled a summary of several important qualitative characteristics that are useful to consider prior to selecting an instrument for use with preschoolers. Table 11.2 provides a definition of each qualitative characteristic as well as guidelines that may be used to evaluate them. For example, this table indicates that test materials should be attractive and colorful in order to maximize the child's interest and participation. Table 11.2 also suggests that test directions should be brief and should be composed of short, simple sentences. Although we have provided our own evaluative judgments of these qualitative characteristics in our description of individual tests, these judgments are based almost exclusively on our knowledge of and experience in preschool assessment. Therefore, our evaluations of the qualitative characteristics of intelligence tests should be used in conjunction with one's own professional judgment and clinical experience.

Relative Influence of North American Culture on Intelligence Test Performance

Many recent theories and/or perspectives on intelligence include a consideration of culture as a critical component in understanding how differing experiences hinder or advance intellectual behavior (e.g., Gardner, 1983; Sternberg, 1997). Although no current test of intelligence has been developed from these or similar theoretical perspectives (Helms, 1992), practitioners often employ a conceptual framework, such as Newland's (1971)

TABLE 11.1   Criteria for Evaluating Quantitative Characteristics of Intelligence Tests for Preschoolers

Psychometric Properties	Criteria	Evaluative Classification
I. Standardization[a]	(1) *Size of normative group*	
	200 persons per each 1-year interval and at least 2,000 persons overall	Good
	100 persons per each 1-year interval and at least 1,000 persons overall	Adequate
	Neither criterion above is met	Inadequate
	(2) *Recency of normative data*	
	Collected in 1988 or later	Good
	Collected between 1978 and 1987	Adequate
	Collected in 1977 or earlier	Inadequate
	(3) *Match of the demographic characteristics of the normative group to the U.S. population*	
	Normative group represents the U.S. population on five or more important demographic variables (e.g., gender, race) with SES included	Good
	Normative group represents the U.S. population on three or four important demographic variables with SES included	Adequate
	Neither criterion is met	Inadequate
Ia. Norm Table Age Divisions	One to two months	Good
	Three to four months	Adequate
	Greater than four months	Inadequate
II. Reliability[a]	(1) *Internal Consistency Reliability Coefficient*	
	Greater than or equal to .90 ($\geq$ .90)	Good
	.80 to .89	Adequate
	Less than .80 ($<$ .80)	Inadequate
	(2) *Test-Retest Reliability Coefficient*	
	Greater than or equal to .90 ($\geq$ .90)	Good
	.80 to .89	Adequate
	Less than .80 ($<$ .80)	Inadequate
	(3) *Sample size and representativeness of test-retest sample*	
	Sample contains at least 100 subjects and represents the U.S. population on at least five or more demographic variables	Good
	Sample contains at least 50 subjects and represents the U.S. population on three or four demographic variables	Adequate
	Neither criterion is met	Inadequate
	(4) *Age range of the test-retest sample*	
	Spans no more than a 1-year interval	Good
	Spans no more than 2 years	Adequate
	Spans more than 2 years or extends beyond the preschool age range (i.e., 3 to 5 yrs.), regardless of interval size	Inadequate

(5) *Length of test-retest interval*[b]		
Interval is 3 months or less		Good
Interval is between 3 and 6 months		Adequate
Interval is greater than 6 months		Inadequate

III. Floors

(1) *Subtests*	
Raw score of 1 is associated with a standard score greater than 2 standard deviations below the normative mean	Adequate
Raw score of 1 is associated with a standard score less than or equal to 2 standard deviations below the normative mean	Inadequate
(2) *Scale and Total Test*[c]	
Scale or total test standard score greater than 2 standard deviations below the normative mean	Adequate
Scale or total test standard score less than or equal to 2 standard deviations below the normative mean	Inadequate

IV. Item Gradients[d]

Item Gradient Violations	
No item gradient violations occur or all item gradient violations are between 2 and 3 standard deviations below the normative mean	Good
All item gradient violations occur between 1 and 3 standard deviations below the normative mean	Adequate
All or any portion of item gradient violations occur between the mean and 1 standard deviation below the normative mean	Inadequate

V. Validity[e]

Presence and Quality of Content, Criterion-Related, and Construct Validity Evidence	
3 types of validity and the authors' evaluation of available data	Good
2 types of validity and the authors' evaluation of available data	Adequate
1 type of validity and the authors' evaluation of available data	Inadequate

[a]An overall rating is obtained as follows: Good = All Goods; Adequate = Goods and Adequates; Inadequate = Goods and/or Adequates, and Inadequates.

[b]The criteria presented here regarding the length of the test–retest interval differ from traditional criteria used with school-age children because young children's abilities change rapidly.

[c]Floors were calculated based on the aggregate of the subtest raw scores that comprised the scale and total test composites, where one item per subtest was scored correctly.

[d]An item gradient is defined as the increase in standard score points associated with a one point increase in raw score values. An item gradient violation occurs when a one point increase in raw score points is associated with a standard score increase of greater than one third of a standard deviation.

[e]Ratings of "Good" or "Adequate" were made only when the available validity evidence was reviewed positively by the authors and corroborated by other reviews in the extant literature.

process-dominant/product-dominant continuum, when interpreting the performance of culturally and linguistically diverse children on any intelligence test. Following from this framework, it is assumed that a child's level of acculturation, or the learning of mainstream North American culture, will impact his or her performance on subtests that depend on accumulated knowledge and environmental experiences (product-dominant) to a greater extent than subtests that are assumed to assess fundamental learning processes (process-dominant) (Newland, 1971).

TABLE 11.2   Qualitative Characteristics of Intelligence Tests for Preschoolers

Qualitative Characteristic	Guidelines for Evaluating Intelligence Tests for Preschoolers
Test Construction and Format	
Test Manual	Test manuals should indicate clearly the theoretical model espoused by the test developer, the abilities that are measured by the instrument, test interpretation guidelines, and intervention strategies to remediate areas of weakness.
Test materials	Test materials should include manipulatives, be attractive and colorful, and maximize the child's interest and participation. The number of small materials should be minimized due to possible ingestion by young children. In addition, test materials should be as universal as possible and not gender- or ethnic-stereotyped (see Appendix 11A).
Administration procedures	The test should contain efficient administration procedures, including alternating subtests (e.g., verbal/nonverbal), beginning the test with a stimulating task that involves manipulatives, and providing guidelines for the average length of time needed to complete a task. These administration characteristics should engage the child and hold his/her interest. Total test time should be kept at a minimum (e.g., one hour or less).
Expressive language requirements	Subtests should require one-word responses versus multiple-word responses unless the test is measuring expressive language ability or verbal fluency. Tests should allow for the use of gestures on the part of the child.
Appropriateness of nonverbal scale	Nonverbal scales of intelligence tests should be multidimensional, allow for a nonverbal administration of each subtest (i.e., through pantomime or gestures only), provide a separate nonverbal score (based on a nonverbal administration), assess higher-order cognitive functions, and emphasize power rather than speed.
Administration	
Length of test directions	All test directions should be brief. Sentences should be short and of simple structure.
Number and complexity of basic concepts	All test directions should use a small number of basic concepts (e.g., less than 15) and these concepts should be understood by at least 75% of same-age peers.
Inclusion of opportunities to "teach the task"	Prior to evaluating a child's performance in a given area there should be opportunities to "teach the task" through the use of sample items, multiple trials per item, alternative wording, and/or examiner demonstration to ensure understanding of task requirements.
Inclusion of alternative stopping rules	Throughout the test there should be alternative means of discontinuing a subtest in order to minimize a young child's frustration. For example, a subtest may contain a set of items for a particular age range (e.g., 2-6 to 3-6), but have several methods of subtest discontinuation within that set of items instead of administration of every item in that age set.
Translation/adaptation in other languages	Tests should be translated in other languages or provide some method(s) to assist in test interpretation of children from culturally diverse backgrounds.

All intelligence tests appear to include subtests that are either product-dominant and process-dominant or some combination thereof. Therefore, no intelligence test is *culture-free* (Humphreys, 1992). Instead, assuming that "cognitive-ability tests measure problem-solving and other skills that result from the interaction between the person's neurophysiology and the *environment* [emphasis added]" (Elliott, 1990b, p. 2), the degree to which they are *culturally loaded* differs. For example, the WPPSI-R and SB:IV include many items that require knowledge of societal conventions (product-dominant) and therefore, may be more culturally loaded than tests that contain items that are assumed to be more process-dominant (e.g., many WJ-R COG subtests). Moreover, like the DAS, the cognitive subtests of the WJ-R appear to be less culturally loaded than the WPPSI-R, for example, since they generally do not contain "country-specific content or questions about social values... [but rather, include] content that is [considered to be] fair in a variety of literate, industrial societies, in which language and communication, reasoning, and memory functions are likely to be widely relevant" (Elliott, 1990b, p. 27).

Even though it is clear that the extent to which North American culture influences test performance is crucial to consider when assessing the cognitive functioning of preschoolers who are culturally and linguistically diverse (e.g., Armour-Thomas, 1992; Helms, 1997; Lopez, 1997) it is perhaps the most difficult test characteristic to evaluate. In order to provide the reader with information regarding the relative influence of North American culture on preschool intelligence test performance, it was necessary to use a contemporary, well-researched theoretical framework for understanding the abilities and processes that are measured by intelligence tests, particularly those that are well known to be strongly influenced by culture.

Based on a review of the most prominent theoretical frameworks discussed in the psychological and educational literature, McGrew and Flanagan (1996) concluded that an integration of the Horn-Cattell *Gf-Gc* Theory (Horn, 1991, 1994; Horn & Noll, 1997) and the Three-Stratum Theory of Cognitive Abilities (Carroll, 1993, 1997) provides the most comprehensive and empirically supported framework of the structure of intelligence to date (see also Messick, 1992, and reviews by Carroll, 1993; Gustafson, 1988; Horn, 1994).

Using this integrated Horn-Carroll framework as a guide, as well as results of several joint factor analyses of cognitive batteries (e.g., Flanagan & McGrew, 1996; McGhee, 1993; Stone, 1992; Woodcock, 1990), McGrew (1997) and McGrew and Flanagan (1996) classified the subtests of all major intelligence batteries according to *Gf-Gc* theory (see Table 11.3 for definitions of *Gf-Gc* abilities). For example, the Information, Similarities, Vocabulary, and Comprehension subtests of the WPPSI-R were classified as measures of Crystallized Intelligence (*Gc*) and the WPPSI-R Arithmetic subtest was classified as a measure of Quantitative Ability (*Gq*). On the DAS, the Copying, Pattern Construction, and Block Building subtests were classified as measures of Visual Processing (*Gv*). Space limitations preclude an in-depth discussion of the classification process as well as how *Gf-Gc* theory can be used as a framework for assessing and interpreting human cognitive abilities (see Flanagan & McGrew, 1997 and McGrew & Flanagan, 1996 for a discussion). Nevertheless, use of this classification scheme provides knowledge of the underlying *Gf-Gc* abilities and processes of all subtests included on the intelligence tests reviewed here, a necessary step prior to considering how culture impacts performance on these subtests.

Like Newland's (1971) process-dominant/product-dominant continuum, the *Gf-Gc* abilities can be thought of as lying on a continuum, with Fluid Intelligence (*Gf*) on one end and Crystallized Intelligence (*Gc*) on the other. *Gf* is defined as the ability to reason, form concepts, and solve problems that typically include novel stimuli and/or procedures (Horn,

TABLE 11.3   *Gf-Gc* Ability Definitions

Gf-Gc Ability	*Gf-Gc* Symbol	Definition
Fluid Reasoning	*Gf*	Ability to reason, form concepts, and problem solve, using novel information and/or procedures.
Crystallized Intelligence	*Gc*	Measures an individual's breadth and depth of general knowledge and knowledge of a culture, including verbal communication and reasoning with previously learned procedures.
Visual Processing	*Gv*	Ability to analyze and synthesize visual information.
Auditory Processing	*Ga*	Ability to analyze and synthesize auditory information.
Processing Speed	*Gs*	Ability to perform automatic cognitive tasks quickly, particularly when under pressure to maintain focused attention.
Short-Term Memory	*Gsm*	Ability to hold information temporarily in immediate awareness and then use it within a few seconds.
Long-Term Retrieval	*Glr*	Ability to store information and retrieve it later through association.
Quantitative Knowledge	*Gq*	Ability to comprehend quantitative concepts and relationships and to manipulate numerical symbols.
Correct Decision Speed	*CDS*	Quickness in providing correct answers to a variety of moderately difficult problems in comprehension, reasoning, and problem solving.

1991). As such, performance on tasks that measure *Gf* ability depends little on direct instruction, formal learning experience, and level of education. On the other hand, *Gc* is defined as a person's breadth and depth of knowledge, including the ability to communicate (especially verbally) as well as the ability to reason through the application of previously learned procedures. *Gc* is highly dependent on level of acculturation. Performance on *Gc* tasks reflects the person's ability to "absorb and incorporate the concepts, ideas, and knowledge of a culture and to reason with this culturally-based information (Horn, 1988)" (see Hessler, 1993, p. 75). The remaining *Gf-Gc* abilities lie somewhere between *Gf* and *Gc* on the continuum, with their location depending on the extent to which they differ vis a vis relative emphasis on process, content, and manner of response (Carroll, 1993).

With this continuum in mind and knowledge of the *Gf-Gc* classifications of cognitive tests, Flanagan and Alfonso (1994) examined each of the subtests included on the major intelligence batteries according to underlying process, nature of the content included, and type of response, to determine the relative influence of culture (i.e., high, moderate, low) on these tests for use with preschoolers (see Appendix 11A). Hessler's (1993) classifications of the relative influence of culture on the WJ-R subtests was also used as a guide. Since the "relative influence of culture" classifications are based solely on our own judgments, we recommend that they be used only as a guide for selecting subtests that most appropriately meet the needs of culturally diverse preschool populations.

A Description and Critical Evaluation of Intelligence Tests for Preschoolers

Stanford-Binet Intelligence Scale: Fourth Edition (SB:IV)

Description.   The SB:IV (Thorndike, Hagen, & Sattler, 1986) is composed of eight subtests that may be used to assess the cognitive functioning of preschoolers as young as 2-0. These subtests form four areas, including Verbal Reasoning, Abstract/Visual Reasoning, Quantitative Reasoning, and Short-Term Memory. The Vocabulary, Comprehension, and Absurdities subtests combine to yield the Verbal Reasoning area score; the Pattern Analysis and Copying subtests combine to yield the Abstract/Visual Reasoning area score; the Quantitative subtest yields the Quantitative area score; and the Bead Memory and Memory for Sentences subtests combine to yield the Short-Term Memory area score. Scores from one or more of these areas are combined to yield the Test Composite which is interpreted as a measure of general intelligence (Thorndike et al., 1986). Descriptions of all SB:IV subtests are found in Delaney and Hopkins (1987) and Glutting and Kaplan (1990).

The SB:IV subtests have a mean of 50 and a standard deviation of 8. All area scores as well as the Test Composite have a mean of 100 and a standard deviation of 16. Several derived scores are available on the SB:IV that aid in test interpretation, including standard scores, percentiles, and age equivalents. According to Delaney and Hopkins (1987), testing

Stanford–Binet Intelligence Scale, Fourth Edition (SB:IV). Copyright © 1986 by The Riverside Publishing Company. Reproduced from the *Stanford–Binet Intelligence Scale, Fourth Edition* by Robert L. Thorndike, Elizabeth P. Hagen and Jerome M. Sattler, with permission of the publisher.

time for preschoolers ranges from 30 to 40 minutes. The SB:IV as well as software for scoring are available from the Riverside Publishing Company.

Quantitative Characteristics.   In general, the standardization sample characteristics of the SB:IV are adequate. The standardization sample included 5,000 individuals, with at least 200 individuals per one-year interval (Thorndike et al., 1986). The sample closely approximated the U.S. population (1980 Census data) on the following variables: gender, geographic region, race/ethnicity, community size, and socioeconomic status (i.e., parent occupation and parent education). However, Glutting and Kaplan (1990) indicated that there was an under-representation of low SES and an over-representation of high SES individuals in the standardization sample. In addition, Flanagan and Alfonso (1995) stated that much of the information regarding the standardization characteristics for the SB:IV was presented for the entire sample rather than by specific age intervals. Thus, the match of the preschool sample of the SB:IV to the U.S. population is not clear. For these reasons, examiners are advised to use caution when making interpretive statements about a preschooler's test performance based on the available norms. The norm tables of the SB:IV are divided in 4-month age blocks for children between the ages of 2-0 and 5-11 which is considered adequate (see Table 11.1). Scores on the SB:IV may overestimate an individual's functioning (by approximately 3 to 4 standard score points) because the norms were obtained in 1985 (i.e., more than a decade ago) (Flynn, 1984).

The total test internal consistency reliability coefficients of the SB:IV were good for the preschool age range, with the lowest coefficient being .95 (see Table 11.1). Conversely, the SB:IV's test–retest reliability is inadequate because the test–retest sample was not representative of the U.S. population on at least three variables (see Table 11.1). However, the age range of the test–retest sample and the test–retest reliability coefficient (i.e., .91) were good. The length of the test–retest interval (i.e., 16 weeks) was adequate. Thus, although the SB:IV's reliability was rated as inadequate overall based on the criteria presented in Table 11.1, it appears to measure reliably what it purports to measure. However, whether the SB:IV measures the same constructs over time is questionable.

The most significant quantitative limitation of the SB:IV is its subtest floors. All of the SB:IV subtests appropriate for preschoolers have inadequate floors at the beginning age level of the test (i.e., 2-0). It is not until age 5-0 that all subtests for preschoolers have adequate floors. Similarly, all clusters (i.e., areas) of the SB:IV as well as the Test Composite have inadequate floors at the youngest age levels (Flanagan & Alfonso, 1995). The SB:IV area with the greatest floor effect is the Quantitative area; its floor does not become adequate until age 5-0. However, the floors of most other areas are adequate at about age 3-6. To illustrate the poor quality of the SB:IV total test floor, a child aged 2-6 who earns a raw score of 1 on all the recommended subtests for this age level will obtain a score in the upper end of the low average range (i.e., 88). Overall, the subtest, scale, and total test floors of the SB:IV are inadequate for the assessment of very young children (2-6 to 3-6).

The item gradients on the SB:IV also represent a major quantitative limitation. For example, six of the eight subtests for preschoolers (i.e., Comprehension, Absurdities, Bead Memory, Quantitative, Copying, and Pattern Analysis) have inadequate item gradients at ages 2-6 to 3-5. Conversely, one subtest (i.e., Comprehension) has adequate item gradients at ages 3-6 to 4-5, whereas two subtests (i.e., Comprehension and Absurdities) have good item gradients at ages 4-6 to 5-5. However, only Vocabulary and Memory for Sentences have good item gradients across the entire preschool age range. This indicates that fine gradations in ability may not be detected on most subtests of the SB:IV, especially for very young children.

Based on the criteria presented in Table 11.1, the validity of the SB:IV is considered adequate. There is evidence of content, criterion-related, and construct validity for the SB:IV. However, the quality of the construct validity evidence has been questioned extensively (e.g., Glutting & Kaplan, 1990; Kaplan & Alfonso, 1997; Laurent, Swerdlik, & Ryburn, 1992). Although there is consensus that the Test Composite of the SB:IV can be interpreted as a measure of general intelligence, there is considerable controversy regarding the factor structure of the instrument. That is, there has been minimal agreement among independent researchers regarding the number of factors that underlie the SB:IV across the age levels of the instrument. The test authors have proposed that the four areas of the SB:IV may be interpreted for all individuals regardless of age (Thorndike et al., 1986). Yet, no study that has employed either exploratory or confirmatory factor analyses has supported the factorial invariance of the SB:IV across age (e.g., Keith, Cool, Novak, White, & Pottebaum, 1988; Kline, 1989; Molfese, Yaple, Helwig, Harris, & Connell, 1992). The reasons for the lack of consensus regarding the number of factors that underlie the instrument may be related to the fact that some of its constructs are *under-represented* at different ages and when different combinations of tests are administered.

Results of joint-factor analyses have shed some light on this issue. That is, when a sufficient breadth of cognitive abilities are represented in a factor analysis, it appears that the SB:IV does in fact measure four areas across the age range of the test (Woodcock, 1990). Thus, when factor analyses are restricted to the subtests included only in the SB:IV battery, two and three-factor solutions may result, depending on the age of the sample and the number and diversity of subtests included. Nevertheless, the factors that are under-represented on the SB:IV at particular age levels should not be interpreted. For example, the Quantitative area should not be interpreted at the preschool age level because it is based on only one subtest (see Kaplan & Alfonso, 1997 and McGrew & Flanagan, 1996 for a discussion).

Despite the lack of agreement regarding the construct validity of the SB:IV across the age range of the test, there is general agreement regarding the structure of the SB:IV for preschoolers. It appears that the SB:IV is a two-factor (or area) test for young children (e.g., Molfese et al., 1992; Ownby & Carmin, 1988). These factors have been labeled Verbal Comprehension and Nonverbal Reasoning/Visualization by Sattler (1992). The subtests that load on the Verbal Comprehension factor are Vocabulary, Comprehension, Absurdities, and Memory for Sentences. The subtests that load on the Nonverbal Reasoning/Visualization factor are Pattern Analysis, Copying, Quantitative, and Bead Memory.

Similarly, in a recent confirmatory factor analysis conducted with more than 400 preschool children with developmental delays, Kaplan and Alfonso (1997) found evidence for a two-factor model similar in composition to that proposed in previous studies (e.g., Sattler, 1992). Therefore, the available evidence suggests that the SB:IV ought to be interpreted as a dichotomy (i.e., verbal–nonverbal) in the preschool population unless cross-battery assessment procedures are employed that would allow for broader measurement of abilities (McGrew & Flanagan, 1996).

The quality of the remaining validity evidence of the SB:IV is less controversial, especially when the Test Composite has been used as the criterion or predictor variable. Dozens of studies have been conducted comparing the SB:IV with other major intelligence tests, such as the WPPSI-R and a variety of populations such as learning disabled, normal, gifted, and mentally retarded (see Laurent et al., 1992 and Thorndike et al., 1986 for details). In general, correlations between the SB:IV and other instruments have been moderate to high (e.g., .74 and .77 with the WPPSI-R and DAS total scores) and test scores for exceptional groups (e.g., gifted, mentally retarded) have been within the expected range of cognitive functioning (see Laurent et al., 1992). Therefore, the SB:IV appears to be a valid measure of general intellectual functioning for most ages and for many exceptional populations.

Qualitative Characteristics.   Overall the "Test Construction and Format" characteristics of the SB:IV are adequate. The SB:IV test kit includes two user-friendly manuals, *The Stanford-Binet Intelligence Scale, Fourth Edition: Guide for Administration and Scoring* and *The Stanford-Binet Intelligence Scale, Fourth Edition: Technical Manual* (Thorndike et al., 1986). These manuals, however, do not provide guidelines for interpreting an individual's test performance and include only limited information on administration procedures. Therefore, practitioners are strongly encouraged to purchase the *Examiner's Handbook: An Expanded Guide for Fourth Edition Users* (Delaney & Hopkins, 1987). In addition, the SB:IV contains some attractive and colorful manipulative materials such as red, white, and blue beads, green cubes, and colored pictures. However, many of its subtests appear to be downward extensions of subtests designed for older children. Therefore, they may not be engaging for the very young child.

The SB:IV effectively employs alternating subtests (e.g., verbal/nonverbal) and may be completed within one hour. However, the administration of most subtests is generally cumbersome and confusing because, with the exception of Memory for Sentences, the item format of subtests changes during administration, often resulting in the need to use different test stimuli. For example, the Vocabulary subtest begins by asking the examinee to label pictures and then changes to asking the examinee to define words. Although the SB:IV subtests usually require minimal verbal expressive language on the part of the child, gestures are not acceptable responses. In addition, the SB:IV does not include a nonverbal scale or nonverbal adaptation for preschoolers.

The "Administration" characteristics of the SB:IV are inadequate. Many subtests contain lengthy directions and there is a large number of basic concepts (i.e., 25) found in the test directions (Flanagan et al., 1995). Only four of the SB:IV's eight subtests for preschoolers have sample items that provide the child with an opportunity to learn the task. There are no alternative stopping rules provided for young children and thus no mechanism to minimize a child's frustration when items become too difficult. Finally, the test directions of the SB:IV as well as correct verbal responses given by the child are not available in other languages and there are no norms for individuals from other cultures.

Relative Influence of North American Culture.   The relative influence of North American culture on the cognitive subtests and clusters of the SB:IV is variable. As expected, the subtests that comprise the Verbal Reasoning cluster are highly influenced by level of acculturation. By contrast, the Abstract/Visual Reasoning cluster is classified as low and the Short-Term Memory cluster is classified as low-moderate. Therefore, the Pattern Analysis and Copying subtests (i.e., Abstract/Visual Reasoning cluster) may provide a more accurate estimate of ability for culturally diverse populations in comparison to other clusters (see Appendix 11A).

Summary of Strengths and Limitations.   The strengths of the SB:IV include adequate standardization and reliability characteristics. In addition, it has been shown to be a valid measure of *general* intellectual functioning. The SB:IV correlates highly with other intelligence tests and has been shown to discriminate among several exceptional groups of children. The SB:IV has two test manuals that describe the theoretical constructs underlying the test and that contain sufficient technical data to evaluate its psychometric properties. In addition, test materials appear to be moderately attractive to young children, subtests have minimal expressive language requirements in general, and testing can be completed within 60 minutes.

The limitations of the SB:IV however, suggest that it should be used cautiously with many preschoolers. First, there is virtually no evidence to substantiate the interpretation of four area scores on the SB:IV for preschoolers. Practitioners are strongly encouraged to interpret only the Test Composite and/or the two factors espoused by Sattler (1992) and corroborated by independent researchers (e.g., Kaplan and Alfonso, 1997; Ownby & Carmin, 1988). Second, the floors and item gradients of many SB:IV subtests are poor. Third, the appropriateness of the SB:IV for use with preschoolers who are culturally or linguistically diverse is questionable. That is, the SB:IV test directions are long and contain many basic concepts, only four subtests include sample items, and it does not have a nonverbal scale. Moreover, there are no alternative stopping rules and no translations or adaptations of the SB:IV in other languages or norms for children from other cultures.

Wechsler Preschool and Primary Scale of Intelligence—Revised (WPPSI-R)

Description.   The Wechsler Preschool and Primary Scale of Intelligence—Revised (WPPSI-R; Wechsler, 1989) is appropriate for the cognitive assessment of children between the ages of 3-0 and 7-3. It contains 10 core battery subtests that combine to form the Verbal and Performance scales. The Verbal scale is comprised of the Information, Comprehension, Arithmetic, Vocabulary, and Similarities subtests. The Performance scale is comprised of the Object Assembly, Geometric Design, Block Design, Mazes, and Picture Completion subtests. The WPPSI-R contains two optional subtests, one verbal subtest (Sentences) and one Performance subtest (Animal Pegs). These optional subtests may be substituted for core battery subtests or given in addition to the core battery. The Verbal and Performance IQs combine to yield the Full Scale IQ which is interpreted as a measure of general intellectual functioning. Descriptions of all WPPSI-R subtests are found in Gyurke (1991) and Wechsler (1989).

The WPPSI-R subtests have a mean of 10 and a standard deviation of 3. The Verbal, Performance, and Full Scales have a mean of 100 and a standard deviation of 15. Standard scores, percentiles, and age equivalents are available for making inter-individual comparisons. Administration time for the WPPSI-R is usually greater than one hour (Psychological Corporation, 1989). The WPPSI-R test kit, as well as software for scoring and report writing, are available from The Psychological Corporation.

Quantitative Characteristics.   Overall, the standardization sample characteristics of the WPPSI-R are adequate. The standardization sample included a total of 1,700 individuals, with 400 individuals included in each one-year interval (Wechsler, 1989). The standardization sample closely approximated the U.S. population (1986 Census data) on the following variables: gender, geographic region, race/ethnicity, and SES (i.e., parent occupation and parent education). The norm tables for the WPPSI-R are divided into three-month age blocks for children between the ages of 3-0 and 7-3, which is considered adequate (see Table 11.1). The norms for the WPPSI-R were collected between 1984 and 1985. Therefore, obtained scores on the WPPSI-R may slightly overestimate cognitive ability (i.e., by approximately 3 standard score points) (Flynn, 1984).

The total test internal consistency reliability coefficients of the WPPSI-R were good (i.e., .95 or greater). Conversely, the WPPSI-R' s test–retest reliability is considered inad-

The Wechsler Preschool and Primary Scale of Intelligence—Revised (WPPSI-R). Copyright
© 1989 by The Psychological Corporation. Reproduced by permission. All rights reserved.
Wechsler Preschool and Primary Scale of Intelligence—Revised and *WPPSI-R* are registered
trademarks of The Psychology Corporation.

equate because approximately 50% of the test–retest sample was comprised of older children (i.e., ≥ 5 years of age), not preschoolers (see Table 11.1). However, the test–retest sample represented the U.S. population on at least three important demographic variables and the test–retest reliability coefficient was good ($r = .91$). Thus, although the WPPSI-R's reliability was rated inadequate overall based on the criteria presented in Table 11.1, it appears to measure what it purports to measure reliably. However, whether it measures the same constructs consistently over time in preschoolers (aged 3 to 5 years) is questionable in light of the broad age range of the test–retest sample (i.e., 3 to 7-year-olds).

A significant quantitative limitation of the WPPSI-R is its subtest floors. All WPPSI-R subtests have inadequate floors at the beginning age level of the test (i.e., 2-11). In addition, the Verbal scale of the WPPSI-R has an inadequate floor for preschoolers aged 2-11 to 3-2. It is not until age 4-9 that all subtests have adequate floors. However, the majority of subtests have adequate floors at about age 3-8 and the Performance and Full scales of the WPPSI-R have adequate floors across the age range of the test. Thus, although all subtests of the WPPSI-R have inadequate floors for very young children, its three global scales provide estimates of ability in the borderline range (i.e., at least 2 sd's below the normative mean). The subtest item gradients of the WPPSI-R are generally adequate. For example, only two subtests have inadequate item gradients at ages 2-6 to 3-5 (i.e., Block Design and Arithmetic). The remaining subtests have adequate or good item gradients at the middle and upper end of the preschool age range (i.e., 3-6 to 5-5). Although the item gradients information of the WPPSI-R demonstrates that this instrument is generally sensitive to fine gradations in ability, given the limited floor of most of its subtests, these gradations are typically discernible only between the mean and one to one and one-half standard deviations below the mean.

The validity of the WPPSI-R is adequate. Information regarding the content, criterion-related, and construct validity of the WPPSI-R is reported in the test manual and the extant literature. Several exploratory and confirmatory factor analyses have been conducted with the WPPSI-R standardization sample (e.g., Stone, Gridley, & Gyurke, 1991; Wechsler, 1989). For example, Gyurke et al. conducted a confirmatory factor analysis with the standardization sample of the WPPSI-R and indicated that a two-factor solution (Verbal-Performance) fit the data better than a one- or three-factor solution. In addition, Stone et al. performed confirmatory factor analyses with the two extreme age groups of the standardization sample (i.e., 3- and 7-year-olds) and also found that a two-factor (Verbal-Performance) solution fit the data best. The results of these and other independent factor analyses support the Verbal-Performance dichotomy purported to underlie the WPPSI-R.

However, the results of joint factor analyses (viz., Woodcock, 1990) demonstrate that more than two constructs underlie the WPPSI-R. That is, when the subtests of the WPPSI-R are factor-analyzed with subtests that adequately represent a broad range of cognitive abilities, at least four constructs are shown to underlie the WPPSI-R. These four constructs are: (1) Crystallized Intelligence (*Gc*), which is comprised of the Information, Similarities, Vocabulary, and Comprehension subtests (i.e., the Verbal scale); (2) Visual Processing (*Gv*), which is comprised of the Picture Completion, Block Design, Mazes, Animal Pegs, and Geometric Design subtests; (3) Quantitative Ability (*Gq*), which is measured by the Arithmetic subtest; and (4) Short-Term Memory (*Gsm*), which is measured by the Sentences subtest (see McGrew, 1997 and McGrew & Flanagan, 1996 for a discussion).

One possible reason that the *Gq* and *Gsm* factors do not emerge in independent factor analytic studies using the WPPSI-R standardization sample may be because there is not a sufficient number of markers (or measures) on the WPPSI-R to represent these factors adequately. Therefore, the WPPSI-R may not provide practitioners with adequate information regarding the young child's cognitive functioning across a variety of abilities. In an attempt to provide a more broad and valid assessment of abilities that is consistent with advances in cognitive theory and research, McGrew and Flanagan (1996) offer theoretically driven, psychometrically sound guidelines for interpreting the WPPSI-R. Although these procedures require that the WPPSI-R be augmented with some additional measures, they are recommended because they provide practitioners with a means of conducting more valid and comprehensive assessments of cognitive abilities.

Although much of the validity evidence provided in the WPPSI-R manual is based on the WPPSI, there is ample support for the criterion-related validity of the WPPSI-R. In addition, there is evidence that the WPPSI-R can differentiate among various exceptional groups (e.g., gifted, mentally retarded), which is the primary purpose of the instrument according to the test manual (Wechsler, 1989).

Qualitative Characteristics.   The "Test Construction and Format" characteristics of the WPPSI-R range from adequate to poor based on the criteria presented in Table 11.2. *The WPPSI-R Manual* (Wechsler, 1989) is adequate, containing information about the development of the instrument, its underlying constructs, administration and scoring procedures, and the interpretation process. The WPPSI-R also contains adequate test materials. It has manipulatives (e.g., puzzles, blocks) and colorful pictures that are likely to stimulate a preschool child. Other positive features of the WPPSI-R include its use of alternating subtests (e.g., verbal/nonverbal) and inclusion of a stimulating initial task (i.e., Object Assembly).

The WPPSI-R also has some qualitative limitations with respect to Test Construction and Format. Administration time for the WPPSI-R is typically greater than 60 minutes, which is exceedingly long for a very young child. Many young children with developmental delays cannot remain focused and attentive for this length of time. In addition, many of the WPPSI-R subtests require extensive expressive language skills (e.g., Comprehension and Vocabulary); gestures are not acceptable responses for these subtests. Finally, although the WPPSI-R Performance scale is interpreted frequently as a measure of "nonverbal" ability, this scale does not allow for nonverbal administration of each subtest (e.g., pantomime), provide a "true" nonverbal score, or emphasize power over speed (see Table 11.2).

The "Administration" characteristics of the WPPSI-R also range from adequate to poor based on the criteria presented in Table 11.2. For example, the WPPSI-R subtests include teaching items, second trials, and allow for demonstrations by the examiner thereby maximizing the child's understanding of the task at hand. However, the directions of the WPPSI-R's subtests are difficult to comprehend, containing 42 basic concepts overall (Flanagan et al., 1995). Moreover, there are no alternative stopping rules provided on the WPPSI-R, which may result in undue frustration in young children. Finally, the WPPSI-R does not provide translations of directions in other languages and there are no norms for children from other cultures.

Relative Influence of North American Culture.   The relative influence of North American culture on the cognitive subtests and clusters of the WPPSI-R ranges from high to low. Performance on the subtests that comprise the Verbal scale is highly influenced by exposure to North American culture, whereas performance on subtests such as Block Design, Mazes, and Geometric Designs appears to be least influenced by exposure to North American culture. Overall, the relative influence of culture on the WPPSI-R Full Scale IQ is moderate to high (see Appendix 11A). Depending on the purpose of assessment, the WPPSI-R may be of limited utility in the assessment of preschoolers from diverse cultural backgrounds.

Summary of Strengths and Limitations.   The main strengths of the WPPSI-R lie in its quantitative characteristics. The WPPSI-R's standardization, reliability, and validity data are generally adequate to good when evaluated against the criteria presented in Table 11.1. According to Kamphaus (1993), in many respects the quantitative characteristics of the WPPSI-R are unparalleled by any other cognitive assessment instrument for preschoolers. However, these positive features may not be sufficient to outweigh the WPPSI-R's limitations. For example, test administration appears to be too long to evaluate the cognitive capabilities of children with mental retardation, autism, and behavioral disorders. In addition, receptive and expressive language demands on the WPPSI-R are excessive and this instrument does not contain a nonverbal scale based on nonverbal administration, which may negate evaluation of linguistically diverse children. The WPPSI-R also does not employ alternative stopping rules to mitigate frustration caused by experiencing multiple failures. The relative influence of North American culture on the subtests and clusters of the WPPSI-R is generally moderate to high, indicating that it may not be appropriate for assessing some cognitive capabilities of culturally diverse children. Finally, the WPPSI-R was not translated, adapted or normed for use with children from diverse cultural and linguistic backgrounds.

Woodcock-Johnson Psycho-Educational Battery— Revised: Tests of Cognitive Ability (WJ-R COG)

Description.   The Woodcock-Johnson Psycho-Educational Battery—Revised Tests of Cognitive Ability (WJ-R COG; Woodcock & Johnson, 1989) is appropriate for use with individuals aged 24 months through 95+ years. It contains 21 tests of cognitive ability that are divided into standard and supplemental batteries. The standard battery contains seven tests, one measure for each of seven *Gf-Gc* factors (i.e., *Gf, Gc, Gv, Ga, Gsm, Glr, Gq*) assessed by the WJ-R COG (see Table 11.3 for definitions of the *Gf-Gc* abilities). The supplemental battery contains 14 tests. Of these, the first seven (i.e., tests 8 through 14) provide complimentary measures of the previously mentioned cognitive factors and constitute the additional tests that are necessary to calculate the seven *Gf-Gc* Cognitive Ability Clusters. The remaining seven tests on the WJ-R COG supplemental battery (i.e., tests 15 through 21) provide mixed measures of *Gf-Gc* abilities and may be administered to derive additional information about an individual's cognitive strengths and limitations. Of the WJ-R's 21 cognitive subtests, only five (i.e., Picture Vocabulary, Memory for Sentences, Visual Closure, Incomplete Words, and Memory for Names) are applicable for children between the ages of 2-0 and 5-11. These subtests measure Crystallized Ability (*Gc*), Short-Term Memory (*Gsm*), Visual Processing (*Gv*), Auditory Processing (*Ga*), and Long-Term Retrieval (*Glr*), respectively, and combine to yield the Broad Cognitive Ability Early Development (BCA-ED) cluster, which is interpreted as an estimate of general intellectual functioning (Woodcock & Mather, 1989).

All WJ-R COG subtests, as well as the BCA-ED cluster, have a mean of 100 and a standard deviation of 15. Several derived scores are available on the WJ-R COG for making inter-individual comparisons, including standard scores, percentiles, and age equivalents. Administration time for the BCA-ED cluster ranges form 20 to 30 minutes (Woodcock & Mather, 1989). The WJ-R test and several supplemental materials, including interpretation books and manuals as well as software for scoring and report writing, are available from the Riverside Publishing Company.

Quantitative Characteristics.   The standardization sample characteristics of the WJ-R COG are good, in general. The standardization sample included 6,359 individuals, with

The Woodcock-Johnson Psycho-Educational Battery—Revised: Tests of Cognitive Ability (WJ-R COG). Reproduced from the *Woodcock-Johnson Psycho-Educational Battery—Revised,* by Richard W. Woodcock and M. Bonner Johnson, with permission of the publisher.

at least 100 individuals per one-year interval (Woodcock & Mather, 1989). The standard-ization sample closely approximated the U.S. population (1988 Census data and later reports) on the following variables: gender, geographic region, race/ethnicity, community size, and socioeconomic status (e.g., educational attainment and occupational status). Although the WJ-R COG has good standardization characteristics for the entire sample, only 705 children were included in the preschool sample, and norming characteristics for this sample were not reported by age (Flanagan & Alfonso, 1995). The norm tables of the WJ-R COG are divided into one-month age blocks (derived from linear interpolations) for children between the ages of 2-0 and 5-11, which is considered good (see Table 11.1). It is likely that scores on the WJ-R COG yield accurate estimates of cognitive functioning because the norms were collected within the past decade (between 1986 and 1988).

The internal consistency reliability coefficients of the WJ-R COG were good, as all coefficients were ≥ .93 across the preschool age range. Conversely, the WJ-R COG's test–retest reliability is considered inadequate because the test–retest sample included very few preschoolers (i.e., the sample included individuals between the ages of 5 and 80+ years) (see Table 11.1). However, the test–retest sample was good because it represented the U.S. population on five important demographic variables. The test–retest interval (i.e., 30 weeks) and the test–retest reliability coefficient ($r = .87$) were adequate. Thus, although the WJ-R COG's reliability was rated inadequate based on the criteria presented in Table 11.1, it appears to measure what it purports to measure reliably. However, whether it measures the same constructs consistently over time in a preschool sample is questionable, given the broad age range of the test–retest sample.

Significant quantitative strengths of the WJ-R COG include its subtest floors and item gradients. All WJ-R COG subtests recommended for preschoolers have adequate floors at the beginning age level of the test (i.e., 2-6) with the exception of Incomplete Words which does not have an adequate floor until age 4-4. The BCA-ED Cluster has an adequate floor across the preschool age range, as it yields scores in the mild and moderate ranges of mental retardation (i.e., IQ range of 35–40 through 50–55). Likewise, all subtests have adequate or good item gradients across the preschool age range. Only one subtest (i.e., Incomplete Words) has item gradients that are considered inadequate at the lower end of the preschool age range (i.e., 2-6 to 3-5). Therefore, the WJ-R COG preschool subtests not only provide estimates of ability in the borderline range (i.e., at least 2 sd's below the normative mean) for very young children, but they are also sensitive to fine gradations in ability between the mean and one to 2 standard deviations below the mean. Moreover, at the middle and upper end of the preschool age range (i.e., 3-6 to 5-6), the five WJ-R preschool subtests can make finely graded distinctions in ability within the borderline and mildly mentally retarded ranges of functioning. The quality of the WJ-R's floors and item gradients is without peer.

The validity of the WJ-R COG for preschoolers is adequate. *The WJ-R Technical Manual* (McGrew, Werder, & Woodcock, 1991), contains ample information in support of the content, construct, and criterion-related validity of the instrument for individuals aged 5 to 80+ years. However, scant validity evidence is available for the WJ-R COG at the pre-school age range. For example, exploratory and confirmatory factor analyses support the Horn-Cattell *Gf-Gc* theoretical model underlying the WJ-R for individuals aged 5 through adulthood (McGrew et al., 1991; Ysseldyke, 1990). Therefore, the WJ-R may be inter-preted from this theoretical model for young children at the upper end of the preschool age range (i.e., 5-year-olds not in kindergarten), but is best interpreted as a measure of general cognitive ability or general intelligence for preschoolers aged 2-6 to 4-11. The lack of investigations of the factor structure of the WJ-R at the preschool age level has serious implications for the interpretation of a child's performance on the separate tests that comprise the BCA-ED Cluster. Moreover, because the five cognitive constructs that are measured at the preschool age range (i.e., *Gc, Gsm, Gv, Ga,* and *Glr*) are under-represented (i.e., only one indicator or subtest per area), caution must be exercised when interpreting performance based on any one of the five subtests recommended for preschoolers.

Investigations that employ contemporary, well-researched theoretical models of intelligence (e.g., Horn, 1991; Carroll, 1993) are needed to understand better the structure of cognitive abilities at the preschool age range. At the older ages, the WJ-R COG has been used in *Gf-Gc* guided joint-factor analyses that have led to a more complete understanding of the cognitive abilities that underlie all intelligence tests (e.g., Woodcock, 1990). Given the broad range of abilities measured by the WJ-R COG at the preschool age range (i.e., 5), it is likely that this instrument will be important in future joint-factor analyses designed to understand the structure of intelligence in preschoolers.

In contrast to its questionable construct validity evidence at the preschool age level, the WJ-R COG has good criterion-related validity evidence. Although the results of the concurrent validity studies conducted with the WJ-R demonstrate a moderate to high degree of similarity among intelligence tests for preschoolers, interpretation of these validity coefficients is difficult in light of the questionable construct validity evidence that is currently available for the WJ-R at the preschool age level.

Qualitative Characteristics.   The "Test Construction and Format" characteristics of the WJ-R COG range from adequate to poor, based on the criteria presented in Table 11.2. The WJ-R COG's *Examiner's Manual* (Woodcock & Johnson, 1989) and *Technical Manual* (McGrew et al., 1991) are comprehensive and well organized, containing information on the test development process and underlying theoretical model of the instrument as well as administration, scoring, and interpretation procedures. In addition, the WJ-R COG can be administered to preschoolers in under one hour (Woodcock & Mather, 1989). Despite these positive features, the WJ-R COG also has some qualitative limitations with respect to "Test Construction and Format." For example, the WJ-R COG battery does not include manipulatives—test stimuli considered important to stimulate a young child or maintain a child's interest throughout test administration. In addition, all WJ-R COG subtests require expressive language on the part of the child and gestures are not acceptable responses. Finally, the WJ-R COG does not have a nonverbal scale.

The "Administration" characteristics of the WJ-R COG range from good to poor, based on the criteria presented in Table 11.2. For example, the WJ-R COG is the only intelligence test that has a parallel Spanish version (Batería-R COG) (Woodcock & Muñoz-Sandoval, 1996) and the WJ-R COG subtests include test directions that contain sentences that are generally brief and of simple structure. In addition, the test directions contain a limited number of basic concepts (i.e., 12) in order to ensure that the child understands the task at hand. However, the WJ-R COG subtests do not provide many opportunities to teach the task or include alternative stopping rules to minimize a young child's frustration that may result from repeated failures.

Relevant Influence of North American Culture.   The relative influence of North American culture on the cognitive subtests of the WJ-R ranges from high to low. As expected, performance on the Picture Vocabulary subtest is highly influenced by exposure to North American culture, whereas performance on the Memory for Names subtest is least influenced (Hessler, 1993). The remaining subtests (i.e., Memory for Sentences, Visual Closure, and Incomplete Words) as well as the BCA-ED Cluster of the WJ-R are moderately influenced by exposure to North American culture. Depending on the purpose of assessment, therefore, the WJ-R COG may be of limited utility in the measurement of cognitive abilities in preschoolers from diverse backgrounds.

Summary of Strengths and Limitations.   The WJ-R COG's greatest strength at the preschool level lies in its quantitative characteristics. Although the norming characteristics of the preschool sample (n = 705) are not reported by age, the WJ-R's standardization features are generally adequate for preschoolers. In addition, the WJ-R has good internal consistency reliability. However, its test–retest reliability is regarded as inadequate because the test–retest sample did not include children aged 2-0 to 4-11. The WJ-R is unique among intelligence tests for preschoolers in that it has subtest floors and item gradients that are generally good throughout the preschool age range, rendering it a sensitive instrument for detecting fine gradations in ability across the average, low average, and borderline ranges of cognitive functioning. The WJ-R has adequate construct validity evidence and good criterion-related validity evidence at the preschool age level. This instrument appears to measure a greater breadth of cognitive abilities than other preschool intelligence tests; however, these constructs are under-represented at the preschool level (i.e., only one subtest is available for each ability). The WJ-R is most useful in preschool evaluations as a general measure of intelligence. Practitioners would need to augment the WJ-R tests with subtests from other batteries prior to generalizing about ability in the five cognitive domains that are represented at the preschool level (see McGrew & Flanagan, 1996).

Although the WJ-R has many quantitative strengths, it is seldom used in the assessment of preschoolers presumably because of its qualitative limitations. That is, the WJ-R does not include manipulatives, all of its subtests require a verbal response from the child, it does not have a nonverbal scale, and its discontinue criteria in individual subtests may be too stringent and thus, result in undue frustration in children with cognitive delays and/or behavioral difficulties.

Differential Ability Scales (DAS)

Description.   The DAS (Elliott, 1990a) is divided into two age levels (Lower and Upper) for preschool children. At the Lower Preschool Level (2-6 to 3-5), the DAS contains four core subtests (i.e., Block Building, Verbal Comprehension, Picture Similarities, and Naming Vocabulary) which combine to yield the General Conceptual Ability (GCA) composite. A Special Nonverbal Composite, comprising the Block Building and Picture Similarities subtests, can be obtained for preschoolers at this age level. At the Upper Preschool Level (3-6 to 5-11), the DAS contains six core subtests (i.e., Verbal Comprehension, Picture Similarities, Naming Vocabulary, Pattern Construction, Copying, and Early Number Concepts) which combine to yield the GCA. The separate assessment of Verbal and Nonverbal abilities can also be made at this age level. The Verbal Comprehension and Naming Vocabulary subtests form the Verbal Cluster and the Picture Similarities, Pattern Construction, and Copying subtests form the Nonverbal Cluster at the Upper Preschool Level. The GCA is interpreted as an estimate of general intelligence (Elliott, 1990b). In addition to these core subtests, the DAS contains diagnostic subtests that allow for measurement of specific cognitive abilities (Elliott, 1990a). For preschoolers at the lower age level, the diagnostic subtests include Recall of Digits and Recognition of Pictures. For preschoolers at the upper age level, the diagnostic subtests include Block Building, Matching Letter-Like Forms, Recall of Digits, Recall of Objects, and Recognition of Pictures. Descriptions of all DAS subtests recommended for preschoolers are found in Elliott (1990a).

All DAS subtests have a mean of 50 and a standard deviation of 10, whereas all composites have a mean of 100 and a standard deviation of 15. Several derived scores are available on the DAS for making inter-individual comparisons, including standard scores, percentiles, and age equivalents. Administration time ranges from 35 to 65 minutes depending on whether or not the diagnostic subtests are given (Elliott, 1990a). The DAS is available from The Psychological Corporation. Software for scoring and report writing were in development at the time that this chapter was being prepared.

Quantitative Characteristics. The standardization sample characteristics of the DAS are good when evaluated against the criteria reported in Table 11.1. The standardization sample included a total of 3,475 individuals, with 200 to 350 individuals per one year interval. In addition, the standardization sample closely approximated the U.S. population (1988 Census data) on the following variables: gender, geographic region, race/ethnicity, enrollment in an educational program, and SES (i.e., parent education) (Elliott, 1990a).

The Differential Abilities Scales (DAS). Copyright © 1990 by The Psychology Corporation. Reproduced by permission. All rights reserved. *Differential Ability Scales* and *DAS* are registered trademarks of The Psychological Corporation.

The norm tables for the DAS are divided into three-month age blocks and, therefore, are considered adequate (see Table 11.1). The norms for the DAS, collected between 1987 and 1989, yield accurate estimates of a child's cognitive functioning.

The reliability of the DAS is considered adequate based on the criteria reported in Table 11.1. The test–retest sample included children between the ages of 3-6 to 4-5 and represented the U.S. population on four variables. The test–retest interval was four weeks, and the test–retest reliability coefficient was .90. Internal consistency reliability coefficients were .90 or higher across the preschool age range, with the exception of ages 3-0 and 4-6 when the coefficients were slightly lower (i.e., 89). Therefore, the DAS generally measures what it purports to measure reliably, and yields consistent estimates of ability over time.

All DAS subtests, except Verbal Comprehension, have inadequate floors at the beginning of both the lower and upper preschool age levels (i.e., 2-6 and 3-6, respectively). It is not until age 3-0 and 4-4 that all subtests have adequate floors at the lower and upper preschool levels, respectively. However, all DAS composites have adequate floors across the preschool age range. Thus, although most subtests of the DAS have inadequate floors for very young children, its various global scales provide estimates of ability well into the borderline range (i.e., at least 2 sd's below the normative mean).

Despite inadequate subtest floors at the early preschool ages, the DAS generally has adequate to good item gradients for most subtests across the preschool age range. For example, all subtests, with the exception of Naming Vocabulary and Copying, have adequate or good item gradients at the middle and upper end of the preschool age range (i.e., 3-6 to 5-5). Conversely, two of the four subtests at the lower preschool age range have inadequate item gradients at ages 2-6 to 3-5 (i.e., Block Design and Naming Vocabulary). Thus, the DAS can detect differences across the average, low average, borderline, and mild mental retardation ranges of ability for most older preschoolers (i.e., ages 3-6 to 5-6) and, with few exceptions, detect fine gradations in ability within these ranges.

Most of the evidence for the content, criterion-related, and construct validity of the DAS is available in the test manual (Elliott, 1990b). Elliott (1990b) conducted several exploratory and confirmatory factor analyses with the DAS standardization sample. Results of these analyses show that a one-factor (general ability) solution provides the best fit of the data for the core subtests for the youngest children (i.e., Lower Preschool Level), and a two-factor (Verbal-Nonverbal) solution provides the best fit of the data for older preschoolers (3-6 to 5-11). Additional factor analyses conducted by Keith (1990) support the underlying factor structure of the DAS. Although the author of the DAS did not develop this instrument from a particular theoretical framework, McGrew and Flanagan (1996) have classified all the subtests of the instrument according to their underlying *Gf-Gc* abilities based on information from both empirical and logical analyses. Their interpretation guidelines may aid practitioners in understanding the abilities and processes that underlie test performance within the context of a contemporary and empirically supported theoretical framework. In addition, the criterion-related validity of the DAS also has been documented adequately, and its manual provides evidence that the DAS differentiates among various exceptional groups (e.g., gifted, mentally retarded) (Elliott, 1990b).

Qualitative Characteristics.   Overall, the "Test Construction and Format" characteristics of the DAS range from good to adequate based on the criteria presented in Table 11.2. First, the DAS *Administration and Scoring Manual* and *Introductory and Technical Handbook* (Elliott, 1990a, b) contain ample information regarding the development and theoretical underpinnings of the instrument as well as its administration, scoring and interpretation procedures and psychometric characteristics. Second, the DAS contains many attractive, stimulating materials that appear to maximize a child's time on task. For example, the DAS contains several toy-like objects, yellow and black foam squares, and multi-colored pictures and chips at the preschool levels. Third, the DAS begins with a stimulating task (i.e., Verbal Comprehension) and uses alternating subtests (e.g., verbal/ nonverbal) which may serve to keep a child engaged throughout test administration.

In addition to these commendable qualitative features, the DAS contains other "Test Construction and Format" features that are generally regarded as adequate (see Table 11.2). For example, administration time for the DAS rarely exceeds one hour and many of the DAS subtests (e.g., Verbal Comprehension and Naming Vocabulary) require minimum expressive language skills (i.e., one word). It should be noted that gestures are not considered acceptable responses on the DAS. The most significant limitation of the DAS with respect to "Test Construction and Format" characteristics is that it lacks a "true" nonverbal scale. That is, although there is a Special Nonverbal Composite for young preschoolers and a Nonverbal Cluster for older preschoolers, these scales are not multidimensional, they do not allow for a true nonverbal administration (e.g., pantomime), and they do not provide a true nonverbal score based on nonverbal norms (see Table 11.1).

The "Administration" characteristics of the DAS also range from good to adequate based on the criteria reported in Table 11.2. For example, most of the DAS subtests include sample and teaching items, second trials, and demonstrations by the examiner to ensure that the child has understood the task. A positive characteristics of the DAS is the inclusion of alternative stopping rules, which were designed to guard against "over-testing" and to minimize a child's frustration (Elliott, 1990a). The most significant qualitative limitation of the DAS with regard to Administration characteristics is the level of complexity of subtest directions. Although many of the DAS subtest directions are short and of simple structure, they contain many basic concepts (i.e., 23) of which several are not understood by very young children (Flanagan et al., 1995). Moreover, the DAS has not been translated in other languages and there are no norms for individuals from other cultures.

Relative Influence of North American Culture.   The relative influence of North American culture on the cognitive subtests and clusters of the DAS ranges from high to low. Performance on the subtests that comprise the Verbal Cluster (i.e., Verbal Comprehension and Naming Vocabulary) is influenced highly by exposure to North American culture, whereas performance on subtests that comprise the Nonverbal Cluster (i.e., Copying, Pattern Construction, and Block Building) and Special Nonverbal Composite (i.e., Block Building and Picture Similarities) appear to be least influenced by exposure to North American culture. Therefore, the subtests of the Nonverbal Cluster appear to be the most appropriate subtests to administer to children who are from culturally and linguistically diverse backgrounds. Overall, the relative influence of culture on the DAS's GCA is moderate to high (see Appendix 11A) and, as such, this total test score may not be the best estimate of ability in preschoolers from diverse backgrounds.

Summary of Strengths and Limitations.   The DAS has several quantitative and qualitative strengths based on the criteria presented in Tables 11.1 and 11.2. For example, the standardization and reliability characteristics of the DAS are exemplary. The DAS is the only instrument reviewed here that had adequate internal consistency *and* test–retest reliability. The item gradients on the DAS, in general, are adequate. In addition, solid evidence for the construct and criterion-related validity of the DAS is mounting. The DAS has varied, colorful manipulatives to maintain a young child's interest and participation in a task. It also includes alternating subtests and can be administered in under 60 minutes. Two additional strengths of the DAS include various opportunities to ensure that a child has understood the task at hand and alternative stopping rules. These characteristics, together with other positive qualitative features mentioned above, assure that the young child will not become unduly frustrated, fatigued, or disinterested when assessed with the DAS.

Despite the many positive features of the DAS, it also has quantitative and qualitative limitations. A major quantitative limitation of the DAS is its subtest floors. As a result, the DAS may yield overestimates of young children's abilities, especially children at the lower end of the preschool age range (i.e., 2-6 to 3-5). A qualitative limitation of the DAS is that its nonverbal scales do not have norms based on a nonverbal administration of their respective subtests. Another qualitative limitation of the DAS is that its subtests contain several basic concepts that are difficult for young children to understand. In addition, many of the DAS subtests are moderately to highly influenced by exposure to North American culture. Therefore, like most other batteries, the DAS should be used with caution when assessing young children who are linguistically and culturally diverse. Finally, the DAS does not provide translations of directions in other languages and there are no norms for children from other cultures. Nevertheless, the DAS, more than any other instrument reviewed here, appears to strike a balance between good quantitative and qualitative characteristics. As a result, unlike other instruments reviewed here, the DAS may have utility in the cognitive assessment of a variety of preschool populations.

Bayley Scales of Infant Development— Second Edition (BSID-II)

Description.   The BSID-II (Bayley, 1993) is designed to assess the cognitive development of infants and toddlers between the ages of 1 and 42 months and represents a *major* revision of the Bayley Scales of Infant Development (BSID; Bayley, 1969). For example, 29 items were deleted from the original Mental scale and 63 new items were added. In addition, the age range of the BSID-II was extended and administration and scoring rules were altered. The BSID-II includes 319 items that comprise the Mental (178 items), Motor (11 items), and Behavior Rating (30 items) scales. The Mental and Motor scales of the BSID-II are similar in content to their corresponding scales of the BSID; however, the Behavior Rating scale differs significantly from the Infant Behavior Record (IBR) of the BSID. Since the present chapter focuses on cognitive assessment, only the BSID-II Mental scale will be reviewed here.

The BSID-II Mental scale is appropriate for children aged 1 to 42 months and includes items that assess memory, habituation, problem solving, early number concepts, language, and other cognitive abilities (Bayley, 1993). The Mental scale yields a Mental Development Index (MDI), having a mean of 100 and a standard deviation of 15. The MDI is interpreted as a measure of overall cognitive development. The Mental scale is also comprised of four "facets" including cognitive, language, motor, and personal/social. However, since there is no factorial validity evidence that supports the division of items within the Mental scale into four areas, interpretation of facets is not recommended. Overall, the BSID-II was not intended to be interpreted as a measure of intelligence, language, or visual perception per se, but rather, a measure of various developmental abilities as well as the acquisition of developmental milestones (Bayley, 1969, 1993). The BSID-II is available from The Psychological Corporation.

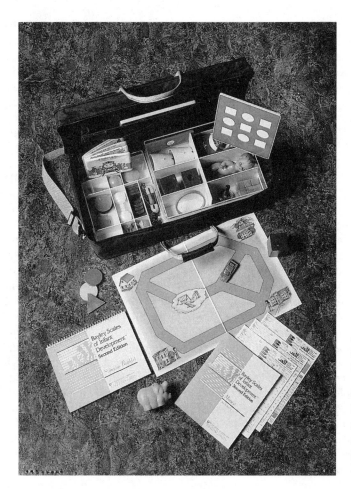

Bayley Scales of Infant Development-2nd Edition (BSID-II). Copyright © 1993 by The Psychological Corporation. Reproduced by permission. All rights reserved. *Bayley Scales of Infant Development* is a registered trademark of the Psychological Corporation.

Quantitative Characteristics. The standardization sample characteristics of the BSID-II are good. The standardization sample included 1,700 individuals, with at least 100 individuals per one-year interval (Bayley, 1993), and closely approximated the U.S. population (1988 Census data) on the following variables: age, gender, geographic region, race/ethnicity, and SES (i.e., parent education). The norm tables for the BSID-II are divided into one-month age blocks for children aged 30 to 36 months (which is considered good), and into three-month age blocks for children aged 36 to 42 months (which is considered adequate) (see Table 11.1). The norms for the BSID-II were collected between 1991 and 1992 and yield accurate estimates of a child's developmental abilities.

The total test internal consistency reliability coefficients of the BSID-II were adequate, ranging from .89 (at age levels 2-6 and 3-0) to .90 (at age level 3-6). Conversely, the BSID-II's test–retest reliability is considered inadequate overall because the test–retest sample was not representative of the U.S. population. However, the age range of the test–retest sample (i.e., 2-0 to 3-0), the test–retest interval (i.e., four days), and the test–retest reliability coefficient ($r = .91$) were all rated as good following the criteria in Table 11.1.

Thus, although the BSID-II appears to measure what it purports to measure reliably, more data are needed to determine whether the BSID-II yields consistent estimates over time.

The Mental scale of the BSID-II has an adequate floor and good item gradients. This scale yields standard scores greater than 2 standard deviations below the mean for children between the ages of 2-6 and 3-6. While most intelligence tests have poor floors for children at the lower end of the preschool age range (i.e., 2-6 to 3-6), the BSID-II has a substantial number of items (i.e., 134) below the entry level for a child aged 2-6. Therefore, it appears that the BSID-II may be more sensitive than other tests to the cognitive capabilities of children suspected of having moderate to severe developmental delays.

Since the BSID-II is a new instrument, a limited amount of validity evidence is available at this time. However, preliminary data suggest that the validity of the BSID-II is adequate. The BSID-II manual includes information about the content, criterion-related, and construct validity of the instrument, although no factor analyses were reported (Bayley, 1993). Because much of the validity evidence presented in the BSID-II manual is based on the BSID, "examiners are cautioned against making too many generalizations from studies of the old Bayley to the new, because the BSID-II is considerably changed from its predecessor" (Nellis & Gridley, 1994, p. 206).

Evidence cited for the construct validity of the BSID-II included professional judgment and age trend, item difficulty, and correlational analyses (Bayley, 1993). For example, more than 25 experts from a variety of developmental fields (e.g., cognitive, language, social) were consulted to create new items for the BSID-II. Age trend and item difficulty analyses were used to determine the placement of items on the Mental scale and to create item sets for children of various ages. Several correlational studies that provide further construct and criterion-related validity evidence for the BSID-II are reported in its test manual. In addition, studies conducted with clinical groups of children (i.e., intra-uterine exposure to drugs, Down syndrome, asphyxia, otitis media, positive HIV, and premature birth) provide preliminary support for the BSID-II's utility in identifying children at risk for developmental delay (Bayley, 1993). However, although scores obtained for these groups were in the expected direction, further data are necessary to evaluate the BSID-II's utility for children with developmental delays.

Qualitative Characteristics.   Overall the "Test Construction and Format" characteristics of the BSID-II range from good to adequate when evaluated against the criteria presented in Table 11.2. *The Bayley Scales of Infant Development-Second Edition Manual* (Bayley, 1993) includes information necessary for practitioners to administer, score, and interpret this instrument as well as evaluate its psychometric properties. The BSID-II contains an extensive amount of attractive and stimulating materials, including many multi-colored objects such as a doll, car, blocks, pegs, formboards, and other "toys." Because of its varied and manipulative materials, it is generally not difficult to maintain a child's focus of attention during assessment. Item types (e.g., language, visual, visual-motor) alternate continually throughout the administration of the BSID-II which aids in keeping a child stimulated and engaged during testing. The BSID-II can be administered within 60 minutes. Most of the BSID-II items require minimum (i.e., one word) expressive language skills; however, gestures are not acceptable responses to language items. The BSID-II does not have a nonverbal scale.

The "Administration" characteristics of the BSID-II also range from good to adequate when evaluated against the criteria presented in Table 11.2. Many of the BSID-II items include multiple trials and allow for examiner demonstration to ensure that the child has understood the task at hand. The BSID-II provides great flexibility regarding the administration and discontinuation of items. The inclusion of various discontinuation rules minimizes the amount of frustration children are likely to experience when they fail multiple items. Although many item directions on the BSID-II are short and of simple structure, they contain many basic concepts (i.e., 28), some of which are not understood by preschool-aged children (Flanagan et al., 1995). Finally, the BSID-II does not have translations of directions in other languages and there are no norms for children from other cultures.

Relative Influence of North American Culture.   Performance on the Mental Scale of the BSID-II appears to be influenced moderately by exposure to North American culture. Therefore, depending on the purpose of assessment, the BSID-II may not be suitable for many children who are culturally and linguistically diverse.

Summary of Strengths and Limitations.   The BSID-II has several quantitative and qualitative strengths based on the criteria presented in Tables 11.1 and 11.2. For example, in general, the standardization, reliability, floor, and item gradient characteristics of the BSID-II are good. In addition, there is preliminary construct and criterion-related validity evidence for the BSID-II. Given its many positive quantitative characteristics, the BSID-II appears to yield reliable and valid estimates of a young child's cognitive development. With regard to qualitative characteristics, the BSID-II has many multi-colored manipulatives to engage young children and maintain their interest and participation during test administration. In addition, the BSID-II has efficient administration procedures, includes a variety of tasks (e.g., verbal, nonverbal, motor), and can be administered in under 60 minutes. Finally, the BSID-II has minimum expressive language requirements for most items.

The BSID-II is not without limitations. For example, item directions contain many basic concepts that typically are not understood by very young children (Flanagan et al., 1995). In addition, performance on the BSID-II generally is influenced moderately by exposure to North American culture and does not include a nonverbal scale. Therefore, the BSID-II may be of limited utility in the assessment of culturally and linguistically diverse children. The BSID-II does not provide translations of directions in other languages and does not have norms for children from other cultures. Despite these limitations, the BSID-II appears to have utility for the cognitive assessment of many preschool populations.

Summary

The present review of the *quantitative* characteristics of intelligence tests for preschoolers demonstrates that these instruments are *not* psychometrically sound for very *young* children (e.g., 2-6 to 3-6). Although the standardization characteristics of most intelligence tests are exemplary, few reliability and validity studies have been conducted with children younger than 4 or 5 years of age. Moreover, the majority of these instruments have inadequate subtest, scale, and total test floors. Also, at the beginning age levels of these intelligence batteries, the majority of subtests have poor item gradients (i.e., are steeply graded). This means that many subtests not only fail to assess cognitive functioning at different levels of ability (i.e., average, low average, borderline, mild mental retardation), but fail to detect fine gradations in ability within these levels. Thus, reliable and valid estimates of a young child's (age 2-6 to 3-6) cognitive abilities cannot be made confidently with most current intelligence tests. Because practitioners use intelligence tests routinely to aid in making diagnostic decisions, the DAS and BSID-II are recommended for this purpose since they have fewer limitations at the *lower* end of the preschool age range than the other instruments reviewed. When using the DAS, BSID-II, or any other instrument with young children, practitioners should interpret a child's performance with caution and integrate other sources of data to substantiate diagnostic decisions.

Unlike the quantitative characteristics of intelligence tests for *young* preschoolers, intelligence tests for children at the *upper* end of the preschool age range (e.g., 4-6 to 5-6) are generally psychometrically sound. Therefore, professionals involved in making diagnostic and educational placement decisions can be confident that most current intelligence tests yield reliable and valid estimates of ability for these children. The WPPSI-R, DAS, and WJ-R COG have good support for their quantitative characteristics at the upper boundary of the preschool age range and are recommended for assessing the cognitive functioning of older preschool children.

The psychometric soundness of intelligence tests for linguistically and culturally diverse preschoolers is questionable. Few studies have been conducted with the instruments reviewed here to support their reliability and validity for use with children from diverse backgrounds. Moreover, the lack of representativeness of many culturally different groups in the standardization samples of intelligence tests renders it difficult to interpret the test performance of children from diverse backgrounds with confidence. Because current intelligence batteries were not developed from a theoretical framework that necessitates an understanding of how culture impacts cognitive development and functioning, the extent to which environmental and/or linguistic factors negatively influence the performance of culturally diverse children on these tests is largely unknown. Therefore, practitioners are strongly encouraged to consider carefully the cultural experiences of the child prior to interpreting test performance. In order to aid practitioners in selecting instruments that are sensitive to the needs of culturally diverse populations, all subtests of the major intelligence batteries for preschoolers were classified here according to the relative degree to which exposure to North American culture is likely to impact performance.

The review of the *qualitative* characteristics of intelligence tests questions further their usefulness for assessing young preschoolers, including those who are from cultures that differ from mainstream North American culture. For example, many intelligence tests contain lengthy and complex subtest directions (e.g., SB:IV, WPPSI-R), require frequent verbalizations from the child (e.g., WJ-R COG), and have limited means for minimizing the child's frustration upon encountering increasingly difficult items (e.g., alternate stopping rules) (e.g., WPPSI-R, WJ-R COG). These characteristics are likely to have an adverse effect on the test performance of any preschool child. However, the negative impact that these characteristics may have on test performance will be exacerbated when interpersonal and sociolinguistic styles (between examiner and examinee) are incompatible. Moreover, because many young preschoolers as well as those who are culturally diverse have difficulty understanding the standardized directions included in intelligence tests, examiners are encouraged to assess a child's understanding of basic concepts prior to evaluating cognitive ability (e.g., Bracken, 1984; Boehm, 1986). This information may be helpful in selecting an appropriate intelligence test and may lead to more accurate and appropriate judgments regarding a child's level of conceptual development and its relationship to test performance. Overall, the DAS and BSID-II appear to have the best qualitative characteristics and are recommended over the other instruments reviewed for the assessment of culturally diverse preschoolers.

Paradoxically, in considering the quantitative and qualitative characteristics of intelligence tests, those that have the best quantitative properties seem to have the poorest qualitative features and vice versa. For example, based on the criteria presented in Tables 11.1 and 11.2 and the information contained in Appendix 11A, the present review showed that the WPPSI-R and WJ-R COG have good validity evidence, internal consistency reliability estimates, and total test floors, but appear to have limited utility for the assessment of very young preschool children and preschoolers who are culturally diverse. That is, due to a lack of positive qualitative characteristics deemed important for assessing preschoolers and, in the case of the WPPSI-R, the great extent to which exposure to North American culture is likely to influence test performance, use of these instruments may inhibit cognitive performance in some children, leading to underestimates of ability. Conversely, the positive qualitative features of the DAS, for example, appear to facilitate the cognitive performance of young children and culturally diverse preschoolers, but some of its subtests have weak quantitative characteristics, such as inadequate floors and poor item gradients, which are likely to result in overestimates of ability.

In sum, *all* current intelligence tests have quantitative and qualitative limitations. However, the DAS is recommended highly for the assessment of children from a variety of preschool populations, because it generally earned favorable ratings across the various quantitative and qualitative characteristics reviewed and its Nonverbal Cluster at the middle and upper preschool age ranges is minimally influenced by exposure to North American culture relative to other cognitive tests. Special consideration is warranted however, when any of these instruments (including the DAS) is used to evaluate very young children (aged 2-6 to 3-6), since the tests' psychometric properties are weakest at this age level. Caution is particularly warranted when using these instruments to assess linguistically and culturally diverse preschoolers because these instruments were not designed specifically for this purpose. That is, they were not developed from a theoretical framework that includes a consideration of culture as a requisite for understanding cognitive functioning. However, because intelligence tests *are* widely used to assess preschoolers as well as children from linguistically and culturally diverse backgrounds, it is incumbent upon the practitioner to consider the quantitative and qualitative characteristics as well as the relative influence of North American culture on test performance when selecting an instrument for use with these children.

A P P E N D I X 1 1 A

Relative Influence of North American Culture on Test Performance within the Context of Contemporary *Gf-Gc* Theory

		Influence of Culture				
Battery	*Subtest (ability measured)* **Scale, Cluster, Composite**	**Low**	**Low-Moderate**	**Moderate**	**Moderate-High**	**High**
SB:IV						
	Vocabulary (*Gc*)					X
	Comprehension (*Gc*)					X

(continued)

APPENDIX 11A   Continued

Battery	Subtest (ability measured) Scale, Cluster, Composite	Influence of Culture				
		Low	Low-Moderate	Moderate	Moderate-High	High
	Absurdities (*Gc*)					X
	Pattern Analysis (*Gv*)	X				
	Copying (*Gv*)	X				
	Quantitative (*Gq*)			X		
	Bead Memory (*Gsm/Gv*)	X				
	Memory for Sentences (*Gsm/Gc*)			X		
	Verbal Reasoning					X
	Abstract/Visual Reasoning		X			
	Quantitative Reasoning		X			
	Short-Term Memory		X			
	Test Composite			X		
WPPSI-R						
	Information (*Gc*)					X
	Similarities (*Gc*)					X
	Vocabulary (*Gc*)					X
	Comprehension (*Gc*)					X
	Picture Completion (*Gv/Gc*)					X
	Block Design (*Gv*)	X				
	Object Assembly (*Gv*)					X
	Mazes (*Gv*)	X				
	Animal Pegs (*Gv*)			X		
	Geometric Design (*Gv*)	X				
	Arithmetic (*Gq*)			X		
	Sentences (*Gsm*)				X	
	Verbal IQ					X
	Performance IQ					
	Full Scale IQ				X	
WJ-R COG						
	Picture Vocabulary (*Gc*)					X
	Memory for Sentences (*Gsm/Gc*)			X		
	Visual Closure (*Gv*)			X		
	Incomplete Words (*Ga*)			X		
	Memory for Names (*Glr*)		X			
	Broad Cognitive Ability			X		
DAS						
	Picture Similarities (*Gf*)			X		
	Verbal Comprehension (*Gc*)					X
	Naming Vocabulary (*Gc*)					X
	Copying (*Gv*)	X				
	Pattern Construction (*Gv*)	X				
	Block Building (*Gv*)	X				
	Early Number Concepts (*Gq*)			X		
	Verbal Cluster (3-6 to 5-11)					X

Battery	*Subtest (ability measured)* **Scale, Cluster, Composite**	Low	Low- Moderate	Moderate	Moderate- High	High
	Nonverbal Cluster (3-6 to 5-11)		X			
	GCA (2-6 to 3-5)					X
	GCA (3-6 to 5-11)			X		

Influence of Culture

Note: All *Gf-Gc* factor classifications are reported in McGrew and Flanagan (1996). Tests in bold are strong indicators of their respective *Gf-Gc* factors as defined empirically. All other *Gf-Gc* classifications are either mixed measures of *Gf-Gc* abilities or logically based due to limited or no adequately designed research studies. "Relative Influence of Culture" classifications were adapted from Hessler (1993) and Flanagan and Alfonso (1994).

12 Assessing the Speech and Language Skills of Preschool Children

TOYA A. WYATT

HARRY N. SEYMOUR

In recent years, there has been increased attention to the early identification and treatment of communication disorders in young children. Accurate identification and remediation of speech and language disorders, however, requires some understanding of normal speech and language development. The purpose of this chapter is to present information on the process of normal speech and language acquisition in early childhood. This information will then be used as a framework for discussing the nature of speech and language disorders as well as current practices in assessing the speech and language skills of preschool children. Issues relevant to the speech and language assessment of preschoolers who are bilingual and/or speakers of non-standard English dialects will also be addressed.

Normal Preschool Speech and Language Development

Speech and Language Defined

In order to understand the nature of speech and language disorders in children, it is important to first understand the nature of normal speech and language development and the process by which children acquire the various aspects of the language(s) to which they are exposed.

Speech and language are two important components of the communication process. The process of communication, as defined by Owens (1995) involves the exchange of information and ideas between two participants. *Language* refers to the communication code that is used for representing the information and ideas to be shared. According to one definition, language can be defined as "a code whereby ideas about the world are expressed through a conventional system of arbitrary signals for communication" (Bloom & Lahey, 1978, p. 2). The specific symbols or signals that are used within any language will vary from *speech community* to speech community, dependent on key cultural, historical, and social factors such as the geographic location or historical origins of a speech community. Regardless of these differences, every language in the world is considered to be rule-governed. Each has rules which govern how sounds or movements, words or signs and sentences or sign combinations are to be ordered so as to form meaningful messages. These rules also dictate how language is to be used in various social situations.

Speech serves as one of the modalities used by human beings for expressing language. The process of speech involves the coordination of several oral structures (articulators) such as the lips, tongue, jaw, teeth, and vocal cords to produce the sounds necessary for forming meaningful words and sentences. Two other modalities that can be used for communication include manual communication (signing) and written language (reading and writing) modes.

The Components of Language

There are several different models of language which have been used to explain what young children must eventually acquire when attempting to master the basic aspects of their native language system. One particularly useful model of language is that proposed by Bloom and Lahey (Bloom & Lahey, 1978; Lahey, 1988). According to Bloom and Lahey, there are three major areas of language which children must eventually master in order to become competent communicators—*form, content,* and *use.*

The first area, form, refers to the structural aspects of language. This includes the sound system (phonology), sentence structure (syntax) and word structuring (morphology) rules of a language.

The *content* dimension of language refers to the underlying meanings or concepts expressed in a language through the use of vocabulary and certain word combinations. During the earliest stages of development, children combine words in a systematic fashion to express meanings, ideas, perceptions and understandings about their world. These early word combinations and expressed meaning are often referred to as *semantic-syntactic relations* (Brown, 1973) or *content categories* (Bloom & Lahey, 1978; Lahey, 1988).

The language *use* or pragmatics dimension of language refers to how utterances are used to accomplish various communicative acts or functions. For example, language can be used to inform, request information, express internal desires and needs, or regulate the behavior of others. It can also be used for other purposes. Children learn quite early the social and instrumental power of these language uses. In addition, children learn how to vary or adjust the nature of their language expressions to suit the needs of their listeners and the social context of the communicative situation.

Cross-Cultural and Language Differences

All languages can be described in terms of form, content, and use. Languages will sometimes differ, however, in how these components are organized or structured. With respect to form, languages can differ in the number and types of sounds that make up their phonological systems. There can also be differing rules as to where sounds can occur within words, and what sound combinations are acceptable. For example, Spanish only has 18 consonants in contrast to English, which has 24 consonants. In addition, English has 14 vowels but Spanish only has 5 (Langdon, 1992). As a result, there are some sounds that occur in English but are not found in Spanish such as the *v* sound as in *violin, th* sound as in *thumb, j* sound as in *jump, sh* sound as in *ship* and the *i* sound in words like *sit*. Sounds that occur in Spanish but not in English include the trilled *r* which is found in Spanish words like *perro*. In addition, although the sounds *b, p, g, m, t, k, ch* and *f* are part of the sound system for both English and Spanish, none of these sounds ever occur in the final positions of words in Spanish. In contrast, they occur in all three word positions (initial, medial, final) in English.

Languages also differ in how word endings such as plural -*s* and past tense -*ed* are used to convey concepts such as plurality and time reference. For example, in Chinese, one does not use something like the English plural -*s* marker on nouns to convey plurality or the English past tense -*ed* marker on verbs to convey past tense. These conceptual meanings are instead inferred from the preceding discourse context (Cheng, 1993).

Finally, languages differ in their rules for how sentences are to be structured. For example, in Spanish, adjectives must follow the noun that they modify. They must also agree in gender and number with the noun which they follow. Therefore, in Spanish, if one wants to talk about a black cat, one would have to say *el gato negro*. However, the literal translation of this phrase in English is *the cat black*. The latter would be considered ungrammatical in English because it violates a very basic syntactic rule of English (the fact that adjectives must precede the nouns that they modify). Similarly, if one wanted to say *the black cats* in Spanish, it would be necessary to mark the gender (masculine) and number (plural) status of the noun (*cat*) on every word in the noun phrase including the article, adjective, and noun. Therefore, it would be necessary to say *los gatos negros* which, literally translated into English, would be produced as *the+s cats blacks*. However, the latter is also incompatible with the *syntactic* or grammatical rules of English because plural markers (e.g., -*s*) are never used with articles (e.g., *the*) and adjectives (e.g., *black*).

Languages also differ in how common objects, events, and meanings are labeled. This results in vocabulary differences between languages. This would explain why a native English speaker may have a difficult time conveying a message to someone who is not familiar with the words of English, and vice-versa. Even within the same speech community, there can be differences in how speakers label common experiences, as a result of dialect differences. *Dialects* are different varieties of a language that differ somewhat in grammar, phonology and/or vocabulary. There are several different dialects of English as well as Spanish and other languages. In many cases, these differences can be attributed to regional or geographical residence distinctions. American English speakers living in the South, for example, generally speak a different dialect of American English than speakers living in Boston, New York, and Philadelphia. In some cases, dialect differences can be attributed to social background differences. For example, *African American English* (also often referred to as *Ebonics* or *Black English*), which is spoken by many but not all African Americans at least some of the time (Wyatt, 1995), is considered by many linguists to be a social dialect. Others have argued that it constitutes an entirely separate language (Smith, 1978). In any event, regardless of whether a dialect is regionally or socially based, speakers from different dialect communities often have differing ways of referring to the same concepts. For example, according to Langdon (1992), there are at least 19 different ways of saying the word *ballpoint pen* in Spanish. Therefore, it would not be unusual for speakers of Mexican-American Spanish to be unfamiliar with some of the terminology or vocabulary used by Puerto Rican Spanish, Castillan Spanish, Cuban Spanish speakers, and vice-versa.

As with every other dimension of language, there are also differences in how individuals from various language or cultural communities use language to accomplish certain communicative acts. This can even result in differing ways for initiating, maintaining, or terminating a conversation. In many English-speaking mainstream American communities, for example, sustained eye-gaze is used by the listener to convey attentiveness and interest. This keeps conversations going. In other communities, sustained eye-gaze can be viewed as a sign of disrespect (Conklin & Lourie, 1983). In these communities, other communicative behaviors such as verbal acknowledgments like *m-hm* serve as the primary means for indicating attentiveness and keeping the conversation going.

Stages of Speech and Language Development

Several developmental milestones characterize the course of normal speech and language development in preschool-aged children. In general, all preschoolers who are developing normally follow a fairly predictable sequence and stages of language development. However, it is important to note that, while normally developing children typically proceed through the various stages of language development in a fairly systematic manner, there is some degree of variability between children in how and when they acquire the various aspects of their native language system(s). Every child should be viewed as an individual who develops at his/her own pace.

In addition, there are some points in development where the forms and behaviors being mastered by children actually vary in frequency or nature of use. This occurs when speech and language behaviors have not been fully mastered. As a result, it is not uncommon for children to produce a grammatical form like the verb *is* in some sentences but not others prior to the age of 3 years.

Despite this variability, it is possible to establish a relatively stable and reliable referent for measuring language development. This referent enables speech and language clinicians to determine a child's stage of language development and to determine whether a child's course of language development is normal. The following section provides a description of the key developmental milestones in each of the three major areas of language that are generally used for accomplishing this goal. A summary of key speech and language developmental milestones can be found in Appendix 12A.

The Development of Form.   The early non-speech vocalizations produced by infants during their first few months of life (e.g., *cooing* and cries) represent the earliest development of language form. At this stage of development, infants are also beginning to produce a limited number of non-crying vowel-like sounds that approximate adult vowel productions (Oller, 1978; Owens, 1995). At about 6 months, *babbling* sounds, which consist of simple consonant-vowel sequences such as "ba-ba-ba-ba" and "da-da," begin to appear. Babbling can continue into the second year and may overlap with the emergence of the child's first few words. Toward the end of the first year, children enter an echolalic stage where they imitate the speech sound productions of others. The extent to which nonspeech and pre-linguistic speech vocalizations serve as precursors to the development of later speech and language forms is not altogether clear, however some language scholars assert that the types of vocalizations produced by infants are highly predictable and can be used to identify infants at risk for later communication delays.

In general, all children, regardless of their language and cultural background, proceed through these same stages of early speech sound development. Research has demonstrated little difference in the speech sound productions and patterns of infants prior to the age of 18 months. Researchers have even found that deaf infants go through the same stages of early babbling as hearing infants, although the frequency of their babbling tends to decrease over time (Bernstein & Tiegerman, 1993). The number and variety of sounds used by deaf infants may also differ (Owens, 1995). This difference has sometimes been attributed to the fact that deaf infants do not receive the same type of auditory feedback and input as hearing infants (Bernthal & Bankson, 1993; Locke, 1994).

As children begin to master the words and grammatical structures of their native language, they are also beginning to master the sounds of their language. There are some sounds, however, which are acquired at earlier stages of development than others. Among English speaking children, for example, the *phonemes* /p, b, m, k, g/ are mastered as early as 3 years of age, while others, such as /r, l, s, z, d_ (j), t_ (ch)/ are not fully mastered until later years. Because these later-emerging phonemes are more difficult to acquire, it is common for normally developing children to make errors when attempting to produce these sounds. The error patterns are fairly predictable in normally developing children. As a child's motor control improves with maturation, however, a greater number of sounds will be produced correctly. The entire phonological system is mastered at approximately 7 years of age.

In addition to making errors on individual speech sounds, children may also exhibit articulation error patterns involving entire classes of sounds. Speech sounds can be classified according to a number of articulatory and acoustic dimensions, such as manner of production, place of articulation, and degree of voicing. Some classes of sounds are mastered earlier than others. In addition, some are more difficult to produce than others for younger children. For example, at a certain stage in their language development, children typically exhibit difficulty with *fricative* sounds such as /s, z, v, th, f, z/. Fricatives are characterized by a hissing quality because airflow through the oral cavity is partially obstructed during their production. It is very common for preschoolers to replace many of these sounds with stops like /d/ or /b/ (saying "dumb" for "thumb" or "biolin" for "violin"). Stops are produced with complete obstruction of airflow. These error patterns are due to early-occurring *phonological processes* that are common during the early stages of phonemic development. These processes, however, typically disappear around the age of 4 in the normally developing child.

To date, there has been very little research on the phonological development of children from language backgrounds other than English. However, some fairly recent studies are beginning to demonstrate that there may be slight differences in how children from non-English language backgrounds acquire the sounds of their language even when they speak a language which contains the same sounds as English. For example, both Acevedo (1988) and Jimenez (1987) have found that Mexican-American Spanish speaking children acquire the /t/ and /l/ sounds at a much earlier age than English speaking children. Researchers have also found that certain phonological processes that tend to disappear in the speech of normally developing Standard English speaking children around the age of 4 years, may persist longer in the speech of children who speak a nonstandard dialect of English such as African American English (AAE). Haynes and Moran (1989) observed, for example, that AAE child speakers essentially go through the same phonological process stages as other English-speaking children. The only difference is that one process known as final consonant deletion (omitting the last sounds of words), which is common in the speech of all preschoolers, persists longer in the speech of AAE child speakers. This process usually disappears around 3 to 4 years of age in most English-speaking children but can continue up until about 8 years of age in AAE child speakers. Haynes and Moran attributed the latter to the fact that these children were acquiring a dialect of English that allows for the "deletion" or absence of many final sounds.

There are also important similarities between the phonological development of children from Standard American English (SAE) and AAE backgrounds. Stockman and Settle (1991), who compared the speech sound development of African American and white chil-

dren, found that both groups of children produced the same *minimal core* of initial consonants (consonants at the beginnings of words) up until the age of 3 years. In another research
study, Seymour and Seymour (1981) found that although African American and white preschoolers make the same types of early speech sound errors, the frequency of certain errors
may differ. For example, the /b/ for /v/ substitution occurred more often in the speech of African American preschoolers, while the /w/ for /r/ substitution was more common in the speech
of white children.

Another important stage of form development is the emergence of children's first
one-word sentences. At this stage of development, children may use a single word like *ball*
to convey the full sentence *I want a ball.* Children often move into this stage of language
development at approximately 10 to 12 months of age. At approximately 18 months of age,
children begin combining words to form two-word utterances. Both are considered to be
universal aspects of language acquisition. Researchers have found, for example, that just as
hearing children begin to produce two-word utterances around 18 months of age, deaf children exposed to ASL as their first language are beginning to produce two-sign utterances
(Meier, 1991).

During the earliest stages of syntactic development, it is common for children to
omit smaller functional words such as *is,* articles *a* and *the,* prepositions (e.g., *in* and *on*),
and key word endings such as past tense *-ed,* plural *-s,* possessive *-s,* and present progressive *-ing* in their sentences. Therefore, it is not unusual for 2- to 3-year-olds to produce
sentences like *That Daddy('s) car, Mommy eat(ing) cookie, I see two cat(s),* and *I pull(ed)
it.* Even though these forms begin to emerge in children's speech around 2 years of age,
most are not mastered until the later preschool years. The mastery of these grammatical
forms and markers enhances children's ability to express additional meanings (e.g., plurality and the time reference of an event).

As previously discussed, it is important to recognize that the rate at which children
acquire these forms can be quite variable. For example, in a study of three English speaking children (Sarah, Adam, and Eve), Brown (1973) noted that the order in which some of
the previously mentioned English grammatical forms were acquired was remarkably similar across the three subjects, but the rate at which syntactic forms were acquired differed
for each child. For example, the present progressive *-ing* marker (e.g., "play*ing*") was
acquired by Sarah by age 2-6 (2 years, 6 months), by Adam at age 2-10, and by Eve at age
1-9. However, all three children still acquired these forms at the same stage of language
development (Brown's Stage II).

Another aspect of syntax which must be mastered by preschoolers is the production of
questions. There are two types of questions that English speaking children must master: the
"yes/no" question and the "wh-" question. The yes/no question requires either a yes or a no
response (e.g., *Can Susan play baseball?*) Wh- questions require information about *when,
where, what, why, which,* or *how* (e.g., *Where does Susan play baseball?*). The response to
this question must involve a stated location (e.g., *in her backyard*).

Children must also learn the word order rules of their language. For example, children acquiring Standard American English as their first language system must learn that
auxiliary (helping) verbs like *can* must be inverted or moved to the front of the sentence
when asking a question such as *Can Bill swim?* In this sentence, the subject noun (*Bill*) and
the auxiliary verb (*can*) have changed places; that is, they have been inverted.

The last major stage of syntactic development involves the acquisition of several
complex sentence phrases such as *embedded phrases and clauses* ("I hope *he likes the
present*), *embedded wh- questions* ("I know *where the toys are*") and *relative clauses* ("The

boy *who ate the apples* is sick"). They must also learn how to produce sentences with *conjoined phrases* or *clauses* through the use of linking words or *conjunctions* such as *and, but,* and *because* ("I ran fast *and* falled down").

In order to capture the changing complexity of children's developing language, several researchers have used measures such as *mean length of utterance (MLU)* to determine a child's level of language development. MLU refers to the average number of morphemes per utterance produced by a child and is calculated by: a) determining the total number of morphemes produced within a set of utterances and b) dividing that sum by the total number of utterances within the sample. MLU was also used by Brown (1973) to delineate five key stages of syntactic development. Each is indexed by a specific MLU range. For example, Stage I (which is associated with an MLU range of 1.0 to 2.0), is characterized by the emergence of children's first words and is commonly achieved by children between the ages of 12 to 26 months. Stage III (MLU range of 2.6 to 3.75) is characterized by the appearance of children's first sentences and typically represents the language skills of children between the ages of 31 to 34 months. The last stage, Stage V (MLU range of 3.76 to 4.25), characterizes the language development of children between the ages of 41 to 46 months. This stage is characterized by the emergence of complex sentences with conjoined clauses. These five stages continue to serve as a useful and important referent in the assessment of child language disorders.

Just as with phonological development, there are some differences between the syntactic development of children acquiring Standard American English as their first language or dialect and those acquiring another language system. These differences become most evident at 3 years of age, when children are beginning to produce sentences that conform to the sentence formation rules of the language to which they have been exposed. For example, while children who are exposed to SAE as their primary language begin to use the verbs *is* and *are* 100% of the time in sentences by age 3 years, children who are exposed to African American English (AAE) continue to use this verb less than 100% of the time in their utterances (Wyatt, 1995; 1996). This is because the rules of AAE allow for variable use of some grammatical forms. However, just as in SAE, there are certain sentence contexts where *is* and *are* must be used all of the time in AAE. These contexts are therefore considered to be obligatory. Examples include past tense contexts where the past tense forms of *is* and *are* (*was* and *were*) are used, and in the final positions of sentences, as in "Yes she *is*." According to the research of Wyatt (1991; 1996), preschool-aged children acquiring AAE as their first dialect demonstrate knowledge of these variable language rules as early as 3 years of age if they are normally developing in their speech and language skills.

Research on Spanish-speaking children has also revealed important differences in the language development of monolingual Spanish and bilingual Spanish/English speakers. For example, according to the research of Kvaal, Shipstead-Cox, Nevitt, Hodson, & Launer (1988), children who are monolingual speakers of Spanish acquire the Spanish articles (*el, la, los, las*) and forms of the verb "to be" (*sera* and *esta*) earlier than English-speaking children acquire the English equivalents (*the, a, is, are*) of these forms. Research by Kvaal et al. (1988) also demonstrated, however, that Spanish-speaking children master the preposition *en* (which means "in" and "on" in English) later than English-speaking children master *in* and *on*.

There has also been a great deal of literature on the type of grammatical errors that one is likely to see in preschool-aged bilingual children acquiring English as a second language (Dulay & Burt, 1992; Gee, 1994; Kayser, 1989). According to this literature, it is very common for children to apply the grammatical rules of their native language to productions in English. This is often referred to as *L1 (language one) interference.* For example, it would not be uncommon for children who are native speakers of Spanish to place adjectives after the nouns that they modify (e.g., *the boy big*) when speaking English because this is the rule in Spanish. Such differences, are a normal part of the second language acquisition process and should not be viewed as a sign of language disorder.

The Development of Content. One of the most significant developments in the acquisition of language meaning occurs when children begin to say their first words. This typically occurs around the age of 10 to 12 months. Most children's early vocabulary consists primarily of nouns, with the most commonly occurring involving names of animals, foods, and toys (Nelson, 1973). Children may vary, however, in the type of words they first use. Nelson (1973), for example, identified two types of early word learners: (1) children who are "referential" (produce a lot of object names like *ball* and *car*) and (2) children who are "expressive" (use more social-related words such as *hi* and *uh-oh*). By 18 months of age, most children have approximately 50 words in their expressive vocabulary. After the emergence of two-word combinations, at approximately 2 years of age, vocabulary development continues at a rapid rate.

During these first months of lexical development, children use single words to achieve a variety of language functions. They use first words to comment on their actions, the actions of others, and the environment around them. They also use words to gain the attention of another, to direct the attention of another to events or objects, and to request information about objects within their immediate environment.

Children are also beginning to use their one-word utterances to express a common core of language meanings and topics. These topics focus on commonly observed events such as the existence of objects, relationships between objects, relationships between objects and events, and relationships between objects and their environment. A list of commonly expressed meanings in children's early one-, two-, and three-word utterances can be found in Table 12.1. These content categories are based on Bloom and Lahey's (1978) and Lahey's (1988) models of language development. Other semantic taxonomies such as Brown's (1973) *syntactic-semantic relations* have also been used to capture children's early expressed language meanings.

The universal appearance of this syntactic-semantic relation in all children's speech has often been explained in terms of cognitive development. Although there are a number of differing views on the relationship between language and cognitive development, most child researchers agree that these two aspects of development are somehow related to each other. One prevailing view, known as a cognitive determinism theory of language learning, asserts that advances in language development are preceded by the achievement of certain *cognitive prerequisites* or milestones. According to this theory, as infants interact with and experience the world of objects, sounds, and movements, they begin to form the ideas and concepts that will later be expressed by language. The language used to represent objects, events, and actions observed around the infant, therefore, is an indirect representation of his or her experiences and/or knowledge of the world.

Given their limited cognitive views of the world, it is not uncommon for children to use their first words to mark meanings which differ from how adults would use the same word to mark meaning. Children often under-extend or over-extend their words on the basis of perceived differences or similarities in the physical characteristics (attributes) or functional uses

TABLE 12.1   Content Category Examples and Phase When They Begin to Emerge

Content Category	Example	Phase
Existence	*boy, ball*	1
Recurrence	*again, more*	1
Nonexistence	*gone, no*	1
Rejection	*no want milk, no sit*	4
Denial	*no*	1
Attribution	*big car*	2
Possession	*mine, my toy*	2
Action	*go, open*	1
Locative action	*out, up*	1
Locative state	*ball here*	3
State	*love you*	3
Quantity	*three cars*	3
Notice	*Hey, look!*	4
Temporal	*Do it now*	4
Additive	*I have a ball and a bat*	5
Specification	*This one mine*	5
Causal	*He's going home 'cause he was bad*	6
Dative	*I gave it to her*	6
Epistemic	*I don't know how*	7
Adversative	*I ate it but it was awful*	7
Communication	*She said go home*	8

Note: From M. Lahey, *Language Disorders and Language Development* (pp. 210–260). New York: Macmillan. Copyright © 1988 by Allyn & Bacon. Adapted by permission.

of objects. For example, a child may initially use the word *dog* to refer only to one specific dog and not to other dogs (*under-extension*). On the other hand, a child may use the word dog to refer to dogs as well as other four-legged animals such as dogs, cows, sheep, and cats (*over-extension*). Both types of errors are the result of normally developing cognitive abilities.

Because cognition is considered to be important in the development of language, the assessment of a child's intellectual abilities is often a very important part of the language assessment process. This is particularly so for young children, for whom the unfolding of language parallels in many ways cognitive-intellectual development.

Perhaps one of the most important cognitive prerequisites for language development is the achievement of *object permanence,* the awareness by children that objects still exist even though they are no longer within the child's perceptual field (Piaget, 1979). Prior to a child's second year of life, there are several stages that a child passes through before reaching complete object permanence. For example, during the first few months of development, infants will not search for hidden objects when they are removed from the infant's visual field. Over a period of months, however, children progress from passive searches for visibly displaced objects to active searching for hidden objects when the hiding place is unknown. Each of the stages marks an advance in cognitive development with possible implications for language. A summary of stages of development for object permanence follows:

Age in months	Activity
0–2	No expectations or searching
2–4	Passive expectations
4–8	Search for partially covered objects
8–12	Search for completely covered objects
12–18	Search for visible displacements
18–24	Search after hidden displacements

Some researchers have attempted to demonstrate a relationship between the development of object permanence and vocabulary development in children. In one study, McCune-Nicolich (1981) noted that at least 50% of words used by toddlers to discuss the non-existence, disappearance, or recurrence of objects (e.g., no ball, gone, again) emerged within one month of their ability to perform certain object permanence tasks. McCune-Nicolich's findings provide additional support for the view that cognitive and language development are intricately related processes.

As with every other area of language development, there are similarities as well as differences in how children from differing cultural and language backgrounds acquire and express meaning in their first utterances. One important similarity is the sequence and order in which content categories emerge. Stockman and Vaughn-Cooke (1982) found that African American children go through the same stages of semantic development as other children. Specifically, these researchers found that African American children acquire the same semantic categories at the same stages of development and in the same sequence as other children. The only difference is the language that is used to code these meanings. Therefore, while AAE and SAE child speakers are both likely to talk about the non-existence of objects (e.g., balls), the SAE child speaker might say *There's no other balls* and the AAE child speaker might say *Ain't no other balls*.

There are also important differences. For example, it is common for bilingual children who are exposed to more than one language before the age of 3 years to mix the two languages when producing some words during the early stages of language development. A good example of this would be the bilingual Spanish-English speaking child who says *kitty-gato* for *kitty-cat* (Kessler, 1984). It is also very common for bilingual children to know the label for some items in one language but not the other. Many bilingual children who are exposed to a second language after the age of 3 years, for example, know the labels for objects generally found at home in their first language but the labels for objects at school in their second language. In some cases, phonological ease may also play a role in determining which label a child is most likely to use. Celce-Muria (1978, cited in Anderson, 1981) who studied the language development of her French-speaking child found that her daughter, who had been exposed to the French (*papillon*) and English (*butterfly*) terms for the insect that is commonly found in the flower garden, tended to avoid the word *butterfly* and favor the use of the word *papillon* because the latter was easier to pronounce. These findings demonstrate some of the differences in the vocabulary development of bilingual and monolingual children.

The Development of Use. The last major component of language is use. Even before children say their first words, they are beginning to become aware of how verbal and nonverbal communication can have an effect on listeners. For example, at approximately 10 months of age, children are already beginning to use nonverbal gestures (e.g., pointing) with or without accompanying vocalizations like *eh* to achieve a number of different language goals such as gaining a listener's attention, requesting objects, rejecting requests, and so forth. Children are also learning that they can use the same vocalization to express a variety of different language meanings, simply by varying the pitch and tone of their productions. As previously discussed, when children move into the one-word stage of development, they are also beginning to realize how to use single words to communicate a variety of different language functions.

As in the content area of language development, several different taxonomies have been proposed for describing children's early emerging language functions. According to Halliday (1973), young language learners demonstrate two different types of language functions in their first years: pragmatic (interpersonal uses of language) and mathetic (intrapersonal uses of language). Pragmatic functions include using language as a tool for regulating the behavior of others (*Stop yelling*). Mathetic functions include using language to ask questions about one's own observations of events, objects, and actions within the environment (*Why this dolly fall down?*). Dore's (1975) model of language development focuses more on the communicative intentions expressed in children's utterances. Dore identified nine primitive speech acts commonly found in children's early utterances: (1) labeling, (2) repeating, (3) answering, (4) requesting action, (5) requesting, (6) calling, (7) greeting, (8) protesting, and (9) practicing.

Another important aspect of pragmatic development occurs when children learn to adjust their language in accordance with the surrounding linguistic and nonlinguistic situational context. *Linguistic context* refers to the linguistic environment in which an utterance occurs, and includes the adjacent utterances (those that precede and follow a particular utterance). Children must eventually learn to produce utterances that are *semantically* or *linguistically contingent* (linked or related in meaning or form to the previous utterance). When a child says *Hit the ball* in response to *Let's play baseball* this response is semantically linked in terms of a shared topic: "baseball."

Children must also learn to adjust their speech to fit the requirements of a given setting. Part of this requires some understanding of the *nonlinguistic context* of discourse. This includes elements such as the nature of any ongoing activity, the physical characteristics of the setting (location), the nature of the communication channel being used (e.g., face-to-face or telephone), accompanying nonverbal communication behaviors of the listener (body position, facial expression, gestures), and the social characteristics of the listener (e.g., adult or peer). Each of these variables has a selective effect on the nature of language to be used. Children must also be able to make correct presuppositions about a listener's needs. For example, they must be able to assess their listener's knowledge or perspective on a given topic. Two types of linguistic devices that reflect children's sensitivity to the latter are deictic words and elliptical utterances.

Deictic words are words such as pronouns and demonstratives that have shifting references within discourse as a function of conversational participant roles. For example, the pronoun *I,* which initially refers to speaker A, can shift from speaker A to listener B when the listener becomes the speaker. Consider the dialogue between Billy and Sammy:

> Billy: *"I want the lollipop."*
> Sammy: *"No, I want the lollipop."*

In the previous example, the pronoun *I* shifted from referring to Billy to indicating Sammy. Children must learn to use words like these to reflect their and others' roles in the discourse situation.

Another important listener presupposition skill that children must eventually master is the use of ellipsis. *Ellipsis* involves the omission of certain words or grammatical structures in sentences for the purpose of reducing redundancy among successive utterances. For example, when a child responds *Let's go* to the question *Do you want to go to the circus?*, he or she is using an elliptical response. If the child had said, *Yes, let's go to the circus* instead, his/her utterance would be considered to contain a great deal of redundancy, since the listener is already familiar with the primary topic of discussion: the circus.

Research studies have documented similarities in the pragmatic development of children from culturally and linguistically different backgrounds. For example, Bridgeforth (1987), who was interested in determining whether African American children display the same general language functions as white children, found that African American children pass through the same stages of pragmatic development in the same sequence as white children. The only difference was the language system (AAE or SAE) used to express these communicative functions.

Some researchers, such as Heath (1986), however, have also observed that some aspects of language use can vary in terms of frequency or nature of use in some cultural communities. In her 1986 study, Heath describes six uses of language (*language genres*) that are commonly found in most mainstream American classrooms. Although all of these language genres are used to some extent in all cultural communities, some—such as label quests (asking a child to label object and pictures in view of both the speaker and listener)—occur less often in some communities. The contexts in which label quests are used may also differ. For example, Heath notes that Mexican American and African American mothers, in contrast to European American mothers, tend to use fewer label quests with their children during book-reading tasks and daily mother–child interactions. In addition, in Mexican American homes, label quests are most likely to occur during large family gatherings, where children are often asked to state the names of family members. These differing language experiences and expectations can create a home–school mismatch situation for some children from minority backgrounds because they will be less familiar with mainstream classroom language use practices. This lack of familiarity, however, should be viewed as the result of language *differences* and not language deficits.

Disorders of Speech and Language

Disorders of speech occur when individuals are unable to perform the motor act of speaking as a result of physically based or functionally based reasons. This results in incorrect pronunciation of age-appropriate sounds. An organically based speech problem would be exemplified by a child who has *cerebral palsy*, a neurologically involved condition that impedes fine motor coordination among the primary articulators (tongue, lips, palate, etc.), or cleft palate—where a child's speech clarity is affected by the absence of palatal tissue or cartilage. There are also some children, however, who display misarticulations for no apparent reason. In other words, there does not appear to be a physical basis for their problem.

A disorder of language usually results from inadequate knowledge of the linguistic rules that make up one's language system and/or the inability to express that knowledge (for reasons other than those associated with speech). Typically, a child with cerebral palsy, for example, has a speech problem due to poor neuromuscular functioning. If this child also exhibits a cognitive/intellectual deficit (a characteristic often associated with mental retardation), he or she more than likely will have a language disorder represented by inadequate knowledge of language rules. In contrast, the child could also exhibit a language disorder resulting from a memory deficit, which limits or impedes the recall and retrieval of stored linguistic information. This latter condition results in an inability to execute linguistic knowledge, as opposed to the former condition where language deficits appear to be related to inadequate or deficient language knowledge. Common signs of language disorder include: using inappropriate word substitutions (e.g., *her* for *she*) or leaving out key grammatical forms (e.g., *the*) after a certain age, using inappropriate word order (word order that does not conform to the rules of the child's native language), producing sentences that are shorter in length than those produced by children of a similar age, responding incorrectly to questions, delayed response to questions, frequent requests for repetition, use of vague versus specific language terms, and frequently talking off topic. Not all children with language disorders will display the same problems, but in general, they are likely to do one or more of the above.

Speech and language disorders may have one or more possible causes. Among the more common are problems with central nervous system functioning (e.g., *language learning disorder*), perceptual deficits (e.g., *hearing loss*), cognitive-intellectual deficits (e.g., *mental retardation*), and social-emotional development (e.g., autism). Each of these categories is made up of a number of behavioral symptoms that, taken together, are sometimes used to classify children with language disorders. This approach to classifying language disorders, based on underlying etiology, is known as a *categorical orientation* to disorder.

The categorical orientation to classifying children with language disorders may have some value in helping to understand a child's language problem in a general sense, but such an orientation provides an inadequate description of the specific speech and language problems exhibited by the child. As a result, more current views of language disorder support the use of a *noncategorical orientation* in assessing, identifying, and treating speech and language disorders. In contrast to the categorical approach for classifying language disorder, a noncategorical orientation focuses more on the actual speech and language problems exhibited by a child, regardless of the underlying etiology. Support for this new approach to classification is based on the recognition that the specific types of language problems exhibited by children with the same shared etiology may still differ. For example, a hearing-impaired child may exhibit the normal cluster of behavioral symptoms associated with hearing impairment, including language disorder, but may also have a central nervous system deficit and/or a psychoemotional problem that is not typically associated with hearing impairment. As a result, this child's language disorder would be different from that of a child with hearing impairment who does not exhibit the latter two disorders. In addition, if one were to list all the common behavioral traits considered to be associated with each of the major categories of disabilities such as autism, mental retardation, and hearing impairment, most, if not all, would overlap.

The Assessment Process: An Assessment Plan

Disorders of speech and language are typically identified through assessment procedures that use normal speech and language developmental profiles as a referent. Consistent with this approach, the assessment process described in this section involves a plan for identifying a speech and language disorder and describing the nature of the disorder. There are at least six major components of a successful assessment plan: (1) referral, (2) collection of background and historical information, (3) observation, (4) formal and informal testing, 5) analysis and interpretation of test data, and (6) making recommendations for intervention. Three questions which are important to answer during the assessment process are as follows:

1. Is there a problem?
2. What is the nature of the problem?
3. What should be the intervention goals?

The first question can be answered from a variety of different sources, including background information obtained from speech screenings, interviews with caregivers, written reports from other healthcare and educational professionals, observation, and formal testing. The first part of the process involves referral of the child with suspected speech and language problems through a speech screening or by individuals such as parents, guardians, teachers, pediatricians, and/or community human and social service agencies. Essential information about the client's personality, health, general well being, and social interactions often can be provided by these referral sources.

Upon referral, an examination must be made of any relevant background or historical information concerning the client's overall speech, language, social/emotional, intellectual, and physical development. Such information is collectively used to identify the existence of a problem and in describing the nature of the problem. This type of information is typically obtained through parental interview, medical records, and previous speech/language or psychological reports. The parent interview provides important information as to the nature of the child's speech/language problem and general course of development (e.g., determining when the child began to babble, sit up, crawl, walk, and talk). Medical records can help identify any relevant health or medical conditions that may precipitate or maintain speech and language disorders. Previous speech/language reports are helpful in demonstrating the success of past intervention efforts.

Clinicians should also routinely observe a child interacting with others in informal play and formal classroom situations. Observations provide an opportunity to speculate about the client's areas of difficulty, which subsequently can lead to a more focused assessment. During informal observations, the diagnostician can evaluate the nature of mother–child and peer communicative interactions. Informal interactions between the diagnostician and the child can also help establish rapport and reduce whatever stranger anxiety the child might otherwise experience. The latter helps a child be as comfortable as possible within the formal test setting and ensures more valid and reliable test results.

In recent years, there has been an increased emphasis on the use of parent interview and observational procedures for identifying children with possible speech and language problems. Part of this emphasis can be attributed to laws such as P.L. 99-457 and the recently passed 105–17 which require greater involvement of the family in a child's clinical assessment, decision making, and intervention plan. The growing awareness of the inherent cultural bias that exists in many of the currently available standardized screening and testing measures when used with children from nonmainstream cultural and language backgrounds has also led many child language researchers to advocate the use of less formal but equally effective identification procedures. In many cases, these two techniques can provide a more accurate and comprehensive view of communication skills, without relying on norms developed for other child populations.

The next step in the assessment process is to conduct a hearing screening. The screening is an important component of the assessment process, because hearing problems can certainly contribute to speech or language deficits. Most screening procedures are conducted at a level of 20 or 25 dB and involve three or four frequencies (500 Hz, 2,000 Hz, 4,000 Hz). When testing the preschool child, it is often necessary to modify the standard testing protocol. For example, the diagnostician may want to have the child drop blocks into a bucket when a tone is heard instead of having the child raise his or her hand. In addition, hand puppets can be used to demonstrate the procedure for the child, and token reinforcers such as colored chips can be used to keep the child on task. Children who fail at any of the tested frequencies should be referred for additional and more in-depth testing.

Following the hearing screening, an *oral-peripheral speech mechanism examination* is typically conducted. The diagnostician assesses the structural and functional integrity of the major articulators involved in speech production: the lips, tongue, jaw, velum, and vocal folds. The child is asked to perform several speech and non-speech tasks designed to elicit imitative and spontaneous oral motor movements. Tasks include activities such as puckering the lips, wiggling the tongue from side to side, opening the jaw against resistance, sustaining productions of sounds such as /a, s, z/, and producing repetitive sequences of simple and multisyllabic consonant-vowel combinations. Any structural or functional abnormalities of the face, head, and oral mechanism are noted.

Because the oral-motor examination can be somewhat intimidating to the preschool-aged child, it is advisable to have some of the following materials on hand to make the procedure more fun and less threatening for the child: (1) sweetened fruit-flavored tongue depressors, (2) a penlight decorated with favorite cartoon characters, (3) a hand puppet used as an assistant in a "Simon Says" adaptation of the normal testing format, and (4) foods such as peanut butter which can be used to assess various lip and tongue functions by observing how well a child can lick peanut butter from around his or her lips.

The next step in the assessment process is to pursue a more detailed evaluation of the child's actual speech and language behavior. More often than not, there is the need to establish how a child compares with speech and language norms of children of a comparable age and/or language level. This comparison usually is accomplished with norm-referenced standardized tests. There is a plethora of standardized tests in the area of speech and language. In selecting the appropriate tests and test batteries, the clinician must be familiar with factors associated with valid instruments. If tests fail to meet the clinician's purpose or standards, alternative testing is advisable.

Formal testing involves a battery of tests covering various aspects of speech and language. There are articulation tests to examine the child's ability to articulate English phonemes, and there are a myriad of tests covering several aspects of language. A list of several commonly used tests is shown in Table 12.2. Some language tests examine only syntax or semantics, whereas others examine multiple language dimensions. Each of the tests has been standardized and reflects normative profiles for the subjects on whom they were standardized. However, the quality of tests varies in terms of their standardization. Clinicians must scrutinize tests for validity and reliability requirements. Also of particular importance is the match between the client under examination and the normative sample of a test. A test normed on New York urban youngsters, for example, may not be appropriate for Iowa farm children.

The test's appropriateness in terms of the standardization sample is of crucial importance for minority children, because so many tests either have no minority children represented in the normative sample or have too few to be truly representative. Also, there is the fallacious assumption among some test developers that, by sampling a presumably representative percentage of minority children (usually matched to the size of the minority population

TABLE 12.2   A List of Some Commonly Used Norm-Referenced Tests in Speech and Language Assessment

Name of Test	Age Range	Standardization Sample	Area(s) of Language		
Language			**Content**	**Form**	**Use**
Assessment of Children's Language Comprehension (Foster, Giddan, & Stark, 1973)	3.0 to 6.5	n = 311 Mixed SES = All levels		X	
Bankson Language Screening Test-2 (Bankson, 1990)	3.0 to 7.0	n = 1200; 19 states Anglo Am, Afro Am, other	X	X	X
Carrow Elicited Language Inventory (Carrow-Woolfolk, 1974)	3.0 to 7.11	n = 311; Texas Anglo Am SES = NR		X	
Clinical Evaluation of Language Fundamental Preschool (Wiig, Secord, & Semel, 1992)	3.0 to 6.11	n = 800 Mixed, Based on 1989 census	X	X	
Expressive One Word Picture Vocabulary Test—Revised (Gardner, 1990)	2.11 to 11.11	n = 1118; California Anglo Am, Afro Am, Hispanic Am SES = NR	X		
Northwestern Syntax Screening Test (Lee, 1971)	3.0 to 7.11	n = 344; IL SE speakers SES = NR		X	
Peabody Picture Vocabulary Test-Revised (Dunn & Dunn, 1981)	2.0 to 4.0	n = 4200; National sample Hispanic Am SES = all levels	X		
Sequenced Inventory of Communication Development-Revised (Hedrick, Prather, & Tobin, 1984)	0.4 to 4.0	n = 252; Washington Anglo Am monolingual SES = All levels	X	X	X
Structured Photographic Expressive Language Test—Preschool (Werner & Kresheck, 1983)	3.0 to 5.11	n = 732; Florida, Illinois, Missouri Anglo Am monolingual SES = Mid		X	
Test for Auditory Comprehension of Language—Revised (Carrow-Woolfolk, 1985)	3.0 to 10.0	n = 1003, National sample Mixed SES = NR	X	X	
Test of Early Language Development—2nd Edition (Hresko, Reid, & Hammill, 1991)	2.0 to 7.11	n = 1274, 30 states Mixed; Based on 1990 census	X	X	
Developmental Indicators for the Assessment of Learning—Revised (DIAL-R) (Mardell-Czudnowski & Goldenberg, 1990)	2.0 to 6.0	Mixed; Based on 1990 census	X	X	

(continued)

TABLE 12.2   Continued

Name of Test	Age Range	Standardization Sample	*Area(s) of Language*		
Language			Content	Form	Use
Preschool Language Scale-3 (PLS-3) (Zimmerman, Steiner, & Pond, 1992)	0.6 to 11	n = 1200 Anglo Am, Afro Am, Hispanic	X	X	X
Detroit Tests of Learning Aptitude—Primary, 2nd edition (Hammill & Bryant, 1991)	3.0 to 9.11	n = 2217, US & Canada	X	X	X
Phonology					
Photo Articulation Test (Pendergast et al., 1969)	3.0 to 12.0	n = 384, Washington Anglo Am SES = Mid		X	
Arizona Articulation Proficiency Scale (2nd Edition) (Fudala, 1986)	1.6 to 13.11	n = 5122; Western states Mixed SES = NR		X	

in society at large), valid representation has been achieved. These approaches to standardization fail to take into account the language variability among nonstandard English and nonnative English speakers. The fact that a test samples 12% black children and 10% Hispanic children does not reveal whether the black children were speakers of African American English, or the degree to which bilingualism was represented among the Hispanic children. Clinicians must be cautious about using such tests with minority children unless the profiles of the children are clearly specified and there is appropriate representation in the normative sample.

In recent years, it should be noted that there are a growing number of speech and language screening and diagnostic tests that have been designed exclusively for children from non-English speaking backgrounds. The majority of these tests, however, have been developed for Spanish-speaking children. In addition, many of these tests fail to eliminate the cultural or language bias concerns found in other English tests (Albertson & Alvarado, 1992; Vaughn-Cooke, 1986). This is because they are often translated versions of English tests which have not been modified to accommodate cultural and language differences. Standardization norms and the underlying theoretical framework of these tests also continue to be based on information obtained on children from white middle class, Standard American English speaking backgrounds.

A cautionary note is also raised here about relying on norm-referenced tests for answering the second diagnostic question for all children: What is the nature of the problem? Norm-referenced standardized tests are often inadequate for this purpose because they simply sample too few speech and language behaviors to be sufficiently representative of the child's language system. Many standardized tests also primarily assess language form. A few tests examine limited aspects of content, and still fewer, if any, examine use (pragmatics). Only through in-depth and more naturalistic observation can one possibly determine a child's areas of strengths and weaknesses and, thus, the nature of the child's speech and language problem. This same precaution extends to tests that are developed for minority language populations as well.

Two assessment methods that are more useful for addressing the nature of communicative difficulties include *language sampling* and *language probing*. Ideally, all assessments should include speech and language sampling and language probing to some degree. Because such methods can be extremely time consuming, however, they may not be carried out in the initial part of an assessment. Most clinicians prefer, instead, to rely on standardized measures that take less time to administer and analyze.

Language sampling, however, is useful in revealing the structures that are absent or the areas where additional information is needed about a child's speech and language behavior. The objective of language sampling is to obtain a sample of conversational speech in as naturalistic a setting as possible. After a language sample is collected, it is then analyzed according to some predetermined language sample analysis profile. Commonly used profiles include Bloom and Lahey (1978), Lee (1974), Lund and Duchan (1993), Miller, (1981); and Tyack and Gottsleben (1977). These profiles are used to determine a child's language level and to identify areas of language weakness.

Some of these same developmental profiles can also be useful in assessing the nature of language problems among minority children, when used with caution. Although data are limited in language acquisition among nonstandard English speakers, there are several aspects of language, as previously discussed, that do not appear to vary as a function of dialect or language difference. This includes early developing content categories, language functions, and non-dialect-specific syntactic forms (those such as the articles *a* and *the*) which are required or obligatory in all dialects of English.

Although language sampling reveals much about a child's speech and language system, there are always some language structures that a child fails to use or uses infrequently because of limited opportunity within the sampling context. Consequently, there is the need to follow up with language probing or criterion-referenced testing in order to complete the speech and language profile. Language probing generally involves the use of nonstandardized tasks to elicit targeted language forms or behaviors. In criterion-referenced assessment, clinicians establish their own criteria for determining whether a form has been mastered or is productive in use. This can involve setting expectations as to the frequency which with a form is used (productivity) or used correctly within obligatory contexts (mastery). Obligatory contexts are those that require the use of a form.

For example, a 4-year-old child who speaks SAE may be tested for the production of the plural -*s* marker in an elicitation task like the following:

CLINICIAN: *"These are two…"* (Clinician holds up two balls)
CHILD'S RESPONSE: *"Balls."*

In this example, the clinician is attempting to determine how often the child correctly uses the plural -*s* form within an obligatory sentence context. At least one use of plural -*s* form would indicate, at minimum, emerging use of the form. Several uses of the form would indicate productivity. The exact number of uses required to indicate the latter, however, is left up to the discretion of the clinician. Correct use of the form the majority of the time would indicate mastery. The criterion of 90%, which is typically used for the latter, is based on previous child language acquisition studies which demonstrate clear mastery of forms when they occur 90% of the time (Brown, 1973).

One advantage of language probing, criterion-referenced assessment and other non-standardized elicitation measures is that they allow a clinician to discern patterns of language weakness and strength without having to use pre-established notions or norms based on white, middle class, SAE child populations. This approach is particularly relevant for children who use language forms that are characteristic of African American English or influenced by normal L1 patterns. As with formal testing, however, it is very important to be aware of the potential cultural bias involved in using certain types of nonstandardized elicitation tasks with children from differing cultural backgrounds. Clinicians must also have the type of training that enables them to clearly discern those language "errors" which appear to be the result of normal language differences versus language disorder.

Answers to the clinical question, "What should be the intervention goals?" often derives from the use of language sample and probe data. Those language behaviors that are missing from the child's repertoire, but which should be present because of the child's age and language level, constitute intervention goals. All aspects of language functioning must be addressed, including content, form, and use. Clinicians should determine whether all are age-appropriate and whether a child is able to integrate all three of these dimensions appropriately. When developing intervention goals, clinicians must also provide information from the assessment that identifies what a child can do linguistically as well as what he or she cannot do. By only focusing on missing language elements, the clinician provides limited and incomplete information. Descriptions that merely establish that the child is not using adult forms also present an incomplete diagnostic profile.

Information obtained from the language assessment is used as a language plan in much the way one would follow a road map to reach a desired destination. This language plan provides all the pieces of a very complicated puzzle, which, when solved, can reveal the direction (intervention goals) a clinician must take in treating a language-disordered child. The extent to which intervention addresses the child's true problems depends on the validity and thoroughness of the assessment process. Whatever goals result from the assessment must be considered tentative, and ongoing assessment should continue concurrently as therapy is being implemented. This apparent overlap between diagnosis and intervention is a recommended practice and has been described variously as "diagnostic teaching" and "diagnostic intervention" (Seymour, 1986).

Because language disorders are extremely varied in terms of the many dimensions of language that may be affected, underlying etiologies, and the type of problems observed, it is very important for professionals to recognize that no one set of procedures can capture the full scope of the process for every child. Therefore, while it is important to follow many of the basic principles of assessment addressed in this chapter, it is also important to remain cognizant of the fact that testing should always be adapted to meet the unique background of the child being assessed when attempting to identify the preschooler with a true communication disorder.

Summary

The assessment of speech and language disorders in preschool children requires an understanding of normal language development. This development involves multidimensional and interactive behavioral components, which include phonology, syntax, semantics, and pragmatics of language. An interactive perspective combines these components so that both structure and function are considered in the assessment process. A current model that achieves this multidimensional and interactive perspective is the form-content-use model.

In assessing disorders of form, content, and use, it is necessary to include in the assessment process referral source information, background developmental data, a hearing screening, an oral mechanism examination, and formal testing. Both norm-referenced and criterion-referenced assessment make up the formal testing component. Norm-referenced tests compare the child with others of similar age and background. Criterion-referenced assessment is conducted in a language-probing format, allowing for in-depth examination of specific domains of language. The assessment process answers three basic diagnostic questions: (1) Is there a problem? (2) What is the nature of the problem? (3) What should be the intervention goals?

APPENDIX 12A

Stages of Speech and Language Development in Preschool-Aged Children

Age	Developmental Milestone
1 to 10 months	Crying serves as one of the earliest forms of communication. Used to signal an infant's internal state (hunger, fatigue, etc.).
	Infants go though a babbling stage at 4 to 6 months. Begin experimenting with several different playful sounds.
10 to 12 months	Toddlers begin to use nonverbal gestures like pointing with or without accompanying vocalizations to communicate intended meanings.
	Deaf infants display patterns of manual babbling similar to the vocal babbling of hearing infants.
	Emergence of first true words. Initial vocabulary consists of approximately 10 words. Understand more words than produced. Are using first words to mark a limited number of language functions and meanings.
18 to 24 months	Hearing children are beginning to produce their first two-word combinations. Deaf children are beginning to produce their first two-sign combinations. These two-word utterances mark old as well as newly emerging semantic categories and pragmatic functions. The same range of meanings and functions are acquired in the same sequence and at the same stages of language development by all normally developing children, regardless of their cultural or language background.
	Hearing children have a vocabulary of approximately 50 words. Nouns constitute the majority of children's words. Frequently over-extend and under-extend the meanings of words.
	Children are still incapable of producing words using adult pronunciation patterns. As a result, they produce simplified and modified versions of these words (e.g., deleting unstressed syllables, omitting final sounds in words, replacing later developing sounds with earlier emerging sounds.) These simplifications and modifications are the result of systematic phonological processes which affect the speech of all children.

(continued)

APPENDIX 12A   Continued

Age	Developmental Milestone
24 to 36 months	English-speaking children are beginning to use key grammatical forms such as "in" and "on," the verb "-ing" ending and the plural "-s" noun marker.
	Early developing pronouns such as "I," "you," "me," "mine," "your," "she," "he," "we" are beginning to appear.
	English-speaking children are beginning to use their first negatives (e.g., "no," "not," "don't," "can't.").
	English-speaking children are beginning to use early developing auxiliary (helping) verb forms such as "do," "can," "be," etc.
	English-speaking children are beginning to ask "what," "where," and yes/no questions. Many of children's first questions are produced with incorrect word order and/or contain missing verb forms.
36 to 48 months	All children are beginning to master the grammatical rules of the language or dialect to which they have been primarily exposed. The language development of children acquiring nonstandard dialects of English begins to look different from that of children acquiring Standard American English as their first dialect. Children are beginning to produce their first three-word utterances. As they move into this stage of development, new grammatical forms (i.e., "a" and "the," "is," possessive "-s," and past tense "-ed") begin to emerge. Use of these forms is inconsistent and it is common for children to make errors in the use of these forms or to leave them out of their sentences (i.e., "I wented to school yesterday" or "My mommy here").
	The majority of English-speaking children are consistently producing the following sounds in at least two word positions (at the beginning and ends of words): "n," "m," "p," "b," "h," "k," "g," "f," "w," "y," "t," "d." Nonstandard-English child speakers produce the same "minimal (shared) core" of initial consonant sounds as Standard English child speakers.
	Children are able to produce words with more adult-like pronunciation patterns as early-developing phonological processes begin to disappear.
	Bilingual children who have been exposed to more than one language before the age of 3 years are becoming effective code-switchers (are able to move between the two languages with ease).
48 to 60 months	English speaking children are beginning to use later developing negatives (e.g., "isn't," "aren't," "didn't," "wasn't," "couldn't," "nobody,"), questions (e.g., "how,", "when," "why"), pronouns (e.g., "they," "them," "their," "herself,"), auxiliary verbs (e.g., "shall," "could"). Questions are produced with appropriate word order.
	The average length of children's sentences is 4 to 5 words although longer and more complex sentences are beginning to appear. Key complex sentence structures such as relative clauses, embedded questions, and conjoined clauses are beginning to emerge.
	English-speaking children are starting to master several later-developing sounds such as "s," "z," "l," "r," "sh," and "ch." However, it is still common for them to make errors such as saying "wing" for "ring." Sounds that continue to be extremely difficult are "v," "th," "ng," and "j."

Children are beginning to master the conversational rules of their speech community. They are becoming much more adept at turn-taking, making requests for clarification, using polite words, and repairing conversational breakdowns. They are also learning the discourse rules associated with the key speech events of their community.

Children are becoming more accurate in their use of deitic terms such as "here/there" and "this/that."

Children are learning to adapt their language to meet the needs of their listener. Bidialectal and bilingual children code-switch between different dialects or languages according to the perceived background of the listener.

13 Assessment of Sensorimotor and Perceptual Development

WINNIE DUNN

The sensorimotor and perceptual systems provide the core mechanism by which young children interact with the environment, and therefore are critical areas to address in assessment and intervention programs. The sensorimotor system comprises the input mechanisms (sensation) and the output mechanisms (motor) that operate to enable children to notice stimuli and react to them. The perceptual system involves those internal actions that enable children to interpret information that will be used in cognitive, motoric, and language tasks. It is important for professionals to know how to assess these systems because these data (1) contribute to an expansive view of the child's overall development, (2) provide information that can be used to interpret other key areas in more detail and more accurately, and (3) sometimes define the child's primary problem area(s).

Although there are some standardized and criterion-referenced tests for young children in this area, much sensorimotor assessment is conducted using skilled observation and interviewing. Like other standardized procedures, observational and interview techniques require practice to ensure that the information that is collected represents the child's actual abilities and performance skills. An important prerequisite to competent, skilled observation is knowledge of the normal developmental processes that occur; this information forms the backdrop against which a child's particular performance is judged and recorded. This chapter addresses knowledge that enables the professional to gather useful data about children and their sensorimotor and perceptual abilities.

Formal Assessment of Sensorimotor and Perceptual Systems

There are several standardized and criterion-referenced measures available to early childhood professionals for assessment of sensorimotor and perceptual systems. Table 13.1 provides a summary of the characteristics of the most common assessments used to evaluate preschool children.

There is a prescribed manner for administering the tests on Table 13.1. When professionals follow these procedures, they can be assured that comparisons between the child being tested and the population used to design the test will yield accurate information

TABLE 13.1 Summary of Standardized and Criterion-Referenced Tests that Evaluate Gross Motor (GM), Fine Motor (FM), and Perceptual (P) Development in Preschoolers

Test Name	Area(s) Tested	Subtest	Areas Covered
Standardized Tests			
Bruininks-Oseretsky Test of Motor Proficiency (Bruininks, 1978)	GM, FM	GM, FM, Visual-Motor	4.5 to 14.5 years
Peabody Developmental Motor Scales (Folio & Fewell, 1983)	GM, FM	GM, FM	0 to 7 years
Miller Assessment for Preschoolers (MAP) (Miller, 1988)	GM, GM, P	Sensory-Motor/ Cognitive Combined	2.75 to 5.67 years
Developmental Test of Visual Motor Integration (3rd rev.) (Beery, 1989)	FM, P	Visual Motor	2 to 15 years
Motor Free Visual Perception Test (Colarusso & Hammill, 1972)	P	Visual Perception Visual–Discrimination Visual–Memory Visual–Spatial Visual–Form Constancy	4 to 11 years
Test of Visual Perceptual Skills (nonmotor) (Gardner, 1988)	P	Visual–Sequential Visual–Closure Visual–Figure-Ground	4 to 13 years
Test of Visual Motor Skills (Gardner, 1995)	FM, P	Visual–Motor Integration	2 to 13 years
Criterion-Referenced Tests			
Hawaii Early Learning Profile (HELP) (Enrichment Project for Handicapped Infants, 1985–1995)	GM, FM, P	Visual-Motor Integration	2 years
BRIGANCE® Test of Early Development (Brigance, 1991)	GM, FM, P	Communication, Cognition, Self-help, GM, FM	0 to 7 years
BRIGANCE® K & 1 Screen (Brigance, 1991)	GM, FM, P	13 areas	K to 1
BRIGANCE® Preschool Screen (Brigance, 1991)	GM, FM, P	11 areas	3 to 4 years
Learning Accomplishments Profile—Revised (Sanford & Zelman, 1981)	GM, FM, P	Personal Social, GM, FM, Reflex, Tactile, Vestibular	3 to 6 years
Developmental Programming for Infants and Young Children (Schafer & Moersch, 1981)	GM, FM, P	Personal Social, Communication, Cognition, Self-Help, GM, FM	0 to 6 years
Gesell Preschool Test (Ames, Gillespie, Haines, & Ilg, 1979)	GM	13 tests Personal Social	2.5 to 6 years
Vulpe Assessment Battery (National Institute on Mental Retardation, 1982)	GM, FM, P	Communication, Cognition	6 years

about the child's development. When professionals change the method for administering the test items, they run the risk of giving the child being tested either an advantage or disadvantage in relation to the children in the test population. This practice can result in incorrect assessment of developmental status.

The standardized and criterion-referenced tests listed in Table 13.1 are based on knowledge of typical development. The items on these tests represent skills we expect of children at particular ages. When early childhood professionals administer one of these tests, they accumulate data about the child's skills related to developmental milestones and determine a developmental age for performance of sensorimotor and perceptual skills.

Informal Assessment of Sensorimotor and Perceptual Systems

The most critical ability that a professional can acquire for assessment of sensorimotor and perceptual development is the ability to perform skilled observations and interviews. Unlike formal assessment, which requires professionals to create a controlled situation for the child's performance, informal assessment enables professionals to determine how the child performs in natural life environments. Informal assessment provides a vehicle for determining a child's functional abilities where those skills matter most—during daily life.

In order to conduct effective skills observations and interviews and interpret information properly, professionals need to understand typical expectations of preschool children. In the following sections, we will review the milestones for perceptual, fine motor, gross motor, and activities of daily living, and discuss ways to conduct informal assessment with this knowledge as a basis for thinking and problem solving.

Perceptual Skills Developed during the Preschool Years

By 2 years of age, the child has created a map of self and environment that can be used for a number of problem-solving tasks. The concepts of sameness and difference enable the child to match simple toys, colors, and shapes to similar models. Additionally, the child applies that perceptual concept to construction of simple formboard puzzles. The concept of *more* emerges, frequently in relation to food items (e.g., "more cookie"), but this is also applied to other situations involving objects, such as the bigger toy or the longer rope (see Table 13.2).

The 3-year-old expands perceptual skills to include sorting and sequencing, while increasing the complexity of discrimination and matching skills. The child completes four- or five-piece puzzles requiring tolerance of multiple-characteristic objects in the task. During this period the child also develops object permanence and so remembers objects when they are taken away and searches for them.

Four-year-olds demonstrate the ability to handle more complex perceptual tasks. They can match objects to pictures, a more abstract form of matching. They fluidly transfer information among the sensory systems for tasks such as identifying objects by touch without vision, or recognizing the picture that matches an animal sound that was heard. Puzzle construction involves more pieces (8 to 12) and pieces that interlock. Memory capacity increases and expands beyond object permanence to include objects from the less

TABLE 13.2 Fine Motor and Perceptual Milestones

	Use of Writing Utensils	Object Manipulation	Manipulation of Self-Care Activities	Perceptual Skills
2 years	Holds crayon with gross grasp. Copies vertical and horizontal lines. Copies circular lines. Imitates a cross. Scribbles spontaneously.	Places small objects into small containers. Builds a tower of three cubes. Imitates a three-block train. Strings three large beads. Unwraps a piece of candy. Manipulates stacking rings. Pulls apart and tries to connect large pop beads. Places six blocks in a form-board in two and a half minutes. Places 16 cubes in box in two minutes. Folds paper in half imprecisely. Snips with scissors.	Feeds self with spoon. Pulls off socks. Pulls pants down with assistance. Assists with washing and drying hands. Assists with tooth brushing.	Matches two simple shapes. Places two simple shapes into foamboard with demonstration. Matches toy animals. Matches one color.
2½ years	Begins to use paint and paintbrush, but strokes are irregular, does not stay on paper, and may quickly paint many pages without definable forms. Enjoys fingerpainting. Copies a cross. Holds crayon with fingers.	Places three shape blocks in formboard (e.g., circle, square, triangle). Builds a three-block bridge. Builds a tower with six cubes. Adds one block chimney to train. Imitates picking up scissors correctly. Snips near line using scissors.	Finds armholes when dressing. Uses fork. Dries hands. Assists with dressing. Buttons large buttons. Assists with pulling pants on. Dons coat.	Matches two colors. Remembers a visual stimulus when it is removed. Places three forms in formboard. Nests four objects correctly. Picks longer line consistently.

(continued)

TABLE 13.2 Continued

	Use of Writing Utensils	Object Manipulation	Manipulation of Self-Care Activities	Perceptual Skills
3 years	Paints pictures with large brush. Vertical and horizontal strokes are easily differentiated. Copies a square and a cross. Traces a diamond.	Builds a 9- or 10-block tower. Places 10 pellets in a bottle in 30 seconds. Places six round and six square pegs in pegboard holes. Cuts with scissors.	Feeds self with little spilling. Undresses self. Pulls pants on and off, but cannot fasten independently. Washes own hands. Brushes teeth. Zips zippers. Holds plastic cup in one hand. Wipes up spills. Approximates lacing shoes. Pours liquid into cup. Unbuttons own clothing. Pulls on sock and shoes. Washes and dries hands and face.	Matches primary colors. Sorts round and square pegs into correct holes. Works a four-piece puzzle. Tells which stimulus is missing from a previously viewed set.
4 years	Holds brush with adult pattern. Draws crude pictures of familiar things. Copies diagonal lines. Draws large circle on chalkboard (15–20 inches). Begins to hold paper with support hand when writing.	Manipulates lacing card to place thread through hole. Builds a six-block pyramid. Picks up scissors correctly. Uses double-handed scissors to cut through small strips of construction paper. Cuts through paper strips. Cuts fringe around a square piece of paper. Cuts between the lines.	Screws and unscrews jar lids. Dresses self. Zips and buttons, coats, shirts. Begins to cut with a knife.	Matches colored shape to colored outline on paper. Works 8–12 piece puzzles. Remembers up to three visual stimuli. Identifies common objects by feeling them (e.g., ball, block, crayon).

5 years	Draws a triangle. Draws a recognizable human figure with head, trunk, legs, arms and features. Draws a simple house with door, windows, roof, and chimney. Prints first name with large irregular letters, and has frequent reversals.	Runs a small car on a one-inch wide path without violating the boundaries. Builds a six-block step. Places 10 pellets in jar in 20 seconds. Buttons two buttons on a button strip. Cuts one-inch strips from large piece of paper. Cuts on lines of increasing length (6–12 inches). Begins to cut curved lines. Folds triangle from six-inch square.	Learns to lace shoes. Uses knife and fork together. Brushes and combs hair. Dresses and undresses alone except for tiny or hard-to-reach fasteners.	Manipulates variable size/shape puzzle pieces. Places 10 forms into formboard. Puts together two cut pieces of simple shapes (e.g., circle, rectangle). Chooses named object from group by feeling without vision. Constructs designs with blocks. Sequences four visual stimuli. Copies dot-to-dot designs.
6 years	Draws human figure with several details and clothing. Imitates an inverted triangle. Imitates horizontal diamond. Writes upper and lower-case letters from memory. Uses pincer grasp to manipulate writing utensils.	Cuts squares on heavy lines from construction paper. Cuts triangles on heavy lines from construction paper. Cuts circles on heavy lines from construction paper. Cuts pictures from magazines.	Blows own nose. Learns to tie own shoes. Spreads with a knife.	Places lines, circles in correct order by size. Finds matching picture from memory. Recognizes left and right sides.

recent past. Children can also organize and remember more details about objects in their environment during this period; this is likely the result of the increasing familiarity of a large number of sensory stimuli within the environment.

By 5 years of age, perceptual constructs are very complex, with combinations of previously developed skills converging to enable the child to face new perceptual and cognitive problems with a wide array of options. Fine motor manipulation skills are also emerging simultaneously, enabling the child to manage multiple properties of objects at the same time. For example, the 5-year-old uses the color, shape, and size of a puzzle piece to determine where it will fit into the puzzle, whereas younger children tend to lock onto one characteristic to make their choices. The child constructs increasingly complex structures with blocks, and can make a block serve as a door in one structure and as a tree or person in the next. Use of writing utensils enables experimentation with two-dimensional space; mazes, dot-to-dot designs, copying, and tracing are all examples of age-appropriate activities that combine perceptual and fine motor skills (see Table 13.2).

By the time the child enters school at 6 years of age, perceptual tasks are more heavily weighted toward those readiness skills necessary for reading and writing (e.g., formation of letters and numbers), recognition of patterns of letters and numbers as units (e.g., *cat, 26, the, from*), and the ability to use language to describe perceptual events. More complex gross motor movements allow a greater variety of action-oriented, problem-solving experiences as well.

Perceptual development does not emerge in isolation, but rather as an integral part of an evolving individual. When a child has difficulties with perceptual skills, this can affect other areas of development; conversely, when other areas of development are impaired, perceptual development can suffer. One must consider the whole child within an age-appropriate context before deciding the exact nature of any developmental concern.

Using Knowledge about Perceptual Development to Conduct Skilled Observations and Interviews

Young children display their perceptual abilities as they participate in their day. It is useful to observe a child during daily home or school routines and during free play. Let's consider an example. Cynthia is a 4-year-old who comes to a parent's day out program each week. When she arrives in the classroom, she puts her blue lunch bag on the blue square that the teacher has secured to the counter for her. She frequently comes to the program with objects from home in her pockets. The teacher asks Cynthia to show her what she brought today, and Cynthia reaches into her pocket and says "a red ball" and pulls out a small, shiny red ball from her bulging pocket. With the ball in her hand, Cynthia then walks to the work table and picks up a red circular wooden bead from the bead stringing bin. She shows the teacher the two objects together.

In this brief observation, we can derive a lot of information about Cynthia's perceptual development. She can match shapes and colors as indicated by the lunch bag placement and the ball and bead matching incident. She was able to identify the ball by touch; with a bulging pocket, it is likely that she had to discriminate the ball from other objects in her pocket. In reviewing the developmental information on Table 13.2 one can deduce that Cynthia's perceptual skill development is commensurate with her chronological age (i.e., 4 years). We can have confidence in this rating of her skills because we observed her during a typical life event in which she was able to call upon her perceptual skills to engage with her teacher and her environment.

Professionals can also ask care providers to describe a child's typical performance at home, and derive meaning about perceptual skill development. In Cynthia's case, we might ask her care provider to describe what objects Cynthia chooses to play with, and how she plays with these objects. For example, with the hypothesis that Cynthia has about 4-year-old level skills, we might expect her care provider to talk about Cynthia's interest in puzzles, since this is a common way that 4-year-old children practice their perceptual skills.

Fine Motor Development

Infancy and Toddlerhood. The most important prerequisite skills that develop during the first 2 years are control over reach, grasp, and release, which enables tool use. By 6 months of age, the infant voluntarily reaches for objects within the visual field. The child also begins to establish voluntary grasp during this period. Initially, fingers are used against the palm in a *palmer* grasp pattern, and then the child uses a *lateral* grasp with the thumb pulled in against the side of the palm (see Figure 13.1). These grasping patterns allow the infant to secure objects in the hand, but they only enable the infant to perform rudimentary movements, such as banging objects together. This is especially distressing when the infant has secured a food item in the palm. The only way to gain access to the object is by letting go of it and letting it drop to the table or floor. Nonetheless, grasp greatly expands the infant's life experiences with objects in the environment (Short-DeGraff, 1988).

Voluntary grasp continues to refine, and voluntary release develops through the first year. The child begins to rotate the thumb around in front of the palm and then can use the thumb as a post for the fingertips; this is called *pincer* grasp (see Figure 13.1). Pincer grasp broadens the child's options. The child can pick up very small objects with the fingertips, and the object remains accessible while in the hand. Just after the development of pincer grasp, voluntary release emerges. It is initially characterized by full hand extension to let go of the object; then, with practice, the child learns to control the releasing movements, and they become smoother and more well timed (Short-DeGraff, 1988). Children are very interested in developing this skill and spend many hours picking up objects and placing them into containers, only to dump them out and begin again.

The Preschool Years. The hallmark of fine motor performance during the preschool years is the development and refinement of tool use. With a variety of reach, grasp, and release patterns available, the child is free to explore new possibilities. Although the hands are incredible tools themselves, their capabilities multiply geometrically when using objects. Hand preference is another important characteristic of manipulation that emerges as tool use improves. Refined tool use and object manipulation requires a contribution by both hands; one hand must hold or stabilize while the other hand moves or acts. In drawing, one hand holds the paper while the other moves the crayon. For bead stringing, one hand holds the bead while the other hand moves the string into the hole. One must consider both components when evaluating fine motor skills. When new fine motor skills are emerging, it is common to see overflow movements in other body parts. Tongue, trunk, or limb movements are commonly part of the observable pattern of performance in emerging skills.

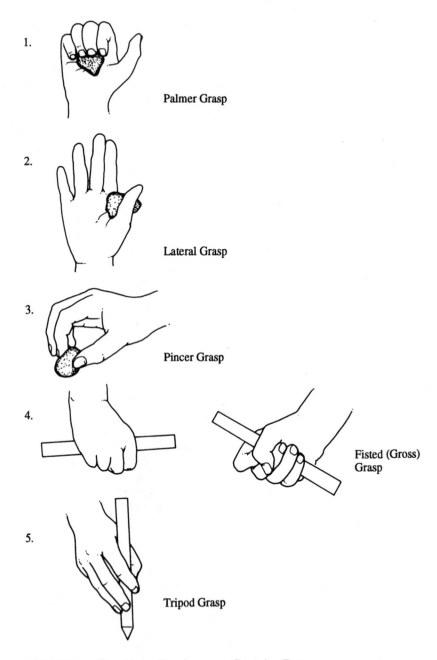

1. Palmer Grasp

2. Lateral Grasp

3. Pincer Grasp

4. Fisted (Gross) Grasp

5. Tripod Grasp

FIGURE 13.1   Fine Motor Development: Grasping Patterns

Use of Writing Utensils.   Initial use of writing utensils occurs during toddlerhood, when the child uses a *fisted grasp* to hold a large crayon and swipes at or scribbles on the paper (see Figure 13.1). During the preschool years, the child learns to use a pincer grasp to hold the writing utensil; the grasping pattern and the movements needed to write or draw become progressively more refined together. Table 13.1 summarizes the preschool milestones attained in the use of writing utensils.

The 2-year-old's use of writing utensils is characterized by large strokes that approximate basic shapes, such as horizontal, vertical, and circular lines. The child spends a lot of time scribbling spontaneously on the writing surface (and on other surfaces, much to the dismay of parents!) without definable forms. This stage of development is characterized by imitation; the child will draw lines after watching someone draw the same lines. Toward the end of the second year, the child begins to use *pincer* or *tripod grasp* (see Figure 13.1) to hold the writing utensil, which allows for the development of more finely tuned movements.

The 3-year-old child demonstrates more control over the writing utensil. Vertical and horizontal lines are more easily differentiated and can be drawn as single strokes. During this period, the child learns how to copy simple forms. Copying provides less input because the child is not able to watch how someone else created the shape and therefore must rely more heavily on internal body maps to identify how the hand might be used to make the form.

By age 4 the child is beginning to combine the shapes learned previously to create new shapes. For example, horizontal and vertical lines can be combined to copy a square. These more complex drawings require greater control of the moving hand but also require greater support from the stabilizing hand. It is very difficult to draw a recognizable square if the paper is moving about with each stroke. Four-year-olds also combine simple shapes to draw simple objects, such as people and houses. The diagonal line is more difficult to create because of the integrated movement required to move both down and over (or up and over) simultaneously; during this period the child learns how to trace and imitate the diagonal line.

Children usually enter public school at 5 years of age; their writing utensil skills are paramount for the readiness activities presented in kindergarten. Five-year-olds combine previously acquired skills to create drawings with some detail. For example, the house may have doors, windows, roof, and chimney; a person may have legs, arms, and facial features. Integration of basic shapes is also necessary for writing. The child learns how to make the alphabet by combining vertical, horizontal, diagonal, and circular lines in the correct patterns. Toward the end of the fifth year, the child writes her or his first name, but the letters are poorly formed, contain reversals, and are large.

Writing utensil skills are well integrated by age 6, enabling the child to write or draw increasingly more complex forms with improved skill and precision. Drawings contain more detail; as noted before, this is also due to the correlate development of body and environmental maps, which allow the child to recognize more details. The child has also begun to remember the letter and number forms, and can draw them from memory.

Manipulation of Other Objects.   Another important area for fine motor development is the ability to manipulate small objects. During infancy and toddlerhood, the child has experimented with reaching, grasping, and releasing objects within the immediate environment, and so is ready in the preschool years to learn more about intricate ways to use objects within the hand (see Table 13.2).

The 2-year-old child can hold objects such as one-inch cubes in the hand, because the thumb has begun to rotate around in front of the fingers, providing three-dimensional support for the object. As controlled releasing is established, the child can let go of objects in a precise way; this skill opens the door for block building. The 2-year-old learns to use this controlled releasing to build block towers, trains, and bridges. The child also uses the grasp and release pattern to complete simple, noninterlocking puzzles, especially puzzles with formboard holes and knobs on each piece. The 2-year-old is not able to rotate objects within the hand very well, so asymmetrical shapes that require special positioning to fit into the formboard pose difficulties. The child can use the hand to fold a paper in half, but the fold is not uniform.

The 3-year-old continues to play with small objects and has enough pincer grasp to pick up small objects such as raisins and release them into a container (or the mouth!). Sensory discrimination skills combine with object manipulation to enable the child to choose the correct forms for a multiple-shape formboard. The child begins to use scissors and makes gross cuts at the paper. Frequently, overflow movements are noted in the tongue and mouth suggesting difficulty with the motor task.

The 4-year-old child spends more time cutting and learns how to hold the scissors correctly. Frequently, preschool teachers use double-handed scissors to teach this skill to young children. The child learns how to make one cut with the scissors but continues to have difficulty with reopening the scissors to cut again, so cutting is characterized by making fringe or cutting across thin strips of paper. Lacing might also be introduced during this period, because the child can stabilize with the nonpreferred hand while pulling the string through the hole with the preferred hand.

By 5 years of age, the child uses the hand to manipulate objects in more complex patterns. Small toys are moved in multiple patterns (airplanes through the air, cars along "roads"). Manipulation of objects for self-care becomes more refined (see the section on self-care), so that the child can button, zip, and manipulate other simple fasteners. Cutting is characterized by repeated, sequential cuts and by following straight and curved lines when cutting. Folding has become more accurate, so that the child can fold a square along the diagonal to create a triangle.

The 6-year-old can cut along heavy lines to create shapes, such as squares, triangles, and circles. Hand strength permits cutting of heavy paper, such as construction paper or magazine pages. School-aged children can also use their hands for many finely tuned manipulations, such as stringing macaroni, clasping a barrette in a doll's hair, replacing the tire on a toy truck or car, or screwing a nut and bolt together. These skills emerge out of earlier hand manipulation practice.

Using Knowledge about Fine Motor Development to Conduct Skilled Observations and Interviews

Young children learn a great deal about their world by manipulating objects with their hands. Watching their attempts to manipulate objects can provide a great deal of information about not only the children's fine motor manipulation skills, but also their problem-solving abilities as they attempt more complex movements across time. Walter is a 29-month old child; he and his mother participate in a "Parents as Teachers" program in which an early intervention specialist visits them once a month. During one of the visits, the specialist sat and talked with the mother as they watched Walter playing. The mother said that recently Walter had become very interested in holding and marking with crayons, pencils, and chalk, and that Walter was marking on not just paper, but also the floor, walls, and cabinets. When she sat with him, Walter could make squares and crosses like the mother's model, but he didn't usually sit very long for this task. As they were talking, Walter sat with blocks and stacked eight blocks on top of each other before knocking them over. When Walter got up to come over to his mother, the specialist handed her blunt scissors and paper, and asked if she would try to get Walter to cut the paper. With mother's help, Walter made several cuts into the paper before he returned to playing with the blocks.

In this vignette, the early intervention specialist was able to combine skilled observation and interviewing to obtain the information he needed to determine a current level of fine motor development. In referring to Table 13.2, it appears that Walter has fine motor skills in the 30–36 month range (see columns 1 and 2). With this knowledge, the specialist can guide the mother regarding appropriate next steps in Walter's play interests and skills development. For example, it might be important to spend more time introducing the scissors to Walter during structured playtime, so he can develop better manipulative skills with this tool. It might also be useful to broaden Walter's repertoire of small objects for play to include formboards, dowel pegs, and other small objects he can place into and out of containers. All of these activities will stimulate Walter's next phases of fine motor development.

Gross Motor Development

Infancy and Toddlerhood.   Many gross motor skill components emerge during the first 2 years. Initially, movements are random and involve the whole body. As the infant develops, movements become more refined. Reflexive patterns or automatic responses characterize early movements; for example, if one taps the bottom of the infant's foot onto the floor, an automatic stepping response is elicited. Sometimes parents think that their infant is walking very early, but this is an involuntary response to the tapping stimulus. This response becomes integrated with other controlled movements as the child grows.

During the first 6 months, the infant learns to sit independently and to roll. In the last 6 months of the first year, the infant crawls, stands, and cruises along the furniture. Each of these skills requires a balance of mobility and stability as the child progressively challenges gravity. The most obvious gross motor skill that emerges during the second year is walking, but in order for the child to walk, transitional skills must also develop. Transitional skills are those movements that enable an individual to move from one position to another—from sitting to standing, or from lying prone (on the stomach) to a supine position (on the back). Some children with motor dysfunction can execute each motor skill component but cannot make the transitions from one position to the next. The child also learns to change position and direction during walking, and increases speed in the later months to run. Children also learn how to walk up and down stairs if they have frequent opportunities to practice the skill.

The Preschool Years.   Preschool gross motor development creates all the basic movement patterns that will be needed for later childhood movements. The child must move about in the environment, learn balance and equilibrium, develop coordination, and learn to interact with objects while performing gross motor movements (e.g., swinging a bat to hit a ball). Nervous system development and maturation support the evolution of these skills (see Table 13.3).

Mobility.   By 2 years of age, walking is the child's primary mode of mobility. Initially, walking is stiff with a wide-based gait, and arms are held over the head or out to the side to assist in balance and protection. As the toddler gets more practice, the arms come down to the side, and the feet move under the trunk for a smaller base of support when walking. When professionals observe early movement, note should be taken of the amount of extraneous effort required to move in an upright posture. When extra effort is required past the age of 2, it is often a sign of difficulties.

The 3-year-old has had a great deal of practice with movement in the upright position and adds reciprocal arm swings to walking. The child also walks down stairs with alternating

TABLE 13.3 Gross Motor Milestones

	Mobility	Balance and Equilibrium	Coordination	Ball Skills
2 years	Walks with feet apart and arms out. Walks upstairs alone with both feet on each step. Walks downstairs holding the railing with both feet on each step. Walks in generally a straight line.	Squats to play with toys and then stands without using hands to push up. Stands in one place with both feet together. Bends at the waist to pick up a toy.	Imitates simple bilateral movements of the body. Walks while pulling pull toy. Climbs up onto furniture to obtain objects or gain a new view.	Can roll and catch a ball when seated on the floor in a group. Pushes the ball with the feet in any manner without losing balance. Stops a large ball with body.
2½ years	Walks upstairs alternating feet while holding hand, wall, or railing. Walks backwards. Walks with arms to sides.	Stands up from the supine position by using a situp. Stands on one foot momentarily. Walks on a line for ten steps. Steps onto a two-inch balance beam.	Jumps from bottom step. Jumps backward. Pushes and pulls large toys skillfully, but is unable to steer them around obstacles. Attempts to jump; poorly coordinated.	Kicks ball forward in any manner. Throws a large ball with both hands. Catches a large ball against body. Tosses a large playground ball into a wastebasket.
3 years	Walks sideways. Walks downstairs alternating feet. Walks using reciprocal arm movement. Walks on tiptoes.	Maneuvers to avoid obstacles in path. Makes successful turns when running. Hops on both feet.	Can move around obstacles while running. Jumps with both feet—somewhat coordinated.	Kicks and throws toward a target. Catches a playground ball with both hands. Throws with an underhanded approach.
4 years	Runs on tiptoes. Gallops. Walks with increased stride length. Displays elementary running patterns.	Hops on one foot. Stands on one foot for 1–5 seconds. Walks forward on the balance beam. Walks sideways on balance beam, sliding feet.	Climbs well. Performs animal walks (e.g., duck, crab, rabbit walks). Jumps over small objects.	Kicks a ball forward while balancing on dominant foot. Keeps a balloon in the air. Throws with an overhanded approach. Catches a bounced ball.

5 years	Skips and marches in elementary way.	Stands on one foot for 5–10 seconds.	Swings self on swing by pumping legs.	Dribbles a large ball with one hand.
	Demonstrates mature running pattern.	Alternates feet to walk on balance beam.	Rides, tricycles, backs and turns.	Bats a ball on a string.
		Walks backwards on balance beam.	Climbs trees and ladders.	Throws a bean bag into a target at six feet.
			Broad jumps using arm swing.	Rolls a ball to a partner with his dominant foot.
				Catches ball with hands more than arms and body.
6 years	Walks or skips to the beat of music.	Walks on tiptoe for 10–15 feet.	Jumps rope.	Catches a ball with one hand. Hits a ball with a bat.
	Demonstrates mature skipping pattern.	Walks backward heel to toe.	Climbs skillfully.	Bounces and catches a tennis ball.
	Demonstrates fluid, well-timed movements.	Hops across room on one foot.	Can maneuver across an overhead ladder with hands.	Kicks ball while running.
			Rides scooter.	
			Successfully uses skates.	
			Begins to master bicycle riding.	
			Plays hopscotch.	

steps. Three-year-olds spend time experimenting with their mobility skills; they try walking on tiptoe and jumping while walking, and have varying degrees of success with these attempts.

Four-year-olds refine mobility by increasing stride length and synchrony of movements. They learn to gallop as a precursor to skipping (while the body is in a sideways position, leaping forward with the front foot and then pulling the other foot up to the first one). Running also becomes a common form of mobility because the children have better balance and coordination. As with the initial patterns of walking, running patterns are often stiff and poorly timed, making the child appear somewhat uncoordinated.

More mature patterns of mobility are expected by age 5. The child integrates arm movements into the running pattern so that it looks very much like an adult pattern. The child experiments with skipping, but the pattern looks more like separate hops and steps than a fully synchronized skip. Because of increased balance on a smaller base of support, the 5-year-old can also march well.

Six-year-olds demonstrate well-integrated mobility patterns. When they skip, run, or walk, it is easy to observe a fluidity in their movements that incorporates all body parts and appears to require little cognitive effort. School-aged children who must expend effort designing and executing these common patterns of movement are significantly out of the normal range of expected performance.

Balance and Equilibrium.   This is the ability to keep the body oriented in space and maintain one's position against gravity. Balance and equilibrium provide the foundation for the other mobility and coordination tasks. Movement cannot create its desired effect if there is no stable base from which to control the distance, direction, and speed of the movement. Problems with movement can frequently be associated with poor stability rather than with difficulty with the movement per se. Equilibrium is an easy phenomenon to observe in young children because it evolves so dramatically in the preschool years.

The 2-year-old is in the upright position most of the time. From the position, the child can *squat down* to obtain a toy and stand back up again (see Figure 13.2). To do this, the child must maintain control over the trunk and head while moving them down over the feet; then, in the squatted position, the child must maintain balance over the trunk, legs, and head while using the arm to reach out for the toy; then, with the new object (which changes the balance requirements), the child must move upward to standing again. A similar challenge to balance and equilibrium occurs when the child attempts to bend forward to pick up an object. Young toddlers are still governed by gravity, and so approach standing up from the supine position in steps. First, they roll from supine (on the back) to prone (on the stomach): then, they move into the crawling position, from there, they move the hips back to sit on the legs, and then can push with the hands to the upright position for standing. As the child gains control over gravity and develops stronger abdominal muscles, a situp can be used to move from supine to sitting, and then the child can raise the entire body up over the feet in a forward motion. This more efficient pattern can be seen as the child approaches 3 years of age. The 2-year-old also likes to try standing on objects, such as a box, a pot, or a pillow; equilibrium is usually not good enough to succeed at these tasks, but the 2-year-old has a great deal of fun trying! A primary reason for failure is that stepping up onto the object requires balancing on one foot, and this skill is only beginning to emerge as the child approaches 3 years of age.

Enough mobility and equilibrium skills have developed by 3 years of age to enable the child to maneuver within the environment successfully. The child can now change

**FIGURE 13.2 Gross Motor
Development: Squat-to-Play
Position**

directions and turn while moving, rather than treating each segment as a separate motoric event. Body organization is such that the child can hop in place, leaving the ground and returning while maintaining balance. The child also more successfully uses fluid arm movements to maintain balance during activities.

The increased fluidity of movement that is seen in the 4-year-old provides evidence that balance and equilibrium are becoming second nature to the child. It is crucial that balance and equilibrium demands be met without extreme cognitive effort; when the child must concentrate heavily on maintaining upright posture, then other perceptual and cognitive events get neglected. Under normal conditions, the lower centers of the brain monitor and respond to equilibrium demands, leaving the higher centers of the brain free to engage in other thinking tasks (deQuiros & Schrager, 1978). Equilibrium has progressed so that the 4-year-old can stand and hop on one foot. Because one foot can leave the ground for a few seconds, the child can walk on narrower surfaces, such as the balance beam or a curb.

By 5 years of age, the child is working to increase and refine previously learned skills. The child can stand on one foot for up to 5 seconds and can alternate feet when walking on the balance beam. Because body scheme is more well defined, the child can also walk backwards on the balance beam. Climbing becomes a favorite activity, with challenges against gravity a common occurrence along the way.

By the time children enter public school at 6 years of age, equilibrium is well integrated into all of their life activities. Hopping, jumping, running, and climbing all begin to contain creative components as the child thinks of ways to combine skills to increase the challenges of movement. Injuries usually occur when the challenge too greatly exceeds the acquired skills at any given moment.

Coordination. Coordination is the ability to organize movements among various body parts. For most life activities, accurate movement of only one body part is not enough to execute the task effectively. Dressing oneself, cooking, and cleaning all require organized movements of both hands and arms, both legs, or a combination of arm and leg movements for task completion. Coordinated movements can be *symmetrical, reciprocal,* or require a *lead-assist* pattern. Symmetrical patterns occur when the involved limbs move in the same way at the same time; rowing a boat and chinning up on a bar are activities that require symmetrical coordination. Reciprocal patterns occur when the limbs move in a complementary way but perform a similar motion; pedaling a bicycle is an example of a reciprocal movement. Lead-assist patterns occur when one limb performs the mobility component of the activity (lead) while the other limb provides stability to enable the movement to be accurate (assist). Cutting paper, hand sewing, stirring batter, and zipping one's coat all require a lead-assist pattern for successful task completion. The lead-assist pattern is the most difficult, and is most frequently used in adult activities.

The 2-year-old uses symmetrical and reciprocal movements to interact with the environment. Both walking and crawling use a reciprocal pattern with the arms and legs. The 2-year-old also uses these patterns of movements to climb onto furniture, such as the couch or an easy chair. Sometimes symmetrical movements are combined with reciprocal movements to push or pull a toy with both hands while walking across the room. Coordination is not yet good enough to manage small or difficult spaces.

Balance and mobility are improved by 3 years of age, to enable the child to maneuver around obstacles. The child attempts to jump but has difficulty because jumping requires a greater challenge of gravity. The 4-year-old child uses coordination skills to climb on furniture and up trees. The child also combines balance and coordination to perform animal walks, such as the duck walk, the bunny hop, and the camel walk. Preschoolers like these activities because they challenge their present skills while helping to develop new ones.

Many more coordination milestones are reached during the fifth year. The child learns to ride a tricycle, pump on a swing, and climb the rungs of a ladder safely. Fluidity of movements seen in mobility patterns also enables the child to use a total body approach to activities such as broad jumping. By 6 years of age, the child can jump rope, use roller skates, play hopscotch, and learn to ride a bicycle. Refinement of skills occurs after this period.

Ball Skills.   Ball play occurs throughout the developmental period and characterizes the many skills being acquired in the gross and fine motor areas. Playing with a ball is a form of object manipulation but requires the use of the large muscles of the body. Perceptual skills are also necessary; the child must be able to predict where the ball is coming from and where it may go, and this requires good maps of the environment. Observation of ball skills provides insight into the integrity of the perceptual and motor systems as a whole.

Since a 2-year-old child is new to the upright position, playing with a ball in this position is difficult. The child is likely to fall if a ball is introduced while standing or walking. While seated with legs out to the side, the child can trap a large playground ball against the trunk and can push the ball away. As the child approaches 3 years of age, increasing balance and coordination enable the child to use a rudimentary kicking motion to push the playground ball away while standing. The child can also let go of the ball, but without accuracy. These ball skills are reflective of the development of other gross motor skills.

By 3 years of age, the child can kick and throw a ball in a specified direction, largely because balance and coordination allow this isolation of movement of one limb to occur, while the rest of the body is controlled. It may be more difficult for the 3-year-old to kick or throw a ball in a specified direction while moving.

The 4-year-old has better one-foot balance and so can kick more accurately. Fluid body movements allow throwing to be integrated with other body movements, and the child can throw more accurately. The child can also bounce and catch a ball independently, but will sometimes trap the ball against the chest. The child can also keep a balloon in the air with pushing movements.

By 5 years of age, the child can maneuver while playing with a ball and can perform repeated movements with the ball. For example, the child can repeat bouncing and catching to dribble a ball. The child also adds tools to ball activities during this stage (e.g., bats, paddles, mallets). Accuracy increases, so that competitive sports can realistically be introduced (e.g., kickball, baseball). By 6 years of age, skills in these same areas have been refined even further.

Using Knowledge about Gross Motor Development to Conduct Skilled Observations and Interviews

Tamela is 4 years, 11 months old, and she and her father are attending the kindergarten preparatory meetings being conducted by the public school district staff. These preparatory meetings are held in the early evening for parents of children who will be eligible to enter kindergarten the next fall. While parents are in a session to learn about their children's development, the children participate in a play experience with district staff and community volunteers (in this case, the volunteer pool includes college students from the early childhood program at the local college). The district and college collaborate on these meetings to provide a service for the families, and to give the college students an opportunity to practice their observational skills in a natural context.

The student assigned to observe Tamela notices that Tamela stays in the open play area, and engages in large movement play. She and another girl march and attempt to skip to the music in the background, but Tamela can only skip 2 to 3 times before she returns to a galloping pattern. When the two children find the playground balls, they engage each other in ball play by kicking it back and forth to each other. Tamela then picks up the playground ball, and throws it to her play partner, who stops the ball, but cannot catch it. When the ball is returned, the child bounces it to Tamela; Tamela is able to catch the ball with her arms and hands, but gets so excited that as she caught the ball, she drops it onto the floor. Tamela and her friend leave the ball, and hop across the play area; Tamela can hop a few times on one foot, but two foot hopping predominates. When they reach the balance beam, they walk on it with their arms out to the side for balance. The college student observer suggests that they try walking backwards, but they can only complete two steps before losing their balance.

In this observation, the college student was able to identify many skills that demonstrate not only Tamela's interest in gross motor activities, but also her skill levels. She is almost 5 years old, and when reviewing the information on Table 13.3, we see that Tamela has 4-year-old skills, and some emerging 5-year-old skills. We would hypothesize that in the gross motor area, Tamela is developing at a rate commensurate with her chronological age. During the parent meetings, her father is learning about the gross motor activities that 5- and 6-year-old children enjoy and are expected to achieve. This will enable her father to consider toys and play activities at home that are the most helpful to Tamela's development.

Motor and Perceptual Components of Activities of Daily Living

The gross motor, fine motor, and perceptual skills that emerge in infancy, toddlerhood, and the preschool years are needed to perform activities of daily living such as eating, dressing, and personal hygiene. Although professionals learn about and evaluate the sensorimotor and perceptual components of development, this information should be considered only in relation to the child's ability to perform age-appropriate daily life tasks.

The 2-year-old has discovered many things about the body and applies them to daily life tasks. Prior to 2 years of age, eating involves only finger foods, but the 2-year-old learns to use a spoon to scoop softer foods such as applesauce or pudding. Eating is messy, with the child spilling the spoon's contents or not capturing all the food from the spoon into the mouth. Eating with a spoon provides an excellent example of the interaction among sensory (weight of the filled spoon, texture of the food on the face), fine motor (grasping the spoon), gross motor (moving the spoon to the mouth), oral motor (opening the mouth and then using the lips to scrape the food from the spoon), and perceptual skills (getting the spoon into the food, watching it come toward the mouth). Problems with any of these areas can interfere with task performance; therefore, decisions regarding the reason for failure should be made cautiously. By observing the toddler in several situations, the professional is better able to determine the specific problem area. The older 2-year-old begins to use a fork to stab firmer foods when eating.

Mastery of dressing tasks begins with undressing, because it requires less skill to pull something off a body part than to put something on. Two-year-olds spend a lot of time undressing, probably because they are fascinated with their own skill development. Children then begin to assist with dressing tasks, such as holding their arms up for sleeves, demonstrating their understanding of the task demands. They also begin to manipulate large buttons, attempting to fasten them, and learn to unzip coat zippers.

By 3 years of age the child eats independently, with little or no spilling. The child holds a cup efficiently and brings the cup to the mouth for a drink. Personal hygiene skills begin to emerge during this period. The child washes and dries hands, brushes teeth, and helps with washing body parts during bath time. Dressing is characterized by donning socks, shoes, and other simple clothing items, all of which requires gross motor and perceptual skills. The child in this age group spends a lot of time practicing with fasteners, thereby improving both dressing and visual motor integration skills at the same time.

The 4-year-old experiments with cutting food with a knife, although early attempts are crude and inefficient. This skill not only requires the fine motor skill to cut with the knife, but also requires bilateral coordination, with one hand holding the food with the fork while the other hand cuts the food. Some children with developmental delays can acquire the more isolated movement skills of spoon and fork use but experience difficulty with these more complex, integrated tasks. Children in this age group establish independence in dressing when using routine types of clothing, but may require assistance for infrequently worn items. Verbal cues are effective to get body parts washed, but help is still needed for hair washing. More sophisticated fine motor skills are applied to manipulation tasks such as screwing and unscrewing jar lids. Well-developed perceptual and body maps enable the child to design strategies for moving about within the environment to acquire materials and supplies for use in daily life tasks (e.g., figuring out how to climb up into the storage closet to get a new tube of toothpaste).

By 5 years of age, the child establishes independence for dressing, except for the more difficult fasteners or unusual clothing (e.g., very small buttons, dresses that button in the back). The child also learns to lace shoes but is clumsy in attempting to tie them. In addition to face and hand washing, the child begins to brush or comb hair and becomes more efficient in toothbrushing. Because so many children enter school at this age, activities of daily living take on a social flavor; children watch and help each other during these tasks and seem to prefer having friends with whom to share during these activities.

Six-year-olds display very sophisticated gross, fine, and perceptual skills, enabling nearly complete independence in the daily life tasks. For example, 6-year-olds tie their own shoes, blow their noses, can prepare a simple meal, locate items in cabinets and closets, attend to personal hygiene needs, and incorporate socialization into daily life tasks.

Using Knowledge about the Perceptual and Motor Aspects of Activities of Daily Living to Conduct Skilled Observations and Interviews

Ms. Ambrose contacted the early intervention helpline because she had concerns about her grandson, Aldus. Ms. Ambrose reported that she had been Aldus' primary caretaker since he was 6 months old; he is currently 3 years old.

When the early intervention specialist, Glen Wieger, interviewed Ms. Ambrose, he discovered that Ms. Ambrose was mostly concerned about Aldus' dressing, eating, and hygiene skills. Ms. Ambrose reported that Aldus seemed to play with other children without trouble, but still required more care during daily routines than other children she had raised. Glen asked Ms. Ambrose to describe Aldus' daily life skills. Ms. Ambrose stated that Aldus used a spoon, and ate finger food during meals, but continued to spill food, and could not use a fork. Ms. Ambrose also reported that Aldus took off his clothing, but continued to resist active participation in dressing each day. She was pleased that he would cooperate with her to wash and dry his hands and face, and seemed to enjoy when they brushed his teeth together.

As Glen and Ms. Ambrose continued to chat, Glen was able to obtain additional helpful information about their living situation. Ms. Ambrose was raising five children currently, and the other four children were older than Aldus. Since Aldus had been disrupted most during his early years with changing living circumstances, the older children had taken on roles of watching out for Aldus. As they talked, Ms. Ambrose revealed that the other children spent a lot of time taking care of Aldus' personal needs, so that Aldus did not have any opportunities or reason for learning some of these daily life skills on his own.

When we examine Table 13.2 (column 3), we see that Aldus has acquired self-care skills at the 2 to 2 and one-half year level. It is likely that he has not acquired additional skills due to the active involvement of the older children in his daily life routines. In their attempts to take care of Aldus, they may have inadvertently reduced his interest in learning more independent skills. Glen's strategy for supporting Ms. Ambrose and Aldus would likely be to talk to the whole family about the importance of Aldus learning skills for himself. Glen could also instruct the other children in how to participate with Aldus while still encouraging him to become more independent. It would be critical for Glen to honor the other children's needs to be part of Aldus' daily routines, but to reconstruct each person's roles so that Aldus can acquire skills without the other children feeling that they are abandoning him.

Patterns of Performance Associated with Abnormal Development

There are two major categories of perceptual and motor performance problems: *delays* and *dysfunction.* A developmental delay occurs when the evaluation reveals sensorimotor and perceptual performance characteristic of a younger child. For example, if a 3-year-old child performs like a 2 year, 3-month-old child, a 9-month delay would be present. The critical feature of a delay in development is that the child demonstrates skills normally present in a younger child; the child is not acquiring skills at the rate of the peer group.

Because developmental progress is quite dynamic in infants, toddlers, and preschoolers, a 3- to 6-month delay in development can be considered significant. Significance must always be related to the child's ability to perform age-appropriate tasks. The presence of a 3-month deficit according to developmental milestones without corresponding difficulty with age-appropriate tasks should not be considered a delay. P.L. 99-457 extends school services to preschoolers and mandates services to infants, toddlers, and families; it directs each state to define what constitutes a significant delay in development for that state. This definition can be inclusionary or exclusionary, depending on how it is constructed. It is important that professionals know their own state's requirements.

A dysfunction is present when a child demonstrates behaviors that are not normally seen during the developmental process. The professional watches for behaviors that are not characteristic of developmental patterns. It is most common for occupational and physical therapists to provide primary data regarding dysfunctional patterns of movement and perceptual processing in the young child. Identification of dysfunctional behaviors generally calls for more expertise in skilled observation. Dysfunctional patterns are more frequently associated with neurological or musculoskeletal problems and therefore require the attention of a more specialized professional. However, there are several observable behaviors that can be used to initiate a referral to an occupational or physical therapist.

The presence of primitive reflex patterns during movement is a common warning signal in young children. A primitive reflex is a predictable pattern of muscle activity in response to a specific stimulus. Primitive reflexes perform a very important function in the early months of development but tend to interfere with movement performance as the child grows older. In normal development, these reflexes become integrated into other movement patterns and therefore cannot be seen during normal life tasks. For example, the asymmetrical tonic neck reflex (ATNR) dictates that when the child's head is turned to the side (chin to shoulder), flexion will increase in the arm closest to the back of the head while extension increases in the area closest to the face; this is called the fencing position. During early infancy this reflex enables the newborn to attend to objects visually while the head and arm move toward them, but this reflexive movement pattern interferes with preschool tabletop activities, which require stabilization with one hand and movement with the other.

Difficulties with muscle tone might also be noted. Children with high muscle tone have extreme tension in the limb muscles and may have a difficult time making transitions from one body position to another. Children with low muscle tone frequently have the appearance of a rag doll. These children spend an excessive amount of time leaning on objects in the environment for support, draping themselves on tables and chairs, or leaning against the teacher; they frequently ask to be held. These children tend to become more fatigued as the day goes on. They are unable to stay at one task for any length of time, especially at tasks requiring body control. Sometimes children with low muscle tone will lock their joints in order to provide additional support, but when one palpates the limbs, the muscles feel very weak.

Tremors are associated with nervous system dysfunction and affect motor performance. Intentional tremors are those that occur when the child "intends" to do something. For example, when the child reaches for a glass of water or points at something in his book, a shaking movement in the hands would be noted. At rest, however, this tremor would not be present. Other tremors are called resting tremors; as the name suggests, they are present whether or not the person is engaged in activity. When any type of tremor is present, a different plan of action must be created because the tremor will interfere with motor performance as the child grows. Professionals who have not been specially trained to observe clinical signs such as these should not make a diagnosis on the basis of their own observations but, rather, should rely on the expertise of other professionals (e.g., occupational therapists, physical therapists, pediatric neurologists) to verify their suspicions.

Summary

The sensorimotor and perceptual systems are important features of young children's development. They provide the vehicle through which the cognitive, language, and socioemotional systems interact with the environment. This chapter introduced basic developmental information regarding the sensory, motor, and perceptual systems, and how skills in these areas evolve through the preschool period. There was a strong emphasis on skilled observation as a mechanism for gathering sensorimotor and perceptual information about a child. Furthermore, the chapter emphasized that isolated skills alone cannot provide adequate data about a child's performance; professionals must also consider the child's ability to use sensorimotor and perceptual abilities within daily activities such as playing, eating, dressing, and writing. Behaviors that indicate more serious sensorimotor or perceptual problems were identified, so that referral to specialized professionals can occur on the child's behalf.

14 Readiness for Academic Achievement in Preschool Children

STAN SCARPATI

PATRICIA G. SILVER

Identifying prerequisite academic ability in young children is a difficult task, often leading to inaccurate and misleading assumptions about how preschoolers will perform later in school. The objectives of this chapter are to guide the reader through a discussion about what constitutes academic readiness—i.e., its history, and how assessing academic readiness is conceptualized and practiced. A review of some current tests follows. Although the review is not exhaustive, the tests presented are considered the most useful and technically sound of those available for young children. These instruments are described to make the reader aware of the test purpose, content, administration, and validity. Included in the discussion is a review of the current trend to use "authentic" tests with children, how that trend applies to preschool children, and its relationship to curriculum-based assessment.

Teaching and Assessing Young Children

The nature of education has become part of the debate concerning appropriate practices for young children (e.g., Boyer 1987; Calkins, 1983; Ferreiro & Teberosky, 1979; Graves, 1983; Howe, 1985; Schickedanz, 1986). As part of this reform, early childhood educators and assessors are considering if "traditional" academic readiness tests are appropriate or able to predict the academic success or failure of young children when they move into formal settings. With the current emphasis on educational reform (e.g., National Goals 2000, 1991; Massachusetts Education Reform Act of 1993), preschool children are part of a movement toward excellence in education. That is usually translated to mean higher expectations about demonstrating basic skills and outcomes on formal assessments. For example, with the movement toward a common core of learning such as seen in Massachusetts Common Core of Learning curricula, guidelines are structured around the content areas of mathematics, language arts, social studies, and so on. Within these frameworks, however, schools are free to develop the curricula scope and sequence and learning activities as they deem appropriate based on a consensus of what they expect their children to know. With the likely potential for differences among schools, can readiness tests assess the academic skills identified in this common core? Furthermore, do they predict performance of future academic achievement (Ellwein, Walsh, Eads, & Miller, 1991; Kagan, 1989; NAEYC, 1988; Meisels, 1987)? Do these tests measure the prerequisite skills necessary for school-based achievement? Do these tests reflect the early childhood curricula? Moreover, do they assess those skills that young children bring to school that have a significant effect on their school learning? Some educators purport that they do not (Harste, Burke, & Woodward, 1981; Schickedanz, 1986).

Because professionals are examining the early childhood curricula in the context of educational reform, the appropriateness of readiness tests has become part of the controversy (Meisels, 1987). The notion of learning readiness evokes a variety of opinions, ranging from the belief that searching for learning indicators in preschool children is an unproductive, often dangerous task, to the conviction that discrete skill analyses in all domains are necessary if future school difficulties are to be diminished. Moreover, in recent years the search for disabilities has become another reason for detailed assessments of preschool children. Some state laws, along with the federal mandate where applicable, promulgated the need through the "child find" process of the *Individuals with Disabilities Education Act* (1997), which now also applies to children with disabilities in private schools.

A recent trend in early childhood education that influences assessment of academic readiness is inclusion (Allen & Schwartz, 1996: McEvoy, Peterson, & McConnell, 1991; Miller, 1996). Inclusion is defined as a philosophy that is "about belonging to a community of friends, a school community, or a neighborhood" (Allen & Schwartz, 1996, p. 2). Inclusive programs often contain elements of developmental curricula and developmentally based evaluation (Miller, 1996). Assessment is viewed as a practice that assists in the inclusion of all children and not one that excludes children because they are not "ready" for a particular academic skill.

© *National Association of School Psychologists. Reprinted by permission of the publisher.*

In an inclusive early childhood program for children ages 6 to 8, basic academic skills in reading, writing, science, and mathematics are introduced. Assessment of children's basic academic skills needed for readiness is also developmental. That is, readiness measures are used to determine the children's individual needs within a developmental curriculum. Assessment of readiness skills is more "contextually based and formative" (Allen & Swartz, 1996, p. 29).

Overview of Readiness Testing

In the United States' educational history, educators and parents have had varied opinions concerning the timing of educating young children, the content in early childhood programs, developmental stages, and measurements for school readiness (Meisels, 1987; Vinovskis, 1987). In New England, for example, in the late 1600s to mid-1800s, parents were expected to be the primary teachers of reading and writing skills (Vinovskis, 1987). Children were expected to have these skills prior to formal schooling. Not until the mid and late 1800s did parents relinquish their major role in academic readiness. By the second World War, educators had assumed the role of teaching reading, writing, and other academic areas to young children (Gesell & Ilg, 1943). Furthermore, these skills were viewed in the context of the cultural heritage of a democratic society (Gesell & Ilg, 1943).

Educators during the 1930s at the Gesell Institute began to develop school readiness measures to determine if children were developmentally ready to learn in this new school environment that consisted of large groups of children with diverse needs. These measures included reading, computation, and writing readiness, because the focus of literacy instruction had shifted from the home to a school environment.

Since the 1930s, educational researchers have conducted many studies to determine what attributes predict school success and what processes and skills are necessary to learn such skills as reading, writing, and math (e.g., Durkin, 1973). Mild to moderate relationships among these processes (e.g., auditory and visual perception) and school success were revealed (see Gillespie-Silver, 1979 for review); however, the components included in these analyses have traditionally comprised academic readiness measures. Recent notions of readiness also take into account *when* children enter formal education, as it appears that the earlier children begin preschool (e.g., ages 3 and 4), the higher they will score on indicators of readiness (Gullo & Burton, 1992).

Academic Readiness and Preschool Children

In this chapter we present definitions of academic or school readiness (these terms are used interchangeably), the perspectives toward how to ascertain academic readiness, and the purpose of school readiness measures. Also discussed are estimates of reading readiness, the range of measures in school readiness, technical aspects of school readiness, examples of school readiness measures, and alternatives.

Definitions

The professionals of the Gesell Institute define school readiness as "the capacity to simultaneously learn and cope with the school environment" (1987, p. 7). Meisels, Wiske, and Tivnan (1984) define academic readiness as "the domain of specific learning and performance" (p. 26). Meisels (1987) draws a distinction between developmental screening tests and readiness tests: Developmental screening tests provide a brief assessment of a child's developmental abilities—abilities that are highly associated with future school success. Readiness tests are concerned with those curriculum-based skills a child has already acquired—skills that are typically prerequisite for specific instructional programs (p. 4). In this chapter, we focus on those measures that determine academic readiness rather than developmental abilities although we consider both measures to be important in developing an effective program to meet individual needs.

Perspectives on Academic Readiness Measures

According to Ysseldyke and Salvia (1982), two different perspectives on readiness have influenced the nature of academic readiness tests. First, readiness can be viewed as the presence of the behavior, skills, and knowledge that are prerequisites to the mastery of skills or information to be taught. Second, readiness may be viewed as the presence of certain processes (intelligence, discrimination, and so on) that are believed to underlie the acquisition of the behaviors or information to be taught.

Most multidimensional and unidemensional readiness measures have used either skill areas, processes, or a combination of both to determine a child's academic or school readiness. Reading assessment, in particular, is currently undergoing a transition from a "mastery learning" (discrete skill) position to one where reading and writing interact and become what is referred to as an "emergent literacy" (see Teale & Sulzby, 1986 for a review). Assessment from this perspective is described in more detail by Teale, Hiebert, and Chittenden (1987). As long as readiness assessment tools are designed in ways that contradict changes in curricula and pedagogy, providing clear indicators of how young children perform will remain a difficult task. The use of standardized readiness tests is routine in many school districts and is legitimate when time and cost factors are considered. The use of such tests, however, is questionable when they are incongruent with what is being taught, with the developmental changes children experience, and with the processes children go through when they learn.

Purpose of Academic Readiness Tests

The purpose of academic readiness tests varies considerably. The Gesell Institute (1987) states that their assessments are "used by schools to gain fuller developmental understanding of the child" (1987, p. 7). They also note that placement decisions can be made on the screening and diagnostic basis of their measurements. These readiness tests have also been used to identify children at risk or in need of special services (Meisels, 1987). Such a purpose may result in a young child being labeled developmentally delayed, learning disabled, and so on. Similar to identification, tests are used to predict future school success—a purpose that is controversial (Meisels, 1987). Another purpose is to "facilitate curriculum planning" (Meisels, 1987, p. 6). Because of the lack of technical adequacy (see next section), these tests should not be used as the sole determinant for identification of special needs, placement decisions, or as predictors of future school success. A more conservative approach is to use them for curricular planning.

Academic readiness tests vary in structure according to their purposes. Tests that screen are used to find, within groups of children, those who may require further testing. They are not used for placement or identification purposes. Tests that diagnose academic difficulties follow a medical model concept, in which the source of the potential difficulty is derived from an analysis of the symptoms. In this way, appropriate treatment—in this case an educational prescription—is employed. Diagnostic instruments generate data that indicate a child's performance on tasks that are assumed related to later learning. The ability to memorize, order, sequence according to size or position, and solve puzzles are examples. However, this approach usually necessitates the use of a label (e.g., processing deficiency, learning disabled, etc.) which in turn identifies a particular theory of why a child is not learning. Diagnosing academic readiness results in a set of predictions of how a young child will perform when engaged in a future task. It does not, however, yield a set of behavioral indicators identifying what the child is doing (e.g., academically) at the time of assessment. The diagnostic-prescriptive teaching model has relied heavily on this approach to assessment. Here, underlying "abilities" are assessed and may be treated with activities that are designed to "fix" the deficits. Strong arguments have been raised against diagnosing symptoms that are generally irrelevant to instruction. In other words, using school-aged children as an example, assessing a reading problem by focusing on short-term memory processes associated with consonant-vowel-consonant patterns as a source of error would provide a list of symptoms related to reading but not an indisputable explanation of why the problem exists. More so, this assessment would provide scant data relevant to teaching reading and is likely to promote instruction around techniques that attempt to train these underlying processes. Results from diagnostic instruments used with preschool children are especially untrustworthy in that their predictive abilities are less reliable and useful than when used with older children. The validity of using standardized readiness measures for placing children in kindergarten programs that have policy implications may be inappropriate, in that they may be the first branching of low SES and minority children into separate placements (e.g., Ellwein, Walsh, Eads, & Miller, 1991).

Although screening and diagnostic instruments are important in the overall assessment process with young children, instruments that guide instruction and direct the instructional process may be the most worthwhile.

Range of Readiness Measurement Components

For the most part, academic readiness tests contain measures of similar content. As noted earlier in this chapter, many of these components have been found to be related to school success, e.g., language and perceptual skills. These components can be classified into the following domains.

Cognitive or Conceptual.   In this category, readiness tests typically include such concepts as color, quantity, size, time, shape, texture, and direction. Also, problem solving, categorization skills, memory, cause and effect, concrete and abstract concepts may be included in this section.

Motor Development.   Gross motor (large muscle) and fine motor skills are two of the major domains of readiness tests. Hopping, skipping, throwing, and catching are examples of the gross motor skills. Usually, perceptual-motor skills are included in the fine motor skills. The child's ability to combine visual perception, for instance, with fine motor muscle movement such as copying a square, is an example.

Language.   The child's receptive and expressive language may be assessed. Vocabulary, sentence structure, use of pronouns, verb tense, negation, functional use of prepositions and plurals, and phonology (e.g., letter sounds) may be included.

Academic Skills.   This category includes those skills that are traditionally taught in kindergarten and first grade. Letter naming, letter recognition, alphabet recitation, counting, numerical recognition, and name writing are examples.

General Knowledge.   Many of these tests include such basic knowledge as a child's address, telephone number, age, body parts, and time awareness as assessment of the child's basic experience and knowledge.

Social Competence and Emotional Development.   More recently, social awareness, social skills, interests, and emotional development have been included on readiness tests. Play skills, self-direction, personal responsibility, recognition of facial expressions of emotions, and "social thinking" are skills learned. For example, the *Help for Special Preschoolers Assessment Checklist: Ages 3–6* (Santa Cruz County, 1987) has an overall category termed "social skills" that includes adaptive skills (e.g., adjusts behavior to fit rules and routines of different situations), responsible behavior (e.g., makes own decision concerning activities with minimal adult supervision), and inter-personal relations (e.g., shows affection for familiar person). Often, self-help skills and personal safety skills are also included.

Process Skills.   A loosely defined category of skills that may cross several domains; e.g., perception (auditory, visual, and motor), attention, concentration, and organization. The *Gesell School Readiness Test*—Complete Battery (Gesell Institute, 1978), has tasks that assess children's ability to organize their thoughts and to attend. The child's ability to follow directions, and to remember two- or three-step commands, for example, are assessed by many readiness tests.

In summary, most multi- and unidimensional readiness tests contain similar components. These components may be skill (e.g., rote naming of the alphabet) or process-related (e.g., visual discrimination of similar and dissimilar visual features). Many of the components have been found to relate, in some degree, to school achievement. The more traditional readiness tests, e.g., the Gesell and the Metropolitan Readiness Test (Nurss & McGauvran, 1986), may not reflect current research concerning children's development with regard to such skills as reading and writing. For example, while a readiness test may assess the child's ability to name the alphabet and to identify initial and final sounds, the test may not determine the child's awareness of how books work (i.e., books begin and end in a certain manner), or the relationship between oral speech and written language (Schickedanz, 1986). When assessing writing, a child's ability to copy figures or to write the alphabet may not disclose the child's knowledge of the audience or the impact of a written message (Schieckedanz, 1986). These untested skills may, in fact, be the ones that determine the child's academic success. As more research is generated in these areas, readiness tests may begin to reflect these findings.

Authentic Assessment of Academic Readiness

Educational reform in recent years has promoted efforts to align assessment and instruction in more meaningful and useful ways. Essentially, educators are seeking ways in which children become fully involved in the evaluation of their own achievements. With notice to the limits of how traditional (standardized) tests can inform the day-to-day curriculum, many are turning to what are commonly referred to as authentic assessments. Heavily influenced by the emergence of constructivism (theory and practice) in education, these assessments utilize techniques that are "alternatives" to traditional means by relying on indicators of "performance" that are "authentic" with respect to the content, the learning context, and to the student alike (e.g., culture, ethnicity, special needs). Authentic assessments immerse educational tests within the context of "real-world" tasks and activities and are being advanced as approaches that will strengthen the validity and utility of educational assessments.

For understanding academic readiness in young children from an authentic perspective, portfolios of student work offer the most promise. A portfolio is an ongoing account of what a child knows, compiled by the child herself and augmented by information from a teacher (and others where appropriate). The portfolio, as described by Arter and Spandel (1992), is a purposeful collection of a student's work, effort, and achievement in a given area. Meisels and Steele (1991) see the widespread use of portfolios to have potential to shift the structure of classrooms to meet the developmental range of student needs.

While this approach may appear quite valid (at least in terms of face validity) will it indeed produce outcomes that accurately reflect if a young child is ready for academics? This question is best answered when notions of validity are framed from the relationship between curricular expectations and the utility of the knowledge acquired. Mesick (1989) considers this relationship to be the heart and soul of construct validity. Mesick feels that this can only be accomplished when teachers use a multitude of sources for evidence and that the indicators of knowledge existing in the portfolio are linked to the construct or intent of the unit around which the portfolio is developed. That is, what is the purpose of the portfolio and is the purpose stated clearly? For readiness, teachers must know how to interpret the pieces that comprise the portfolio in terms of a clear "agreement" of what constitutes academic readiness. Not only what work samples (and drafts of work samples) should be included, but how do children get the opportunity to select items to place in their portfolios and reflect upon them? Also, serious consideration needs to be given to how the portfolios are to be used. Since they are essentially a "within student" assessment (i.e., a child's performance is sequentially developed and compared to herself) can accurate "between student" and eventually "between school" comparisons be made?

The performance activities of the portfolio should contain the skills a child will need to be successful when encountering future academic tasks. The authentic nature of portfolios is enhanced when (1) they allow children to demonstrate what they know in relationship to the objectives of a unit, (2) they give children ample opportunities to express the skills they know and the processes they use that relate the skills to concepts, (3) they have agreed-upon indicators that are reliable and valid, and (4) children themselves understand the purpose of the portfolio, and the expectations that teachers have about what should be included.

Curriculum-Based Assessment and Academic Readiness

Closely related to authentic assessment for academic readiness is *curriculum-based assessment* (CBA). Models for CBA focus on the interrelated aspects of specific skills and instruction and the sequence of skills and knowledge within a broad content domain to which a child is exposed. This content domain is typically prescribed by the class or school curriculum, and a student's ability is referenced against the curricular requirements. The strength of CBA is its direct relevance to the existing curriculum, and that the skills and knowledge applicable to the curriculum comprise the assessment measures (Deno, 1985). In many ways, CBA could be considered the cornerstone on which portfolios and other forms of authentic assessment are based. That is, an authentic representation of readiness does not exist in a vacuum but is a construction based on an amalgam of existing basic skills and knowledge.

CBA techniques for readiness have the advantage of being keyed to the curriculum, unlike many standardized tests, and therefore they enable teachers to evaluate a child's readiness according to local norms. Children can be compared to their peers or other local reference groups. Also, CBA offers more relevant information about gaps in instruction or other basic skills that are missing from a child's repertoire that the teacher can use when planning lessons and activities. More objective assessment information about student progress results from teachers who utilize CBA, and this evidently contributes to gains in achievement for students (Fuchs, 1986; Fuchs, Fuchs, & Strecker, 1989).

A CBA approach to academic readiness would involve developing a sample of readiness activities that are evaluated repeatedly over time, perhaps as often as two to three times each week. The results of each evaluation or "probe," would be recorded and charted, and aligned with the results of preceding probes of the same skill. While the general structure of CBA enables teachers and administrators to view a child's readiness to learn based on local norms, it also enables teachers to develop instruction and assessment in a way such that children's growth is compared to themselves, or is *criterion-referenced*. Curriculum-based assessment is driven by clear goals and objectives that are written in observable and measurable terms.

Readiness for mathematics using CBA might be developed in the following way. For example purposes, consider math readiness skills to include understanding sets and number concepts (obviously there are many more). A CBA would start with clear objectives about each readiness skill, e.g., to be able to recognize the one-to-one correspondence between one object and the number one, two objects and the number two, three objects and the number three, and so on. A series of activities would be designed where children would be expected to identify numbers of objects, place them in sets, and count aloud as they work through the tasks. The activities would logically begin in an ascending sequence of complexity; once they were mastered, they would be arranged randomly to test for maintenance and generalization. Prior to implementing the activities a teacher would predetermine the number of activities of each variety to take place, the number of trials for each activity, and when data about a child's performance would be collected. At these points, measures of performance would be calculated, e.g., the percent correct of number–object correspondences identified. These data would be chartered, monitored, and compared to previous data to determine progress and to make decisions, i.e., the need to shift the pace or complexity of the activities, or when to move on to new objectives.

Format of Readiness Tests

Academic or school readiness tests vary considerably in format; i.e., administration, examiners, time requirements, response requirements, means of gathering information, scoring, and actual test kit material.

Readiness tests are either group or individually administered, a factor that may be an important consideration in test selection. For example, *the Gesell School Readiness Screening Test* (Gesell Institute, 1978) and the *BRIGANCE® K & 1 Screen Test* (Brigance,

1987) are individually administered, while the *Metropolitan Readiness Tests* (MRT) (Nurss & McGauvran, 1986) are suitable for group use.

Means of information gathering vary considerably with a range that includes structured interview questions, checklists for behaviors a caregiver can recall while observing the child perform, formal observation techniques, specific task performance, oral and written observation responses concerning skills, and structured interactions in controlled settings. Some tests may include a combination of these formats, such as structured observations of tasks and interviews with parents and teachers. Time requirements are affected by these varying information-gathering techniques. For example, a checklist of basic school skills based on prior knowledge of the child's performance may require no more than 5 to 8 minutes to complete. A more extensive performance based on task-specific readiness tests may require 100 minutes to complete (e.g., the Metropolitan Readiness Test). Also, the number of items may range from 15 (e.g., the Meeting Street School Screening Test, Hainsworth & Siqueland, 1986) to over 100 items (e.g., Clymer-Barrett Readiness Test, Clymer-Barrett, 1967).

Examiner qualifications also vary. In many cases, the tests may be administered by early childhood teachers. Some checklists or observational systems may be completed by parents; other tests require a trained examiner (e.g., Gesell). Test contents also vary. Most tests include a manual with test items and sets of tests booklets. Some tests include such materials as a storage box, picture cards, building blocks, scissors, beanbags, letter and number charts, and so on. Some manuals include videotapes to assist in administration and scoring and technical data if available.

Another important component to consider in the selection of an academic readiness test is its reflection of the child's culture. Several academic readiness tests are available in languages other than English. If young children from linguistically diverse backgrounds are enrolled in the school, early childhood educators should select tests that are translated into the appropriate language. Unfortunately, because most of these academic readiness tests reflect an Anglo American culture, the young child may be unfamiliar with some concepts, vocabulary, and experiences presented. Also, simply translating test items into another language without restandardizing the test on children from that culture may provide unreliable scores. Chapter 16 in this text provides a further discussion on cultural differences and assessment.

In summary, the choice of an academic or school readiness test may depend on such factors as whether the tests are individual or group tests, type of administration, number of items, and time requirements.

Multidimensional Academic Readiness Tests

In this section, we present a review of selected multidimensional academic readiness tests offering a list of norm-referenced and criterion-referenced tests that are popular among early childhood educators and provide useful results.

A norm-referenced test compares a child's performance against the performance of a group. The following norm-referenced academic readiness tests are reviewed: (1) Woodcock-Johnson Psycho-Educational Battery—Revised (WJ-R; Woodcock & Johnson, 1989); (2) Mullen Scales of Early Learning (MSEL; Mullen, 1995); (3) the Metropolitan Readiness Test (MRT; Nurss & McGauvran, 1986), (4) Comprehensive Test of Basic Skills (CTBS; McGraw-Hill, 1990), (5) Peabody Individual Achievement Test—Revised (PIAT-R; Markwardt, 1989), (6) Test of Early Reading Ability (TERA; Reid, Hresko, & Hammill, 1989), (7)

Key Math Diagnostic Inventory of Mathematics—Revised (Connolly, 1988); and (8) Test of Early Mathematics Ability (TEMA; Ginsburg & Baroody, 1990).

With criterion-referenced tests, content areas are arranged according to curriculum scope and sequence with selected items representing each area. Test results provide teachers with information about where to begin instruction, in which areas or domains children are deficient, and the progress of individual children. Criterion-referenced tests are designed on the assumption that learning occurs along a skill continuum, with performance criteria available at any point. With criterion-referenced tests, skill attainment is referenced against the examinee's previous performance and not against another individual or group. These tests are an outgrowth of the behavioristic or task analytic approach and its attempts to individualize instruction. Representative criterion-referenced tests presented are: (1) the BRIGANCE® Inventory of Early Development—R (Brigance, 1991) and (2) the Portage Classroom Curriculum Checklist (Brinkerhoff & Portage Staff Associates, 1987).

Norm-Referenced Tests

The Woodcock-Johnson Psycho-Educational Battery—Revised (WJ-R). The Woodcock-Johnson Psycho-Educational Battery—Revised (WJ-R) was first developed in 1977 and revised in 1989. This test is a set of wide-age-range, individually administered standardized activities that measure cognitive abilities, scholastic aptitudes, achievement, and interests. The cognitive ability portion of the test is based on the theory that intelligence is comprised of fluid and crystallized abilities (Woodcock, 1990) suggested by Horn and Cattell (1966). It is designed for individuals from age 2 to adult and grades K–12, and college. The cognitive battery consists of 21 subtests, with 7 subtests comprising the standard battery and 14 subtests the supplemental battery. The battery may be administered in its entirety, or single subtests or clusters of subtests may be administered to meet specific appraisal needs. A variety of scores are available for the entire battery and for the clusters.

Normative data for the revised test were gathered from more than 6,300 children and adults ranging in age from 2 to 90+. The sample was proportional to national representations of region, sex, community size, race, and ethnicity. Children whose sole placement was in special education or who had less than one year's experience within an English-language classroom were excluded.

The WJ-R has psychometric properties that make it useful for assessing preschool children. For one, it is among the better technical instruments (along with the Bayley Scales of Infant Development) that measure intelligence, through it (like the Bayley) loses power at the lower end of the preschool years (Flanagan & Alfonso, 1995). While the WJ-R is a popular member of the assessment battery used to identify a learning disability, some research questions its use in that there may be subtest overlap for students with learning disabilities (e.g., McGue, Shinn, & Ysseldyke, 1982) and the overall test may indeed be comprised of only two highly correlated factors, one involving the use and comprehension of language and the other, number skills (e.g., Sinnett, Rogg, Benton, Downey, & Whitfill, 1993).

The following subtests included in the WJ-R *Early Development Scale* are most likely to yield information about a young child's cognitive ability. The standard battery for the Early Development Scale includes the following subtests.

Memory for Names Children demonstrate their ability to make associations between familiar and unfamiliar auditory and visual stimuli. Each step requires a child to view a "space creature" and is told its name. A page of nine space creatures is then presented and the child is asked to point to the creature just introduced, and to previously introduced pictures. Theoretically, this subtest measures long-term storage and retrieval.

Memory for Sentence Using an auditory tape, children are required to repeat single words, sentences, and phrases. Sentence meaning can be used to aid recall. This subtest measures short-term memory and attention.

Incomplete Word A child is asked to listen to an auditory tape of words that have missing phonemes and then complete the word. This subtest measures auditory closure and auditory processing.

Visual Closure This subtest measures visual processing by having children identify a drawing or picture that is altered in one or several ways, such as missing lines or areas, superimposed patterns, or other distortions.

Picture Vocabulary This subtest primarily measures comprehension knowledge by asking children to recognize or name familiar and unfamiliar pictured objects. For very young children, entry level items are multiple choice and only require a pointing response.

From the WJ-R supplemental battery, the following subtests can be included in the Early Development Cluster.

Visual–Auditory Learning. Rebus symbols are used to measure a child's ability to associate new visual symbols with familiar words. Words are expressed orally and translated into verbal sentences. This subtest contributes to understanding a child's long-term memory ability.

Memory for Words. Short-term memory and attention are measured by requiring a child to repeat lists of unrelated words in the correct sequence. Words are presented from an auditory tape. The list begins with single words and increases to eight-word sentences.

Sound Blending. An audio tape presents syllables and phonemes of words. The child must then say the whole word. Auditory processing ability can be determined from this subtest.

Picture Recognition. This subtest requires a child to recognize a subset of previously presented pictures within a field of distractors. Since this subtest intends to measure visual processing, a number of distractors and stimuli are presented in order to reduce the likelihood that verbal mediation strategies are being used to assist recall.

The achievement portion of the WJ-R (standard and supplemental batteries) is available in forms A and B. Skills measured are associated with reading, mathematics, written language, broad knowledge of science social studies, humanities, skills for letter–word identification, applied problem solving, and dictation. For young children, as with the cognitive battery, an Early Development Scale is available. This scale includes the standard subtests for the following curricular areas:

Reading

Letter–Word Identification: The first items involve symbolic learning by having a child match pictograph representations of words with actual pictures of objects. Subsequent items begin with isolated letter identification and become more difficult as the test advances.

Mathematics

Applied Problems: This subtest measures a child's ability to analyze and solve practical math problems. The child must first recognize the procedure to follow, then perform the calculation. The first items have children identifying the number of fingers and of objects (e.g., how many apples?).

Knowledge

Science: This subtest asks a child about his/her knowledge of biological and physical science. Eight of the early items require only a pointing response and the remaining items require an oral response.

Social Studies: This subtest measures a child's knowledge of history, geography, government, economics, and aspects of social studies. Six of the early items only require a pointing response.

Humanities: This measures a child's knowledge of areas of art, music, and literature. Five of the early items only require a pointing response and the remaining items require an oral response.

Mullen Scales of Early Learning (MSEL). The Mullen Scales of Early Learning (MSEL; Mullen, 1995) is an individually administered measure of the cognitive functioning of very young children, infants, and preschoolers from birth to 68 months. This edition of the test combines the original Mullen Scale of Early Learning (MSEL) and the Infant MSEL into a single test with continuous norms. Testing time should range from 15 minutes for very young children to 60 minutes for 5-year-olds.

A representative national sample of 1,849 children ranging in age from 2 days to 69 months was used to develop test norms. African American, Hispanic, and white children from urban and rural settings participated in the standard setting process. The internal median reliability coefficients ranged from .75 to .83; standard error of measurement for the five scales ranged from 4.1 to 5.0 T score points; test–retest for the younger group was .96; median test–retest coefficients for the cognitive scales ranged from .82 to .85 for younger children and from .71 to .79 for the older children; concurrent validity with the *Bayley Scales of Infant Development* (Mental Development Index) ranged from .53 to .59 for the Cognitive Scales and from .21 to .52 with the *Bayley Psychomotor Development Index.* Other validity data are reported, such as comparisons to *Preschool Language Assessment, Peabody Developmental Motor Scales,* and the original *Mullen Scales.* One study reported in the manual indicates the validity of Mullen to predict school readiness for preschool and kindergarten achievement.

The test kit is replete with materials that are common to tests of cognition for young children. Among the many items are rubber balls, nesting cups, plastic spoons, wooden blocks, shoelaces, and a formboard, to name a few. An administration booklet is included and the directions for each scale list the exact manipulatives needed. Obviously, the use of so many manipulatives while testing young children demands that the examiner maintain a high degree of vigilance to keep the unused items away from the child. All scoring for the Mullen requires the conversion of raw scores to T scores where they are positioned within confidence intervals. The manual directs the examiner in how to establish 90 and 95% confidence intervals using the standard error of measurement.

Normative data can be derived from five specific scales.

Gross Motor Scale.   This test, given only to children from birth to 33 months, measures central motor control and mobility in various sitting and upright positions and unilateral and bilateral control.

Visual Reception Scale.   This assesses a child's ability to process visual information (discrimination and memory) found within patterns.

Fine Motor Scale.   This provides a measure of visual-motor ability associated with laterality, manipulation, and writing readiness.

Receptive Language Scale.   This tests a child's ability to process linguistic input such as auditory sequencing, comprehension, and memory.

Expressive Language Scale.   This measures language output, production, complexity, and verbal concept formation.

A summary, composite score based on the T scores from the four cognitive scales represents general intellectual ability.

Metropolitan Readiness Test (MRT).

The Metropolitan Readiness Test (MRT; Nurss & McGauvran, 1986) is the fifth edition (original test, 1933) in a series of group-administered tests that measure fundamental competencies for reading, mathematics, and language-based activities in young children. The test requires children to respond directly on a form and will take a typical child 80 to 90 minutes to complete the entire battery, although the test is not timed. The current MRT has evolved in response to critics of the readiness construct. That is, sound arguments have criticized readiness tests for their brevity and lack of predictive ability. The MRT is thorough, and newer test items more accurately related to the linguistic properties of reading (e.g., Nurss, 1980), for example, have improved its ability to predict a child's reading capability.

Level I of the test is designed for preschool children (4 years old) prior to entering kindergarten and for children beginning and in the middle of kindergarten. Level I subtests are:

Auditory Memory.   This uses familiar pictures in which the child marks the response that contains the same sequence of nouns read by the teacher.

Beginning Consonants.   The child is shown a picture with four objects and is required to match a given sound to one of the objects.

Letter Recognition.   The child is given four letters and is required to mark the letter named by the teacher.

Visual Matching.   The child matches printed shapes to upper and lower case letters.

School Language and listening.   The child marks from a response array the action or object that describes what the teacher has read.

Quantitative Language.   This measure a child's ability to perform simple arithmetic and to understand one-to-one correspondence and concepts such as "more."

Level II consists of eight subtests and is intended for use with children at the end of kindergarten and the beginning of first grade. These subtests are similar to the Part I subtest and for the purposes of this chapter will simply be listed (see Nurss & McGauvran, 1986 for details). They are Beginning Consonants, Sound-Letter Correspondence, Visual Matching,

Finding Patterns, School Language, Listening, Quantitative Concepts and Quantitative Operations.

Both Level I and Level II provide optional subtests that assess a child's ability to copy names and sentences printed on a sheet. Performance is then compared to samples and rated on a scale from one to five. An *Early School Inventory* (ESI), for children ages 5 to 7, assesses a child's understanding of written language and print. The *Early School Inventory (ESI)-Developmental* is completed by parents and teachers who either "observe" or "not observe" physical, language, cognitive, and socio-emotional related behaviors.

Comprehensive Test of Basic Skills (CTBS). The *Comprehensive Test Of Basic Skills, 4th Edition Forms U and V* (CTBS/McGraw Hill, 1990) is a popular test used with kindergarten through twelfth-grade students. This test is used primarily for gathering achievement measures of students in learning basic skills. Major changes in the latest version include 11 subtests instead of 10, higher ceilings for some tests, two test levels (instead of one) covering ages 4-6 to 6-9, and a new locator or pretest to determine where to start testing. Additionally, the three-parameter Item Response Theory (IRT) is used to develop the test items and for scaling purposes. This theory differs from classical test development methods in that item difficulty (ability), discrimination, and guessing are estimated in ways that are independent of a particular group of examinees (Hambleton, Swaminathan, & Rogers, 1991). This should yield more accurate and unbiased test items.

For this review, portions of the test suitable for children in grades K–1.6 (Levels A and B) are discussed. These children are required to place responses in a test booklet and will take approximately 102 minutes to complete the entire battery (about 20 minutes for each individual test). The areas tested are:

Reading. At the beginning levels orally presented items measure visual and sound recognition of letters, words, vowels, and consonants. Comprehension is measured from sentences read by the examiner. Vocabulary, word attack, and the structural analyses of words are also assessed.

Mathematics. This measures addition, subtraction, multiplication and division. Math application items are included.

Language. This measures the mechanics of language; i.e., capitalization, punctuation, and various expressive language and speech skills.

The CTBS is standardized on a large sample of school aged children and efforts were made to represent minority and ethnic groups. However, the percentages of ethnic minorities or children in large urban settings are not included (Hopkins, 1992). According to the publishers, low item bias for black and Hispanic sample groups were obtained for the latest version. A variety of scoring formats are available, and using the publisher's scoring service is recommended for large data sets. Few special needs children were included in the norm sample and the use of this test with these children would require a criterion-referenced rather than norm-referenced interpretation.

Peabody Individual Achievement Test—Revised (PIAT-R). The *Peabody Individual Achievement Test—Revised* (PIAT-R; Markwardt, 1989) is a norm-referenced test (ages 5-0 to 18-11) that is administered individually and consists of assessment in six content areas: general information, reading recognition, reading comprehension, mathematics, spelling, and written expression. The test results are presented by two composites: *Total Reading* is a combination of the two reading subtests and the total reading test score. *Written expression,* which is a new subtest, is given and scored differently from the other subtests. For Level I, which may be of interest to early childhood educators and assessors because it is appropriate for kindergarten and first grade students, pre-writing skills are measured—"copying and writing letters, words, and sentences from dictation" (p. 1). A written language score may be derived from the Spelling and Written Expression scores combined.

The test may be used to obtain an overall picture of the child's educational attainment; however, it is not designed to be used for diagnostic purposes. Any teacher who spends time learning how to administer the test may become proficient in administering the test; however, the author cautions against interpretations by individuals untrained in psychometrics.

The test was standardized nationally with a representative sample of 1,563 students (K–12) in 33 communities. Also, an additional 175 kindergarten children were tested to add data for beginning kindergarten year performance. Students in special education classes were not included in the standardization. The standardization was representative of geographic region, sex, socioeconomic status, and race or ethnic group. Reliability coefficients for all the subtests exceed the minimal requirement of .80. Most are above .90 with the exception of mathematics at the kindergarten level (.84). The test's validity, as measured by correlation with other tests, is presented in the manual via a number of studies relating the test to the *Wide Range Achievement Test,* Key Math, K-ABC, and so on. The grade equivalent scores may differ significantly from some levels in the Wide Range Achievement Test-Revised (Swanson & Watson, 1989).

The Test of Early Reading—2 (TERA).   *The Test of Early Reading—2* (TERA; Reid, Hresko, & Hammill, 1989) is an individually administered norm-referenced test that, according to the authors, was designed to assess early reading behaviors that are not considered to be reading readiness but, in fact, early literary behavior (p. 2). Sample behaviors are included that relate to the following components: Construction of meaning, print awareness in figural/situational contexts, relational vocabulary, discourse, and knowledge of the alphabet and its functions (pp. 3 to 4). Letter naming, which is considered to be a strong predictor of reading success, and oral reading are also included with other conventions of text, i.e., book handling, left-right orientation, and proofreading. The authors draw heavily on the research of Clay (1979); Yetta and Kenneth Goodman (1979) and Holdaway (1979).

The test may be used with children ages 3 to 9. The test was standardized on a sample of 1,454 children from 15 states. Race, urban–rural, geographic region, age, and sex were appropriately represented. According to the manual, the test has a stability reliability of .89, which exceeds minimum acceptable levels (.80).

The test authors caution against using the TERA-2 to diagnose reading difficulties and/or to plan specific interventions. They note that while the test may indicate "that children are advanced or lagging behind their peers in the acquisition of reading behaviors and knowledge" (p. 19), ongoing assessment is important for determining children's reading acquisition skills. The authors note that validity of a test is a matter of "personal preference" (p. 28). They do present two studies relating the TERA to two other tests, *The Basic School Skills Inventory-Diagnostic (BSSI-D), Reading Sub-test* with a correlations of .61 for Form A and .52 for Form B, and the Paragraph Reading Subtests of the *Test of Reading Comprehension* with coefficients of .36 for Form A and .34 for Form B. Also, the test is based on a whole language perspective, which has drawn a great deal of criticism, especially with recent research that indicates that phonological awareness is highly correlated with determining readiness for reading achievement (Stanovitch, 1994).

Key Math Diagnostic Inventory of Mathematics (Revised). *Key Math Diagnostic Inventory of Mathematics—Revised* (Connolly, 1988) measures an individual's understanding and application of math skills and concepts. Developed for children from kindergarten through grade nine, the Key Math offers both norm-referenced and content-referenced (criterion-referenced) information. Sequences of skills are organized according to the domains of *Basic Concepts, Operations,* and *Application.* Basic Concepts are numeration, rational numbers, and geometry. Operations are addition, subtraction, multiplication, division, and mental computation. Application domains consist of measurement, time and money, estimation, interpreting data, and problem solving. The scope and sequence for each domain was garnered from existing mathematics curricula, national professional organizations for mathematics education, and various research articles.

The revised version of the Key Math was standardized using a national sample of 1,637 subjects, adjusting for regional, ethnic, socioeconomic, and racial proportions. There is ample evidence to demonstrate it has moderate to high content and construct validity with similar mathematics tests. Reliability has also been established using a one-parameter item response model. Essentially, the Key Math measures what it purports to measure and does it in a reliable and trustworthy fashion.

The revised version offers two forms, each of which should take approximately 30 to 40 minutes to administer to young children, and 40 to 50 minutes with older children. Each form yields a variety of scores and comparisons that offer diagnostic, placement, and instructional information. These are norm-referenced scores (e.g., standard scores, percentiles, confidence intervals, grade equivalents, stanines), area scores (between domain comparisons), and subtest, domain, and item analyses. Scoring is relatively straightforward and the protocol yields a score profile for easy analysis.

The utility of the Key Math with young children may be limited due to the nature of the items at the beginning of each domain and the number of these items available that can give an accurate picture of what a child knows. These limits, although more applicable to some domains than others, should be taken seriously when looking for math readiness skills in young children. For instance, the first items in the Numeration Subset of Basic Concepts have to do with counting and ordering numbers form 1 to 5 and from 1 to 9 (a total of 7 items). A child's readiness skills for counting can be generally understood from looking at these items. However, other domains and subsets require knowledge of concepts that may go untapped in young children, not in terms of the child not possessing the concepts per se, but that the limited number of items and the types of items are incapable of uncovering the information. The first two items in the Division subset, for example, require understanding the concepts of "left over" and "equal" and how to organize objects in "sets." These items may not be adequate to fully assess this information. Understanding the subset items in terms of how they ask a young child to respond, the language used, and the number of items available, should be taken into consideration. Otherwise, the Key Math (Revised) has been shown to be a useful tool for developing a profile of math skills in children that relate to how well they will perform when dealing with day-to-day math activities in school. The test results also can provide information that is diagnostic and directly related to instruction—information that can be extremely useful when developing education plans for children with special needs.

Test of Early Mathematics Ability (TEMA-2).   The *Test of Early Mathematics Ability-2* (Ginsburg & Baroody, 1990) is the latest version of a test that intends to provide useful information about children who have learning problems in mathematics or are likely to develop problems. The TEMA-2 has added items more appropriate for preschool children ages 3 to 4. Norms extend until age 8–11. The TEMA-2 is individually administered and, with a few exceptions, is untimed and should be completed within 20 minutes.

The TEMA-2 was standardized on a national sample of children ages 3 to 8 years exhibiting proportional characteristics for sex, residence, race, ethnicity, and geographic area for the general population. The sample was comprised of 75 3-year-old, 173 4-year-old, 182 5-year-old, 209 6-year-old, 147 7-year-old, and 110 8-year-old children. Overall internal consistency reliability was .94; the standard error of measurement was 4 raw score points; the test–retest reliability was .94. In addition, the criterion-related validity was with the original *TEMA* and with two groups of children taking the Math Calculation subtest of the *Diagnostic Achievement Battery.* These coefficients were .93, .40, and .59, respectively.

The TEMA-2 is constructed to assess a child's thinking about mathematics, referred to as informal mathematics, and a child's formal mathematics competence. Informal assessment consists of concepts of relative magnitude, counting, and calculation skills. Formal mathematical competence involves items about knowledge of conventions (reading and writing numbers), number facts, calculation, and base-ten concepts. Scoring requires only the entry of a 1 for correct or 0 for incorrect. The sum of the raw scores correct can be converted to a Math Quotient and Percentile Score.

Criterion-Referenced Academic Readiness Tests (BDIED)

The Revised BRIGANCE® Diagnostic Inventory of Early Development (BDIED).   The BRIGANCE® (Brigance, 1991) is an individually administered criterion-referenced or curriculum-based test for ages ranging from birth to second grade. The new test contains most of the original version. However, a new section, Social and Emotional Development, has been added. The readiness items are based on developmental data (e.g., Gesell & Ilg, 1943) and instructional tasks and curricula typical of the early grades. The readiness sections include reading, math, and manuscript writing. In the reading readiness section are such categories as responses to books, visual discrimination, alphabet recitation, letter identification, and such correlates of reading achievement as auditory discrimination. Also, sight recognition of basic vocabulary (e.g., color words, common signs) is included. In math, number concepts, rote counting, numeral recognition, comprehension, and dictation are included. The test also assesses the child's ability to print his or her name and recognize upper case letters.

The author states that the test is well researched; however, no information is provided concerning reliability and validity (Bagnato, 1985; Carpenter, 1994). In the manual, the examiner is reminded continually that the items represent typical kindergarten, first, and second grade curricula. Also, age norms are provided for some items. The examiner is encouraged to use interview, observations, and formal structured tasks to acquire the information. The test is also in Spanish. While the test results may be beneficial for instructional purposes (instructional objectives are provided), this test also represents what teachers must often teach, rather than how children learn.

The BRIGANCE® K & 1 Screen (Brigance, 1987) is a shorter version of the BDIED. Many of the same items are included in this screening instrument. While the test is individually administered, some of the subtasks may be adapted for small group administration (e.g., visual-motor skills). Parent and teacher rating forms are included for kindergarten and first grade. The items were field tested in the same manner as the BDIED.

Portage Guide and Portage Checklist. The *Portage Guide to Early Childhood Education* (Bluma et al., 1976) and the *Portage Classroom Curriculum Checklist* (Brinkerhoff et al., 1987) are criterion-referenced checklists that were designed originally for assisting in home-based instruction and for the ongoing assessment of skill acquisition. The Portage Project was a federally funded early childhood project based in Wisconsin to serve the needs of children in rural environments. Since 1969, the Project that has served the needs of rural Wisconsin has been replicated nationally and internationally. The checklists are in the areas of motor, self-help, cognitive, social, and language skills and range from infancy to 6 years old. A curriculum accompanies the checklist. Other assessments may be administered to accompany the checklists. The tests also provide a database for a precision-teaching approach which targets specific areas for instruction and conducts ongoing assessment. As with other criterion-referenced tests, especially checklists, technical adequacy is a problem. Since criterion-referenced tests are not generally standardized, reliability information is not available. Also, performance standards are more likely set arbitrarily than empirically (McLoughlin & Lewis, 1990).

Other Criterion-Referenced Tests. Other criterion-referenced checklists for academic readiness are available. For example, the *Help for Special Preschoolers Assessment Checklist* (1987); Ages 3–6 assesses more than 600 skill areas that are developmentally sequenced; the age ranges represent normal developmental milestones.

In summary, criterion-referenced tests and checklists for academic school readiness can best serve the purpose of instructional intervention. These instruments can guide instruction and allow continual data gathering in specific content areas. When a young child's rapidly changing cognitive and social development are considered, this method of assessment may provide the most trustworthy and applicable results. Assessment that is closely related to instruction may allow children to proceed to the next skill level when they are ready and assist teachers to more accurately identify subskills and appropriate materials.

Summary

We have presented an overview of academic readiness testing and a description of the structure and use of many readiness tests. We briefly addressed the technical aspects of readiness and highlighted the general failing of most tests to validly predict how children will perform. It is our contention, however, that assessing academic readiness in young children cannot take place independent of the decision-making process about how, when, and where these children will be educated. It is clear that these decisions require choices.

Choices made when readiness testing is implemented must begin with a serious consideration of how applicable the assessment will be, not only to the curriculum, but to a child's learning process. Identifying specific skills is necessary but not sufficient for a precise insight into how young children actively engage the demands of a classroom and mediate their own learning. There is little doubt that providing learning opportunities during the preschool years with activities that treat all aspects of children, and that recognize their prior experiences and how they function as learners, will better prepare them for future schooling. Readiness measures need to reflect the developmental changes in language and cognition as well as the developmental changes in young children's beliefs and judgments about what they are expected to learn. Readiness testing must embrace this position if assessments are expected to accurately predict how children will become the readers, writers, and calculators of tomorrow. Given the current trend to analyze how children personalize the construction of knowledge while they engage in academics, it may be time to think of assessing readiness from the perspective of dynamic interaction, that is, to focus on the strategies used to accomplish a task (e.g., Heywood, Brown, & Wingenfield, 1990) rather than on a single, unidimensional outcome that is characteristic of many readiness tests. While authentic measures are appealing in how they allow children to build their own representations of what they interpret as meaningful to them, these representations will continue to be held to the same standards for reliability and validity we have come to expect from all assessment techniques and instruments. This is no small task, but the challenge should ultimately result in more useful and worthwhile information about young children and when they are ready to learn and to gain insight and understanding of what they know about themselves as learners.

15 Neuropsychological Assessment of Preschool Children

CELIANNE REY-CASSERLY*

Neuropsychological assessment of the preschool child presents a unique challenge to the clinician in terms of the need for integration of knowledge bases from child development, neurology, developmental neurobiology, child clinical psychology, measurement theory, and traditional neuropsychology. Children with neurological or neurodevelopmental disorders constitute a large subgroup of children referred for assessment at preschool age, since many of these disorders are present congenitally or diagnosed in early childhood. For the preschool population, special approaches to diagnosis and management are required which emphasize developmental theory and accommodate specific psychometric issues.

The field of child neuropsychology developed from adult neuropsychology. Early on, techniques of assessment for children were limited to downward extensions of adult instruments. Whereas this strategy may be employed fairly comfortably (although challenged) with the older school age population, extrapolation to younger children or pre-schoolers is much less productive. Because of the inherent variability in behavior in young children, often especially pronounced in the youngster with neurological compromise, the neuropsychological assessment of preschool children demands an approach which incorporates a developmental perspective. Children are not smaller or less competent adults, but are qualitatively different from adults (Hooper, 1991).

Preschool children in particular are ever-changing with respect to developmental competencies; variability is the hallmark of the young child. Not only do typically developing children vary in their behavior relative to same-age peers, the individual child's behavior varies from day to day. Children's behavior is dynamic and responsive to a range of influences, both internal and external. As our knowledge of development has become more sophisticated, we have come to realize that a linear approach to development, which implies a steady continuum between infancy and adulthood, fails to reflect the variability inherent in children and does not accurately conceptualize the course of their journey from early childhood to adulthood. Consequently, neuropsychological evaluation of preschool children requires a theoretical foundation that includes not only an understanding of brain–behavior relationships, but also, critically, developmental theory. In addition, understanding of neurodevelopmental factors needs to take place in conjunction with an appreciation

*The author wishes to acknowledge Jane Holmes Bernstein for her thoughtful editorial assistance.

281

of an array of social, cultural, and environmental factors. Taylor and Fletcher (1995) argue that although the pediatric neuropsychologist focuses on neurological and cognitive factors, interpreting the impact of these on a child's development, adjustment, and behavior requires an integration of social influences.

Issues in Assessment of Preschool Children

The Nature of the Child

Preschool children present specific challenges which are related to the nature of the child in this age group. (For this chapter, preschool age refers to children aged 3 to 6 years, with occasional inclusion of 2-year-old children.) This period is an intensely active one with respect to brain development, behavioral repertoire, and cognitive change. Typically developing children demonstrate a wide range of variation with respect to developmental timetables (Wolff, 1981). The variable and unpredictable nature of the preschool child has important implications when it comes to issues of reliability and validity of test findings, the interpretation of which can be quite limited unless a comprehensive approach is employed that integrates observations from the test setting and the natural environment. As noted by Wilson (1986) and Hooper (1991), reliability of assessment measures is less certain in the preschool population because of developmental factors, test construction issues, and effects of state, variable concentration, and physiological status. Preschool children with some sort of brain compromise are even more vulnerable to difficulties with regulation of behavior, attention, and stamina (Hooper, 1991), which can profoundly affect quality of test data. Limited test performance is characteristic of the young child; in conducting an evaluation, it is more often the rule than the exception to have few valid, formal test scores available.

The assessment of preschool children requires a flexible approach that can quickly adapt to changing circumstances. Test sessions often require a balancing act, in that materials need to be presented efficiently in order to maintain the young child's interest and cooperation while simultaneously minimizing "empty time" which can promote off-task behavior and interfere with effort. The examiner–child dyad must be analyzed carefully such that the child is provided with the type of support and encouragement to which he or she would be most likely to respond. Limited stamina, variable concentration, increased vulnerability to physiological factors (fatigue, hunger), and lack of experience with the school-related tasks may all interfere with valid assessments of neurodevelopmental status. Preschool children often have not been socialized into dealing with a teacher or evaluator and may respond unpredictably to the testing experience. In addition, preschool children experience particular developmental issues such as separation, individuation, and independence; these may affect or limit cooperation. With the preschool child, the approach to assessment needs to be responsive to the child's developmental status and thus more flexible than the approach used in the more structured school-age or adult settings. This flexibility can only be effected successfully if the neuropsychologist has extensive knowledge of assessment instruments, neuropsychology, and child development.

Developmental Theory

Children grow from the toddler stage of gesturing and few-word utterances to competent, talkative, and creative youngsters who are ready to take on the challenges of formal schooling (Dworkin, 1988). There are qualitative changes in the behavioral repertoire as well as in thinking skills and sense of self (Harris, 1995). Over the course of this time period, postnatal brain development progresses in conjunction with increased elaboration and sophistication of the child's behavior and competencies (Risser & Edgell, 1988). From a developmental perspective, it is important to understand that changes in one arena set the stage for elaboration in the other and vice versa. Fischer and Rose (1994) argue that developing brain functions and behavior move through periods of rapid change that engender periods of discontinuities which are followed by intervals of reorganization and coordination. Developmental change is now interpreted in a more synthetic manner which has promoted a more comprehensive understanding of how behavior emerges. This approach has yielded rich rewards in the areas of motor (Thelen, 1995) and cognitive development (Diamond, 1991). As Thelen cogently argues, this perspective has changed the focus from the structure-function debate, to an appreciation of the dynamic process involved in developmental change. This understanding of the mutually dependent and dynamic nature of the relationship between structure and function needs to be integrated into the neurodevelopmental theory which guides neuropsychological assessment. For example, in the case of the child with early acquired or congenital brain compromise, development proceeds as the disorder is incorporated into the developmental course and affects interactions with the world on multiple levels. From a neuropsychologist's point of view, the impact of a particular neurodevelopmental disorder needs to be understood in the context of the multiple systems which have an impact on the child and in the context of the systems the child impacts. This systemic view is elegantly expressed by Dawson and Fischer (1994, p. xiii):

> ...complexities of human nature can be understood best by examining interfaces among systems at several levels, including the neurophysiological, behavioral, and social-contextual levels...People are biological organisms, after all, and our activities and thoughts can be understood only by situating us properly with a brain in a body in an eventful world abounding with objects and people.

Psychological clinicians dealing with young children also need to be concerned with the issue of development in the context of the timing and impact of neurodevelopmental deficits. As Bernstein and Waber (1990) point out, in developmental neuropsychology the crucial questions are not related to localizing brain damage but to ascertaining how the child has been affected during which period of development. With respect to the goals of assessment, the neuropsychologist's focus, in many ways, is concordant with the parent's concern with the overall adaptation of the child, and not merely on test performance. Given the nature of the particular compromise, a child may present "on developmental track," i.e., functioning more or less appropriately in the natural environment, or "off developmental track" and limited in adaptive functioning (Bernstein, Prather, & Rey-Casserly, 1995). A dynamic understanding of development underlies this categorization; the child who is "off developmental track" as a consequence of neurodevelopmental deficits is forging a new and unique path whose hills and valleys cannot be understood without a neurodevelopmental theory that is dynamic and systemic (Bernstein & Waber, 1990). Even the child who is "on developmental track" overall, but demonstrates specific neuropsychological issues, will face different challenges as he or she travels through development. It is the role of the developmental neuropsychologist to understand "the whole child" and guide interventions and management to optimize functional adaptation over time.

Psychometric Considerations

There has been little focused attention in neuropsychology on the preschool population and there has been a lag in the development of appropriate assessment instruments (Wilson, 1986). Although a comprehensive children's battery has just been published (Korkman, Kirk, & Kemp, 1998), the fact that there has not been a standardized "neuropsychological assessment battery for preschool children" available has fostered the conception that neuropsychology does not apply to this population. This narrow conceptualization of neuropsychology implies that the field is limited to tests, and is not based on an integrated understanding of brain–behavior relationships. Tests are essentially one component of assessment but do not comprise the totality of the endeavor. As Taylor (1988) aptly states "...any test that neuropsychologists or others are willing to use to make CNS inferences qualifies as neuropsychological" (pg. 795).

The issue of the appropriateness of testing in the preschool population is a controversial topic in the field of early intervention. Some have urged that intelligence tests in particular be banned from use in early intervention assessments. Neisworth and Bagnato (1992) argue that intelligence test findings with young children are unstable, vulnerable to misuse, insensitive to individual differences, and generally of limited usefulness. Certainly, intelligence tests have been misused to inappropriately label children and thereby limit opportunities. This has been most detrimental when dealing with children from culturally diverse backgrounds. Instead of eliminating intelligence tests, the focus should be on devising more appropriate and comprehensive assessment strategies. Neisworth and Bagnato's argument presumes that the goal of an assessment strategy is to obtain an IQ score and not to provide an integrated and comprehensive picture of the whole child. In reply to Neisworth and Bagnato, Gyurke (1994) points out that the authors are assuming that all intelligence tests are the same (infant and preschool) and that they have over-emphasized the importance of IQ scores and minimized the contribution of the evaluator. Neuropsychologists need to understand the difficulties inherent in making predictions from early childhood assessment instruments and limitations in the tests themselves. It has been demonstrated that predictability is greatly enhanced if multiple assessment points are used, timing of assessment is addressed, and other variables are integrated in the assessment process. For example, in a study of a sample of low-birth-weight children, the ability to predict outcome was significantly increased when data from multiple assessment points and social factors were factored into the equation (Rey-Casserly, 1982).

Valid assessments also require in-depth knowledge of test instruments and how they function with particular populations or contexts. Although several tests purport to assess general intellectual ability in the preschool period, they are not interchangeable. The tests vary with respect to normative data, composition of subtests, item selection, item gradients, test demands, and statistical factors (Kamphaus, Dresden, & Kaufman, 1993). These tests have particular strengths and limitations that vary according to context. Consequently, when dealing with special populations, the tests must be carefully selected and not used without attention to these complex variables. Furthermore, the assessment needs to be broad-based and not just produce an IQ score. The IQ score is a global measure that cannot provide specific information with respect to the pattern of processing skills in a particular individual. IQ tests fail to capture specific areas of competence such as information processing skills and social adaptation (Fletcher, Taylor, Levin, & Satz, 1995) and the tests do not assess aspects of "real world" functioning which are crucial to adaptation; the ecological validity of certain instruments can be quite limited. Furthermore, IQ test findings may be unduly biased when dealing with children from diverse cultural and linguistic backgrounds. For children from culturally diverse backgrounds the use of standardized measures presents problematic issues such as inappropriate standardization samples, insufficient test floors, multiple language backgrounds and inadequate translations, sampling bias, item difficulty differences, and poor predictive validity (Mellor & Ohr, 1996).

Preschool intelligence tests vary with respect to a range of factors including technical characteristics, interface with the child, item selection and order, and psychometric properties. There has been serious concern over floor and ceiling effects of these instruments in the preschool population. In a recent review of intelligence tests for preschool children (Flanagan & Alfonso, 1995), the weakest areas identified were inadequate test floors and item gradients. These difficulties have been reported in the Stanford-Binet Intelligence Scale: Fourth Edition (Thorndike, Hagen, & Sattler, 1986), which—though it purports to be applicable to children as young as 2 years of age—can be insensitive to variations in ability in the younger child. A review of the test (Reynolds & Kamphaus, 1990) notes that the Stanford-Binet Composite score is unable to diagnose mild deficits before the age of 4 years and can fail to detect moderate retardation until the child is well into preschool age (5 years old). These data argue for careful consideration of test characteristics before selecting a specific test of intellectual ability.

In addition to the limitations of IQ scores in particular, a rigidly test- or score-based diagnostic strategy is likely to limit diagnostic and outcome information. Relying, for example, on tests and on an "additive" strategy, that is, a summation of information provided by level of performance across tests in order to localize the source of behavioral dysfunction, can be effective within adult models of brain–behavior relationships but, in the developmental context, can lead to "false negative" conclusions. It can also contribute to a picture of the child as a "bundle of deficits" instead of an active, developing individual. It is important to note that there are no neuropsychological tests that target specific brain areas exclusively. Even in the intact adult brain, very few tasks are domain- or brain system-specific (Weintraub & Mesulam, 1985). Thus, a low score on a specific task is not diagnostic by itself nor does it always indicate compromise in a given system. A child's low score on a test may reflect the functioning of a spared system or the effects of compensatory strategies, since the child may have had to learn to solve a given functional problem by alternate means. This is a salient issue in the preschool population, in that an early neurodevelopmental disorder is considered likely to derail normal functional development, yet test performance may reflect adaptation or establishment of compensatory pathways in response to the neurological insult. Alternatively, early neurological compromise may lead to deficits that can only be readily seen later in development in the context of changing environmental demands. Tests elicit different data in varying contexts due to test construction factors and differences in demand (interface with the child). Children in particular may do very well under the highly structured conditions of testing and with specific test materials. They may nonetheless demonstrate deficits in performance in less structured situations or when skills are to be demonstrated in the natural environment.

Reliability and predictability are active areas of investigation in the area of preschool assessment. Nevertheless, despite extensive efforts in this area, findings pertaining to the ability of preschool measures to predict educational success or failure remain contradictory. Hooper (1988) argues that this has occurred because of simplistic goals (attempting to find a single "best" or group of predictors), limited conceptualizations of outcome, and, most importantly, failure to incorporate and be guided by a comprehensive neurodevelopmental theory: "...prediction of learning disabilities during the preschool years is complex and, consequently, any neuropsychological assessment strategy must be dynamic and multifaceted" (p. 334).

Models of Assessment

There are few formal diagnostic strategies in the literature specifically designed for the preschool child. In the early days, neuropsychological approaches were limited to downward extensions of adult batteries and the use of single, global measures of outcome were common. Flexible or informal batteries are now the rule as fixed battery approaches have been found to be limited and narrow, especially in the context of children with complex medical disorders (Baron, Fennel, & Voeller, 1995). These informal or flexible batteries are created to tap a range of behaviors using developmentally appropriate instruments. Specific inferences or assumptions are made regarding a test's ability to measure a particular neuropsychological construct. Hooper (1991) presents a range of preschool assessment instruments available to assess neuropsychological functioning in the areas of lateral dominance, motor, attention, sensory-perceptual, language, memory, problem solving, preacademic skills, and behavior. He also distinguishes two types of flexible approaches that have been developed for use with preschool children—clinical and empirical. The clinical approaches generally follow a flexible battery approach and select tests to assess the range of neuropsychological constructs. The specific tests that comprise the battery are not the critical issue here; rather, one is interested primarily in how the tests are employed to generate a diagnostic picture. Empirical approaches generally employ factor-analytic strategies to quantify the contribution of specific variables to a particular outcome measure, usually academic performance or reading competence, at later school age. Though the latter approaches contribute significantly to our understanding of possible precursors of reading disorders, their usefulness in the context of neurologically compromised children can be limited (Hooper, 1991).

A clinical approach to preschool assessment based on a branching model has been applied to preschool children with language disorders (Wilson, 1986; Wilson & Risucci, 1986; VanSanten, Black, Wilson, & Risucci, 1994). The clinical examination is guided by a hypothesis testing strategy based on the child's pattern of responses. Neuropsychological constructs are broken down into component factors which are assessed individually to ascertain the relative contribution of specific areas of functioning to performance in a given area. These factors are then profiled to describe a pattern of performance that then can be grouped within a typological system. Wilson's approach is basically a diagnostic one that tends to focus on areas of weakness, which are examined in detail to ascertain the purported basis of the deficit. It can be argued that detailed examination of areas of strength could provide just as meaningful information for the diagnostic profile. Wilson also recognizes that the model cannot function without clinical observational data, but that techniques for operationalizing or quantifying such data are yet to be developed.

Bernstein and Waber (1990) describe a developmental systems approach to neuropsychological assessment that is particularly applicable to the challenges presented by the preschool child. The focus of the approach is to understand the role of developmental change and neurobehavioral compromise within a systems model. In the area of preschool assessment, this is particularly important in that these children often demonstrate very early brain insults which can disrupt normal brain processes and thus change the development of the neural substrate subserving behavioral development. Bernstein and Waber present a diagnostic strategy which integrates development and neuropsychological theory with clinical-observational and test data in a broad, multifaceted manner which not only assists in generating a diagnosis but also provides a strategy for management and risk assessment. In this model, neurobehavioral systems are reviewed much in the manner developed in behavioral neurology but in the context of the systems affecting the child's development. The strategy emphasizes integration of data from various sources and does not rely exclusively on test data. History is reviewed in detail; observations are obtained from the test setting and from a range of sources (direct and indirect) to provide a more complete picture of the "whole child" within his or her environment; and tests and techniques are selected to tap basic domains of behavior (neurobehavioral systems) and to test specific hypotheses generated by the integration of observational and historical data. Quantitative (level of performance) and qualitative data (approach to solution) are analyzed in a complementary fashion. The information thus obtained is integrated with neuropsychological and developmental theory and databases to generate a diagnostic behavioral cluster which then guides strategies for management.

Within this model, the history is examined with a view towards examining the multiple systems which have an interactive impact on the child and the family. One attends to the child's cultural and linguistic experiences and attempts to understand how this interacts with the child's neurological disorder, the family's adaptation, the specific developmental challenges the child faces, and the particular demands presented by the various test materials. For example, it is important to know about a particular family's philosophy with respect to independence and self-help skills before one assesses this area with a standardized interview instrument such as the Vineland Adaptive Behavior Scales (Sparrow, Balla, & Cicchetti, 1984).

It is critical to assess neurodevelopmental factors and address not only "what" has happened to the child but "when" and in what context (Bernstein, 1994). The timing of developmental deviations can be crucial; these can occur at any point in a child's life, in utero, perinatally, or in childhood. The timing factor is also important with respect to "when" the assessment takes place (immediately following brain injury, during recovery, etc.). The intersection between the child's neuropsychological compromise and developmental challenges can reveal different data as a function of the timing issue. A clear example of this comes from current approaches to the study of specific groups of children at risk for neuropsychological compromise. Waber and McCormick (1995) report that in a sample of low-birth-weight premature children, visual motor deficits appear to resolve over time but difficulties with integration and organization of complex visual motor materials emerge later in development. Following a brain injury, children may develop compensatory systems that support recovery and adaptation; conversely, they may also develop different difficulties as a function of changing expectations and requirements for higher order, complex information processing. They may be seen to "grow into deficits" and this may be interpreted as regression or deterioration if a developmental neuropsychological perspective is not employed.

A comprehensive view of the child's functioning in the real world can provide valuable clues to assist in generating a diagnosis and an intervention plan. This is especially important when dealing with the preschool child, since formal test data may be of limited value. Therefore, it is important to obtain information from the natural environment (through interviews, questionnaires, and collateral contacts) and assess the preschool child on more than one occasion. In addition, many behavioral changes noted in preschool children with neurological compromise may be observable in certain contexts, but not apparent in structured, one-to-one testing situations nor captured by specific tests. Direct observations provide crucial data and can be validated when supported by concordance with indirect observations of parents, teachers, and other professionals. In this regard, psychological expertise and training play an important role in the evaluation and interpretation of the observational data obtained from other parties. A trained clinician can assess the "history-giving" potential of an interviewee (parent, teacher) and make clinical judgements regarding the material provided. It is often more useful to elicit actual vignettes of behavior (examples or descriptions) rather than editorial comments.

This systemic model is particularly useful in the assessment of the preschool child because it emphasizes and integrates information from a broad range of sources such that the clinician can look for concordant findings in test data, observations, and history. The characteristic variability of the preschool child need not be as limiting if findings can be validated across domains. The attention to context, development, and multiple inter-related systems can help with making predictions regarding outcome and determining the risks faced by the child in different environments and in the future.

The Tripartite Model of Preschool Assessment

A comprehensive assessment strategy is critical for obtaining a valid and meaningful evaluation of the preschool child that will generate relevant and appropriate intervention strategies, not just for the immediate future but anticipating more long-term risks as well. In the systemic approach to pediatric neuropsychological assessment, clinical information derived from history and observations is accorded comparable weight to the test findings in the diagnostic process. In this model, information is obtained from the history, from observations in the clinical setting and natural environment, and from test performance (quantitative and qualitative analysis). These three areas are all tapped to obtain data regarding functioning in specific domains of behavior. Consequently, the emerging analysis of the neurobehavioral functioning of the child is organized around these functional categories and not solely on the basis of test performance.

Traditional approaches to neuropsychological assessment organize test findings around behavioral domains. What is added in the tripartite model is an integration of information contributed by three sources: history, observations, and testing. Table 15.1 summarizes this matrix of behavioral domains by sources of data. The domains are listed and relevant diagnostic information is described under each heading. "History" refers to material obtained from the clinical developmental history as well as an understanding of the child's social and cultural context. "Observations" include both direct and indirect reports of the child's behavior and focuses on specific competencies as well as weaknesses. "Testing" refers to instruments and formal procedures. Table 15.1 lists tests and procedures that are frequently used in the preschool population; these are referenced in Appendix 15A. This table is not meant to present an exhaustive or ideal list; rather, the goal is to demonstrate the usefulness and structure of the tripartite model of assessment. The history is not conceptualized as a static, moderator variable, but rather as a dynamic process in a developmental context. The view of observations is also broader than in traditional approaches to assessment. The focus here is to understand systemic interactions and to develop a view of how the child functions in different environmental contexts, with the understanding that each places a specific demand on the child–world interaction. Observations are not obtained exclusively in the context of the testing situation, but also include information from parents, teachers, other professionals, and so on. For example, teacher reports of how the child behaves in play, small group, and large group situations can provide information regarding social development, peer relationships, communication skills, and executive functions.

The model also emphasizes rigorous observation in the clinical context. The child's behavioral repertoire is assessed in the office and in the waiting room. The examiner can observe how the child relates to parents and other children as well as how the separation from parents is managed. The examiner also closely observes his or her own behavior. For example, one could identify what types of interventions facilitate separation from the examiner before the testing session. Within the testing situation, some children require modification of language and instructions to improve comprehension. The examiner can focus on which types of changes are required to garner clues about the quality of the child's communicative skills. Observation of problem-solving skills across the evaluation can provide useful data in the area of emerging executive functions. Since there are few well-validated instruments that directly assess problem-solving skills in the preschool child, noting the quality of problem-solving skills throughout the assessment can help identify the types of difficulties faced by the child and the sorts of interventions which can support adaptive performance. In sum, the goal of this model is to promote overall adjustment for the child and not merely to identify a set of difficulties.

Case Example

The following case study presents a young child referred for neuropsychological assessment at preschool age. Principles from the developmental systems model are employed to achieve a comprehensive understanding of this child's current neurobehavioral status and to make predictions about future risks and the need for intervention. This case study presents a child with myelodysplasia and hydrocephalus. Hydrocephalus often accompanies neural tube defects (Wills, 1993). The myelodysplasias are congenital disorders involving malformations of the brain or spinal cord early in gestation. Children with myelodysplasia and hydrocephalus have been the focus of active neuropsychological research. Whereas older studies have emphasized overall IQ as a measure of outcome, more recent studies have focused on examining changes in adaptation over time (Holler, Fennell, Crosson, Boggs, & Mickle, 1995) and on delineating the qualitative patterns of neuropsychological functioning in different domains (Dennis & Barnes, 1993; Yeates, Enrile, Loss, Blumenstein, & Delis, 1995). Myelodysplasia can be seen as a neurodevelopmental disorder that affects neuropsychological, physical, social, and family systems and one that is further complicated by the physical and psychosocial impact of multiple medical procedures and hospitalizations. This case study highlights the complexity of evaluating a preschool child with a significant medical disorder that has implications for physiological and cognitive functions.

"Katie" is a 4-year-old girl who was born with a lumbar level (L5) myelomeningocele, a spinal lesion resulting from a failure of closure of the neural tube. A brainstem malformation (Arnold Chiari type II) frequently seen in children with spina bifida, which is associated with obstruction of cerebrospinal fluid flow, was noted as well. In the neonatal period, Katie underwent surgical closure of the spinal defect and a shunt was placed to correct hydrocephalus.

Myelodysplasia is associated with significant physical complications affecting sensory and motor functions. Katie has paraplegia and limitations in bowel and bladder control. She requires braces or a wheelchair for ambulation. Her development was within

TABLE 15.1 Domains of Behavior—Techniques for Assessment for Preschool Children

History	Observations	Testing
General Cognitive Abilities		
Specifics of developmental history	Reasoning and problem-solving skills across the evaluation	*Wechsler Preschool and Primary Test of Intelligence—Revised (WPPSI-R)*[24]
Acquisition of preacademic skills	Quality of interaction with examiner, parents, peers, siblings	*Differential Ability Scale-Preschool Core (DAS)*[9]
Ability to generalize from one situation to another in language, concepts, experiences	Curiosity and exploratory behavior	*Stanford-Binet Intelligence Scale: Fourth Edition*[22]
Interests/skill in specific activities	Level of imaginary/representative play	*McCarthy Scales of Children's Abilities*[17]
		Kaufman Assessment Battery for Children (K-ABC)[16]
		Woodcock-Johnson Psychoeducational Test Battery—Revised (WJ-R)[27]
		Bayley Scales of Infant Development-II[3]
		Less commonly used:
		Hiskey-Nebraska Test of Learning Aptitude[15]
		Leiter-R Intelligence Scale[19]
		Columbia Mental Maturity Scale[5]
		Pictorial Test of Intelligence (PTI)[12]
		Merrill-Palmer Scale of Mental Tests[21]
Language and language related processing		
Language developmental milestones	Speech parameters: articulation, prosody, pragmatics, semantics, syntax	*Peabody Picture Vocabulary Test-Third Edition* (PPVT-III)*[8]
History of oral-motor development	Quality of conversation with parents or caretaker	*Preschool Language Scale—Third Edition* (PLS-3)*[28]
Quality of communication with peers, parents, teachers	Quality of spontaneous vs. elicited language	*Test of Language Development-Second Edition (TOLD-2)*[18]
Interest and behavior around books, stories	Ability to follow commands	*Gardner Expressive One-Word Vocabulary Test—Revised**[13]
Use of language to generate ideas	Ability to describe experiences, ideas	Verbal subtests of standardized intellectual batteries
Ability to generate language structures and generalize to new situations	Mean length of utterance on informal conversation or language sample	Tests of symbolic play[10,11]
Degree of use of gesture, pantomime	Difference in response to open-ended vs. more structured verbal tasks	*Vineland Adaptive Behavior Scales*-Communication Domain*[20]

Non-verbal processing:

Interest in puzzles, constructional and building toys, video games, etc.
Imitative behavior

Developmental Test of Visual Motor Integration (VMI)[4]
Motor Free Visual Perception Test-Revised[7]
K-ABC Simultaneous Scale[16]
Non-verbal subtests of *DAS, WPPSI-R, McCarthy, Binet*
Wide Range Assessment of Visual Motor Abilities-Drawing, Matching[2]

Visual acuity
Quality of scanning
Navigation in space; exploratory activity
Visual locomotor functioning
Quality and coordination on manipulative tasks
Attention to details of visual materials

Executive functions

Regulation of state
Sleep patterns
Self-soothing capacity
Behavioral problems
Distractibility, impulsivity
Ability to sit still, stick with an activity
Ability to control aggression
Frustration tolerance
Medication history

Level of alertness (arousal)
Observation of problem solving behaviors across the evaluation
Ability to deal with frustration
Attention/behavior regulation
Quality of goal directed behavior
Active coping skills
Ability to inhibit inappropriate or irrelevant responses (inhibitory controls)
Ability to respond and adjust to changing environmental parameters (shift set)

WPPSI-R Animal Pegs[24]
Preschool continuous performance tasks
Goodman Lock Box[14]
Tests requiring auditory-verbal retention or short-term memory (sentence memory, bead memory, etc.)
Disc-Ring Transfer Task (Tower of Hanoi)[25]

Memory

Reported acquisition of knowledge
Ability to learn names, places, and events associated with each

Parent or school reports regarding acquisition of general information and ability to retain over time

Differential Ability Scale: Recall of Digits, Recall of Objects[9]
McCarthy Memory Scale[17]
Wide Range Assessment of Memory and Learning (WRAML)[1]
Binet 4 Bead Memory, Sentence Memory[22]
K-ABC Face Recognition, Hand Movements, Number Recall, Word Order, Spatial Memory[16]

(continued)

TABLE 15.1   Continued

History	Observations	Testing
Social/emotional adjustment		
History of overall adjustment—developmental tasks: separation, toilet training, social interactions, behavior regulation	Play observation by teachers, parents Behavior questionnaires and rating scales Observation of affect regulation, mood, social interaction in the evaluation Social cognition and language pragmatics	Interview with child Analysis of themes of play and social interaction Analysis of narrative information[23] *Home Observation for Measurement of the Environment (HOME)*[6] *Vineland Socialization Domain*[20] Drawings
Preacademic skills		
History of adjustment to school-type settings Interest in books, letters, numbers Ability to recognize familiar letter patterns (signs, names, etc.)	Observation of understanding of number concepts, colors, letters, emerging sound-symbol relationships, language and relational concepts	*Achievement Scale (K-ABC)*[16] *WJ-R Achievement*[27] *WPPSI-R Arithmetic, Information*[16] *DAS Matching Letter Like Forms; Early Number Concepts*[9]
Motor		
Developmental history; activity preferences and opportunities Reports of occupational or physical therapy evaluations and treatment	Observation of gait, balance, bimanual coordination, negotiation of obstacles Quality of motor output, manipulation of materials	*Purdue Pegboard*[26] *Vineland Motor Domain*[20] *McCarthy Motor Scale*[17] *WRAVMA-Pegboard*[2] *Motor Coordination (Beery)*[4]

*Spanish version available

normal limits with respect to acquisition of language and social skills. Fine motor difficulties have been noted in addition to the gross motor disability. She was involved in early intervention and currently attends an integrated preschool setting where she receives physical and occupational therapy.

Katie lives in a middle class home with both parents and two siblings. Her parents have been very involved with her school and have participated in support groups for parents of children with spina bifida. They have been able to develop a positive relationship with the early childhood teachers and special educational personnel of the local school system.

For the assessment, Katie's parents were interviewed and teachers were contacted to provide historical and observational data. The goal here was to obtain actual descriptions of the child's behavior or narratives of actual vignettes describing situations that are particularly problematic for Katie or situations that reveal her special competencies or strengths. Katie's mother described her daughter as a very verbal, outgoing, and happy youngster who remembers everything. She also described specific situations in which Katie had difficulty following instructions. Her teacher noted that Katie is very talkative to the extent that talking gets in the way of her ability to complete her work.

Katie was seen for two sessions and a broad range of psychological tests were administered in the areas of general cognitive ability, language, visual-spatial processing, memory, motor skills, and adaptive functioning. Due to her motor difficulties, it was important to select tests that required different types of responses. Timed tests or tests that require efficient motor planning and output would have to be interpreted with caution.

During the assessment, Katie was friendly and very sociable. Her vocabulary was well developed and language use was fairly sophisticated. Some problems in generating responses to open-ended questions were seen. She was also very active and distractible. She alerted to sounds in the corridor and frequently interrupted her work. Difficulties in sustaining effort were noted, as well as an impulsive and poorly planned approach to problems. "Stimulus bound" errors were common; that is, Katie often responded to a salient part of a stimulus, ignoring more relevant and critical elements. In addition, she would often lose interest in a particular task, withdraw effort prematurely, or become distracted.

Formal assessment revealed a wide variability in skills with higher scores noted on verbal tasks, and more deficient performance on nonverbal tasks. Although her performance on language tasks was generally better than on nonverbal tests, language skills were, in fact, uneven. For example, on a task requiring repeating sentences verbatim, Katie did well for a short while and then began talking about words in the sentences instead of repeating them. This behavior mirrored other situations in which Katie's difficulties with inhibitor controls interfered with her performance.

Performance on language tasks was analyzed with respect to formal scores as well as quality of performance and differential task demands. By attending to these interactions, it was also clear that specific language tasks proved more difficult for Katie. Whereas she performed very well when material was presented in a highly organized, rule-oriented manner, her performance deteriorated when she was asked to independently organize or plan her verbal responses, particularly when faced with unfamiliar or novel situations.

The pattern of lower nonverbal performance relative to intact verbal skills is often noted in children with myelodysplasia. Difficulties with visual motor tasks are not unexpected, given the motor coordination deficits of these children. Katie also encountered significant difficulties on nonverbal tasks that did not require a motoric response (visual discrimination, analysis, and reasoning). It has been argued that children with myelodysplasia have neuropsychologically-based visual perceptual and organizational deficits which account for depressed performance on nonverbal tasks (Fletcher, Francis, Thompson, Davidson, & Miner, 1992). From a developmental systems perspective, this finding is not surprising if one understands that due to motor development problems, children with myelodysplasia experience and interact with the world in unique ways which affect how the brain organizes and processes types of information and stimuli (Thelen, 1995).

Katie's neuropsychological evaluation revealed significant difficulties in the areas of executive functions, fine motor coordination, and organizational skills. Concordant findings were noted in the history, parental and teacher reports, behavioral observations, and qualitative and quantitative analysis of test performance. She had problems with focused attention, inhibition of inappropriate or irrelevant responses, flexibility in shifting set as a response to task demands, ability to sustain effort, and capacity to deal with more complex tasks. She was noted to do best on verbal tasks or in situations that were very structured and in which the organization of the task was obvious or explicitly taught.

In the area of social-emotional functioning, Katie was described by her parents as being too dependent and demanding of attention. She also had developed certain fears, especially of doctors and medical procedures. Socially, she preferred to play with older children; one can hypothesize that she could engage them verbally with more success than very young children.

With this neuropsychological profile, Katie is at risk for encountering problems in academic, social, and home contexts. By employing a developmental perspective that incorporates both what is known about the natural history of her neurological compromise, her specific history, and her neurobehavioral status, we can make predictions regarding the kinds of difficulties Katie will face over the course of development. She has made significant progress and was functioning very well with the support of her family and a coordinated educational intervention program. It was important to highlight the issues that Katie would be facing and assist both her parents and the school in making modifications that would most effectively foster her continued progress and adaptation.

A developmental systems perspective to the neuropsychological assessment process provides a principled method for assessing the preschool child. It avoids using a purely "number-based" strategy that can be unproductive and potentially damaging for young children. In the case of Katie, cognitive skills were not the only focus of the assessment; the quality of exploratory and self-regulation abilities were addressed. Her particular strengths in verbal abilities and social responsivity could be capitalized on to generate specific intervention schemes. Attention to context and factors that promote the most effective and efficient performance also helps guide the overall management program.

Summary

The neuropsychological assessment of preschool children presents a set of difficult but not insurmountable challenges. The nature of the child, the psychometric issues, and the dynamic quality of development all need to be addressed in the evaluation process. The importance of a broad-based assessment approach cannot be overstated when dealing with young children, especially those who have neurological disorders and are forging unique developmental pathways for adaptation and growth. A model of neuropsychological assessment is proposed.

APPENDIX 15A

References for Tests from Table 15.1

Adams, W., & Sheslow, D. (1990). *Wide Range Assessment of Memory and Learning.* Wilmington, DE: Jastak.

Adams, W., & Sheslow, D. (1995). *Wide Range Assessment of Visual Motor Abilities.* Wilmington, DE: Wide Range, Inc.

Bayley, N. (1993). *Bayley Scales of Infant Development-II.* San Antonio, TX: The Psychological Corporation.

Beery, K. E. (1997). *Beery-Buktenica Developmental Test of Visual Motor Integration, Fourth Edition.* Parsippany, NJ: Modern Curriculum Press.

Burgemeister, B. B., Blum, L. H., & Lorge, I. (1972). *Columbia Mental Maturity Scale.* San Antonio, TX: The Psychological Corporation.

Caldwell, B. M., & Bradley, R. H. (1984). *Home Observation for Measurement of the Environment.* Little Rock, AR: Center for Research on Teaching and Learning, University of Arkansas.

Colarusso, R. P., & Hammill, D. D. (1995). *Motor Free Visual Perceptual Test-Revised.* Novato, CA: Academic Therapy Publications.

Dunn, L. M., & Dunn, L. M. (1981). *Peabody Picture Vocabulary Test-Revised.* Circle Pines, MN: American Guidance Service.

Elliott, C. (1990). *The Differential Ability Scale.* San Antonio, TX: The Psychological Corporation.

Fewell, R. R., & Glick, M. P. (1993). Observing play: An appropriate process for learning and assessment. *Infants and Young Children, 5,* 35–43.

Fewell, R. R., & Rich, J. S. (1987). Play assessment as a procedure for examining cognitive, communication, and social skills in multihandicapped children. *Journal of Psychoeducational Assessment, 2,* 102–118.

French, J. L. (1964). *Pictorial Test of Intelligence.* Montreal, Canada: Institute of Psychological Research, Inc.

Gardner, M. F. (1990). *Expressive One-Word Picture Vocabulary Test-Revised.* Novato, CA: Academic Therapy Publications.

Goodman, J. (1981). *The Goodman Lock Box.* Chicago: Stoelting.

Hiskey, M. S. (1966). *Hiskey-Nebraska Test of Learning Aptitude.* Lincoln, NE: Hiskey-Nebraska Test.

Kaufman, A. S., & Kaufman, N. L. (1983). *Kaufman Assessment Battery for Children (K-ABC).* Circle Pines, MN: American Guidance Service.

McCarthy, D. (1972). *McCarthy Scales of Children's Abilities.* San Antonio, TX: The Psychological Corporation.

Newcomber, P. L., & Hammill, D. D. (1988). *Test of Language Development-2.* Austin, TX: Pro-Ed, Inc.

Roid, G., & Miller, L. (1997). *Leiter-R Intelligence Scale.* Wood Dale, IL: Stoelting Company.

Sparrow, S. S., Balla, D. A., & Cicchetti, D. V. (1984). *Vineland Adaptive Behavior Scales.* Circle Pines, MN: American Guidance Service.

Stutsman, R. (1932). *Merrill Palmer Scale.* Wood Dale, IL: Stoelting Company.

Thorndike, R. L., Hagen, E. P., & Sattler, J. M. (1986). *The Stanford-Binet Intelligence Scale: Fourth Edition.* Chicago, IL: The Riverside Publishing Company.

Trad, P. (1992). Use of developmental principles to decipher the narrative of preschool children. *Journal of the American Academy of Child and Adolescent Psychiatry, 31(4),* 581–592.

Wechsler, D. (1989). *Wechsler Preschool and Primary Scale of Intelligence-Revised.* San Antonio, TX: The Psychological Corporation.

Welsh, M. C., Pennington, B. F., & Grossier, D. B. (1991). A normative-developmental study of executive function: A window on prefrontal functions in children. *Developmental Neuropsychology, 7,* 131–149.

Wilson, B. C., Iacoviello, J. M., Wilson, J. J., & Risucci, D. (1982). Purdue Pegboard performance in normal preschool children. *Journal of Clinical Neuropsychology, 4,* 19–26.

Woodcock, R. W., & Johnson, M. B. (1989,1990). *Woodcock-Johnson Psychoeducational Battery-Revised.* Allen, TX: DLM Teaching Resources.

Zimmerman, I. R., Steiner, V. G., & Pond, R. E. (1992). *Preschool Language Scale-3.* San Antonio, TX: The Psychological Corporation.

16 Preschool Evaluation of Culturally and Linguistically Diverse Children

CHIEH LI

JOAN RILEY WALTON

ENA VAZQUEZ NUTTALL

The population now entering the U.S. school system is more culturally diverse than ever before. By the year 2000, it is predicted that one out of every three children will come from a non-mainstream group. As reported by the U.S. Department of Education, the 1993 national estimate for public school enrollment was 54,803,000, of which 34% were minority (U.S. Department of Education, 1995). In large city school systems, minority children are already a majority. By the year 2030, culturally and linguistically diverse children will constitute the majority of the school population (Hodgkinson, 1992).

Because of these demographics, because preschoolers are closely bound to their families, and because Federal Public Law (99-457 of 1986, amendments to the Education for All Handicapped Children Act in 1991, retitled the Individuals with Disabilities Education Act, or IDEA, Public Law 102-119 and reauthorized in 1997 as P.L. 105-17) requires a family plan, school personnel will have closer working relationships with culturally different families. These regulations require that evaluation of preschoolers be racially and culturally nondiscriminatory, and be conducted in the child and family's native language or mode of communication, unless it is clearly not feasible to do so. To be effective, clinicians must evaluate differently.

This chapter focuses on the evaluation of culturally different preschoolers. Included are (1) guidelines and steps for evaluating culturally diverse children, (2) a selected list of tests with specific cultural and linguistic data, (3) informal alternative procedures for evaluation, and (4) suggestions for culturally appropriate report writing.

Assessing Culturally and Linguistically Diverse Preschoolers

The Challenge

Psychologists and other early childhood specialists are expected to assess all children. However, many of them have not been trained to conduct culturally appropriate assessments of culturally and linguistically diverse preschoolers. In the assessment process these professionals may face cultural, linguistic, and class barriers. Very often, clinicians have to evaluate a child but do not speak or are not familiar with the child's language or culture. In addition, in many states, standard scores are required for evaluation of a child's special education needs (except for children 0 to 3 years old), but few appropriately normed tests are available for diverse preschoolers. Most instruments are primarily designed to meet the needs of middle class, English-speaking, majority children. In practice, evaluators are left to deal with all these deficiencies, assuming that they are multiculturally competent.

Multicultural Competence

Multicultural competence includes multicultural awareness, knowledge, and skills. The American Psychological Association (APA) *Guidelines for Providers of Psychological Services to Ethnic, Linguistic, and Culturally Diverse Populations (1993, p. 45)** state:

> Psychological service providers need a sociocultural framework to consider diversity of values, interactional styles, and cultural expectations in a systematic fashion. They need knowledge and skills for multicultural assessment and intervention, including abilities to:
> —recognize cultural diversity;
> —understand the role that culture and ethnic/race play in the sociopsychological and economic development of ethnic and culturally diverse populations;
> —understand that socioeconomic and political factors significantly impact the psychosocial, political, and economic development of ethnic and culturally diverse groups;
> —help clients to understand/maintain/resolve their own sociocultural identification; and
> —understand the interaction of culture, gender, and sexual orientation on behavior and needs.

A positive multicultural orientation in the school and service systems, and professionals with appropriate skills, are the necessary context for culturally competent evaluation of diverse preschoolers. The rest of this chapter assumes this context and focuses on practical and specific strategies.

How to approach an evaluation referral for preschoolers from diverse cultures? APA Guidelines (1993)* "for *evaluating* linguistically and culturally diverse populations require that:

2. Psychologists are cognizant of relevant research and practice issues as related to the population being served....

2c. Psychologists recognize the limits of their competencies and expertise. Psychologists who do not possess knowledge and training about an ethnic group seek consultation with, and/or make referrals to, appropriate experts as necessary.

2d. Psychologists consider the validity of a given instrument procedure and interpret resulting data, keeping in mind the cultural and linguistic characteristics of the person being assessed. Psychologists are aware of the test's reference population and possible limitations of such instruments with other populations.

3a. Psychologists, regardless of ethnic/racial background, are aware of how their own culture background/experiences, attitudes, values, and biases influence psychological processes. They make efforts to correct any prejudices and biases. . . .

3e. Psychologists consider not only differential diagnostic issues but also the cultural beliefs and values of the client and his/her community in providing intervention.

4. Psychologists respect the roles of family members and community structures, hierarchies, values, and beliefs within the client's culture.

5. Psychologists respect client's religious and/or spiritual beliefs and values, including attributions and taboos, since they affect world view, psychosocial functioning, and expressions of distress. . . .

5b. Effective psychological intervention may be aided by consultation with and/or inclusion of religious/spiritual leaders/practitioners relevant to the client's cultural and belief systems.

6. Psychologists interact in the language requested by the client and, if this is not feasible, make an appropriate referral. . . .

9. Psychologists working with culturally diverse populations should document culturally and sociopolitically relevant factors in the records. These may include, but are not limited to a. number of generations in the country, b. number of years in the country, c. fluency in English, d. extent of family support (or disintegration of family), e. community resources, f. level of education, g. change in social status as a result of coming to this country (for immigrant or refugee), h. intimate relationship with people of different backgrounds, i. level of stress related to acculturation. (pp. 46–47).

As practitioners, how shall we translate the APA guidelines into our assessment of preschoolers from diverse cultures? To answer this question, we have developed a *Decision-Making Tree for Special Education Referrals* (see Figure 16.1) to share with colleagues who want to conduct culturally appropriate assessments for diverse preschoolers and seek specific suggestions.

Specific Suggestions for Decision Making, Steps 3 to 6

Step 3: Use of Interpreters.   Interpreters should be used only when a competent psychologist who speaks the native language of the child cannot be found within reasonable distance from the home or school district (see Figure 16.2, for *Qualifications of Interpreters*).

Training of Interpreters.   If you cannot find a psychologist who speaks the native language of the child and you are forced to use an interpreter you should meet, train, and establish rapport with the interpreter before using him or her. If you plan to use an interpreter frequently, you should invest time in training the interpreter well in psychological assessment.

1. Interpreters should be trained as most psychology students are currently trained in assessment. Tests to be used should be taught and demonstrated. Interpreters should be able to observe psychologists while they test another child so that they become aware of the testing situation from beginning to end.

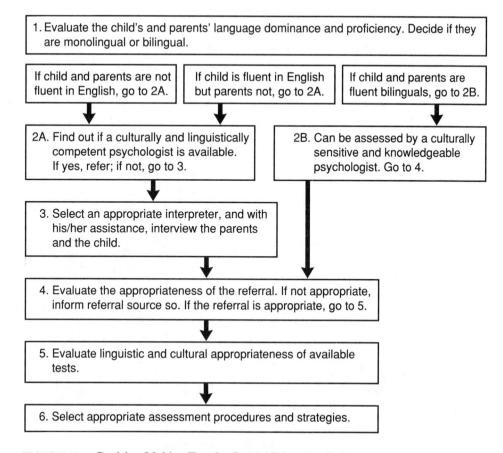

FIGURE 16.1   Decision-Making Tree for Special Education Referrals

2. Use tests that have language adaptations in the language of the child to be tested. A linguistically adapted test is a translated test that has been tried with a small sample of people from that language group to ensure cultural and linguistic appropriateness of the test. Any culturally and linguistically inappropriate items, scales, and procedures should be eliminated from the test. If an adapted test is not available, use good translations. If adaptations or translations are not available, give the test to the translator so that he or she can study and translate it ahead of time. Ask the translator if there are terms or items that cannot be translated or are culturally inappropriate. If test items or directions are to be translated or if informal tests in the minority language are created, this should be done before the session begins. Avoid direct translations while testing (See Figure 16.2 for Suggestions 3–8).

It should be noted that the presence of two adults testing and speaking to each other is likely to be confusing to the child or family and may alter the results. Testing done with translators is likely to take more time and can become burdensome to the child and family; several short sessions may be required.

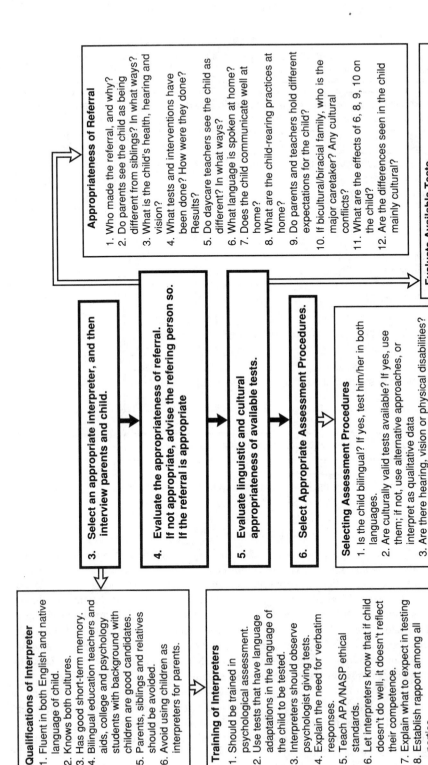

FIGURE 16.2 Decision-Making Tree: Branches

Precautions

1. Remember that you, as the professional, are ethically and legally responsible for the assessment since it is conducted under your supervision.

2. Before starting the assessment, consult with the interpreter on how to avoid verbal and nonverbal communications that may be offensive to the child and family.

3. The region, social class, race, gender, or ethnic group that the interpreter comes from may play an important role in the assessment process. Use of mismatched interpreters may cause tension and affect assessment results negatively. For example, a recent immigrant family from mainland China may not feel comfortable with an interpreter from Taiwan because of different political backgrounds. An interpreter who can communicate well with parents may not necessarily be able to communicate with a preschooler with the same success. For instance, despite the different choice of words of various regions, adult Mandarin speakers from mainland China, Taiwan, Singapore, Hong Kong, and Malaysia can communicate with each other well because most adults have been exposed to some extent to the dialects of other regions. However, preschoolers are not yet used to the synonymous words used in other regions. Their test scores may be depressed because the examiner or interpreter uses unfamiliar words. Another example is with White Hmong and Blue Hmong. Although both groups speak Hmong, they speak different dialects and can only understand each other about 50% of the time. These recommendations are developed from the authors' clinical experiences and the work of Wilen (1989). For *supervision* and other suggestions for using interpreters, see *Assessing Bilingual and LEP Students: Practical Issues in the Use of Interpreters* (Hallberg, 1996).

Step 4. Evaluate Appropriateness of Referral. To avoid over-referring caused by lack of knowledge of the culture that the child comes from, we need to consider the twelve questions in Step 4 (see Figure 16.2).

See Figure 16.2 for the specific questions in Step 5, *Evaluate Appropriateness of Available Tests*. The brief review of formal assessment measures in the next section provides information on cultural appropriateness of some tests. For information on how to select appropriate assessment procedures refer to Step 6 in the same figure. See Figure 16.2 for questions in Step 6, *Select Appropriate Assessment Procedures*.

Brief Review of Formal Assessment Measures

Selected instruments for use in the evaluation of culturally diverse preschoolers are presented in Tables 16.1 through 16.6. These instruments were selected because their standardization sample included diverse populations of preschoolers, or they have specific translations (sometimes adaptations with norms) in languages other than English, or because reliability or validity studies with diverse preschoolers have been conducted. Most of the tests include minority populations in their standardization sample in proportion to the national census. However, this still can mean small numbers of some particular ethnic groups. Inclusion of minorities does not establish that the test is unbiased for these groups.

Instruments older than thirty years were not included in the tables unless there was new research indicating their value. Areas of measurement include screening, general cognitive ability, specific cognitive ability, language, perceptual, adaptive and social development, and curriculum-based measures.

Screening Instruments

As indicated in Table 16.1, seven screening measures were found that fit the criteria. For example, the Children's Developmental Scale of China (1991) comprehensively measures verbal, cognitive, social and motor skills, and was normed on Chinese urban children with validity and reliability reported. This would be appropriate in evaluating a recently arrived Chinese preschooler.

Research with the BRIGANCE® K & 1 Screen (Manzicopoulos & Jarvinen, 1993) examining a low socio-economic population suggests that there are really only five factors measured rather than the twelve subtests indicated in the manual. Caution should be used in reporting subtest scores and differences.

General Cognitive Instruments

Seven nationally standardized and frequently used measures of general cognitive development are listed in Table 16.2.

Batería Woodcock-Muñoz: Pruebas de Habilidad Cognitiva—Revisada.   The Batería Woodcock-Muñoz: Pruebas de Habilidad Cognitiva—Revisada (Batería-R COG) (Woodcock & Muñoz-Sandoval, 1996) is the parallel Spanish version of the Woodcock-Johnson Test of Cognitive Ability-Revised (WJ-R COG) (Woodcock-Johnson, 1989, 1990). It has been included in this chapter as it is one of the few comprehensive cognitive abilities tests available for preschoolers in the Spanish language. Although normative data were not obtained from a sample of Spanish-speaking children, the Batería-R COG underwent a careful translation/adaptation process to make the instrument appropriate across different Spanish-speaking groups. The authors utilize the concept of "Equated U.S. Norms", which means, Spanish norms equated to English norms as substitute for normative data. The manual describes that the calibration-equating data for each Spanish test was obtained from approximately 2,000 native Spanish-speaking subjects, ranging from two years of age to university graduate students.

Bayley Scales of Infant Development—Second Edition.   The Bayley Scales of Infant Development—Second Edition (Bayley, 1993) is included because the 1988 norms represent majority and minority populations. There is, as yet, no reliability or validity data with diverse preschoolers.

Differential Ability Scales.   The Differential Ability Scales (DAS, Elliott, 1990) is included because careful item selection was used, items discriminating against minority groups were excluded, and the standardization sample included proportional minority populations. Testers are instructed to teach the sample items.

Kaufman Assessment Battery for Children.   The Kaufman Assessment Battery for Children (K-ABC, Kaufman & Kaufman, 1983) is included because most cognitive subtests can be given in Spanish (translations are in the manual and were used in the standardization), and because it yields a nonverbal cognitive estimate for older preschoolers. Careful item discrimination was conducted before standardization. Norms for different socio-economic groups and African Americans are included. The test separates out crystalized knowledge, such as vocabulary, from more fluid thinking, which may better measure abilities of children

TABLE 16.1 Screening Instruments

Name	Ages	Psychometric Data	Description	Administration Time	Year/Author/Publisher
BRIGANCE® Early Preschool Screen	2 to 2-6	Suggested cutoff points, standardized scores Reliability and validation reports available.	Measures gross motor, fine motor, social skills, self-help skills, cognitive skills, pre-academic, expressive, receptive language, articulation, and behavioral/self control. Has Spanish directions, which were used in the norming.	15 minutes	1995, Curriculum Associates Inc.
BRIGANCE® Preschool Screen	3 to 4	Suggested cutoff points. Reliability and validity reports available.	Same as early preschool. Has Spanish directions, which were used in the norming.	15 minutes	1985, Curriculum Associates Inc.
Children's Developmental Scale of China	3 to 6	Normed on Chinese urban children. Gives percentiles. Reports on reliability and validity available.	Measures verbal, cognitive, social, and motor skills. Reliability and validity reports available.	60 minutes	1994 Hòcàn Zhang, Beijing Normal University Beijing, P. R. China
Denver Developmental Screening Test—R	2 weeks to 6 years	Validity and reliability reported for the English form. Normed in Denver with diverse population.	Screens personal-social, fine-motor, language, and gross motor. Has Spanish forms.	15 to 20 minutes	1981 Denver Developmental Materials
Developmental Indicator for Assessment of Learning—Revised	2 to 5	Percentiles and cutoff points given for total norming group representing U.S. population, 1980, and for white and nonwhite populations.	Measures motor, concepts, and language.	30 minutes	1990 American Guidance Service, Circle Pines, MN
Early Screening Inventory (Inventorio para Detección Temprana)	3, and 4 to 6	Recommended cutoff points for each age for referral.	Measures visual-motor, adaptive, language, cognitive, gross motor, and body scheme; includes a parent questionnaire. Has Spanish version.	30 minutes	1991 Meisels et al. University of Michigan at Ann Arbor
Preschool Screening System	2-6 to 6-6	Norm-referenced with 3,000 preschoolers representing U.S. population. Reliability and validity only for the English form.	Measures body awareness, visual-motor perception, language, general information. Includes a parent questionnaire. Translations into Spanish, Chinese, French, Vietnamese, Portuguese, Samoan, Laotian, Cambodian, Cape Verdean, Ilocano, Tagalog and Eskimo; none with specific validity or reliability.	20 minutes to 1 hour	1980 Hainsworth & Hainsworth, Pawtucket, R.I.: Erisys

*BRIGANCE® is a registered trademark of Curriculum Associates®, Inc.

TABLE 16.2 General Cognitive Assessment Instruments

Name	Ages	Psychometric Data	Description	Administration Time	Year/Author/Publisher
Batería Woodcock-Muñoz: Pruebas de Habilidad Cognitiva—Revisada	2-0 to 90+	Equated U.S. norms, calibration-equating data for each Spanish test obtained from 2,000 native Spanish-speaking subjects from U.S., Mexico, Cuba, Nicaragua, Dominican Republic, Puerto Rico, Honduras, Colombia, Spain and other Latin American countries. Reliability and validity studies reported in the manual.	Provides standard and percentile scores as well as grade equivalents. Includes a measure of overall intellectual functioning based on an average of seven different cognitive abilities (short-term memory, comprehension-knowledge, visual processing, auditory processing, long-term retrieval, fluid reasoning and processing speed).	Depends on age and battery administered (standard vs. supplementary)	1996 Woodcock, R. W., & Muñoz-Sandoval, A. F. Riverside Publishing
Bayley Scales of Infant Development—2nd Edition	1 month to 42 months	National norms including African American, Latin American and other minority children using 1988 census. Item bias checked for African American and Latin American children. No reliability or validity studies for minorities.	Has standard scores for mental skills, motor skills, and a behavior rating scale.	25 to 60 minutes	1993 Nancy Bayley The Psychological Corporation
Differential Ability Scales	2-6 to 17-11	National norms including African American, Latin American and other minority children from 1988 census. Item bias checked for African American children. General reliability and validity data reported.	Standard scores for general cognitive ability for young preschoolers. Verbal and nonverbal and general scores for older preschoolers.	30 to 60 minutes depending on age and number of subtests used.	1990 Colin D. Elliott The Psychological Corporation
Kaufman Assessment Battery for Children	2-6 to 12-0	National norms including African American, Latin American and other minority children using 1980 census. Reliability and validity data offered. Item bias checked for African American children. Norms for different SES groups, blacks and whites. Spanish directions used in the norming.	Includes a Mental Processing Index, a Sequential and a Simultaneous score; a Nonverbal Score, and an Achievement Score.	About 60 minutes	1983 Kaufman & Kaufman American Guidance Services

Test	Age Range	Standardization	Description	Administration Time	Date/Publisher
Leiter International Performance Scale—Revised	2-0 to 20	Normed based on the 1993 census figures with proportional inclusion of African American, Latin American, Asian American and other minorities. Item bias checked. Standand scores. Reliability and validity data for the norming sample.	Measures global intelligence, with scores for visualization, reasoning, memory, and attention. Uses a nonverbal mode, with no verbal instructions required.	Depends on age and ability level	1996 Gale Roid & Lucy Miller Stolting Company Woodale, IL.
McCarthy Scale of Children's Abilities, Chinese Revision	2-6 to 8-6	Large city norms, with standardized scores. Reliability and validity data reported.	Measures, verbal performance and quantitative skills; includes a general score.	60 minutes	1991 Psychology Dept. Eastern China Normal University of Shanghai, P. R. China
Wechsler Preschool and Primary Scale of Intelligence—R	3 to 7-3 years	National norms including minority children based using the 1980 census. Reliability and validity data offered for general population. Item bias checked.	Measures general cognitive ability with verbal and nonverbal problems.	45 minutes	1989 The Psychological Corporation

from diverse backgrounds. Early items in nearly every subtest are taught as well as tested. The test generally has lower difference scores between white, and black and Latino children. It is important to note, however, that the sample of Latino children used in norming was higher in SES than the total Latino population in the United States (Bracken, 1985). Glutting (1986) found that scores on the K-ABC from minority children and white children predicted equally well for each group on later achievement tests and teacher grades. Flanagan (1995) found that children of various linguistic backgrounds who were proficient in conversational English had higher scores on the K-ABC than the WISC-R. It was suggested that caution should be used to avoid over-interpreting inter-subtest differences of the K-ABC in a study with white and black preschoolers in Tennessee (Bracken, Howell, Harrison, Stanford, & Zahn, 1991).

Leiter International Scale—Revised.   The Leiter International Scale—Revised (LIS-R, 1996), may prove to be a major addition to tests available for diverse preschoolers. LIS-R standard scores are normed using the 1993 census, including African American, Latin American, Asian American and "other" minority children. Item bias was examined by trial testing of those minority populations. Data from a special sampling of English-as-a-Second-Language Latin American children and Asian American children are reported. The test is nonverbal and uses new manipulatives.

Wechsler Preschool and Primary Scale—Revised.   The Wechsler Preschool and Primary Scale of Intelligence—Revised (WPPSI-R, 1989) Performance Scale may be helpful in giving an estimate of perceptual thinking skills for diverse preschoolers who speak at least conversational English. The Verbal Scale of the WPPSI-R and the directions for the Performance Scale can be translated with careful use of a translator. However translated verbal scales should not be interpreted as verbal intelligence, but as an informal measure of some verbal skills. The Verbal Scale, given in English, is best used for informal evaluation of English achievement, assimilation, and/or second-language learning for most linguistically diverse children.

The English version of the McCarthy was not included because the norms are too old. However, the new adaptation in Chinese will be useful for newly immigrating Chinese students (McCarthy Scale of Children's Abilities, Chinese Version, 1991).

Specific Area Cognitive Instruments

Two tests, described in Table 16.3, focus on the measurement of specific cognitive skills. The Boehm Test of Basic Concepts—Preschool Version (1986) had wide trial testing of its items in urban day care centers. Therefore the construction may be less biased for diverse preschoolers who speak English. It tests verbal concepts and relationships. The Bracken Basic Concepts Scale (BBCS, 1984), measuring the same areas, has a Spanish version which used the "back translation" method and includes validity data (Bracken & Fouad, 1987). However, the BBCS was given to black and white preschoolers with similar age, sex, and father's education and resulted in African American scores that were lower than European American scores by 0.5 standard deviation (Bracken, Sabers, & Insko, 1987).

The Columbia Mental Maturity Test (CMMT, 1972) is a nonverbal measure for older preschool children, measuring only classification skills. The verbal directions consist of one simple sentence, easy to translate into any language. It is not appropriate for young

TABLE 16.3 Specific Area Cognitive Instruments

Name	Ages	Psychometric Data	Description	Administration Time	Year/Author/Publisher
Boehm Test of Basic Concepts	3 to 5	Normed with over 400 children representing the national population. Item trial done with urban day care children, including 342 minority children. Standard scores. Reliability and validity data presented	Measures 26 verbal concepts.	15 minutes	1986 Ann Boehn The Psychological Corporation
Columbia Mental Maturity Test— 3rd Edition	3-6 to 10	Standard scores. No specific reliability or validity data with diverse children.	Measures categorization in a nonverbal way by asking children to look at four pictures and find the picture that does not belong. Instruction available in Spanish.	10 to 15 minutes	1972 Burgenmeister The Psychological Corporation

children who do not have the concept of "different" or "does not belong." Gómez-Benito and Forns-Santacana (1993) found that CMMT scores correlated well (.74) with McCarthy scores for Perceptual-Performance but not so well with McCarthy Verbal scores (.15) with a group of kindergartners in Barcelona, Spain.

Language Instruments

Eight instruments are selected as possible measures of language skills for diverse children (see Table 16.4). In our opinion, English language tests can be given to limited-English-speaking students and minority children if it is remembered that:

- These tests should be used to informally measure acquisition of a second or majority language. They will yield qualitative data, not reliable, valid quantitative data.
- Data obtained from language tests in a second language, or that are translated without reliability, validity, or norming data relevant to a bilingual person, cannot be considered a valid indicator of a language deficit or disability.
- Norms for monolingual speakers of a language are not appropriate for children with varying degrees of bilingual development.

Bing and Bing (1984) showed that 57% of a group of African American rural children had nine or more points difference on the two forms, L and M, of the Peabody Picture Vocabulary Test. Form L was significantly harder for them, despite generally good correlations between forms (McCallum & Bracken, 1981). Pena, Quin, and Iglesias (1992) concluded (from research with another similar vocabulary test) that lower scores in receptive/expressive vocabulary tests do not tap the cultural pattern in African American and Latino cultures for using verbal description rather than labeling. This could possibly account in some part for the lower scores achieved by Native American children as well (Naglieri & Yazzie, 1984). Pena, Quin, and Iglesias (1992) suggest that comprehension tests rather than labeling tests are more appropriate for these cultural groups. Cuban preschoolers in Miami did not do as well as expected on the Test Vocabulario de Imagenes-Peabody, which was not normed on Cuban children. Fernández, Pearson, Umbel, and Oller (1992) concluded that the word order was wrong for this population. They also found that word concepts were known in one language, but not in the other, about one-third of the time. Tests in only one of the languages spoken by bilingual preschoolers will underestimate the total receptive vocabulary of the children in both languages.

Two studies used the Preschool Language Scale-R (PLS-R) with diverse children. The PLS-R in English and Spanish successfully measured language growth in Spanish-speaking preschoolers who received an intergenerational literacy learning program with their mothers (Thornburg, 1993). Hilton and Mumma (1991) found that rural children were disadvantaged in the Verbal section of the PLS-R test, presumably because they were culturally more quiet and nonverbal. This could have ramifications for other cultural groups who do not value verbosity in their young children.

One new study described the use of the Illinois Test for Psycholinguistic Ability (ITPA) with Japanese preschoolers. Yamamoto (1990) reported that the ITPA subtest for receptive language was sensitive to finding a difference in favor of first-born children in Japan, who may be advantaged by greater exposure to parental speech than are later-born children.

TABLE 16.4 Language Instruments

Name	Ages	Psychometric Data	Description	Administration Time	Year/Author/Publisher
Del Rio Language Screening Test—English and Spanish	3-0 to 6-11	Normed with groups of normal students in Del Rio, Texas for Anglos, Spanish-Speaking Mexicans and English-Speaking Mexicans. Reliability data presented. Has percentile ranks for age groups.	Measures receptive vocabulary, sentence repetition for length and for complexity, oral commands, and story comprehension in both languages. Can be used to measure bilingual proficiency and language development.	30 minutes	1975 A. Toronto San Felipe-Del Rio Consolidated School District SPED Department Del Rio, Texas
Expressive One-Word Picture Vocabulary Test-Revised—Spanish Version	2-0 to 11-11	Spanish record forms available. No norms, reliability and validity studies available.	Measures expressive vocabulary by showing a picture and asking the child to name the picture.	20 minutes	1990 M. F. Gardner Novato, CA: Academic Therapy Publications
Illinois Test of Psycholinguistic Abilities—Spanish Version, Japanese Version	2-6 to 10-0	Standard Scores. Spanish Version normed with monolingual children in Mexico, Peru, Columbia, Chile, and Puerto Rico who attended school. Adapted Japanese version offers some monolingual norms.	Measures language in expressive and receptive modes and in three phases: input, meaning, output.	one hour	Spanish Version, 1980 Von Isler & Kirk University of Arizona, Tucson Japanese Version, 1973 Honkomagome 6-15-17 Bunnkyou-ku, Tokyo-to, Japan (113)
Peabody Picture Vocabulary Test—Test de Vocabulario de Imágenes	2-0 to adult	Standard Scores. Normed with monolingual children in Mexico City and in San Juan, Puerto Rico who were in school. No validity or reliability reported in manual.	Measures receptive vocabulary by asking children to listen to a word and to chose the matching picture from a group of four.	20 minutes	1986 Dunn, Lugo, Padilla, & Dunn American Guidance Services
Preschool Language Scale—III, Spanish Version	birth to 3 years	Development with Spanish-speaking children in the U.S. Standard scores and percentiles. No norms, reliability, or validity data for the Spanish form.	Measures auditory and expressive communication	30 minutes	1992, Zimmerman, Steiner, and Pond The Psychological Corporation

(continued)

TABLE 16.4 Continued

Name	Ages	Psychometric Data	Description	Administration Time	Year/Author/Publisher
Prueba del Desarrollo Inicial del Lenguaje	3 to 7	Normed on an undescribed population of Spanish-speaking children in Mexico, Puerto Rico, and the United States. No reliability or validity for the translation presented.	Measures content and form of language in both receptive and expressive modes. Includes 38 items.	20 minutes	1982, Hresko, Reid, & Hammill Pro-Ed
The Sequenced Inventory of Communication Development—R Spanish	4 months to 4 years	Criterion-referenced. Age norms from normal children in Miami and Detroit. Manual includes African American norms from Detroit study. Cuban adaptation. No norms, validity, or reliability for the Spanish form.	Measures language development	Depends on the number of domains assessed	1984 L. Rosenberg Slosson Educational Publications, Inc.
Toronto Test of Receptive Vocabulary (Spanish and English)	4-0 to 10-0	Percentile scores for a norming group in Texas of Anglo, Spanish-speaking Mexican, and English-speaking Mexican children.	Measures receptive language by asking children to listen to a word and pick the correct picture for it out of three choices. Can measure dominant language.	15 minutes for each form	1977 A. Toronto San Felipe-Del Rio Consolidated School District Del Rio, Texas

Social, Emotional, and Adaptive Behavior Instruments

Six instruments were selected in this area as tools to be used with culturally diverse children. All depend upon teacher or parental report (see Table 16.5). Vig and Jedrysek (1995) used the Vineland with urban children (mostly African American and Latin American) and found a high correlation between scores on this measure and normed measures of intelligence. Xin, Chen, Tang, Lin, and McConville (1992) report that Achenbach scores correlated as expected with demographic data on Chinese children: only children were more socially withdrawn, delinquency and hyperactivity were found more in boys than in girls, and somatic complaints, schizoid behavior, anxiety, or depression were more frequent among girls.

Curriculum-Based Instruments

A different approach to preschool assessment that does not focus on labels or classifications of preschoolers was advocated by Oakland and Matuszek (1977), Piaget and Nagle (1986), and Neisworth and Bagnato (1986). This approach, called curriculum-based assessment, focuses on carefully sequenced developmental tasks and asks whether the child has or has not mastered the particular task. Assessment and learning are clearly linked. Unfortunately, the validity of the developmental sequence for culturally diverse groups has not been well researched. Four examples of this type of assessment/intervention system are described in Table 16.6.

Alternative Assessment Approaches

Transdisciplinary Play-Based Assessment

Transdisciplinary Play-Based Assessment (TPBA) seems to be a promising alternative approach for assessing culturally diverse preschoolers because it is a natural, holistic, functional, and dynamic approach that includes parents in the assessment process and allows cross-disciplinary analysis of developmental level, learning style, interaction patterns, and other factors (Linder, 1993). For a detailed description of TPBA, see Chapter 10 by Linder.

TPBA involves the child in structured and unstructured play situations with, at varying times, a facilitating adult, the parent(s), and another child or children. Designed for children functioning between infancy and 6 years of age, TPBA provides an opportunity for developmental observations of the cognitive, social-emotional, communication and language, and sensorimotor domains. The particular advantages of TPBA are its ease for children with language difficulties and its flexibility in testing. These advantages may decrease assessment bias against children who are less verbal, and who come from a different cultural or linguistic background.

However, TPBA was developed for use with children with various disabilities. Conducting culturally sensitive assessment of diverse children was not an emphasis in TPBA. The *Observation Guidelines* in TPBA mainly reflect the expected functioning/behaviors of English-speaking children from mainstream culture. Cultural issues are not addressed in the book, despite the fact that there are cultural differences in children's play behavior (Williams & Beeson, 1983). Since TPBA is a young assessment approach, data from research studies on the validity of TPBA for assessing culturally diverse preschoolers are

TABLE 16.5 Social, Emotional and Adaptive Behavior Instruments

Name	Ages	Psychometric Data	Description	Administration Time	Year/Author/Publisher
Achenbach Preschool Child Behavior Checklist, Chinese and Spanish Versions	age 4 to 5 ages 2–3 & 4–18	Standardized for norms in Shanghai using 3,000 cases. No norms or adaptation in Spanish.	Measures social withdrawal, depression, immaturity, somatic complaints, sex problems, schizoid behavior, aggression, delinquent syndromes, anxious behavior, obesity, hyperactivity.	30 minutes	1992 Shanghai Mental Health Center, Shanghai, P. R. of China 1995 Child Behavior Checklist 1 S. Prospect St. Burlington VT 05401-3456
Adaptive Behavior Index for Children— Spanish Version	5–10 years	Norms for a California population, including African American norms and Latino norms.	The ABIC measures the child's social role performance in the family, the peer group, and the community by interviewing a caretaker. Spanish form included.	30 to 40 minutes	1979 Mercer Sompa System Psychological Corp
Inventario de Comportamiento Pre Escolar (IDC-PRE). [Preschool Behavior Inventory]	4–5 years	T-scores and percentiles. Norms developed from the administration to preschool teachers of 415 Puerto Rican children. Reliability and validity data included in the manual.	Includes scales on social withdrawal, anxiety, activity-impulsivity-distraction and irritability-hostility. Has a follow-up version to be administered repeatedly at different times to evaluate effectiveness of treatment for ADHD.	15 to 20 minutes	1995 Bauermeister Atención, Inc. 177 Las Caobas, San Juan, PR 00927
Penn Interactive Peer Play Scale	3 to 5	Built using data from urban Head Start teachers and parents. Normed on 312 African American children in Head Start programs in Philadelphia. Validity and reliability data reported.	Measures three factors of child interaction: Disruption, Disconnection, and Peer Interaction. Based on teacher checklist.	20 minutes	1995 Fantuzzo et al. Graduate School of Ed, University of Penn. Philadelphia

Test	Age	Standardization	Description	Time	Date / Authors / Publisher
Vineland Adaptive Behavior Scales—R, Spanish Edition	0 to 18-11	Standard Scores. Spanish translation used during standardization. Norming group represents the 1980 U.S. population. Reliability and validity data given for the normed version.	Measures development in communication, daily living, socialization, and motor skills, as reported by a caretaker. Style of interview is open-ended and flexible. Spanish version of the Interview Edition Survey only.	30 to 40 minutes	1984 Sparrow, Balla, & Cicchetti American Guidance Service
Woodcock Johnson Scales of Independent Behavior (Spanish Translation)	3 months to 3 years	Standard scores, age equivalents, percentiles. National norms with African American, Latin American and other minority children proportionately represented. No validity or reliability data for the Spanish translation.	Measures motor, social communication, and personal independence skills through interview with a caretaker.	10 to 15 minutes	1984 Brunininks, Woodcock, Weatherman, & Hill DLM Teaching Resources

313

TABLE 16.6 Curriculum-Based Assessment Instruments

Name	Ages	Psychometric Data	Description	Administration Time	Year/Author/Publisher
Battelle Developmental Inventory	0 to 8 years	Criterion-based, with standard scores. Minority children in norming group proportionately. Reliability and validity data reported.	Describes child development in personal-social, adaptive, motor, communication, and cognitive domains. Includes a screening component.	10 minutes to 2 hours	1984 Newburg, Stock, Wnek, Guidubaldi, & Svinicki DLM Teaching Resources
Spanish Version	0 to 8 years				1989 Tans. Isabel Llasat Funació Catalina per a la síndrome de down. Valencia, 229, 08007 Barcelona, Spain
BRIGANCE ® Diagnostic Inventory of Early Development—Revised	0 to 7 years	Criterion-referenced with suggested age equivalents.	Measures growth in motor, self-help, language, knowledge, social skills, and early learning skills	Depends on the number of areas to be evaluated	1991 Curriculum Associates, Inc. N. Billerica, MA
Hawaii Early Learning Profile—Revised	0 to 3 3 to 6	Criterion-referenced with home and school materials.	Measurement and intervention materials for cognition, gross and fine motor, social and self-help.	Depends on the number of areas to be evaluated	1996 Vort Corporation Palo Alto, CA
Portage Guide to Early Education—Spanish adaptation	0 to 6 years	Criterion-referenced. Offers a plan for home based instruction. Validation of sequence in England and Peru and the U.S. Keyed to a curriculum.	Covers areas of infant stimulation, socialization, language, self-help, cognition, and motor skills.	one hour	1994 Portage-CESA 5 Portage Project Materials, Portage, Wisconsin

314

not available yet. When using the TPBA with a culturally diverse preschooler, it is imperative to review the cultural appropriateness of the Observation Guidelines item by item and interpret the child's behavior from a cultural perspective, because developmental expectations of young children vary greatly from one culture to another.

Dynamic Assessment

There has been growing concern about standardized testing of preschoolers' intelligence because of their young age, their diversity, and their variability in testing situations (Bagnato & Neisworth, 1994). From Vygotsky (1929, 1962, 1978) to Budoff (1967) to Feuerstein, Rand, and Hoffman (1979), attempts have been made to modify assessment procedures and to suggest different models and goals for assessment. Vygotsky and Feuerstein responded to social conditions, in Russia and Israel, respectively, that demanded the incorporation of minority groups into a majority culture. Both emphasized the role of culture in determining intelligence test scores in children. Both are optimistic about the modifiability of cognitive structures with proper interventions including assessments.

Assessment and teaching materials and instruments were developed using the theories of Feuerstein and his associates. They visualize the examiner as a mediator or teacher who fosters new patterns of thought in the examinee. The methods rely on a test–teach–test approach where the examiner directly observes the results of teaching. The child's ability, or cognitive modifiability, is inferred from the increase in learning with mediation (teaching).

Clinically, only the teaching phase needs to be used to gather qualitative data and make judgments about cognitive and affective strengths and weaknesses. Judgments may be made on the basis of two or three subtests. These judgments lead directly to educational suggestions. These methods are aimed at helping the practitioner distinguish students with true handicaps from those who only lack traditional educational experiences.

Recently three devices for older preschoolers have been developed: The Children's Analogical Thinking Modifiability Test (CATM, Tzuriel & Klein, undated), the Frame Test of Cognitive Modifiability (FTCM, Tzuriel & Klein, undated) and the Children's Inferential Thinking Modifiability Test (CITM, Tzuriel, undated). All three are available from the School of Education, Ramat Gan 52900, Israel. The accompanying manuals are undated but the authors report research about these instruments (Tzuriel & Haywood, 1992; Lidz, 1987; Tzuriel & Klein, 1985). The CATM involves thinking in analogies with blocks of three shapes, three colors, and two sizes. The FTCM uses frames to observe and teach serial and patterning skills. The CITM uses a game of placing objects correctly into houses, which requires inferential thinking. These devices may tap cognitive skills that are just emerging in 3-, 4-, and 5-year-olds. They may not be appropriate for immature, cognitively handicapped, or younger preschoolers.

Sewell (1979) found that kindergarten posttest scores from a Learning Potential instrument predicted African American student's first grade achievement better than Stanford Binet IV (1986) scores. Glutting & McDermott's (1990) general review of research on this approach did not find support for the reliability and validity of dynamic assessment. Laughton (1990) reviewed the research and suggested the use of dynamic assessment only when traditional methods are inappropriate, for example, when children are young and bilingual. She reported appropriate reliability and validity data for the dynamic method, but was concerned about tester-to-tester reliability.

Lidz and Thomas (1987) reported their use of this "dynamic" method with standardized measures. They described careful, planned pretesting, teaching, and posttesting with appropriate subtests of the K-ABC (Matrices and Triangles). This method is an elaboration of the testing-the-limits approach regularly used by many practitioners. The pretest gives the practitioner a standardized score. Other practitioners trained in the method (Provost & Broderick, 1996) use the McCarthy Scale subtests of puzzles and blocks. The use of the Draw-A-Person procedure with a test–teach–test method is appropriate for older preschoolers. Observing children solving problems with toys, mediating, and observing the results gives the trained practitioner qualitative data for making judgments about style of learning and which teaching methods are effective.

Dynamic assessment has promise because it was devised with multicultural children in mind, it allows the examiner to interact with the child in a positive, teaching mode, and it fosters reporting of educational strategies. The practitioner is cautioned that research is mixed about the cultural "fairness" of the method and its effectiveness. Inter-tester reliability remains a concern. Where states require standardized scores for placement it will not be practical. Since most normed tests are not valid for young, bilingual, and diverse children, this method of acquiring qualitative information will often be the only available choice.

Report Writing for Culturally Diverse Preschoolers

When writing psychological assessment reports for culturally diverse preschoolers, the following factors should be considered in the traditional sections included in most case reports.

A. Referral.   Include who made the referral and why. If it was not made by parents, indicate whether parents share the concern and what is the parents' view of the problem.

B. Background Information.   In addition to the usual information, the cultural background, the languages spoken at home, English proficiency, learning style (description of how the child learns), family structure (pre- and post-immigration), parents' attitudes toward school and the suspected disability, and the acculturation levels of the child and family should be included. Acculturation level can be estimated through assessing a) language use and preferences, b) identification with ethnic vs. dominant culture, and c) ethnic social relations (Bash, 1981).

C. Source of Information.   Document efforts to ensure that the child's language and communication mode have been considered. Report if tests were adapted and how the items were modified. The cultural and linguistic competency of the evaluator, use of and interpreter and his/her qualifications, and his/her effect on assessment should also be included.

D. Observations and Test Behaviors.   Observation should include the child's behavior both in natural settings such as home or school, and in testing sessions. When observing a child, one should check for appropriate dress, appearance, height, weight, body build, activity level, attention, curiosity, interest level, creativity, concentration, impulsivity, affect, and anxiety. If it is not possible to compare the child directly to others in the same cultural group as the child, the teacher or caregiver should be asked about ways in which the child being examined is different from other children in the family. It is helpful to check with someone from the culture if you have misinterpreted any nonverbal cross-cultural communication.

E. Test Results and Interpretation.   Interpret test results and other data collected, taking into consideration linguistic, cultural, and socio-economic context. Note any major differences between the standardization sample and the child being tested. Does the child have similar access to the information tested by specific items—for example, experience playing with puzzles as other children? To answer this question, ask the parents about what toys the child has, and what games the child plays. Test results obtained through the use of interpreters should be evaluated with great caution. Norms for tests are usually not obtained through the use of interpreters. Thus, it is more appropriate to use the test results as descriptive measures of current functioning. For most minority preschoolers, if they do not have sensory-motor difficulties, more weight should be given to nonverbal estimates of general ability.

F. Recommendations.   Discuss with parents, and bilingual teachers if applicable, the cultural and linguistic appropriateness of the recommendations before writing them in the formal report. Ideally, develop intervention recommendations together with the parents. If the child needs therapy or further assessment, a culturally competent professional should be recommended.

Summary

The purpose of this chapter is to increase the readers' competence in assessing culturally and linguistically diverse preschoolers. Included are guidelines and step-by-step procedures for assessing diverse children. A review of the psychometric and clinical characteristics of important measures in the realms of screening, cognition, language, socio-emotional functioning, and alternative assessment approaches are presented.

Because of the increasing numbers of culturally diverse children, most professionals who want to serve preschoolers will need to develop skills in cross-cultural assessment. Preschool children present a great challenge to evaluators because they are less socialized in mainstream culture than school-age children. Assessment practice in the twenty-first century will require knowledge not only of the theory and practice of assessment, but also of the culture and language of the children to be tested and their families.

17 Assessment of Preschool Children with Developmental Disabilities and At-Risk Conditions

JAYNE E. BUCY

TINA SMITH

STEVEN LANDAU

Vicki's parents became concerned about her development after noticing she was slower at learning to walk and talk than her same-age cousins. Though she is 3 years old, Vicki communicates her wants and needs by pointing and making sounds. Her parents describe her behavior as increasingly difficult to manage. They are very worried because at times she bangs her head or flaps her hands rapidly in front of her face. They find they avoid taking Vicki to public places like restaurants or shopping malls because she has temper tantrums and begins kicking and screaming, sometimes for no apparent reason. Around unfamiliar adults, Vicki is shy and clings to her parents. She does not seem interested in the same toys as other children her age and Vicki's parents worry that she will not be ready to start school in a couple of years.

The assessment of preschool children like Vicki is a challenge to most practitioners, even those with experience testing young children. With the passage of Public Law 99-457 in 1986, and its 1991 and 1997 reauthorizations (P.L. 102-119 and P.L. 105-17), Vicki and other young children with disabilities became entitled to a free and appropriate public education. These children are also entitled to nondiscriminatory assessment procedures ensuring that tests are (a) administered in the child's native language, (b) valid for their selected purpose, (c) administered by appropriately trained personnel, (d) selected to reflect the child's aptitude and abilities rather than just the child's disabilities, and (e) that no single procedure is used to determine eligibility or services to be delivered. This is quite a challenge for early childhood professionals assessing young children with disabilities. In a recent national survey of preschool psychologists, Bagnato and Neisworth (1994) underscored the difficulty of assessing these children. The survey respondents described a number of child characteristics that limit the use of traditional assessment methods including (a) language deficits, (b) sensory impairments, (c) behavior that interfered with performance, (d) multiple disabilities, and (e) social skill deficits. Most of these respondents found it necessary to supplement or abandon the traditional assessment methods typically successful with school-aged children.

The intent of this chapter is to provide the reader with assessment strategies to utilize when faced with a child like Vicki or any preschooler with a disability, regardless of severity. We will begin with a discussion of the purposes of assessment, how the determination of assessment goals leads to development of an assessment plan addressing the individual needs of the child, and description of a multidimensional model of assessment that currently reflects best practice in preschool assessment. Practical assessment strategies will be offered for assessing children with mental retardation, multiple disabilities, autism, orthopedic impairments, and traumatic brain injury. Finally, we will offer advice when assessing young children with other health conditions that may impact development, including pediatric HIV/AIDS, lead poisoning, *in utero* exposure to drugs or alcohol, and prematurity. Throughout the chapter we will offer recommendations to address the individual needs of preschool children with disabilities.

Determining the Purpose of Assessment

Assessment of young children is undertaken for an array of reasons, although all reasons share a common goal, to solve the psychological problems of clients. For practitioners serving young children with, or suspected of having, a disability, assessment is designed to answer questions about the child and develop interventions that will treat (perhaps solve) the child's problems. These questions may lead us to assess for purposes of screening, diagnosis, eligibility determination, intervention planning, and/or program monitoring (McLean, 1996). The purpose of the assessment is driven by the type of questions to be answered about the child. For Vicki, the assessment may answer these questions: (a) Does Vicki have a disability and if so, what impact may it have on her development? (b) Does Vicki meet the eligibility requirements for early childhood special education in her state of residence? (c) What is Vicki's current level of functioning and what are her strengths and weaknesses? and (d) What intervention/treatment services does Vicki need and where should those services be provided? Prior to the assessment, a practitioner will determine the questions to be answered through assessment, guiding the selection of assessment instruments and the areas of development to be assessed.

A multidimensional assessment will include a variety of assessment methods, measure multiple developmental domains, and accumulate data from multiple sources and across multiple settings (Bagnato & Neisworth, 1991; Paget & Nagle, 1986). Each measure is specifically chosen to document development, though there are many different approaches to doing so. Standardized, norm-referenced assessment approaches are not appropriate or desirable for all young children with disabilities. Other assessment methods (criterion-referenced, judgement-based, or qualitative/developmental) will yield important information that is useful for identifying strengths and weaknesses, planning interventions, and documenting developmental change. Play-based methods such as those described by Linder (Chapter 10, this volume) are another alternative to consider for young children.

It is sometimes necessary to adapt traditional, norm-referenced assessment for young children with disabilities. This is called 'testing of limits' and allows the evaluator to go beyond standard test procedures to obtain a more accurate picture of the children's strengths and weaknesses (Sattler, 1992). This break with standardized protocol occurs after the complete administration of the measure and does not change the child's scores, which should be reported based on the standardized administration. The early childhood professional may find testing of limits to be useful when, for example, a child is able to, perform on a cognitive measure like the Wechsler Primary and Preschool Scale of Intelligence-Revised (WPPSI-R; Wechsler, 1989), but failed all the items of the Block Design subtest. Sattler suggests that the examiner may wish to revisit the subtest and provide additional time for the child to assemble the designs that were previously missed. For young children, testing of limits may include modifications of the assessment task or of the response required by the child (Salvia & Ysseldyke, 1991). An example of modifications that may be attempted when testing limits is presented in Table 17.1.

Again, the goal of testing of limits is to gain additional information about the child and his or her strengths and weaknesses. The report generated from the assessment must include a description of the modifications and the resulting performance. Standardized scores should not be computed for performances achieved by testing of limits, as this is a clear break from standardized assessment procedures.

For preschool children, the developmental domains to be measured are defined by Part B of IDEA amendments, 1997, and include physical development (gross and fine motor), cognitive development, communication development (receptive and expressive), social or emotional development, and adaptive development. Though eligibility criteria for preschool special education vary by state, the assessment of these developmental domains provides a clear and comprehensive description of the child's development and guides selection of the assessment tools. Another consideration is whether to use a measure that assesses multiple developmental domains or one that assesses a single domain. Generally,

TABLE 17.1   Testing of Limits with Young Children

Modification of task demands	Modification of required response
Make test pieces easier to handle by adding pegs to puzzle pieces or using larger blocks.	Make a verbal task nonverbal by crediting pointing rather than naming a picture.
Teach the child a strategy for solving the problem.	Change modality of a task.
Provide additional cues to the correct response.	If child cannot isolate a finger to point, allow pointing with a fist.
Make an abstract item concrete (e.g., use real blocks rather than a picture of the design to be copied).	If the child cannot generate an answer, make the item multiple choice by offering three or four answer choices.
Break task into smaller segments.	Eliminate time limits for tasks.
Ask parent or familiar adult to administer items.	Solve part of the problem for the child, (e.g., put two of five puzzle pieces together for the child).
Enlarge items by photocopy.	Allow child to indicate correct answer by eye gaze.
Repeat instructions or include gestures with instructions.	Readminister items giving the child cues to the correct response.

Note: Adapted from *Assessment* (fifth edition) by J. Salvia & J. E. Ysseldyke, 1991, Boston: Houghton Mifflin and *Assessment of children* (Revised and updated 3rd edition) by J. Sattler, (1992), San Diego: Jerome M. Sattler.

single-domain measures provide a more comprehensive evaluation of the domain than multi-domain measures, but their use requires that more time and a greater number of instruments be invested in the assessment.

Data should be acquired from different sources to obtain an accurate and full picture of a child's strengths and weaknesses. For young children, this typically includes the parents and other family members, preschool teachers, and paraprofessionals. Parent involvement in the assessment process is particularly valuable because the parents are best able to put the child's performance into the perspective of daily life and developmental history. Parents should be encouraged to identify the level of involvement that is best suited for themselves and their child.

A multidimensional assessment of the preschool child is not complete without the recognition of the importance of the child's environment to his or her present behavior and developmental outcome. Judgement-based assessment of the preschool environment provides a systematic way to evaluate setting variables such as personal care routines, physical plant, creative activities, and opportunities for social and motor development (Harms & Clifford, 1980). This assessment will assist in determining and selecting an appropriate preschool environment to facilitate development.

General Considerations for Testing Young Children with Disabilities

Careful planning is required when assessing a young child. In addition to the assessment procedures described in Chapter 5 (this volume), additional considerations are necessary when the child has or is suspected of having a disability.

Preparing for the Assessment

Gathering Information.   The unique behaviors and characteristics of a young child with a disability influence the selection of the assessment instruments and the need for evaluator preparation before the testing session. Ideally, the evaluator has observed the child in a variety of settings. These observations, along with a careful review of records and consultation with adults who know the child, will identify child variables that may impact the assessment. Once these variables are identified, the evaluator should determine strategies to accommodate the child's needs. Variables that should be considered include:

Medical Needs and Effects of Medication.   Is the child currently taking medication (prescription or over-the-counter) and how does the medication affect the child's alertness, attention, motor activity, and behavior? Does the child have seizures? If so, what do they look like and how should the evaluator respond?

Child's Ability to Perceive Test Stimuli.   Have the child's hearing and vision been assessed? Does the child have any sensory impairments? How might they affect the evaluation session and what accommodations will be necessary?

Special Positioning Needs.   Does the child have special positioning needs? Does the child use special adaptive equipment? Will it be available during the assessment?

Child's Ability to Use Reciprocal Communication.   How does the child communicate? Is the child verbal? How effective is that communication with unfamiliar adults? What type of writing tool does the child use, if any?

Child's Behaviors that May Interfere with Evaluation Performance.   Does the child have any problematic behavior? How are those behaviors responded to at home? At preschool or daycare? What is the child's best time of day? What environment is most conducive to the child's performance? How does the child typically respond to strangers?

Parental Involvement in Assessment.   There is consensus that family involvement is a necessary and worthwhile component of early childhood assessment. Best practice mandates that preassessment activities include (a) professional contact with families to share and review existing information about the child, (b) identification of family questions and concerns that will guide test selection and assessment procedures, (c) collaboration between professionals and families to determine who will participate as assessment team members, and (d) determination of the role of family members in the assessment (DEC Task Force on Recommended Practices, 1993).

Early childhood professionals are strongly encouraged to include one or both parents during the assessment sessions. This avoids the anxiety of separation that can be disruptive with young children. Parents should be prepared for the assessment session with a careful explanation of the types of tasks that will be presented to the child, a description of standardized assessment, if it will be used, the need for items to be presented in a prescribed manner and reasons for asking the child to attempt tasks that will be too difficult. Parents should be assured that they will have an opportunity to demonstrate or readminister tasks to the child if they like. This will diminish interruptions during the session and allow the parent to demonstrate the child's best performance. Parents who observe or participate in the assessment are an excellent "validity check" for the test results and will likely have more confidence in the results when they have been a part of the process.

A secondary gain to parent involvement in the assessment process becomes apparent when it is recognized that the assessment frequently acts as an intervention. Parents will see their child's competence in some areas and recognize unknown weaknesses in others. Assessment also provides parents with new play ideas. Some parents who never thought to offer paper and crayons or scissors to their three-year-old may soon be providing their child with these opportunities.

The Testing Session.   On the day of the assessment, it is recommended that the evaluator contact the caregiver, confirm the appointment, and determine that the child is healthy. Many young children with disabilities have frequent illnesses (as do youngsters who are not disabled). Comfortable dress is necessary so that the evaluator is prepared to sit on the floor or child-sized chair. Take along stickers or small toys as reinforcers. A puppet will facilitate interaction with even the shyest child. A switch toy will prove useful for a child with severe orthopedic or multiple disabilities. After each session, sterilize all the assessment items to protect the health of the next child using the toys.

The evaluator should prepare a test environment that minimizes distractions. Test in short sessions with frequent breaks. Interspersing work and play is often an effective manner of structuring the sessions. See the child in multiple settings and on more than one occasion. All children are influenced by their environment; a shy, quiet child at preschool may be talkative and energetic at home. Begin the sessions with tasks that ensure success. Many children enjoy visual-motor tasks such as drawing and coloring. Early success may ensure continued effort when tasks become more difficult.

Suggestions for Assessing Preschoolers with Special Needs

Each child brings his or her own unique characteristics to the evaluation session. Children with disabilities have additional individual attributes that interact with the evaluation session, the evaluator, and the selected assessment instruments. Though each child is unique, certain disabilities involve characteristics that are generally consistent across children with that disability. Table 17.2 summarizes some unique assessment challenges that young children with disabilities may bring to the assessment setting. Specific recommendations to facilitate the assessment process with these children follow.

Assessing the Child With Mental Retardation

The new definition of mental retardation developed by the American Association on Mental Retardation (AAMR) impacts both assessment and intervention planning provided for children who fall within this category (AAMR, 1992). This definition includes children with IQs from 70 to 75 (to allow for measurement error) with deficits in at least 2 of 10 areas of adaptive behavior (communication, social skills, health and safety, work, self-care,

TABLE 17.2 Disability-Specific Assessment Considerations

	MR	A	OI	TBI	HIV/ AIDS	Lead	Drug- exposed	Premature
Easily fatigued			X	X	X			X
Easily distracted	X	X	X	X		X	X	X
Communication deficits	X	X	X	X			X	X
Difficulty maintaining attention to task	X	X	X	X	X	X	X	X
Motivation deficits	X	X		X				X
Unique positioning needs			X	X	X			X
Establishing/maintaining rapport	X	X						
Difficulty maintaining alertness	X			X	X			X
Failure to understand contingencies	X	X						
Uneven skill development		X	X	X				X
Difficulty with social rules		X						
Negative effects of medication				X	X	X	X	X	X
Stereotypes	X	X						

Note: **MR**—Mental Retardation; **A**—Autism; **OI**—Orthopedic Impairment; **TBI**—Traumatic Brain Injury community use, functional academics, home living, self-direction, and leisure-time activities). In addition, severity classifications (mild, moderate, severe, and profound) were replaced with a system that describes the level of support needed by the individual to function within their community. These levels of support intensity are described as: intermittent (as needed), limited (regularly occurring though time-limited), extensive (ongoing and regular), and pervasive (constant and highly intense) (AAMR). This new definition is not without its critics. Gresham, MacMillan, and Siperstein (1995) analyzed its implications and identified a number of measurement concerns. These include (a) changing the IQ cutoff will increase (perhaps double) the number of individuals who will meet the IQ score criterion for mental retardation, (b) potentially greater impact upon African Americans, who are already over-represented among those classified as mildly mentally handicapped, (c) the lack of adequate norm-referenced measures of the 10 adaptive skill areas, (d) no established measures to differentiate among the four levels of support intensity, and (e) little utility when identifying mental retardation in children, particularly the very young.

Practical Considerations.   In spite of the above controversy, early childhood professionals will continue to provide comprehensive assessment of young children with mental retardation. The following recommendations are provided to assist in this process:

Carefully Examine Each Developmental Domain.   The evaluation should address each of the domains with a careful examination of cognitive development, adaptive behavior, and academic readiness (discussed extensively in Chapters 9, 10, and 14, respectively, this volume).

Consider the Child's Cultural Context.   Unfortunately, despite our sophisticated diagnostic instruments and growing awareness of cultural bias in assessment, there continues to be an over-representation of minorities among individuals diagnosed as mildly mentally retarded. Careful assessment of adaptive behavior within the child's cultural context will be necessary to guard against mislabeling children (see Chapter 16, this volume, on testing culturally and linguistically different children).

Obtain a Complete History.   A thorough interview with the parents will also be necessary to carefully document prenatal history and development (including drug or alcohol use by the mother), attainment of developmental milestones, history of illnesses or head injuries, and early environmental experiences (Semrud-Clikeman & Hynd, 1993).

Assess Maladaptive Behavior.   Families and teachers should also be encouraged to identify maladaptive behaviors that interfere with development or challenge parenting. Adaptive behavior instruments may include a behavioral domain which allows identification of problematic behaviors that may interfere with educational and social development and can provide a baseline for intervention development and monitoring. A selection of instruments that are particularly useful for assessing young children with developmental disabilities is provided on Table 17.3.

Assessing the Child with Multiple Disabilities

For the most part, children with severe/profound mental retardation or multiple disabilities are identified at birth, though some of these children may have experienced an illness or

TABLE 17.3   Selected Assessment Instruments for Children with Developmental Disabilities

Instrument	Description	Special Population
Assessment of Developmental Level by Observation (Wolf-Schein, 1993)	Performance assessment of behavior in relationship to adults, expressive/receptive language, gross and fine motor, and self-help. For the most difficult-to-assess child.	MR, PDD, MD
Bracken Basic Concept Scale (Bracken, 1984)	Measure of basic concepts of color, letter and number identification, counting and quantity, comparisons, shape, direction/position, size, texture, and time/sequence	MR, PDD
Carolina Record of Individual Behavior (Simeonsson, 1979)	Observational measure of behavioral state, orientation to objects and persons, communication, and stereotypes.	Children at sensorimotor level
Childhood Autism Rating Scale (Schopler, Reichler, & Renner, 1988)	Behaviorally based rating system of autistic behavior.	PDD
Early Coping Inventory (Zeitlin, Williamson, & Szczepanski, 1988) Coping Inventory (Zeitlin, 1985)	Criterion-referenced observation measures of the effectiveness of strategies for coping with both self and the environment.	MR, PDD, OI, TBI, MD
Ordinal Scales of Psychological Development (Uzgiris & Hunt, 1975)	Individually administered measure of sensorimotor development.	MR, PDD
Social Skills Rating System (Gresham & Elliot, 1990)	Multirater measure of prosocial (cooperation, assertion, self-control) and problem behaviors (externalizing, internalizing) and rating of intervention priority.	MR, PDD, TBI
Vineland Adaptive Behavior Scales (Sparrow, Balla & Cicchetti, 1984)	Multirater inventory of personal and social development. Includes rating of problem behavior.	MR, PDD, TBI, OI, MD

Note: **MR**—Mental Retardation; **PDD**—Pervasive Developmental Disorder; **MD**—Multiple Disabilities; **OI**—Orthopedic Impaired; **TBI**—Traumatic Brain Injury accident that caused catastrophic damage after birth. Many will have additional medical complications that affect development and/or sensory or motor impairments in addition to mental retardation. Young children with severe/profound or multiple disabilities will require a specially designed assessment battery that is extensively modified. For children with multiple disabilities, it is imperative that assessment be designed to contribute to intervention planning. Unfortunately, it is all too common for professionals to describe young children who are not successful in a traditional, standardized assessment situation as "untestable." Children with multiple disabilities, particularly those with communication, motor, and sensory impairments, are more likely to receive this label. This is due in great measure to the inexperience of the evaluator, inappropriate reliance upon standardized assessment techniques, and improper selection of test measures, rather than the true nature of the child's disabilities (Marcus & Baker, 1986).

Behavioral States.   In order to accurately assess the abilities of young children, particularly those with severe or multiple disabilities, the child's behavioral state during testing must be taken into account. *Behavioral state* refers to the child's levels of arousal or consciousness. State falls along a continuum from deep sleep to active/alert to agitated (See Table 17.4 for a description of this continuum). Consideration of the child's state and his or her ability to control state is an important component of a thorough evaluation.

Given that behavioral states "mediate the child's ability to respond to the environment and to stimulation," (Helm, 1989, p. 203) the behavioral state or range of states demonstrated

TABLE 17.4   Behavioral States as Defined by the Carolina Record of Individual Behavior

State	Description
1	Deep sleep; eyes closed, regular respiration, no body movements.
2	Intermediate sleep, eyes closed, few minor facial, body, and/or mouth movements; respiration is "periodic" alternating periods of deep and shallow breathing.
3	Active sleep, eyes closed, irregular respiration, some gross motor activity (stirring, writhing, grimacing, mouthing, or other facial expression).
4	Drowsiness, eyes open and closed intermittently, fluttering eyelids, eyes have glassy appearance, frequent relaxation followed by sudden jerks.
5	Quiet awake, relatively inactive, eyes open and appear bright and shiny, respiration regular.
6	Active awake, eyes open, diffuse motor activity of limbs or whole body, vocalizations of a content nature.
7	Fussy awake, eyes open, irregular respirations, diffuse motor activity, vocalizations of a fussy, cranky variety.
8	Mild agitation, eyes open, diffuse motor activity, moderate crying, tears may or may not be present.
9	Marked uncontrollable agitation, screaming, eyes open or closed, tears may or may not be present.

Note: From Simeonsson, R. J. (1979). *Carolina Record of Individual Behavior.* Chapel Hill, NC: University of North Carolina.

by a child during testing will either enhance or severely limit the validity of an assessment. Factors such as medication or disorders of the central nervous system (CNS) may lead to overarousal (hyperactivity) or underarousal (drowsiness), both of which interfere with examiner attempts to obtain an optimal performance. Documentation of the child's range of state can serve to qualify the overall assessment findings to account for the child's level of responsivity (Simeonsson, 1986).

In the same way that inadequate state control can interfere with assessment, it can interfere in an even more profound way with the child's daily functioning. Research has demonstrated that children with profound disabilities may experience the active/alert state for as little as 20% of the day, making them unavailable to others and to experiences in their environment (Guess et al., 1993). Therefore, the assessment of state control provides important information for intervention planning. Given that children with severe CNS impairments or those on medication regimens may lack adequate state control, maximizing the child's naturally occurring alert states can be a vital intervention goal. Parents and teachers may need to develop strategies for manipulating the environment to facilitate alertness. Interventions such as speech therapy or attendance at preschool should be timed to correspond with the child's "best periods." For example, a child who is always drowsy in the morning because of medication effects may be better served by attending afternoon preschool.

Another compelling argument for assessment of children's state is that state control is a developmental process that provides important information about the functioning of the CNS (Thomas, 1990). In typically developing children, the organization of states begins in early infancy, as periods of sleeping and wakefulness become increasingly differentiated and of longer duration. Research suggests that the developmental process of state organization may be disrupted in children with disabilities. Similarly, disrupted state organization may reflect CNS dysfunction (MacLean, MacLean, & Baumeister, 1995).

Assessment of State Organization.   To examine state organization during infancy, researchers have utilized a number of methods, ranging from the simple (e.g., naturalistic observation) to the sublime (e.g., video solmography) (MacLean et al., 1995). For the practitioner, however, rating scales are the method of choice. Most scales designed to assess state were developed for use with infants (e.g., Brazelton Neonatal Assessment Scale, Brazelton, 1984; Assessment of Preterm Infants' Behavior, Als, Lester, Tronick, & Brazelton, 1982). However, the Carolina Record of Individual Behavior (CRIB) (Simeonsson, 1979) rates the range and predominant states observed during an assessment and is intended for use with any individual functioning in the sensorimotor stage of development. The specific criteria for rating state as specified in the CRIB is outlined in Table 17.4. Behavioral observations at different times of the day and in different settings as well as interviews with parents and caregivers about the child's levels of arousal are also important sources of information. Ongoing and frequent assessment of behavioral state in early childhood is recommended to document change, increase active/alert states, and optimally time interventions when the child is most likely to benefit (Guess et al., 1993).

Strategies to Help the Child Maintain an Optimal State.   Apart from assessing state in its own right, to some extent examiners can facilitate the maintenance of optimal states for assessment. The following strategies are recommended:

1. In planning the assessment, ask the caregiver to identify the best time of day for the child and schedule accordingly.

2. Ask the caregiver or, with the caregiver's permission, the child's physician about medications and their effects on the child's arousal. It may be possible to delay administration of some medications if they will interfere with the child's ability to concentrate. On the other hand, if the child regularly takes a medication (e.g., Ritalin) designed to improve concentration, the medication could affect the assessment in a positive way. In these cases, the practitioner (in consultation with the child's parent and physician) should decide whether or not taking the medication will enhance or limit the validity of the assessment. The practitioner should carefully document in the assessment report any medications taken prior to the session and their possible effects on state control and arousal.

3. During the assessment, the examiner will need to systematically vary the nature and extent of stimulation to maintain the child's attention. A child who is overaroused may require a laid back style, fast-paced delivery of items, and stimulus-free environment. On the other hand, the underaroused child may benefit from a more animated examiner.

4. If the child has difficulty maintaining an optimal state either because of under- or over-arousal, the assessment should be conducted over a series of shorter segments, possibly over the course of several days.

Augmentative and Alternative Communication.   Children with multiple disabilities are likely to have sensory and/or motor impairments that will interfere with effective communication. The presence of severe speech impairments may also necessitate incorporating augmentative or alternative communication strategies. Children with multiple disabilities incorporate a number of different strategies to communicate with others. A recent survey of caregivers of children and young adults with severe speech impairments associated with disabilities (e.g., cerebral palsy, traumatic brain injury, mental retardation, and sensory deficits) described their use of augmentative and alternative communication (Allaire, Gressard, Blackman, & Hostler, 1991). Their strategies included crying/cooing (35%), gesturing/pointing (45%), eye pointing (33%), moving body/face (29%), sign language (25%), communication boards (13%), and other electronic systems (19%). The majority (81%) used more than one strategy to communicate. Given that some of these systems are informal, parents and/or teachers should be consulted to determine the most reliable means of communicating with the child.

The early childhood professional must also determine whether the child's response is reliable and purposeful—a difficult proposition when the child is nonverbal, orthopedically impaired, or when reciprocal interactions are uncertain, as with autism. A range of response modes can be incorporated and a child assessed to determine their response reliability. If necessary, training to develop new response strategies may be necessary. Duncan, Sbardellati, Maheady, and Sainato (1981) suggested this continuum of response modes: (a) expressive language response, (b) pointing response, or (c) an existing motor response. If these are not present, they recommend training an existing response that is inconsistent or teaching a new response. If necessary, the evaluator should attend to involuntary responses. These may include changes in color, respiration, or movement.

The Developmental Domains.   Though the practitioners will want to consider each of the developmental domains, for the child with multiply disabilities these domains may be redefined or expanded to provide a more useful description of the child. An assessment report may forgo descriptions within the developmental domains and instead include descriptions of the following (Rogers, 1986; Reavis, 1990; Sternberg, 1994; Davidson & Dolins, 1993):

Awareness of Environment.   Document the child's recognition, exploration, and control of objects and the environment. What efforts does the child make to obtain and manipulate objects? This may indicate problem-solving abilities. Can the child be taught a new behavior such as activating a switch toy? Remove the toy and reintroduce it later to see if the child remembers how it is activated.

Awareness and Response to Others.   Can the child discriminate familiar persons from strangers? What does the child do to communicate this awareness? Does the child make eye contact? Assessment of receptive language will be influenced by the degree to which the child's sensory systems are intact. In general, the evaluator should consider how the child demonstrates understanding of the communication of others.

Communication.   How does the child communicate needs and wants? Can the child indicate by pointing, eye gaze, or vocalizing? Can the parents differentiate the child's cries to know when he/she is hungry, tired, in pain? Does the child imitate sounds, movements, or facial expressions? Does the child use sign or an augmentative or alternative communication system? If so, describe the system and its effectiveness.

Movement.   Begin by assessing the child's ability to move independently and whether the child can ambulate about the environment. Is movement purposeful? Note the use of adaptive equipment and how it facilitates movement. What positions best facilitate participation in the assessment? Next, describe the child's fine motor movements. Note how the child interacts with the environment and whether that interaction is functional and purposeful. Is grasp voluntary? Can the child reach for, obtain, and manipulate objects? How does the child coordinate both hands? If the child is not able to grasp or manipulate objects, how does he/she interact with objects?

Adaptive Behavior.   This section should describe how the child is able to cope with change in the environment. Does the child require rigid adherence to a routine? How well does the child tolerate transitions?
   Next, describe the child's self-care, including:

■ The child's ability to self-feed and respond to caregivers' feeding. Many children with medical problems have special diets or alternative means of nutritional intake (e.g., gastrostomy tube). Though special skills are necessary for a comprehensive assessment of feeding, the evaluator can describe the daily feeding routines with special attention to problems and concerns noted by the parents. Problems may include coordinating suck, swallow and breathing, gagging, vomiting and rumination, or difficulties with digestion or constipation (Eicher, 1992). Feeding times may be stressful for parents who must balance the child's need for nutrition with the length and intensity of the sessions.

■ Note the degree of independence in toileting and any special concerns. Some motor impairments such as spasticity may cause diapering problems as the child's hypertonicity interferes with the ability to separate the legs. Is the child aware of being wet or soiled? Can the child indicate the need to toilet? Is there an established routine?

■ How independent is the child in bathing and dressing? Does the child cooperate in dressing? How does the child tolerate bathing, tooth brushing, and hair care?

Assessment of Behaviors that May be Problematic or Maladaptive.   This should include stereotypic, self-stimulatory, and injurious behavior. A behavioral assessment of frequency, intensity, and duration is most useful for establishing a baseline and measuring the effects of intervention.

Assessing the Child with Pervasive Developmental Disorders

The recent revision of the *Diagnostic and Statistical Manual* (DSM-IV; American Psychiatric Association, 1994) includes diagnostic criteria for five Pervasive Developmental Disorders (PDD's) including autism and Asperger's Disorder. Autism, the most commonly recognized of these disorders, is characterized by impairments of communication and social interaction, accompanied by stereotypical behavior, interests, or activities. As with autism, children with Asperger's show impaired social interactions and unusual or a restricted range of interests. On the other hand, children with Asperger's generally demonstrate no significant delay in language development, though they may have unusual communication behaviors such as robot-like speech. Social interactions show marked impairment. Teachers and family members may describe these children as "eccentric." Asperger's is thought to be more prevalent than autism, though the differential diagnosis is very difficult, particularly in the preschool years. There is some evidence to suggest that children with Asperger's are initially slow to develop language, but that these delays remit during the later preschool years (Bucy & Foust, 1996). Therefore, it is sometimes the case that a child is diagnosed as autistic, then, after language develops, the diagnosis is changed to Asperger's. Though the diagnosis may have implications over time, in many cases, intervention designs will be much the same for young children with Asperger's and those with high functioning autism.

Assessment of young children with PDD is particularly challenging because the nature of the assessment process is both social and communicative. These children also are likely to demonstrate behaviors that interfere with the evaluation (e.g., hand flapping, perseveration, echolalia). Accommodation for the child can be made in the following manner (Marcus & Baker, 1986; Marcus, Lansing, & Schopler, 1993; Waterman, 1982).

Practical Considerations

Minimize the social aspects of the evaluation session.   When assessing a child with PDD, it is advisable to minimize both eye contact and interpersonal interactions. Keep verbal communication to a minimum. Use hand movements, gestures, and physical prompts to facilitate understanding of task instructions.

Ensure early success.   Begin the assessment session with tasks that ensure the child's success. Visual-motor tasks are often more rewarding and enjoyable than tasks which require verbal interaction.

Establish an assessment routine.   Quickly establish an assessment routine and maintain it. Intersperse assessment activities with play breaks. For some children, it may be helpful to allow self-stimulatory behavior as a tension-relief and reward for task completion.

Establish a routine for task completion. Marcus et al. (1993) suggest using a "Finished Box," a special place for the child to place a task after its completion.

Try nonverbal measures to assess cognitive functioning. Many children with PDD are by definition nonverbal or limited in their communication skills. The evaluator may have more success measuring cognitive performance with nonverbal procedures.

Document your observations. Immediately following the assessment, rate the child's behavior with a scale designed to measure autistic behavior like the Childhood Autism Rating Scale (Schopler, Reichler, & Renner, 1988).

Assessing the Child with Orthopedic Impairments

Many children with orthopedic impairments have normal cognitive skills, though their physical disabilities may interfere with their demonstration of these abilities during assessment. Motor impairments may prevent the child from completing assessment tasks in a standardized fashion, resulting in a gross underestimate of the child's abilities, particularly in cognitive and communication domains. Children with motor impairments may also demonstrate poor development of visual-perception. Young children with orthopedic impairments may not have complete head control, sitting balance, or upright ambulation (Copeland & Kimmel, 1989). They may be delayed in their ability to reach, grasp, and manipulate objects or use both hands together. In addition, adaptations to standardized tests are likely to be necessary. Specific recommendations for assessing children with orthopedic impairments are presented next.

Practical Considerations

Gain information about positioning needs. Parents of young children with cerebral palsy, neural tube defect, or other movement disorders frequently receive training regarding the correct positioning and handling of their children. Evaluators should consult with parents and/or a physical or occupational therapist familiar with the child. Identify specific positioning strategies or adaptive equipment needs that will maximize the child's balance and coordination and improve test performance.

Allow frequent changes in position. The child with neural tube defects may need frequent changes in position and movement tasks that are interspersed throughout the assessment period, as decreased sensations of pain or pressure in the buttocks and lower extremities can lead to injury.

Allow extra time to respond. Allow the child additional time to respond to both verbal and motoric tasks. In addition to longer processing time, the child may be slower to determine a response or have difficulty initiating independent movement. Be sure to separate item choices sufficiently when the child is using eye gaze or pointing with a fist to indicate a selection. Assessment instruments that allow for flexible test conditions, such as the Ordinal Scales of Intellectual Development (Uzgiris & Hunt, 1975) are particularly desirable (Cioni, Paolicelli, Sordi, & Vinter, 1993).

Determine whether the child uses augmentative or alternative communication. Allow the child to use their communication system during the evaluation. (Additional discussion of AAC is presented in Chapter 12.) If the child is able to communicate effectively orally, verbal tests will be preferable to visual-motor tasks.

Be skeptical of assessment results.   Tests may underestimate true abilities. Be aware, however, that the *halo effect* may unduly influence assessment procedures and produce interpretations of performance that may be inaccurately positive (Wilhelm, Johnson, & Eisert, 1986).

Assessing the Child with Traumatic Brain Injury (TBI)

According to the National Head Injury Foundation (NHIF, 1985), a traumatic brain injury is "an insult to the brain, not of a degenerative or congenital nature, but caused by an external force, that may produce a diminished or altered state of consciousness." An "external force" may consist of a blow to the head resulting in either an open or closed injury. In an open head injury, the skull is penetrated and generally leads to very specific deficits. Damage from a closed head injury occurs as a result of the mechanical force on the brain and generally results in more diffuse deficits than an open head injury (Kolb & Whishaw, 1990). While it is important to distinguish an "external force" from a degenerative disorder that leads to decline in functioning, it is also important to remember that the force does not have to consist of a direct blow to the head. For example, in the case of a "shaken baby" there is no physical contact to the head, but damage occurs nonetheless as a result of the acceleration-deceleration of the brain within the skull (Snow & Hooper, 1994).

A number of factors—severity of injury, type of injury, and associated medical complications (e.g., cerebral hemorrhage, infections)—contribute to the differential developmental outcomes of pediatric TBI. However, the factor that is perhaps most salient for this discussion is the age at which the injury occurred. While studies of children 5 years of age and older find no relationship between the age at which the injury occurred and recovery, studies that include infants and preschoolers report more severe outcomes are found for younger children (Snow & Hooper, 1994).

Practical Considerations.   Because of the complexity of the issues surrounding brain development during the preschool years and recovery from early insult, evaluation of children with TBI should be conducted by or in close consultation with a pediatric neuropsychologist. Additional considerations in the assessment of this population include:

Utilize a neuropsychological approach.   In taking a "neuropsychological approach" to psychological assessment, the clinician addresses a wide array of characteristics and abilities, including the following areas: gross and fine motor functioning, sensory and perceptual abilities across modalities (i.e., visual, auditory, tactile and kinesthetic); visual-motor abilities and visual processing; receptive and expressive language abilities including auditory processing; memory, planning; attention and concentration; and behavior. Because there are no widely used neuropsychological batteries for preschoolers (Hooper, 1991), the clinician who would conduct such an assessment must have a sophisticated understanding of early neurodevelopment as well as the ability to adapt and utilize formal and informal assessment techniques appropriate for young children. Additional discussion of neuropsychological assessment is presented in Chapter 15 of this volume.

Look at quality, not just quantity.   The characteristics of preschoolers, as well as the nature of TBI, compel the evaluator to consider the *quality* as well as the *quantity* of behavior. Particularly because TBI may lead to very specific deficits, the way that a child approaches or completes a task may have substantial implications for treatment and prognosis. Problem-solving behavior is more important than the product of the performance.

Attempt to obtain an estimate of preinjury functioning.   To estimate the effects of a TBI, current functioning must be compared to pre-injury functioning. If no formal assessment was conducted prior to the injury (as is likely the case), estimates of global functioning can be obtained through interviews with parents or preschool teachers or examining early school records. In addition, most pediatricians globally assess their patients' developmental status and record information such as when milestones were achieved.

Conduct an evaluation as soon as possible following the injury and at frequent intervals, particularly during the first year post-injury.   The existing evidence suggests that recovery following a TBI continues for one year after the accident, with the bulk of the gains occurring within the first 6 months (Snow & Hooper, 1994).

Other Conditions Affecting Preschool Development

In addition to the disabilities of mental retardation, autism, orthopedic impairments, and traumatic brain injury, there are a number of health-related events that may compromise the developmental outcome of children. Though they are too numerous to address in this chapter, we have included some conditions that are unfortunately becoming more prevalent and have greater impact during early childhood. These are pediatric HIV/AIDS, lead poisoning, prenatal exposure to drugs or alcohol, and the effects of prematurity.

Pediatric HIV/AIDS

As of the summer of 1995, at least one-half million Americans were reported to have contracted AIDS since the onset of this dreaded illness (CDC, 1995a). HIV infection among children is growing at an alarming rate: The 12-month period July, 1994 to June, 1995 witnessed almost 1,000 new cases in the pediatric setting (CDC, 1995a). Because treatment drugs continue to enhance the longevity of patients, an increasing number of HIV-infected children are living to reach school age (Palfrey et al., 1994).

It is important to acknowledge that AIDS attacks entire families. It is projected that, by the year 2000, more than 80,000 children and adolescents in the U.S. will have been orphaned by maternal deaths attributable to HIV and AIDS (Michaels & Levine, 1992). Even if the preschool-age child does not present medically with the disease, children who have a family member with AIDS may be subjected to social stigma and intense emotional strain (Pryor & Reeder, 1993). Clearly, HIV/AIDS is a growing concern for professionals who serve the preschool setting. As such, early childhood practitioners need to become familiar with issues surrounding HIV infection and its psychoeducational and psychosocial sequelae, to meet the growing needs of involved children and their families.

Epidemiology of HIV/AIDS.   Even though an exhaustive review of epidemiological information is well beyond the scope of this chapter (see Landau, Mangione, & Pryor, in press), important trends related to young children need to be discussed. Approximately 90% of infected children have acquired HIV through perinatal transmission (CDC, 1995b).

Modes of perinatal transmission include intrauterine or transplacental (e.g., during early or late pregnancy), intrapartum (e.g., at delivery), and postpartum (e.g., through breast feeding) (Levenson & Mellins, 1992). All babies born of HIV-infected mothers carry maternal antibodies to HIV; however, only about one-third are actually infected with the virus. Distinct groups exist representing the spectrum of HIV disease in infants (CDC, 1994b). Infants born to known-infected mothers are classified in a transitional category and not clinically confirmed as to their HIV status. These infants will test positive to HIV antibody tests because they carry maternal antibodies until 15 months of age. At this time, they will lose the passively acquired maternal antibodies. Approximately 70% of these infants will test negative when their own antibodies are tested. The classification for these infants is called seroreverters. If the infant's antibodies continue to test positive for the HIV infection, four classifications are possible: Category N (Not Symptomatic) is used to classify those infants testing positive who will remain relatively healthy and asymptomatic for a number of years. However, when an infant or child becomes symptomatic (e.g., progressive neurological disease, pneumonia), a classification of Category A (Mildly Symptomatic), B (Moderately Symptomatic), or C (Severely Symptomatic) is used.

Medical Symptoms.   HIV attacks the cells that activate the body's immune response and manifests itself as a series of life-threatening viral and bacterial infections which the body's immune system is unable to fight (Batshaw & Perret, 1992). Pediatric cases infected prenatally are distinguished from those infected later in life by virtue of their dramatically shorter incubation period. Eighty percent of children infected by their mothers develop frank symptoms by two years of age. In contrast, older patients experience an 8- to 10-year lag between infection and the conspicuous presence of symptoms.

Common medical problems for children with HIV infection include chronic illness, intermittent fever, recurrent diarrhea, failure to thrive, and acute weight loss (Batshaw & Perret, 1992). In addition, pediatric HIV patients are at high risk for developing bacterial infections such as meningitis or pneumonia. As such, common childhood illnesses, such as measles or chicken pox, can become deadly (Burroughs & Edelson, 1991). These children are also susceptible to minor infections of the ears, eyes, and mouth which can interfere with hearing, vision, and eating, respectively.

Neurological Sequelae.   In children, the HIV virus directly affects brain development which results in neurological damage (Fletcher et al., 1991). Indeed, this consequence is one of the most common causes of death in children with AIDS (CDC, 1995b). Children with HIV present extensive brain damage, including cerebral atrophy, enlarged ventricles, and microcephaly, all of which are related to compromised intellectual functioning. Due to the progressive nature of the disease and high likelihood of brain infection, the cognitive abilities of most children deteriorate over the course of the illness (Batshaw & Perret, 1992). Because the HIV virus has potentially profound effects on multiple areas of brain development, subsequent impairments become evident in the attainment of motor, intellectual, and developmental milestones (Cohen, Papola, & Alvarez, 1994). In addition, the infection may cause auditory and visual short-term memory difficulties, speech, and language delays, as well as severe attention deficits (Butler, Hittelman, & Hauger, 1991). Most children with pediatric HIV show delays in motor milestones. Thus, the HIV-infected child who lives to reach school age is likely to have a variety of profound academic difficulties. Needless to say, each of these domains of impaired function must serve as a potential target in the assessment protocol for pediatric HIV.

Psychosocial Sequelae.   The psychological and social consequences associated with HIV are compelling. Children with HIV present higher rates of depression and anxiety (Spiegel & Mayers, 1991). Some HIV-infected children have been labeled "autistic-like" because they present severely withdrawn behaviors (Seidel, 1991). It is not clear whether these behavioral outcomes are due to the disease itself, or other environmental stressors commonly found with HIV-infected children. Indeed, recent (and alarming) data indicate that an infected child's exposure to psychological stressors can have a deleterious effect on the medical course of pediatric HIV (Bose, Moss, Brouwers, Pizzo, & Lorion, 1994).

The stigma associated with AIDS presents a major problem for families with an HIV-infected child. Once diagnosed, the family may be ostracized. Other family members may fear catching AIDS, remain distant, and offer little support. These family-related phenomena may significantly reduce the infected child's resilience to his or her vulnerability status (see Masten, Best, & Garmezy, 1990). It is also likely in pediatric HIV cases that multiple family members are actually infected, thus contributing a host of additional psychological and social concerns. Each of these must serve as a potential focus during the assessment process.

Confounding this discussion is the fact that HIV-infected children are typically from ethnic minorities, inner cities, and poverty. These factors alone put any child at risk for social and economic hardship. Unfortunately, HIV-infected infants are more likely to have been exposed to deficient prenatal and postnatal care, and are at greater risk for *in utero* exposure to heroin, cocaine, alcohol, and nicotine (Landau, Pryor, & Haefli, 1995). Each of these factors alone could impair the development of the child; the combination may eventually prove lethal.

Practical Considerations.   From an assessment perspective, it is important to recognize that children with HIV will show individual differences regarding HIV-related CNS disease as well as a changing pattern of functioning across time (Meyers, 1994). Most children infected prenatally will present an advanced state of HIV disease by the time they reach school age. Their impairments will differ greatly depending on the areas of the brain affected by HIV-related CNS disease.

Take a longitudinal perspective.   When undertaking an assessment of preschoolers with HIV/AIDS, it is important to engage a longitudinal perspective due to the progressive nature of the disease and deteriorating CNS functioning over time (Wolters, Brouwers, & Moss, 1995). Regular and comprehensive assessments will detect changes in CNS functioning plus related areas of impairment. Batshaw and Perret (1992) recommend that HIV-positive infants be thoroughly assessed by 2 months of age and followed at least every 6 months for the first 2 years of life. If a child remains asymptomatic after 2 years of age, regular assessments should be undertaken at least yearly. If there is any delay or decline in skills, more frequent reevaluations should occur.

Neuropsychological disabilities may be global or specific.   A thorough neurodevelopmental assessment is important to determine the exact areas of impaired functioning. Early childhood programs should be flexible to account for changes in cognitive functioning across time. Monitoring these changes will aid in the decision-making process of the multidisciplinary team when deciding on developmental and educational interventions, as well as the efficacy of drug therapies.

Work within a multidisciplinary team.   Though assessment and intervention services to young children and their families are generally multidisciplinary, this is particularly important for the young child with HIV. The psychoeducational assessment protocol should also target neurodevelopmental impairment, current cognitive functioning, psychosocial functioning, physical impairments, and the many abilities known to be affected by HIV. These include receptive and expressive language, attention, memory, perceptual-motor skills, academic skills, and adaptive behavior (Wolters et al., 1995). The reader is encouraged to consult Wolters et al. (1995) for details regarding an excellent pediatric HIV psychoeducational assessment protocol.

Obtain a complete family and developmental history.   This is necessary, especially given the prevalence of poverty and drug use among mothers of pediatric HIV patients (Brouwers, Belman, & Epstein, 1991).

Lead Poisoning

Researchers have investigated the effects of lead poisoning and low level exposure to lead and its impact upon children for decades (Berney, 1993). Increased understanding of this environmental hazard has led to efforts to reduce lead exposure through legislation such as the Lead Paint Poisoning Prevention Act of 1970 and the Clean Air Act. Though lead poisoning has been described as the "... largest preventable childhood health problem in the nation" (Berney, p. 15), it continues to adversely impact the development of children. At greatest risk are poor children living in inner cities.

Children may also be exposed to lead prenatally as a result of maternal blood levels. This exposure may lead to decreased birth weight or smaller head circumference (Boivin & Giordani, 1995). Though not conclusive, low level exposure to lead in the preschool years has been shown to have a continuing impact upon child development. Needleman, Schell, Bellinger, Leviton, and Allred (1990) completed a follow-up study of children with low level lead exposure assessed through dentin lead levels. Eleven years later, the lead-exposed young adults had histories of reading difficulties and academic failure. They were noted to have reduced eye-hand coordination and reaction time and poor fine motor skills.

Practical Considerations.   When assessing young children with lead exposure, consider the following:

Refer children at risk for medical assessment.   Early detection and treatment will lessen the continued effect of the exposure on the child's brain and nervous system. Treatment may include removal of the lead from the body with drugs such as edetate calcium disodium (EDTA) and penicillamine (Batshaw & Perret, 1992). Additional environmental interventions such as removal of lead paint will diminish further exposure.

Assess for behavior and learning problems.   For the child exposed to lead, a careful evaluation of behavior will be necessary. Many children with lead exposure display behavioral and regulatory deficits resulting in diagnosis such as hyperactivity (Boivin & Giordani, 1995).

Assess hearing and language development.   Many children with lead poisoning will experience hearing loss and associated deficits in expressive and receptive language development. Careful monitoring of sensory abilities will allow early detection and prevention or reduction of subsequent developmental delays.

Prenatal Drug and Alcohol Exposure

In recent years, prenatal exposure to drugs, cocaine in particular, has received a great deal of public attention, verging, at times, on hysteria. The lay public, fueled by the popular press, seems to have assumed that the outcome for children prenatally exposed to cocaine and other drugs is particularly bleak. However, in the face of widespread pessimism, the existing literature on infants prenatally exposed to cocaine and other illegal drugs suggests differences in temperament and specific cognitive abilities, but not in global cognitive abilities (Barone, 1995; Mayes, Bornstein, Chawarska, & Granger, 1995; Edmondson & Smith, 1994).

In contrast to prenatal cocaine exposure, fetal alcohol syndrome (FAS) is among the top three known causes of mental retardation and is characterized by a well-documented pattern of craniofacial and central nervous system anomalies, including mental retardation and microcephaly. An additional cluster of characteristics has been identified as Fetal Alcohol Effects (FAE). Children with FAE demonstrate milder forms of the problems associated with FAS such as hyperactivity, short attention span, learning problems, language problems, and poor social skills (Autti-Ramo et al., 1992; Streissguth et al., 1991).

Although the effects of full-blown FAS on a child's cognitive abilities have been well researched, much less is known about the more subtle risks faced by children exposed *in utero* either to lower quantities of alcohol or to alcohol in combination with other drugs. However, the existing literature about the effects of prenatal substance exposure suggests the following general assessment considerations:

Practical Considerations

A global IQ score may not accurately reflect the child's abilities.   With the exception of heavy alcohol exposure, the prenatal substance exposure has not been linked to significant global cognitive impairment. However, subtle learning problems that are not likely to be reflected in a global IQ score are more likely to be problematic. In particular, language-based difficulties have been identified and should be given particular attention as part of developmental evaluations. Other factors such as behavioral dyscontrol and chaotic home environment that are associated with prenatal substance exposure also may interfere with a child's performance on a standardized test of ability.

Address behavioral characteristics.   In the research literature, prenatal exposure to drugs and alcohol has consistently been associated with behavior problems such as hyperactivity and difficult temperament. Therefore, child temperament and behavior should be assessed across settings, perhaps through parent and teacher questionnaires.

Use a contextual approach as a framework for the evaluation.   The caregiving environment and other environmental factors are particularly important considerations with the population (Phelps & Cox, 1993; Singer, Farkas, & Kliegman, 1992). Children who were prenatally exposed to an illicit substance are more likely to live in homes that deviate from traditional middle class norms. Additionally, such children are more likely to have been in foster care or have other contact with social services. Therefore, their behavior is best understood in the context of their caregiving environment, and behavioral observations across settings is recommended before a child's behavior is labeled deviant (Phelps & Cox, 1993).

Effects of Prematurity

Infants born prior to the 36th week after conception are considered to be premature. Over the past 20 years, the number of children born prematurely who survive has increased drastically. Notably the extent to which such children are disabled as a result of their early birth has decreased with improvements in technology as well. Among children with a history of premature delivery, outcomes range from no detectable effects to profound disability. Given such a heterogeneous group, planning for the evaluation of children born prematurely must be done on a case by case basis. However, a review of the literature suggests a number of general considerations for assessment planning.

Practical Considerations.   For the most part, premature birth does not imply subaverage overall intellectual functioning. A meta-analysis by Aylward, Pfeiffer, Wright, and Verhulst (1989) found that the mean IQ for children born prematurely was 95.85, clearly within the average range. However, the meta-analysis also revealed that premature infants were at significant greater risk for more subtle learning and behavioral problems. In addition, complications associated with prematurity may place a child at increased developmental risk. Based on these findings, the following practices are recommended:

Supplement measures of global IQ with measures of specific abilities.   A global IQ measure may be inadequate for describing the learning capabilities of children born prematurely (Aylward et al., 1989). In addition to assessing overall cognitive abilities, the early childhood professional should also assess visual-motor and visual-spatial skills, attention, concentration, language, planning, academic achievement, and behavior.

Consider perinatal and prenatal health risks.   Although the wide range of developmental outcomes for children born prematurely has not been explained fully, a number of factors have been associated with less than optimal development and therefore should be considered when the assessment is planned. This information could be gathered in an interview with the parents or by reviewing the child's medical records. Whenever possible, the following questions should be answered prior to the assessment.

■ How early was the child born? Obviously the closer to term, the lower the risk of developmental disability. It is no longer unusual for infants born as young as 24 weeks postconception (about 16 weeks early) to survive. During this stage of prenatal development, a week is crucial. Thus, although there is considerable variability among premature infants at all ages, an extra week *in utero* can make a tremendous difference in the child's prognosis.

■ What was the child's birth weight and was it appropriate for the child's gestational age? Independent of gestational age, the infant's size has implications for development. A normal weight for a healthy full-term newborn is 2000 grams. In the literature, infants whose birth weight is less than 1500 grams are referred to as very-low-birth-weight and those whose weight is less than 1000 grams are referred to as extremely-low-birth-weight.

■ Did the child have additional medical risks, such as intraventricular hemorrhage (IVH), bronchopulmonarly dysplasia (BPD)? Because a number of medical complications associated with prematurity have been linked to developmental disability and learning problems (Smith, Ulvind, & Lindemann, 1994; Weisglas-Kuperus, Baerts, Fetter, & Sauer, 1992; Aylward et al., 1989) practitioners planning assessments of children born prematurely would do well to familiarize themselves with the medical complications that commonly occur among this group. An excellent reference for this and other medical complications associated with childhood is Batshaw and Perret (1992).

Address effects of technology-dependence.   Severe respiratory problems in preterm infants often means lengthy hospitalizations. Even after the child is sent home, he or she may be dependent on a respirator or other equipment that significantly limits activities and mobility. If the child is dependent on such equipment at the time of the assessment, the assessment may need to occur in the child's home. Even if the child is no longer technology-dependent, the effects of prolonged hospitalization or immobility may interfere with the child's developmental skills and performance on assessment measures. Therefore, interpretation of assessment results under such conditions should be made cautiously and with an awareness that the child's developmental pattern may differ as a result of abnormal restriction in early motor and social activity.

Assess the child's relationship with the primary caregiver.   At least one study (Cohen, Parmelee, Sigman, & Beckwith, 1988) suggests that the relationship between parents and their preterm child is an important consideration when trying to predict developmental outcome. Prolonged hospitalization and difficult infant behaviors may interfere with attachment, which in turn leads to decreased environmental stimulation.

Summary

The assessment of young children with atypical development represents one of the greatest challenges for early childhood professionals. A multidimensional model of assessment incorporates multiple methods to assess developmental domains from multiple sources across a variety of settings. Creative and flexible assessment planning with the goal of accommodating the child's individual attributes will facilitate diagnosis, eligibility determination, identification of both strengths and weaknesses, and the development and monitoring of intervention/treatment strategies.

18 Assessment of the Preschool Child with a Hearing Loss

YVONNE MULLEN

A hearing loss in a young child implies much more than simply the lack of hearing. The significance of this disability lies not in being cut off from sound, but in the effect this has on the child's development of language and communication skills, as well as the potentially limiting influence it can have on the child's developing experiential base. Thus, the preschool-aged child who is deaf or hard of hearing presents a unique challenge in assessment.

Given the relatively low incidence of deafness or significant hearing loss in children (approximately one per thousand) (Clark, 1989), few professionals have specific training and/or experience in working with this specialized population. When considering the preschool-aged child with a hearing loss, the field of expertise narrows even further. Yet changing special education laws require the assessment of preschool children with special needs in order to provide appropriate early intervention and educational programming.

Early, appropriate, specialized intervention has long been viewed as crucial to the growth and development of children who are deaf or hard of hearing (Ross, 1989). A comprehensive assessment can provide better understanding of the many factors affecting development and can help target the most appropriate intervention strategies. However, those involved in providing these assessments for a preschooler with a hearing loss must fully understand the profound effects this complex disability can have on the child's functioning and development. Many factors need to be considered in collecting and interpreting all the necessary information in order to provide an assessment that is both valid and useful.

The purpose of this chapter is to help the evaluator develop some understanding of the issues the presence of a hearing loss raises for the assessment process. Crucial components for the comprehensive evaluation of preschool children who are deaf or hard of hearing will be presented, along with a review of selected assessment instruments.

Special Considerations in the Assessment Process

Providing a valid and comprehensive assessment of a preschool child who is deaf or hard of hearing can be a complex and time-consuming process. Despite some of the common issues raised by the presence of a hearing loss, these children represent a very heterogeneous group. Like all children, they vary with regard to a full range of significant background and personal variables (family size, parental education, socioeconomic status, minority group membership, intelligence, personality, additional disabilities, etc.). They also vary with regard to a number of factors related to the hearing loss itself (degree and type of hearing loss, communication mode and competence, hearing status of parents, etc.). All of these factors, particularly those related to auditory functioning and communication, need to be given special consideration when evaluating a child who is deaf or hard of hearing.

Hearing Loss: Definitions and Implications

In general, the terms most frequently used in reference to an individual with a hearing loss are *deaf, hard of hearing,* and *hearing impaired.* The generic term *hearing-impaired* has often been used to connote the entire range of auditory impairments, from the totally deaf person whose experience of sound is presumed to be purely tactile all the way to the individual with a mild loss who still understands speech without difficulty. However, the term hearing impaired has come to be considered pejorative by some deaf people and thus tends to be used with less frequency today by many professionals in the field. Educationally, IDEA (1997) has defined *deafness* as having a hearing impairment that is so severe that the child is impaired in processing linguistic information through hearing, with or without amplification, that adversely affects educational performance. Hearing impairment means an impairment of hearing (section 300.7 [3]), whether permanent or fluctuating, that adversely affects the child's educational performance but is not included under the definition of deafness in this section (300.7 [5]). The terms *mild, moderate, severe,* and *profound* are often used to provide more specific descriptive categories based primarily on the degree of decibel loss.

In practice, however, these terms all tend to be diagnostically simplistic, and medically, rather than educationally, oriented. Numerous other factors, in addition to audiometric functioning, seem to be related to how well a particular child will actually perform. In addition to factors such as the degree and type of hearing loss, the etiology and age of onset of the loss, the use of amplification and residual hearing, variables such as intellectual capacity, personality, and family and educational background all appear to play at least some role in determining the outcome. It is important for the evaluator to be aware that there is usually much more to understanding the functioning of a child who is deaf or hard of hearing than the label used or even the audiometric measurement of the hearing loss itself. The only valid criterion must be the individual child's actual performance. Labels and their definitions should be accepted only within very broad limits.

It is not so much a matter of how much hearing is absent, but what the child is able to do with whatever remains. The functional behavior of most significant concern in a child with a hearing loss is *communication.* This includes both receptive and expressive abilities as well as the overall level of language development. Not only does the actual degree of hearing loss have implications for the development of language and communication skills, factors such as the age of onset of the hearing loss and how early the loss was identified can be equally important (see Ross, 1989). These factors all have significant effects on the child's communication competence as well as what modes the child will utilize.

Communication Modes

A child with a hearing loss may communicate through a variety of means. Some preschool-aged children with severe to profound losses, who have not yet received much intervention, may rely primarily on informal gestures or pantomime. However, others will have begun to develop their aural/oral abilities through the combined use of residual hearing, speechreading, and speaking abilities. Still others will communicate primarily through the language of signs. Sign systems themselves vary widely, from American Sign Language (ASL), which has its own grammar and syntax, to Manual English and Siglish, which more closely approximate English word order; to fingerspelling, where one hand configuration equals one letter (rather than a single word or concept as in other systems). Total Communication is the term used to indicate the combined usage of aural/oral methods with signs or fingerspelling. (For additional information regarding various options in communication, see Schwartz, 1987.)

Public Law 94-142, its extension P.L. 99-457, the Individuals with Disabilities Act (IDEA), and later reauthorizations P.L. 101-476 and P.L. 105-17, all mandate assessment appropriate to a child's needs. Tests and other evaluation materials are to be "provided and administered in the child's native language or other mode of communication." Thus, evaluators should be skilled in the child's primary communication system. Although technically, the use of a sign interpreter might be considered when necessary to meet the mandate of the law, in practice, the results are unlikely to be satisfactory. Particularly in the case of a young, preschool-aged child, the probable negative effects on building rapport and natural interaction when attempting to communicate through a third party are obvious.

Issues in Instrumentation

The mandates of federal regulations also have important implications for the selection and administration of assessment instruments. According to the laws, tests and other evaluation materials utilized in the assessment process are to have been "validated for the specific purpose for which they are used" and are to be "administered by trained personnel in conformance with the instructions provided by their producer" (IDEA (1997) Section 300.532, 2, C). The laws further mandate that tests be

> selected and administered so as best to ensure that when a test is administered to a child with impaired sensory, manual, or speaking skills, that the results accurately reflect the child's aptitude or achievement level or whatever other factors the test purports to measure rather than reflecting the child's impaired sensory, manual, or speaking skills (except when those skills are the factors which the test purports to measure). (IDEA, 1997, Section 300.532, 2, E)

Clearly these mandates all raise serious issues for the evaluation of a child with a hearing loss, particularly at the preschool level.

As will be examined later in this chapter, when specific assessment tools are evaluated more closely, the available test instruments appropriate for use with young children who are deaf or hard of hearing are limited in number. Furthermore, few of the instruments which are most frequently employed have actually been standardized for use with this population. The results produced are then compared to *hearing* norms, which may be questionable in terms of their validity when applied to a child with a hearing loss. Examiners also frequently "adapt" tests to make them more suitable for use with children who are deaf or hard of hearing by simplifying verbal instructions, gesturing or pointing, demonstrating and/or providing extra practice items to clarify the tasks. This, too, breaks standardization. While the results may produce useful information to the assessment process regarding the child's specific skills functioning, the formal test "scores" must again be viewed as questionable in terms of their validity and thus interpreted with caution. When used with a young child with a significant hearing loss, most tests are better treated as "structured observations."

In an effort to minimize the degree to which test results are confounded by the effects of the hearing loss itself, evaluators frequently rely heavily on nonverbal instruments which do not require verbal directions or responses, or draw on the child's language processing (unless, of course, those are the skills they are specifically trying to measure). However, this significantly reduces the range of behavior sampled as part of the assessment process. Again, the validity of generalizations made based on these more narrow and limited samples must be considered tenuous at best. Valid assessments of preschool children who are deaf or hard of hearing, which are in full accordance with the mandates of the law, are still far more a goal to be achieved rather than an established fact.

Ecological Assessments

Many evaluators, particularly those experienced in working with preschool-aged populations, emphasize the importance of utilizing an ecological approach to the assessment process. *Any* test is merely a sample of behavior. In the assessment process, selected samples of behavior are gathered, interpreted and used to make generalizations about an individual's overall functioning. The better the quality and broader the range of behavioral samples, the more confidence one can put in the validity of the generalizations made.

It is difficult when evaluating any preschool-aged child, hearing or deaf, to get as broad a range of behavioral samples as can be obtained from an older child or adult primarily because the preschooler's knowledge base and level of skills development is so much more limited. This issue is compounded further in the case of a preschooler who is deaf or hard of hearing when most verbal and language loaded items or instruments are eliminated. Evaluators need to find ways of broadening their information base by utilizing different techniques and sources to gather assessment data. This is where the "team" approach to evaluation can be most useful. Working together with other members of the evaluation team, observing or perhaps even helping to facilitate the assessment process in domains other than one's own, expands the number and breadth of observations used to make generalizations. While more is not always better, convergent findings from a variety of sources can help to increase the confidence level in the validity of the results.

Helpful Hints and Practical Considerations

Background noise should be kept to a minimum during the assessment activities. Check to see if the child is wearing hearing aids or has a cochlear implant and determine if the device is working properly. It is important to include a few cautionary words about hearing aids and cochlear implants at this point. Although these devices can be very helpful in allowing a child to more fully capitalize on his or her auditory potential, unlike eye glasses, these devices usually do not "correct" the problem. Hearing aids amplify *all* sound in the environment, not only desired sound (i.e., speech) but unwanted sound (i.e., background noises) as well. If the sound signal is distorted as well as weakened by the child's particular type of hearing loss, the hearing aid will only make this distorted sound louder. Rather than amplifying the sound itself, a cochlear implant converts sound into electrical stimulation within the inner ear which the child then must interpret. While these devices may provide the child with important additional information, they do not, by themselves, help the child "make sense" of what he hears.

Visual distractions should also be kept to a minimum in the room used for testing. Look directly at the child and wait for his or her glance. The lighting source should illuminate the materials and the examiner's face without undue glare or shadows. Speak clearly, and at a natural rate, without exaggerated mouth movements. Be aware that obstructions—such as untrimmed mustaches, items in mouth, or hands on face—may interfere with the child's ability to understand. Also, be sensitive to your own nonverbal communications (nods, frowns, directional gazes) and the effects these may have on the child's responses.

Given the effect a hearing loss is likely to have on a child's language development, avoid, at least initially, more expanded and/or complex language structures as well as idioms. Children who are deaf or hard of hearing often learn very early to facilitate the flow of social interaction by smiling and nodding, even when they have absolutely no idea about what is being said. Check on the child's understanding regularly by asking questions and having him or her demonstrate or repeat back directions. Note the child's response style. How are breakdowns in communication dealt with? Does the child ask for repetition or clarification, withdraw, or perhaps attempt to direct and control the interaction? These behavioral observations are important in understanding how a particular child copes.

In summary, providing a valid assessment of a preschool child who is deaf or hard of hearing requires some very specialized skills. Evaluators need to have a solid foundation and understanding of the implications of hearing loss and have competence in the child's primary mode of communication. They also need to understand the limitations of the assessment tools available and be willing to take the time to gather the additional samples of behavior that will help increase the validity of their assessment. Sensitivity to the many practical considerations that must be taken into account comes through experience. It is difficult for the general practitioner, who perhaps receives a referral to evaluate a child who is deaf or hard of hearing every two or three years, to develop the necessary experiential base. In such cases, it may be better to refer out to others who specialize in working with this low-incidence population or perhaps to work with someone who already has the appropriate training, skills, and experience.

Crucial Components for Comprehensive Assessment

Given the complexities involved, it should be apparent that no one individual would be able to gather sufficient information nor have the necessary range of expertise to provide a truly comprehensive assessment of a child with a significant hearing loss. In order for all relevant factors to be evaluated objectively, the assessment needs to draw on a multidisciplinary diagnostic team. It is with good reason that the federal laws mandate such an approach. Critical components for the comprehensive assessment of a preschool child with a hearing loss include assessments of audiological functioning, language and communication skills, cognitive development, adaptive behavior, and social-emotional functioning (see Table 18.1). In the case of a child with additional disabilities, additional specialist assessments may also be required. Those providing the assessments should have training and experience in working with young children with significant hearing losses.

Audiological Functioning

The audiologist is clearly best qualified to provide specific information regarding the child's hearing sensitivity and appropriate audiological management. An educational audiologist can help interpret information regarding degree, type, configuration, and stability

TABLE 18.1   Crucial Components for Comprehensive Assessment

I. *Audiological*

- Degree and type of hearing loss
- Configuration of hearing loss
- Etiology of hearing loss
- Age of onset of hearing loss
- Stability of hearing loss
- Speech discrimination ability
- Amplification history

II. *Language and communication*

- Oral and/or manual receptive language ability
- Oral and/or manual expressive language ability
- Speech reading ability
- Speech intelligibility

III. *Cognitive functioning*

- General cognitive development
- Specific cognitive processes (i.e., memory, reasoning, problem solving)
- Knowledge of basic concepts
- Learning and response styles (i.e., attention, perseverance, self-monitoring, need for reinforcement)

IV. *Social-emotional development and adaptive behavior*

Background history data
- Birth history
- Developmental milestones
- Medical history
- Additional disabilities
- Family history
- Hearing status of parents and siblings
- Parent-infant work and/or prior interventions

Interviews
- Parents
- Teachers
- Other caregivers

Behavioral observation data
- Checklists and/or inventories
- Behavioral techniques (i.e., time sampling, anecdotal, event or interval recording)
- Diagnostic play techniques

Sources: Some of the information presented here was adapted from the following materials:

Mullen, Y., & Spragins, A. (1998). Deaf children and schools: Choosing and using appropriate assessment instruments. Paper presented at National Association of School Psychologists Convention, Orlando, Florida.

Spragins, A. B., Blennerhassett, L., & Mullen, Y. (1998). Reviews of four types of assessment instruments used with the deaf and hard of hearing students. Workshop materials presented at the National Association of School Psychologists Convention, Orlando, Florida.

Spragins, A. B., & Blennerhassett, L. (1989). *Intellectual, adaptive behavior, social-emotional, developmental/criterion-based, language and basic concept assessment instruments used with preschool deaf children.* Workshop materials presented at the National Association of School Psychologists Convention, Boston, Massachusetts.

of the hearing loss, as well as speech discrimination ability, and can discuss the possible implications for the child's functioning in other domains.

What was the cause of the hearing loss? Is the etiology one that is associated with additional handicapping conditions such as maternal rubella or Rh factor? Is the loss believed to be congenital or did the onset occur later? (The later the onset, the more opportunity the child had to begin to lay the foundations for language development and speech discrimination abilities.) How early was the loss identified? When was the child fitted with amplification, and has any type of early intervention support been provided? Late diagnosis and/or intervention can often result in significantly delayed skill development. Each member of the evaluation team needs to be aware of how this additional audiological information may influence the interpretation of assessment data in their own domain. (For more comprehensive information on hearing loss and auditory functioning in children, see Boothroyd, 1982, and/or Northern & Downs, 1991.)

Language and Communication Functioning

Full evaluation of all aspects of language and communication skills development will be necessary in order to obtain a better overall picture of the child's performance and, again, to provide perspective on the data gathered in other domains. It is crucial that the specialists responsible for evaluating this aspect of the child's functioning be knowledgeable of language development in children who are deaf or hard of hearing. (See Kretschmer & Kretschmer, 1978, for more comprehensive coverage of language development.) The assessment might best be provided by an experienced teacher of the deaf and/or a speech and language specialist with specific background in working with young deaf and hard of hearing children.

The effects of the child's hearing loss on the complex process of language acquisition need to be thoroughly assessed. In order to target appropriate objectives and strategies for intervention, detailed information must be gathered regarding the child's current functioning levels in various language skill areas. Evaluation of the child's receptive and expressive language abilities in his or her preferred mode of communication, as well as the child's speech reading and intelligibility, are all crucial components of this part of the assessment.

As in most areas of assessment for the preschool child who is deaf or hard of hearing, the number of instruments available for formal evaluation in these critical areas is limited. Table 18.2 provides an overview of some of the tools that may be appropriate in assessing communication skills as well as basic concept development with this population. However, the skilled evaluator is likely to adapt or supplement some of these tools with a variety of more informal techniques for sampling language and assessing the child's oral and/or signing abilities. Flexibility, creativity, and experience can all be major assets to the evaluator in the assessment process.

The assessment of communication functioning can be further complicated in a child who is deaf or hard of hearing when the primary language spoken in the home is other than English. The often difficult questions regarding what is the child's "dominant" language, what is the appropriate language for the evaluation, and at what point to involve an interpreter are more confusing and challenging in the presence of a hearing loss. Recent statistics clearly reflect significant increases in the numbers of preschool-aged children with significant hearing losses who come from bilingual/bicultural backgrounds (Schildroth, Rawlings, & Allen, 1989). This suggests that today these issues are being confronted with greater frequency. (For more information on the assessment of culturally different children, see Chapter 16).

TABLE 18.2   Selected Language and Basic Concept Assessment Instruments[1]

Categories

A. Name of instrument

B. Age range, availability of norms for deaf and/or hard of hearing

C. Psychometric data

D. Description

E. Evaluation

F. Year, author, publisher

A. *Assessment of Children's Language Comprehension*

B. 3-0 to 6-5, no norms for deaf/hard of hearing.

C. Standardized on 311 nursery and elementary children. Limited statistical data provided.

D. Designed to assess comprehension of utterances one to four "critical elements" in length. Examiner reads word or phrase and child points to one of four pictures on test plate.

E. Provides practical information about length of utterance child can comprehend and if he or she tends to miss particular parts. Test can be signed and used as a criterion-based versus norm-referenced test. May be evaluating lipreading (speechreading) skills in children who do not use sign language.

F. 1973, Foster, Gidden, and Stark, Consulting Psychologists Press.

A. *Bare Essentials in Assessing Really Little Kids (BEAR)*

B. Developmental assessment process, not normed.

C. Criterion-referenced. No reliability or validity data.

D. Based on developmental models of language acquisition, BEAR is designed to assess language mastery. Includes: concept analysis, syntactic/morphological analysis, phonological analysis, and semantic/pragmatic analysis.

E. Yields developmental information useful in program planning, but no standard scores.

F. 1982, Hasenstab and Laighton (in Hasenstab & Horner, 1982). Rockville, MD: Aspen Systems.

A. *Bracken Basic Concept Scale*

B. 2-6 to 7-11, no norms for deaf/hard of hearing.

C. Standardized on nationally representative sample ($N = 1,109$). Reliability and validity data presented.

D. Measures receptive vocabulary thought to be essential to success in kindergarten, with a conceptual sentence format ("Show me..."; Which is..."; Who is..."). Includes color, letter identification, numbers, counting, comparisons, shapes, direction/position, size, social/emotional, time/sequence, and texture/material concepts.

E. Language demands of test may be too difficult for many deaf children. Difficult to determine if child does not understand language or not know actual concept being tested. However, limited response requirements (i.e., pointing or short verbal response) are an advantage assuming the child understands verbal questions. Provides potential information for programming. May be signed if used as criterion-referenced test, but iconicity of signs in some categories (e.g., shapes) may prove problematic.

F. 1984, Bracken, Psychological Corporation.

(continued)

TABLE 18.2   Continued

A. *Carolina Picture Vocabulary Test for Deaf and Hearing Impaired*

B. 2-6 to 16-0, norms for deaf/hard of hearing provided.

C. Standard scores, age equivalents, percentiles. Standardized on 767 children with hearing impairment. Reported standard error considerably larger for children below age 6.

D. Designed to measure receptive sign vocabulary. Examiner signs a word and child points to one of four pictures on test plate.

E. Good tool for assessment of preschool children who have been exposed to sign language. Limited usefulness below age 4. Although test author suggests that stop-action pictures depicting sign production allow for administration by examiners inexperienced in signing, this practice is not recommended.

F. 1985, Layton and Holmes, Modern Education Corporation.

A. *Environmental Language Inventory (ELI)*

B. Developmental assessment instrument, not normed.

C. Manual reports results of three research studies using ELI. Standard score comparisons not provided but frequency, proportion, and rank-ordering of the semantic/grammatical forms is available.

D. Designed to assess early semantic/grammatical expressive rules through imitation, conversation, and free play. Included are: agent–action, action–object, modifier–possession, negation, location–agent, location–object, and introducer.

E. Assumes some level of receptive understanding. ELI can yield diagnostic information about expressive skills for use in program development. Designed for use with a variety of children, including autistic, mentally retarded, and deaf/hard of hearing.

F. 1978a, MacDonald and Horstmeier, Charles E. Merrill Publisher.

A. *Environmental Pre-Language Battery (EPB)*

B. Behavioral assessment process, not normed.

C. Criterion-referenced, no reliability or validity data.

D. Designed to yield behavioral descriptions of very early language skills (one-word stage or below) primarily through structured play situations. Skills included are: nonverbal skills of object permanence, attention, gesture communication, picture and object identification, and following directions; verbal skills of naming objects, naming actions, repeating, two-word imitations, and two-word answers to questions. Can be adapted for use with children with a variety of disabilities.

E. Yields criterion-referenced information for use in program development. Teaching strategies built into assessment process can be helpful in developing intervention strategies.

F. 1978b, MacDonald and Horstmeier, Charles E. Merrill Publisher.

A. *Grammatical Analysis of Elicited Language, Pre-Sentence Level (GAEL-P), Simple Sentence Level (GAEL-S), and Complex Sentence Level (GAEL-C)*

B. 2-6 to 11-11, Norms for deaf/hard of hearing provided.

C. GAEL-P standardized on 150 children with hearing impairments ages 3-0 to 5–11, and 75 hearing ages 2-6 to 3-11. GAEL-S standardized on 200 orally educated children, severe to profoundly deaf ages 5-0 to 7-6, and 200 hearing children ages 2-6 to 5-0. Norms for children using total communication on GAEL-S are reported in Geers, Moog, and Schnick (1984). GAEL-C standardized on 270 orally educated, severe to profoundly deaf ages 8-0 to 11-11, and 240 hearing ages 3-0 to 5-11.

D. Designed to elicit and evaluate spoken or signed English through both prompted and imitated utterances. (GAEL-P assesses communication concepts versus English skill.)

E. Good tools for communication assessment and among few normed for deaf/hard of hearing. GAEL-P provides good communication baseline for young children without testing English skills. Levels S and C test English syntax and allow comparisons of both hearing and deaf/hard of hearing children. However, neither pragmatics nor semantics are directly measured at the S and C levels. Length of administration can be a drawback.

F. 1983, Moog, Kozak, and Geers (GAEL-P), 1979, Moog and Geers (GAEL-S) and 1980, Moog and Geers (GAEL-C), Central Institute for the Deaf.

A. *Scales of Early Communication Skills for Hearing Impaired Children*

B. 2–0 to 8–11, norms for deaf/hard of hearing provided.

C. Standardized on 372 orally educated hearing-impaired from 14 different programs across six states. Means and standard deviations provided in seven age groups. Data provided on reliability but not validity.

D. Teacher-administered instrument designed to measure speech and language development in hearing-impaired. Includes four scales: receptive language, expressive language, nonverbal receptive and nonverbal expressive.

E. Useful and easily administered screening instrument.

F. 1975, Moog and Geers. Central Institute for the Deaf.

Sources: Some of the information presented here was adapted from the following materials:

Mullen, Y., & Spragins, A. (1998). *Deaf children and schools: Choosing and using appropriate assessment instruments.* Paper presented at National Association of School Psychologists Convention, Orlando, Florida.

Spragins, A. B., Blennerhassett, L., & Mullen, Y. (1998). *Reviews of four types of assessment instruments used with the deaf and hard of hearing students.* Workshop materials presented at the National Association of School Psychologists Convention, Orlando, FL.

Spragins, A. B., & Blennerhassett, L. (1989). *Intellectual, adaptive behavior, social-emotional, developmental/criterion-based, language and basic concept assessment instruments used with preschool deaf children.* Workshop materials presents at the National Association of School Psychologists Convention, Boston, Massachusetts.

Cognitive Functioning

The primary challenge in evaluating cognitive development in a child with a significant hearing loss is to somehow differentiate linguistic competence from other areas of cognitive functioning. Tests that are in any way verbal in nature, requiring the child either to comprehend directions or to provide a verbal response, may give the examiner useful information regarding verbal skills development but are totally useless for assessing the quality of the child's thinking and reasoning abilities.

Valid efforts to measure the child's general level of cognitive development require assessment tools that are primarily nonverbal in nature. Table 18.3 provides an overview of selected instruments often used in evaluating young children with significant hearing losses. However, the cautionary notes often raised with regard to the poor validity of infant and preschool tests of "ability" for predicting future performance need to be emphasized even more strongly when dealing with a child with a hearing loss. Labels and differential diagnoses should generally be avoided at this stage.

The purpose of any formal testing should be to provide information regarding the child's current level of development of basic concepts and specific cognitive processes (memory, reasoning, problem solving) for use in planning appropriate programming. Behavioral

TABLE 18.3   Selected Cognitive Assessment Instruments

Categories

A. Name of instrument
B. Age range, availability of norms for deaf/hard of hearing
C. Psychometric data
D. Description
E. Evaluation
F. Year, author, publisher

A. *CID Preschool Performance Scale (CID)*
B. 2-0 to 5-5, norms for deaf/hard of hearing provided.
C. Standard scores. Reliability and validity data available. Standardized on 978 children, hearing and hearing-impaired.
D. Totally nonverbal measure of cognitive functioning. Subtests include: Manual Planning, Manual Dexterity, Form Perception, Perceptual Motor, Preschool Skills, and Part/Whole Relations.
E. Generally a good tool for the assessment of young hearing- or language-impaired children. Some drawbacks are test's length and failure to accommodate for the refusal or omission of items when used with children who are difficult to test.
F. 1984, Moog and Lane, Stoelting.

A. *Columbia Mental Maturity Scale, Third Edition (CMMS)*
B. 3-6 to 9-11, no norms for deaf/hard of hearing.
C. Standard scores. Reliability and validity data available for hearing population. Standardized on nationally representative stratified sample.
D. Totally nonverbal test of reasoning abilities. Consists of a series of pictorial or figural classification items with demonstration and/or pantomime directions.
E. Nonverbal format, sample/teaching items, and brief administration time make CMMS good supplemental tool. Should not be used in isolation, given the limited range of cognitive processes sampled. Particularly useful in evaluating children with motor problems, as test is untimed and child need only point or nod for response. However, heavy loading of test with visual-perceptual items makes CMMS a poor choice for children with perceptual problems.
F. 1972, Burgemeister, Blum, and Lorge, The Psychological Corporation.

A. *Differential Ability Scales (DAS)*
B. 2-6 to 17-11, no norms for deaf/hard of hearing.
C. Standard scores. Reliability and validity data provided. DAS standardized on nationally representative stratified sample of 3,475 children, including some special education students (category includes 2.4% speech-impaired but no listing for deaf/hard of hearing).
D. The DAS is a comprehensive battery of cognitive and achievement tests. The Cognitive Battery includes a range of subtests divided into overlapping levels. Lower Preschool (ages 2-6 to 3-5) subtests include Block Building and Picture Similarities. Upper Preschool (ages 3-6 to 5-11) subtests include Picture Similarities, Pattern Construction, and Copying. At the School-Age Level (ages 6-0 to 17-11) subtests include Recall of Designs, Pattern Construction, Matrices, and Sequential & Quantitative Reasoning. The DAS is designed to yield a composite score of General Conceptual Ability (GCA), cluster scores, and also includes a Special Nonverbal scale.

E. The DAS manual specifically indicates that subtests having verbal content or requiring oral responses may not be appropriate for children with hearing impairments, speech problems, or language problems. Instead, it recommends that a battery composed of nonverbal subtests be administered, and a Special Nonverbal Composite score be obtained. Relatively new in its development, research is still lacking on use of the DAS with deaf and hard of hearing students. However, some examiners experienced with this special population report finding it a useful tool, particularly with preschool-aged children.

F. 1990, Elliott, The Psychological Corporation.

A. *Hiskey-Nebraska Test of Learning Aptitude (H-NTLA)*

B. 3-0 to 16-6, norms for both hearing and deaf/hard of hearing provided.

C. Standard scores. Reliability and validity data available for both hearing and deaf/hard of hearing populations.

D. Performance-based test of learning aptitude consisting of 12 subtests sampling a variety of areas, including visual attention, matching memory, classification, spatial reasoning, eye–hand coordination, and so on.

E. Developed, standardized, new and normed specifically for use with deaf/hard of hearing children, H-NTLA is still used by some evaluators to assess this population, despite dated norms and materials. Test samples fairly broad behavioral base. Most subtests are untimed or have very generous time limits. Tasks hold interest of young children. However, test's length is sometimes problematic. Beware, small differences in raw scores may translate into significant differences in "learning age." Also scores may be low for preschool children compared to their performance on other tests. Best used in conjunction with other assessment techniques.

F. 1966, Hiskey, Mr. M. S. Hiskey.

A. *Kaufman Assessment Battery for Children (K-ABC)—Nonverbal Scale*

B. 4-0 to 12-6, no norms for deaf/hard of hearing.

C. Standard scores. Reliability and validity data provided. Small number of children with hearing losses included in the standardization sample for proportional representation.

D. K-ABC taps two different thinking styles. Nonverbal scale can be used to derive separate Mental Processing Composite scale score based on selected subtests from Simultaneous and Sequential Processing Scales.

E. Nonverbal scale of K-ABC appears generally appropriate for use in assessing deaf and hard of hearing children aged 4 years or above. Not recommended at younger age levels, as number of nonverbal subtests is too small to constitute scale. Most subtests are untimed and role of language is kept to a minimum. Pantomime instructions provided. Teaching items included in standardization.

F. 1983, Kaufman and Kaufman, American Guidance Service.

A. *Leiter International Performance Scale—Arthur Adaptation (AALIPS)*

B. 3-0 to 8-0, no norms for deaf/hard of hearing.

C. Mental age and ratio IQ scores. Limited norms, reliability, and validity data provided.

D. Age scale with four items at each level. Test items and instructions totally nonverbal with some demonstration. Subtests untimed with constant response format as task complexity increases. Yields measure of nonverbal intelligence based on traditional IQ formula.

(continued)

TABLE 18.3   Continued

E. Despite significant psychometric weaknesses (see Ratcliff & Ratcliff, 1979), AALIPS is still used with some frequency in assessing young children with hearing losses. There is greater variability in scores of this population relative to the standardization sample. Scores for some preschool-aged deaf/hard of hearing appear inflated, while scores tend to be lower than other tests (Wechsler) for low-functioning children. AALIPS should never be used in isolation, and obtained scores need to be interpreted with great caution.

F. 1952, Arthur, Stoelting.

A. *Leiter International Performance Scale—Revised (LIPS-R)*

B. 2-0 to 20-11, no norms for deaf/hard of hearing.

C. Standard scores. Reliability and validity data provided. Norms based on a sample of over 1,750 children and adolescents, nationally stratified based on the 1993 census including age, gender, ethnicity, SES, and geographic region. Data also available for a number of special populations including hearing- and speech-impaired.

D. Completely nonverbal in both its administration and required responses, the LIPS-R includes 20 subtests and uses new manipulative materials to measure nonverbal mental abilities in four domains: Reasoning, Visualization, Memory, and Attention. Scores are provided for each subtest and domain, as well as a composite IQ score. New "growth" scores are also provided in all domains to help show the progression of improvement across time, irrespective of age-based standard scores.

E. The LIPS-R test materials have only recently become available. However, preliminary prepublication data suggests that this new edition of the test has been designed to eliminate many of the psychometric weaknesses of the old LIPS and will provide a more comprehensive profile of a child's cognitive strengths and weaknesses. The LIPS-R may prove to be a major addition to the instruments available for assessing preschoolers from diverse backgrounds with a wide variety of special needs.

F. 1997, Roid and Miller, Stoelting.

A. *Merrill-Palmer Scale of Mental Tests (MPSMT)*

B. 1-6 to 6-0, no norms for deaf/hard of hearing.

C. IQ score. Dated norms. Reliability and validity data lacking.

D. Test of general intelligence, including both visual-motor and language items.

E. Helpful supplemental tool. Possible to eliminate verbal items and still obtain total score for child with hearing loss. Flexibility in format allows for demonstration and some reordering of item administration, and does not penalize child for items refused or omitted. Useful with some hard-to-test children. However, a large number of motor and/or timed tasks makes MPSMT inappropriate for evaluating children with motor difficulties.

F. 1931, Stutsman, Stoelting.

A. *Mullen Scales of Early Learning*

B. Birth to 5-8, no norms for deaf/hard of hearing.

C. Standard scores, percentile ranks, and age equivalents provided for each of the five scales, as well as a composite standard score based on the four cognitive scales. Standardization and reliability data also provided.

D. Five scales provide a developmentally integrated system for assessing functioning in gross motor, visual reception, fine motor, expressive and receptive language skill areas.

E. Scales include a variety of cognitive reasoning activities appropriate for use with young deaf and hard of hearing children. Possible to omit verbal items and still obtain useable scores in many domains. Test's range and flexibility appear to be major assets in dealing with the variability in functioning of young deaf and hard of hearing children.

F. 1995, Mullen, American Guidance Service.

A. *Smith-Johnson Nonverbal Performance Scale (SJNPS)*

B. 2-0 to 4-0, norms provided for hearing-impaired.

C. Test performance in each of 14 categories is compared to normative sample and scored as above, below, or within the average range for children of similar age, sex, and hearing status. Yields no global score. Reliability data provided. Validity data lacking. However, test items are drawn from other well-established and standardized tests.

D. Nonverbal developmental assessment instrument consisting of 14 different categories of items tapping broad range of skills and cognitive processes. Tasks require minimal instruction and appear to hold the interest of children.

E. Though limited in age range, SJNPS is a very useful tool for assessing young children who are deaf or hard of hearing. Provides data about individual strengths and weaknesses, as well as giving a general sense of the child's overall performance level, despite lack of global score.

F. 1977, Smith and Johnson, Western Psychological Service.

A. *Wechsler Preschool and Primary Scale of Intelligence (WPPSI): Performance Scale—Ray & Ulissi Adaptation*

B. 4-0 to 6-6, no separate norms for deaf/hard of hearing provided.

C. Standard scores. Sample of 120 children with hearing losses matched proportionally for demographic characteristics to original standardization sample of WPPSI (Wechsler, 1967). No significant differences found between hearing and deaf/hard of hearing when adapted instructions are used. Reliability and validity data available for hearing populations.

D. Ray and Ulissi provide modified instructions simplifying complexity of language and including practice items for the original WPPSI Performance Scale.

E. Despite its nonverbal format, the original WPPSI-PS is usually not the instrument of choice among experienced evaluators of young deaf and hard of hearing children because of the complexity of language of instructions and difficulty in conveying tasks. Ray and Ulissi attempt to circumvent these difficulties in administration, and present data suggesting use of standard norms may be appropriate with deaf/hard of hearing.

F. 1982, Ray and Ulissi, Steven Ray Publishing; 1967, Wechsler, The Psychological Corporation.

Sources: Some of the information presented here was adapted from the following materials:

Mullen, Y., & Spragins, A. (1998). *Deaf children and schools: Choosing and using appropriate assessment instruments.* Paper presented at National Association of School Psychologists Convention, Orlando, Florida.

Spragins, A. B., & Blennerhassett, L. (1989). *Intellectual, adaptive behavior, social-emotional, developmental/ criterion-based, language and basic concept assessment instruments used with preschool deaf children.* Workshop materials presents at the National Association of School Psychologists Convention, Boston, Massachusetts.

Spragins, A. B., Blennerhassett, L., & Mullen, Y. (1998). *Reviews of four types of assessment instruments used with the deaf and hard of hearing students.* Workshop materials presented at the National Association of School Psychologists Convention, Orlando, FL.

observations can supplement the more structured measures of skills functioning and provide information regarding the child's response style (attention, perseverance, self-correction, need for reinforcement).

Although the psychologist typically assumes a significant role in assessing the level of cognitive development in a child with a hearing loss, special educators, preschool teachers, early intervention specialists, parents, and other caregivers can often provide valuable observational data in this process. However, it is crucial that the evaluator integrating and interpreting the information fully understands the possible implications of the child's hearing loss for cognitive functioning.

Adaptive Behavior and Social-Emotional Functioning

As in the assessment of cognitive functioning, the experienced psychologist can often play an important role in helping to integrate and interpret information regarding the social-emotional development and adaptive behavior of a child with a hearing loss. However, preschool teachers and/or other caregivers, early intervention specialists, special educators, parent educators, social workers, and, of course, the parents themselves are frequently in positions to contribute significantly to the assessment process, either by actually gathering data or perhaps by serving as important informants regarding the child's daily functioning.

Detailed background information related to the child's birth, development, and medical and family histories can help put other data gathered into some perspective. Is there evidence of possible additional disabilities that need to be explored? How is the family coping? The diagnosis of a hearing loss can put tremendous physical, emotional, and financial strains on even the strongest of families. Understanding how a particular family adapts, addressing its concerns as well as expectations, are necessary pieces of information for developing an appropriate intervention plan for the child and the entire family. For additional information on deafness and the family, see Luterman (1979, 1987) and Moores (1996). Ninety percent of children with significant hearing losses are born to hearing parents, who typically have no previous knowledge of or experience with deafness (Moores, 1996). Thus, information regarding the hearing status of parents and siblings, as well as what modes of communication are currently used in the home, is vital to planning appropriate intervention strategies. Parent education and support have long been viewed as crucial components in most early intervention programs with young children who are deaf or hard of hearing.

In addition to gathering data from background histories and interviews, direct behavioral observations can also serve as an important source of information regarding the child's general adjustment, interpersonal skills, and adaptive behavior. This might include data from time-sampling, anecdotal, event, and interval recording, as well as information from behavioral checklists or other assessment instruments. Diagnostic play techniques can also be useful in gathering additional observational data regarding the child's emotional functioning. Table 18.4 provides an overview of a selected number of assessment tools often used to evaluate social-emotional development and/or adaptive behavior in young children who are deaf or hard of hearing.

Additional Assessments

As noted previously, it is difficult to gather a sufficiently broad range of behavioral samples when evaluating a young child who is deaf or hard of hearing, not only because of the

TABLE 18.4   Selected Social-Emotional and Adaptive Behavior Scales

Categories

A. Name of instrument
B. Age range, availability of norms for deaf/hard of hearing
C. Psychometric data
D. Description
E. Evaluation
F. Year, author, publisher

A. *Joseph Pre-School and Primary Self Concept Screening Test*
B. 3-6 to 9-11, No norms for deaf/hard of hearing.
C. Normed on 1,200 children from Illinois. No deaf/hard of hearing reported in sample, but some children receiving special education services were included.
D. Scale consists of 15 items and provides a general measure of self concept. Child chooses between two pictures: "Which is most like you?" Instructions can be pantomimed (although process is not standardized), and scoring allows for both a "don't know" and/or a "confusion" response.
E. Despite limited data on use with deaf/hard of hearing, appears to provide good format for structured interview in screening for potential difficulties. However, should only be used by examiners skilled in communication with young deaf and hard of hearing children.
F. 1979, Joseph, Stoelting.

A. *Meadow/Kendall Social-Emotional Assessment Inventories for Deaf and Hearing-Impaired Students Preschool Form*
B. 3-0 to 6-11, norms for deaf/hard of hearing provided.
C. Percentiles. Normed on a population of 857 preschool deaf/hard of hearing children in a variety of residential and day school programs. Reliability and validity provided for school-aged but not for preschool form.
D. Rating scale of observable behaviors, including some specific to hearing loss. Yields scores on four scales: communicative behaviors, dominating behaviors, developmental lags, and compulsive behaviors.
E. Despite lack of reliability and validity data for preschool form, Meadow/Kendall appears to be a very useful assessment tool and is one of the few with deaf/hard of hearing norms. Can be used to gather information fairly easily from multiple informants working with a child in different settings, providing a more complete, though often varied, picture of a child's functioning. Geared to identify developmental problems, may bias focus towards pathology versus normal development.
F. 1983, Meadow, Gallaudet University.

A. *Scales of Independent Behavior*
B. Developmental scale, no norms for deaf/hard of hearing.
C. Standard scores, percentiles, age scores, adaptive level. Normed on representative sample of 1,764 regular education children, infants, preschoolers, and adults. Reliability and validity data available for hearing population. No deaf/hard of hearing reported in sample.
D. Measures motor, social/communication, personal independence, and community independence skills through interview with a caregiver.

(continued)

TABLE 18.4 Continued

E. Although data still limited on use with deaf/hard of hearing, seems potentially useful as assessment tool. Relatively few questions involve auditory or communication behavior.

F. 1984, Bruininks, Woodcock, Weatherman, and Hill, DLM Teaching Resources.

A. *Vineland Adaptive Behavior Scales Revised—Survey Form*

B. 0 to 18-11, no norms for deaf/hard of hearing below age 6 years.

C. Standard scores, percentiles, age scores, adaptive level. Standardized on nationally representative sample of 3,000. (Supplemental norms provided based on sample of 300 deaf/ hard of hearing children aged 6 to 12 in residential facilities.) Reliability and validity data available.

D. Assesses communication, daily living skills, socialization, and motor skills based on semi-structured interview of caregiver.

E. Survey Form recommended over other formats for assessing preschool deaf/hard of hearing as it includes fewer items related to communication. Manual provides procedure for excluding individual domain score (i.e., Communication) in Adaptive Behavior Composite. However, individual domain scores are generally more useful than composite score with this population, allowing communication to be viewed independently from other skill areas. Length is a drawback.

F. 1984, Sparrow, Balla, and Cicchetti, American Guidance Service.

Sources: Some of the information presented here was adapted from the following materials:

Mullen, Y., & Spragins, A. (1998). *Deaf children and schools: Choosing and using appropriate assessment instruments.* Paper presented at National Association of School Psychologists Convention, Orlando, Florida.

Spragins, A. B., Blennerhassett, L., & Mullen, Y. (1998). *Reviews of four types of assessment instruments used with the deaf and hard of hearing students.* Workshop materials presented at the National Association of School Psychologists Convention, Orlando, Florida.

Spragins, A. B., & Blennerhassett, L. (1989). *Intellectual, adaptive behavior, social-emotional, developmental/ criterion-based, language and basic concept assessment instruments used with preschool deaf children.* Workshop materials presented at the National Association of School Psychologists Convention, Boston, Massachusetts.

age and limited knowledge base but also because of the results of the hearing loss itself. Taking the time to gather whatever additional information is needed to provide a clear and detailed picture of the child's functioning is essential to the assessment process. The more specific the evaluator can be about the child's needs and what skills he has or has not developed, the more targeted the goals can be for early intervention support. Table 18.5 lists a number of developmental/criterion-based scales that can be used to provide supplemental information for use in program development.

Approximately 20% of the children under age 6 in the 1984 Annual Survey of Hearing Impaired Children and Youth were reported as multiply handicapped (Schildroth, 1986). Within the school-aged population, the identification rate rises to 30% (Wolff & Harkins, 1986). Obviously, in the case of a deaf or hard of hearing child with additional disabilities, referrals for additional specialist assessments may be required. Again, it is important that the professionals providing these additional assessments have some background and experience in working with young children with significant hearing losses and understand the impact a hearing loss may have on the assessment of their particular domain.

Summary

Providing a valid and comprehensive assessment of a preschool-aged child who is deaf or hard of hearing can present even the most experienced team of evaluators with a significant challenge. Evaluators need to fully understand the pervasive nature of a hearing loss and the implications it can have for a child's overall functioning. They must have competence in the child's primary mode of communication and be sensitive to the many practical considerations that must be taken into account in the communication process. Finally, they must understand the limitations of the available assessment tools and must be willing to spend extra time gathering the additional samples of behavior that can help to increase the validity of their results.

However, it is also important that, in considering all of the issues related to the hearing loss, one not lose sight of the rest of the child. A child with a hearing loss has the same developmental needs as a hearing child, and more. A well-integrated comprehensive assessment is a crucial first step in ensuring that each important developmental need will indeed be met.

TABLE 18.5 Selected Developmental/Criterion-Based Scales

Categories

A. Name of instrument
B. Age range
C. Description and psychometric information
D. Evaluation
E. Year, author, publisher

A. *Battelle Developmental Inventory*
B. 0 to 8 years.
C. Provides assessment of personal-social, adaptive, motor, communication, and cognitive domains. Yields standard scores, percentile ranks, and age equivalents.
D. Modified instructions provided for use with deaf/hard of hearing. Appears to have good potential for use with this population.
E. 1984, Newborg, Stock, Wnek, Guidubaldi, and Svinicki, DLM.

A. *Callier-Azusa Scale*
B. 0 to 8 years.
C. Developmental scale designed specifically for assessment of deaf-blind and children with severe disabilities. Areas assessed include motor, perceptual, cognitive, social, communication and language development, and daily living skills. Scale not normed. Developmental ages for items drawn from other sources. Limited reliability and validity information.
D. Useful in assessment of children with severe multiple disabilities.
E. 1978, Stillman, Callier Center.

A. *Developmental Activities Screening Inventory (DASI-II)*
B. 1 month to 5 years.

(continued)

TABLE 18.5   Continued

C. Provides assessment of fine-motor coordination, cause–effect and means–end relationships, association, number concepts, size discrimination, memory, spatial relationships, object function, and seriation. Scores provide developmental age and a developmental quotient. No norms given.
D. Useful in assessing specific skills development of children who are deaf or hard of hearing, particularly those suspected of having additional disabilities.
E. 1984, Fewell and Langley, Pro-Ed.

A. *Developmental Profile II*
B. 0 to 9 years.
C. Developmentally sequenced items provide assessment of physical skills, self-help ability, social competence, academic skills, and communication ability primarily through parent interview and direct observation. Children with disabilities were purposely excluded from standardization sample in order to represent normal developmental expectations.
D. Can provide useful information in assessing specific skills development, despite some items which may be inappropriate for children who are deaf or hard of hearing (i.e., telephone use).
E. 1986, Alpern, Boll, and Shearer, Western Psychological Services.

A. *Inventory of Early Development—Revised* (BRIGANCE®)
B. 0 to 7 years.
C. Combines norm- and criterion-based elements in a developmental task-analytic model. Links assessment to curriculum goals. Developmental age norms for items are drawn from other sources. Allows for pragmatic modification of tasks and response styles.
D. Useful in assessing skill development for educational planning.
E. 1991, Brigance, Curriculum Associates.

A. *Southern California Ordinal Scales of Development*
B. N/A (Piagetian type developmental scales).
C. Provides assessment of cognitive, communicative, fine motor, gross motor, social-affective, and life skills behaviors. Scales not normed but general developmental ages/stages drawn from other sources. Deaf/hard of hearing children included in the standardization process.
D. Useful tool in assessment of children with various disabilities because of the flexibility in procedures. Use of sign language encouraged if appropriate.
E. 1985, Ashurst et al., Foreworks.

A. *Transdisciplinary Play-Based Assessment (TPBA)*
B. 6 months to 6 years.
C. Dynamic, play-based, developmental format for a multidimensional, team approach to assessing young children. TPBA involves child in a variety of structured and unstructured play situations and provides and opportunity for developmental observations of cognitive, social-emotional, communication and language, and sensorimotor domains. Parent actively participates in the team process, both as an observer and facilitator. TPBA provides information about child's developmental level, learning style, interactional patterns, and other relevant behaviors for use in individual program development.

(continued)

TABLE 18.5   Continued

D. Flexibility in structure allows for adaptation to the needs of an individual child. Useful, holistic approach to the assessment of young children, with or without disabilities. While not much data is yet available, it seems promising for use with deaf or hard of hearing. However, play-facilitator obviously needs to be fluent in communication mode of child (as well as the parents) and knowledgeable of child development. Time required may be drawback.

E. 1993, Linder, Brookes Publishing.

A. *Uniform Performance Assessment System*

B. 0 to 6 years.

C. Criterion-referenced. Provides assessment of pre-academic/fine motor, communication, social/ self help, and gross motor skills for use in educational program development. Adaptations, such as providing support or signing, are coded on answer sheet.

D. Potentially useful in assessing deaf/hard of hearing children and those with more limited functioning levels.

E. 1981, White & Haring, Psychological Corporation.

Sources: Some of the information presented here was adapted from the following materials:

Mullen, Y., & Spragins, A. (1998). *Deaf children and schools: Choosing and using appropriate assessment instruments.* Paper presented at National Association of School Psychologists Convention, Orlando, Florida.

Spragins, A. B., Blennerhassett, L., & Mullen, Y. (1998). *Reviews of four types of assessment instruments used with the deaf and hard of hearing students.* Workshop materials presented at the National Association of School Psychologists Convention, Orlando, Florida.

Spragins, A. B., & Blennerhassett, L. (1989). *Intellectual, adaptive behavior, social-emotional, developmental/ criterion-based, language and basic concept assessment instruments used with preschool deaf children.* Workshop materials presented at the National Association of School Psychologists Convention, Boston, Massachusetts.

19 Assessing the Preschool Child with Visual Impairment

MARCIA COLLINS MOORE*

Professionals responsible for psychosocial and psychoeducational assessment are confronted with numerous challenges when assessing a preschooler with visual impairment. The effects of visual impairment on development and learning are complex and not fully understood. Furthermore, there is often a lack of fit between the child's developmental status and the psychometric and clinical tools available to assess that status. Specialized training about development and assessment of children with visual impairment is seldom if ever included in typical assessment courses. Even if it were, there is little research-based information available regarding the development of preschool children with visual impairment, and few formal assessment instruments have been specifically designed for them. Evaluators often find it necessary to adapt and modify available tools, a practice that significantly limits interpretation of results from tests that were not standardized on children with visual impairment. Therefore, special expertise in nonstandard evaluation and clinical judgment, as well as a multidisciplinary approach, are necessary to yield valid and relevant conclusions from assessment. This chapter provides an overview of research findings regarding variations in development of infants and preschoolers with visual impairment and discussion of unique considerations in assessing these children, including the selection of procedures and instruments, adaptation and modification of instruments, and interpretation of findings. The focus is limited to children with moderate and severe visual impairment who may have one or more additional handicaps but who are not severely multihandicapped. The intent is to provide practical information to increase the knowledge and comfort level of professionals with limited exposure to or familiarity with such children.

Overview of Visual Impairment and Blindness

Terminology

The population of children with visual impairment is highly heterogeneous with respect to degree of visual impairment. Numerous definitions are used for specific purposes by various agencies; only those most generally used are included here.

*The author wishes to thank Lisa McLaughlin who assisted with the original version of this chapter.

Visual Acuity.   This term refers to a clinical measurement of the sharpness and clarity of vision for discrimination of fine details at a specified distance. Measurements for distance vision are given in feet (e.g., 20/20) or meters (e.g., 6/6), both of which indicate normal vision. The first number refers to what the person sees, the second to what a normally sighted person can see at that same distance. A child with 20/100 vision sees at 20 feet what a normally sighted child sees at 100 feet. Near-vision measurements are generally given in inches, meters, or Jaeger chart numbers that pertain to type size.

Visual Impairment.   This term refers to any optically or medically diagnosable condition of the eye(s) or visual system that affects the structure or functioning of the tissues so that less than normal vision is the result (Barraga & Erin, 1992).

Visually Impaired.   In the field of vision/visual impairment, this term has come to mean the same thing as visually disabled or visually handicapped, and is probably the most common term used (Bishop, 1996). Barraga and Erin (1992) use the term visually handicapped to denote the total group of children with visual impairments which cause a limitation that, even with the best possible correction, interferes with incidental or normal learning through the visual sense and therefore constitutes an educational handicap. Optimal learning and achievement require adaptations in the methods of presenting learning experiences, in the nature of the materials and devices used, and/or in the learning environment.

Blind.   Children who have only light perception without projection or who are totally without vision are blind. *Blind* and *legally blind* are not synonymous. Educationally, children who are blind learn through tactile and sensory channels other than vision, although perception of light may be present and useful in orientation and movement (Barraga & Erin, 1992).

Low Vision.   This term denotes less than normal visual acuity even with corrective lenses for distance and/or near visual functioning under ordinary conditions. Most children with low vision can use vision for many educational activities, including visual reading, but some may require the use of some tactile materials, possibly even braille, to supplement printed and other visual materials (Barraga & Erin, 1992).

Legally Blind.   This term refers to central visual acuity of 20/200 or less in the better eye with corrective lenses or central visual acuity of more than 20/200 if there is a visual field defect in which the widest diameter of the field of vision is no greater than 20 degrees in the better eye (Koestler, 1976). Only distance vision is measured. This definition became part of federal law in 1935 and is used to determine eligibility for public assistance.

Deaf-Blind.   P.L. 105-17 defines this group as having "concomitant hearing and visual impairments, the combination of which causes such severe communication and other developmental and educational problems that they cannot be accommodated in special programs solely for deaf or blind children" (Federal Register, Oct. 22, 1997, p. 55069). The term *multiple disability* "does not include deaf-blind children" (Federal Register, Oct. 22, 1997, p. 55069).

Prevalence

Visual impairment is a low-prevalence handicap in children. Reliable data on the number of children with visual impairment are unavailable because of the lack of a nationally uniform definition for educational placement. In addition, the U.S. Department of Education is not collecting statistics by disabilities for preschool children with handicaps (Bishop, 1991).

In 1990, the estimated number of visually impaired children in the United States from birth through age 17 years was 1.5 per 1,000 persons. This estimate, equaling 95,410 children nationwide, is the midpoint of a range of estimates based on the 1977 data of the Health Interview Survey (HIS) conducted by the National Center for Health Statistics. For children under six, the data represents the caregiver's (usually the mother's) report that the child lacks useful vision. Although the 1977 HIS contained procedural problems resulting in rates that were too low, this data remains the most recent source of prevalence rates for children birth through 17 years (Nelson & Dimitrova, 1993).

Bishop (1991) conducted a study that examined a number of demographic factors related to the population of preschoolers with visual impairment. Among the data collected were the number of children in two age groups (birth to age 2 and ages 3 to 5), their visual diagnoses, and the most common additional handicaps among children who were identified as multiply handicapped. All 50 states were contacted in at least one capacity, and of the 48 responses, 30 states were represented. The more than 4,000 children who were reported were almost evenly divided between the two age groups—birth to 2 years (group 1) and 3 to 5 years (group 2). Forty percent of group 1 and 60 percent of group 2 were identified as multiply handicapped.

The most common additional impairments reported among multiply handicapped preschoolers with visual impairment in Bishop's (1991) study were mental retardation, speech-language deficits, and neurological involvement. Other handicapping conditions commonly mentioned were cerebral palsy, orthopedic defects, and hearing impairment. The visual defects or diseases that were identified as common included "cortical blindness," congenital malformations (including colobomas), retinopathy of prematurity (ROP) formerly called retrolental fibroplasia (RLF), optic nerve involvement (both optic atrophy and optic nerve hypoplasia), cataracts, and retinal defects or diseases.

Variations in Development of Children with Visual Impairment

In general, the development of children with visual impairment tends to be more similar to than different from that of nonhandicapped children. For example, auditory and tactual development appear to be entirely normal (Warren, 1994). It has been demonstrated that numerous obstacles in the early development of blind and low-vision children may be overcome by specific interventions. It has been argued that certain developmental differences simply ought to be considered normal for children with visual impairment (Barraga, 1983; Warren, 1984). Thus, Warren (1984) questioned the value of comparative research between these children and sighted children and called for a longitudinal, broad-based study of infants and young children with visual impairment that would incorporate the many environmental and demographic variables that may affect their development. Ferrell and her associates (Ferrell et al., 1990) at the University of Northern Colorado are conducting such a longitudinal research study, which has the potential to validate or refute speculations of 50 years. Hopefully, the report, which will be published within the next few years, will give more definitive evidence regarding the question of whether blind children have a different sequence of developmental milestones which is "normal" for them, or do they acquire the same milestone skills that sighted children achieve, but take longer (Bishop, 1996)? Although the research with this population in the age range between infancy and 5 or 6 years continues to increase, sample sizes remain small and the reader is often cautioned about generalizing the results.

Visual Impairment, Development, and Functioning.   Vision is the most dominant sense in development. It has been estimated that as much as 90% to 95% of the perceptions of sighted children originate in the visual sense. Sight gives continuous contact with the environment, enables us to anticipate events, and provides constant information, immediate verification, and the means for understanding oneself and others in space. Vision has been described as the "coordinating sense," which organizes and synthesizes sensory impressions and sequential perceptions into an understandable whole (Barraga, 1983).

Visual impairment interferes with and/or interrupts the relatively automatic and spontaneous process of attachment to the environment and imitation of appropriate behavior. It severely limits the child's incidental, casual learning and the ability to bring meaning to the various experiences of living. Visual functioning may be affected physiologically by reduced visual acuity, restricted field of vision, defective color vision, and fixation problems.

The patterns of visual development in children have been studied extensively in recent years, and findings indicate that visual acuity, visual skills, and visual perception may progress at a faster rate than was thought previously. An excellent model of visual development proposed by Barraga and Erin (1992) indicates that the sequence of visual behaviors and functions may be assumed to develop in a similar pattern for all children. They also provide a developmental sequence of visual age behaviors (See Barraga & Erin, 1992, pp. 93–96, for the developmental model and sequence.)

For low-vision children, however, the process is seldom, if ever, spontaneous and automatic, and the sequence of perceptual development may emerge quite unevenly. Most babies and preschoolers with visual impairment have some degree of vision, from object perception to very useful near vision. The limitations in quantity and quality of visual information necessitate that all children with visual impairment ask questions and discuss visual impressions with normally sighted persons so that valid visual perceptions can be organized and remembered. Although research suggests that the low vision child is potentially at an advantage over the blind child, being able to realize that potential requires early, concentrated attention to learning how to use the impaired vision (Barraga & Erin, 1992).

Congenital visual impairment is present at birth or shortly thereafter, whereas *adventitious impairment* occurs after visual learning has begun. The child with congenital visual impairment has a complete lack or limitation of visual orientation and input of visual impressions, but is not aware that his vision is impaired or that he is any different from others. His parents need to initiate the process of adjustment and compensation with guided sensory stimulation to develop curiosity about the world within and beyond his reach. The child who sustains visual impairment after he has experienced the world visually and has acquired visual memories is able to retain and build upon visual concepts such as space and distance with encouragement.

Specific characteristics of the visual impairment in addition to age at onset have implications for a child's development, including the etiology, type and degree of vision, stability, and prognosis. Although the etiology of the visual impairment is significant in that, for example, some eye conditions are accompanied by pain, photophobia, or brain damage, typically there are insufficient numbers of children in the different etiology groups to allow detailed analysis of possible differences. However, some relatively consistent differences have been found in retinopathy of prematurity with a pattern of social-emotional characteristics that has an autistic-like quality, and retinoblastoma in which intelligence scores may be bimodally distributed, with a small portion in the weak normal range and a larger distribution centered about a mean well above average (Warren, 1994).

The type and degree of visual loss determine the amount and clarity of vision as well as how vision is used for learning and functioning. The stability and prognosis of the visual impairment have other implications. Because seeing is a learned process, the child needs time to relearn with each change in visual acuity and functioning. If the child's vision is currently or potentially deteriorating, he will need help in adjusting to and preparing for the visual loss, and learning strategies may be affected.

Visual functioning and efficiency are contingent on physiological, psychological, intellectual, and environmental factors. Accordingly, the same diagnosis and degree of visual impairment may affect each low-vision child uniquely. Furthermore, visual acuity has minimal if any relationship to the capacity for visual development or for actual visual functioning (Faye, 1984; Jose, 1983). The greater the visual impairment, however, the earlier the child needs special educational services and visual stimulation if development is to progress in relation to capacity.

Psychosocial Development.   Social relationships may be affected from early infancy since the infant with visual impairment is at risk for inadequate attachment. Several potentially counterproductive behaviors have been noted in the study of the dynamics of attachment between visually impaired infants and their mothers. However, a review of the literature suggests that the risks for inadequate attachment are not necessary consequences of the infant's visual impairment (Warren, 1994). Clearly, the parental reactions and adjustment to the child's visual impairment have implications for the social-emotional as well as the physical environment and the opportunities and encouragement offered the child throughout infancy, the preschool years and beyond.

In the normal developmental progression from egocentric to limited social to extended social interactions, the child with visual impairment is at a disadvantage as he or she moves into the social sphere to play with available persons and things. Visual impairment decreases awareness of and attraction to objects and people and limits acquisition of information about them. In reviewing the literature regarding characteristics of the play of young children with visual impairment, Rettig (1994) reported that their play was found to be more solitary, more engaged with adults, less varied, less active, less exploratory and involving significantly more stereotypical behaviors than that of their sighted peers. The children with visual impairments who were most likely to engage in symbolic play were those who had developed personal pronouns, such as "I," and asserted some individuality by using the word "no." In comparison to sighted peers, these children demonstrated a different approach and style to learning about toys. They spend much more time mouthing and looking, and they display less functional play behavior (repetition of appropriate uses of toys).

As with social skills, the development of self-help skills is accomplished primarily through visual observation and incidental learning. For visually impaired preschoolers, development of daily living (self-help) skills are often delayed, and many skills, such as finger feeding and scooping, require guided instruction for mastery. Insecurity may contribute to delayed toilet training and tactile defensiveness may affect acquisition of tooth-brushing.

Though significant, visual functioning may not be the most salient characteristic contributing to the child's psychosocial development. As with sighted children, development and adjustment are most likely the product of the interaction of the child's cognitive resources, other genetic endowments, and the demands and expectations of the environmental context in which the child is placed.

Motor Development. For children with visual impairment, movement may be the most accurate replacement for vision in clarifying information about the world (Barraga & Erin, 1992). The motor system remains a major skill area during the preschool years and a focus of instruction for these children (Bishop, 1996).

Review of the literature indicates general agreement that selective lags occur in certain aspects of manual (midline bimanual coordination) and locomotor development (crawling, walking) in blind infants and young children (Warren, 1984, 1994). Observation and Piagetian-like experiments have demonstrated that congenitally blind infants do not reach for objects until the last quarter of the first year, and they do not begin to walk until about 18 months (Bigelow, 1986). Late reaching to sound has been attributed to lack of visual stimulation (ear-hand coordination substituting for eye-hand coordination), to motor factors relative to blind infants' resistance to lying in the prone position, and to conceptual and affective factors. Late crawling and walking patterns primarily have been attributed to lack of opportunity and encouragement, such that restriction of opportunity causes inadequacy or delays in motor and locomotor development (Warren, 1994). Also, the delay or absence of creeping and crawling which has been observed in blind children may result in lack of fluidity when walking and/or delay in fine motor and tactual development (Ferrell, 1985, 1986). Interpreting previous research, Ross and Tobin (1987) indicate that lags in motor behavior may have profound effects on other areas of development, including acquisition of intellectual abilities, perceptual-motor functioning, and affective reorganization of the mother–infant dyad.

Furthermore, due to the aforementioned limitations inherent in severe visual impairment, blind and many low-vision children require specialized training in concepts and skills needed to orient themselves within space and to achieve purposeful, safe, independent travel through the environment. This training area is called orientation and mobility, or O & M, and requires assessment and intervention by an orientation and mobility instructor. The definition of O & M specific to the unique training needs of infants and preschoolers includes sensory skill development, concept development, motor development, formal orientation skills, environmental and community awareness, and formal mobility skills (Hill et al., 1984).

Language Development. Blind and low-vision infants babble and speak their first words at the expected times, according to most research, but there is much variation, just as with sighted infants (Warren, 1994). Although there appears to be little difference between the language development of blind and low vision children (Dunlea, 1989; Urwin, 1983), significant differences have been observed between their language development and that of sighted children.

For these infants, the visual impairment appears to impose limitations on the observation of gestures, on the "shared frame of reference" with their parents, and on mutual attention to external events (Urwin, 1983). Since the development of communicative language is based on shared experience, the evidence for differences in certain aspects of their early language development should not be surprising.

Review of the research suggests that prelinguistic vocal activity, as well as early language development, of children with visual impairment is significantly impacted by parental responsiveness and language patterns (Dote-Kwan, 1995; Dote-Kwan & Hughes, 1994; Kekelis & Andersen, 1984; Rowland, 1984; Urwin, 1983). Parents' behaviors significantly affect the patterns of prelinguistic communication developed by parents and infants.

It has been demonstrated that parents' speech with infant and preschool blind children includes an unusually high number of single-word labels, questions, and limited explanations, with input that is often directive, repetitive, child-centered, and routine based (Kekelis

& Andersen, 1984). Accordingly, the children's tendency to use labels, ask questions, repeat questions of adults without providing an answer, and speak or question in apparently unrelated situations or totally out of context may not be unusual, given their early conditioning (Ferrell, 1986). Recent data (Kekelis & Prinz, 1996) suggest that even when mothers of preschool blind children do not ask more questions or provide more directives, the conversational patterns and responses of these children differ from sighted children with comparable linguistic levels. They responded to fewer of their mothers' questions or directives with contingent responses and contributed considerably fewer utterances than their mothers. However, the mothers produced series of questions and directives that afforded the blind children fewer opportunities to respond. Also, they were more likely to ask their children questions that tested their knowledge and that are less likely to encourage children to talk about their interpretations of events and feelings.

In Mulford's (1988) integration of several studies that analyzed the 50-word vocabularies of small numbers of children with visual impairments and in Bigelow's (1990) study, the children rarely overgeneralized words and had a relatively large number of words that refer to specific objects or events, rather than to classes of objects or events. They persisted in use of action words mainly to describe their own actions, with less frequent reference to actions of other persons. Bigelow (1990) also found that the blind children's acquisition of their 50-word vocabularies was within the norms of sighted children and that the differences in their language are not caused by delay in object permanence.

Cognitive Development.   Gallagher's (1975) summary of research suggests that preschool children interpret the world primarily in a perceptual rather than a conceptual manner. However, adequate percepts must be formed to enable realistic concepts to develop. If there is a visual impairment, auditory and tactual kinesthetic stimuli are most emphasized for learning, and the visual percepts are either lacking or limited. Children with visual impairment are more dependent on secondhand experience or on mediation, with information introduced by a sighted companion and verbally transmitted.

It is generally agreed, as Lowenfeld (1971) posited, that a visual impairment places children at a disadvantage in cognitive development as a result of limitations on their range and variety of experience, mobility, and control of interaction with the environment. Initially, the world of young blind children extends no further than arm's length. As a result of limitations of their perceptual base, blind and low-vision children perceive from part to whole, whereas sighted children perceive a gestalt, from whole to part. In analyzing parts of objects, blind children's perceptual base is limited to the pads of their fingers. For the low-vision child, however, even when visual information is blurred, distorted, or incomplete, as long as the brain is able to combine the images with auditory and other sensory information, the child can use vision to contribute to cognitive development (Barraga & Erin, 1992).

There is little research on perceptual development and executive functions such as attention and memory with visually impaired infants. As with sighted infants, those with visual impairments move beyond the constraints of immediate perception into the realm of cognition with the development of concepts, which requires memory. The concept of object permanence is one of the early concepts, and, as originally discussed by Piaget, it relies heavily on vision. In his review of the literature, Warren (1994) observed substantial variation among blind infants in the timetable, though not in the sequence, of acquisition of various criterion behaviors in the six stages of object permanence as defined by Piaget. Research evidence with blind infants showed reasonable progression through the stages of object permanence up to Stage 6, but failure at that point. Warren (1994) suggested that this failure may not have so much to do with weakness in the concept itself, but in inadequate understanding of the spatial structure of the environment to be searched. Their difficulty in moving from Stage 5 to Stage 6 suggests a problem in making the transition from egocentrically to externally organized space. This is consistent with observations noted in the previous section regarding the differences in the early language development of children with visual impairment. Specifically, Bigelow (1990) found delay in object permanence of blind children and interpreted the delay and the differences in language of the blind and low-vision children in her study and others (Dunlea, 1984; Urwin, 1983) as dependent on difficulties with a more fundamental ability that is critical to both areas of development: decentering or taking a non-egocentric perspective.

In terms of Piaget's theory, the first differences in cognitive development of blind infants become evident at about 4 months of age, when hand-watching is an important component, and continue through the last stage of the sensorimotor period with delay in achievement of object constancy (normally emerging at 8 to 12 months) by a year or more.

In summary, the process through which children with visual impairment form concepts and develop cognitive styles is not fully understood. Barraga (1986) proposes that there may be differences in early childhood related primarily to the time required to store enough mental images for processing and coding. She emphasizes the importance of providing a range and variety of concrete experiences in the preschool years and attention to language interaction with meaningful vocabulary. "There is no evidence, however, to indicate that the nature and quality of cognitive organization, once achieved, is significantly different from that of sighted children" (p. 97).

Current Issues and Assessment Approaches

As part of the national initiative lead by the U.S. Department of Education to bring about lasting and effective education reform within the United States by the year 2000, *The National Agenda for the Education of Children and Youths with Visual Impairments, Including Those with Multiple Disabilities* (Corn et al., 1995), (hereafter called the *National Agenda*) was created to address the components of education for children with visual impairment that are most in need of improvement and to provide goals and strategies for effecting the needed changes. Eight goal statements were generated from input by representatives from parent groups, specialized schools for children with visual impairments, private agencies serving visually impaired children and their families, university programs for training teachers of visually impaired students, and state departments of education. Goal statement 6 reads as follows: "Assessment of students will be conducted, in collaboration with parents, by personnel having expertise in the education of students with visual impairments" (p. 11).

According to the *National Agenda* (Corn et al., 1995), quality assessment of children with visual impairments requires that the professional conducting or orchestrating the assessment have a high level of expertise in the effects of visual impairment on learning. Most often, this professional will be "the teacher of students with visual impairments or the orientation and mobility instructor" (p. 11). It is recommended that assessments must be comprehensive and include all areas of the core curriculum for children with visual impairments.

Although no national guidelines for selection, administration, and interpretation of assessment instruments currently exist, several trends in special education have resulted from the nondiscriminatory provisions originally required by P.L. 94-142 and expanded with the advent of P.L. 99-457 (reauthorized as P.L. 105-17 in 1997). These trends include the move away from standardized instruments that emphasize a comparison with norms toward a more functional assessment through non-test-based approaches, and increasing use of the ecological approach (assessing children in relationship to their environment) (Hall, Scholl, & Swallow, 1986).

Few standardized instruments are available for assessing the capabilities and adaptive skills of preschool children with visual impairment. The examiner must be knowledgeable about the various instruments and how the standardization was obtained. When tests designed and standardized on nonhandicapped children or on those with other categories of handicaps are used with preschoolers with visual impairment, interpretation of results must include consideration of the impact of visual impairment on performance.

One response to the use of standardized tests or test items that may discriminate against these children has been to use them in nonstandardized ways by modifying or adapting administration procedures. If adaptations or modifications are made, however, results cannot legitimately be compared with the norms. Separate norms for children with visual impairment are generally unavailable for commonly used instruments because disagreement exists among professionals in the field of visual impairment regarding the development of such norms.

Tests designed for children with visual impairments often have norms based on small numbers or biased by institutional populations. Furthermore, no age norms exist for developmental milestones of infants and preschoolers with visual impairment (Ferrell, 1986). Therefore, criterion-referenced tests are generally more useful than norm-referenced tests for this population. Diagnostic tests that measure the skills the child has and identify what skills need to be learned have proved valuable in assessing educational needs and problems. The child's approach to each task is as important as whether the answer is right or wrong. Observing *how* the child attempts a task helps the examiner to determine what adaptations or compensatory strategies the child has developed for problem solving. In addition, non-test-based and ecological approaches to assessment are necessary and appropriate with this population.

Ecological and Non-Test-Based Approaches to Assessment

The ecological approach expands conventional child-centered assessment to include assessment of the child's functioning within her total environmental system. It assumes a reciprocal interaction and influence between the child and the environment, and recognizes that situational factors that initiate and maintain behavior must be examined also. The examiner "gathers information about a variety of variables, compares competencies across situations, and examines the context in which behaviors take place" (Oka & Scholl, 1984, p. 44). The HOME Inventory Infant–Toddler and Early Childhood versions have been used successfully with visually impaired children and their families (Rock, Head, Bradley, Whiteside, & Brisby, 1994).

Observation, a non-test-based approach, is an important basic tool in ecological assessment. Direct, systematic observation of the child's behavior, the environment, and the behavioral interactions is an integral part of any assessment of a child with visual impairment. Fortunately, the procedures for carrying out direct observation are no different for children with visual impairment than for sighted children. However, the behaviors of concern may be different, including the stereotypic behaviors discussed earlier. For example, if eye pressing were a problem, interval recording would be a viable assessment method to employ (Bradley-Johnson, 1986).

A useful place to begin observation of young children with visual impairment is the Checklist for Home Observation of Visually Impaired and Blind Infants and Preschoolers (Bradley-Johnson, 1986). This information may serve as a reliability check of the information obtained from parent interviews, and items also can be used to observe children enrolled in a preschool program.

As with any young child, observation and assessment of the child with visual impairment in his or her home is preferable for obtaining the most valid and useful results. For children who participate in a preschool program and will be assessed outside of the home, classroom observation prior to undertaking a formal child-centered assessment is necessary in order to determine the child's sensory, motor, and communications limitations and abilities in the natural setting.

Another non-test approach to assessment based on observation involves the use of videotape in some situations. Although videotape has been used more for research projects and evaluating the effect of intervention procedures, there is increasing use of it in both natural and clinical settings to record behavior for later review. The examiner may then utilize chronolog, frequency recording, frequency tally, and other recording methods, taking into account antecedent and consequent behaviors and situational factors that may be overlooked by an on-site observer. Other non-test or informal assessment techniques include task analysis and discrepancy analysis.

Preparation for Assessment

A comprehensive assessment includes information from a variety of sources; representative samples of the child's behavior in numerous situations; and both observational and objective data from parents, medical specialists, teachers, and other professionals who provide services to the child and family. A prediagnostic staffing is advisable to design an overall plan for assessment of a preschool child with visual impairment.

As with any child with handicaps, information from hospital charts, previous assessments, and preschool records need to be reviewed prior to assessment. Of special importance with a child who has a visual impairment is information from an eye report and a functional vision evaluation. No psychosocial or psychoeducational assessment should take place until recent ophthalmological and functional vision evaluations have been completed and the results communicated among the assessment team (Spungin, 1981). Also, since neurological involvement is a common additional impairment reported among preschoolers with visual impairment (Bishop, 1991), a neurological examination has been recommended as an integral part of the assessment of visually impaired children (Groenveld & Jan, 1992).

Assessment Procedures

Assessment of a preschool child with visual impairment is challenging and requires special expertise in nonstandard evaluation, as well as keen clinical judgment. Once the examiner knows the objective and specific questions to be answered, the sessions must be structured to gain and maintain rapport with the child and to gather representative samples of his or her functioning. This section provies information regarding unique considerations for assessment, an overview of assessment instruments, suggestions for adapting and modifying instruments, and guidelines for analyzing and interpreting results.

Assessment of a child with visual impairment involves unique considerations about the environment and interactions with the child. Table 19.1 is a compilation of suggested guidelines for assessment of children with visual impairments (Bauman, 1974; Collins-Moore & Osborn, 1984; Genshaft, Dare, & O'Malley, 1980; Hall, Scholl, & Swallow, 1986; Langley, 1979; Scholl & Schnur, 1976).

The examiner provides the key stimulus in the assessment environment. How the examiner presents himself or herself has an important effect on the child's performance in the

TABLE 19.1   Assessment Guidelines

1. Prior to assessment, verify that the child is wearing or has in his (or her) possession the glasses or contact lenses that are regularly used during visual activities.
2. Speak as you approach so that the child will be aware of your presence.
3. Offer the child your hand or initiate other appropriate physical contact such as a pat on the shoulder.
4. Speak in a normal tone of voice, unless the child has a confirmed hearing loss.
5. If the room is unfamiliar to the child, allow him or her to explore; assist in the exploration as necessary.
6. Guide the child to the assessment area table and chair and provide time for the child to become familiar with the setting.
7. Position the child to promote comfort, alertness, maximum range of motion, and optimal use of vision.
8. Explain what you will be doing and answer the child's questions about activities and materials.
9. Define the work space. Materials may be placed on a tray that provides a perimeter, or on a large piece of construction paper outlined with masking tape.
10. For the low-vision child, provide the most favorable lighting conditions and avoid glare on materials and work surface.
11. Provide adequate contrast between the working surface and test objects. Use black construction paper or flannel fabric with light-colored objects and white with dark objects. Demonstrate test materials against a plain background rather than near the examiner's body.
12. Provide children with low vision with a bookstand or other raised surface to bring test materials closer to their eyes and reduce postural fatigue.
13. Provide verbal and tactual information about all test materials and procedures that a normally sighted child would observe visually during assessment.
14. Allow the child to explore and manipulate any materials that will be used in the assessment prior to beginning each test; tap the object, cue verbally, or touch the child slightly to assist in locating materials.
15. Allow time for initial contact and for organization of behavioral responses, including physical manipulation.
16. Prompt the child to ensure that he understands the demands of the task and to help focus the child's attention on the task.
17. Provide verbal and tactual guidance to imitate body actions when assessing motor or self-care skills.
18. Add sound elements to tasks when possible to stimulate interest.
19. Do not feel uncomfortable about using sight-oriented words such as *look* and *see.*
20. Use tactile and verbal reinforcements frequently.

interactional process of assessment. Examiners are encouraged to address any bias or fear they may have regarding blindness, since it has been identified as the most feared disability within the United States (Gallup, 1988). The examiner's attitude and affect are important. The preschooler is sensitive to one's sense of urgency or time pressure; pleasure or displeasure in the interaction; comfort or discomfort with the testing situation; nervousness; and genuineness in establishing a caring, sensitive, and responsive relationship with the child. The degree of rapport may be affected by these and other subtle visceral cues. To avoid inadvertently interfering with the child's performance, the examiner needs to avoid wearing heavy colognes or perfume. With low-vision children, bright or patterned clothes and dangling, glittery jewelry may create visual distractions that interfere with the child's attention.

It is advisable for the examiner and child to spend some time together before actual testing. Also, in selecting the time of day for assessment, the examiner should take into account any therapeutic medications taken by the child and inquire about side effects and peak effect times, since peak levels may produce either high or low levels of performance. Every attempt should be made to time assessment so that it coincides with a child's optimal-functioning interval for the medication. For a review of medications used by children with visual and multiple impairments, see Kelley and Wedding (1995).

Because the child with visual impairment is unable to see nonverbal communication such as smiles and facial cues clearly—if at all—the examiner must provide guidance and convey approval through what is said, tone of voice, and touch. Auditory noise in the assessment environment such as music, telephones, intercom interruptions, and other loud sounds that create competition for the child's attention must be controlled. Visual distractions, such as the clutter of irrelevant objects in the room, should be kept to a minimum. Only functional furniture, arranged to provide adequate space and mobility in the room, is advisable.

To promote optimal lighting for the low-vision child, recommendations from the functional vision assessment should be implemented. In general, low-vision children may require 3 to 10 times the usual room illumination even when working in familiar surroundings and with known materials. Incandescent, fluorescent, and natural light must be taken into consideration. Children with visual impairments such as albinism, aniridia, and some cataracts may require minimum light, whereas those with optic atrophy and juvenile macular degeneration usually require more.

Glare should be avoided because it reduces visibility and interferes with visual efficiency. Directed light should come from a closed-hood lamp with an adjustable stand, which is placed so that light is shed only on the working surface. Placing the lamp to direct the light over the child's shoulder on the side of the better eye is helpful. The child should face away from the bright light of windows.

Fatigue is a final factor to be considered. Low-vision children often experience visual and general fatigue more quickly during assessment because of the effort and attention required to employ usable vision. Scheduling short breaks at regular intervals may avoid excessive fatigue, or the examiner may rely on behavioral cues of fatigue such as rubbing eyes or apparent strain to focus.

Overview of Assessment Instruments

The assessment instruments included are designed to be individually administered and are able to be adapted to ensure that the child with visual impairment will be capable of making the required response. Functional vision and orientation and mobility assessment instruments are not included because use of these tools with young children requires extensive knowledge of the impact of visual impairment on development, specialized training in their assessment, and prior experience in working with visually impaired children. Such tests should be administered only by low-vision specialists, certified teachers of the visually impaired, or orientation and mobility instructors.

Because of the diverse knowledge base of professionals who may be involved in a multidisciplinary assessment, Table 19.2 provides a chart of assessment instruments for use with young children with visual impairment. A wide variety of instruments for use with children from birth through 5 years of age are reviewed. For instruments that have an age range beginning at 5 years, only those for which a useful basal level can be established were included.

Only assessment instruments with which the examiner has had prior experience should be administered to children with visual impairment. The American Printing House for the Blind will print, in large type, short runs of any special achievement tests used in a school district.

Adaptation and Modification of Instruments

Adaptation and modification of assessment procedures and materials are major issues when evaluating children of any age with visual impairment. When using tests that have been standardized on nonhandicapped children or on those with handicaps other than visual impairment, it may be advantageous to use portions of numerous instruments that are appropriate for assessing specific domains even when an entire test is not applicable. Estimates of a child's abilities may be made by using age-referenced items that do not require vision or that can be adequately modified to circumvent visual requirements and still measure the same skills. The clinician should analyze information gained from selected items/subtests diagnostically, with the focus on functional aspects of what the child can do and how he solves problems adaptively. These subtests or selected items can help provide checks and balances on results obtained from other intact assessment instruments utilized. Modifications of administration require changing the stimulus items, the instructions, and/or the response modes. Since no two blind or low-vision children respond in the same way to their impairment, modifications are often individualized. Therefore, it is essential that any deviations from standardized procedures be recorded for later inclusion in the written report.

In modifying assessment items, it is critical that the intent and purpose of the original item not be altered. Standard instructions that may be inappropriate or confusing to the child should be clarified with precise and concise explanation; possible item modifications include changing the format to multiple or forced (yes/no) choice, lengthening or eliminating time limits, providing additional cues, altering the size of the object or picture, modifying visual designs for tactual presentation, replacing models/miniatures or words with real objects, and liberalizing scoring to take experiential differences into account.

The general rule for increasing time limits is one and a half the allotted time for the low-vision child and twice the time for blind children. Because of visual or tactile fatigue, it may be necessary to divide the test administration into two or more sessions. Using real objects whenever possible should ensure that *concepts* are assessed and not the familiarity with two-dimensional representations of concrete objects. In assessing play skills, the use

TABLE 19.2 Commonly Used and Additional Assessment Instruments for Use with Young Children with Visual Impairment

Commonly Used Assessment Instruments for Use with Young Children with Visual Impairment

Test Name	Publication Year; Author(s)	Comments
Adaptive Behavior Measure		
Scales of Independent Behavior (SIB)—Revised	1996; R. H. Bruininks, R. W. Woodcock, R. F. Weatherman, & B. K. Hill	Part of the Woodcock-Johnson Psycho-educational Battery; available separately. Standardization sample limited in number of visually impaired subjects.
Vineland Adaptive Behavior Scales Expanded Form	1984; S. S. Sparrow, D. Balla, & D. Cicchetti	A norm-referenced, standardized test with supplementary norms for a relatively large visually impaired sample aged 6 years to 12 years 11 months. Various items in all domains are inappropriate for visually impaired preschoolers or require careful adaptation.
Cognitive/Conceptual Understanding Measures		
Kaufman Assessment Battery for Children	1983; A. S. Kaufman & N. L. Kaufman	The only subtests appropriate for blind children are Number Recall and Riddles. Subtests that may be appropriate for low-vision children include Hand Movements, Number Recall, Triangles, Word Order, Expressive Vocabulary, Faces & Places, Arithmetic, and Riddles. Careful modifications or adaptations may be required for low-vision children, depending on functional vision. Minimum developmental level of 3.5 to 4 years is advised for use with visually impaired children.
Stanford-Binet Intelligence Scale, Fourth Edition	1986; R. L. Thorndike, E. P. Hagen, & J. M. Sattle	Norm-referenced, standardized test that assesses intelligence. Adaptations for children with visual impairment are general and were not field-tested. Handbook recommends attempting to administer all tests in standard format to low-vision children, modifying Vocabulary, Quantitative, Comprehension, Number Series, Verbal Relations, and Equation Building as necessary. For blind children, only present Memory for Sentences and Memory for Digits without modifications. The type of discriminations required with Braille are different and sometimes more difficult.
Developmental Measures		
Battelle Developmental Inventory (BDI)	1984; J. Newborg, J. R. Stock, L. Wnek, J. Guidubaldi, & J. Svinicki	Modifications and adaptations for children with visual impairments are included, but were not field-tested and no score adjustments are given. For severely low-vision and blind, each domain contains items that must be scored 0; most are in Cognitive, thus invalidating this domain for other than criterion-referenced information and the total score. Valid scores may be obtained only for low-vision children with good usable vision.
BRIGANCE® Diagnostic Inventory of Early Development: APH Tactile Supplement	1991; A. Brigance	The APH Tactile Supplement, designed to be used with the print edition, provides alternative procedures and tactile materials for items which involve visual stimuli, with additional directions and suggestions where appropriate.

(continued)

373

TABLE 19.2 Continued

Test Name	Publication Year; Author(s)	Comments
Developmental Measures		
The Callier-Azusa Scale	1978; R. Stillman	Criterion-referenced test for deaf-blind and severely impaired children designed to provide information for planning instructional programs. Form G is a revision of the Cognitive domain published in 1984.
Growing Up: A Developmental Curriculum—Revised	1991; N. B. Croft & L. W. Robinson	An informal criterion-referenced assessment procedure accompanying a curriculum guide based on Piaget's work originally developed for use with infants and preschoolers with visual impairments, designed to provide information for planning instructional programs. Six areas of development are assessed: Physical, Fine-Motor, Self-Help Skills, Social Personal, Language, and Intellectual Development. Items available in Spanish.
Informal Assessment of Developmental Skills for Visually Handicapped Students	1978; R. Swallow, S. Mangold, & P. Mangold	Part Two: Informal Assessment of Developmental Skills for Younger Visually Handicapped and Multihandicapped Children was developed to aid in assessment and formulation of teaching objectives for infants and preschoolers with visual impairment. Part Two provides five checklists: Self-Help, Psychomotor, Social-Emotional, Language, and Cognition.
Oregon Project for Visually Impaired and Blind Preschoolers—Revised	1991, Fifth Edition; 1994, in Spanish; S. Anderson, S. Boigon, and K. Davis	A criterion-referenced instrument designed for assessment and educational program planning for young children with visual impairments. The Skills Inventory is organized into eight developmental areas: Cognitive, Language, Socialization, Vision, Compensatory, Self-Help, Fine-Motor, and Gross-Motor. Each area contains skills that have been developmentally sequenced and arranged in approximate age categories for sighted children; estimated delay for visually impaired children is provided.
Reynell-Zinkin Scales	1980; J. Reynell & P. Zinkin	These developmental scales were designed for use with visually impaired babies and preschool children, including those who have multiple disabilities. Six areas of development are assessed: Social Adaptation, Sensorimotor, Exploration of Environment, Response to Sound/Verbal Comprehension, Expressive Language, and Non-Verbal Communication.
Ecological Measures		
Early Childhood Environment Rating Scale	1980; T. Harms & R. M. Clifford	A field-tested, criterion-referenced, observational inventory to assess the quality of caregiver environments and interpersonal interactions outside the home. Minimal, if any, adaptations are necessary. Thirty-seven items are rated on a seven-point scale with all criteria specifically defined, to develop a profile for each room observed. The seven subscales are Personal Care Routines of Children, Furnishings and Display for Children, Language-Reasoning Experiences, Fine and Gross Motor Activities, Creative Activities, Social Development, and Adult Needs.

Home Observation for Measurement of the Environmental Inventory for Children with Severe Handicaps	1987; R. H. Bradley, B. M. Caldwell, S. L. Rock, J. A. Brisby, & P. T. Harris	A field-tested, criterion-referenced, observational inventory to assess the stimulation potential and quality of early developmental environment within the home. The Preschooler with Severe Handicaps version includes items to assess presence of adaptive aids for children with visual, hearing, orthopedic, and mental impairments, such that more than one handicapping condition can be included as necessary. The seven subscales are Physical Environment, Emotional and Social Responsivity, Acceptance of Child's Behavior, Organization of Environment, Provision of Play Materials, Parental Involvement with Child, and Opportunities for Variety in Daily Stimulation.
Language		
Receptive Expressive Language Assessment for the Visually Impaired	1979; G. Anderson & A. Smith	A three-dimensional adaptation of the Preschool Language Scale (Zimmerman, Steiner, & Pond, 1979) and language items for the Maxfield-Buchholz Scale of Social Maturity for Preschool Blind Children (Maxfield-Buchholz, 1957). Designed to measure receptive and expressive language of young children with visual impairments through predominantly auditory and tactile responses. Real objects are utilized and an audio cassette tape of environmental sounds is provided. Limited field testing with sighted children and a small number of children with visual impairments dictates judicious interpretation.
Reynell Developmental Language Scales	1980; J. Reynell & P. Zinkin	Assesses expressive language and verbal comprehension utilizing miniature objects. Use real objects as possible.

Other Selected Assessment Instruments for Use with Young Children with Visual Impairment

Bayley Scales of Infant Development—Second Edition (BSID-II)	1993; N. Bayley	Heavy emphasis on vision and audition; selected adaptations are advisable. Mental scale is well suited for longitudinal study of visually impaired children (Leguire, Fellows, & Bier, 1990).
Behavioral Characteristics Progression—Revised	1997; Vort Corporation	Includes orientation and mobility strands.
The Body Image of Blind Children	1978; R. Swallow, S. Mangold, & P. Mangold (Eds.)	Scale available in Informal Assessment of Developmental Skills for the Visually Handicapped.
Boehm Test of Basic Concepts—Preschool Version	1986; A. E. Boehm	Pictures may need adaptation or enlargement.
Bruininks-Oseretsky Test of Motor Proficiency	1978; R. H. Bruininks	Complete battery or short form; some subtests not appropriate for children with visual impairment.

(continued)

TABLE 19.2 Continued

Other Selected Assessment Instruments for Use with Young Children with Visual Impairment

Instrument	Year; Author	Description
Burks Behavior Rating Scales: Preschool and Kindergarten Edition—Revised	1996; H. F. Burks	Descriptive statements to be rated by parent or teacher; measures adjustment and social conduct.
Child Behavior Checklist: 2–3 years (CBCL/2-3)—Revised	1992; T. M. Achenbach	Behavioral rating scale; no norms for physically or perceptually impaired children.
Detroit Tests of Learning Aptitude—Primary Second Edition (DTLA-P2)	1991; D. D. Hammill & B. R. Bryant	A new version of the DTLA-3 for children ages 3 to 9; pictures may need enlargement.
Developmental Activities Screening Inventory—II (DASI-II)	1984; R. R. Fewell & M. B. Langley	Adaptations listed for Visually Impaired (no score adjustments). Screening only.
Developmental Programming for Infants and Young Children	1981; D. S. Shafer & M. S. Moersch	Adaptations listed for Visually Impaired. Heavy emphasis on visual tasks in fine motor area.
Expressive One-Word Picture Vocabulary Tests—Revised (EOWPVT-R)	1990; M. F. Gardner	Objects may be substituted for pictures with blind and severely low vision.
Leiter International Performance Scale—Revised	1997; G. H. Roid & L. J. Miller	May be appropriate according to quality and quantity of available vision for children from 2 years 0 months and older to assess nonverbal intelligence and cognitive abilities.
Mangold Developmental Program of Tactile Perception and Braille Letter Recognition	1976; S. S. Mangold	Criterion checklists to determine current functioning; appropriate only as part of a total reading program.
Mullen Scales of Early Learning	1995; E. M. Mullen	Pictures may need enlargement.
Peabody Developmental Motor Scales	1983; M. R. Folio & R. R. Fewell	Few adaptations needed for low vision. Not sufficient for motor-impaired child.
Peabody Picture Vocabulary Test—Revised (PPVT-R)—Third Edition	1981; L. M. Dunn & L. M. Dunn	Few adaptations needed for low vision.
Preschool Language Scale—Third Edition (PLS-3)	1992; I. L. Zimmerman, V. G. Steiner, & R. E. Pond	Administered by speech-language pathologist; may be adapted for blind children by substituting objects for pictures. Original edition used with success in research with low-vision children.

Test	Author/Year	Notes
Receptive-Expressive Emergent Language Test—Second Edition (REEL-2)	1991; K. R. Bzoch & R. League	Administration by speech-language pathologist preferred. Based on parent interview and observation.
Receptive One-Word Picture Vocabulary Test (ROWPVT)	1985; M. F. Gardner	Objects may be substituted for pictures with blind children and those with severely low vision.
Social Climate Scales; Family Environment Scale (FES)	1981; R. H. Moos & B. S. Moos	No adaptations necessary; diverse norming sample. Measures family's interpersonal relationships; emphasis on personal growth and organizational structure.
Slosson Intelligence Test—Revised	1991; R. L. Slosson	Screening instrument for evaluating crystalized verbal intelligence 2 years and above. Assesses visually impaired children over age 30 months.
Test of Early Language Development: Second Edition (TELD-2)	1981; H. Resko, Reid, & Hammill	Generates an overall language score.
Wechsler Preschool and Primary Scale of Intelligence—Revised (WPPSI-R)	1989; D. Wechsler	Verbal section are more appropriate for visually impaired children.
Woodcock-Johnson Psychoeducational Battery—Revised (WJ-R)	1989; R. W. Woodcock & M. B. Johnson	Instead of composite IQ scores, regard subtests individually as indicators of strategies for intervention (Groenveld & Jan, 1992). Pictures may need enlargement. Omit selected subtests according to visual functioning.

of toys that provide auditory stimulation and are relatively large, such as ones available from the American Printing House for the Blind, will help the child locate and use them.

Great care must be taken in modifying visual designs for tactile presentation to the blind child. Tactile graphics cannot be used to represent pictures because tactile representations do not take the place of discrete visual information or pictures. Modifications can be accomplished by using geometric shapes or designs with simple structure and only essential details. The examiner can trace the design and then outline it with a line of glue, or glue and string or yarn, to produce a raised line drawing. Also, thermoform copies of tactile material may be obtained from a teacher of the visually impaired.

Large-print words and adequately enlarged pictorial materials can be used for the low-vision child with adequate vision. However, enlarging visual material is not a panacea, because not all children benefit. Special care must be taken when making enlargements for children with visual field deficits such as peripheral field loss or scotomas, because it is easy to magnify the image beyond the child's visual field.

When enlarging pictorial material, pictures with only clear and essential details should be selected. Pictures can be enlarged through bold reproduction with a copying machine or by hand. Visual aids, such as a large lighted magnifier or a closed-circuit television, may be used to enlarge printed materials from one to sixty times the original size. Visual aids should be considered only when the child is sufficiently mature to use them and has had experience with them prior to assessment.

Few response modifications have been suggested. Two such modifications include allowing gestures and other action responses, and allowing oral responses to be substituted for visually mediated responses such as pointing or manipulating objects.

Interpretation of Results and Communication of Assessment Findings

Extreme caution must be exercised in interpreting assessment results of children with visual impairment. These results may be taken from a combination of intake information, ecological assessment, observation of the child, performance on standardized tests, and/or the outcome of criterion-based assessments. It is especially important that the interpretation process go beyond mere reporting of scores. This synthesis of information must objectively report assessment outcomes, provide detailed information of the child's performance, and yet remain concise and functional.

Taking into account the original purpose of the assessment, the interpretation of findings should include a brief discussion of the methods of assessment used. Description of deviations from standardized assessment procedures, including modifications employed, should be carefully reported. Specific descriptions provide useful information on how particular tasks were approached as well as guidelines for future intervention and assessment.

Deviations from standard test administration dictate that normative data should not be used for interpretation of test results. Furthermore, unless a standardized test has normative data for blind and low-vision children, it is recommended that results should not be interpreted using the norms published with the test (Hall, Scholl, & Swallow, 1986). Since no age norms exist for developmental milestones of infants and preschoolers with visual impairment (Ferrell, 1986), the examiner should report only approximate developmental age ranges and then use a criterion-referenced approach to specify abilities and deficits within a given age equivalent.

Interpretation of all test performance must include behavioral descriptions of how the child approached and completed tasks as well as the level of mastery achieved. Note any factors that may have negatively affected the child's performance, such as lack of familiarity with test materials, separation anxiety, visual fatigue, and so on. In some instances, observational reports may be the most appropriate method for drawing inferences from a child's performance. Behavioral observations are of particular importance when specific measurement of a response is not attainable by any other means.

Scores on certain types of assessments may be significantly inflated or depressed in low-vision and blind children. For example, on verbal tests, the "verbal veneer" previously discussed may give an impression of advanced verbal ability, where in fact it may be an indication of a form of delayed echolalia. Significantly depressed scores of verbal ability may be predicted for minority children with limited English proficiency. Likewise, tests containing motor performance items may penalize the child with visual impairment. Bradley-Johnson (1986) provides an in-depth view on the use of motor performance age-referenced items and identifies specific behaviors that the child with visual impairment often takes more time to learn.

Drawing conclusions on the basis of test performance requires special attention to the validity of not only the tests but also individual items within tests. One should ascertain that items reflect assessment of desired skills, not information unrelated to the concept being tested. For example, a preschooler's inability to complete a simple, low-contrast form board may indicate that the child lacks the visual acuity to complete the task, rather than a conceptual deficit.

Although interpretation of test results requires consideration of the impact of visual impairment on performance, it is extremely difficult at best to quantify the extent to which a visual impairment interferes with optimal performance. It is important to remember, for example, that under stress, low-vision children's visual efficiency is compromised, especially that of children with nystagmus or limited field of vision. Secondary handicaps such as expressive language delay and apparent mental retardation may not necessarily indicate limited potential; rather, they may be attributed to a failure to attain certain concepts that are typically acquired through incidental visual learning (Ferrell, 1986).

Diagnosis of mental retardation in preschoolers with visual impairment cannot be justified unless there is substantial evidence of neurological damage through the use of CT scans and other medical evaluations (Ferrell, 1987). Likewise, the use of developmental assessments for predicting the child's potential intellectual functioning is a dangerous practice and is strongly discouraged when working with these young children. Certain components of cognitive development typically emerge at later stages in blind children, and their potential is prone to be underestimated by any measure (Warren, 1984). Accordingly, the use of "serial evaluations" at three-month intervals will yield multiple data points to estimate progress of cognitive development in the first few years of life (Davidson & Legouri, 1986).

The examiner is the primary tool in the assessment process. Keeping this in mind, there is a need to think critically about the following questions:

1. Do I have a firm knowledge base about how visual impairment affects various areas of development?

2. Do I have sufficient expertise and experience with a variety of instruments in order to select, adapt, and administer both standardized and nonstandardized evaluation instruments?
3. Does my interpretation of the assessment results go well beyond mere score reporting, to consider the use of norms as appropriate or notation of adaptations and deviations from standardized procedures?
4. Have I considered all relevant sources of information as I summarize observations and draw conclusions from the data?

When communicating assessment findings, provide clear and concise descriptions of functional performance, a summary of strengths and weaknesses, and specific recommendations.

Summary

Consideration must be given to the unique variations in the development of preschoolers with visual impairments when determining their eligibility for services as well as when making recommendations for program planning. Accordingly, the *National Agenda for the Education of Children and Youths with Visual Impairments, Including Those with Multiple Disabilities* (Corn et al., 1995) recommends that quality assessment (1) requires the professional conducting or orchestrating the assessment to have a high level of expertise in the effects of visual impairment on learning, and that assessment (2) is comprehensive, to include all areas of the core curriculum for children with visual impairments. The use of nonstandardized, non-test-based and ecological approaches to assessment are of special significance because very few formal assessment instruments have been specially designed for young children with visual impairments.

20 Assessment of Maltreatment and Neglect in the Preschool Child

ANN H. TYLER

VICKIE R. GREGORY

The first recorded case of child abuse occurred in 1874 in New York City. Neighbors became concerned about Mary Ellen Wilson, a 9-year-old girl living with foster parents, when they noticed that she was being severely maltreated. Frustrated that no law existed to protect the child from further abuse, the neighbors appealed to the American Society for the Prevention of Cruelty to Animals. The case was brought to court and the foster parents were charged with cruelty to an animal and were convicted on the premise that little Mary Ellen, a member of the animal kingdom, deserved the same justice as a common cur. As a result of the publicity generated by the case, the first law recognizing the rights of children was passed in New York State (Tyler, 1978).

It was not until the early 1970s, when federal funds for child abuse programs were made available, that child abuse and neglect statutes were drafted in all 50 of the United States, and only within the last 18 years have national child abuse incidence statistics been recorded. The problem of child sexual abuse rudely awakened the nation in the early 1980s with the realization that perhaps one-quarter of our children will be victims of sexual exploitation before reaching legal maturation.

There are variations in the reporting rate of child abuse from state to state, probably due to differences in definitions, legal policies, public awareness, and availability of resources. It is noteworthy, however, that across states, similar major patterns are emerging. The number of children alleged to have been maltreated increased from 2.6 million in 1990 to 2.9 million in 1994. The number of "substantiated" cases increased from 798,318 in 1990 to 1,104,628 in 1994. Almost 50% of the victims were under the age of eight. Forty-six percent were male children and 52% were female children. There were 5,400 deaths attributed to child maltreatment, with parents and relatives comprising 90% of the perpetrators. (U.S. Department of Health and Human Services, 1994).

Definitions of Maltreatment

For purposes of this review, the definitions of abuse under Utah state law will be used. This law (Utah Code, 1994, pp. 90, 91; 1996a, pp. 90, 91) states as follows:

"Child" means a person under 18 years of age.

"Child abuse or neglect" means causing harm or threatened harm to a child's health or welfare...and welfare of a child, through neglect or abuse, and includes causing non-accidental physical or mental injury, incest, sexual abuse, sexual exploitation, molestation, or repeated negligent treatment or maltreatment.

"Incest" means having sexual intercourse with a person whom the perpetrator knows to be his or her ancestor, descendant, brother, sister, uncle, aunt, nephew, niece, or first cousin.

"Molestation" means touching the anus or any part of the genitals of a child or otherwise taking indecent liberties with a child.

"Sexual abuse" means acts or attempted acts of sexual intercourse, sodomy, or molestation directed towards a child.

"Sexual exploitation of minors" means knowingly employing, using, persuading, inducing, enticing, or coercing any minor to pose in the nude for the purpose of sexual arousal of any person or for profit, or to engage in any sexual or simulated sexual conduct for the purpose of photographing, filming, recording, or displaying in any way the sexual or simulated sexual conduct, and includes displaying, distributing, possessing for the purpose of distribution, or selling material depicting minors in the nude or engaging in sexual or simulated sexual conduct.

Psychological Maltreatment

Psychological maltreatment is now recognized as a core issue in all forms of abuse and neglect. The term *psychological* has replaced the term *emotional* in many states' child abuse statutes because it is more inclusive, better explaining the affective, cognitive, and behavioral conditions embedded in this type of maltreatment. Psychological maltreatment can occur in isolation; however, children who are sexually abused, physically abused, or neglected are also likely to suffer psychological abuse. Psychological maltreatment can take the form of: *spurning* (behaviors that are rejecting, degrading, shaming); *terrorizing* (behaviors that threaten harm or actually physically harm); *exploiting/corrupting* (acts that encourage child in development of inappropriate, self-destructive or criminal behaviors through modeling or coercion); *denying emotional responsiveness* (acts of ignoring a child's basic needs for affection and attention); *isolating* (acts that isolate child physically, mentally, or emotionally from other possible care givers or peers); *mental health, medical and educational neglect* (acts that ignore or refuse to provide for these important needs) (Brassard, Germain, & Hart, 1987).

Reporting Law

It is absolutely essential that professionals know their state reporting law. Every state has statutes mandating who must report child abuse, stating penalties for negligence to do so and granting immunity for any civil or criminal liability that could result from such actions. When any person has reason to believe that a child has been abused, he or she must immediately notify the police or child protective service agency.

> Any person making this report in "good faith" is immune from any liability, civil or criminal, that otherwise might result by reason of such actions.

> Failure to report can result in the negligent person, official, or institution being charged with a Class B misdemeanor. (Utah Code, 1996a, p. 94)

Professionals who are assessing children must be competent in detecting signs of maltreatment and must also be able to make appropriate referrals for services once a report is made to proper authorities.

Familial and Societal Impacts of Abuse

Child abuse is considered a generational phenomenon in cases where the parents were victims of abuse themselves (Tyler, 1986). Thus, treatment evaluations for the entire family may be indicated. Family dysfunction may be associated with marital disorder, poor parenting models, significant situational stressors, mental illness, and social isolation (Lusk & Waterman, 1986; Tyler & Brassard, 1984). Sometimes only one child in a family is targeted for abuse; however, our clinical experience indicates that the identified victim's siblings are usually also affected.

Retrospective studies of samples of delinquent youth resulted in several significant findings. A significant number of juveniles who had contact with the juvenile court system were abused as children (McCord, 1983). Children neglected by their families had a higher rate of delinquency. Families of delinquent youth who were abused used more community agency programs (such as those for drug and alcohol abuse). The incidence of prostitution, drug abuse, and runaway youth was significantly correlated with sexual abuse victimization (Brown & Finkelhor, 1986). Indeed, child abuse trauma affects every fiber of our society (Briere, 1992a; Briere & Runtz, 1991).

Impact on the Child

Sexual Abuse.   In a review of the research on the impact of child sexual abuse, it has been concluded that most sexual abuse experiences can be defined as traumatic and emotionally damaging, with common results. First, preschoolers tend to regress when abused. Sexual abuse frequently leads to regression in toilet training, with frequent "accidents" or bedwetting. In addition, children will revert to baby talk or thumb-sucking. Second, a change in the child's manner of interacting with the environment is a red flag for abuse. Children may appear depressed and withdrawn or may act out in unacceptable ways (e.g., temper tantrums, obstinate behavior). They may exhibit impaired self-concepts and guilt. Third, young children frequently experience sleep disturbances—inability to sleep, nightmares, refusal to go to bed, and insistence on sleeping with the parent. Fourth, an increase in somatic symptoms is commonly seen, with children complaining of a variety of aches and pains. Finally, children who have been sexually abused are frequently eroticized (James, 1989), and an increase in sexual behavior occurs (Brassard, Tyler, & Kehle, 1983; Brown & Finkelhor, 1986; Goodwin, Sokal, & Rada, 1982).

Many symptoms of child abuse satisfy the diagnostic criteria for Post-Traumatic Stress Disorder (PTSD) in the Diagnostic and Statistical Manual of Mental Disorders, Fourth Edition, revised (DSM-IV; American Psychiatric Association, 1994):

1. Child sexual abuse constitutes a recognizable stressor that would evoke stress symptoms.
2. Re-experiencing of the trauma occurs, as evidenced by recurrent dreams and intrusive recollection of the abuse.
3. There is reduced involvement with the external world, marked by signs of social withdrawal and contradiction of affect.
4. Symptom formation is often manifested as a sequel to sexual abuse and includes hyper vigilance, nightmares, avoidance of stimuli that might re-traumatize, problems in concentrating or remembering, and symptom intensification during exposure to events that resemble the abusive situation.

In addition to the psychological and behavioral effects of abuse, some victims suffer from physical effects, including bladder infections, rectal and vaginal tears, lacerations and bruising, and sexually transmitted diseases (Brassard, Tyler, & Kehle, 1983).

Physical Abuse. Physical abuse can result in direct injuries such as burns, welts, bruises, broken bones, and injuries to internal organs. Some of the psychological effects are similar to those found in the sexually abused child with noncompliant, withdrawn, or aggressive behaviors exhibited to a marked degree. These children often demonstrate significant difficulties with peer interactions and academic learning.

Psychological Maltreatment and Neglect. For purposes of this chapter, effects of neglect are considered as those derived from acts of omission, whereas the effects of emotional maltreatment result from acts of commission. The impact of both forms is significant. The child feels unwanted, bad, fearful, alone and has great difficulty empathizing or reading social cues. These children appear to either internalize their problems, becoming apathetic, depressed, withdrawn and anxious, or to externalize, becoming aggressive, violent, and delinquent. In sum, child maltreatment produces acute and long-term effects which must be assessed in order to implement appropriate intervention and treatment.

Overview of Assessment Process

Psychological evaluations of preschool victims of child maltreatment and neglect are relevant to both diagnostic and legal issues. First of all, the collection and analysis of clinical and test data provide information relevant to diagnosis, appropriate treatment interventions, and, ultimately, to the development of prevention programs. Second, the psychological evaluation is a central component to child protective service investigations, civil proceedings such as child custody cases, and criminal prosecutions of the perpetrators of the maltreatment. The application of psychological evaluations to child protective and legal proceedings is the focus of this chapter.

Psychological evaluations completed in the forensic arena differ from those directed solely towards treatment. For instance, addressing the reliability and credibility of the victim as a witness is essential. Toward this end, the examiner needs to understand critical areas of relevant psychological research, including evaluation of memory skills in the preschooler. Several other factors are included in this evaluation of memory. For instance, language development, knowledge of sexuality, and vulnerability toward suggestion require consideration. Specifics related to the clinical interview and the assessment of cognitive and developmental skills will be addressed later in this chapter.

Memory

In recent years, investigators have focused on the memory skills of preschool children. Literature reviews indicate that a variety of memory skills improve with age (Kail, 1989; Schneider & Pressley, 1989). Several developmental trends in the literature have also been noted (Ornstein, Larus, & Clubb, 1991). For instance, younger children make more omission errors than do older children or adults when the task requires recall (Brown, 1979; Chi, 1983). Similarly, studies suggest that preschool children provide less information when responding to open-ended questions than do older children (Baker-Ward, Hess, and Flanagan, 1990; Ornstein, Gordon, and Larus, 1992). Further, preschool children's performance improved when tasks required recognition as opposed to recall (Perlmutter & Myers, 1975), although their recall performance was enhanced when cues were used (Perlmutter & Ricks, 1979). Preschool children were not able to accurately state the number of times an event happened, or to identify the time of the event (Marshall, Marquis, & Oskamp, 1971). Further, young children do not rehearse memories in a strategic fashion as older children and adults do (Brown, 1979). Despite these difficulties, some evidence indicates that when young children are asked to recall experiences with which they are familiar, their recall can be good, even after a period of time (Fivush & Hammond, 1990), and in some cases was equivalent to that of adults (Chi, 1978; Lindberg, 1980).

Recent literature has emphasized the importance of language development in memory performance (Saywitz, Nathanson, & Snyder, 1993). Children cannot answer questions they do not understand. Children's memory is also dependent upon what they have attended to and encoded into their memory (Saywitz et al., 1993). Recent research suggested the differences in memory development of preschool children may be related to the increasing ability to use narrative skills that develops with age (Mandler, 1990). In addition, preschool children have accumulated little experience to assist them in organizing their memories into coherent and relevant scenarios (Johnson & Foley, 1984). Thus, accurate recall is more difficult for them because they have little understanding of the relevant factors. For instance, in one study, preschool children erroneously related the sequence of events surrounding a fire drill because they failed to understand the causal connection between the ringing of the fire alarm and the leaving of the building (Pillemer, Picariello, and Pruett, 1994).

Despite memory deficits due to lack of development, the literature is replete with instances in which young children have recalled personal, traumatic events. Terr (1988) observed behavioral memories of trauma in children under one year of age. Hewitt (1994) described two case studies in which young children exhibited the capacity to recall sexual abuse that occurred when they were two years old. In another case study, investigators (Jones, Psych, & Krugman, 1986) reported that a 3-year-old girl, Susie, was abducted, sexually molested, and left for dead in an outhouse. After receiving medical attention, during which the physicians concluded her genital examination was "normal," she was interviewed by police and was able to describe the kidnaping in detail. In addition, she identified the assailant from photographs provided by the police. Ten days after the ordeal, she identified the assailant from a police line-up. Two weeks after the abduction, a psychiatrist interviewed her and assessed her suggestibility by deleting the photograph of the defendant from the photographs shown to her. She "firmly stated he was not among the photographs" (Jones et al., 1986, p. 254). Susie withstood further attempts to question her memory and credibility. She testified by videotaped interview. Fifteen months after the sexual molestation, the defendant confessed to the crime.

Clinicians have also reported preschool children can recall and relate traumatic events they witness (Fivush & Hammond, 1990; Terr, 1988). For example, Pynoos and Eth (1984) reported a case study of a 4-year-old girl, Julie, who witnessed the fatal stabbing of her mother. Julie was able to describe significant portions of the murder and of her father's attempt to clean the house prior to leaving.

In summary, language development has an impact on memory encoding and recall. Preschool children exhibit good recognition skills, with performance at visual memory tasks exceeding that of verbal tasks. It is more difficult for them to use free recall memory in laboratory experiments. Data indicate, however, that if the information is part of their normal repertoire or, conversely, is personalized and traumatic, they have the ability to recall pertinent information and to relate it to adults. Recent reviews (Fivush, 1993; Goodman, Batterman-Faunce, & Kenney, 1992) provide further information on the strengths of preschool children's memories. As a caveat, the literature also suggests that children are less likely to review traumatic material as time passes (Terr, 1983).

Suggestibility

The concerns of the criminal justice system about the memory skills of children has led to speculation that children are more suggestible than adults—that they can be convincingly coached to falsely accuse others of maltreatment. As delineated previously, children's memory is different from that of adults in many ways. In an early review of the literature, Loftus and Davies (1984) concluded:

> The results of the studies support the conclusion that adults spontaneously recall more about events they have witnessed than do children, but not the simple notion that children are always more suggestible than adults...No clear developmental trend emerges...on the effects of leading questions. This may surprise those who believe that suggestibility is a general characteristic of childhood. (p. 62)

They go on to state that age alone is not the answer to the difficult question about the suggestibility of children. Other relevant factors include the child's ability to understand the event, the delay between the event and the disclosure, the interest value of the stimulus to the child, and language sophistication.

More recent investigations regarding the factors related to suggestibility are contradictory. For instance, Ceci and Bruck (1993), in a review of sixteen studies comparing preschoolers, older children, and adults, concluded that young children were the most suggestible. In contrast, Zaragoza (1991) conducted four experiments involving more than 260 subjects and was unable to identify salient factors influencing preschool children's suggestibility. Zaragoza (1991) concluded that the evidence is insufficient to support a general conclusion that preschool children are more suggestible than adults.

Language Development

Preschool children have limited verbal skills. Prior to the interview regarding abuse, the examiner needs to obtain some measure of the child's language ability. This can be accomplished through an interview with the child, an interview with the parents, and formal testing. Assessment of a preschool child's verbal skills is necessary for two reasons. First of all, using language which a child does not understand can lead to erroneous reporting. For instance, in a study in which 3-year-old children were asked if a man touched their "private parts," they inaccurately answered yes (Goodman & Aman, 1990). The inaccurate report stemmed from the children's confusion regarding the meaning of "private parts."

Second, because regression is one of the behavioral symptoms frequently observed in children who have been abused, it is common for them to regress in verbal skills during interviews regarding the abuse. Thus, data demonstrating that a verbally articulate child is reduced to one-word responses or mutism, supports the allegation of maltreatment.

Knowledge of Sexuality

Preschool children's knowledge of anatomy and sexual interactions varies considerably as a function of the attitudes of the adults who care for them. Observations of young children reveal that they are curious about the differences between the sexes. Some children ask questions about where babies come from or why boys' bodies are different from girls' bodies. However, preschoolers are not typically curious about sexual intercourse or other types of sexual interactions unless they have had some exposure to such activities, through pornography, observation of adults engaged in sexual activity, or molestation. Therefore, mental health professionals should interview parents regarding their methods of teaching about sexuality—that is, the terminology they use and their attitudes toward nudity and exposure to sexual activity.

Bernstein (1976) interviewed 60 boys and girls and asked them where people get babies. A consistent developmental pattern emerged, with most 3- and 4-year-olds believing that babies exist somewhere and people simply go and get them. Some children at this age reported, "You go to a baby store and buy one." Children at the next level believed babies were manufactured or made, although the process varied. At the next stage of knowledge, children began to realize that a mother and father are necessary. Consistent with Bernstein's (1976) findings, play interviews with children revealed that very few children from ages 4 to 5 years of age connected sexual intercourse with babies (Cohen & Parker, 1977).

In a thorough review of the literature regarding children's sexual behaviors, Johnson and Friend (1995) concluded little empirical data exists regarding the significance of children's sexual behaviors. Many children engage in sexual behaviors whether or not they have been sexually abused. Johnson and Friend (1995) provide detailed clinical information regarding the specifics of evaluating children's sexual behaviors, with emphasis on behaviors which should concern the clinician.

Critical Issues Related to the Disclosure of Child Abuse

Accommodation Syndrome.   Disclosure of child sexual abuse is often difficult for both the child and the examiner. Several factors increase the already difficult task of disclosing the abuse. Frequently, the perpetrator has threatened the child and continued exposure to the perpetrator causes the child to be frightened. Further, children are often disbelieved by adults, which adds to their confusion, especially if the adult is a primary caretaker or in a trusted relationship with the child. In cases where the perpetrator is a primary caretaker, the child's disclosure is problematic because it often results in the dissolution of the family, for which the child is often blamed. Children face rejection by the perpetrator who is also a primary caretaker. In most cases, the victimized child is abandoned by the adults whom he or she needs the most.

These factors result in a syndrome which Summit (1983) calls the "child sexual abuse accommodation syndrome." The syndrome includes the most commonly observed behaviors in victims of sexual abuse, which fall into five categories: (1) secrecy; (2) helplessness; (3) entrapment and accommodation; (4) delayed, conflicted, and unconvincing disclosure; and (5) retraction (Summit, 1983, p. 181).

Secrecy.   Child sexual abuse is almost always posed to the child as "a secret" or "our little game," which the child must not tell anyone about. Typically, the perpetrator accompanies the abuse with a threat of dire outcome if the child does not keep the secret. The child has only the perpetrator to rely on in assessing the situation. This is especially true of younger children who have a limited knowledge of sex.

Helplessness.   By virtue of their tender age, preschoolers are helpless. They depend on their parents for nourishment, shelter, comfort, and love. Unfortunately, the statistics clearly reveal that children are more likely to be sexually molested by an adult in a position of trust (Finkelhor, 1979, 1980). This dramatically increases the helplessness of the child, for he or she has nowhere to turn.

Entrapment and Accommodation.   Early intervention and protection of the child is a critical issue in cases of child abuse. If these steps are not taken, the child becomes entrapped in the abusive dynamics and resorts to accommodation, the third category delineated by Summit (1983). More simply stated, the child must survive. Survival usually occurs by the child "accommodating not only to escalating sexual demands but to an increasing consciousness of betrayal and objectification by someone who is ordinarily idealized as a protective, altruistic, loving parental figure" (Summit, 1983, p. 194). Inherent in this model are the guilt and self-blame that the child feels for the abuse. Many forms of psychopathology observed in adults can be traced to incidences of sexual abuse as children and can be viewed as the children's attempts to accommodate and accept the reality of the ongoing abuse.

Disclosure.   Given this explanation of the factors that control children's disclosure, it is no surprise that disclosure, if it ever occurs, is delayed and conflicted. Children who have kept the "secret" sometimes disclose it during the dissolution of a marriage because it is deemed safe. In some cases, the secret is divulged during adolescence, when the child is better able to question the authority of the abusing parent. These circumstances cause the criminal justice system to look skeptically upon the disclosing adolescent. Thus, when the child is most in need of support and reinforcement, he or she is least likely to obtain it.

Retraction.   If the child's statement is viewed skeptically, retraction is likely. The parents' prediction has come true: The child was not believed. The ramifications now become more difficult to live with than the abuse. Retractions are so prevalent in cases of child sexual abuse that they have been rated as a criterion for judging the truthfulness of the child's statement (Green, 1986).

False Allegations

Methodologically sound studies of false allegations of child sexual abuse concluded that false allegations are relatively rare (Everson & Boat, 1989; Jones & McGraw, 1987), although the rates of false reporting across all studies varied dramatically, ranging from 2% to 50% (Everson & Boat, 1989). In a well-documented study, only 8% of the sexual abuse allegations over a period of one year were deemed fictitious (Jones & McGraw, 1987; Ney, 1995). The majority of cases in which allegations are false occurs within the context of a custody dispute. Although it is important to realize that custody or visitation issues may give rise to false allegations, it is equally essential to recall the accommodation syndrome and to realize that divorce is one of the circumstances in which disclosure is common.

A careful review of videotapes, clinical notes, and transcripts of interviews is imperative in evaluating claims of false allegations. The use of suggestive techniques (e.g., "I've heard he does bad things to you."), or leading questions may result in erroneous reports of maltreatment. Characteristics of techniques which produce accurate reporting include a neutral tone on the part of the interviewer, limited use of misleading questions and suggestive techniques, and the lack of a motive to produce distorted reports of abuse.

The Interviews

Concern over the false reporting of child abuse makes it imperative to secure information about the family history: relationships, guardianship issues, situational stresses, previous history of abuse of any family member, and the child's history (medical, developmental, physical, and emotional).

Typically, by the time the mental health professional sees the child, others have interviewed him or her. It is useful to review records of those interviews after examining the child. To reduce preconceived opinions, the child should be interviewed before the case is discussed with parents, police, or caseworkers. The interviewer needs just enough information to be able to conduct an interview. It is essential that the examiner not enter the interviewing situation with a bias or opinion as to the alleged abuse of the child.

Interviewing with preschool children can be difficult, depending on their age and developmental level. Ideally, the victim would be able to provide a detailed narrative of the abuse. A good strategy is to give the child the opportunity to tell about the abuse without interrupting with questions. However, because many children this age do not provide detailed information, questions are often necessary. The examiner needs to be careful not to lead the child through questioning. Given the research described earlier indicating that children profit through cuing, some direct questions will undoubtedly help the child recall the event. Another opinion in constructing questions is to provide the child with choices. For instance, rather than saying, "The bad touches happened after dinner, didn't they?" the examiner could ask, "Did the bad touches happen before dinner or after dinner?"

Another concern in interviewing preschoolers is the possibility of a response set. Often children will automatically respond "no" or "yes," depending on their stage of development. Everyone has observed the 2-year-old who constantly says "no." Some children will consistently respond "yes" regardless of the content of the question. Therefore, the interviewer needs to determine if the child has a tendency to respond affirmatively or negatively. A response set is particularly likely to occur toward the end of the interview, when the child is tired and ready to quit. It is a wise interviewer who attends to the child's cues that the interview is over. In closing the interview, the child should be thanked for his or her cooperation; however, the examiner should not extract promises from the child regarding his or her testifying because undue emphasis on the trial will have little meaning and will often frighten the child, causing nightmares and apprehension.

After concluding the interview process, the examiner should review the records of other professionals involved. Often the detectives, caseworkers, and parents have audio taped the interviews with the child. Written reports can be obtained from other mental health professionals, physicians, and detectives. If the child has been interviewed by numerous people prior to the examination by the mental health professional, it is important to check for contamination of the data. In other words, the examination of the child's statement is important, but it is also necessary to review the types of questioning used by these professionals. Often, detectives or caseworkers will insist that the child use adult terminology for anatomical parts. When leading questions have been used by previous interviewers, it is more difficult to determine the veracity of the child's statement. Indeed, multiple interviews by untrained interviewers pose one of the most difficult problems encountered in the corroborative evaluations.

The Use of Anatomical Dolls

Anatomical dolls are often very helpful when used by an experienced professional who is trained in their use. Although dolls cannot be used as a test for abuse, they can be effective as an additional investigative or diagnostic interview tool. Current research does not support the criticism that the dolls are sexually stimulating or too suggestive (Everson & Boat, 1994, 1990). In fact, studies have found that, when used with the 3- to 7-year-old child, the dolls facilitate accurate recall (Katz, Schonfeld, Carter, Leventhal, & Cichetti, 1995). Documentation of the interview is important. The interviewer's questions and the child's verbal, nonverbal, and emotional responses should be videotaped or well documented in writing. It is absolutely essential that professionals who interview children be highly skilled and well trained. Child abuse and neglect cases are often lost or won depending upon the quality of the first interview.

Videotaping

The initial clinical interviews are often videotaped in order to document details, provide against a future recantation by the child, and/or be used at the preliminary hearing or trial in lieu of the child's testimony. As an example of the unique aspects of this process, 15 standards define what must be done to videotape the interview (Tyler & Gully, 1988):

1. No attorneys may be present.
2. The tape must be visual and aural.
3. It must be an accurate record of the interview with the child.
4. It must be filmed by a competent operator.
5. Voices of each person on the tape must be identified.
6. The interviewer must be able to testify.
7. The videotape cannot have been edited *in any way*.
8. Only the videotapes of children under 12 may be used in lieu of appearance.
9. Only one child may be in the room at a time.
10. Quality lighting must be used.

11. The videotape must be secured when complete to ensure that no one could alter, lose, copy, or mar the tape.
12. The interviewer must be able to meet the test as an expert.
13. The videotape must have a determination of the ability to determine truth and falsity.
14. The videotape must have specific details of the acts in question.
15. The tape must not have any other recording on it, over it, or under it.

Examination of the Child's Statement

Following the interview, the examiner analyzes the child's statement. There are three hallmarks of a true allegation that need to be explored. The first characteristic is the child's ability to describe the *context* in which the events took place. Details surrounding the alleged abuse are crucial. For instance, it is helpful to understand the context in which the alleged abuse occurred. Was the alleged perpetrator giving the child a bath? Putting the child to bed?

The second hallmark of a true allegation is the child's ability to give an *explicit description* of the abuse. The more details that are provided, the more likely the child is to be judged credible. If the child displays knowledge of sexual activity that is not age-appropriate, the child's statement is more believable. For example, many girls do not know about the vaginal opening unless it has been pointed out to them in some way.

The third hallmark is *congruence of affect,* between the child's affect and the nature and scope of the abuse—both when the abuse occurred and the child's emotional reactions as he or she tells about it. Children are typically withdrawn and appear distressed by recounting the abuse. In cases where children are smiling and laughing, the truthfulness of the statement is questionable. Indeed, the affect of the child distinguished between true and false allegations in the study by Jones and McGraw (1987).

Other factors are also important in examining the child's statement. Most cases of abuse are accompanied by threats or coercion. The consistency with which the child tells the story over time is an important element in the credibility of the statement. All interview data should be reviewed for consistency. Also, when children are asked to demonstrate the abuse with anatomically correct dolls, their rendition of the abuse can be validated against their verbal description. Thus, consistency of description across different media can be reviewed.

Expert Witness Preparation

Preparation for the role of expert witness is extremely important. Because of the Hearsay Statute in many states, the prosecution may rely almost entirely on the expert for documentation and validation of the abuse. The expert must make certain that his or her curriculum vita is current and includes evidence of experience in child abuse cases. He or she must be prepared to withstand the defense attorney's attempts to impugn or impeach witness credibility. The expert must be knowledgeable about court procedure, prepared with sufficient data to make informed statements, and capable of defending the reliability and validity of the assessment results.

Documentation

Careful note-taking is imperative. Dates of interview and client contact must be recorded. Documenting who is responsible for what statement, using direct quotes wherever possible, is important. Only the examiner and the child should be present during the evaluation. Videotapes used to record the clinical interview must be secured when complete to ensure that no one can alter, lose, copy, or mar the tape. The tape must have a determination of the ability of the child to determine truth and falsity, and it must not have any other recording on it, over it, or under it.

Psychological Tests

Psychological testing provides an objective measure of cognitive and developmental deficits and emotional and behavioral problems associated with child abuse. This information can be used for substantiation of the abuse and for treatment planning. In addition, psychological testing provides relevant data with which to evaluate the child's ability to provide an accurate account of the abuse. The most commonly used tests are listed next, with a review of the relevant research in the area. For a comprehensive description of these tests, see chapters 9, 10, and 11.

Developmental Testing

There are a variety of instruments that yield data regarding developmental domains for preschool children. The best known tests include the Bayley Scales of Infant Development—Second Edition (Bayley, 1993), the Battelle Development Inventory (BDI; Newborg, Stock, Wnek, Guidubaldi, & Svinicki, 1984), and the Denver Developmental Screening Test—Revised (DDST-R, Frankenburg, Dodds, Fandal, Kazuk, & Cohrs, 1975). To measure language development, the Peabody Picture Vocabulary Test—Revised (PPVT-R, Dunn & Dunn, 1981) is frequently used. Finally, the Developmental Test of Visual Motor Integration (VMI-3R; Beery & Butkenica, 1997) is a test of visual-motor perception skills.

Few controlled studies exist that test the development of children who have been physically abused. However, Applebaum (1977) conducted a well-controlled study on the developmental concomitants of physical child abuse. Thirty children who were physically abused were compared to 30 nonabused children on the Bayley Scales of Infant Development (Bayley, 1969) and the DDST-R. The abused children scored significantly lower on the cognitive and motor development scales of the Bayley and on three of the four mental age levels of the DDST-R (personal-social, language, and gross motor).

In a similar fashion, other researchers have described the concomitants of sexual abuse. It is reported that children who have been sexually abused frequently regress in their behavior. They also suffer from cognitive deficits (inability to concentrate) and emotional problems that will have an impact on their developmental skills.

Cognitive Testing

Frequently used cognitive tests include the Kaufman Assessment Battery for Children (K-ABC; Kaufman & Kaufman, 1983a, 1983b) the Stanford-Binet Intelligence Scale, Fourth Edition (SB:IV; Thorndike, Hagen, & Sattler, 1986a, 1986b), and the Wechsler Preschool and Primary Scale of Intelligence—Revised (WPPSI-R; Wechsler, 1989).

Investigators (Hoffman-Plotkin & Twentyman, 1984) compared 42 preschoolers who had been physically abused, neglected, or not been maltreated on a number of tests, including the Stanford-Binet (Form L-M) and the PPVT-R. On both measures, the abused and neglected preschool children scored significantly lower than the control group, indicating that abused children might tend to exhibit cognitive deficits.

It should be noted that these tests are especially effective tools for assessing the abilities of the preschool child to report abuse. Specifically, the tests include measures of both visual and verbal memory, language ability, and concept formation. The Stanford-Binet includes age-equivalency tables that are useful for communicating the child's ability to the criminal justice system. Interpretation of the relationship between the test results and the child's statement can provide insight into the veracity of the statement. For instance, an articulate child who scores in the superior range of intellectual functioning on the Stanford-Binet may, as a result of the emotional trauma, be reduced to one-word sentences or even mutism during an interview session. The testing in this case illustrates the child's ability level and reinforces his or her ability to report the events. Yet, in the interview, the child appears unable to do so. The depressive and withdrawn affect is consistent with abuse. In a different situation is a child scoring within this range who expresses affect during the interview that is positive and happy, speaks in one- or two-word sentences, and frequently expresses the inability to remember. In this latter situation, the superior intellectual ability combined with the positive affect suggest the abuse is fictitious.

Behavioral Testing

The Child Behavior Checklist (CBCL; Achenbach, 1988; Achenbach & Edelbrock, 1983) a frequently used behavioral inventory which is useful to delineate the problems associated with sexual abuse, such as sexual acting out, depression, and regression.

The Child Sexual Behavior Inventory (CSBI) (Friedrich, Grambsch, Damon, Hewitt, Koverola, Lang, & Wolfe, 1992) was specifically designed to assess sexual behavior in children. The CSBI is designed for use with children from age 2 to age 12. The CSBI has been revised twice (CSBI-R and CSBI-3). The 36-item inventory is completed by the child's primary female caregiver. The caregiver rates the numerical frequency of the child's behavior over the previous 6 months. The CSBI ratings cover various sexual behaviors, including self-stimulation, sexual interest, sexually intrusive behavior towards others, boundary permeability, and gender related behaviors.

Empirical studies of the sexual behavior of children are limited. Clinical experience and the existing research support the general conclusion that maltreatment and sexual abuse of children results in a higher frequency of sexual behavior than occurs in comparable samples of nonabused children. (Finkelhor, 1979; Friedrich, 1993; Friedrich, Beilke, & Urquiza, 1988; Friedrich, Grambsch, Broughton, Kuiper, & Beilke, 1991; Friedrich et al., 1992). Research indicates that the CSBI and CSBI-R discriminated abused from nonabused children (Friedrich, 1991). Similarly, Hewitt and Friedrich (1991) found significantly different levels of sexual behavior in a group of young children categorized as "probably abused" when compared to a group who were "probably not abused."

Projective Testing

The Plenk Storytelling Test (PST; Plenk, Hinchey, & Davies, 1985) consists of nine projective picture storytelling cards. The child is asked to tell a story about what is happening in the picture, how he or she feels about it, and what is going to happen next. The test provides information about the child's anxieties, fears, peer and family relationships, and approach to life. The PST should be used with children whose verbal skills are well developed.

Simple sentence completion tasks can also be used with preschool children as indicators of emotional functioning. For instance, the following types of questions can be answered by most preschool children:

> "I like…,"
> "I am afraid of…,"
> "I want…,"
> "The thing that scares me the most…,"
> "My daddy…,"
> "At daycare I…,"
> "My mommy…,"
> "My favorite person is…,"
> "I don't like…".

Projective drawings are also useful with preschool children. The Human Figure Drawing (HFD; Koppitz, 1968), House-Tree-Person drawings (H-T-P; Hammer, 1954), and Kinetic Family Drawing (KFD; Burns & Kaufman, 1972) are useful diagnostic tools and also build rapport with children. It should be noted that the HFD also provides information about the child's cognitive development (e.g., the Koppitz Scoring System; Koppitz, 1968).

Projective drawings have been useful in discriminating children who have been both sexually and physically abused from children who are emotionally disturbed and who have not been abused. Investigators (Blain, Bergner, Lewis, & Goldstein, 1981) found that six items on the House-Tree-Person drawings discriminated between physically abused, emotionally disturbed, and well-adjusted children. The six items were smoke present from chimney (House), absence of windows from the ground floor (House), size of limbs noticeably different (Person), human figure drawn with geometric shapes (Person), feet deleted (Person), and a head more than one-quarter of the total size of the figure (Person).

Chase (1987) conducted a pilot study on the discriminative power of the Human Figure Drawing and the Kinetic Family Drawing. She concluded that the Human Figure Drawing was a powerful test for discrimination between sexually abused, emotionally disturbed, and well-adjusted children. The figures were analyzed on 76 different measures according to the Sidun and Chase (1986) Human Figure Drawing Code Manual. The sexually abused children differed from the emotionally disturbed children on the following details: hands, fingers, and clothing were omitted; phallic objects were present; and developmental scores differed significantly. When the children who had been sexually abused were compared with children who were well-adjusted, the following details were significant: hands, fingers, and clothing were omitted; phallic objects were present; sexuality of the figure was undifferentiated; large circular eyes were present, mouth was emphasized; a long neck was present; and developmental scores were different. The developmental scores for the children who were sexually abused were significantly lower than those for the other two groups, indicating regression in the abused group.

Summary

Reports of child abuse have been steadily increasing through the past decade. But have incidents of such abuse really increased, or have more stringent child protection laws drawn this nation's attention to an age-old problem? The fact that statistics continue to suggest that child abuse is prevalent and widespread, even across all socioeconomic levels, is a good indication that it has been around for a long time. Why is this so? Because although it is difficult to find patterns of similarity among abusers and perpetrators, a major pattern that consistently emerges is that abuse, particularly intrafamilial abuse, tends to repeat itself across generations. The goals in assessing child victims of abuse are typically to assist in protective service investigations; but, on a more encompassing level, the purpose becomes to facilitate breaking the cycle of abusive behavior. For this reason, the crucial issues in the assessment process become proper identification and verification of the victim(s) and offender(s), followed by implementation of recommendations for treatment of the child and family and rehabilitation or incarceration of the offender.

21 Writing Assessment Results

ENA VAZQUEZ NUTTALL

JENNIFER L. DEVANEY

NANCY A. MALATESTA

ANAT HAMPEL

In the previous chapters, different assessment approaches that can be used to collect data from preschool children and their families have been described. After collecting data from the parents, the referred child, teachers, and other sources, the practitioner must synthesize and describe the findings in a well written report. Writing case reports is one of the most crucial parts of the evaluation process. However, many students and practitioners find this component of the assessment process difficult and time-consuming. Writing case reports requires knowledge of the content and technical properties of norm-referenced and informal assessment measures, knowledge of normal and exceptional development, and knowledge of educational and psychological intervention strategies. Foremost, it requires good writing and editing skills, including the ability to organize materials and decide what is important and ethical to include and what to exclude.

Writing assessment findings should accomplish the following goals: (1) to organize, analyze and synthesize the collected data and then translate it into intervention plans; (2) to communicate to other professionals and to parents findings and recommendations; and (3) to keep a record of the developmental status of the child who was tested and the recommended plans.

This chapter focuses on practical, technical, and ethical aspects of writing traditional, individual case reports. Writing can be made easier and case reports can become more valuable if appropriate training is provided to the writer. Within the limits of its brevity, this chapter tries to provide such training by discussing the major points of case report writing and presenting a sample case report. However, achieving excellence in case report writing also needs in vivo and close supervision from competent and experienced professionals.

Audiences

One of the most important factors to consider when writing a case report is the audience for whom it is intended. Case report writers should make sure they know who needs to receive the information and for what purposes. The receiving audience will determine the type of

"I have taken care of the error in your report writing program."

© National Association of School Psychologists.
Reprinted by permission of the publisher.

language used in the report, the content covered, the tone, and the recommendations. In many instances, two or more reports may need to be written: one for the general public and one for the professional. However, if practitioners only have time to write one case report, they should use plain English for the bulk of the report and include technical terms only when necessary. When using technical terms, brief explanations should be included.

Before testing, parents of preschool children should be informed of the purpose and intended use of the tests and information gathered, in terms that they can understand. During the initial visit, it is important to explain to parents that the relevant information regarding family history that is obtained will be summarized in a case report and that they should identify any information they wish to keep confidential. Beyond this, parents must also be told who will have access to the report. Open disclosure of this information is crucial for making informed decisions about what, if any, information should be kept out of the report. Parents have a right to know the results of the evaluation and the right to have test data kept confidential within the limits promised when consent is obtained (Keith-Spiegel & Koocher, 1985).

Parents' rights to have access to their children's records pose two challenges for practitioners. The first is to present information with tact and sensitivity without revealing information that the parents do not wish to make public. Second, the practitioner must frame the report in language that is intelligible to parents and, as much as possible, phrased using positive terms that are not frightening or easily misunderstood (Keith-Spiegel & Koocher, 1985). In addition to being aware of the parents' and adults' rights to see reports, practitioners should keep in mind that case reports tend to be kept in schools and agencies for many years and may be sent to many other professionals and agencies over which they will have no control. Given the potential for circulation of records, practitioners must be extremely careful about how they conduct evaluations and what they put in writing. They should also be prepared to defend their work in a court of law if necessary.

The Traditional Case Report

Because of its flexibility and wide applicability, the traditional individual case report is the focus of this chapter. Those readers interested in other styles of case report writing should consult Tallent (1976). The traditional model of case report writing usually includes the following sections:

- Identifying Information
- Reason for Referral
- Background History
- Sources of Information
- Behavioral Observations
- Assessment Results and Interpretations
- Summary and Recommendations

In the following pages, each of these sections is discussed.

Identifying Information

Most reports include the following information for identification purposes: name of the child, the date of birth, the age at time of testing, the dates on which the testing was conducted and the report was written, the school or center the child was attending, the name of the evaluator, the name of the supervisor (if appropriate), and the professional status of the practitioners involved. This information is "boiler plate" in most reports; its major function being record keeping. The age at which a child was tested and who did the testing are important data to have in conducting future assessments. It is also important for recipients of the case report to know the qualifications of the evaluators. Evaluators should be sure that their professional titles and bilingual abilities, if appropriate, are correctly indicated. The supervisor's name should be included when a student, noncertified, or nonlicensed person has conducted the assessment. According to the ethical standards of the American Psychological Association (Keith-Spiegel & Koocher, 1985), psychologists should not put their signatures on case reports that they have not completed themselves or supervised.

Reason for Referral

The most important initial steps in the assessment process include clarifying the exact concern(s) prompting the referral, identifying who is referring the child, and understanding what they want from the assessment. This information should be stated clearly and comprehensively unless there are confidentiality issues to be considered. The reason for referral guides the assessment process and helps organize the case report. Case report writers should focus the report around the referral question(s) and should re-address the referral question(s) in the Summary and Recommendations sections. Close coordination between the referral question(s) and the other parts of the report is crucial for producing a cohesive and well-integrated narrative.

Background History

Only *relevant* background information concerning the problems experienced by the child and the family should be included in this section. This part should include information about family size and structure, education and employment of parents, sibling order, and a developmental, health, social, treatment, and educational history of the child. Previous test results should be summarized in this section if available and relevant. If the child is on any medications or already receiving services, it should be stated in this section. The privacy of the family should be protected, and delicate information that the family does not want revealed should not be disclosed. Family information should be presented tactfully and sensitively.

Sources of Information

All the sources of information should be identified in this section. The writer should be careful to capitalize and spell test names properly, specify the edition, indicate whether a partial administration of a test was employed, and, if relevant, whether the test was administered in another language. Observation sessions and interviews held with parents, teachers, and other professionals, and any records and past case reports that have been examined should also be noted. This information is helpful for determining the comprehensiveness of the assessment and reveals the plan of action that was followed in order to directly address the referral question.

Behavioral Observations

The physical appearance and manner of dressing of the child should be described because it is a helpful indicator of the care that a child receives, and the cultural background and present economic condition of the family. The way a child moves or walks is important developmental information and should be included. If any family members accompany the child to the testing session, their physical appearance and manner of dressing, as well as their interaction with the child, should be reported. If the adult who brought the child stayed for the testing session, a description of the interaction between the child and adult should be included.

The way children respond to test items and to the examiner is as important as how they actually score on a test. The degree of *rapport* established between the child and the examiner is extremely important and should be described. Was the child friendly and at ease with the examiner, or uncomfortable and distrusting? Was the child helpful with the test materials? Introverted or extroverted? Did she converse easily with the examiner? If rapport was poor, the examiner should indicate the degree to which the results are valid and a true measure of the child's abilities. If the evaluator was testing a limited English proficient child, the language(s) used during the testing should be noted. If an interpreter was used, the qualifications and training or preparation given to the interpreter should be described. Modifications and adaptations of the tests made by the examiner also should be reported.

It is important to describe how *attentive* the child was. Was the child able to sit down in her seat for a reasonable period of time or was she running around the room, climbing the walls, and standing up on chairs? Was the child's attention span appropriate for her age?

The degree of *self-confidence* exhibited by the child should be reported. Was the child self-assured or lacking in self-confidence? How did she handle failure and success? Was she able to recuperate? Did the child make remarks indicating her feelings about herself?

Was the child *persistent,* or did she give up easily without trying? What parts of the testing did she seem to enjoy or dislike? Which parts were difficult for the child and which were easier?

What was the *language* of the child like? Did she have difficulty organizing responses? Did she speak in one-word sentences, two-words, or other combinations? Was her articulation age-appropriate? Did she speak a foreign language or a mixture of English and a foreign language? If examples of the child's language were recorded, they should be cited in this section.

Assessment Results and Interpretations

The findings and interpretations are the crux of the case report. It is imperative in this section that the examiner comment about the appropriateness of the tests used for the particular child being tested. If the child is from a minority group the examiner should explain the applicability of the tests used for his or her particular group. If the test norms do not include the child's ethnic group, specific disabilities, or level of English proficiency, the examiner should caution the reader about the validity of the findings and focus more on qualitative rather than quantitative information.

As Sattler (1988a) recommends, organize assessment findings by identifying common themes within and across tests and procedures. Findings are easier to read and remember if they are organized by areas such as cognitive, social-adaptive, fine motor, gross motor, language, and academic achievement or readiness. In presenting specific tests, the content of the tests should be described briefly. Any results that are expressed in standard scores or grade equivalent scores also should be indicated in percentile ranks or age equivalent scores. These scores should be indented, presented in vertical columns, and labeled clearly.

High, average, and low scores should be discussed. Consistency and inconsistency between and within tests and other sources of information should be described. Strengths and weaknesses of the profile should be indicated. If test results can be interpreted using factors such as the K-ABC Sequential and Simultaneous factors (Kaufman & Kaufman, 1983b) or Bannatyne's factors (1971), these factors should be presented and discussed. The degree to which the child differs from the average for his or her age level should also be noted. Clearly present any information that may help clarify referral questions that were raised.

Summary and Recommendations

At this point, the writer should return to the section titled Reason for Referral and decide how the evidence collected clarifies the initial referral question. Returning to the beginning question is necessary if the report is going to be coherent, well integrated, and useful. What do the results have to say about the initial referral? Do they clarify the nature of the difficulties described by the family or teacher? Is the presenting problem of an organic or functional origin? Can the child's profile be subsumed under a DSM-IV category? Are the results clear and consistent or are they confusing and ambiguous? Findings should be integrated and a theoretical focus found, to the extent possible (Sattler, 1988).

If the child is a member of a minority group or a special population (i.e., deaf, blind, or severely disabled), the writer should discuss the validity of the findings and the role culture and language played in the results obtained.

Once the nature of the difficulties is clearly described, plans for intervention can be prescribed. Recommendations should be organized by area, such as provision of physical therapy, parent training or family counseling, and so on. The best thing to do is to provide an action sentence which is underlined and preferably starts with a verb—for example, *"Provide parent training services,"* and then discuss why, how, and by whom these services should be provided. The more specific the recommendations, the more useful they will be. Specific names of several possible therapists or medical practitioners, teaching materials, booklets, parent training programs, treatment programs, or agencies should be given if appropriate. Professionals should take into account the cultural and linguistic background of the family when making recommendations for therapists or any other treatment that is not familiar to the parents.

Presentation of a Case Report

In this section, a case report will be presented. The report is typical of those written at a public school setting. Reports vary in length depending on the time available to the practitioners and the needs and functions of the different settings. School case reports tend to be shorter because of the lack of personnel to meet high demands, while university assessment reports tend to be longer because the mission of the university is to train students in as many measures as possible and according to the highest standards. Professionals intending to serve preschoolers should learn to write all types of reports so that they can adapt their style to the demands of the many settings in which they may work.

Sample Case Report
Anywhere Public Schools
Confidential Psychological Assessment

Name:　Bill Jones

D.O.B.:　2/10/94

Age:　5 years, 4 months

School:　Anywhere School

Grade:　Preschool

Examiner:　Jane Smith, M.S.
　　　　　School Psychologist

Date of testing:　6/10–12/99

Date of report:　6/13/99

Parents:　Jack and Jill Jones

Address:　10 Main St.
　　　　　Flower City, MA 55555

Reason for Referral

Bill is a 5-year, 4-month-old child who has been receiving special education services for three years. Academic testing conducted by Bill's preschool teacher and other professional staff at this site revealed that Bill is performing well below his same-age peers. When asked, Bill could not give personal information such as age, address, or date of birth. He was unable to write his first name or form any letters of the alphabet. He was unable to follow one-step directions and had difficulty with visual discrimination tasks. His expressive language was unintelligible with features of perseveration. Fine and gross motor skills were informally assessed and appeared delayed. Bill did not show any understanding of numbers, number concepts, or one-to-one correspondence when asked to count.

As a result of his performance, the current referral was initiated through a joint effort by Bill's preschool teacher and his mother. This psychological assessment was requested in order to provide more information regarding Bill's current level of functioning and assist in making appropriate recommendations regarding academic placement for the next school year.

Background History

Bill lives with his mother, maternal grandfather, and younger brother. His father has recently been released from a drug treatment program and is living in a nearby town. Both parents completed high school and are from Irish-American background. The boys visit their father regularly on weekends. There is a family history of language, attention, and emotionally-based learning disabilities. His father and paternal uncles reportedly had undiagnosed speech and language difficulties. Bill's mother reported that her attention problems may have been overlooked as a child.

Bill's medical history indicates a normal pregnancy, a natural childbirth delivery, and a full-term birth weight at 6 pounds 8 ounces. At birth, Bill was found to have a heart murmur which subsided without medical intervention. Bill has a history of chronic ear infections that were medically treated with ear tubes and adenoid surgery. His general health is good and he is not currently taking any medications. As a result of the early medical complications, Bill's progress has been closely monitored by his pediatrician.

At the age of two, Bill's pediatrician contacted Child Find Services on behalf of the family and identified him as a child in need of services, as his development was not commensurate with expected milestones. Particular areas of concern included delays in expressive and receptive language skills and motor delays. As a result of this action, Bill received Early Intervention Services until the age of 3. At that time, Bill entered the special education preschool operated through the public school system, which serves children with multiple needs.

Bill's mother commented that attendance at the preschool program between the ages of 3 and 5 "did him a world of good." In the structured preschool environment, Bill's behavior was age-appropriate. In contrast, his mother reports his behavior to be quite different at home. Bill is aggressive toward his brother, lacks impulse control, and becomes easily frustrated.

Between the ages of 2 and 4, Bill and his mother received counseling to address behavioral issues related to exposure to abuse, neglect, and domestic violence. She reported to the psychologist that she was trying to lessen the negative impact of Bill's early tumultuous years. She was also concerned about Bill's father's discipline style and commented that he would often taunt the children.

Sources of Information

Wechsler Preschool and Primary Scale of Intelligence—Revised (WPPSI-R)
Developmental and Family History Interview
Developmental Test of Visual Motor Integration
Human Figure Drawing
Vineland Adaptive Behavior Scales
Developmental Play Assessment (Partial Administration)
Informal Play-Based Assessment
Observations in child's home, preschool classroom, and psychologist's office
Record Review

Behavioral Observations

The examiner was able to spend time with Bill in his home environment, in a preschool classroom, and also in the psychologist's office. Bill is a child of average height and weight with dark brown hair and brown eyes. In the home, Bill greeted the psychologist with a friendly and eager smile. He was very outgoing and demanded her attention from the onset. Bill presented as an extremely verbal child although his expressive speech was unintelligible. He was observed playing with his younger brother. The two boys incessantly argued; yelling and crying until their mother intervened.

Bill came to the evaluation session with his mother. He had no difficulty separating from his mother for the testing session. Rapport was easily established and his eye contact was good. He was able to attend to the formalized testing for over an hour and gave a consistent, diligent effort. He responded well to praise and encouragement and wanted to please the examiner. He enjoyed the one-on-one attention and appeared content and comfortable during testing.

Throughout the testing, Bill needed directions repeated and rephrased frequently to ensure comprehension. At times, he would subvocalize verbal subtest directions. His pattern of speech was challenging to decipher due to atypical characteristics such as perseveration, awkward phrasing, inappropriate word choice, and rapid rate. He would often switch the topic without giving the listener enough background information to follow his train of thought. Bill's language was representative of a much younger child.

Assessment Results and Interpretation

Cognitive Skills. The WPPSI-R was administered in order to assess Bill's cognitive strengths and weaknesses. This test assesses verbal skills, as well as visual-perceptual and fine motor skills. Bill's performance on the WPPSI-R places his current functioning in the Intellectually Deficient range when compared to same-age peers. There appear to be many factors that influenced his scores and overall performance on this cognitive assessment. In the nonverbal domain, Bill's performance suffered as a result of his difficulty handling both the test tasks and materials presented such as puzzles, holding a pencil, manipulating blocks, and matching items. Bill's expressive and receptive language deficits greatly compromised his performance on both verbal and nonverbal tasks. Despite the visual discrimination concerns that were noted after his academic screening, visual perceptual skills appear to be areas of relative strength.

Bill's performance on this cognitive test fell within the Intellectually Deficient Range according to the classifications specified by the instrument. He achieved a verbal IQ of 57, a Performance IQ of 67 and a Full Scale IQ of 58. Subtest scores are presented below:

WPPSI-R

Verbal Scale	Scaled Scores and Percentiles		Performance Scale	Scaled Scores and Percentiles		
Information	(5)	5%	Object Assembly	(7)	16%	
Comprehension	(2)	1%	Geometric Design	(4)	2%	
Arithmetic	(1)	1%	Block Design	(7)	16%	
Vocabulary	(4)	2%	Mazes	(4)	2%	
Similarities	(2)	1%	Picture Completion	(1)	1%	(w)
(Sentences)	(2)	1%	(Animal Pegs)	(4)	2%	

(w) = weakness
(s) = strength

Caution should be used when interpreting these results as an estimate of Bill's true potential. His language difficulties and lack of experience with educational materials seriously impaired his performance. Given this, it would be more beneficial to interpret Bill's performance using a qualitative rather than a quantitative approach. Bill's cognitive performance across the verbal domain revealed depressed abilities. Again, this performance supports the existence of serious language difficulties which may suggest that cognitive difficulties also exist. His performance domain revealed some scatter, with relative strengths in tasks requiring visual perceptual analysis, and a significant weakness in visual attention to detail.

Expressive and Receptive Language Skills.   The WPPSI-R Verbal Scale subtests measure how well Bill expresses himself and understands language. All of his skills in this domain fell markedly below the average range and these appear to be his greatest areas of weakness. Similar to his performance during the screening, Bill had a difficult time recalling and relaying factual information that he would have learned from his environment. His ability to comprehend "wh" question forms such as who, what, why, and where, was severely delayed. These question forms appeared foreign to Bill and he showed no ability to draw conclusions or respond. He exhibited no understanding of math terms such as "biggest" or "tallest," nor could he count by rote or when using manipulatives. Even when guided with visual assists during the Arithmetic subtest, he could not comprehend the questions asked. When shown a picture, he could identify it correctly by name. However, when asked what specific words meant, he was unable to use language to express his understanding of word meanings. He was unfamiliar with the verbal concepts of same and different. His short-term auditory recall skill was also weak. Despite good eye contact and attention, Bill was only able to repeat up to 3-word sentences, which is considered below average for his chronological age.

Visual-Perceptual and Motor Skills.   Overall, Bill performed better on subtests involving perceptual organization skill, fine motor control, speed and accuracy, as well as visual organization and planning ability. Two areas of relative strength were evidenced on the Object Assembly and Block Design subtests. These tasks involve visual perceptual skill with commonly known and abstract items, forming closure, analyzing, and synthesizing visually presented information. When given the opportunity to use manipulatives, Bill's performance was enhanced with the examiner modeling and adding structure to guide his performance. He was observed "talking" his way through these subtests, paying close attention to the tasks. Too much visual information appeared to overwhelm Bill. When the nonverbal problem-solving tasks became more complex, Bill had difficulty making the cognitive shift from the concrete to the abstract.

Formal testing was combined with Bill's mother's observations using the Vineland Adaptive Behavior Scales to assess Bill's fine and gross motor development. He appears to be right-hand dominant but exhibited an awkward pencil grasp, particularly when asked to copy designs. He was able to draw singular and intersecting line segments, but was unable to copy circles or multi-angled designs. Bill's performance on the Developmental Test of Visual Motor Integration and the Human Figure Drawing placed him within the late 4-year range. Visual motor integration and fine motor skills appear below average. In contrast, Bill used an appropriate pincer grasp to place pegs into a formboard.

During the play assessment, Bill was unable to tiptoe, jump in succession, broad jump, and jump from a chair. Bill's balance appeared weak, which compromised his ability to hop, gallop and skip. His demonstrated skill level in these areas fell between the 4 to 4-6 year level. His eye–hand and eye–foot coordination are more age-appropriate. He was able to throw, catch, and kick a ball with control and accuracy.

Social/Interpersonal Domain. Bill was observed in a preschool classroom to assess his play and social behavior skills in an authentic setting. This behavioral analysis is based upon direct observation of spontaneous play. Bill approached these play activities in an enthusiastic and confident manner that was consistent with his performance on the cognitive battery.

Bill was presented with specific toys during a 30-minute session. While interacting with the toys, Bill was able to master differentiating among singular objects while preserving their unique characteristics. He displayed many discriminative actions such as walking farm animals, pouring from a pitcher, and looking at himself in a mirror. He was also able to relate these objects to himself by pretending to drink from a cup and comb his own hair.

When presented with combinations of toys such as simple form puzzles and trucks with drivers, he was able to successfully take them apart and recreate them according to their original configuration. Bill created play combinations suggesting that he has mastered a variety of learned relations that are solely dependent on physical characteristics of objects and conventional social behavior. Bill approached the play materials in a manner that was dependent on the concrete characteristics of the objects. Bill used his atypical expressive language to comment on the physical characteristics of the toys. Overall, his play can be summarized as consistent with a child who has serious cognitive and expressive/receptive language delays.

Bill's social interactions within a preschool setting were appropriate when given structure and routine. During free play, Bill sought out other children and played alongside them without signs of aggression or frustration. He was observed augmenting his unintelligible speech with gesturing and nonverbal modes of communication. Bill was able to follow the routine and responded well to songs and visual cues used within the classroom setting.

On the Vineland, his mother ranked his social behavior as follows:

Play and Leisure	5-0 year old level
Interpersonal	3-5 year old level
Community	3-6 year old level

These scores reflect Bill's struggles with many of the developmental social tasks expected of a child his age. Specifically, he lacks a solid understanding of street safety, stranger awareness, and what to do in emergency situations. Socially, his mother observes that when playing with his younger sibling, Bill has difficulty cooperating and initiating effective social communication.

Summary

Bill was evaluated in order to provide more information regarding his current level of functioning and to assist in making appropriate recommendations regarding academic placement for the next school year. Based on his performance on the WPPSI-R, a cognitive assessment battery, Bill's present estimated cognitive development falls in the Intellectually Deficient range when compared to his same-age peers. His expressive and receptive language are well below age level. His relative strength was in the visual-perceptual area. He performs better socially in structured routine situations. *Caution should be used when interpreting these results as an estimate of his true potential as his language difficulties and lack of experience with educational materials seriously impaired his performance.* Considering his results, Bill presents as a 5-year, 4 month old child who is in need of a kindergarten placement with intensive support services.

Recommendations

1. *Place in an inclusion-model language-based kindergarten classroom.* This program will provide intensive exposure to structured language learning and skill development, accompanied with frequent rewards and praise. Bill would also benefit from exposure to peers in the classroom who are good language models.
2. *Provide individual speech and language therapy to address expressive and receptive language delays.* Despite his expressive difficulties, Bill demonstrates a strong desire to communicate verbally. He attempts to compensate for auditory weaknesses by subvocalizing verbal information. This strategy should be reinforced in his classroom and at home. In addition, use of simple pictures aids his comprehension and improves communication. Multimodal teaching strategies should be used. His teacher should capitalize on his good attention span and sustained effort.
3. *Use his relative strengths in visual-perceptual skills and nonverbal problem solving to enhance learning.* Presenting material visually and concretely should be a strategic teaching modality. Hand-over-hand guided modeling appears to help him learn new tasks.
4. *Promote home/school communication.* The use of a daily notebook journal will facilitate communication between home and school and serve to track his progress. Child management resources in the community should be identified and facilitated by the school psychologist.

Summary

This chapter focused on the writing of traditional case reports. For additional sources on case report writing, the following authors are recommended: Anastasi (1988), Knoff (1986), Maloney and Ward (1976), Sattler (1992), and Tallent (1976). For general writing techniques, Strunk and White's (1979) *The Elements of Style* is an excellent resource which concisely covers the essentials of writing.

When writing case reports, it is good to outline the major points obtained from the data before starting to write formally. After a first draft of the report is written, it is often helpful to allow time to pass before returning to edit. Asking a friend or colleague to review the report is also a good practice and provides the consultation and supervision that is beneficial for all psychologists. Sometimes a lay person is a better judge of report clarity than a colleague because laypeople are not accustomed to the technical language. Writing case reports using a word processor facilitates the editing process and helps produce well-written and clearly presented reports. Being a good case report writer is a lifelong process. This chapter was intended to provide the foundations for this challenging task.

22 Implementing the Results of Preschool Assessments

Transforming Data and Recommendations into Action

MARIANNE LAROCHE

LOUIS J. KRUGER

Once a team assessment is completed, recommendations are made, and appropriate interventions agreed upon, it becomes a matter of how best to get these results implemented quickly and effectively. Many special service personnel, however, receive no specific training in ways to facilitate the implementation process. It therefore seems important to consider how this process occurs, and what skills and techniques must be employed in order for it to be accomplished successfully.

In this chapter, the implementation of assessment results is broadly conceptualized as a two-phase process consisting of (1) planning and (2) service delivery. The first half deals with the planning phase, outlining the interdisciplinary team process and the steps involved in developing an individualized service plan from assessment results. The second half of the chapter discusses how the services specified in such a plan might be delivered most effectively. Indirect services, such as consultation and collaboration with families, teachers, and outside agencies, are emphasized as being crucial components of the implementation process.

Phase One: Planning

Though planning occurs throughout the assessment and intervention process, it takes on particular significance after the requested assessments of a referred child have been completed. The first task of this phase involves the sharing of information obtained from each of the discipline-specific assessments. The second step, assuming a special need is identified, consists of developing an individualized plan that specifies goals and interventions tailored to that particular child's strengths and needs.

Step One: Sharing Assessment Results

The Team Approach.   A multidisciplinary team (MDT) approach to assessment, intervention, and follow up with preschool-aged children is mandated under the provisions of P.L. 102-119, the Individuals with Disabilities Education Act (IDEA) and its re-authorization, P.L. 105-17. This involves professionals from several disciplines, each of whom performs his or her own particular assessment of the referred child (medical, social, speech and language, educational, psychological, etc.). They then come together, along with the child's parent or guardian, to share the results of their assessments, determine whether the child has a significant special need, and, if so, to recommend the services and interventions needed in order to meet those needs effectively.

Although it is agreed that professionals from multiple disciplines should be involved in the evaluation and planning process for children with special needs, questions have been raised about the effectiveness of the MDT model (see, for example, Huebner & Gould, 1991; Knoff, 1984; Silverstein, 1989; Yoshida, 1980). The MDT deficiencies most frequently cited include weak coordination of team personnel and services, redundant responsibilities, infrequent communication among team members, and inflexible roles. In efforts to alleviate some of these shortcomings, variations of the MDT model have been developed, including the interdisciplinary team (IDT) and transdisciplinary team (TDT) approaches. These were designed to include more consultation and collaboration among team members, thus hopefully improving the coordination and efficiency of the team process (Paget, 1985). These alternatives might be considered especially appropriate for the preschool-aged population, since there is often a good deal of overlap among the various professional disciplines in assessing the developmental functioning of a young child.

McCollum and Hughes (1988) provided a more detailed overview of the structure and functioning of these various team models, classifying them on a continuum from minimal interaction (multidisciplinary) to maximal interaction (transdisciplinary). An MDT is described as a group of professionals from different disciplines who are all evaluating and/or providing services to the same individual, but with no ongoing coordination of information among team members. An IDT approach also involves a group of professionals who perform their tasks independently of one another, but in this model they would consult with each other on some sort of an ongoing basis in order to share information and coordinate their efforts. A TDT is the most highly interactive and flexible of these three team models, however it is not as well known or commonly practiced as the others.

The TDT approach stresses the involvement of parents in planning, implementing, and evaluating their child's service plan. Parental participation is both an ethical imperative and an important pragmatic strategy for implementing the best possible plan. Not only do parents have ideas and information that can enhance the problem-solving process, their cooperation and commitment can help ensure that the plan is implemented as intended. The TDT approach also provides greater flexibility in how duties are assigned, which is intended to help the team make the best possible use of its human resources. This is perhaps best exemplified by the concept of role release. This involves TDT members (including parents) releasing specific aspects of their traditional role to one or more of the other team members, in the interest of efficiency or practicality (Broder & Bologna, 1993).

In the absence of empirical data to support the efficacy of one team model over another, we propose an eclectic approach to teamwork that poses the following question: Given the organization's resources, the needs of the case, and the abilities and attitudes of the team members, what is the optimal team approach for this particular case? In answering this question, it is possible that an optimal approach might be some combination of models, such as MDT during the assessment and planning process and TDT for implementing aspects of the service plan.

Whatever the approach taken, there are several factors that are important to a team's performance. These factors are represented by the acronym PERFORMS (Kruger & Kaplan, 1994; Kruger & Harington, in press). (See Table 22.1). For example, an important purpose (the 'P' in PERFORMS) of a preschool team should be to integrate all of the data obtained on the referred child and form a set of conclusions that will lead to appropriate recommendations for services and implementation. After reviewing the PERFORMS factors, if the team members believe that their team is deficient in one or more areas they can develop a plan to improve those areas (Kruger & Harrington, in press).

Communicating Results. The sharing of information obtained from the various assessments is the first step toward effectively identifying and obtaining appropriate services for a child with special needs. It is thus crucial that the data obtained be clearly communicated to all those taking part in the decision-making process. Therefore, team members who have completed assessments of the child should carefully consider how their findings might be presented most effectively.

Effective communication of results may be facilitated by fostering a comfortable, supportive atmosphere; by using descriptive behavioral terms or developmental levels rather

TABLE 22.1 PERFORMS: Factors Important to Team Success

Factor	Description
Purpose	The team has a well-articulated and important purpose, as well as goals that further specify the purpose.
Empowerment	Team members are able to assume a leadership role when they have skills or knowledge relevant to tasks.
Relationships (Internal)	Team members trust and respect one another. They collaborate and frequently communicate with other members.
Feedback	Team members assess their progress on tasks. They seek feedback on goal attainment, consumer reactions, and group process.
Organization	The team has an appropriate structure which includes methods for attaining goals, roles for members, regular meeting times, and timelines for task completion.
Relationships (External)	The team has support from its parent organization. The team frequently monitors the environment for opportunities and threats that might impact its functioning.
Motivation	Team members have a strong sense of obligation to meet and exceed team goals. They are motivated to continually improve their performance.
Skills	Team members have skills and knowledge relevant to team tasks.

For a review of the literature and research on factors important to team success, see Swezy and Salas (1992) and Cannon-Bowers, Tannebaum, Salas, and Volpe (1995).

than diagnostic labels; and by eliminating professional jargon as much as possible. An integrated presentation of the data is generally preferable to a test-by-test analysis, and it is often very helpful to share one's behavioral observations of the child, as well as verbatim or anecdotal material. The more one is able to translate assessment findings into easily comprehensible, useful statements about the child's functioning and needs, the more likely it is that the team will be able to develop an optimally appropriate and effective service plan.

Parents. It is especially important to ensure that the parents of the referred child are completely informed about the various assessment results in a sensitive manner. This may be the first exposure the parents of a preschool-aged child have had to the technical terms and diagnostic labels that may be used in reference to their child, and this can cause intense anxiety and defensiveness. Both the manner in which the assessment results are presented and the rapport established between the parents and the other team members may make the difference between parental cooperation and resistance to the recommendations for intervention offered by the team.

Facilitating an Effective Meeting. A comprehensive discussion of running effective team meetings is beyond the scope of this chapter; nonetheless, there are a few aspects that seem particularly important to mention. First, there should be a facilitator who is able to keep the participants focused on the task, while also maintaining a comfortable social envi-

© *National Association of School Psychologists. Reprinted by permission of the publisher.*

ronment. An agenda is useful for orienting participants to important issues and limiting tangential discussions. When an agenda item is completed, the facilitator should summarize the main points before moving the group on to the next topic. This relatively simple strategy can help prevent misunderstandings that later might interfere with the implementation of the individualized plan. The facilitator must also be sensitive to issues that might arouse negative feelings among the participants and thereby create resistance to the implementation of the plan. For example, some people may participate too much and monopolize the meeting, whereas others might silently wait for an invitation to share their opinions that never comes. In these instances, the facilitator must be tactful but assertive in ensuring that everyone who wants to speak has the opportunity. The facilitator must also be aware of time constraints and set the appropriate tempo for the meeting. If it becomes apparent that all of the agenda items cannot be adequately covered during the allotted time, the facilitator should reserve sometime at the end for the team to discuss how the remaining items will be addressed. The major outcomes and decisions should be summarized, and there should be a clear plan for what will happen next. If possible, the meeting should end on a positive note, with people feeling that that they made worthwhile contributions.

Regardless of how successful a meeting is, unfinished business is inevitable. There is never enough meeting time, and people's schedules are difficult to coordinate. Therefore, if communication is to occur frequently, other means must be used to supplement face-to-face meetings. These might include telephone, mail, or electronic mail. Indeed, as models develop of how team communication can be enhanced by means of technology, computers and related technology will take on an increasingly important role in teamwork (Kruger, Cohen, Marca, & Matthews, 1996).

Step Two: Developing the Service Plan

Description. If it has been determined at the team meeting that the child has a handicapping condition, the next step is to decide what services will be required to address his or her specific needs. For children age 3 and older, an individualized education plan (IEP) will be developed; for children younger than 3, an individualized family service plan (IFSP) must be developed. Both types of plans have been sanctioned by legislation, the IEP in 1975 by Public Law 94-142, and the IFSP in 1986 by Public Law 102-119 and their reauthorizations, P.L. 105-17. Both types of plans are prescriptive and are concerned with establishing goals and devising interventions that will help remediate the child's areas of need and maximize his or her development (Bluth, 1987; Sandall, 1993).

Both the IEP and the IFSP are based on a comprehensive assessment of the child conducted by professionals from multiple disciplines, and both must be signed by a parent or legal guardian before they can be implemented. All of the components of a good individualized plan are relevant to both the IEP and IFSP. These generic components include: a statements of the child's current level of functioning, including both needs and strengths; specific goals and objectives; the types of services that will be provided, the location and the staff responsible; the methods, activities, and materials that will be used to provide these services; projected dates and duration of services; and a plan for reviewing progress.

Despite the similarities between the IEP and IFSP, there are also some important differences. Whereas the IEP is focused primarily on the child and his or her educational needs, the IFSP is family-centered (Safer & Hamilton, 1993). Therefore, a comprehensive assessment of the entire family's strengths and needs is central to the development of an appropriate IFSP.

Furthermore, whereas educational personnel take primary responsibility for implementing an IEP, the service agency that is most germane to the child's and family's needs takes a leadership role in implementing an IFSP. Thus, in contrast to the IEP which is usually school-based, the location of IFSP services can be quite varied.

Since an IFSP ends when a child reaches the age of 3, it must contain a plan for follow-up services, which typically includes the development of an IEP. However, the transition from IFSP to IEP may be poorly planned or coordinated, and the IEP by itself generally provides few, if any, services for the family. Agency directors and school administrators need to give more consideration to the question of how agencies and schools might collaborate in order to help families make a smooth transition from one set of services and providers to another.

Developing Recommendations.   Identification of services and methods to address the needs of a child is an important decision that is worthy of considerable reflection by the team. Often there may be multiple methods and activities that can meet the same need. The team should structure the process so that participants not only carefully consider the advantages and disadvantages of each alternative, but also endeavor to think creatively about the universe of alternatives. One way this can be accomplished is to allow the participants to brainstorm the different means that might be used to meet the plan's goals. After the group has narrowed the options to the most promising two or three, the participants can systematically evaluate the strengths and weaknesses of each alternative (for a more detailed discussion, see Kruger & Harrington, in press).

Disagreements might arise during the decision-making process, but, as noted by Linder (1990), they can be an important resource to the team. If the disagreements are openly acknowledged, and if they are viewed as substantive and not personal, then there is the possibility that differences of opinion might lead team members to achieve deeper insights about the child. Such an understanding might in turn lead to a better individualized plan.

In developing recommendations for an individualized plan, it is best if they are designed to offer teachers, parents, and others involved in service provision *specific* strategies for accomplishing the plan's objectives. The extent to which a plan is implemented appropriately has been shown to increase substantially as a function of the specificity of the suggested interventions and methods to be used, together with a means of providing feedback to the service providers regarding their adherence to the strategies outlined in the plan (Lidz, 1980). Yoshida (1980) emphasized the importance of *all* team members participating in the development of an individualized plan, as this increases the likelihood of cooperation and contributes to optimal implementation. Instructional personnel and parents often tend to have less input than other team members in the development of the plan, yet often bear most of the responsibility for implementing team decisions. It is therefore important to actively solicit and encourage their full participation in the planning process in order to maximize the chances for efficient and effective implementation.

One recommendation that sometimes emerges from a team meeting is to conduct further assessments in order to clarify aspects of the case that are not well understood (Linder, 1990). Thus, assessment might continue to occur during the planning phase. For the purposes of clarity, assessment, planning and implementation have been discussed as separate phases, but they do (and should) overlap in practice. Rigid boundaries between phases would only reduce the flexibility needed to plan and implement effective services.

Phase Two: The Service Delivery Phase

Implementation has been defined by Bluth (1987) as the actual delivery of services prescribed in an individualized plan (IEP or IFSP). It is obvious that even the best recommendations and interventions generated as a result of the assessment process and written into such a plan are of no benefit to the child unless they are accurately and consistently implemented by the designated service providers. Having a specific plan in place to facilitate implementation has been cited as a "critical" factor in the success or failure of service plans (Berman & McLaughlin, 1978). One such structured plan for facilitating program implementation, known by the acronym DURABLE, was developed by Maher and his colleagues (Maher, 1989; Maher & Bennett, 1984; Maher & Illback, 1984; Maher & Illback, 1985); they found that training team members to utilize the DURABLE approach led to greater involvement in evaluating the implementation process and increased positive outcomes of the intervention plans. Unfortunately, it is more commonly the case that there is no specific strategy in place to ensure the accurate and consistent implementation of an individualized service plan.

One of the major challenges often involved in implementing an IEP or IFSP is that of influencing service providers to follow through on the recommended interventions (Tombari & Davis, 1979). Those responsible for ensuring that plans are appropriately implemented must therefore be prepared to offer indirect services, such as regular communication, consultation, training, and so on, to the parents and professionals who are designated as the direct service providers. The goals are not only to ensure that the required services are effectively delivered, but also to support and enhance the efforts of these team members. As was noted by Conoley and Gutkin (1986b), inadequate attention to the adults who are to provide the recommended services to a particular youngster may well lead to inadequate, and ultimately ineffective, implementation of the plan.

This section of the chapter will emphasize the knowledge and skills needed to successfully support the implementation of an IEP or IFSP. It is divided into three sections: (1) the consultant role, (2) working with parents and families, and (3) collaborating with outside agencies.

The Consultant Role

Consultation has been defined as an interactive process of collaborative problem solving between a specialist (the consultant) and one or more persons (the consultees) who are responsible for providing some sort of service or assistance to another person (the client) (Medway, 1979; West & Idol, 1990). Thus, in the implementation of an individualized plan resulting from the referral and assessment of a preschool-aged child, the child is the client and the designated service providers are the potential consultees. The consultant is most often a professional who is already employed within the agency or educational setting where services are being delivered (Ellis & Osowski, 1990; Marks, 1995).

Unfortunately, the implementation of a service delivery plan is seldom facilitated in a systematic fashion. Direct communication between the planning team and those who are ultimately responsible for providing services may occur haphazardly, or not at all. Sometimes the written IEP or IFSP document is the sole means of communicating to service providers the nature of the child's needs and the specific interventions that have been recommended and incorporated into the plan. The assumption appears to be that teachers, parents, and other service providers will naturally accept and be able to implement the treatment recommendations. However the service providers must be *motivated* to implement the recommendations, and they must be *informed* as to the specific correct procedures for implementation. These tasks can be accomplished through the process of collaborative consultation between the specialist and the service provider (Conoley & Gutkin, 1986; Gutkin & Curtis, 1990). A good consultant can make things happen by energizing and motivating others to become more effective, and by making every effort to remove or reduce any barriers to achieving the ultimate goal of consultation—that of enabling the consultee to provide optimal services to the child client (An American Teacher, 1992; Brown, 1988). Consultation is probably most critical to effective program implementation when parents, paraprofessionals, and/or regular classroom teachers are the primary service providers.

Basic Characteristics of Consultation.

Certain "ground rules" must be followed in order to achieve a maximally effective consulting relationship. These include establishing an open trusting relationship with the consultee, emphasizing the collaborative nature of the consulting relationship, engaging the active involvement of the consultee in the consultation process, affirming the consultee's right to reject the consultant's suggestions, and adhering to the basic rules of confidentiality within the consulting relationship. The consultant also needs to have excellent skills in listening, problem solving, and communication in order to be effective.

According to Sandoval and Davis (1984), school-based consultation is essentially comprised of three overlapping phases: rapport building, data gathering, sharing, and problem solving; and review and disengagement. In the first phase, counseling skills such as negotiating entry, active, empathic listening, and understanding and dealing with the consultee's expectations are used to establish rapport. The goal of maintaining rapport is to validate the consultee's experience with the child client, and to reinforce the idea that any problem encountered can be talked over with the consultant.

In the second phase, the consultant and consultee must establish their goals for the consultation and deal with any resistances that may be present (which may have to do with lack of knowledge, skill, objectivity, or self-confidence). After resistances are addressed, both participants can then plan how to proceed in order to achieve their goals, deciding when and where to start, and when to change tactics if necessary. It is crucial that the consultant later support the intervention by following up on the plan, providing support to the consultee without encouraging dependence, and fostering an "experimental attitude" of trying, testing, and, if necessary, readjusting or rejecting various approaches.

During the final phase, the task is to evaluate the progress of the consultation. If consultation has led to a successful outcome, the follow-up meeting should focus on the steps the consultee took to achieve this end. If it has not, the meeting can be used to work through feelings of frustration and failure, and plan for some other form of intervention.

It is critically important that consultation occurs regularly, and over a sufficient period of time (Zins & Ponti, 1990). A one-time consultation meeting with a particular service provider is not sufficient. Treatment recommendations may not be carried out adequately for many reasons, one being that consultees may not be aware that they lack the skills necessary to carry out the recommendations effectively until they actually try to implement them. Or, some of the concepts presented may have been misunderstood by the consultee, and therefore the treatment is not executed as intended. In some instances a consultee may realize after trying to implement the recommendations that one or more necessary resources are missing or unavailable. Some consultees may lack awareness and/or objectivity about their own interactions with a child. Additionally, it may turn out that the recommendations and interventions themselves may not be optimal for the child.

Scheduled follow-up meetings allow these and similar issues to be addressed as they emerge. When an intervention is being implemented smoothly and effectively, follow-up meetings give the consultant an opportunity to reinforce the service provider for a job well done, thus helping to maintain motivation for current and future endeavors. When failures occur, they enable the consultant to share frustration and provide support and encouragement to the consultee. Making it a routine practice to follow up on initial consultations also facilitates a consultant's professional growth, helping him or her learn what is effective and what is not, the underlying reasons for successes and failures, the most efficient ways for communicating with others, and how to best work with particular individuals and systems.

Suggestions for Effective Consultation. Conoley and Gutkin (1986) offered several suggestions that may enable a specialist to act in the role of consultant more effectively. These include establishing and maintaining interpersonal relationships with those working in the system, projecting an image of professional competence, scheduling planning meetings with those who will be implementing the educational program of a child before any direct services take place, trying to ensure that service providers are included in the assessment and planning process whenever possible, and anticipating what sort of indirect services might be needed to facilitate program implementation (training and instruction in techniques, case management, supervision, family and/or teacher consultation, and so on).

Dorr (1977) noted that beginning consultants often must learn by trial and error how to approach consultees, how to present ideas, and how to circumvent problems. He outlined some practical guidelines for consulting with teachers, parents, and other service providers. They are:

1. Avoid jargon, even if it means being less precise than you can be when you use technical terms.

2. Your manner, style, and the way you present yourself to consultees is important in forming an effective consultation relationship. Colorful, warm, flexible, and funny are better than cold, formal, mechanistic, or rigid when trying to engage someone's participation and cooperation. Don't argue with consultees, don't overstate your case, and don't be overly subtle or academic in your interactions. Consultees' attention can usually be engaged more effectively by using examples or real-life anecdotes to illustrate the ideas you are trying to get across to them.

3. Remember that parents, teachers, and others with whom you may be consulting are a very heterogeneous group, and their levels of competence, cooperativeness, insight, and skill will understandably vary widely. Adopt a nonevaluative stance, and be prepared to adapt to each consultee as an individual with his or her own particular style, strengths, and weaknesses.

4. Unless a particular consulting relationship is a very close one, it is unwise to get into arguments of any sort—because even if you win a battle, you are at great risk of losing the war. It is more productive to focus on the positive aspects of the situation by acknowledging what the consultee is doing right, and by stressing positive attributes of the child that can be built upon. In general, maintain a positive, constructive approach and avoid confrontations, arguments, and other negative interactions.

5. Remember not to lecture to consultees. Exaggerating your knowledge and adequacy by lecturing (and, by implication, the lack of knowledge and adequacy of the person being lectured to) violates the egalitarian nature of collaborative consultation and is counter to one of the major aims of consultation, which is to foster the independence and confidence of the consultee. Also, although consultees may acquire facts via lecture, it in no way guarantees that they will acquire the skills necessary for a successful intervention—it is far better to rely on coached practice, or modeling and imitation strategies for that.

Often, the best strategy may be for the consultant to model the appropriate procedures for working with the child. Basic procedures can be communicated much more rapidly and effectively through modeling, as opposed to verbal presentation. Also, when the consultee has the opportunity of observing the consultant working with the child, it tends to have a disinhibitory effect, often facilitating more rapid implementation of the procedures being modeled. The consultee becomes less intimidated and less afraid to try the interventions when they see that the so-called "experts" are human and can make mistakes too! Another advantage to this strategy is that it allows the consultee to observe directly that the approaches modeled can be effective with the child they are working with, and the positive response of the child tends to be highly reinforcing and motivating,

6. Finally, whatever your own favorite strategies for implementation may be, it is far wiser to use procedures that are palatable for the individual consultee you are working with, even if they are not always elegant or orthodox in the academic sense.

Barriers to Effective Consultation.   Any number of factors can interfere with the effectiveness of the consultation process and therefore make it less likely to succeed as an implementation strategy. For example, systemic support or funding for consultation practices might be lacking. Consultants or consultees may feel stretched too thin already by their efforts to handle unrealistic caseloads, and lack both the willingness and the time to participate in an ongoing consultation relationship (Friend & Bauwens, 1988; Johnson, Pugach, & Hammitte, 1988). They may also be undertrained in the necessary skills (Dyke & Dettmer, 1989; Huefner, 1988).

Consultees may have had prior negative experiences with consultation, or may harbor unrealistic expectations of the consultation process or of the consultant. In cases such as these it is especially important to clarify what the consultee's expectations are, to find out what may have gone wrong in previous consultation experiences, to do more listening than talking in order to reinforce the consultee's ownership of the consultation process, and to set limited goals initially (Erchul, 1991; Schmuck, 1990). More experienced teachers or other service providers may be less likely to find consultants' suggestions acceptable (Witt & Elliot, 1985), and consultants may in fact be unaware of the types of suggestions that are most likely to be accepted by consultees—those that are positive, require little time to implement, and are perceived to be practical for that particular combination of service provider, child, and setting (Elliot, 1988; Whinnery, Fuchs, & Fuchs, 1991).

Working with Parents and Families.   The importance of parents and families to the development of children is commonly accepted, and family involvement is a recognized principle in early intervention (Bailey et al., 1987; Paget, 1985; Weiss, 1987; Zigler, Kagan, & Muenchow, 1982). A partnership of shared responsibility between service providers and parents is more likely to occur when: (1) the parents are willing and able to make a commitment to participate actively in the planning and implementation of their child's individualized plan; (2) the professionals are prepared to meet parents as equals in the team process; and (3) the child is offered real alternatives in programming based on *all* available resources.

Other suggestions for encouraging collaboration between parents and professionals include taking pains to explain the assessment and intervention process thoroughly to parents; informing parents about various educational options; empowering parents to participate actively in team meetings and to become effective advocates for their child; and providing opportunities for on-going parent education, support, and counseling services (Christenson, Avery, & Weinberg, 1986). Paget (1985) offered for consideration a series of questions that are helpful to keep in mind when working with the parents of a child with special needs: What roles are best for particular parents, and what objectives are most appropriate? Where and how often should contact with parents occur? Who should be the primary contact person for parents? How should objectives and activities be altered to meet the needs of working parents, parents of varying socioeconomic and educational status, minority parents, and parents who are handicapped, single, or very young? How should parent involvement be evaluated?

Educators and other service providers who are in contact with the parents and families of children with special needs should continually try to think of ways to support and enhance parents' confidence. For example, it is *always* possible to find something positive to say about the way a parent is relating to their child or managing family routines. At times it may be necessary to provide immediate and relevant advice or assistance to parents, in order to help them deal with a crisis, an unexpected turn of events, or simply with the inevitable stressors on the family unit that arise from their efforts to provide what is needed for their child (Blumberg, 1987). Educating school or agency personnel about the inherent physical and emotional demands experienced by the parents of a child who is handicapped can also help to promote understanding and cooperation between parents and service providers (Harris & Fong, 1985).

In summary, in order to help assure the effective implementation of a young child's IEP or IFSP it is best to not simply take family considerations into account when planning and implementing interventions, but rather to engage the parents of the child in a collaborative partnership with the school and/or other agencies providing services, and involve them directly in the planning and implementation of their child's program.

Collaborating with Outside Agencies.   Intervention with preschool-aged children often involves a number of different agencies as service providers, so it is obviously very important that efforts be coordinated so that all of the needed services will be delivered efficiently. Additionally, one of the ways in which a shortfall of funds may be overcome and services expanded is through gaining the cooperation of various agencies that serve young children, in order to pool resources and avoid duplication of efforts. However, collaboration between agencies for the coordination of services is frequently not attempted in an organized fashion. There is often no systematic method for sharing information among all the professionals and agencies who may be working with a particular child and family, and there tends to be a lack of awareness among professionals about the availability of various program and service options.

Unfortunately, it can take an extraordinary amount of time to build and sustain an effective system of interagency collaboration. Activities such as making contacts, providing verbal and written explanations of data, talking with parents and agency personnel, scheduling and participating in meetings, keeping track of the delivery of services, doing follow-up work, writing reports and memos, and making phone calls are typically required (Mearig, 1982). In rural areas, integrating services can be even more time consuming, as the parties involved may be spread over a wide geographical area, making contacts, meetings, and follow-up activities more difficult to arrange and coordinate.

Effective interagency collaboration is more likely to occur when the individuals responsible for negotiating collaboration are knowledgeable about the purpose and function of each participating agency, and careful to attend to both administrative and direct service concerns of all those involved. The importance of good communication in establishing and maintaining effective interagency collaboration cannot be overemphasized. There is also a need to recognize and be aware of individual differences when prescribing and coordinating services—programs that work well with one family or in one setting may be impractical or ineffective with another. It is also important that service coordinators be aware of the existence and functions of other agencies in the community who might be called upon to provide services. In general, the implementation of services involving multiple agencies needs to be carefully monitored—and revised or simplified as needed to ensure maximum compatibility between the service system and the child and family (Hall, 1980).

Under the provisions of P.L. 102-119 and its re-authorization, P.L. 105-17, schools have been officially designated as the lead agencies for servicing 3- to 5-year-olds. However it must be kept in mind that service coordinators who are employed by a school system owe their primary allegiance to the child rather than to the school as an institution. Their main task is to make every effort to ensure that all of the required services are effectively obtained and integrated into the child's educational program.

Real Versus Ideal

In actual practice, *optimal* implementation of an individualized service plan is most likely a somewhat rare occurrence. There can be many reasons for this, which may vary from state to state, town to town, and person to person. Some of these reasons appear to be fairly universal, however, and bear further delineation and discussion.

Lack of Resources

What appears to be the most common reason for inefficient or inadequate program implementation is lack of resources, both lack of funding to hire or train needed personnel and to purchase necessary equipment and materials, and the chronic lack of time experienced by virtually all practitioners and educators. Societal risk factors such as poverty, substance abuse, and family disruption, as well as increased parent awareness, more stringent and far-reaching legislative mandates for special education services, and more aggressive and efficient child find and early intervention programs appear to result in the identification of young children with special needs in ever increasing numbers. In many places, service providers are finding themselves overwhelmed by increased caseloads, additional paperwork, and insufficient support. Although some systems do hire personnel whose sole function is to serve as case managers and service coordinators, it seems that many more have no specifically designated person or systematic process in place for coordinating and monitoring the implementation of IEPs or IFSPs. A school psychologist, preschool teacher, speech therapist, or special education teacher may be assigned to these tasks, but each of them typically has a long list of other job duties to attend to as well. Under these circumstances, "optimal" implementation is likely to be an ideal that gets lost in the shuffle.

Role Confusion

Another somewhat related issue has to do with role confusion. When there is no established procedure for implementing and following up on IEPs or IFSPs, there may tend to be confusion about who is responsible for seeing that the plan is implemented appropriately. Along with its many advantages, the mandated team approach can have the disadvantage of diffusing the sense of "ownership" or responsibility for a referred child and his or her needs. It becomes far too easy to assume that someone else will take responsibility, particularly when team members' time is at such a premium.

Uncoordinated Teamwork

A third factor which may interfere with optimal implementation concerns team functioning. Teams are often not well-coordinated, even *within* a single school or early childhood center, much less when numerous outside agencies or professionals may be involved. Rather than functioning as a cooperative unit, the team may adopt a fragmented approach, with each service provider essentially working in isolation. Inadequate communication and collaboration are probably the primary factors that contribute to team disorganization and ineffectual implementation. However politics and personalities may also be involved, such as organizational alliances, territoriality, differing values and philosophies, idiosyncratic likes and dislikes, and other similar issues among team members.

Lack of Training and Expertise

A lack of training and expertise in relevant skills appears to be another common impediment to effective implementation. Many training programs for school psychologists, teachers, and therapists tend to be too narrowly focused in their content areas, with little emphasis placed on training or practicing indirect service delivery techniques. Practitioners may therefore emerge from graduate programs with excellent skills in assessment, diagnosis, teaching and treatment strategies, and other forms of technical expertise, but lacking the skills in dissemination of information and influencing others that would help ensure that diagnostic data is used appropriately (Conoley & Gutkin, 1986). Service coordination, consulting, working with families, and other such relevant activities often must be learned "on the job" if at all, presumably with varying degrees of competence and success.

Although readers may find the apparent gap between "optimal" and "actual" implementation practices discouraging or disturbing, we should bear in mind that such gaps between the ideal and the real exist in nearly every facet of life and work—the important thing is to keep a conception of the ideal in mind, and work at narrowing the gap to the best of one's ability. As Conoley and Gutkin (1986) asserted:

> The challenges are not only to know what the realities of the field are, but also to know how to continually strive toward more perfect situations. Neither challenge is trivial. (p. 457)

Summary

Once an interdisciplinary assessment of a preschool child has been completed and a special need identified, the work of implementation gets underway. In this chapter implementation was conceptualized as a two-stage process, consisting of a planning phase and a service delivery phase. Issues relevant to each of these phases were discussed, and strategies were reviewed that may contribute to the optimal planning and implementation of a child's individualized plan for services. Finally, the point was made that optimal implementation is a goal to strive for, while coping with the realities of service delivery in actual practice.

APPENDIX

Selected Screening Measures

Instrument	Age Range	Administration Time	Technical Data	Content	Multicultural Applicability
BRIGANCE® Preschool Screen (1985) Curriculum Associates Inc.	3 years to 4 years	10–15 minutes	*Validity:* correlates (.46) with the Slosson Intelligence Test, correlates (.49) with the Child Development Inventory expressive language domain *Reliability:* TR* = .97 IC** = .82	motor language body parts colors personal data	Directions are available in Spanish. Normed on 408 students in 4 states ages 2 years to 6 years.
Denver II (1990) Denver Developmental Material Inc.	1 month to 6 years	15–20 minutes	*Validity:* no specific information provided. *Reliability:* TR = .90 IR*** = .98	personal social motor language adaptive	Has Spanish forms. Normed on 2,096 children across 21 counties in Colorado. Ethnic groups included black, Hispanic, and white.
Developmental Indicators for the Assessment of Learning—Revised (DIAL–R) (1990) American Guidance Services	2 years to 6 years	30 minutes	*Validity:* correlates (.79) with the Learning Accomplishment Profile-Diagnostic *Reliability:* TR = .87.	motor language concepts	Only available in English. Normed on 2,447 children at 8 sites across the United States: 1,358 white children and 1,089 nonwhite children.
Early Screening Inventory (ESI-P) (1988) Rebus Inc.	3 years to 6 years	20–25 minutes	*Validity:* correlates (.73) with the McCarthy Scales *Reliability:* TR = .98 IR = .99	motor adaptive language cognitive	Available in Spanish and Korean. Normed across 3 states on 997 children aged 3 years to 4 years 5 months: 410 white children, 162 black children, and 198 other.

(continued)

Instrument	Age Range	Administration Time	Technical Data	Content	Multicultural Applicability
Early Screening Profile (1990) AGS	2 years to 6.11 years	30 minutes	*Validity:* cognitive and language domains correlate (.68–.84) with the Kaufman Assessment Battery for Children *Reliability:* TR = .78 – .89	cognitive language motor self-help social	Only available in English. Normed on 1,149 children: 797 white, 197 black, 116 Hispanic, and 39 other.
McCarthy Screening Test (MST) (1978) The Psychological Corporation	4 years to 6.5 years	20 minutes	*Validity:* correlates well with the Metropolitan Readiness Test *Reliability:* TR = .32 – .69	motor cognitive language mathematics	Only available in English. Norms based on the McCarthy Scales using 1,032 children: 862 white, 154 black, and 16 other (1969–1970 census).
Miller Assessment for Preschoolers (MAP) (1988) The Psychological Corporation	2.9 years to 5.8 years	25–30 minutes	*Validity:* 84% accuracy in identifying children at risk *Reliability:* TR = .81 – .98	motor language cognition	Only available in English. Normed on 1,204 children: 86% white, 12% black, 2% other (1979–1980 census).
Preschool Development Inventory (PDI) (1988) Behavior Science Systems	3 years to 5.5 years	25 minutes	*Validity:* identification rates are similar to those of the DIAL (88%) *Reliability:* not reported	language motor self-help personal social	Only available in English. Normed on 220 children in South St. Paul, Minnesota, aged 3-7 through 4-9 years (predominantly white children).

*TR = Test-Retest Reliability

**IC = Internal Consistency

***IR = Inter-rater Reliability

REFERENCES AND ADDITIONAL READINGS

Aboud, F. (1988). *Children and prejudice.* New York: Basil Blackwell.

Acevedo, M. A. (1988, November). *Development of Spanish consonants in three to five year olds.* Paper presented at the annual meeting of the American Speech-Language-Hearing Association, Boston, MA.

Achenbach, T. M. (1966). The classification of children's psychiatric symptoms: A factor analytic study. *Psychological Monographs, 80* (7, Whole No. 615).

Achenbach, T. M. (1988). *Child Behavior Checklist.* Burlington, VT: University Associates in Psychology.

Achenbach, T. M. (1991). *Manual for the Child Behavior Checklist and Revised Child Behavior Profile.* Burlington, VT: University of Vermont Department of Psychiatry.

Achenbach, T. M., & Edelbrock, C. S. (1981). Behavioral problems and competencies reported by parents of normal and disturbed children aged four to sixteen. *Monographs of the Society for Research in Child Development, 46* (Serial No. 188).

Achenbach, T. M., Edelbrock, C. S., & Howell, C. T. (1987). Empirically-based assessment of the behavioral/emotional problems of 2–3 year old children. *Journal of Abnormal Child Psychology, 15,* 629–650.

Achenbach, T. M., Howell, C. T., Quay, H. C., & Conners, C. K. (1991). National survey of problems and competencies among 4- to 16-year-olds: Parents' reports for normative and clinical samples. *Monographs of the Society for Research in Child Development, 225*(3), 1–20.

Ainsworth, M. D. S., Blehar, M. C., Waters, E., & Wall, S. (1978). *Patterns of attachment: A psychological study of the stranger situation.* Hillsdale, NJ: Erlbaum.

Albertson, L. L., & Alvarado, D. Y. (1992). *An evaluation of Spanish speech and language assessment tools used by speech and language specialists in Orange County.* Unpublished master's project, California State University, Fullerton.

Alessi, G. J. (1980). Behavioral observation for the school psychologist: Responsive-discrepancy model. *School Psychology Review, 9,* 31–45.

Alessi, G. J. (1988). Direct observation methods for emotional/behavioral problems. In E. S. Shapiro & T. R. Kratochwill (Eds.), *Behavioral assessment in schools: Conceptual foundations and practical applications* (pp. 14–75). New York: Guilford Press.

Alessi, G. J., & Kaye, J. H. (1983). *Behavioral assessment for school psychologists.* Washington, DC: National Association of School Psychologists.

Allaire, J. H., Gressard, R. P., Blackman, J. A., & Hostler, S. L. (1991). Children with severe speech impairments: Care-givers survey of AAC use. *ACC Augmentative and Alternative Communication, 7,* 248–255.

Allen, B. A., & Boykin, A. W. (1992). African American children and the educational process: Alleviating cultural discontinuity through prescriptive pedagogy. *School Psychology Review, 21,* 586–596.

Allen, D. A., & Hudd, S. S. (1987). Are we professionalizing parents? Weighing the benefits and pitfalls. *Mental Retardation, 25*(3), 133–139.

Allen, K. E., & Schwartz, I. S. (1996). *The exceptional child: Inclusion in early childhood education* (3rd ed.). Albany, NY: Delmar.

Allessandri, S. M. (1992). Attention, play, and social behavior in ADHD preschoolers. *Journal of Abnormal Child Psychology, 20*(3), 289–302.

Alpern, G. D., Boll, T. J., & Shearer, M. (1986). *Developmental Profile II (DP–II).* Los Angeles, CA: Western Psychological Services.

Als, H., Lester, B. M., Tronick, E. Z., & Brazelton, T. B. (1982). Towards a research instrument for the assessment of preterm infants' behavior (APIB). In H. E. Fitzgerald, B. M. Lester, & M. W. Yogman (Eds.), *Theory and research in behavioral pediatrics, 1* (pp. 35–132). New York: Plenum Press.

American Association on Mental Retardation. (1992). *Definitions, classifications, and systems of supports* (9th ed.). Washington DC: Author.

American Professional Society on the Abuse of Children. (1995). *Use of anatomical dolls in child sexual abuse assessments.* Chicago: Author.

American Psychiatric Association. (1994). *Diagnostic and statistical manual of mental disorders (DSM–IV)* (4th ed.). Washington, DC: Author.

American Psychiatric Association. (1994). *The diagnostic criteria from DSM–IV.* Washington, DC: Author.

American Psychological Association. (1992). *Ethical Principles of Psychologists and Code of Conduct.* Washington, DC: Author.

American Psychological Association. (1993). Guidelines for providers of psychological services to ethnic, linguistic, and culturally diverse populations. *American Psychologist 48*(1), 45–48.

Ames, L. B., Gillespie, C., Haines, J., & Ilg, F. L. (Eds.). (1980). *Gesell preschool test for evaluating motor, adaptive, language, and personal-social behavior in children ages 2½–6.* Rosemont, NJ: Programs for Education.

An American teacher—A profile. (1992, September). *NEA Today,* pp. 12–13.

Anastasi, A. (1988). *Psychological testing* (6th ed.). New York: Macmillan.

Anderson, M., & Goldgerg, P. F. (Eds.). (1991). *Cultural competence in screening and assessments: Implications for services to young children with special need ages birth through five.* Minneapolis, MN: PACER Center.

Anderson, S., Boigon, S., & Davis, K. (1991). *Oregon project for visually impaired and blind preschoolers-Revised.* Medford, OR: Jackson County Education Service District.

Annie E. Casey Foundation (1995). *Kids count data book: State profiles of child well-being.* Baltimore: Author.

Antley, T. R., & DuBose, R. F. (Eds.). (1981). *A case for early intervention: Summary of program findings.* Unpublished manuscript, University of Washington, Experimental Education Unit, Seattle.

APA (1993). Guidelines for Providers of Psychological Services to Ethnic, Linguistic, and Culturally Diverse Populations. *American Psychologist, 48*(1), 45–48.

Applebaum, A. S. (1977). Developmental retardation in infants as a concomitant of physical abuse. *Journal of Abnormal Child Psychology, 5*(4), 416–423.

Arizona Department of Education. (1992). *Quality preschool screening: How to get there from here.* Phoenix, AZ: Division of Special Education.

Armour-Thomas, E. (1992). Intellectual assessment of children from culturally diverse backgrounds. *School Psychology Review, 21,* 552–565.

Arter, J. A., & Spandel, V. (1992). NCME instructional module: Using portfolios of student work in instruction and assessment. *Educational Measurement: Issues and Practice, 11,* 36–44.

Arthur, G. (1952). *Arthur Adaptation of the Leiter International Performance Scale.* Chicago: Stoelting.

Ashurst, D. I., Bamberg, E., Barrett, J., Bisno, A., Burke, A., Chambers, D., Fentiman, J., Kadish, R., Mitchell, M., Neeley, L., Thorne, T., & Wents, D. (1985). *Southern California Ordinal Scales of Development.* North Hollywood, CA: Foreworks.

Autti-Ramo, I., Korkman, M., Hilakivi-Clarke, L., Lehtonen, M., Halmesmaki, E., & Granstrom, M. (1992). Mental development of 2-year-old children exposed to alcohol in utero. *Journal of Pediatrics, 120,* 740–746.

Axline, V. (1947). *Play therapy.* Boston: Houghton-Mifflin.

Aylward, G. P., Pfeiffer, S. I., Wright, A., & Verhulst, S. J. (1989). Outcome studies of low birth weight infants published in the last decade: A meta-analysis. *Journal of Pediatrics, 115*(4), 515–520.

Bagnato, J. (1985). The BRIGANCE® Diagnostic Inventory of Early Development (BDIED). In J. V. Mitchell (Ed.), *The ninth mental measurement yearbook* (p. 21). Lincoln, NE: University of Nebraska Press.

Bagnato, S. J., & Neisworth, J. T. (Eds.). (1991). *Assessment for early intervention: Best practices for professionals.* New York: Guilford Press.

Bagnato, S. J., & Neisworth, J. T. (Eds.). (1991). How does the preschool psychologist stage an assessment? In S. J. Bagnato & J. T. Neisworth (Eds.), *Assessment of Early Intervention: Best practices for professionals* (pp. 36–53). New York: Guilford Press.

Bagnato, S. J., & Neisworth, J. T. (1994). A national study of the social and treatment "invalidity" of intelligence testing for early intervention. *School Psychology Quarterly, 9,* 81–102.

Bagnato, S. J., Neisworth, J. T., & Munson, S. (1989). *Linking developmental assessment and early intervention: Curriculum-based prescriptions* (Rev. ed.). Rockville, MD: Aspen.

Bailey, D. B. (1989). Issues and directions in preparing professionals to work with young handicapped children and their families. In J. J. Gallagher, P. L. Trohanis, & R. M. Clifford (Eds.), *Policy implementation & P.L. 99–457: Planning for young children with special needs* (pp. 97–132). Baltimore: Paul H. Brookes.

Bailey, D. B. (1991a). Building positive relationships between professionals and families. In M. J. McGonigel, R. K. Kaufmann, & B. H. Johnson (Eds.), *Guidelines and recommended practices for the individualized family service plan* (2nd ed., pp. 29–38). Chapel Hill, NC: National Early Childhood Technical Assistance System.

Bailey, D. B., Clifford, R. M., & Harms, T. (1982). Comparison of environments for handicapped and non-handicapped children. *Topics in Early Childhood Special Education, 2,* 9–20.

Bailey, D. B., & Simeonsson, R. J. (1988). *Family assessment in early intervention.* Columbus, OH: Merrill.

Bailey, D. B., Simeonsson, R. J., Winton, P. J., Huntington, G. S., Comfort, M., Isbell, P., O'Donnell, K. J., & Helm, J. M. (1987). Family-focused intervention: A functional model for planning, implementing, and evaluating individualized family services in early intervention. *Journal of the Division for Early Childhood, 10*(2), 156–171.

Bailey, D. B., & Wolery, M. (1992). *Teaching infants and preschoolers with disabilities* (2nd ed.). New York: Macmillan.

Baker-Ward, L. E., Hess, T. M., & Flanagan, D. A. (1990). The effects of involvement on children's memory for events. *Cognitive Development, 5,* 55–70.

Bankson, N. W. (1990). *Bankson Language Screening Test* (2nd ed.). Austin, TX: Pro-Ed.

Bankson, N. W., & Bernthal, J. E. (1990). *Quick Screen of Phonology.* Chicago: Riverside.

Barker, R. G., & Associates. (1978). *Habitats, environments, and human behavior.* San Francisco: Jossey-Bass.

Barnard, K. E., Morisset, C. E., & Spieker, S. (1993). Preventive interventions: Enhancing parent–infant relationships. In C. Zeanah (Ed.), *Handbook of infant mental health* (pp. 386–401). NY: Guilford Press.

Barnett, D. W., & Carey, K. T. (1992). *Designing interventions for preschool learning and behavior problems.* San Francisco, CA: Jossey-Bass.

Barnett, W. S. (1995). Long-term effects of early childhood programs on cognitive and school outcomes. *The Future of Children (Long-Term Outcomes of Early Childhood Programs), 5*(3), 25–50.

Baron, I. S., Fennell, E. F., & Voeller, K. K. S. (1995). *Pediatric neuropsychology in the medical setting.* New York: Oxford.

Barona, M. S., & Barona, A. (1991). The assessment of culturally and linguistically different preschoolers. *Early Childhood Research Quarterly, 6,* 363–376.

Barone, D. (1995). "Be very careful not to let the facts get mixed up with the truth." Children prenatally exposed to crack/cocaine. *Urban Education, 30,* 40–55.

Bash, H. (1981). *Sociology, race, and ethnicity.* New York: Gordon and Breach.

Batsche, G. M., & Knoff, H. M. (1995). Best practices in linking assessment to intervention. In A. Thomas & J. Grimes (Eds.), *Best practices in school psychology* (3rd ed., 569–585). Washington, DC: National Association of School Psychologists.

Batshaw, M. L. (1997a). *Children with disabilities* (4th ed.). Baltimore: Paul H. Brookes.

Batshaw, M. L. (1997b). Fragile X syndrome. In M. L. Batshaw (Ed.), *Children with disabilities* (4th ed., pp. 377–388). Baltimore: Paul H. Brookes.

Batshaw, M. L., & Conlon, C. J. (1997). Substance abuse: A preventable threat to development. In M. L. Batshaw (Ed.), *Children with disabilities* (4th ed., pp. 143–162). Baltimore: Paul H. Brookes.

Batshaw, M. L., & Perret, Y. M. (1992). *Children with disabilities: A medical primer* (3rd ed.). Baltimore: Paul H. Brookes.

Batshaw, M. L., & Shapiro, B. K. (1997). Medical retardation. In M. L. Batshaw (Ed.), *Children with disabilities* (4th ed., pp. 335–359). Baltimore: Paul H. Brookes.

Bauermeister, J. (1995). *Manual: Inventario de comportamiento pre escolar.* San Juan, PR: Atención.

Bayley, N. (1969). *Manual for the Bayley Scales of Infant Development.* San Antonio, TX: The Psychological Corporation.

Bayley, N. (1993). *Manual for the Bayley Scales of Infant Development* (2nd ed.). San Antonio, TX: The Psychological Corporation.

Bayley, N. (1933). *The California First Year Mental Scale.* Berkeley, CA: University of California Press.

Beeghly, M., & Cicchetti, D. (1981). A organizational approach to symbolic development in children with Down syndrome. In D. Cicchetti & M. Beeghly (Eds.), *New directions for child development, no. 36: Symbolic development in atypical children* (pp. 5–29). San Francisco: Jossey-Bass.

Beeghly, M., Weiss-Perry, B., & Cicchetti, D. (1990). Beyond sensorimotor functioning: Early communicative and play development of children with Down syndrome. In D. Cicchetti & M. Beeghly (Eds.), *Children with Down syndrome: A developmental perspective,* (pp. 329–368). Cambridge, England: Cambridge University Press.

Beery, K. E. (1989). *The VMI: Developmental Test of Visual Motor Integration* (Rev. ed.). Cleveland, OH: Modern Curriculum Press.

Beery, K. E., & Butkenica, N. A. (1997). *Developmental Test of Visual Motor Integration.* Columbus, OH: Modern Curriculum Press.

Belsky, J., & Most, R. K. (1981). From exploration to play: A cross-sectional study of infant free play behavior. *Developmental Psychology, 17*(5), 630–639.

Belsky, J., Garduque, L., & Hrncir, E. (1984). Assessing performance, competence, and executive capacity in infant play. *Developmental Psychology, 20,* 1163–1178.

Benner, S. M. (1992). *Assessing young children with special needs: An ecological perspective.* New York: Longman.

Berman, P., & McLaughlin, M. W. (1978). *Federal programs supporting educational change: Implementing and sustaining innovations.* Santa Monica, CA: Rand Corporation.

Berney, B. (1993). Round and round it goes: The epidemiology of childhood lead poisoning, 1950–1990. *The Milbank Quarterly, 71*(1), 3–39.

Bernheimer, L., & Keogh, B. (1986). Developmental disabilities in preschool children. In B. Keogh (Ed.), *Advances in special education: Vol. 5. Developmental problems in infancy and the preschool years* (pp. 61–91). Greenwich, CT: JAI Press.

Bernstein, A. C. (1976, January). How children learn about sex and birth. *Psychology Today,* pp. 31–35, 66.

Bernstein, D. K., & Tiegerman, E. (1993). *Language and communication disorders in children* (3rd ed.). New York: Macmillan.

Bernstein, J. H. (1994). Assessment of developmental neurotoxicity: Neuropsychological batteries. *Environmental Health Perspectives, 102*(Suppl. 2), 141–144.

Bernstein, J. H., & Waber, D. P. (1990). Developmental neuropsychological assessment: The systemic approach. In A. A. Boulton, G. B. Baker, & M. Hiscock (Eds.), *Neuromethods: Neuropsychology* (Vol. 17, pp. 311–371). Clifton, NJ: Humana Press.

Bernstein, J. H., Prather, P. A., & Rey-Casserly, C. (1995). Neuropsychological assessment in preoperative and postoperative evaluation. *Neurosurgery Clinics of North America, 6*(3), 443–454.

Berruata-Clement, J. R., Schweinhart, L. J., Barnett, W. S., Epstein, A. S., & Weikart, D. P. (1984). *Changed lives: The effects of the Perry Preschool Program on youths through age 19.* Ypsilanti, MI: High/Scope Press.

Bersoff, D. N., & Hofer, P. T. (1990). The legal regulation of school psychology. In C. Reynolds & T. Gutkin (Eds.), *Handbook of School Psychology* (2nd ed.). New York: Wiley.

Best, S., Bigg, J., & Sirvis, B. (1990). Physical and health impairments. In N. Haring & L. McCormick (Eds.), *Exceptional children and youth: An introduction to special education* (5th ed., pp. 283–324). Columbus, OH: Merrill.

Bigelow, A. E. (1990). Relationship between the development of language and thought in young blind children. *Journal of Visual Impairment and Blindness, 84,* 414–418.

Bijou, S. W., Peterson, R. F., Allen, K. F., & Johnston, M. S. (1969). Methodology for experimental studies of young children in natural settings. *The Psychological Record, 19,* 177–210.

Bing, J., & Bing, S. (1984). Alternate form reliability of the PPVT-R for Black Headstart preschoolers. *Psychological Reports, 54,* 235–238.

Bishop, V. E. (1991). Preschool visually impaired children: A demographic study. *Journal of Visual Impairment and Blindness, 85,* 69–74.

Blain, G. H., Bergner, R. M., Lewis, M. L., & Goldstein, M. A. (1981). The use of objectively scoreable House–Tree–Person indicators to establish child abuse. *Journal of Clinical Psychology, 37*(3), 667–673.

Bloom, L. (1973). *One word at a time.* The Hague: Mouton.

Bloom, L. (1974). Talking, understanding, and thinking: Developmental relationship between receptive and expressive language. In R. Schiefelbusch & L. Lloyed (Eds.), *Language perspectives—Acquisition, retardation, and intervention* (pp. 285–312). Baltimore: University Park Press.

Bloom, L. (1993). *The transition from infancy to language: Acquiring the power of expression.* New York: Cambridge University Press.

Bloom, L., & Lahey, M. (1978). *Language development and language disorders.* New York: Wiley.

Blum, N. J., & Mercugliano, M. (1997). Attention-deficit Hyperactivity Disorder. In M. L. Batshaw (Ed.), *Children with disabilities* (4th ed., pp. 449–470). Baltimore: Paul H. Brookes.

Bluma, S., Shearer, A., Frohman, A., & Hillard, J. (1976). *Portage Guide of Early Education Checklist.* Portage, WI: Portage Project, Cooperative Educational Services.

Blumberg, T. L. (1987). Parent counseling and training. In M. Esterson & L. Bluth (Eds.), *Related services for handicapped children* (pp. 69–77). Boston: College Hill Press.

Bluth, L. F. (1987). The individualized education program and related services. In M. Esterson & L. Bluth (Eds.), *Related services for handicapped children* (pp. 9–13). Boston: College Hill Press.

Boehm, A. E. (1986). *Manual for the Boehm Test of Basic Concepts.* San Antonio, TX: The Psychological Corporation.

Boivin, M. J., & Giordani, B. (1995). A risk evaluation of the neuropsychological effects of childhood lead toxicity. *Developmental Neuropsychology, 11*(2), 157–180.

Bond, L. A., Creasey, G. L., & Abrams, C. L. (1990). Play assessment: Reflecting and promoting cognitive competence. In E. D. Gibbs & D. M. Teti (Eds.), *Interdisciplinary assessment of infants: A guide for early intervention professionals.* Baltimore: Paul H. Brookes.

Bond, L. A., Kelly, L. D., Teti, D. M., & Gibbs, E. D. (1983, April). *Longitudinal analyses of infant free play with familiar and unfamiliar toys.* Paper presented at the biannual meeting of the Society for Research and Child Development, Detroit.

Boothroyd, A. (1982). *Hearing impairments in young children.* Englewood Cliffs, NJ: Prentice-Hall.

Bose, S., Moss, H. A., Brouwers, P., Pizzo, P., & Lorion, R. (1994). Psychologic adjustment of human immunodeficiency virus–infected school-age children. *Developmental and Behavioral Pediatrics, 15,* S26–S33.

Bowen, E. (1988, February). Getting tough. *Time,* pp. 52–58.

Bowlby, J. (1951). *Maternal care and child health.* Geneva, Switzerland: World Health Organization.

Boyle, G. (1989). Confirmation of the structural dimensionality of the Stanford–Binet Intelligence Scale (4th ed.). *Personality and Individual Differences, 10,* 709–715.

Bracken, B. A. (1984). *Bracken Basic Concepts Scale.* San Antonio, TX: Psychological Corporation.

Bracken, B. A. (1985). Critical review of the Kaufman Assessment Battery for Children (K–ABC). *School Psychology Review, 14,* 21–36.

Bracken, B. A. (1986). Incidence of basic concepts in the directions of five commonly used American tests of intelligence. *School Psychology International, 7,* 1–10.

Bracken, B. A. (1987). Limitations of preschool instruments and standards for minimal levels of technical adequacy. *Journal of Psychoeducational Assessment, 4,* 313–326.

Bracken, B. A. (1991). The clinical observation of preschool assessment behavior. In B. A. Bracken (Ed.), *The psychoeducational assessment of preschool children* (pp. 40–52). Boston: Allyn & Bacon.

Bracken, B. A., & Fouad, N. (1987). Spanish translation and validation of the Bracken Basic Concepts Scale. *School Psychology Review, 16,* 94–102.

Bracken, B. A., Howell, K. K., Harrison, T. E., Stanford, L. D., & Zahn, B. H. (1991). Ipsative subtest pattern stability of the Bracken Basic Concept Scale and the Kaufman Assessment Battery for Children in a preschool sample. *School Psychology Review, 20,* 315–330.

Bracken, B. A., Sabers, D., & Insko, W. (1987). Performance of black and white children on the Bracken Basic Concepts Scale. *Psychology in the Schools, 24,* 22–27.

Bracken, B. A., & Walker, K. C. (1997). The utility of intelligence tests for preschool children. In D. P. Flanagan, J. L. Genshaft, & P. L. Harrison (Eds.), *Contemporary intellectual assessment: Theories, tests, and issues* (pp. 484–502). New York: Guilford Press.

Bradley, R. H., Caldwell, B. M., Rock, S. L., Brisby, J. A., & Harris, P. T. (1987). *Addendum to HOME manual: Use of the HOME inventory with children with handicaps.* Little Rock, AR: University of Arkansas, Center for Research on Teaching and Learning.

Brambring, M., & Tröster, H. (1992). On the stability of stereotyped behaviors in blind infants and preschoolers. *Journal of Visual Impairment and Blindness, 86,* 105–110.

Brambring, M., & Tröster, H. (1994). The assessment of cognitive development of blind infants and preschoolers. *Journal of Visual Impairment and Blindness, 88,* 9–18.

Bramlett, R. K., & Barnett, D. W. (1993). The development of a direct observation code for use in preschool settings. *School Psychology Review, 22,* 49–62.

Brandon, K. A., Kehle, T. J., Jenson, W. R., & Clark, E. (1990). Regression, practice, and expectation effects on the Revised Conners' Teacher Rating Scale. *Journal of Psychoeducational Assessment, 8,* 456–466.

Brassard, M. R., Germain, R., & Hart, S. N. (Eds.). (1987). *Psychological maltreatment of children and youth.* Elmsford, NY: Pergamon.

Brassard, M. R., Tyler, A. H., & Kehle, T. J. (1983). Sexually abused children: Identification and suggestions for intervention. *School Psychology Review, 12,* 93–97.

Brazelton, T. B. (1984) *Neonatal Behavioral Assessment Scale* (2nd ed.). London: Spastics International Medical Publications.

Brazelton, T. B., Koslowski, B., & Tronick, E. (1976). Neonatal behavior among urban Zambians and Americans. *Journal of the American Academy of Child Psychiatry, 15,* 97–107.

Briere, J. (1992a). *Child abuse trauma: Theory and treatment of the lasting effects.* Newbury Park, CA: Sage.

Briere, J., & Runtz, M. (1991). The long-term effects of sexual abuse: a review and synthesis. In J. Briere (Ed.), *Treating victims of child abuse.* San Francisco, CA: Jossey-Bass.

Brigance, A. H. (1991). *BRIGANCE® Diagnostic Inventory of Early Development—Revised.* North Billerica, MA: Curriculum Associates.

Brigance, A. H. (1991). *BRIGANCE® K and 1 Screen for Kindergarten and First Grade.* North Billerica, MA: Curriculum Associates.

Brim, O. G. (1975). Macrostructural influences on child development and the need for childhood social indicators. *American Journal of Orthopsychiatry, 45,* 517–524.

Brinkerhoff, J., & Portage Project Staff Associates. (1987). *The Portage classroom curriculum checklist.* Portage, WI: Portage Project.

Bronfenbrenner, U. (1977). Toward an experimental ecology of human development. *American Psychologist, 32,* 513–531.

Bronfenbrenner, U. (1979). The ecology of human development. Cambridge, MA: Harvard University Press.

Bronfenbrenner, U. (1986). Ecology of the family as a context for human development. *Developmental Psychology, 22,* 723–742.

Bronfenbrenner, U. (1991). What families do? *Family Affairs, 4*(1), 237–248.

Bronson, M. B., Hauser-Cram, P., & Warfield, M. E. (1995). Classroom behaviors of preschool children with and without developmental disabilities. *Journal of Applied Developmental Psychology, 16,* 371–390.

Brouwers, P., Belman, A. L., & Epstein, L. G. (1991). Central nervous system involvement: Manifestation and evaluation. In P. A. Pizzo & C. M. Wilfert (Eds.), *Pediatric AIDS: The challenge of HIV infection in infants, children, and adolescents* (pp. 318–335). Baltimore: Williams & Wilkins.

Brown, A., & Finkelhor, D. (1986). Impact of child sexual abuse: A review of the research. *Psychological Bulletin, 99,* 66–77.

Brown, A. L. (1979). Theories of memory and the problem of development: Activity, growth, and knowledge. In L. Cermak & F. I. M. Craik (Eds.), *Levels of processing in memory* (pp. 133–137). Hillsdale, NJ: Erlbaum.

Brown, C., Goodman, S., & Kupper, L. (1993). The unplanned journey: When you learn that your child has a disability. *NICHCY News Digest, 3*(1), 5–15.

Brown, D. (1988). Empowerment through advocacy. In D. J. Kirpius & D. Brown (Eds.), *Handbook of consultation: An intervention for advocacy and outreach* (pp. 5–17). Alexandria, VA: Association for Counselor Education and Supervision.

Brown, L. W. (1997). Seizure disorders. In M. L. Batshaw (Ed.), *Children with disabilities* (4th ed., pp. 553–593).

Brown, R. (1973). *A first language, the early stages.* Cambridge, MA: Harvard University Press.

Bruder, M. B., & Bologna, T. (1993). Collaboration and service coordination for effective early intervention. In W. Brown, S. K. Thurman, & L. F. Pearl (Eds.), *Family-centered early intervention with infants and toddlers: Innovative cross-disciplinary approaches* (pp. 103–127). Baltimore: Paul H. Brookes.

Bruininks, R. H. (1978). *Bruininks–Oseretsky Test of Motor Proficiency.* Circle Pines, MN: American Guidance Service.

Bruininks, R. H., Woodcock, R. W., Weatherman, R. F., & Hill, B. K. (1984). *Scales of Independent Behavior (SIB).* Allen, TX: DLM Teaching Resources.

Bucy, J. E., & Foust, J. (1996, March) *Asperger's Disorder: A rose by another name?* Paper presented at the annual meeting of the National Association for School Psychologists, Atlanta, GA.

Budoff, M. (1967). Learning potential among institutionalized young adult retardates. *American Journal of Mental Deficiency, 72,* 404–411.

Burgemeister, B. B., Blum, L. H., & Lorge, I. (1972). *Columbia Mental Maturity Scale.* New York: Psychological Corporation.

Burks, H. F. (1977). *Burks' Behavior Rating Scales: Preschool and kindergarten edition.* Los Angeles: Western Psychological Services.

Burks, H. F. (1996). *Burks' Behavior Rating Scales-Revised.* Los Angeles: Western Psychological Services.

Burns, R. C., & Kaufman, S. H. (1972). *Actions, styles, and symbols in kinetic family drawings.* New York: Brunner/ Mazel.

Burroughs, M. H., & Edelson, P. J. (1991). Medical care of the HIV-infected child. *Pediatric Clinics of North America, 38,* 45–67.

Butler, C., Hittelman, J., & Hauger, S. B. (1991). Approach to neurodevelopmental and neurological complications in pediatric HIV infection. *Journal of Pediatrics, 119,* S41–S46.

Calhoun, M. L., & Newson, E. (1984). Parents as experts: An assessment approach for hard-to-test children. *Diagnostique, 9*(4), 239–244.

Calkins, L. M. (1983). *Lessons from a child: On the teaching and learning of writing.* Portsmouth, NH: Heinemann.

Campbell, F. A., & Ramey, C. T. (Eds.). (1993). *Mid-adolescent outcomes for high risk students: An examination of the continuing effects of early intervention.* Paper presented at the Society for Research in Child Development, New Orleans.

Campos, J. J., Svejda, M. J., Campos, R. G., & Bertenthal, B. (1982). The emergence of self-produced locomotion: Its importance for psychological development in infancy. In D. D. Bricher (Ed.), *Intervention with at-risk and handicapped infants: From research to application* (pp. 195–217). Baltimore: University Park Press.

Carey, S. (1977). The child as word learner. In M. Halle, J. Bresman, & G. A. Miller (Eds.), *Linguistic theory and psychological reality.* (pp. 264–293). Cambridge, MA: MIT Press.

Carpenter, C. D. (1994). Review of the Revised BRIGANCE® Diagnostic Inventory of Early Development. In J. C. Connely & J. C. Impera (Eds.), *Supplement to the eleventh mental measurement yearbook* (pp. 352–353). Lincoln, NE: University of Nebraska Press.

Carroll, J. B. (1993). *Human cognitive abilities: A survey of factor-analytic studies.* Cambridge, England: Cambridge University Press.

Carroll, J. B. (1997). The three-stratum theory of cognitive abilities. In D. P. Flanagan, J. L. Genshaft, & P. L. Harrison (Eds.), *Contemporary intellectual assessment: Theories, tests, and issues* (pp. 122–130). New York: Guilford Press.

Carrow-Woolfork, E. (1974). *Carrow Elicited Language Inventory.* Chicago: Riverside.

Carrow-Woolfork, E. (1985). *Test for Auditory Comprehension of Language.* Chicago: Riverside.

Carta, J. J., Greenwood, C. R., & Atwater, J. B. (1985). *Ecobehavioral system for the complex assessment of preschool environments: ESCAPE.* Kansas City, KS: Juniper Gardens Children's Project, Bureau of Child Research, University of Kansas. (ERIC Document Reproduction Service Nos. ED 288 268, EC 200 587).

Case, R., & Okamoto, Y. (1996). The role of central conceptual structures in the development of children's thought. *Monographs of the Society for Research in Child Development.* Serial No. 246, Vol. 61, Nos. 1–2.

Case-Smith, J. (1994). The relationships among sensorimotor components, fine motor skill, and functional performance in preschool children. *The American Journal of Occupational Therapy, 49*(7), 645–652.

Casey Foundation, Center for the Study of Social Policy (1992). *Kids count data book: State profiles of child well-being.* Washington, DC: Author.

Casto, G., & Mastropieri, M. (Eds.). (1986). The efficacy of early intervention programs for handicapped children: A meta analysis. *Exceptional Children, 52*(5), 417–424.

Ceci, S. J., & Bruck, M. (1993). The suggestibility of the child witness: A historical review and synthesis. *Psychological Bulletin, 113,* 403–439.

Ceci, S. J., & Bruck, M. (1995). *Jeopardy in the courtroom: A scientific analysis of children's testimony.* Washington, DC: American Psychological Association.

Celce-Murcia, J. (1978). The simultaneous acquisition of English and French in a two-year-old. In E. Hatch (Ed.), *Second language acquisition* (pp. 38–53). Rowley, MA: Newbury House.

Centers for Disease Control. (1995a). First 500,000 AIDS cases—United States, 1995. *Journal of the American Medical Association, 274,* 1827–1828.

Centers for Disease Control. (1995b). U.S. Public Health Service recommendations for human immunodeficiency virus counseling and voluntary testing for pregnant women. *Morbidity and Mortality Weekly Report, 44* (RR-1).

Chapin, H. D. (1915). Are institutions for infants necessary? *Journal of the American Medical Association, 64,* 1–3.

Chase, D. A. (1987). *An analysis of human figure and kinetic family drawings of sexually abused children and adolescents.* Unpublished doctoral dissertation, University of Massachusetts, Amherst.

Chattin, S. H., & Bracken, B. A. (1989). School psychologists' evaluation of the K–ABC, McCarthy Scales, Stanford–Binet IV, and WISC–R. *Journal of Psychoeducational Assessment, 7,* 112–130.

Cheng, L. R. (1993). Asian-American cultures. In D. Brattle (Ed.), *Communication disorders in multicultural populations.* Boston: Andover Medical Publishers.

Chi, M. T. H. (1978). Knowledge structures and memory development. In R. S. Siegler (Ed.), *Children's thinking: What develops?* (pp. 37–52). Hillsdale, NJ: Erlbaum.

Chi, M. T. H. (1983). *Trends in memory development.* Basel, Switzerland: Karger.

Children's Defense Fund (1989). *A vision for America's future.* Washington, DC: Author.

Children's Defense Fund (1994). *The state of America's children yearbook 1994.* Washington, DC: Author.

Christenson, S., Abery, B., & Weinberg, R. A. (1986). An alternative model for the delivery of psychological services in the school community. In S. Elliott & J. Witt (Eds.), *The delivery of psychological services in schools* (pp. 349–391). Hillsdale, NJ: Erlbaum.

Church, R. P., Lewis, M. E. B., & Batshaw, M. L. (1997). Learning Disabilities. In M. L. Batshaw (Ed.), *Children with disabilities* (4th ed., pp. 471–497). Baltimore: Paul H. Brookes.

Cicchetti, D., & Beeghly, M. (Eds.). (1990). *Children with Down syndrome: A developmental perspective.* Cambridge, England: Cambridge University Press.

Cioni, G., Paolicelli, P. B., Sordi, C., & Vinter, A. (1993). Sensorimotor development in cerebral-palsied infants assessed with the Uzgiris-Hunt Scales. *Developmental Medicine and Child Neurology, 35,* 1055–1066.

Clarke, D. A. (1989). Neonates and infants at risk for hearing and speech language disorders. *Topics in Language Disorders, 10*(1), 1–12.

Clarke, K. L. (1988). Barriers or enablers? Mobility devices for visually impaired and multihandicapped infants and pre-schoolers. *Education of the Visually Handicapped, 20,* 115–132.

Clay, M. (1979). *The early detection of reading difficulties: A diagnostic survey with recovery procedures.* Portsmouth, NH: Heinemann.

Clymer, T., & Barrett, T. (1967). *Clymer-Barrett Prereading Battery.* Boston: Personal Press.

Coe, D. A., Matson, J. L., Craigie, C. J., & Gossen, M. A. (1991). Play skills of autistic children: Assessment and instruction. *Child and Family Behavior Therapy, 13*(3), 13–40.

Cohen, B., & Parker, W. (1977). Sex information among nursery school children. In E. K. Oremland & J. D. Oremland (Eds.), *The sexual and gender development of young children: The role of the educator* (pp. 142–159). Cambridge, MA: Ballinger.

Cohen, S. E., Parmalee, A. H., Sigman, M., & Beckwith, L. (1988). Antecedents of school problems in children born preterm. *Journal of Pediatric Psychology, 113*(4), 493–508.

Cohen, H. J., Papola, P., & Alvarez, M. (1994). Neurodevelopmental abnormalities in school-age children with HIV infection. *Journal of School Health, 64,* 11–13.

Colarusso, R. P., & Hammill, D. D. (Eds.). (1995). *Motor-Free Visual Perception Test.* Novato, CA: Academic Therapy Publications.

Cone, J. D. (1978). The Behavioral Assessment Grid (BAG): A conceptual framework and a taxonomy. *Behavior Therapy, 9,* 882–888.

Congressional Record 132 (1986). (100 STAT 1145-1177).

Conklin, N. F., & Lourie, M. A. (1983). *A host of tongues: Language communities in the United States.* New York: The Free Press.

Conners, C. K. (1990). *Conners' Rating Scales manual.* North Tonawanda, NY: Multi-Health Systems.

Connolly, A. (1988). *Key Math Diagnostic Inventory of Essential Mathematics—Revised.* Circle Pines, MN: American Guidance Service.

Conoley, J. C., & Gutkin, T. B. (1986a). Educating school psychologists for the real world. *School Psychology Review, 15*(4), 457–465.

Conoley, J. C., & Gutkin, T. B. (1986b). School psychology: A reconceptualization of service delivery realities. In S. Elliot & J. Witt (Eds.), *The delivery of psychological services in the schools* (pp. 393–424). Hillsdale, NJ: Erlbaum.

Coopersmith, S. (1967). *The antecedents of self-esteem.* San Francisco: W. H. Freeman.

Copeland, A. P., & White, K. M. (1991). *Studying families.* Newbury Park, CA: Sage.

Copeland, M. E., & Kimmel, J. R. (1989). *Evaluation and management of infants and young children with developmental disabilities.* Baltimore: Paul H. Brookes.

Corn, A. L., Hatlen, P., Huebner, K. M., Ryan, F., & Siller, M. A. (1995). *The national agenda for the education of children and youths with visual impairments, including those with multiple disabilities.* New York: American Foundation for the Blind Press.

Costenbader, V. K., & Keller, H. R. (1990). Behavioral ratings of emotionally handicapped, learning disabled, and non-referred children: Scale and source consistency. *Journal of Psychoeducational Assessment, 8,* 485–496.

Crawford, L., & Lee, S. W. (1991). Test-retest reliability of the CBCL ages 2–3. *Psychological Report, 69,* 496–498.

Crocker, A. D., & Orr, R. R. (1996). Social behaviors of children with visual impairments enrolled in preschool programs. *Exceptional Children, 62*(5), 451–463.

Croft, N. B., & Robinson, L. W. (1991). *Growing up: A developmental curriculum-Revised.* Ogden, UT: Parent Consultants.

CTB/McGraw-Hill (1977). *Comprehensive Test of Basic Skills.* Monterey CA: Author.

Curcio, F., & Piserchia, E. A. (1978). Pantomimic representation in psychotic children. *Journal of Autism and Childhood Schizophrenia, 8*(2), 181–189.

Damon, W. (1988). *The moral child.* New York: The Free Press.

Damon, W. (1977). *The social world of the child.* San Francisco: Jossey-Bass.

Danaher, J. (1995). *Preschool special education eligibility classifications and criteria.* Chapel Hill, NC: National Early Childhood Technical Assistance System.

Davidson, P. W., & Dolins, M. (1993). Assessment of the young child with visual impairments and multiple difficulties. In J. L. Culbertson & D. J. Willis (Eds.), *Testing young children: A reference guide for developmental, psychoeducational and psychosocial assessments* (pp. 237–261). Austin, TX: Pro-Ed.

Davis, Z. T. (1987). Effects of time-of-day of instruction on beginning reading achievement. *Journal of Educational Research, 80*(3), 138–140.

Dawson, G. (1989). *Autism: Nature, diagnosis, and treatment.* New York: Guilford Press.

Dawson, G., & Fischer, K. (1994). *Human behavior and the developing brain.* New York: Guilford Press.

DEC Task Force on Recommended Practices. (1993). *DEC recommended practices: Indicators of quality in programs for infants and young children with special needs and their families.* Reston, VA: Council for Exceptional Children.

Delaney, E., & Hopkins, T. (1987). *Examiner's handbook: An expanded guide for fourth edition uses.* Chicago: Riverside.

DeMers, S. T. (1986). Legal and ethical issues in child and adolescent personality assessment. In H. Knoff (Ed.), *The assessment of child and adolescent personality* (pp. 35–55). New York: Guilford Press.

DeMers, S. T., & Bersoff, D. N. (1985). Legal issues in school psychological practice. In J. Bergan (Ed.), *School psychology in contemporary society: An introduction* (pp. 319–339). Columbus, OH: Merrill.

Dennis, M., & Barnes, M. A. (1993). Oral discourse after early-onset hydrocephalus: Linguistic ambiguity, figurative language, speech act, and script based inferences. *Journal of Pediatric Psychology, 18,* 639–652.

Deno, S. L. (1985). Curriculum-based measurement: The emerging alternative. *Exceptional Children, 52,* 219–232.

DeQuiros, B., & Schrager, L. (Eds.). (1978). *Visual and auditory foundations of learning: Neuropsychological fundamentals in learning disabilities.* San Rafael, CA: Academic Publishers.

deVilliers, P. A., & deVilliers, J. G. (1979). *Early language.* Cambridge, MA: Harvard University Press.

Diamond, A. (1991). Neuropsychological insights into the meaning of object concept development. In S. Carey & R. Gelman (Eds.), *The Epigenesis of mind: Essays on biology and cognition* (pp. 67–110). Hillsdale, NJ: Erlbaum.

Diamond, K. E. (1993). The role of parents' observations and concerns in screening for developmental delays in young children. *Topics in Early Childhood Special Education, 13*(1), 68–81.

Dore, J. (1975). Holophrases, speech acts and language universals. *Journal of Child Language, 2,* 21–40.

Dormans, J. P., & Batshaw, M. L. (1997). Muscles, bones and nerves: The body's framework. In M. L. Batshaw (Ed.), *Children with disabilities* (4th ed., pp. 315–332). Baltimore: Paul H. Brookes.

Dorr, D. (1977). Some practical suggestions on behavioral consulting with teachers. *Professional Psychology, 8,* 96–102.

Dote-Kwan, J. (1995). Impact of mothers' interactions on the development of their young visually impaired children. *Journal of Visual Impairment and Blindness, 89,* 46–58.

Dote-Kwan, J., & Hughes, M. (1994). The home environment of young blind children. *Journal of Visual Impairment and Blindness, 88,* 31–42.

Dreisbach, M., & Keogh, B. K. (Eds.). (1982). Testwiseness as a factor in readiness test performance of young Mexican-American children. *Journal of Educational Psychology, 74*(2), 224–229.

Drew, C. J., & Turnbull, H. R. (1987). Whose ethics, whose code: An analysis of problems in interdisciplinary interventions. *Mental Retardation, 25*(2), 113–117.

Dulay, H., Burt, M., & Krashen, S. (1992). *Language two.* New York: Oxford University Press.

Duncan, D., Sbardellati, E., Maheady, F., & Sainato, D. (1981). Nondiscriminatory assessment of severely physically handicapped individuals. *Journal of the Association of the Severely Handicapped, 6*(2), 17–22.

Dunlea, A. (1984). The relationship between concept formation and semantic roles: Some evidence from the blind. In L. Fegans, C. Gravey, & R. Golinkoff (Eds.), *The origins and growth of communication.* Norwood, NJ: Albex.

Dunlea, A. (1989). *Vision and the emergence of meaning.* Cambridge, England: Cambridge University Press.

Dunn, L. M., & Dunn, L. M. (1981). *Peabody Picture Vocabulary Test—Revised.* Circle Pines, MN: American Guidance Service.

Dunn, L. M., & Williams, D. T. (1997). *Peabody Picture Vocabulary Test* (3rd ed.). Circle Pines, MN: American Guidance Service.

Dunst, C. J. (1991). Implementation of the Individualized Family Service Plan. In M. J. McGonigel, R. K. Kaufmann, & B. H. Johnson (Eds.), *Guidelines and recommended practices for the Individualized Family Service*

Plan (2nd ed., pp. 67–78). Bethesda, MD: Association for the Care of Children's Health.

Dunst, C. J., McWilliam, R. A., & Holbert, K. (1986). Assessment of preschool classroom environments. *Diagnostique, 11,* 212–232.

Dunst, C. J., & Trivette, C. M. (1985). *A guide to measures of social support and family behaviors.* Chapel Hill, NC: Technical Assistance Development System.

Dunst, C. J., & Trivette, C. M. (1990). Assessment of social support in early intervention programs. In S. Meisels & J. Shonkoff (Eds.), *Handbook of early childhood intervention* (pp. 326–349). New York: Cambridge University Press.

Dunst, C. J., Trivette, C. M., & Thompson, R. (1991). Supporting and strengthening family functioning: Toward a congruence between principles and practice. *Prevention in Human Services, 9*(1), 19–43.

Durkin, D. (1973). What does research say about the time to begin reading instruction? In R. Karlin (Ed.), *Perspectives on elementary reading: Principles and strategies of teaching* (pp. 135–145). New York: Harcourt Brace Jovanovich.

Dworkin, P. H. (1988). The preschool child: Developmental themes and clinical issues. *Current Problems in Pediatrics, 18*(2), 73–134.

Dyer, K., Santarcangelo, S., & Luce, S. (1987). Developmental influences in teaching language forms to individuals with developmental disabilities. *Journal of Speech & Hearing Disorders, 52,* 335–347.

Dyke, N., & Dettmer, P. (1989). Collaborative consultation: A promising tool for serving gifted students with learning disabilities. *Journal of Reading, Writing, and Learning Disabilities International, 5*(3), 253–264.

Edelbrock, C. S. (1983). Problems and issues in using rating scales to assess child personality and psychopathology. *School Psychology Review, 12,* 293–299.

Edmondson, R., & Smith, T. M. (1994). Temperament and behavior of infants prenatally exposed to drugs: Clinical implications for the mother–infant dyad. *Infant Mental Health Journal, 15*(4), 368–379.

Edwards, C. P. (1987). *Promoting social and moral development in young children: Creative ideas for the classroom.* New York: Teachers College Press.

Eicher, P. M. (1992). Feeding the child with disabilities. In M. L. Batshaw & Y. M. Perret (Eds.), *Children with disabilities: A medical primer* (pp. 197–211). Baltimore: Paul H. Brookes.

Elliott, C. D. (1990a). *Differential Ability Scales: Administration manual.* San Antonio, TX: The Psychological Corporation.

Elliott, C. D. (1990b). *Differential Ability Scales: Introductory and technical handbook.* San Antonio, TX: The Psychological Corporation.

Elliott, C. D. (1997). The Differential Ability Scales. In D. P. Flanagan, J. L. Genshaft, & P. L. Harrison (Eds.), *Contemporary intellectual assessment: Theories, tests, and issues* (pp. 183–208). New York: Guilford Press.

Elliott, C. D., Daniel, M. H., & Guiton, G. W. (1991). Preschool cognitive assessment with the Differential Ability Scales. In B. A. Bracken (Ed.), *The psychoeducational assessment of preschool children* (2nd ed., pp. 133–153). Boston: Allyn & Bacon.

Elliot, S. N. (1988). Acceptability of behavioral treatments: Review of variables that influence treatment selection. *Professional Psychology: Research and Practice, 19,* 68–80.

Elliott, S. N., Barnard, J., & Gresham, F. M. (1989). Preschoolers' social behavior: Teachers' and parents' assessments. *Journal of Psychoeducational Assessment, 7,* 223–234.

Elliott, S. N., Racine, C. N., & Bruce, R. T. (1995). Preschool social skills training. In A. Thomas & J. Grimes (Eds.), *Best practices in school psychology-III* (pp. 1009–1020). Washington, DC: National Association of School Psychologists.

Ellis, J., & Osowski, J. V. (Eds.). (1990). *A plan to revise special education in New Jersey: An overview of pilot project outcomes.* Trenton, NJ: New Jersey Department of Education.

Ellwein, M. C., Walsh, D. J., Eads, G. M., & Miller, A. K. (1991). Using readiness tests to route kindergarten students: The snarled intersection of psychometrics, policy, and practice. *Educational Evaluation and Policy Analysis, 13,* 159–175.

Enrichment Project for Handicapped Infants. (1985). *Hawaii Early Learning Profile (HELP).* Palo Alto, CA: VORT Corporation.

Erchul, W. P. (1991, March). An interview with Gerald Caplan. *National Association of School Psychologists Communique, 20*(6), 18–19.

Erikson, E. H. (1963). *Childhood and society* (2nd ed.). New York: Norton.

Erwin, E. J. (1993). Social participation of young children with visual impairments in specialized and integrated environments. *Journal of Visual Impairment and Blindness, 87,* 138–142.

Everson, M. D., & Boat, B. W. (1989). False allegations of sexual abuse by children and adolescents. *Journal of the American Academy of Child and Adolescent Psychiatry, 28*(2), 230–235.

Everson, M. D., & Boat, B. W. (1990). Sexualized doll play among young children: Implications for the use of anatomical dolls in sexual abuse evaluations. *Journal of the American Academy of Child and Adolescent Psychiatry, 29,* 736–742.

Everson, M. D., & Boat, B. W. (1994). Putting the anatomical doll controversy in perspective: An examination of the major uses and criticisms of the dolls in child sexual abuse evaluations. *Child Abuse and Neglect, 18,* 113–129.

Fallen, N. H., & Unmansky, W. (Eds.). (1985). *Young children with special needs* (2nd ed.). Columbus, OH: Merrill.

Family Educational Rights and Privacy Act of 1974. 20 U.S.C.A. Section 123g with accompanying regulations set down in 45 C.F.R. part 99.

Farber, A. F., Yanni, C. C., & Batshaw, M. L. (1997). Nutrition: Good and bad. In M. L. Batshaw (Ed.), *Children with disabilities* (4th ed., pp. 183–210). Baltimore: Paul H. Brookes.

Faye, E. E. (Ed.). (1984). *Clinical low vision* (2nd ed.). Boston: Little, Brown.

Federal Register. (1997, October 22), *62* (204). Part V. Department of Education. 34 CFR Parts 300, 301, and 303. Assistance to States for the Education of Children with Disabilities, Preschool Grants for children with Disabilities, and Early Intervention Programs for Infants and Toddlers with Disabilities; Proposed Rule.

Fein, G., & Apfel, N. (1979). Some preliminary observations on knowing and pretending. In M. Smith & M. B. Franklin (Eds.), *Symbolic functioning in childhood* (pp. 87–100). Hillsdale, NJ: Erlbaum.

Fernández, M., Pearson, B., Umbel, V., & Oller, D. (1992). Bilingual receptive vocabulary in Hispanic preschool children. *Hispanic Journal of Behavioral Sciences, 68,* 214–287.

Ferreiro, E., & Teberosky, A. (1979). *Literacy before schooling.* Portsmouth, NH: Heinemann.

Ferrell, K. A., Trief, E., Dietz, S. J., Bonner, M. A., Cruz, D., Ford, E., & Stratton, J. M. (1990). Visually impaired infants research consortium (VIIRC): First year results. *Journal of Visual Impairment and Blindness, 84,* 404–410.

Feuerstein, R., Rand, Y., & Hoffman, M. (1979). *The dynamic assessment of retarded performers: The Learning Potential Assessment Device: Theory, instruments, and techniques.* Baltimore: University Park Press.

Fewell, R. R. (1984). *Play assessment scale* (4th ed.). Unpublished document. Seattle: University of Washington.

Fewell, R. R. (1986). The measurement of family functioning. In L. Bickman & D. Weatherford (Eds.), *Evaluating early intervention programs for severely handicapped children and their families* (pp. 263–307). Austin, TX: Pro-Ed.

Fewell, R. R., & Kaminski, R. (1988). Play skills development and instruction for children with handicaps. In S. L. Odom & M. B. Karnes (Eds.), *Early intervention for infants and children with handicaps* (pp. 145–157). Baltimore: Paul H. Brookes.

Fewell, R. R., & Langley, M. B. (1984). *Developmental Activities Screening Inventory (DASI-II).* Austin, TX: Pro-Ed.

Field, T. M., Sostek, A. M., Vietze, P., & Leiderman, P. H. (1981). *Culture and early interactions.* Hillsdale, NJ: Erlbaum.

Fillmore, E. A. (1936). Iowa Tests for young children. *University of Iowa Studies in Child Welfare, 11,* 4.

Finkelhor, D. (1979). *Sexually victimized children.* New York: Free Press.

Fischer, K. W. (1980). A theory of cognitive development: The control and construction of hierarchies of skills. *Psychological Review, 87,* 477–531.

Fischer, K. W., Hand, H. H., Watson, M. W., Van Parys, M. M., & Tucker, J. L. (1984). Putting the child into socialization: The development of social categories in preschool children. In L. Katz (Ed.), *Current topics in early childhood education* (Vol. 5, pp. 27–72). Norwood, NJ: Ablex.

Fischer, K. W., & Lazerson, A. (1984). *Human development: From conception through adolescence.* New York: Freeman.

Fischer, K. W., & Rose, S. P. (1994). Dynamic development of coordination of components in brain and behavior: A framework for theory and research. In G. Dawson, & K. W. Fischer (Eds.), *Human behavior and the developing brain.* New York: Guilford Press.

Fivush, R. (1993). Developmental perspectives on autobiographical recall. In G. S. Goodman & B. Bottoms (Eds.), *Child victims and child witnesses: Understanding and improving testimony* (pp. 1–24). New York: Guilford Press.

Fivush, R., & Hammond, N. (1990). Autobiographical memory across the preschool years: Toward reconceptualizing childhood amnesia. In R. Fivush & J. Hudson (Eds.), *Knowing and remembering in young children.* New York: Cambridge University Press.

Flanagan, D. P., & Alfonso, V. C. (1994, May). *A critical review of intelligence tests for culturally diverse preschoolers.* Paper presented at the annual convention of the New York State Psychological Association, Bolton Landing, NY.

Flanagan, D. P., & Alfonso, V. C. (1995). A critical review of the technical characteristics of new and recently revised intelligence tests for preschool children. *Journal of Psychoeducational Assessment, 13*(1), 66–90.

Flanagan, D. P., Alfonso, V. C., Kaminer, T., & Rader, D. E. (1995). Incidence of basic concepts in the directions of new and recently revised American intelligence tests for preschoolers. *School Psychology International, 16,* 345–364.

Flanagan, D. P., & Miranda, A. H. (1994). Best practices in working with culturally different families. In A. Thomas (Ed.), *Best practices in school psychology* (3rd ed., pp. 1049–1060). Washington, DC: National Association of School Psychologists.

Flanagan, D. P., & McGrew, K. S. (1996). *Interpreting intelligence tests from contemporary Gf-Gc theory: Joint confirmatory factor analysis of the WJ-R and KAIT.* Manuscript submitted for publication.

Flanagan, D. P., & McGrew, K. S. (1997). A cross-battery approach to assessing and interpreting cognitive abilities: Narrowing the gap between practice and cognitive science. In D. P. Flanagan, J. L. Genshaft, & P. L. Harrison (Eds.), *Contemporary intellectual assessment: Theories, tests, and issues* (pp. 315–325). New York: Guilford Press.

Flanagan, R. (1995). The utility of the K-ABC and the WISC-R for linguistically different children: Clinical considerations. *Psychology in the Schools, 32,* 5–11.

Fletcher, J. M., Francis, D. J., Pequegnat, W., Raudenbush, S. W., Bornstein, M. H., Schmitt, F., Brouwers, P., & Stover, E. (1991). Neurobehavioral outcomes in diseases of childhood: Individual change models for pediatric human immunodeficiency viruses. *American Psychologist, 46,* 1267–1277.

Fletcher, J. M., Francis, D. J., Thompson, N. M., Davidson, K. C., & Miner, M. E. (1992). Verbal and nonverbal skills discrepancies in hydrocephalic children. *Journal of Clinical Experimental Neuropsychology, 14,* 593–609.

Fletcher, J. M., Taylor, H. G., Levin, H. S., & Satz, P. (1995). Neuropsychological and intellectual assessment of children. In H. I. Kaplan & B. J. Sadock (Eds.), *Comprehensive textbook of psychiatry/VI: Volume I.* Baltimore: Williams & Wilkins.

Flynn, J. R. (1984). The mean IQ of Americans: Massive gains 1932 to 1978. *Psychological Bulletin, 95,* 29–51.

Foley, G. M. (1990). Portrait of an arena evaluation: Assessment in the transdisciplinary approach. In E. D. Gibbs & D. M. Teti (Eds.), *Interdisciplinary assessment of infants: A guide for early intervention professionals* (pp. 271–286). Baltimore: Paul H. Brookes.

Foster, R., Gidden, J. J., & Stark, J. (1973). *Assessment of children's language comprehension.* Palo Alto, CA: Consulting Psychologists Press.

Foster, R., Gidden, J. J., & Stark, J. (1983). *Assessment of children's language comprehension* (Rev. ed.). Palo Alto, CA: Consulting Psychologists Press.

Fraiberg, S. (1977). *Insights from the blind.* London: Souvenir Press.

Fraiberg, S., & Anderson, E. (1977). Self-representation in language and play. In S. Fraiberg (Ed.), *Insights from the blind: Comparative studies of blind and sighted infants* (pp. 248–270). New York: Basic Books.

Frankenburg, W. K., Dodds, J., Archer, P., Boesnick, B., Meschka, P., Edelman, N., & Shapiro, H. (Eds.). (1992). *Denver II training manual* (2nd ed.). Denver, CO: Denver Developmental Materials.

Frankenburg, W. K., Dodds, J. B., Fandal, A. W., Kazuk, E., & Cohrs, M. (1975). *Denver Developmental Screening Test* (Rev. ed.). Denver, CO: Denver Developmental Materials.

Friedli, C. R. (1994) Transdisciplinary play-based assessment: A study of reliability and validity. Dissertation Abstracts International, 55(11), p. 3405a. (University Microfilms, No. AAC 95–0633).

Friedrich, W. N. (1991). Sexual behavior in sexually abused children. In J. Briere (Ed.), *Treating victims of child sexual abuse* (pp. 15–27). San Francisco, CA: Jossey-Bass.

Friedrich, W. N. (1991). Sexual victimization and sexual behavior in children: A review of recent literature. *Child Abuse and Neglect, 17,* 59–66.

Friedrich, W. N. (1995). The clinical use of the Child Sexual Behavior Inventory. *The ASPAC Advisor, 8*(1), 1, 17–20.

Friedrich, W. N., Beilke, R., & Urquiza, A. (1988). Behavior problems in young sexually abused boys. *Journal of Interpersonal Violence, 3*(1), 21–27.

Friedrich, W. N., Grambsch, P., Broughton, D., Kuiper, J., & Beilke, R. (1991). Normative sexual behavior in children. *Pediatrics, 88*(3), 456–464.

Friedrich, W. N., Grambsch, P., Damon, L., Hewitt, S., Koverola, C., Lang, R., Wolfe, V., & Broughton, D. (1992). The Child Sexual Behavior Inventory: Normative and clinical comparisons. *Psychological Assessment, 4*(3), 303–311.

Friend, M., & Bauwens, J. (1988). Managing resistance: An essential consulting skill for learning disabilities teachers. *Journal of Learning Disabilities, 21*(9), 556–561.

Frisby, C. L. (1992). Issues and problems in the influence of culture on the psychoeducational needs of African American children. *School Psychology Review, 21,* 532–551.

Froebel, F. (1887). *The education of man.* (W. H. Hailmann, Trans.). New York: Appleton. (Original work published in 1826).

Fuchs, D., Featherstone, N., Garwick, D. R., & Fuchs, L. S. (Eds.). (1984). *The importance of situational factors and task demands to handicapped children's test performance* (Research Report No. 54). Minneapolis, MN: University of Minnesota, Institute for Research on Learning Disabilities.

Fuchs, D., & Fuchs, L. S. (Eds.). (1986). Test procedure bias: A meta-analysis of examiner familiarity effects. *Review of Educational Research, 56*(2), 243–262.

Fuchs, D., Fuchs, L. S., Dailey, A. M., & Power, M. H. (Eds.). (1985). The effect of examiners' personal familiarity and professional experience on handicapped children's test performance. *Journal of Educational Research, 78*(3), 141–146.

Fuchs, D., Fuchs, L. S., Garwich, D. R., & Featherstone, N. (Eds.). (1983). Test performance of language-handi-

capped children with familiar and unfamiliar examiners. *Journal of Psychology, 114,* 37–46.

Fuchs, D., Zern, D. S., & Fuchs, L. S. (Eds.). 1983. *A microanalysis of participant behavior in familiar and unfamiliar test conditions* (Research Report No. 70). Minneapolis, MN: University of Minnesota, Institute for Research on Learning Disabilities.

Fuchs, L. S. (1986). Monitoring progress among mildly handicapped pupils: Review of current practice and research. *Remedial and Special Education, 7,* 5–12.

Fuchs, L. S., Fuchs, D., & Strecker, P. M. (1989). Effects of curriculum-based measurement on teacher's instructional planning. *Journal of Learning Disabilities, 22,* 51–59.

Fudala, J. B. (1986). *Arizona Articulation Proficiency Scale.* (2nd ed.). Los Angeles: Western Psychological Services.

Furth, H. (1971). Linguistic deficiency and thinking: Research with deaf subjects, 1964–1969. *Psychological Bulletin, 96,* 58–72.

Gallagher, J. (1990). The family as a focus for intervention. In S. Meisels & J. Shonkoff (Eds.), *Handbook of early childhood intervention* (pp. 540–559). New York: Cambridge University Press.

Gallup Surveys. (1988). New York: Research to Prevent Blindness.

Garbarino, J., & Stott, F. M. (1989). *What children can tell us.* San Francisco, CA: Jossey-Bass.

Garcia-Preto, N. (1982). Puerto Rican families. In M. McGoldrick, J. Pearce, & J. Giordano (Eds.), *Ethnicity and family therapy* (pp. 164–186). New York: Guilford Press.

Gardner, H. (1983). *Frames of mind: The theory of multiple intelligences.* New York: Basic Books.

Gardner, M. F. (1982). *Test of Visual-Perceptual Skills (Non-Motor).* Seattle, WA: Special Child Publications.

Gardner, M. F. (1985). *Receptive One-Word Picture Vocabulary Test (ROWPVT).* Novato, CA: Academic Therapy Publications.

Gardner, M. F. (1986). *Test of Visual–Motor Skills.* San Francisco: Children's Hospital of San Francisco.

Gardner, M. F. (1990). *Expressive One Word Picture Vocabulary Test-Revised.* Novato, CA: Academic Therapy.

Garland, C. W., McGonigel, M. J., Frank, A., & Buck, D. (1989). *The transdisciplinary model of service delivery.* Lightfoot, VA: Child Development Resources.

Garmezy, N. (1988). Stressors of childhood. In N. Garmezy & M. Rutter (Eds.), *Stress, coping, and development in children.* Baltimore: The Johns Hopkins University Press.

Garvey, C. (1977a). *Play.* Cambridge, MA: Harvard University Press.

Gee, B. (1994). *English as a second language aquisition in Taishan child speech.* Unpublished master's project, California State University, Fullerton.

Geers, A., Moog, J., & Scheck, B. (1984). Acquisition of spoken and signed English by profoundly deaf children. *Journal of Speech and Hearing Disorders, 49,* 378–388.

Gesell, A. (1925). *The mental growth of the preschool child: A psychological outline of normal development from birth to the sixth year.* New York: Macmillan.

Gesell, A., & Ilg, F. L. (1943). *Infant and child in the culture of today.* New York: Harper & Brothers Publishers.

Gesell Institute of Child Development. (1978). *School Readiness Screening Test.* Rosemont, NJ: Programs for Education.

Gesell Institute of Child Development. (1987). The Gesell Institute responds. *Young Children, 42,* 7–8.

Gillespie-Silver, P. H. (1979). *Teaching reading to children with special needs.* Columbus, OH: Merrill.

Ginsburg, H. P., & Baroody, A. J. (1990). *Test of Early Mathematics Ability* (2nd ed.). Austin, TX: PRO-ED.

Glascoe, F. P., MacLean, W. E., & Stone, W. L. (Eds.). (1991). The importance of parents' concerns about their child's behavior. *Clinical Pediatrics, 30,* 8–11.

Glutting, J. (1986). Potthoff bias analysis of the K-ABC, MPC, and nonverbal scale IQ's among Anglo, Black, and Puerto Rican kindergarten children. *Professional School Psychology, 1,* 225–234.

Glutting, J., & Kaplan, D. (1990). Stanford–Binet Intelligence Scale: Fourth Edition: Making the case for reasonable interpretations. In C. R. Reynolds & R. W. Kamphaus (Eds.), *Handbook of psychological and educational assessment of children: Intelligence and achievement* (pp. 277–296). New York: Guilford Press.

Glutting, J., & McDermott, P. (1990). Childhood learning potential as an alternative to traditional ability measures. *Journal of Consulting and Clinical Psychology, 2,* 398–403.

Goldfried, M. R. (1977). Behavioral assessment in perspective. In J. D. Cone & R. P. Hawkins (Eds.), *Behavioral assessment: New directions in clinical psychology* (pp. 3–22). New York: Brunner/Mazel.

Goldman, J. A. (1981). Social participation of children in same- versus mixed-aged groups. *Child Development, 52,* 644–650.

Gómez-Benito, J., & Forns-Santacan, M. (1993). Concurrent validity between the Columbia Mental Maturity Scale and the McCarthy Scales. *Perceptual and Motor Skills, 76,* 1177–1178.

Goodman, J. F., & Cameron, J. (1978). The meaning of IQ constancy in young retarded children. *Journal of Genetic Psychology, 132,* 109–119.

Goodman, K., & Goodman, Y. (1979). Learning to read is natural. In L. B. Resnick & P. A. Weaver (Eds.), *Theory and practice of early reading, Vol. 1.* Hillsdale, NJ: Erlbaum.

Goodenough, F. L. (1926). *Measurement of intelligence by drawings.* Chicago: World Book.

Goodenough, F. L. (1949). *Mental testing.* New York: Rinehart.

Goodenough, F. L., Maurer, K. M., & Van Wagene, M. J. (1940). *Minnesota Preschool Scales: Manual of instructions.* Minneapolis, MN: Educational Testing Bureau.

Goodman, G., & Aman, C. (1990). Children's use of anatomically detailed dolls to recount an event. *Child Development, 61,* 1859–1871.

Goodman, G. S., Batterman-Faunce, J. M., & Kenney, R. (1992). Optimizing children's testimony: Research and social policy issues concerning allegations of child sexual abuse. In D. Cichetti & S. Toth (Eds.), *Child abuse, child development, and social policy.* Norwood, NJ: Ablex.

Goodman, J. F., & Cameron, J. (1978). The meaning of IQ constancy in young retarded children. *Journal of Genetic Psychology, 132,* 109–119.

Goodwin, J., Sokal, D., & Rada, R. (1978). Incest hoax: False accusation, false denials. *Bulletin of the American Academy of Psychiatric Law, 6,* 269–276.

Graves, D. H. (1983). *Writing: Teachers and children at work.* Portsmouth, NH: Heinemann.

Green, A. H. (1986). True and false allegations of sexual abuse in child custody disputes. *Journal of the American Academy of Child Psychiatry, 25,* 449–456.

Gresham, F. M. (1995). Social skills training. In A. Thomas & J. Grimes (Eds.), *Best practices in school psychology* (3rd ed., pp. 1021–1030). Washington, DC: National Association of School Psychologists.

Gresham, F. M., & Elliott, S. N. (1990). *Social Skills Rating System manual.* Circle Pines, MN: American Guidance Service.

Gresham, F. M., MacMillan, D. L., & Siperstein, G. N. (1994). Critical analysis of the 1992 AAMR definition: Implications for school psychology. *School Psychology Quarterly, 10*(1), 1–19.

Groenveld, M., & Jan, J. E. (1992). Intelligence profiles of low vision and blind children. *Journal of Visual Impairment and Blindness, 86,* 68–71.

Guess, D., Seigel-Causey, E., Roberts, S., Guy, B., Ault, M. M., & Rues, J. (1993). Analysis of state organizational patterns among students with profound disabilities. *Journal of the Association of Persons with Severe Handicaps, 18*(2), 93–108.

Gullo, D. F., & Burton, C. B. (1992). Age of entry, preschool experience, and sex as antecedents of academic readiness in kindergarten. Special issue: Research on kindergarten. *Early Childhood Research Quarterly, 7,* 175–186.

Guralnick, M. J., Connor, R., Hammond, M., Gottman, J., & Kinnish, K. (1996). The peer relations of preschool children with communication disorders. *Child Development, 67,* 471–490.

Guralnick, M. J., & Groom, J. M. (1987). The peer relations of mildly delayed and nonhandicapped preschool children in mainstreamed play groups. *Child Development, 58,* 1556–1572.

Gustafson, J. E. (1984). A unifying model for the structures of intellectual abilities. *Intelligence, 8,* 179–203.

Gustafson, J. E. (1988). Hierarchical models of individual differences in cognitive abilities. In R. J. Sternberg (Ed.), *Advances in the psychology of human intelligence* (Vol. 4, pp. 35–71). Hillsdale, NJ: Erlbaum.

Gutkin, T. B., & Curtis, M. J. (1990). School-based consultation: Theory, techniques, and research. In C. R. Reynolds & T. B. Gutkin (Eds.), *Handbook of school psychology* (2nd ed., pp. 577–613). New York: Wiley.

Gyurke, J. S. (1991). The assessment of preschool children with the Wechsler Preschool and Primary Scale of Intelligence—Revised. In B. A. Bracken (Ed.), *The psychoeducational assessment of preschool children* (2nd ed., pp. 86–106). Boston: Allyn & Bacon.

Gyurke, J. S. (1994). A reply to Bagnato and Neisworth: Intelligent versus intelligence testing of preschoolers. *School Psychology Quarterly, 9*(2), 109–112.

Gyurke, J. S., Stone, B., & Beyer, M. (1990). A confirmatory factor analysis of the WPPSI-R. *Journal of Psychoeducational Assessment, 8,* 15–21.

Hainsworth, P. K., & Siqueland, J. L. (1986). *Early identification of children with learning disabilities: The Meeting Street School Screening Test.* Providence, RI: Easter Seal Society of Rhode Island.

Hall, H. B. (1980). The intangible human factor: The most critical coordination variable. In J. Elder & P. Magrab (Eds.),

Coordinating services to handicapped children (pp. 45–62). Baltimore: Paul H. Brookes.

Hallberg, Gay Robb. (1996). Assessing bilingual and LEP students: Practical issues in the use of interpreters. *Communique of the National Association of School Psychologists,* September, 16–18.

Halliday, M. A. (1973). *Explorations in the functions of language.* London: Arnold.

Halpern, R. (1993). Poverty and infant development. In C. Zeanah (Ed.), *Handbook of infant mental health.* New York: Guilford Press.

Hambleton, R. K., Swaminathan, H., & Rogers, J. (1991). *Fundamentals of item response theory.* Newbury Park, CA: Sage.

Hamburg, D. A. (1992). *Today's children: Creating a future for a generation in crisis.* New York: Random House.

Hamill, P., Drizd, T., Johnson, C., Reed, R., Roche, A., & Moore, W. (1979). Physical growth: National Center for Health Statistics percentiles. *Clinical Nutrition, 32,* 607–629.

Hammer, E. S. (1954). House–Tree–Person technique (H-T-P): A qualitative and quantitative scoring manual. *Journal of Clinical Psychology, 4,* 317–396.

Hammes, J., & Langdell, T. (1981). Precursors of symbolic formation and childhood autism. *Journal of Autism and Developmental Disorders, 11*(3), 331–346.

Hammill, D. D., Brown, L., & Bryant, B. R. (1992). *A consumer's guide to tests in print* (2nd ed.). Austin, TX: Pro-Ed.

Hammill, D. D., & Bryant, B. R. (1991). *Detroit Test of Learning Aptitude* (3rd ed.). Austin, TX: Pro-Ed.

Hanson, M. J. (1992). Ethnic, cultural, and language diversity in intervention settings. In E. Lynch & M. Hanson (Eds.), *Developing cross-cultural competence: A guide for working with young children and their families* (pp. 3–18). Baltimore: Paul H. Brookes.

Hanson, M. J., & Lynch, E. W. (1992). Family diversity: Implications for policy and practice. *Topics in Early Childhood Special Education, 12*(3), 283–306.

Harley, R. K., Long, R., Merbler, J. B., & Woods, T. A. (1986). *The development of a program in O & M for multihandicapped blind infants. Final report.* Nashville, TN: George Peabody College Press.

Harms, T., & Clifford, R. M. (1980). *Early Childhood Environment Rating Scale.* New York: Teachers College Press.

Harris, J. C. (1995). *Developmental neuropsychiatry: Vol. I and Vol. II.* New York: Oxford University Press.

Harris, S. L., & Fong, P. L. (1985). Developmental disabilities: The family and the school. *School Psychology Review, 14,* 162–165.

Harrison, P. L., Flanagan, D. P., & Genshaft, J. L. (1997). An integration and synthesis of contemporary theories, tests, and issues in the field of intellectual assessment. In D. P. Flanagan, J. L. Genshaft, & P. L. Harrison (Eds.), *Contemporary intellectual assessment: Theories, tests, and issues* (pp. 533–562). New York: Guilford Press.

Harst, J., Burke, C. L., & Woodward, V. (1981). *Children, their language, and the world: Initial encounters with print*

(Project # NIE G-79–0132). Washington, DC: National Institute of Education.

Hart, B., & Risley, T. R. (1975). Incidental teaching of language in the preschool. *Journal of Applied Behavior Analysis, 8,* 411–420.

Hart, S. N. (1991). From poverty to person status: Historical perspective on children's rights. *American Psychologist, 46,* 53–60.

Hasenstab, M. S., & Horner, J. S. (1982). *Comprehensive intervention with hearing-impaired infants and preschool children.* Rockville, MD: Aspen.

Haviland, J. (1976). Looking smart: The relationship between affect and intelligence in infancy. In M. Lewis (Ed.), *Origins of infant intelligence* (pp. 353–377). New York: Plenum.

Haynes, W. O., & Moran, M. J. (1989). A cross-sectional developmental study of final consonant production in southern Black children from preschool through third grade. *Language, Speech, and Hearing Services in Schools, 20*(4), 400–406.

Hayward, H., Brown, A., & Wingenfeld, S. (1990). Dynamic approaches to psychoeducational assessment. *School Psychology Review, 19,* 411–422.

Heath, S. B. (1986). Sociocultural contexts of language development. In *Beyond language: Social and cultural factors in schooling language minority students.* Los Angeles: Evaluation, Dissemination, and Assessment Center, California State University, Los Angeles.

Hedrick, D., Prather, E., & Tobin, A. (1984). *Sequenced Inventory of Communication Development* (Rev. ed.). Seattle, WA: University of Washington Press.

Helm, J. M. (1989) Assessment of behavioral state organization. In D. B. Bailey & M. Wolery (Eds.), *Assessing infants and preschoolers with handicaps.* Columbus, OH: Merrill.

Helms, J. E. (1992). Why is there no study of cultural equivalence in standardized cognitive ability testing? *American Psychologist, 47,* 1083–1101.

Helms, J. E. (1997). The triple quandary of race, culture, and social class in standardized cognitive ability testing. In D. P. Flanagan, J. L. Genshaft, & P. L. Harrison (Eds.), *Contemporary intellectual assessment: Theories, tests, and issues* (pp. 517–532). New York: Guilford Press.

Help for special preschoolers assessment checklist: Ages 3–6. (1987). Santa Cruz, CA: Santa Cruz County.

Here they come, ready or not. (1986, May) *Education Week,* p. 31.

Hessler, G. (1993). *Use and interpretation of the Woodcock-Johnson Psycho-Educational Battery-Revised.* Chicago: Riverside.

Hewitt, S. (1994). Preverbal sexual abuse: What two children report in later years. *International Journal of Child Abuse and Neglect, 18*(10), 819–824.

Hewitt, S., & Friedrich, W. N. (1991). Effects of probable sexual abuse on preschool children. In M. Q. Patton (Ed.), *Family Sexual Abuse* (pp. 57–74). Newbury, CA: Sage.

Heywood, H. C., Brown, A. L., & Wingenfield, S. (1990). Dynamic approaches to psychoeducational assessment. *School Psychology Review, 19,* 411–422.

Hill, E. W., Dodson-Burk, B., & Talor, C. R. (1992). The development and evaluation of an orientation and mobility screening for preschool children with visual impairments. *RE:view, 23,* 165–176.

Hill, E. W., Rosen, S., Correa, V. I., & Langley, M. B. (1984). Preschool O & M: An expanded definition. *Education of the Visually Handicapped, 16,* 58–71.

Hill, P., & McCune-Nicolich, L. (1981). Pretend play and patterns of cognition in Down's syndrome children. *Child Development, 52,* 611–617.

Hilton, L., & Mumma, K. (1991). Screening rural and suburban children with the Preschool Language Scale. *Journal of Communication Disorders, 24,* 111–122.

Hiskey, M. S. (1966). *The Hiskey–Nebraska Test of Learning Aptitude.* Lincoln, NE: Union College Press.

Hodgkinson, H. L. (1992). *A demographic look at tomorrow.* Washington, DC: Institute for Educational Leadership, Center for Demographic Policy.

Hodgkinson, H. L., & Outtz, J. H. (Eds.). (1992). *The nation and the states: A profile and data book of America's diversity.* Washington, DC: Institute for Educational Leadership, Center for Demographic Policy.

Hoepfner, R., Stern, C., & Nummedal, S. G. (1971). *CSE-ECRC preschool kindergarten test evaluations.* Los Angeles: UCLA Graduate School of Education.

Hofferth, S. L., West, J., Henke, R., & Kaufman, P. (Eds.). (1994). *Access to early childhood programs for children at risk.* Washington, DC: National Center for Educational Statistics.

Hoffman-Plotkin, D., & Twentyman, C. T. (1984). A multimodal assessment of behavioral and cognitive deficits in abused and neglected preschoolers. *Child Development, 55,* 794–802.

Holdaway, D. (1979). *The foundations of literacy.* New York: Ashton.

Holler, K. A., Fennell, E. B., Crosson, B., Boggs, S. R., & Mickle, J. P. (1995). Neuropsychological and adaptive functioning in younger versus older children shunted for early hydrocephalus. *Child Neuropsychology, 1*(1), 63–73.

Hooper, S. R. (1988). The prediction of learning disabilities in the preschool child: A neuropsychological perspective. In M. G. Tramontana & S. R. Hooper (Eds.), *Assessment Issues in Child Neuropsychology* (pp. 313–335). New York: Plenum Press.

Hooper, S. R. (1991). Neuropsychological assessment of the preschool child: Issue and procedures. In B. A. Bracken (Ed.), *The psychoeducational assessment of preschool children* (pp. 465–485). Boston: Allyn & Bacon.

Hopkins, K. D. (1990). Review of the comprehensive test of basic skills (4th ed.). In J. Kramer & J. C. Coneley (Eds.), *Eleventh mental measurement yearbook* (pp. 213–217). Lincoln, NB: University of Nebraska Press.

Horn, J. L. (1988). Thinking about human abilities. In J. R. Nesselroade & R. B. Cattell (Eds.), *Handbook of multivariate psychology* (Rev. ed., pp. 645–865). New York: Academic Press.

Horn, J. L. (1991). Measurement of intellectual capabilities: A review of theory. In K. S. McGrew, J. K. Werder, & R. W. Woodcock (Eds.), *WJ-R technical manual* (pp. 197–232). Chicago: Riverside.

Horn, J. L. (1994). Theory of fluid and crystallized intelligence. In R. J. Sternberg (Ed.), *Encyclopedia of human intelligence* (pp. 443–451). New York: Macmillan.

Horn, J. L., & Cattell, R. B. (1966). Refinement and test of the theory of fluid and crystallized intelligence. *Journal of Educational Psychology, 57,* 253–270.

Horn, J. L., & Noll, J. (1997). Human cognitive capabilities: Gf-Gc theory. In D. P. Flanagan, J. L. Genshaft, & P. L. Harrison (Eds.), *Contemporary intellectual assessment: Theories, tests, and issues* (pp. 53–91). New York: Guilford Press.

Horner, T. M., & Guyer, M. J. (1993). Infant placement and custody. In C. Zeanah (Ed.), *Handbook of infant mental health* (pp. 462–479). New York: Guilford Press.

Howard, J. (1982). The role of the pediatrician with young exceptional children and their families. *Exceptional Children, 48,* 316–322.

Howe, H. (1987). Giving equity a chance in the excellence game. In B. Gross & R. Gross (Eds.), *The great school debate* (pp. 281–297). New York: Simon & Schuster, Inc.

Howes, C. M., & Matheson, C. C. (1992). Sequences in the development of competent play with peers: Social and social pretend play. *Developmental Psychology, 28*(5), 961–974.

Hresko, W., Reid, K., & Hammill, D. (1991). *Test of Early Language Development* (2nd ed.). Austin, TX: Pro-Ed.

Hresko, W. P., Miguel, S. A., Sherbenou, R. J., & Burton, S. D. (1994). *Developmental Observation Checklist System (DOCS).* Austin, TX: Pro-Ed.

Huang, L. N., & Gibbs, J. T. (1992). Partners or adversaries? Home-school collaboration across culture, race, and ethnicity. In S. Christenson & J. Conoley (Eds.), *Home–school collaboration* (pp. 81–109). Silver Spring, MD: National Association of School Psychologists.

Huebner, E. S., & Gould, K. (1991). Multidisciplinary teams revisited: Current perceptions of school psychologists regarding team functioning. *School Psychology Review, 20*(3), 428–434.

Huefner, D. S. (1988). The consulting teacher model: Risks and opportunities. *Exceptional Children, 54*(5), 403–414.

Humphreys, L. G. (1992). Commentary: What both critics and users of ability tests need to know. *Psychological Science, 3,* 271–274.

Hunt, J. M. (1961). *Intelligence and experience.* New York: Ronald Press.

Hutinger, P. L. (1994). Integrated program activities for young children. In L. J. Johnson, R. J. Gallagher, M. J. LaMontagne, J. B. Jordan, J. J. Gallagher, P. L. Hutinger, & M. B. Karnes, (Eds.), *Meeting early intervention challenges: Issues from birth to three* (2nd ed., pp. 59–94). Baltimore: Paul H. Brookes.

Individuals with Disabilities Education Act of 1990 (IDEA), 20 U.S.C.A. Section 1400 as amended by P.L. 102–119. Regulations implementing IDEA-Part B appear in 34

C.F.R. Part 300 (1993) and IDEA-Part H, *Federal Register,* July 30, 1993.

Individuals with Disabilities Education Act Amendments of 1997, 20 U.S.C.A. Section 1400 as amended by P.L. 105-17. Regulations implementing IDEA appear in 34 C. F. R., Part 300, 301, & 303, *Federal Register,* October 22, 1997.

Ireton, H. (1988). *Preschool Development Inventory (PDI).* Minneapolis, MN: Behavior Science Systems.

Ireton, H., & Thwing, E. (1992). *Child Development Inventory (CDI).* Minneapolis, MN: Behavior Science Systems.

Izard, C. E. (1978). On the ontogenesis of emotions and emotion-cognition relationships in infancy. In M. E. Lewis & L. A. Rosenblum (Eds.), *The development of affect* (pp. 389–413). New York: Plenum Press.

Jacob-Timm, S., & Hartshorne, T. (1994). *Ethics and Law for School Psychologists.* Brandon, VT: Clinical Psychology Publishing.

James, B. (1989). *Treating traumatized children.* Lexington, MA/ Toronto, Canada: Lexington Books.

Jencks, C., & Peterson, P. (Eds.). (1991). *The urban underclass.* Washington, DC: Brookings Institute Press.

Jimenez, B. C. (1987). Acquisition of Spanish consonants in children aged 3–5 years, 7 months, *Language, Speech, and Hearing Services in the Schools, 18*(4), 357–361.

Johnson, C. M., Sum, A. M., & Weill, J. D. (1992). *Vanishing dreams: The economic plight of America's young families.* Washington, DC: Children's Defense Fund and Northeastern University's Center for Labor Market Studies.

Johnson, C. R., Lubetsky, M. J., & Sacco, K. A. (1995). Psychic and behavioral disorders in hospitalized preschoolers with developmental disabilities. *Journal of Autism and Developmental Disorders, 25*(2), 169–182.

Johnson, L. J. (1994). Challenges facing early intervention: An overview. In L. J. Johnson, R. J. Gallagher, M. J. LaMontagne, J. B. Jordan, J. J. Gallagher, P. L. Hutinger, & M. B. Karnes (Eds.), *Meeting early intervention challenges: Issues from birth to three* (2nd ed., pp. 1–12). Baltimore: Paul H. Brookes.

Johnson, L. J., & LaMontagne, M. J. (1994). Program evaluation: The key to quality programming. In L. J. Johnson, R. J. Gallagher, M. J. LaMontagne, J. B. Jordan, J. J. Gallagher, P. L. Hutinger, & M. B. Karnes (Eds.), *Meeting early intervention challenges: Issues from birth to three* (2nd ed., pp. 1–12). Baltimore: Paul H. Brookes.

Johnson, L. J., Pugach, M. C., & Hammitte, D. J. (1988). Barriers to effective special education consultation. *Remedial and Special Education, 9*(6), 41–47.

Johnson, M. K., & Foley, M. A. (1984). Differentiating fact from fantasy: The reliability of children's memory. *Journal of Social Issues, 40,* 33–50.

Johnson, T. C., & Friend, C. (1995). Assessing young children's sexual behaviors in the context of child sexual abuse evaluations. In T. Ney (Ed.), *True and false allegations of child sexual abuse* (pp. 44–72). New York: Brunner/Mazel.

Jones, D. P. H., & McGraw, J. M. (1987). Reliable and fictitious accounts of sexual abuse to children. *Journal of Interpersonal Violence, 2,* 27–45.

Jones, D. P. H., Psych, M. R. C., & Krugman, R. D. (1986). Can a three-year-old child bear witness to her sexual assault and attempted murder? *Child Abuse and Neglect, 10,* 253–258.

Jose, R. T. (1983). *Understanding low vision.* New York: American Foundation for the Blind.

Joseph, J. (1979). *Joseph Preschool and Primary Self Concept Screening Test.* Chicago: Stoelting.

Kagan, J. (1984). The idea of emotion in human development. In C. E. Izard, J. Kagan, & R. B. Zajonc (Eds.), *Emotions, cognition, and behavior* (pp. 38–72). New York: Cambridge University Press.

Kagan, J. (1988). Stress and coping in early development. In N. Garmezy & M. Rutter (Eds.), *Stress, coping, and development in children* (pp. 191–216). Baltimore: The Johns Hopkins University Press.

Kagan, S. L. (1989). *ASHA Reports.* American speech, language, and hearing association. Nov. 17, 13–17.

Kagan, S. L., Moore, E., & Bredekamp, S. (Eds.). (1995). *Considering children's early development and learning: Toward shared belief and vocabulary.* Washington, DC: National Education Goals Panel.

Kahler, C. T. (1983). *The language use and language development of blind and sighted preschool children.* Unpublished doctoral dissertation, University of North Carolina, Greensboro.

Kai, J. (1994). "Baby Check" in the inner city: Use and value to parents. *Family Practice, 11*(3), 245–250.

Kail, R. V. (1989). *The development of memory in children* (Rev. ed.). New York: Freeman.

Kalverboer, A. F. (1977). Measurement of play: Clinical applications. In B. Tizard & D. Harvey (Eds.), *Biology of play* (pp. 100–122). Philadelphia: J. B. Lippincott.

Kamphaus, R. W. (1993). *Clinical assessment of children's intelligence.* Boston: Allyn & Bacon.

Kamphaus, R. W., Dresden, J., & Kaufman, A. S. (1993). Clinical and psychometric considerations in the cognitive assessment of preschool children. In J. L. Culbertson & D. J. Willis (Eds.), *Testing young children: A reference guide for developmental, psychoeducational, and psychosocial assessments* (pp. 55–72). Austin, TX: Pro-Ed.

Kamphaus, R. W., & Kaufman, A. S. (1991). The assessment of preschool children with the Kaufman Assessment Battery for Children. In B. A. Bracken (Ed.), *The psychoeducational assessment of preschool children* (2nd ed., pp. 154–186). Boston: Allyn & Bacon.

Kamphaus, R. W., Kaufman, A. S., & Harrison, P. (1990). Clinical assessment practice with the Kaufman Assessment Battery for Children (K-ABC). In C. R. Reynolds & R. W. Kamphaus (Eds.), *Handbook for the psychological and educational assessment of children: Intelligence and achievement* (pp. 359–276). New York: Guilford Press.

Kamphaus, R. W., & Reynolds, C. R. (1987). *Clinical and research applications of the K-ABC.* Circle Pines, MN: American Guidance Service.

Kanfer, F. H., & Grimm, L. G. (1977). Behavior analysis: Selecting target behaviors in the interview. *Behavior Modification, 1,* 7–28.

Kanfer, F. H., & Saslow, G. (1969). Behavioral diagnosis. In C. M. Franks (Ed.), *Behavior-therapy: Appraisal and status.* New York: McGraw-Hill.

Kaplan, S. L., & Alfonso, V. C. (1996). *Confirmatory factor analysis of the Stanford–Binet Intelligence Scale: Fourth*

Edition with preschoolers with developmental delays. Manuscript submitted for publication.

Kaplan-Sanoff, M., & Nigro, J. (1988). The educator in a medical setting. *Infants & Young Children, 1*(2), 1–10.

Katz, S., Schonfeld, D. J., Carter, A. S., Leventhal, J. M., & Cichetti, D. V. (1995). The accuracy of children's reports with anatomically correct dolls. *Developmental and Behavioral Pediatrics, 16*(2), 71–76.

Kaufman, A. S. (1990). *Assessing adolescent and adult intelligence.* Boston: Allyn & Bacon.

Kaufman, A. S., & Kaufman, N. L. (1983). *Kaufman Assessment Battery for Children.* Circle Pines, MN: American Guidance Service.

Kayser, H. (1989). Speech and language assessment of Spanish-English speaking children, *Language, Speech, and Hearing Services in the Schools, 20*(3), 242–244.

Kearsley, R. B. (1984). *The systematic observation of children's play.* Unpublished scoring manual. (Available from author, Child Health Services, Manchester, NH).

Keith, T. Z. (1985). Questioning the K-ABC: What does it measure? *School Psychology Review, 14,* 9–20.

Keith, T. Z. (1990). Confirmatory and hierarchical confirmatory analysis of the Differential Ability Scales. *Journal of Psychoeducational Assessment, 8,* 391–405.

Keith, T. Z., Cool, V. A., Novak, C. G., White, L. J., & Pottebaum, S. M. (1988). Confirmatory factor analysis of the Stanford–Binet Fourth Edition: Testing the theory–test match. *Journal of School Psychology, 26,* 253–274.

Kekelis, L. S., & Pring, P. M. (1996). Blind and sighted children with their mothers: The development of discourse skills. *Journal of Visual Impairment and Blindness, 90,* 423–436.

Kekelis, L. S. (1988). Peer interactions in childhood: The impact of visual impairment. In S. Z. Sacks, L. S. Kekelis, & R. J. Gaylord-Ross (Eds.), *The development of social skills by visually impaired children.* San Francisco: San Francisco State University.

Keller, H. R. (1986). Behavioral observation approaches to assessment. In H. M. Knoff (Ed.), *The assessment of child and adolescent personality* (pp. 353–397). New York: Guilford Press.

Kelley, P., & Wedding, J. A. (1995). Medications used by students with visual and multiple impairments: Implications for teachers. *Journal of Visual Impairment and Blindness, 89,* 38–45.

Kennedy, M. D., Sheridan, M. K., Radlinski, S. H., & Beeghly, M. (1991). Play–language relationships in young children with developmental delays: Implications for assessment. *Journal of Speech and Hearing Research, 34,* 112–122.

Keogh, B. K. (1977). Early identification: Selective perception or perceptive selection? *Academic Therapy, 7*(3), 267–274.

Keogh, B. K., & Daley, S. E. (Eds.). (1983). Early identification: One component of comprehensive services for at-risk children. *Topics in Early Childhood Special Education, 3*(3), 7–16.

Kerbow, D. (1996). *Pervasive student mobility: A moving target for school improvement.* Chicago: Chicago Panel on School Policy.

Kirschenbaum, D. S., Steffen, J. J., & D'Orta, C. (1978). An easily mastered Social Competence Classroom Behav-ioral Observation System. *Behavioral Analysis and Modification, 2,* 314–322.

Kitayama, S., & Markus, H. R. (1994). *Emotion and culture.* Washington, DC: American Psychological Association.

Kjerland, L., & Kovach, J. (1987). *Structures for program responsiveness to parents.* Eagan, MN: Project Dakota.

Klein, S. D., & Schleifer, M. J. (Eds.). (1993). *It isn't fair! Siblings of children with disabilities.* Westport, CT: Bergin & Garvey.

Klerman, L. (1991). *Alive and well?* New York: National Center for Children in Poverty.

Kline, R. B. (1989). Is the Fourth Edition Stanford Binet a four-factor test? Confirmatory factor analyses of alternative models for ages 2 through 23. *Journal of Psychoeducational Assessment, 7,* 4–13.

Knapp, S., & Vandecreek, L. (1987). *Privileged communication in the mental health professions.* New York: Van Nostrand, Reinhold.

Knoff, H. M. (1984). The practice of multi-modal consultation: An integrating approach for consultation service delivery. *Psychology in the Schools, 21,* 83–91.

Knoff, H. M. (Ed.). (1986). *The assessment of child and adolescent personality.* New York: Guilford Press.

Knoff, H. M. (1988). Effective social interventions. In J. L. Graden, J. E. Zins, & M. J. Curtis (Eds.), *Alternative educational delivery systems: Enhancing instructional options for all students* (pp. 431–453). Washington, DC: National Association of School Psychologists.

Knoff, H. M. (1990). Evaluation of projective drawings. In C. R. Reynolds & R. W. Kamphaus (Eds.), *Handbook of psychological and educational assessment of children: Volume 2, Personality, behavior, and context* (pp. 89–146). New York: Guilford Press.

Knoff, H. M. (1995). Best practices in personality assessment. In A. Thomas & J. Grimes (Eds.), *Best practices in school psychology-III* (pp. 849–864). Washington, DC: National Association of School Psychologists.

Knoff, H. M., & Batsche, G. M. (1991). *The referral question consultation process: Addressing system, school, and classroom academic and behavioral problems.* Tampa, FL: Authors.

Kochanek, T. T. (1992). *Developmental surveillance for infants and toddlers: The application of knowledge to public policy and program initiatives.* Providence, RI: Rhode Island College, Department of Special Education.

Kochanek, T. T., & Hennen, F. (Eds.). (1988). Prediction of special education need from preschool screening data: A two-year follow-up investigation. *Special Services in the Schools, 4*(3/4), 23–35.

Kochanek, T. T., Kobacoff, R. I., & Lipsitt, L. P. (Eds.). (1990). Early identification of developmentally disabled and at-risk preschool children. *Exceptional Children, 56* (6), 528–538.

Kohlberg, L. (1981). *Essays on moral development* (Vols. 1–2). New York: Harper & Row.

Kolb, B. & Whishaw, I. (1990). *Fundamentals of human neuropsychology,* (3rd ed.). New York: Freeman.

Konner, M. (1991). *Childhood.* Boston: Little, Brown.

Kopp, C. (1983). Risk factors in development. In P. Mussen (Series Ed.), M. Haith & J. Campos (Vol. Eds.), *Manual of Child Psychology: Vol. 2. Infancy and the biology of development* (pp. 1081–1188). New York: Wiley.

Kopp, C., Baker, B., & Brown, K. (1992). Social skills and their correlates: Preschoolers with developmental delays. *Journal on Mental Retardation, 96*(4), 357–366.

Koppitz, E. M. (1968). *Psychological evaluation of children's Human Figure Drawings.* New York: Grune & Stratton.

Korkman, M., Kirk, U., Kamp, S. (1997). NEPSY: A developmental neuropsychological assessment. San Antonio, TX: Psychological Corporation.

Krakow, J., & Kopp, C. (1983). The effect of developmental delay on sustained attention in young children. *Child Development, 54,* 1143–1155.

Kramer, S., McGonigel, M. J., & Kaufmann, R. K. (1991). Developing the IFSP: Outcomes, strategies, activities, and services. In M. J. McGonigel, R. K. Kaufman, & B. H. Johnson (Eds.), *Guidelines and recommended practices for the Individualized Family Service Plan* (2nd ed., pp. 57–66). Bethesda, MD: Association for the Care of Children's Health.

Krauss, M. W., & Jacobs, F. (1990). Family assessment: Purposes and techniques. In S. Meisels & J. Shonkoff (Eds.), *Handbook of early childhood intervention.* New York: Cambridge University Press.

Kretschmer, R. R., & Kretschmer, L. W. (1978). *Language development and intervention with the hearing-impaired.* Baltimore: University Park Press.

Kruger, L. J., & Kaplan, S. (1994, March). *Multi-modal team leadership skills.* Paper presented at the National Association of School Psychologists Conference, Seattle, WA.

Kruger, L. J., Cohen, S., Marca, D., & Matthews, L. (1996). Using the INTERNET to extend training in team problem solving. *Behavioral Research Methods, Instrumentation, and Computers, 28,* 248–252.

Kruger, L. J., & Harrington, T. (1997). A team approach to program planning. In T. Harrington (Ed.), *Handbook of career planning with special needs students* (pp. 383–410). Austin, TX: Pro-Ed.

Kvaal, J. T., Shipstead-Cox, N., Nevitt, S. G., Hodson, B. W., & Launer P. B. (1988). The acquisition of 10 Spanish morphemes by Spanish speaking children. *Language, Speech, and Hearing Services in the Schools, 19*(4), 384–394.

Lahey, M. (1988). *Language disorders and language development.* New York: Macmillan.

Lambert, N. M., Nihira, K., & Leland, H. (1993). *AAMR Adaptive Behavior Scales-School: Second Edition (ABS-S:2).* Austin, TX: Pro-Ed and Los Angeles, CA: Western Psychological Services.

Lambert, N. M., Windmiller, M., Tharinger, D., & Cole, L. J. (1981). *AAMD Adaptive Behavior Scale-School Edition.* Monterey, CA: CTB/McGraw-Hill.

Landau, B., & Gleitman, L. (1985). *Language and experience: Evidence from the blind child.* Cambridge, MA: Harvard University Press.

Landau, S., Mangione, C., & Pryor, J. B. (in press). HIV/AIDS. In G. Bear, K. Minke, & A. Thomas (Eds.), *Children's needs II: Psychological perspectives.* Washington, DC: National Association of School Psychologists.

Landau, S., Pryor, J. B., & Haefli, K. (1995). Pediatric HIV: School-based sequelae and curricular interventions for infection prevention and social acceptance. *School Psychology Review, 24,* 213–229.

Langdon, H. W. (Ed.), with Cheng, L. L. (1992). *Hispanic children and adults with communication disorders.* Gaithersburg, MD: Aspen.

Laughon, P. (1990). The dynamic assessment of intelligence: A review of three approaches. *School Psychology Review, 19,* 459–470.

Laurent, J., Swerdlik, M., & Ryburn, M. (1992). Review of validity research on the Stanford–Binet Intelligence Scale: Fourth Edition. *Psychological Assessment, 4,* 102–112.

Layton, T. L., & Holmes, D. W. (1985). *Carolina Picture Vocabulary Test for Deaf and Hearing-Impaired.* Tulsa, OK: Modern Education Corporation.

Lazarus, A. A. (1981). *The practice of multi-modal therapy.* New York: McGraw-Hill.

Lee, L. L. (1971). *Northwestern Syntax Screening Test.* Evanston, IL: Northwestern University Press.

Leguire, L. E., Fellows, R. R., & Bier, G. (1990). Bayley mental scale of infant development and visually impaired children. *Journal of Visual Impairment and Blindness, 84,* 400–404.

Lehr, C. A., Ysseldyke, J. E., & Thurlow, M. L. (Eds.). (1986). Assessment practices in model early childhood education programs. *Psychology in the schools, 24,* 390–399.

LeLaurin, K., & Risley, T. R. (1972). The organization of day-care environments: "Zone" versus "man-to-man" staff assignments. *Journal of Applied Behavior Analysis, 5,* 225–232.

Lennenberg, E. H. (1967). *Biological foundations of language.* New York: Wiley.

Leong, S. (1996). Preschool orientation and mobility: A review of the literature. *Journal of Visual Impairment and Blindness, 90,* 145–153.

Lerner, J., Mardell-Czudnowski, C., & Goldenberg, D. (1987). *Special education for the early childhood years* (2nd ed.). Englewood Cliffs, NJ: Prentice-Hall.

Levenson, R. L., & Mellins, C. A. (1992). Pediatric HIV disease: What psychologists need to know. *Professional Psychology: Research and Practice, 23,* 410–415.

Levitt, H., McGarr, N., & Geffner, D. (1987). *Development of language and communication skills in hearing-impaired children* (ASHA Monograph #26). Washington, DC: American Speech-Language-Hearing Association.

Lewis, M., & Brooks, J. (1974). Self, other, and fear: Infants' reactions to people. In M. Lewis & L. A. Rosenblum (Eds.), *The origins of fear* (pp. 195–228). New York: Wiley.

Li, A. K. F. (1981). Play and the mentally retarded. *Mental Retardation, 19,* 121–126.

Lichtenstein, R., & Ireton, H. (1984). *Preschool screening: Identifying young children with developmental and educational problems.* Orlando, FL: Grune & Stratton.

Lidz, C. S. (1980). Assessment for development and implementation of the individual education program. *School Psychology Review, 9*(3), 207–211.

Lidz, C. S. (1983). Issues in assessing preschool children. In K. D. Paget & B. A. Bracken (Eds.), *The psychoeducational assessment of preschool children* (pp. 17–27). New York: Grune & Stratton.

Lidz, C. S. (Ed.). (1987). *Dynamic assessment.* New York: Guilford Press.

Lidz, C. S., & Thomas, C. (1987). The Preschool Learning Assessment Device: Extension of a static approach. In C. Lidz (Ed.), *Dynamic assessment* (pp. 288–325). NY: Guilford Press.

Lifter, K. (1996). Assessing play skills. In M. McLean, D. B. Bailey, & M. Wolery (Eds.), *Assessing infants and preschoolers with special needs* (2nd ed., pp. 435–461). Englewood Cliffs, NJ: Merrill.

Lifter, K., & Bloom, L. (1989). Object play and the emergence of language. *Infant Behavior and Development, 12,* 395–423.

Lifter, K., & Bloom, L. (1998). Intentionality and the role of play in the transition to language. In A. M. Wetherby, S. F. Warren, & J. Reichle (Eds.), *Transitions in prelinguistic communication: Preintentional to intentional and presymbolic to symbolic* (pp. 161–195). Baltimore: Paul H. Brookes.

Lifter, K., Pierce-Jordan, S., Campbell, S., Considine, M., Foley, C., Pedi, R. A., Small, C., & Windham, J. (1997, November). *PROJECT PLAY: Integrating language and play objectives to support full inclusion.* Paper presented at the International Early Childhood Conference on Children with Special Needs, New Orleans, LA.

Lifter, K., Sulzer-Azaroff, B., Anderson, S., & Cowdery, G. (1993). Teaching play activities to preschool children with disabilities: The importance of developmental considerations. *Journal of Early Intervention, 17*(2), 139–159.

Lindberg, M. (1980). Is knowledge base development a necessary and sufficient condition for memory development? *Journal of Experimental Child Psychology, 30,* 401–410.

Linder, T. W. (1983). *Early childhood special education: Program development and administration.* Baltimore: Paul H. Brookes.

Linder, T. W. (1990). *Transdisciplinary play-based assessment: A functional approach to working with young children.* Baltimore: Paul H. Brookes.

Linder, T. W. (1993a). *Transdisciplinary play-based assessment: A functional approach to working with young children* (Rev. ed.). Baltimore: Paul H. Brookes.

Linder, T. W. (1993b). *Transdisciplinary play-based intervention: Guidelines for developing a meaningful curriculum for young children.* Baltimore: Paul H. Brookes.

Linder, T. W. (1994). The role of play in early childhood special education. In R. L. Safford, B. Spodek, & O. N. Saracho (Eds.), *Yearbook in early childhood education: Early childhood special education* (Vol. 5). New York: Teacher's College Press, Columbia University.

Linder, T. W., Green, K., & Friedli, C. (1996). *Validity of transdisciplinary play-based assessment.* Unpublished manuscript.

Liptak, G. S. (1997). Neural tube defects. In M. L. Batshaw (Ed.), *Children with disabilities* (4th ed., pp. 529–552). Baltimore: Paul H. Brookes.

Loan, C. (1992). Keys to caregiving: Knowledge improves quality of adolescents' interactions with their infants. *NCAST National News, 8*(3), 6–7.

Loftus, E. F., & Davies, G. M. (1984). Distortions in the memory of children. *Journal of Social Issues, 40,* 51–67.

Lohman, D. F. (1989). Human intelligence: An introduction to advances in theory and research. *Review of Educational Research, 59,* 333–373.

Lopez, E. C. (1997). The cognitive assessment of limited English proficient and bilingual children. In D. P. Flanagan, J. L. Genshaft, & P. L. Harrison (Eds.), *Contemporary intellectual assessment: Theories, tests, and issues* (pp. 503–516). New York: Guilford Press.

Lorimier, S., Doyle, A., & Tessier, O. (1995). Social coordination during pretend play: Comparisons with non-pretend play and effect on expressive content. *Merrill-Palmer Quarterly, 41*(4), 497–516.

Lovell, K., Hoyle, H. W., & Siddall, M. C. (1968). A study of some aspects of the play and language of young children in delayed speech. *Journal of Child Psychology and Psychiatry, 9,* 41–50.

Lowe, M., & Costello, A. J. (1976). *Manual for the Symbolic Play Test.* Windsor, England: NFR-Nelson.

Luehr, R. E., & Hoxie, A. (Eds.). (1995). *Early childhood screening: Program administration manual.* St. Paul, MN: Minnesota Department of Education.

Lund, N., & Duchan, J., (1983). *Assessing children's language in naturalistic context* (3rd ed.). Englewood Cliffs, NJ: Prentice-Hall.

Lusk, R., & Waterman, J. (1986). Effects of sexual abuse on children. In K. MacFarlane, J. Waterman, S. Connerly, L. Damon, M. Durfee, & S. Long (Eds.), *Sexual abuse of young children: Evaluation and treatment* (pp. 122–126). New York: Guilford Press.

Luterman, D. (1979). *Counseling parents of hearing-impaired children.* Boston: Little, Brown.

Luterman, D. (1987). *Deafness in the family.* Boston: Little, Brown.

Lutz, C. (1982). The domain of emotion words on Ifaluk. *American Ethnologist, 9,* 113–128.

Lynch, E. W., & Hanson, M. J. (1992). *Developing cross cultural competence: A guide for working with young children and their families.* Baltimore: Paul H. Brookes.

Lynch, E. W., & Hanson, M. J. (1996). Ensuring cultural competence in assessment. In M. McLean, D. B. Bailey, Jr., & M. Wolery (Eds.), *Assessing infants and preschoolers with special needs* (2nd ed., chapter 4). Englewood Cliffs, NJ: Prentice-Hall.

Lyon, M. A., & Smith, D. K. (1986). A comparison of at-risk preschool children's performance on the K-ABC, McCarthy Scales, and Stanford–Binet. *Journal of Psychoeducational Assessment, 4,* 35–43.

Maccoby, E. E. (1980). *Social development.* New York: Harcourt Brace Jovanovich.

MacDonald, J. D., & Horstmeier, D. (1978a). *Environmental Language Inventory.* Columbus, OH: Merrill.

MacDonald, J. D., & Horstmeier, D. (1978b). *Environmental Pre-language Battery.* Columbus, OH: Merrill.

MacLean, L. F., MacLean, W. E., & Baumeister, A. A. (1995). Infant sleep–wake characteristics: Relation to neurological status and the prediction of developmental outcome. *Developmental Review, 15,* 255–291.

Maher, C. A. (1984). Implementing programs and systems in organizational settings: The DURABLE approach. *Journal of Organizational Behavior Management, 6*(3), 69–98.

Maher, C. A., & Bennett, R. E. (1984). *Planning and Evaluating Special Education Services.* Englewood Cliffs, NJ: Prentice-Hall.

Maher, C. A., & Illback, R. J. (1984). An approach to implementing IEP evaluation in public schools. *School Psychology Review, 13,* 519–525.

Maher, C. A., & Illback, R. J. (1985). Implementing school psychological service programs: Description and application of the DURABLE approach. *Journal of School Psychology, 23,* 81–89.

Mahler, M. S., Pine, F., & Bergman, A. (1975). *The Psychological birth of the human infant: Symbiosis and individuation.* New York: Basic Books.

Mahoney, G., Glover, A., & Finger, I. (1981). Relationship between large and sensorimotor development of Down Syndrome and nonretarded children. *American Journal of Mental Deficiency, 86*(1), 21–27.

Mandler, J. M. (1990). Recall and its verbal expression. In R. Fivush & J. A. Hudson (Eds.), *Knowing and remembering in young children* (pp. 317–330). New York: Cambridge University Press.

Mangold, S. S. (1976). *Mangold developmental program of tactile perception and braille letter recognition.* Castro Valley, CA: Exceptional Teaching Aids.

Mantzicopoulos, P., & Jarvinen, D. (1993). *An analysis of the BRIGANCE® K & 1 Screen with a disadvantaged preschool sample.* Paper presented at the Annual Meeting of the American Educational Research Association, Atlanta, GA. (ERIC Document Reproduction Service No. ED 363377).

Marcus, L. M., & Baker, A. (1986). Assessment of autistic children. In R. Simeonsson (Ed.), *Psychological and developmental assessment of special children* (pp. 279–304). Boston: Allyn & Bacon.

Marcus, L. M., Lansing, M., & Schopler, R. (1993). Assessment of children with autism and pervasive developmental disorders (pp. 319–344). In J. L. Culbertson & D. J. Willis (Eds.), *Testing young children: A reference guide for developmental, psychoeducational and psychosocial assessments.* Austin, TX: Pro-Ed.

Mardell-Czudnowski, C., & Goldenberg, D. S. (1990). *Developmental indicators for the assessment of learning* (Rev. ed.). Circle Pines, MN: American Guidance Service.

Mardell-Czudnowski, C., & Goldenberg, D. S. (Eds.). (1990). *Dial-R manual.* Circle Pines, MN: AGS.

Marks, E. S. (1995). *Entry strategies for school consultation.* New York: Guilford Press.

Markwardt, F. C. (1989). *Peabody Individual Achievement Test—Revised.* Circle Pines, MN: American Guidance Service.

Marner, E. (1991). Love's labors (E. Marner, Director). In E. Marner (producer), *Childhood: Seven-part video series* (Part 3). New York: Ambrose.

Marner, E. (1991). In the land of the giants (E. Marner, Director). In E. Marner (producer), *Childhood: Seven-part video series* (Part 4). New York: Ambrose.

Marshall, J., Marquis, K. H., & Oskamp, S. (1971). Effects of kind of question and atmosphere of interrogation on accuracy and completeness of testimony. *Harvard Law Review, 84,* 1620–1643.

Martin, R. P. (1986). Assessment of the social and emotional functioning of preschool children. *School Psychology Review, 15,* 216–232.

Martin, R. P. (1988). *The Temperment Assessment Battery for Children.* Brandon, VT: Clinical Psychology Publishing.

Mash, E. J., & Terdal, L. G. (1988). Behavioral assessment of child and family disturbance. In E. J. Mash & L. G. Terdal (Eds.), *Behavioral assessment of childhood disorders* (pp. 3–65). New York: Guilford Press.

Mash, E. J., Terdal, L. G., & Anderson, K. (1973). The response-class matrix: A procedure for recording parent–child interactions. *Journal of Clinical Psychology, 40,* 303–305.

Massachusetts Education Reform Act. (1993). *Great and general court of the commonwealth of Massachusetts.*

Massachusetts Department of Education. (1994). *Massachusetts common core of learning* (State Publication No. 17608–14–100, 000–9/94-DOE).

Masten, A. S., Best, K. M., & Garmezy, N. (1990). Resilience and development: Contributions from the study of children who overcome adversity. *Development and Psychopathology, 2,* 425–444.

Mauk, J. E., Reber, M., & Batshaw, M. L., (1997). Autism: And other Pervasive developmental disorders. In M. L. Batshaw (Ed.), *Children with disabilities* (4th ed., pp. 425–447). Baltimore: Paul H. Brookes.

Mayes, L. C., Bornstein, M. H., Chawarska, K., & Granger, R. H. (1995). Information processing and developmental assessments in 3-month-old infants exposed prenatally to cocaine. *Pediatrics, 95,* 539–545.

McAlpine, L. M., & Moore, C. L. (1995). The development of social understanding in children with visual impairments. *Journal of Visual Impairment and Blindness, 89,* 349–358.

McAnaney, K. D. (1992). *I wish: Dreams and realities of parenting a special needs child.* Sacramento, CA: United Cerebral Palsy Association.

McCallum, R. S. (1991). The assessment of preschool children with the Stanford–Binet Intelligence Scale: Fourth Edition. In B. A. Bracken (Ed.), *The psychoeducational assessment of preschool children* (2nd ed., pp. 107–132). Boston: Allyn & Bacon.

McCallum, R., & Bracken, B. (1981). Alternate form reliability of the PPVT–R for white and black preschool children. *Psychology in the Schools, 18,* 422–425.

McCarthy, D. A. (1972). *Manual of the McCarthy scales of children's abilities.* New York: The Psychological Corporation.

McCartney, K. (1984). Effect of quality of day care environment on children's language development. *Developmental Psychology, 20,* 244–260.

McCollum, J. A., & Hughes, M. (1988). Staffing patterns and team models in infancy programs. In J. Jordan, J. Gallagher, P. Hutinger, & M. Karnes (Eds.), *Early childhood special education: Birth to three.* Reston, VA: Council for Exceptional Children.

McCollum, J. A., & Thorp, E. K. (1988). Training of infant specialists: A look to the future. *Infants and Young Children, 1*(2), 55–65.

McCord, J. (1983). A forty-year perspective on effects of child abuse and neglect. *Child Abuse and Neglect, 7,* 265–270.

McCune, L. (1995). A normative study of representational play at the transition to language. *Developmental Psychology, 31*(2), 198–206.

McCune-Nicolich, L. (1981). The cognitive bases of relational words and the single word period. *Journal of Child Language, 8*, 15–34.

McCune-Nicolich, L. (1983). *A manual for analyzing free play.* New Brunswick, NJ: Douglas College, Rutgers University.

McDonough, S. C. (1993). Interaction guidance: Understanding and treating early infant–caregiver relationship disturbances. In C. Zeanah (Ed.), *Handbook of infant mental health* (pp. 414–426). New York: Guilford Press.

McEvoy, M. A., Peterson, C., & McDonnell, S. (1991). Early education: Which part of inclusion? *Impact Institute on Community Integration.* Feature issue on inclusive Education (Preschool–First grade). Vol. 4, Summer.

McGhee, R. (1993). Fluid and crystallized intelligence: Confirmatory factor analysis of the Differential Abilities Scale, Detroit Test of Learning Aptitude-3, and Woodcock-Johnson Psycho-educational Battery-Revised. *Journal of Psychoeducational Assessment, WJ-R Monograph,* 20–38.

McGoldrick, M., Pearce, J. K., & Giordano, J. (1996). *Ethnicity and family therapy* (2nd ed.). New York: Guilford Press.

McGonigel, M. J. (1991). Philosophy and conceptual framework. In M. J. McGonigel, R. K. Kaufmann, & B. H. Johnson (Eds.), *Guidelines and recommended practices for the Individualized Family Service Plan* (2nd ed., pp. 7–14). Bethesda, MD: Association for the Care of Children's Health.

McGonigel, M. J., & Garland, C. W. (1988). The Individualized Family Service Plan and the early intervention team: Team and family issues and recommended practices. *Infants and Young Children, 1*(1), 10–21.

McGonigel, M. J., Kaufmann, R. K., & Johnson, B. H. (1991). A family-centered process for the individualized family service plan. *Journal of Early Intervention, 15*(1), 46–56.

McGonigel, M. J., Woodruff, G., & Roszmann-Millican, M. (1994). The transdisciplinary team: A model for family-centered early intervention. In L. J. Johnson, R. J. Gallagher, P. L. Hutinger, & M. B. Karnes (Eds.), *Meeting early intervention challenges: Issues from birth to three* (2nd ed., pp. 95–132). Baltimore: Paul H. Brookes.

McGrew, K. S. (1997). Analysis of the major intelligence batteries according to a proposed comprehensive Gf-Gc framework. In D. P. Flanagan, J. L. Genshaft, & P. L. Harrison (Eds.), *Contemporary intellectual assessment: Theories, tests, and issues* (pp. 151–180). New York: Guilford Press.

McGrew, K. S., & Flanagan, D. P. (1996). The intelligence test desk reference (ITDR): Gf-Gc cross-battery assessment. Boston: Allyn & Bacon.

McGrew, K. S., Werder, J. K., & Woodcock, R. W. (1991). *Woodcock-Johnson Technical Manual.* Chicago: Riverside.

McGue, M., Shinn, M., & Ysseldyke, J. (1982). Use of cluster scores on the Woodcock-Johnson Psychological Battery with learning disabled students. *Learning Disability Quarterly, 5,* 274–287.

McLean, M. (1996). Procedural considerations in assessing infants and preschoolers with disabilities. In M. McLean, D. B. Bailey, & M. Wolery (Eds.), *Assessing infants and preschoolers with special needs* (second ed., pp. 46–65). Englewood Cliffs, NJ: Merrill.

McLean, M., & McCormick, K. (1993). Assessment and evaluation in early intervention. In W. Brown, S. K. Thurman, & L. F. Pearl (Eds.), *Family-centered early intervention with infants and toddlers: Innovative cross-disciplinary approaches* (pp. 43–77). Baltimore: Paul H. Brookes.

McLoughlin, J. A., & Lewis, R. B. (1990). *Assessing special students (3rd ed.).* Columbus, OH: Merrill.

McReynolds, P. (1968). *Advances in psychological assessment, Vol. 1.* Palo Alto, CA: Science and Behavior Books.

McWilliam, R. A., & Dunst, C. J. (1985). *Preschool assessment of the classroom environment.* Morganton, NC: Western Carolina Center, Family, Infant, and Preschool Program.

McWilliams, R. J., & Winton, P. J. (1990). *Brass tacks.* Chapel Hill, NC: Frank Porter Graham Child Development Center, University of North Carolina at Chapel Hill.

Meadow, K. P. (1983). *Meadow/Kendall Social-Emotional Assessment Inventory for Deaf and Hearing-Impaired Students-Preschool Form.* Washington, DC: Gallaudet University.

Mearig, J. S. (1982). Integration of school and community services for children with special needs. In C. Reynolds & T. Gutkin (Eds.), *The handbook of school psychology.* New York: Wiley.

Medway, F. J. (1979). How effective is school consultation: A review of recent research. *Journal of School Psychology, 17,* 275–282.

Meier, R. P. (1991). Language acquisition by deaf children. *American Scientist, 79*(1), 62–64.

Meisels, S. J. (1984). Prediction, prevention, and developmental screening in the EPSDT program. In H. W. Stevenson & A. E. Siegel (Eds.), *Child development research and social policy* (pp. 267–317). Chicago: University of Chicago Press.

Meisels, S. J. (1985). *Developmental screening in early childhood: A guide* (Rev. ed.). Washington, DC: National Association for the Education of Young Children.

Meisels, S. J. (1987). Uses and abuses of developmental screening and school readiness testing. *Young Children,* January, 4–9.

Meisels, S. J., Henderson, L., Marsden, D., Browning, K., & Olson, K. (1991). *Inventario para detección temprana.* Assessment Projects. University of Michigan, Ann Arbor.

Meisels, S. J., & Shonkoff, J. P. (Eds.). (1990). *Handbook of early childhood intervention.* New York: Cambridge University Press.

Meisels, S. J., & Provence, S. (Eds.). (1989). *Screening and assessment: Guidelines for identifying young disabled children and their families.* Washington, DC: National Center for Clinical Infant Programs.

Meisels, S. J., & Steele, D. (1991). *The early childhood portfolio collection process.* Ann Arbor, MI: Center for Human Growth and Development, University of Michigan.

Meisels, S. J., Wiske, M. S., & Tivnan, T. (1984). Predicting school performance with the early screening inventory. *Psychology in the Schools, 21,* 25–33.

Melaville, A. I., & Blank, M. J. (1991). *What it takes: Structuring interagency partnerships to connect children and families with comprehensive services.* Washington, DC: Education and Human Services Consortium.

Mellor, P. J., & Ohr, P. S. (1996). The assessment of culturally diverse infants and preschool children. In L. A. Suzuki, P. J. Mellor, & J. G. Ponterotto (Eds.), *Handbook of multicultural assessment: Clinical, psychological, and educational applications* (pp. 509–559). San Francisco: Jossey-Bass.

Menacker, S. J., & Batshaw, M. L. (1997). Vision: Our window to the world. In M. L. Batshaw (Ed.), *Children with disabilities* (4th ed., pp. 211–239). Baltimore: Paul H. Brookes.

Mercer, R. T. (1990). *Parents at risk.* New York: Springer.

Messick, S. (1989). Validity. In R. L. Linn (Ed.), *Educational Measurement* (pp. 13–103). Washington, DC: American Council on Education.

Messick, S. (1992). Multiple intelligences or multilevel intelligence? Selective emphasis on distinctive properties of hierarchy: On Gardner's *Frames of Mind* and Sternberg's *Beyond IQ* in the context of theory and research on the structure of human abilities. *Psychological Inquiry, 3,* 365–384.

Messick, S. (1995). Validity of psychological assessment: Validation of inferences from persons' responses and performances as scientific inquiry into score meaning. *American Psychologist, 50,* 741–749.

Meyers, A. (1994). Natural history of congenital HIV infection. *Journal of School Health, 64,* 9–10.

Michaels, D., & Levine, C. (1992). Estimates of the number of motherless youth orphaned by AIDS in the United States. *Journal of the American Medical Association, 268,* 3456–3461.

Michaud, L., Duhaime, A., & Lazar, M. F. (1997). Traumatic brain injury. In M. L. Batshaw (Ed.), *Children with disabilities* (4th ed., pp. 595–617). Baltimore: Paul H. Brookes.

Miki, Y., Taguchi, T., Ueno, K., & Ochi, K. (1973). *Examiner's manual for Japanese ITPA (Illinois Test of Psycholinguistic Abilities).* Tokyo, Japan: Nihonbunkakagakusha.

Miller, J. F. (1981). *Assessing language production in children: Experimental procedures.* Baltimore: University Park Press.

Miller, L. J. (1988). *Miller Assessment for Preschoolers.* San Antonio, TX: The Psychological Corporation.

Miller, R. (1996). *The developmentally appropriate inclusive classroom in early childhood education.* Albany, NY: Delmar.

Molfese, V., Yaple, K., Helwig, S., Harris, L., & Connell, S. (1992). Stanford–Binet Intelligence Scale (4th ed.): Factor structure and verbal subscale scores for three-year-olds. *Journal of Psychoeducational Assessment, 10,* 47–58.

Montes, F., & Risley, T. R. (1975). Evaluating traditional day care practice: An empirical approach. *Child Care Quarterly, 4,* 208–215.

Moog, J., & Geers, A. (1975). *Scales of Early Communication Skills for Hearing-Impaired Children.* St. Louis, MO: Central Institute for the Deaf.

Moog, J., & Geers, A. (1979). *Grammatical analysis of elicited language: Simple sentence level.* St. Louis, MO: Central Institute for the Deaf.

Moog, J., & Geers, A. (1980). *Grammatical Analysis of Elicited Language: Complex Sentence Level.* St. Louis, MO: Central Institute for the Deaf.

Moog, J., Kozak, V., & Geers, A. (1983). *The Grammatical Analysis of Elicited Language: Pre-Sentence Level.* St. Louis, MO: Central Institute for the Deaf.

Moog, J., & Lane, H. (1984). *Central Institute for the Deaf Preschool Performance Scale.* Chicago: Stoelting.

Moore, G. T. (1987). The physical environment and cognitive development in child-care centers. In C. S. Weinstein & T. G. David (Eds.), *Spaces for children: The built environment and child development* (pp. 41–72). New York: Plenum Press.

Moore, H. B. (1983). Person-centered approaches. In H. T. Prout & D. T. Brown (Eds.), *Counseling and psychotherapy with children and adolescents* (pp. 225–286). Tampa, FL: Mariner Press.

Moores, D. F. (1996). *Educating the deaf: Psychology, principles, and practices.* Boston: Houghton Mifflin.

Moos, R. L., & Moos, B. S. (1981). *Family Environment Scale Manual.* Palo Alto, CA: Consulting Psychologists Press.

Morgan, G. A., Harmon, R. J., & Bennett, C. A. (1976). A system for coding and scoring infants' spontaneous play with objects. *JSAS Catalog of Selected Documents in Psychology, 6*(105), (Ms. No. 1355).

Motti, F., Cichetti, D., & Sroufe, L. A. (1983). From infant affect expression to symbolic play: The coherence of development in Down Syndrome children. *Child Development, 54,* 1168–1175.

Mulford, R. (1988). First words of the blind child. In M. D. Smith & J. L. Locke (Eds.), *The emergent lexicon: The child's development of a linguistic vocabulary* (pp. 293–338). San Diego, CA: Academic Press.

Mullen, E. M. (1995). *Mullen Scales of Early Learning.* Circle Pines, MN: American Guidance Service.

Mullen, Y., & Spragins, A. (1998, April). *Deaf children and schools: Choosing and using appropriate assessment instruments.* Paper presented at National Association of School Psychologists Convention, Orlando, FL.

Musick, J. (1993). *Poor, hungry, and pregnant: The psychology of high-risk adolescence.* New Haven, CT: Yale University Press.

Myers, C. L., McBride, S. L., & Peterson, C. A. (1996). Transdisciplinary, play-based assessment in early childhood special education: An examination of social validity. *Topics in Early Childhood, 16,* 102–126.

NAEYC. (1988). Position statement on standardized testing of young children 3 through 8 years of age: Adopted November 1987. *Young Children, 43,* 42–47.

Naglieri, J. A., & Yazzie, C. (1984). Comparison of the WISC-R and PPVT-R with Navajo children. *Journal of Clinical Psychology, 39,* 598–600.

Najman, J., Dor, W., Morrison, J., Andersen, M., & Williams, G. (1992). Child developmental delay and socioeconomic disadvantage in Australia: A longitudinal study. *Journal of Scientific Medicine, 34,* 829–835.

National Association of School Psychologists (1992). *Principles for Professional Ethics.* Washington, DC: Author.

National Center for Children in Poverty (1990). *Five million children.* New York: Author.

National Center for Education Statistics. (1993). *Public school kindergarten teachers' views on children's readiness for school.* Washington, DC: U.S. Department of Education.

National Center on Child Abuse and Neglect (NCCAN). (1988). *Study findings: Study of national incidence and prevalence of child abuse and neglect* (DHSS Publication No. OHPS). Washington, DC: Government Printing Office.

Needleman, H. L., Schell, A., Bellinger, D., Leviton, A., & Allread, E. N. (1990). The long-term effects of exposure to low doses of lead in childhood: An 11-year follow-up report. *The New England Journal of Medicine, 322*(2), 83–88.

Neisworth, J., & Bagnato, S. (1988). Assessment in early childhood special education: A typology of dependent measures. In S. Odom & M. Karnes (Eds.), *Early intervention for infants and children with handicaps: An empirical base* (pp. 23–49). Baltimore: Paul H. Brookes.

Neisworth, J. T., & Bagnato, S. J. (1986). Curriculum-based developmental assessment: Congruence of testing and teaching. *School Psychology Review, 15,* 180–199.

Neisworth, J. T., & Bagnato, S. J. (1992). The case against intelligence testing in early childhood. *Topics in Early Childhood Special Education, 12*(1), 1–20.

Nellis, L., & Gridley, B. E. (1994). Reviews of the Bayley Scales of Infant Development-Second Edition. *Journal of School Psychology, 32,* 201–209.

Nelson, K. (1973). Some evidence for the cognitive primacy of categorization and its functional basis. *Merrill-Palmer Quarterly, 19,* 21–39.

Nelson, K. A., & Dimitrova, E. (1993). Severe visual impairment in the United States and in each state, 1990. *Journal of Visual Impairment and Blindness, 87,* 80–85.

Newborg, J., Stock, J. R., Wnek, L., Guidubaldi, J., & Svinicki, J. (1984). *Battelle Developmental Inventory (BDI)*. Allen, TX: DLM Teaching Resources.

Newland, T. E. (1971). Psychological assessment of exceptional children and youth. In W. Cruickshank (Ed.), *Psychology of exceptional children and youth* (pp. 115–172). Englewood Cliffs, NJ: Prentice-Hall.

Newman, B. M., & Newman, P. R. (1995). *Development through life: A psychosocial approach* (6th ed.). Pacific Grove, CA: Brooks/Cole.

Newson, E., & Head, E. (1979). Play and play-things for handicapped children. In E. Newson & J. Newson (Eds.), *Toys and play things in development and remediation*. New York: Penguin Books.

Ney, Tara (Ed.). (1995). *True and false allegations of child sexual abuse: Assessment & case management*. New York: Brunner/Mazel.

NICHCY News Digest (1991). Children with disabilities: Understanding sibling issues. *National Information Center for Children and Youth with Handicaps, 11,* 1–10.

Nicolich, L. (1977). Beyond sensorimotor intelligence: Assessment of symbolic maturity through analysis of pretend play. *Merrill-Palmer Quarterly, 23,* 89–99.

Nihira, K., Foster, R., Shellhaas, M., & Leland, H. (1974). *AAMD Adaptive Behavior Scale* (Rev. ed.). Washington, DC: American Association on Mental Deficiency.

Northern, J. L., & Downs, M. P. (1991). *Hearing in children*. Baltimore: Williams & Wilkins.

Nurss, J. (1980). Linguistic awareness and learning to read. *Young Children, 35,* 57–66.

Nurss, J., & McGauvran, M. (1986). *Metropolitan Readiness Assessment Program*. San Antonio, TX: The Psychological Corporation.

Nuttall, E. V. (1997). *Pre-testing activities*. Revised unpublished manuscript.

Nuttall, E. V., DeLeon, B., & Valle, M. (1990). Best practices in considering cultural factors. In A. Thomas & J. Grimes (Eds.), *Best practices in school psychology-II,* (pp. 221–233). Washington, DC: National Association of School Psychologists.

Nuttall, E. V., & Ivey, A. E. (1986). The diagnostic interview process. In H. M. Knoff (Ed.), *The assessment of child and adolescent personality* (pp. 195–140). NY: Guilford Press.

Nuttall, E. V., Landurand, P. M., & Goldman, P. (Eds.). (1984). A critical look at testing and evaluation from a cross-cultural perspective. In P. C. Chinn (Ed.), *Education of culturally and linguistically different exceptional children* (pp. 42–62). Reston, VA: Council for Exceptional Children.

Oakland, T., & Matuszek, P. (1977). Using tests in nondiscriminatory assessment. In T. Oakland (Ed.), *Psychological and educational assessment of minority children* (pp. 52–68). New York: Brunner/Mazel.

Odom, S. L., McConnell, S. R., & McEvoy, M. A. (1992). *Social competence of young children with disabilities: Issues and strategies for intervention*. Baltimore: Paul H. Brookes.

Odom, S. L., Strain, P. S., Karger, M. A., & Smith, J. D. (1986). Using single and multiple peers to promote social interaction of preschool children with handicaps. *Journal of the Division for Early Childhood, 10,* 53–64.

Office of Research. (1993). *Review of research on achieving the nation's readiness goal*. Washington, DC: U. S. Department of Education.

Olds, A. R. (1979). Designing developmentally optimal classrooms for children with special needs. In S. J. Meisels (Ed.), *Special education and development: Perspectives on young children with special needs*. Baltimore: University Park.

Olds, A. R. (1987). Designing settings for infants and toddlers. In C. S. Weinstein & T. G. David (Eds.), *Spaces for children: The built environment and child development* (pp. 91–138). Baltimore: University Park.

Oller, D. (1978). Infant vocalization and the development of speech. *Allied Health and Behavior Sciences, 1,* 523–549.

Orelove, F. P., & Sobsey, D. (1991). *Educating children with multiple disabilities: A transdisciplinary approach* (2nd ed.). Baltimore: Paul H. Brookes.

Ornstein, P. A., Gordon, B. N., & Larus, D. M. (1992). Children's memory for a personally experienced event: Implications for testimony. *Applied Cognitive Psychology, 6,* 49–60.

Ornstein, P. A., Larus, D. M., & Clubb, P. A. (1991). Understanding children's testimony: Implications of research on the development of memory. In R. Vasta (Ed.), *Annals of child development* (Vol. 8, pp. 145–176). London, England: Kingsley.

Owens, R. E. (1992). *Language development: An introduction*. New York: Merrill/Macmillan.

Owens, R. E. (1995). *Language development: An introduction* (4th ed.). Boston: Allyn & Bacon.

Ownby, R. L., & Carmin, C. N. (1988). Confirmatory factor analysis of the Stanford–Binet Intelligence Scale—Fourth Edition. *Journal of Psychoeducational Assessment, 6,* 331–340.

Overcast, T., Sales, B., & Sacken, D. M. (1990). The legal rights of students in the elementary and secondary schools. In C. Reynolds & T. Gutkin (Eds.), *Handbook of school psychology* (2nd ed.). New York: Wiley.

Paget, K. D. (1983). The individual examining situation: Basic considerations for preschool-age children. In B. A. Bracken (Ed.), *The psychological assessment of preschool children* (pp. 51–61). Boston: Allyn & Bacon.

Paget, K. D. (1985). Preschool services in the schools: Issues and implications. *Special Services in the Schools, 2*(1) 3–25.

Paget, K. D. (1991). The individual examining situation: Basic considerations for preschool-age children. In B. A. Bracken (Ed.), *The psychoeducational assessment of preschool children* (pp. 32–39). Boston: Allyn & Bacon.

Paget, K., & Nagle, R. (1986). A conceptual model of preschool assessment. *School Psychology Review, 15*(2), 154–165.

Palfrey, J. S., Fenton, T., Lavin, A. T., Porter, S. M., Shaw, D. M., Weill, K. S., & Crocker, A. C. (1994). Schoolchildren with HIV infection: A survey of the nation's largest school districts. *Journal of School Health, 64,* 22–26.

Palmer, J. O. (1970). *The psychological assessment of children.* New York: Wiley.

Parten, M. (1932). Social participation among preschool children. *Journal of Abnormal and Social Psychology, 27,* 243–269.

Patton, J., Beirne-Smith, M., & Payne, J. (1990). *Mental retardation* (3rd ed.). Columbus, OH: Merrill.

Pellegrino, L. (1997). Cerebral palsy. In M. L. Batshaw (Ed.), *Children with disabilities* (4th ed., pp. 499–528). Baltimore: Paul H. Brookes.

Pena, P., Quinn, R., & Iglesias, A. (1993). The application of dynamic methods to language assessment: A nonbiased procedure. *Journal of Special Education, 26*(3), 269–280.

Pendergast, K., Dickey, S., & Selman, J. W. (1969). *Photo Articulation Test.* Danville, IL: Interstate.

Pennsylvania Department of Education. (1992). *Pennsylvania early intervention guidelines.* Harrisburg, PA: Author.

Perlmutter, M., & Myers, N. A. (1975). Young children's coding and storage of visual and verbal material. *Child Development, 46,* 215–219.

Perlmutter, M., & Ricks, M. (1979). Recall in preschool children. *Journal of Experimental Child Psychology, 27,* 423–436.

Perry, D. G., & Bussey, K. (1984). *Social development.* Englewood Cliffs, NJ: Prentice-Hall.

Peters, J. (1976). Children who are victims of sexual assault and the psychology of offenders. *American Journal of Psychotherapy, 30,* 398–421.

Peterson, D. R. (1968). *The clinical study of social behavior.* New York: Appleton-Century-Crofts.

Peterson, N. L. (1987). *Early intervention for handicapped and at-risk children: An introduction to early childhood-special education.* Denver, CO: Love.

Phelps, L., & Cox, D. (1993). Children with prenatal cocaine exposure: Resilient or handicapped? *School Psychology Review, 22,* 710–724.

Piaget, J. (1948). *The moral judgment of the child.* Glencoe, IL: Free Press.

Piaget, J. (1979). Piaget's theory. In P. H. Mussen (Ed.), *Carmichael's manual of child psychology: Vol. 1* (3rd ed., pp. 703–732). New York: Wiley.

Piaget, J. (1983). Piaget's theory. In P. H. Mussen (Ed.), *Handbook of child psychology* (4th ed., pp. 103–128). New York: Wiley.

Piaget, J., & Inhelder, B. (1969). *The psychology of the child.* New York: Basic Books.

Piaget, K., & Nagle, R. (1986). A conceptual model of preschool assessment. *School Psychology Review, 15*(2), 154–165.

Pianta, R. C., & Reeve, R. E. (Eds.). (1993). Preschool screening of ethnic minority children and children of poverty: Issues for practice and research. In A. Barona & E. E. Garcia (Eds.), *Children at risk: Poverty, minority status, and other issues in educational equity* (pp. 259–268). Silver Spring, MD: National Association of School Psychology.

Pillemer, D. B., Picariello, M. L., & Pruett, J. C. (1994). Very long term memories of a salient event. *Applied Cognitive Psychology, 8,* 95–106.

P.L. 94-142, The Education of All Handicapped Children's Act. *Federal Register,* November 29, 1975.

P.L. 99-457, The Amendments to the Education for All Handicapped Children's Act. *Federal Register,* October 8, 1986.

P.L. 101-476, Individuals with Disabilities Education Act (IDEA). *Federal Register,* 1992.

P.L. 102-119, The amendment to P.L. 94-142, The Individuals with Disabilities Education Act (IDEA). *Federal Register,* 1991.

Plenk, A. M., Hinchey, F. S., & Davies, M. U. (1985). *Plenk Storytelling Test.* Salt Lake City, UT: The Children's Center.

Pogrund, R. L., Fazzi, D. L., & Lampert, J. S. (Eds.). (1992). *Early focus: Working with young blind and visually impaired children and their families.* New York: American Foundation for the Blind.

Pope-Edwards, C. (in press). Development in the preschool years: The typical path. In E. V. Nuttall, I. Romero., & J. Kalesnik (Eds.), *Assessing and screening preschoolers* (2nd ed.). Boston, MA: Allyn & Bacon.

Powell, T., & Gallagher, P. A. (Eds.). (1993). *Brothers and sisters: A special part of exceptional families* (2nd ed.). Baltimore: Paul H. Brookes.

Prasse, D. (1983). Legal issues underlying preschool assessment. In K. Paget & B. Bracken (Eds.), *The psychoeducational assessment of preschool children* (pp. 29–50). New York: Grune & Stratton.

Preator, K. K., & McAllistor, J. R. (1995). Best practices assessing infants and toddlers. In A. Thomas & J. Grimes (Eds.), *Best practices in school psychology III* (pp. 775–788). Washington, DC: National Association of School Psychologists.

Provence, S., & Naylor, A. (Eds.). (1983). *Working with disadvantaged parents and their children: Scientific issues and practice.* New Haven, CT: Yale University Press.

Pryor, J. B., & Reeder, G. D. (1993). Collective and individual representations of HIV/AIDS stigma. In J. B. Pryor & G. D. Reeder (Eds.), *The social psychology of HIV infection* (pp. 263–286). Hillsdale, NJ: Erlbaum.

Psychological Corporation (1989). *WPPSI-R: A technical report* (Vol. 1, No. 1). San Antonio, TX: Harcourt, Brace, Jovanovich.

Pugmire-Stoy, M. C. (1992). *Spontaneous play in early childhood.* Albany, NY: Delmar.

Pynoos, R. S., & Eth, S. (1984). The child as witness to homicide. *Journal of Social Issues, 40,* 87–108.

Rapin, I. (1996). Practitioner review: Developmental language disorder: A clinical update. *Journal of Child Psychology & Psychiatry, 37*(6), 643–655.

Ratcliff, K. J., & Ratcliff, M. W. (1979). The Leiter scales: A review of validity findings. *American Annals of the Deaf, 124,* 38–45.

Ray, S., & Ulissi, S. M. (1982). *An adaptation of the Wechsler Preschool and Primary Scale of Intelligence for Deaf Children.* Northridge, CA: Steven Ray.

Reavis, D. (1990). *Assessing students with multiple disabilities: Practical guidelines for practitioners.* Springfield, IL: Charles C. Thomas.

Reid, K. D., Hresko, W. P., & Hammill, D. (1989). *Test of Early Reading Ability-II.* Austin, TX: Pro-Ed.

Research and Policy Committee of the Committee for Economic Development (1987). *Children in need: Investment strategies for the educationally disadvantaged.* New York: Author.

Restall, G., & Magill-Evans, J. (1994). Play and preschool children with autism. *The American Journal of Occupational Therapy, 49*(2), 113–120.

Rettig, M. (1994). The play of young children with visual impairments: Characteristics and interventions. *Journal of Visual Impairment and Blindness, 88,* 410–420.

Rey-Casserly, C. (1982). *Neuropsychological status of low birth weight children at preschool age.* Unpublished doctoral dissertation. Boston University, Boston, MA.

Reynell, J., & Zinkin, P. (1980). *Reynell-Zinkin Scales.* Chicago, IL: Stoelting.

Reynolds, C. R., & Clark, J. (1983). Assessment of cognitive abilities. In K. Paget & B. Bracken (Eds.), *The psychoeducational assessment of preschool children* (pp. 163–190). New York: Grune & Stratton.

Reynolds, C. R., & Kamphaus, R. W. (Eds.). (1990). *Handbook of psychological and educational assessment of children: Intelligence and achievement.* New York: Guilford Press.

Reynolds, C. R., Kamphaus, R. W., & Rosenthal, B. (1988). Factor analysis of the Stanford–Binet—Fourth Edition for ages 2 through 23. *Measurement and Evaluation in Counseling and Development, 21,* 52–63.

Rice, F. P. (1992). *Human development: A life-span approach.* New York: Macmillan.

Ricks, D., & Wing, L. (1975). Language, communication, and the use of symbols in normal autistic children. *Journal of Autism and Childhood Schizophrenia, 5*(3), 191–221.

Risser, A. H., & Edgell, D. (1988). Neuropsychology of the developing brain: Implications for neuropsychological assessment. In M. G. Tramontana & S. R. Hooper (Eds.), *Assessment issues in child neuropsychology* (pp. 41–65). New York: Plenum Press.

Rock, S. L., Head, S. N., Bradley, R. H., Whiteside, B. L., & Brisby, J. (1994). Use of the HOME inventory with families of young visually impaired children. *Journal of Visual Impairment and Blindness, 88,* 140–151.

Rogers, S. (1977). Characteristics of the cognitive development of profoundly retarded children. *Child Development, 48,* 837–843.

Rogers, S. J. (1982). Assessment of cognitive development in the preschool years. In G. Ulrey & S. Rogers (Eds.), *Psychological assessment of handicapped infants and young children* (pp. 45–53). New York: Thieme-Stratton.

Rogers, S. J. (1982). Cognitive characteristics of handicapped children's play. In R. Pelz (Ed.), *Developmental and clinical aspects of young children's play.* Mammoth, OR: Westar series paper, No. 17.

Rogers, S. J. (1986). *Play observation scale.* Unpublished document. Denver, CO: University of Colorado Health Sciences Center.

Rogers, S. J., & Puchalski, C. B. (1984). Social characteristics of visually impaired infants' play. *Topics in Early Childhood Education, 3,* 52–56.

Rogers-Warren, A. K. (1982). Behavioral ecology in classrooms for young, handicapped children. *Topics in Early Childhood Special Education, 2,* 21–32.

Rogoff, B., & Chavajay, P. (1995). What's become of research on the cultural basis of cognitive development? *American Psychologist, 50,* 859–877.

Roid, G. H., & Miller, L. J. (1997). *Leiter International Performance Scale-Revised.* Chicago: Stoelting.

Roizen, N. J. (1997). Down syndrome. In M. L. Batshaw (Ed.), *Children with disabilities* (4th ed., pp. 183–210). Baltimore: Paul H. Brookes.

Rosenkoetter, S. E., & Wanska, S. K. (1992). *Best practice in preschool screening.* Paper presented at the annual convention of the Council for Exceptional Children, Baltimore.

Rosenshine, B. (1977). Review of teaching variables and student achievement. In G. D. Borich (Ed.), *The appraisal of teaching: Concepts and process* (pp. 114–120). Reading, MA: Addison-Wesley.

Ross, M. (1989). Implications of delay in detection and management of deafness. *The Volta Review, 92*(2), 69–80.

Ross, S., & Tobin, M. J. (1997). Object permanence, reaching, & locomotion in infants who are blind. *Journal of Visual Impairment and Blindness, 91,* 25–32.

Roth, M., McCaul, E., & Barnes, K. (Eds.). (1993). Who becomes an "at-risk" student? The predictive value of a kindergarten screening battery. *Exceptional Children, 59* (4), 348–358.

Rubenstein, J., & Howes, C. (1976). The effects of peers on toddler interactions with mothers and toys. *Child Development, 47,* 597–605.

Rubin, K. N., Fein, G. G., & Vandenberg, B. (1983). Play. In E. M. Hetherington (Ed.) & P. H. Mussen (Series Ed.), *Handbook of child psychology: Socialization, personality, and social development* (Vol. 4, pp. 698–774). New York: Wiley.

Rurstein, R. M., Conlon, C. J., & Batshaw, M. L. (1997). HIV and AIDS: From mother to children. In M. L. Batshaw (Ed.), *Children with disabilities* (4th ed., pp. 163–183). Baltimore: Paul H. Brookes.

Sackett, G. P. (1978). Measurement in observational research. In G. P. Sackett (Ed.), *Observing behavior: Volume II: Data collection and analysis methods* (pp. 25–43). Baltimore: University Park Press.

Safer, N. D., & Hamilton, J. L. (1993). Legislative context for early intervention services. In W. Brown, S. K. Thurman, & L. F. Pearl (Eds.), *Family-centered early intervention* with infants and toddlers: Innovative cross-disciplinary approaches (pp. 1–20). Baltimore: Paul H. Brookes.

Salvia, J., & Ysseldyke, J. E. (1991). Assessment (5th ed.). Boston: Houghton Mifflin.

Salvia, J., & Ysseldyke, J. E. (1995). Assessment (6th ed.). Boston, MA: Houghton Mifflin.

Sameroff, A. J. (1986). Environmental context of child development. Journal of Pediatrics, 109, 192–200.

Sandall, S. R. (1993). Curricula for early intervention. In W. Brown, S. K. Thurman, & L. F. Pearl (Eds.), Family-centered early intervention with infants and toddlers: Innovative cross-disciplinary approaches. (pp. 129–172). Baltimore: Paul H. Brookes.

Sandoval, J., & Davis, J. M. (1984). A school-based mental health consultation curriculum. Journal of School Psychology, 22, 31–43.

Sanford, A. R., & Zelman, J. G. (1995). Learning Accomplishment Profile (Rev. ed.). Winston-Salem, NC: Kaplan Press.

Santa Cruz County (1987). Help for Special Preschoolers Assessment Checklist: Ages 3–6. Santa Cruz, CA: Author.

Sattler, J. M. (1992). Assessment of children (3rd ed.-Revised). San Diego, CA: Author.

Sattler, J. M. (1998). Clinical and forensic interviewing of children and families. San Diego, CA: Author.

Saywitz, K. J., Nathanson, R., & Snyder, L. (1993). Credibility of child witnesses: The role of communicative competence. Topics in Language Disorders, 13, 59–78.

Scarborough, H. (1990). Very early language deficits in dyslexic children. Child Development, 61.

Schafer, D. S., & Moersch, M. S. (Eds.). (1981a). Developmental programming for infants and young children. Ann Arbor, MI: The University of Michigan Press.

Schickedanz, J. A. (1986). More than the abc's: The early stages of reading and writing. Washington, DC: National Association for the Education of Young Children.

Schildroth, A. N. (1986). Hearing-impaired children under age 6: 1977 & 1984. American Annals of the Deaf, 131(2), 85–90.

Schildroth, A. N., Rawlings, B. W., & Allen, T. E. (1989). Hearing-impaired children under age 6: A demographic analysis. American Annals of the Deaf, 134(2) 63–69.

Schmuck, R. A. (1990). Organizational development in the schools: Contemporary concepts and practices. In T. B. Gutkin & C. R. Reynolds (Eds.), The handbook of school psychology (pp. 899–919). New York: Wiley.

Schneider, W., & Pressley, M. (1989). Memory development between 2 and 20. New York: Springer-Verlag.

Schopler, E., Reichler, R. J., & Renner, B. R. (1988). The Childhood Autism Rating Scale. Los Angeles: Western Psychological Services.

Schreibman, L., Koegel, L., & Koegel, R. (1989). Autism. In M. Hersen (Ed.), Innovations in child behavior therapy (pp. 395–428). New York: Springer.

Schwartz, S. (Ed.) (1987). Choices in deafness: A parent's guide. Kensington, MD: Woodbine House.

Schweinhart, L. J., & Weikart, D. P. (Eds.). (1981). Effects of the Perry Preschool Program on youth through age 15. Early Childhood, 4, 29–39.

Seidel, J. F. (1991) The development of a comprehensive pediatric HIV developmental service program. In A. Rudigier (Ed.), Technical report on developmental disabilities and HIV infection. (No. 7, pp. 1–4). Silver Spring, MD: American Association of University Affiliated Programs.

Semrud-Clikeman, M., & Hynd, G. W. (1993). Assessment of learning and cognitive dysfunction in young children. In J. L. Culbertson & D. J. Willis (Eds.), Testing young children: A reference guide for developmental, psychoeducational and psychosocial assessments (pp. 167–191). Austin, TX: Pro-Ed.

Sewell, T. (1979). Intelligence and learning tasks as predictors of scholastic achievement in black and white first-grade children. Journal of School Psychology, 17, 325–332.

Seymour, H. N. (1986). Clinical intervention for language disorders among nonstandard speakers of English. In O. L. Taylor (Ed.), Treatment of communication disorders in culturally and linguistically diverse populations (pp.135–153). San Diego, CA: College Hill Press.

Seymour, H. N., & Seymour, C. M. (1981). Black English and standard American English contrast in consonantal development for four- and five-year-old children, Journal of Speech and Hearing Disorders, 46(3), 276–280.

Shepard, L. A. (1994). The challenges of assessing young children appropriately. Phi Delta Kappan, 76(3), 206–212.

Shonkoff, J., & Marshall, P. (1990). Biological bases of developmental dysfunction. In S. Meisels & J. Shonkoff (Eds.), Handbook of early childhood intervention (pp. 35–52). New York: Cambridge University Press.

Shonkoff, J. P., & Meisels, S. J. (1990). Early childhood intervention: The evolution of a concept. In S. J. Meisels & J. P. Shonkoff (Eds.), Handbook of early childhood intervention (pp. 3–31). New York: Cambridge University Press.

Short-DeGraff, M. A. (1988). Human development for occupational and physical therapists. Baltimore: Williams & Wilkins.

Sidun, N. M., & Chase, D. A. (1986). Human Figure Drawing (H-F-D) coding manual and coding sheet. Unpublished manuscript.

Sigelman, C. K., & Shaffer, D. R. (1994). Life-span human development. Pacific Grove, CA: Brooks/Cole.

Sigman, M., & Mundy, P. (1987). Symbolic processes in young autistic children. In D. Cicchetti & M. Beeghly (Eds.), New directions for child development: No. 36. Symbolic development in atypical children (pp. 31–46). San Francisco: Jossey-Bass.

Sigman, M., & Ungerer, J. (1984). Cognitive and language skills in autistic, mentally retarded, and normal children. Developmental Psychology, 20(2), 293–302.

Silverstein, J. (1989). Fostering parent-professional involvement in special education: A role for school psychology educators. Trainer's Forum, 9(2), 4–7.

Simeonsson, R. J. (1979). Carolina Record of Individual Behavior. Chapel Hill, NC: University of North Carolina at Chapel Hill, Frank Porter Graham Child Development Center.

Simeonsson, R. J. (1986). Psychological and developmental assessment of special children. Boston: Allyn & Bacon.

Singer, L., Farkas, K., & Kliegman, R. (1992). Childhood medical and behavioral consequences of maternal cocaine use. Journal of Pediatric Psychology, 17, 389–406.

Simpson, P. (1990). *Living in poverty: Coping on the welfare grant.* New York: Community Service Society.

Sinnett, E. R., Rogg, K. L., Benton, S. L., Downey, R. G., & Whitfill J. M. (1993). The Woodcock-Johnson Revised— Its factor structure. *Educational and Psychological Measurement, 53,* 763–769.

Skellenger, A. C., & Hill, E. W. (1991). Current practices and considerations regarding long care instruction with preschool children. *Journal of Visual Impairment and Blindness, 85,* 101–104.

Slobin, D. (Ed.). (1982). *The cross-cultural study of language acquisition.* Hillsdale, NJ: Erlbaum.

Slosson, R. L. (1991). *Slosson Intelligence Test (SIT-R).* East Aurora, NY: Slosson Educational Publications.

Smilansky, S. (1990). Sociodramatic play: Its relevance to behavior and achievement in school. In E. Klugman and S. Smilansky (Eds.), *Children's play and learning: Perspectives and policy implications* (pp. 18–42). New York: Teacher's College Press.

Smith, A. J., & Johnson, R. E. (1977). *Smith-Johnson Nonverbal Performance Scale.* Los Angeles: Western Psychological Services.

Smith, D. K., & Lyon, M. A. (1987). *K-ABC/McCarthy performance for repeating and non-repeating preschoolers.* Paper presented at the meeting of the National Association of School Psychologists, New Orleans, LA.

Smith, L., Ulvind, S. E., & Lindemann, R. (1994). Very low birth weight infants at double risk. *Developmental and Behavioral Pediatrics, 15,* 7–13.

Smith, P. K. (1977). Social and fantasy play in young children. In B. Tizard & D. Harvey (Eds.), *Biology of Play* (pp. 123–145). Philadelphia: Lippincott.

Smith, P. M. (1993). You are not alone: For parents when they learn that their child has a disability. *NICHCY News Digest, 3*(1), 1–4.

Snow, J. H., & Hooper, S. R. (1994). *Pediatric traumatic brain injury.* Thousand Oaks, CA: Sage.

Snow, R. W. (1986). Individual differences and the design of educational programs. *American Psychologist, 41,* 1029–1039.

Snyder, P., Bailey, D. B., & Auer, C. (1994). Preschool eligibility determination for children with known or suspected learning disabilities under IDEA. *Journal of Early Intervention, 18*(4), 380–390.

Sparrow, S., Balla, D., & Cicchetti, D. (1984). *Vineland Adaptive Behavior Scales.* Circle Pines, MN: American Guidance Service.

Spiegal, L., & Mayers, A. (1991). Psychosocial aspects of AIDS in children and adolescents. *Pediatric Clinics of North America, 38,* 153–167.

Spitz, R. (1946). Anaclitic depression: An inquiry into the genesis of psychiatric conditions in early childhood. *Psychoanalytic study of the child, 2,* 53–74.

Spragins, A. B., & Blennerhassett, L. (1989). *Intellectual, adaptive behavior, social-emotional, developmental/criterion-based, language and basic concept assessment instruments used with preschool deaf children.* Materials presented at the National Association of School Psychologists Convention, Boston, MA.

Spragins, A. B., Blennerhassett, L., & Mullen, Y. (1998). *Reviews of four types of assessment instruments used with deaf and hard of hearing students.* Materials presented at the National Association of School Psychologists Convention, Orlando, FL.

Spungin, S. J. (Ed.). (1981). *Guidelines for public school programs serving visually handicapped children* (2nd ed.). New York: American Foundation for the Blind.

Squires, J. K., Nickel, R., & Bricker, D. (1990). Use of parent-completed developmental questionnaires for child-find and screening. *Infants and Young Children, 3*(2), 46–57.

Stacey, K. (1994). Contextual assessment of young children: Moving from the strange to the familiar and from theory to practice. *Child language teaching and therapy, 10*(2), 179–198.

Stanovitch, K. E. (1994). Constructivism in reading education. *The Journal of Special Education, 28,* 259–274.

Stark, R. (1979). Prespeech segmental feature development. In P. Fletcher & M. Garman (Eds.), *Language acquisition* (pp. 15–32). Cambridge, England: Cambridge University Press.

Stein, M. A., Szomowski, E., Blondis, T. A., & Roizen, N. J. (1995). Adaptive skills dysfunction in ADD and ADHD children. *Journal of Child Psychology and Psychiatry, 36*(4), 663–670.

Steinberg, A. G., & Knightly, C. A. (1995). Hearing: Sounds and silences. In M. L. Batshaw (Ed.), *Children with disabilities* (4h ed., pp. 241–274). Baltimore: Paul H. Brookes.

Stephens, B., Smith, R. E., Fitzgerald, J. R., Grobe, C., Hitt, J., & Daly, M. (1977). *Training manual for teachers of the visually impaired.* Richardson, TX: University of Texas at Dallas.

Sternberg, L. (1994). Individuals with profound disabilities: Definitions, characteristics and conceptual framework (pp. 3–20). In L. Sternberg (Ed.), *Individuals with profound disabilities: Instructional and assistive strategies.* Austin, TX: Pro-Ed.

Sternberg, R. J. (1984). Evaluation of the Kaufman Assessment Battery for children from an information-processing perspective. *Journal of Special Education, 18,* 269–280.

Sternberg, R. J. (1985). *Beyond IQ: A triarchic theory of human intelligence.* New York: Cambridge University Press.

Sternberg, R. J. (1997). The triarchic theory of intelligence. In D. P. Flanagan, J. L. Genshaft, & P. L. Harrison (Eds.), *Contemporary intellectual assessment: Theories, tests, and issues* (pp. 92–104). New York: Guilford Press.

Stillman, R. (1978). *The Callier-Azusa Scale.* Dallas, TX: University of Texas, Callier Center for Communication Disorders.

Stixrud, W. R. (1982). *Plaintalk about early education and development.* Minneapolis, MN: University of Minnesota, College of Education, Center for Early Education and Development.

Stockman, I. J., & Settle, S. (1991, November). *Initial consonants in young Black children's conversational speech.* Poster session presented at the annual convention of the American Speech-Language-Hearing Association, Atlanta, GA.

Stockman, I. J., & Vaughn-Cooke, F. B. (1982). Semantic categories in the language of working class Black children. In C. Johnson & C. Thew (Eds.), *Proceedings from the second international child language conference* (Vol. 1, pp. 312–327). Washington, DC: University Press of America.

Stone, B. J. (1992). Joint confirmatory factor analyses of the DAS and the WISC-R. *Journal of School Psychology, 30,* 185–195.

Stone, B. J., Gridley, B. E., & Gyurke, J. S. (1991). Confirmatory factor analysis of the WPPSI-R at the extreme end of the age range. *Journal of Psychoeducational Assessment, 9,* 263–270.

Stone, B. J., Gridley, B., & Treloar, J. (Eds.). (1992). Validation of a battery of preschool screening tests for predicting special education placement. *Diagnostique, 17*(4), 289–297.

Stoneman, Z., & Gibson, S. (Eds.). (1978). Situational influences on assessment performances of developmentally disabled preschool children. *Exceptional Children, 45,* 166–171.

Strain, P. (1985). Social and nonsocial determinants of acceptability in handicapped preschool children. *Topics in Early Childhood Special Education, 4*(4), 47–58.

Streissguth, A. P., Barr, H. M., Sampson, P. D., Darby, B. L., & Martin, D. C. (1989). IQ at age four in relation to maternal alcohol use and smoking during pregnancy. *Developmental Psychology, 25,* 3–11.

Streissguth, A. P., Grant, T. M., Barr, H. M., Brown, Z. A., Martin, J. C., Mayock, D. E., Ramey, S. L., & Moore, L. (1991). Cocaine and the use of alcohol and other drugs during pregnancy. *American Journal of Obstetrics and Gynecology, 164,* 1239–1243.

Strunk, W., & White, E. (1979). *The elements of style.* New York: Macmillan.

Stutsman, R. (1931). *Merrill-Palmer Scale of Mental Tests.* Chicago: Stoelting.

Sue, D. W., Ivey, A. E., & Pederson, P. B. (1996). *A theory of multicultural counseling and therapy.* New York: Brooks/Cole.

Sue, D. W., & Sue, D. (1990). *Counseling the culturally different: Theory and practice* (2nd ed.). New York: Wiley.

Suen, H. K., & Ary, D. (1989). *Analyzing quantitative behavioral observation data.* Hillsdale, NJ: Erlbaum.

Summit, R. (1983). The child sexual abuse accommodation syndrome. *Child Abuse and Neglect, 7,* 177–193.

Suzukamo, L. B. (1996, January 9). Screening of children falls short. *St. Paul Pioneer Press,* pp. 1A, 6A-7A.

Swanson, H. L., & Watson, B. L. (1989). *Educational and psychological assessment of exceptional children.* Columbus, OH: Merrill.

Sylva, K. (1977). Play and learning. In B. Tizard & D. Harvey (Eds.), *Biology of Play* (pp. 59–73). Philadelphia: Lippincott.

Szatmari, P., Archer, L., Fisman, S., Streiner, D. L., & Wilson, F. (1995). Asperger's syndrome and autism: Differences in behavior, cognition, and adaptive function. *Journal of the American Academy of Child & Adolescent Psychiatry, 34*(12), 1662–1671.

Tager-Flusberg, H. (1989). A psycholinguistic perspective on language development in the autistic child. In G. Dawson (Ed.), *Autism: Nature, diagnosis, and treatment* (pp. 92–115). New York: Guilford Press.

Tallent, N. (1976). *Psychological report writing.* Englewood Cliffs, NJ: Prentice-Hall.

Tanner, J. M. (1978). *Fetus into man: Physical growth from conception to maturity.* Cambridge, MA: Harvard University Press.

Taylor, H. G. (1988). Neuropsychological testing: Relevance for assessing children's learning disabilities. *Journal of Consulting and Clinical Psychology, 56*(6), 795–800.

Teale, W. H., Hiebert, E. H., & Chittenden, E. A. (1987). Assessing young children's literacy development. *The Reading Teacher, 40,* 772–777.

Teale, W. H., & Sulzby, E. (Eds.). (1986). *Emergent literacy: Writing and reading.* Norwood, NJ: Albex.

Terr, L. (1983). Chowchilla revisited: The effects of psychiatric trauma five years after a school bus kidnapping. *American Journal of Psychiatry, 140,* 1543–1550.

Terr, L. (1988). What happens to early memories of trauma? A study of twenty children under age five at the time of documented traumatic events. *Journal of the American Academy of Child and Adolescent Psychiatry, 27,* 96–104.

Teska, J. A., & Stonebruner, R. L. (Eds.). (1980). The concept and practice of second-level screening. *Psychology in the Schools, 17,* 192–195.

Thelen, E. (1995). Motor development: A new synthesis. *American Psychologist, 50*(2), 79–95.

Third International Mathematics and Science Study (TIMSS). (1998). *Highlights February 1998.* TIMSS International Study Center, Boston College, Chestnut Hill, MA.

Thomas, A., & Chess, S. (1977). *Temperament and development.* New York: Brunner/Mazel.

Thomas, E. B. (1990). Sleeping and waking states in infants: A functional perspective. *Neuroscience and Biobehavioral Reviews, 14,* 93–107.

Thompson, R. A. (1994). Emotion regulation: A theme in search of definition. In N. A. Fox (Ed.), *The development of emotion regulation: Biological and behavioral considerations. Monographs of the Society for Research in Child Development, 59,* (2–3), Serial No. 240.

Thompson, T., & Berkson, G. (1985). Stereotyped behavior of severely disabled children in classroom and free-play settings. *American Journal of Mental Deficiency, 89*(6), 580–586.

Thornburg, D. (1993). Intergenerational literacy learning with bilingual families: a context for the analysis of social mediation of thought. *Journal of Reading Behavior, 25,* 323–352.

Thorndike, R. L., Hagen, E. P., & Sattler, J. M. (1986). *Stanford–Binet Intelligence Scale: Fourth Edition.* Chicago: Riverside.

Thorndike, R. M. (1990). Would the real factors of the Stanford–Binet Fourth Edition please come forward? *Journal of Psychoeducational Assessment, 8,* 412–435.

Thurlow, M. L. (1992). Issues in the screening of preschool children. In E. V. Nuttall, I. Romero, & J. Kalesnik (Eds.), *Assessing and screening preschoolers: Psychological and educational dimensions* (pp. 67–82). Boston: Allyn & Bacon.

Thurlow, M. L., O'Sullivan, P. J., & Ysseldyke, J. E. (Eds.). (1986). Early screening for special education: How accurate? *Educational Leadership, 44*(3), 93–95.

Thurlow, M. L., & Ysseldyke, J. (1979). Current assessment and decision making practices in model LD programs. *Learning Disabilities Quarterly, 2,* 15–24.

Thurlow, M. L., Ysseldyke, J. E., & O'Sullivan, P. (Eds.). (1985). *Preschool screening in Minnesota: 1982–83* (Research Report No. 1). Minneapolis, MN: University of Minnesota, Early Childhood Assessment Project. (ERIC Document Reproduction Service No. ED 269 950).

Thurman, S. K., & Widerstrom, A. H. (1985). *Young children with special needs: A developmental and ecological approach.* Boston: Allyn & Bacon.

Tizard, B. (1977). Play: The child's way of learning? In B. Tizard & D. Harvey (Eds.), *Biology of Play* (pp. 199–208). Philadelphia: Lippincott.

Tombari, M., & Davis, R. A. (1979). Behavioral consultation. In G. Phye & D. Reschly (Eds.), *Educational psychology* (pp. 281–307). New York: Academic Press.

Trawick-Smith, J. (1994). *Interactions in the classroom: Facilitating play in the early years.* New York: Merrill.

Tröster, H., Branbring, M., & Belman, A. (1991). Prevelence and situational causes of stereotyped behaviors in blind infants and preschoolers. *Journal of Abnormal Child Psychology, 19,* 569–590.

Turnbull, A. P. (1991). Identifying children's strengths and needs. In M. J. McGonigel, R. K. Kaufmann, & B. H. Johnson (Eds.), *Guidelines and recommended practices for the individualized family service plan* (2nd ed., pp. 39–55). Bethesda, MD: Association for the Care of Children's Health.

Turnbull, A. P., Patterson, J. M., Behr, S. K., Murphy, D. L., Marquis, J. G., & Blue-Banning, M. J. (Eds.). (1993). *Cognitive coping, families, and disability.* Baltimore: Paul H. Brookes.

Turnbull, A. P., & Turnbull III, H. R. (Eds.). (1990). *Families, professionals, and exceptionality: A special partnership* (2nd ed.). Columbus, OH: Merrill.

Tyack, D., & Gottsleben, R. (1977). *Language sampling, analysis, and training* (Rev. ed.). Palo Alto, CA: Consulting Psychologists Press.

Tyler, A. H. (1978). *The conceptualization and development of a model crisis nursery.* Unpublished master's thesis, University of Utah.

Tyler, A. H. (1986). The abusive father. In M. E. Lamb (Ed.), *The father's role: Applied perspectives* (pp. 256–275). New York: Wiley.

Tyler, A. H., & Brassard, M. R. (1984). Abuse in the investigation and treatment of intrafamilial child sexual abuse. *Child Abuse and Neglect, 8,* 47–53.

Tyler, A. H., & Gully, K. J. (1988). Intervention and treatment of child sexual abuse. In O. C. S. Tzeng & J. J. Jacobsen (Eds.), *Sourcebook for child abuse and neglect: Intervention, treatment and prevention through crisis programs* (pp. 345–377). Springfield, IL: Thomas.

Tzuriel, D., & Haywood, H. (1992). The development of interactive-dynamic approaches to assessment of learning potential. In H. Haywood & D. Tzuriel (Eds.), *Interactive assessment* (pp. 3–37). New York: Springer-Verlag.

Tzuriel, D., & Klein, P. (1985). Analogical thinking modifiability in disadvantaged, regular, special education, and mentally retarded children. *Journal of Abnormal Child Psychology, 13,* 539–552.

Tzuriel, D., & Klein, P. (1987). Assessing the young child: Children's analogical thinking modifiability. In C. Lidz (Ed.), *Dynamic assessment* (pp. 268–282). New York: Guilford Press.

Ulrey, G. (1982). Influences of preschooler's behavior on assessment. In G. Ulrey & S. J. Rogers (Eds.), *Psychological assessment of handicapped infants and young children* (pp. 25–34). New York: Thieme-Stratton.

Ulrey, G., & Schnell, R. R. (Eds.). (1982). Introduction to assessing young children. In G. Ulrey & S. J. Rogers (Eds.), *Psychological assessment of handicapped infants and young children* (pp. 1–13). New York: Thieme-Stratton.

Ungerer, J., & Sigman, M. (1981). Symbolic play and language comprehension in autistic children. *Journal of the American Academy of Child Psychiatry, 20,* 318–337.

United Cerebral Palsy National Collaborative Infant Project. (1976). *Staff development handbook: A resource for the transdisciplinary process.* New York: United Cerebral Palsy Association of America.

Urwin, C. (1978). The development of communication between blind infants and their parents. In A. Lock (Ed.), *Action, gesture and symbols: The emergence of language* (pp. 79–108). London, England: Academic Press.

Urwin, C. (1983). Dialogue and cognitive functioning in the early language development of three blind children. In A. E. Mills (Ed.), *Language acquisition in the blind child: Normal and deficient.* London, England: Croom Helm.

U.S. Department of Education. (1987). *Ninth Annual Report to Congress on the Implementation of the Education of the Handicapped Act.* Washington, DC: Author.

U.S. Department of Education. (1991). *America 2000.* Washington, DC: Author.

U.S. Department of Education. (1995). *Seventeenth annual report to Congress on the implementation of the Individuals with Disabilities Education Act.* Washington, DC: Author.

U.S. Department of Education. (1995). Public elementary and secondary school enrollment by state: 1993. *Digest of Education Statistics, 1995.* Washington, DC: Author.

U.S. Department of Health and Human Services, National Center on Child Abuse and Neglect, Child Maltreatment, 1994. *Reports from states to the National Center on Child Abuse and Neglect* (Washington, DC: U.S. Government Printing Office, 1996).

Utah Code Annotated, Section 62A-4a-402 (90, 91) (1994). IN: Allen Smith.

Utah Code Annotated, Section 62A-4a-403 (91) (1994). IN: Allen Smith.

Utah Code Annotated, Section 62A-4a-410 (1994). IN: Allen Smith.

Utah Code Annotated, Section 62A-4a-411 (94, 95) (1994). IN: Allen Smith.

Uzgiris, I. C., & Hunt, J. McV. (1975). *Assessment in infancy: Ordinal scales of psychological development.* Urbana, IL: University of Illinois Press.

VanSanten, J. P. H., Black, L. M., Wilson, B. C., & Risucci, D. A. (1994). Modeling clinical judgement: A reanalysis of data from Wilson and Risucci's (1986) paper "A model for clinical-quantitative classification Generation I: Applications to language-disordered preschool children." *Brain & Language, 46*(3), 469–481.

Vaughn-Cooke, F. (1986). The challenge of assessing the language of nonmainstream speakers. In O. L. Taylor (Ed.), *Treatment of communication disorders in culturally and linguistically diverse populations.* San Diego, CA: College Hill Press.

Vazquez Nuttall, E., & Nuttall, R. L. (1979, March). *Families as support systems and psychological helpers.* Paper presented at the annual convention of the American Personnel and Guidance Association, Atlanta, GA.

Vellutino, F. (1987). Dyslexia. *Scientific American, 256*(3), 34–42.

Vernon, P. E., Jackson, D. N., & Messick, S. (1988). Cultural influences on patterns of abilities in North America. In S. H. Irvine & J. W. Berry (Eds.), *Human abilities in cultural context* (pp. 208–231). New York: Cambridge University Press.

Vig, S., & Jedrysek, E. (1995). Adaptive behavior of young urban children with developmental disabilities. *Mental Retardation, 33,* 90–98.

Vinovski, M. A. (1987). Family and schooling in colonial and nineteenth-century America. *Journal of Family History, 12,* 19–37.

Vort Corporation (1997). *Behavioral Characteristics Progression-Revised.* Palo Alto, CA: Vort.

Vulpe, S. G. (1982). *Vulpe Assessment Battery.* Toronto, Canada: National Institute on Mental Retardation.

Vygotsky, L. (1929). The problem of cultural development of the child. *Journal of Genetic Psychology, 36,* 515–534.

Vygotsky, L. (1962). *Thought and language.* Cambridge, MA: MIT Press.

Vygotsky, L. (1967). Play and its role in the mental development of the child. *Soviet Psychology, 12,* 62–76.

Vygotsky, L. (1978). Mind in society: The development of higher psychological processes (M. Cole, V. John-Steiner, S. Scribner, & E. Souberman, Eds. and Trans.). Cambridge, MA: Harvard University Press.

Waber, D., & McCormick, M. (1995). Late neuropsychological outcomes in preterm infants of normal IQ: Selective vulnerability of the visual system. *Journal of Pediatric Psychology, 20*(6), 721–735.

Wahler, R. G., & Cormier, W. H. (1970). The ecological interview: A first step in outpatient child behavior therapy. *Journal of Behavior Therapy and Experimental Psychiatry, 1,* 279–289.

Walker, H. M., & Hops, H. (1976). Use of normative peer data as a standard for evaluating classroom treatment effects. *Journal of Applied Behavior Analysis, 9,* 159–168.

Wallerstein, J. S. (1991). The long-term effects of divorce on children: A review. *Journal of the American academy of child and adolescent psychiatry, 30,* 349–360.

Warren, S. F., Yoder, P. J., Gazdag, G. E., Kim, K., & Jones, H. A. (1993). Facilitating prelinguistic skills in young children with developmental delay. *Journal of Speech and Hearing Research, 36,* 89–97.

Waterman, J. (1982). Assessment consideration with the emotionally disturbed child. In G. Ulrey & S. J. Rogers (Eds.), *Psychological assessment of handicapped infants and young children* (pp. 142–148). New York: Thieme-Stratton.

Watson, M. W., & Fischer, K. W. (1980). Development of social roles in elicited and spontaneous behavior during the preschool years. *Developmental Psychology, 16,* 483–494.

Weber, C. U., Foster, P. W., & Weikart, D. P. (Eds.). (1978). *An economic analysis of the Ypsilanti Perry Preschool Project.* (Monographs of the High/Scope Educational Research Foundation No. 5). Ypsilanti, MI: High/Scope Foundation.

Wechsler, D. (1967). *Wechsler Preschool and Primary Scale of Intelligence.* New York: Psychological Corporation.

Wechsler, D. (1989). *Manual for the Wechsler Preschool and Primary Scale of Intelligence—Revised.* San Antonio, TX: The Psychological Corporation.

Weiner, E. J., Ottinger, D. R., & Tilton, J. R. (1969). Comparisons of toy play behavior of autistic, retarded, and normal children: A reanalysis. *Psychological Reports, 25,* 223–227.

Weintraub, S., & Mesulam, M. M. (1985). Mental state assessment of young and elderly adults in behavioral neurology. In M. M. Mesulam (Ed.), *Principles of Behavioral Neurology* (pp. 71–123). Philadelphia: F. A. Davis.

Weisglas-Kuperus, N., Baerts, W., Fetter, W. P. F., & Sauer, P. J. J. (1992). Neonatal cerebral ultrasound, neonatal neurology, and perinatal conditions as predictors of neurodevelopmental outcome in very low birth weight infants. *Early Human Development, 31,* 131–148.

Weiss, H. M. (1987, December). Family/school collaborative efforts: Systemic approaches to problem solving. *National Association of School Psychologists Communiqué, 16*(4), 18.

Weiss, R. (1981). INREAL Intervention for language handicapped and bilingual children. *Journal of the Division for Early Childhood, 4,* 40–51.

Werner, E. (1986). The concept of risk from a developmental perspective. In B. Keogh (Ed.), *Advances in special education: Vol. 5. Developmental problems in infancy and the preschool years* (pp. 1–23). Greenwich, CT: JAI Press.

Werner, E. E., & Smith, R. S. (Eds.). (1992). *Overcoming the odds: High risk children from birth to adulthood.* Ithaca, NY: Cornell University Press.

Werner, E. O., & Kreshcheck, J. D. (1983). *Structured Photographic Expressive Language Test-Preschool.* Sandwich, IL: Janelle.

West, J., Wright, D., & Hausken, E. G. (Eds.). (1995). *Statistics in brief: Child care and early education program participation of infants, toddlers, and preschoolers* (NCES 95–824). Washington, DC: National Center for Education Statistics.

West, J. F., & Idol, L. (1990). Collaborative consultation in the education of mildly handicapped and at-risk students. *RASE: Remedial and Special Education, 11*(1), 22–31.

Westby, C. E. (1980). Assessment of cognitive and language abilities through play. *Language, Speech, and Hearing Services in the Schools, 11,* 154–168.

Westby, C. E. (1986). Cultural differences in caregiver-child interaction: Implications for assessment and intervention. In L. Cole & V. Deal (Eds.), *Communication disorders in multicultural populations.* Rockville, MD: American Speech-Language-Hearing Association.

Whinnery, K. W., Fuchs, L. S., & Fuchs, D. (1991). General, special, and remedial teachers' acceptance of behavioral and instruction strategies for mainstreaming students with mild handicaps. *RASE: Remedial and Special Education, 12*(4), 6–17.

White, K. R., & Greenspan, S. P. (1986). An overview of the effectiveness of preventive intervention programs. In R. Berlin & J. Noshpitz (Eds.), *Basic handbook of child psychiatry* (p. 5). New York: Basic Books.

White, O. R., & Haring, N. G. (1981). *Uniform Performance Assessment System (UPAS).* New York: Psychological Corporation.

Whiting, B. B., & Edwards, C. P. (1988). *Children of different worlds: The formation of social behavior.* Cambridge, MA: Harvard University Press.

WHO (World Health Organization). (1994). *ICD-10 Classification of mental and behavioral disorders: Clinical descriptions and diagnostic guidelines.* Geneva: Author.

WHO (World Health Organization). (1992). *ICD-10 Classification of mental and behavioral disorders: Clinical descriptions and diagnostic guidelines.* Geneva: Author.

Wigg, E. H., Secord, W., & Semel, E. (1992). *Clinical Evaluation of Language Rudimentals-Preschool.* San Antonio, TX: Psychological Corporation.

Wilder Foundation. (1996). *Social outcomes for our community: Entering the 21st century.* St. Paul, MN: Wilder Research Center.

Wilen, D. K. (1989). Working with language minority students. *Communique of the National Association of School Psychologists,* May, p. 20.

Wilhelm, C., Johnson, M., & Eisert, D. (1986). Assessment of motor-impaired children. In R. J. Simeonsson (Ed.), *Psychological and developmental assessment of special children* (pp. 241–278). Boston: Allyn & Bacon.

Williams, R. (1980, February). *Symbolic play in young language handicapped and normal speaking children.* Paper presented at the International Conference on Piaget and the Helping Professions, Los Angeles.

Williams, R., & Beeson, B. (1983). *Monograph of Play Research.* Muncie, IL: Ball State University, Elementary Education Department (ERIC Document Reproduction Service No. ED221–290).

Wills, K. E. (1993). Neuropsychological functioning in children with spina bifida and/or hydrocephalus. *Journal of Clinical Child Psychology, 22*(2), 247–265.

Wilson, B. C. (1986). An approach to the neuropsychological assessment of the preschool child. In S. B. Filskov & T. J. Boll (Eds.), *Handbook of clinical neuropsychology* (Vol. 2, pp. 121–171). New York: Wiley.

Wilson, B. C., & Risucci, D. A. (1986). A model for clinical-quantitative classification Generation I: Applications to language-disordered preschool children. *Brain and Language, 27,* 281–309.

Winnicott, D. W. (1987). *The child, the family, and the outside world.* Reading, MA: Addison-Wesley.

Wirt, R. D., Lachar, D., Klinedinst, J. K., & Seat, P. D. (1984). *Multidimensional description of child personality: A manual for the Personality Inventory for Children.* Los Angeles: Western Psychological Services.

Witt, J. C., & Elliot, S. N. (1985). Acceptability of classroom intervention strategies. In T. R. Kratochwill (Ed.), *Advances in school psychology* (Vol. IV, pp. 251–288). Hillsdale, NJ: Erlbaum.

Wolery, M. (1989). Using direct observation in assessment. In D. B. Bailey, Jr., & M. Wolery (Eds.), *Assessing infants and preschoolers with handicaps* (pp. 64–96). Columbus, OH: Merrill.

Wolery, M., & Bailey, D. B. (1989). Assessing play skills. In D. B. Bailey & M. Wolery (Eds.), *Assessing infants and preschoolers with handicaps.* (pp. 428–446). New York: Merrill.

Wolf-Schein, E. G. (1993). Assessing the "untestable" client: ADLO. *Developmental Disabilities Bulletin, 21*(2), 52–70.

Wolff, A., & Harkins, J. (1986). Multiple handicaps. In A. N. Schildroth & M. A. Karchmer (Eds.), *Deaf children in America* (pp. 55–81). San Diego, CA: College-Hill Press.

Wolff, P. H. (1981). Normal variation in human maturation. In K. J. Connolly & H. F. R. Prectl (Eds.), *Maturation and development: Biological and psychological perspectives* (1977–1978 edition). Philadelphia: Lippincott.

Wolters, P. L., Brouwers, P., & Moss, H. A. (1995). Pediatric HIV disease: Effects on cognition, learning, and behavior. *School Psychological Quarterly, 10,* 305–328.

Wood, F. H., Smith, C. R., & Grimes, J. (1985). *The Iowa assessment model in behavioral disorders: A training manual.* Des Moines, IA: State Department of Public Instruction.

Wood, M. E. (1981). Costs of intervention programs. In C. Garland, N. Stone, J. Swanson, & G. Woodruff (Eds.), *Early intervention for children with special needs and their families: Findings and recommendations* (pp. 15–26). Seattle, WA: University of Washington, Western States Technical Assistance Resource (WESTAR).

Woodcock, R. W. (1990). Theoretical foundations of the WJ-R measures of cognitive ability. *Journal of Psychoeducational Assessment, 8,* 231–258.

Woodcock, R. W., & Johnson, M. B. (1989). *Woodcock-Johnson Psycho-Educational Battery-Revised.* Allen, TX: DLM.

Woodcock, R. W., & Johnson, M. B. (1989). *Woodcock-Johnson-Revised.* Chicago: Riverside.

Woodcock, R. W., & Mather, N. (1989). *WJ-R tests of cognitive ability standard and supplemental batteries: Examiner's manual.* Chicago: Riverside.

Woodcock, R. W., & Muñoz-Sandoval, A. F. (1996). *Batería Woodcock-Muñoz: pruebas de habilidad cognitiva—revisada.* Chicago: Riverside.

Woodcock, R. W., & Muñoz-Sandoval, A. F. (1996). *Batería Woodcock-Muñoz: pruebas de habilidad cognitiva: revisada, Supplemental Manual.* Chicago: Riverside.

Woodruff, G. (1980, June). Transdisciplinary approach for preschool children and parents. *The Exceptional Parent,* pp. 13–15.

Woodruff, G., Hunson, C. R., McGonigel, M., & Sterzin, E. D. (1990). *Community-based services for children with HIV infections and their families: A manual for planners, service providers, families, and advocates.* Brighton, MA: South Shore Mental Health Center.

Woodruff, G., & McGonigel, M. (1988). Early intervention team approaches: The transdisciplinary model. In J. B. Jordan, J. J. Gallagher, P. L. Hutinger, & M. B. Karnes (Eds.), *Early childhood special education: Birth to three* (pp. 163–181). Reston, VA: Council for Exceptional Children.

Wortham, S. C. (1990). *Tests and measurement in early education.* Columbus, OH: Merrill.

Wright, H. F. (1967). *Recording and analyzing child behavior.* New York: HarperCollins.

Wyatt, T. A. (1991). *Linguistic constraints on copula production in Black English child speech.* Unpublished doctoral dissertation, University of Massachusetts, Amherst, MA.

Wyatt, T. A. (1995). Language development in African American English child speech, *Linguistics in Education, 7*(1), 7–22.

Wyatt, T. A. (1996). Acquisition of the African-American English copula. In A. G. Kamhi, K. E. Pollock, & J. L. Harris (Eds.) *Communication development and disorders in African-American children.* Baltimore: Paul H. Brookes.

Xin, R., Chen, S., Tang, H., Lin, X., & McConville, B. (1992). *Behavioral problems among preschool age children in Shanghai: Analysis of 3000 cases.* Shanghai: Shanghai Mental Health Center.

Yamamoto, M. (1990). Birth order, gender differences, and language development in modern Japanese preschool children. *Psychologia, 33,* 185–190.

Yarrow, L. J., McQuiston, S., MacTurk, R. H., McCarthy, M. E., Klein, R. P., & Vietze, P. M. (1983). Assessment of mastery motivation during the first year of life. Contemporaneous and cross-age relationships. *Developmental Psychology, 19,* 159–171.

Yeates, K., Enrile, B., Loss, N., Blumenstein, E., & Delis, D. (1995). Verbal learning and memory in children with myeolomeningocele. *Journal of Pediatric Psychology, 20*(6), 801–815.

Yoshida, R. K. (1980). Multidisciplinary decision making in special education: A review of issues. *School Psychology Review, 9*(3), 221–227.

Ysseldyke, J. E. (1987). Classification of handicapped students. In M. C. Wang, M. C. Reynolds, & H. J. Walberg (Eds.), *Learner characteristics and adaptive education* (pp. 253–272). New York: Pergamon Press.

Ysseldyke, J. E. (1990). Goodness of fit of the Woodcock-Johnson Psycho-Educational Battery-Revised to the Horn-Cattell Gf-Gc theory. *Journal of Psychoeducational Assessment, 8,* 268–275.

Ysseldyke, J. E., & Algozzine, B. (1982). *Critical issues in special and remedial education.* Boston: Houghton Mifflin.

Ysseldyke, J. E., & Algozzine, B. (1990). *Introduction to special education* (2nd ed.). Boston: Houghton Mifflin.

Ysseldyke, J. E., Algozzine, B., & Thurlow, M. L. (1992). *Critical issues in special education.* Boston: Houghton Mifflin.

Ysseldyke, J. E., & O'Sullivan, P. J. (1987). Predicting preschool screening referral rates from district demographic data. *Journal of School Psychology, 25,* 119–129.

Ysseldyke, J. E., & Salvia, J. (1982). *Assessment in special and remedial education* (2nd ed.). New York: Houghton Mifflin.

Ysseldyke, J. E., Thurlow, M. L., & Gilman, C. J. (1993a). *Educational outcomes and indicators for early childhood (age 3).* Minneapolis, MN: University of Minnesota, National Center on Educational Outcomes.

Ysseldyke, J. E., Thurlow, M. L., & Gilman, C. J. (1993b). *Educational outcomes and indicators for early childhood (age 6).* Minneapolis, MN: University of Minnesota, National Center on Educational Outcomes.

Ysseldyke, J. E., Thurlow, M. L., Lehr, C. A., Nania, P. A., O'Sullivan, P. J., Weiss, J. A., & Bursaw, R. A. (1986). *An ecological investigation of assessment and decision making for handicapped children prior to school entrance*

(Research Report No. 10). Minneapolis, MN: University of Minnesota, Early Childhood Assessment Project.

Ysseldyke, J. E., Thurlow, M. L., & O'Sullivan, P. J. (1987). The impact of screening and referral practices in early childhood special education: Policy considerations and research directions. *Journal of Special Education, 21*(2), 85–96.

Ysseldyke, J. E., Thurlow, M. L., O'Sullivan, P. J., & Bursaw, R. A. (1986). Current screening and diagnostic practices in a state offering free preschool screening since 1977: Implications for the field. *Journal of Psychoeducational Assessment, 4,* 191–201.

Ysseldyke, J. E., Thurlow, M. L., Weiss, J. A., Lehr, C. A., & Bursaw, R. A. (1985). *An ecological study of school districts with high and low preschool screening referral rates* (Research Report No. 6). Minneapolis, MN: University of Minnesota, Early Childhood Assessment Project. (ERIC Document Reproduction Service No. ED 269 955).

Yussen, S. R., & Santrock, J. W. (1982). *Child development: An introduction.* Dubuque, IA: W. C. Brown.

Zahn-Waxler, C., McKnew, D. H., Cummings, E. M., Davenport, Y. B., & Radke-Yarrow, M. (1984). Problem behaviors and peer interactions of young children with a manic-depressive parent. *American Journal of Psychiatry, 141,* 236–240.

Zaragoza, M. S. (1991). Preschool children's susceptibility to memory impairment. In J. Doris (Ed.), *The suggestibility of children's recollections.* Washington, DC: American Psychological Association.

Zeanah, C. H. (Ed.). (1993). *Handbook of infant mental health.* New York: Guilford Press.

Zeitlin, S. (1985). *Coping Inventory.* Bensenville, IL: Scholastic Testing Services.

Zeitlin, S., Williamson, G. G., & Szczepanski, M. (1988). *Early Coping Inventory.* Bensenville, IL: Scholastic Testing Services.

Zero to Three. (1992). *Head start: The emotional foundations of school readiness.* Arlington, VA: National Center for Clinical Infant Programs.

Zero to Three/National Center for Clinical Infant Programs. (1994). *Diagnostic Classification: 0–3. Diagnostic classification of Mental Health and Developmental Disorders of Infancy and Early Childhood.* Arlington, VA: National Center of Clinical Infant Programs.

Zigler, E., & Balla, D. (1982). Introduction: The developmental approach to mental retardation. In E. Zigler & D. Balla (Eds.), *Mental retardation: The developmental–difference controversy* (pp. 3–8). Hillsdale, NJ: Erlbaum.

Zigler, E., Kagan, S. L., & Muenchow, S. (1982). Preventive intervention in the schools. In C. Reynolds & T. Gutkin (Eds.), *The handbook of school psychology* (pp. 774–795). New York: Wiley.

Zill, N., Moore, K. A., Smith, E. W., Stief, R., & Coiro, M. A. (Eds.). (1991). *The life circumstances and development of children in welfare families: A profile based on national survey data.* Washington, DC: Child Trends.

Zimmerman, I. L., Steiner, V. G., & Pond, R. E. (1992). *Preschool Language Scale-3.* San Antonio, TX: Psychological Corporation.

Zins, J. E., & Ponti, C. R. (1990). Strategies to facilitate the implementation, organization, and operation of system-wide consultation programs. *Journal of Educational and Psychological Consultation, 1*(3), 205–218.

INDEX